Library and Information Science

For NET, SLET and Other Competitive Examinations

(Objective Type Questions)

Third Revised and Enlarged Edition

Dr. D.K. Pandey
Assistant Librarian
Rajiv Gandhi University

ATLANTIC
PUBLISHERS & DISTRIBUTORS (P) LTD

Published by
ATLANTIC
PUBLISHERS & DISTRIBUTORS (P) LTD
7/22, Ansari Road, Darya Ganj, New Delhi-110002
Phones : +91-11-40775252, 40775214, 23273880, 23275880
Fax : +91-11-23285873
Web : www.atlanticbooks.com
E-mail : orders@atlanticbooks.com

Branch Office: Chennai
Phones : +91-44-48531784, 28291383
E-mail : chennai@atlanticbooks.com

First Edition, 2002
Second Edition, 2015
Third Edition, 2021

Printed & bound in India by Atlantic Print Services

Preface

It has been the need of present-day students of Library and Information Science to compete in the objective type of examination pattern for absorption into different posts. On behalf of the UGC, the National Eligibility Test (NET) is conducted for determining the eligibility of Indian nationals for Assistant Professors only or Junior Research Fellowship & Eligibility for Assistant Professor. Both in Indian Universities and College still recently, the CBSE conducted the NET in 84 subjects at 91 selected Cities of spread across the country.

From Dec. 2018 onwards, the UGC-NET (for Eligibility for Assistant Professor only or Junior Research Fellowship & Eligibility for Assistant Professor both), is being conducted by the NTA. This book covers objective type questions with answers given at the end of each chapter. This makes the book more suitable on the subject to meet the requirements of the students appearing for NET, SLET and JRF. It will be helpful for the candidates as well as for those who want to get jobs as Librarian in Kendriya Vidayalaya, Navodaya Vidayalaya, and Staff Selection Commission etc. Question papers of NET. from 1991-2019 have been included with answers. The book has been divided into fourteen chapters in such a way that all the 10 Units are covered.

I have precisely tried to provide the solutions for the objective type of tests to meet the need of the students in the field of Library & Information Science. Different questions in objective mode have been properly classified in the normal sub-divisions. Each sub-division provides the details of the units covered in the UGC-NET format. Since it is necessary to provide solutions for UGC-NET mode, question papers of the last three decades have been included along with other preferential questions considering the modern changes in the new syllabus and pattern of the subject.

Utmost care has been taken in providing correct solutions, However, any suggestion and submission for further improvement are from the experts in the field is highly welcome.

I hope that the book will act not only as a question bank on the subject, but also serve as a good tool for appearing in the interviews.

D.K. Pandey

Acknowledgements

I would like to acknowledge the contribution of a number of persons during the preparation of the book. There has been feed backs from different corners to enrich the subject matter.

Since the compilation of question papers, and finding their solutions from the authentic sources were necessary, a large number of people engaged in various libraries were consulted in the process. I offer my deep gratitude to them.

I express my sincere thanks to former Librarian Dr. M. Maltesh, Dr. V.R. Tiwary (Librarian) Indian Institute of Science Education of Research (IISER) Kolkata for their valuable guidance and constructive suggestions. I also thanks to Prof. A.R. Parhi, Dr. Miyaji Hazam of the Department of English, for his valuable inputs. Mr. Rahul Sharma, Mr. Bhaskar Saikia, Ms. Sabita Kalita and Ms. Gayatri Dey also deserve my thanks for the timely suggestion in this regard.

I have great pleasure to acknowledge the contribution of my wife Smt. Niru Pandey, my daughter Priya Pandey and son Bholu, without whose encouragement, it would not have become a reality.

I am grateful to all the persons who have helped me directly or indirectly in the process.

I record my thankfulness to M/s Atlantic Publishers and Distributors (P) Ltd., for bringing out this publication, and hope it will become an effective tool for the aspirants appearing in the different examinations in the subject of Library and Information Sciences.

D.K. Pandey

Contents

	Preface	*iii*
	Acknowledgments	*iv*
	Syllabus	*vi*
1.	Abbreviations	1
2.	Books and Authors/Editors	9
3.	Academic Library	12
4.	Bibliography and Reference Service	30
5.	Catalogue and Cataloguing	71
6.	Classification	105
7.	Information Service and Research Methodology	135
8.	Information Technology and Library Automation	195
9.	Library Management	268
10.	Library and Society	312
11.	Periodicals	349
12.	Important Personalities	361
13.	Important Dates in Library Science	362
14.	Plagiarism	365
	NET Exam 2018	371
	NET Exam June 2019	385
	NET Exam December 2019	395

Syllabus

ALL THE QUESTIONS OF PAPER–I AND PAPER–II WILL BE COMPULSORY, COVERING ENTIRE SYLLABUS

PAPER – II

Unit-I

Data, Information, Knowledge and Wisdom. Information Life Cycle: Generation, Collection, Storage and Dissemination. Role of Information in Planning, Management, Socio-economic, Cultural, Educational and Technological Development. Information Science: Relationship with other subjects, Information Society and Knowledge Society. Communication: Concept, Types, Theories, Models, Channels and Barriers; Trends in Scholarly Communication. Information Industry: Generators, Providers and Intermediaries. IPR and Legal Issues: Categories, Conventions, Treaties, Laws. Plagiarism: Concept and Types. Right to Information Act (RTI); Information Technology Act. National Knowledge Commission; National Mission on Libraries.

Unit-II

Historical Development of Libraries in India; Committees and Commissions on Libraries in India. Types of Libraries: Academic, Public, Special and National. Library Legislation and Library Acts in Indian States; The Press and Registration of Books Act; The Delivery of Books and Newspapers (Public Libraries) Act. Laws of Library Science. Library and Information Science Profession: Librarianship as a Profession, Professional Skills and Competences; Professional Ethics. Professional Associations: National—ILA, IASLIC, IATLIS; International—IFLA, ALA, CILIP, ASLIB, SLA; Role of UGC, RRRLF and UNESCO in Promotion and Development of Libraries. Library and Information Science Education in India. Library Public Relations and Extension Activities. Type of Users: User Studies, User Education. Information Literacy: Areas, Standards, Types and Models; Trends in Information Literacy.

Unit-III

Information Sources: Nature, Characteristics, Types and Formats. Sources of Information: Primary, Secondary and Tertiary; Documentary and NonDocumentary. Primary Information Sources (Print and Electronic): Journals, Conference Proceedings, Patents, Standards, Theses & Dissertations, Trade Literature. Secondary Information Sources (Print and Electronic): Dictionaries, Encyclopedias, Bibliographies, Indexing & Abstracting, Statistical sources, Handbooks and Manuals.

Tertiary Information Sources (Print and Electronic): Directories, Year Books, Almanacs. Reference Sources: Bibliographical, Biographical, Educational, Language and Geographical. Electronic Information Resources: Subject Gateways, Web Portals, Bulletin Boards, Discussion Forums /Groups. Databases: Bibliographic, Numeric, Full text, Multimedia; Open Access Databases. Institutional and Human Resources. Evaluation of Reference Sources and Web Resources

Unit-IV

Community Information Services. Reference Service: Concept and Types; Referral Services Alerting Services: CAS, SDI, Inter Library Loan and Document Delivery. Mobile based Library

Services and Tools: Mobile OPAC, Mobile Databases, Mobile Library Website, Library Apps, Mobile Library Instructions, Augmented Reality, SMS Alerts, GeoLocation, Reference Enquiry. Web 2.0 and 3.0 Library 2.0: Concept, Characteristics, Components; Instant Messaging, RSS Feeds, Podcasts, Vodcasts, Ask a Librarian Collaborative Services: Social Networks, Academics Social Networks, Social Tagging, Social Bookmarking. Web: Scale Discovery Services National Information Systems and Networks: NISCAIR, DESIDOC, SENDOC, ENVIS, INFLIBNET, DELNET, NICNET, ERNET, National Knowledge Network (NKN), Biotechnology Information System Network International Information Systems and Networks: INIS, AGRIS, INSPEC, MEDLARS, BIOSIS, ERIC, Patent Information System (PIS), Biotechnology Information System (BIS). Library Resource Sharing and Library Consortia: National and International.

Unit-V

Universe of Knowledge: Nature and Attributes; Modes of Formation of Subjects. Knowledge Organisation: Classification: Theories, Cannons, and Principles; Simple Knowledge Organisation System (SKOS), Taxonomies, Folksonomy, Trends in Classification. Mapping of Subjects in Library Classification Schemes: DDC, UDC and CC. Knowledge Organisation: Cataloguing: Cannons and Principles; Centralized and Cooperative Catalogue; Library Cataloguing Codes: CCC and AACR-II. Standards of Bibliographic Record Formats and Description: ISBD, MARC 21, CCF, RDA, FRBR, Bibframe. Standards for Bibliographic Information Interchange and Communication: ISO 2709, Z39.50, Z39.71. Metadata Standards: Dublin Core; MARC21, METS, MODES, EAD. Indexing Systems and Techniques: Assigned: Pre-coordinate; Post-Coordinate; DerivedTitle-based; Vocabulary Control. Abstracting: Types and Guidelines. Information Retrieval System: Features, Components, Models and Evaluation.

Unit-VI

Management: Principles, Functions and Schools of thought. Library and Information CentersManagement: Book Selection Tools and Principles; Library Acquisition, Technical Processing, Circulation, Serial Control, Maintenance and Stock Verification; Preservation and Conservation; Hazards and Control Measures of Library Materials. Human Resource Management: Planning, Job Analysis, Job Description, Job Evaluation, Selection, Recruitment, Motivation, Training and Development, Performance Appraisal; Staff Manual.

Financial Management in Libraries: Sources of Finance, Resource Mobilisation, Budgeting Methods; Cost Effective and Cost Benefit Analysis, Annual Reports and Statistics; Library Authority and Committee. Project Management: SWOT, PEST, PERT / CPM. Total Quality Management (TQM): Concepts, Principles and Techniques, Six Sigma; Evaluation of Services of Libraries and Information Centers. Library Building, Furniture and Equipments; Green Library Building; Information Commons; Makers Space; Security and Safety. Management Information System (MIS), MBO, Change Management, Disaster Management, Crisis Management. Knowledge Management: Principles, Tools, Components and Architecture. Marketing of Library Products and Services: Plan, Research, Strategies, Mix, Segmentation, Pricing and Advertising; Management Consultancy.

Unit-VII

Computer Technology: Character Representation (ASCII, ISCII, Unicode); Computer Hardware, Software; Storage Devices; Input and Output Devices. Types of Software: System Software, Application Software. Programming Languages: Object Oriented, Procedural, High Level, Scripting; Web Languages. Telecommunication: Transmission Channels, Mode, and Media, ISDN, PSDN,

Multiplexing, Modulation, Standards and Protocols. Wireless Communication: Media, Wi-fi, Li-fi, Satellite Communication, Mobile Communication. Computer Networks: Topologies, Types of Networks—LAN, MAN, WAN. Internet: Web browsers, WWW, E-mail; Search Engines, Meta and Entity Search engines.

Internet Protocols and Standards: HTTP, SHTTP, FTP, SMTP, TCP/IP, URI, URL. Hypertext, Hypermedia, Multimedia, Video conferencing, Virtual Reality, Augmented Technologies. Data Security, Network Security, Firewalls, Cryptographic Techniques, Anti-virus software, Anti-spyware, Intrusion Detection System.

Unit-VIII

Library Automation: Areas, Planning, Selection of Hardware and Software, Implementation and Evaluation; Standards for Library Automation. Barcode, RFID, QR Code, Biometric, Smartcard: Features and Applications. Digitization: Planning, Selection of Materials, Hardware, Software, Process, Issues. Digital Library: Genesis, Characteristics, Types, Architecture; Standards, Formats and Protocols, DOI. Digital Preservation: Need, Purpose, Standards, Methods, Techniques, Projects (National and International). Digital Library Initiatives: National and International. Institutional Repositories: Need, Purpose, Types and Tools; Institutional Repositories in India; ROAR, DOAR, SHARPA-ROMIO. Content Management Systems: Architecture, Data Integration, CMS Software—Selection, Implementation and Evaluation. Application of Artificial Intelligence, Expert Systems and Robotics in Libraries; Social Mobile Analytics Cloud (SMAC); Cloud Computing. Ontology: Tools (RDF, RDFS, Potege); Semantic Web, Linked Data, Big Data, Data Mining, Data Harvesting.

Unit-IX

Research: Concept, Purpose, Functions, Scope and Ethics; Types of Research—Basic and Applied, Interdisciplinary and Multidisciplinary. Research Methods: Historical, Descriptive, Experimental and Delphi. Research Design: Selection of Research Problem, Review of Literature; Formulation of Research Problem; Hypothesis-Formulation, Types and Testing; Sampling Techniques. Methods of Data Collection: Questionnaire, Interview, Observation, Library Records, Scales and Checklist. Data Analysis and Interpretation: Presentation of Data; Statistical Methods/Techniques. Statistical Packages: Spreadsheet, SPSS, Bibexcel, 'R' Statistics. Research Report Writing and Citation Tools: Structure, Style, Contents, Guidelines; Style Manuals; Online Citation Tools; Reference Style Management Tools; Antiplagiarism Tools; Evaluation of Research Report. Metric Studies in LIS: Bibliometrics, Scientometric, Webometrics, Altmetrics; Impact Factors: Journal, Institutional and Authors; h-Index, g-Index, i10 Index. Trends in Library and Information Science Research.

Unit-X

TAcademic Library and Information System. Public Library and Information System. Special Library and Information System. Health Science Library and Information System. Corporate Library and Information System. Agricultural Library and Information System. Engineering and Technological Library and Information System. Archive, Museums and Oriental Libraries. Community Information System. Information Services and System for Persons with Disability, Children and Women.

Chapter 1
Abbreviations

AACOBS : Australian Advisory Council on Bibliographical Services

AACR : Anglo American Cataloguing Rule

AACR2 : Anglo-American Cataloguing Rules, Second edition

AAL : Association of Assistant Librarian (Great Britain)

AALL : The American Association of Law Libraries

AASL : American Association of School Librarians

AALS : The Association of American Library School

AAMBP : Association of American Medical Book Publishers

AAMC : Association of American Medical Colleges. Established in 1959

AAUP : Association of American University Press

ABC : Abridged Bibliographic Classification

ABLISS : Association of British Library and Information Science Schools

ABN : Australian Bibliographic Network

ACRL : Association of College and Research Libraries (United States)

ADI : American Documentation Institute

ADONIS : The Article Delivery Over Network Information System

ADP : Automated Data Processing

AFSARI : Automation for Storage and Retrieval of Information

AGRIS : Agricultural Information System or International Information System for the Agricultural Science & Technology

AIBA : Agricultural Information Bank of Asia (Philippines)

ALA : American Library Association

ALGOL : Algorithmic Language

ALS : Automated Library System

ALSD : Academy of Library Science and Documentation (Hyderabad)

ALTA : American Library Trustees Association

ALU : Arithmetic Logic Unit

AMI : Association of Medical Illustrators

AMIC : Asian Mass Communication and Research Centre

AMULA : Aligarh Muslim University Libraries Association

AOC : Army Ordnance Corps

APA : American Psychological Association.

APALA : Asian Pacific American Librarians Association

APCTT : Asian Pacific Centre for Transfer of Technology

APIN : Asia and Pacific Information Network

APINESS : Asia-Pacific Information Network in Social Sciences

APINMAP : Asian and Pacific Information Network on Medicine and Aromatic Plants

APPLE : Ariane Passenger Pay Load Experiment

APSDEP : Asian and Pacific Skill Development

ARIC : Agricultural Research Information Centre (New Delhi)

ARIST : Annual Review of Information Science and Technology (USA)
ARLIS : Art Libraries Society
ARPANET : Advanced Research Project Network
ASA : American Standard Association
ASCII : Americans Standard Code for Information Interchange
ASLIB : Association of Special Libraries and Information Bureaux (Great Britain). It was founded on 1926.
ASM : American Society for Metals
ATIS : Appropriate Technology Information Service
AUBC : All Union Book Chamber (USSR). It was founded on 10 May 1917.
AUDACIOUS : Automatic Direct Access to Information with an On-line UDC System
BA : Biological Abstracts
BANKNET : Computer Network for Bank
BANSDOC : Bangladesh National Scientific and Technical Documentation Centre
BARC : Bhabha Atomic Research Centre
BASIC : Beginners All Purpose Symbolic Instruction Code
BBIP : British Book in Print
BC : Bibliographic Classification (Bliss)
BCA : Bliss Classification Association
BCR : Bibliography of Current Reports
BHI : British Humanities Index
BA : Biological Abstracts
BHULSA : Banaras Hindu University Library Science Students Association
BIOSIS : Bioscience Information Service (Philadelphia)
BI : Bibliographic Instruction
BIP : Books in Print
BIS : (The) Bureau of Indian Standard
BISA : Bibliographic Information on South-East Asia (Australia)
BITNET : Because It is Time Network (USA)
BL : British Library
BLACMP : Birmingham Library Co-operative Mechanisation Project
BLAISE : British Library Automated Information Service (UK)
BLLD : British Library Lending Division
BLRD : British Library Research and Development
BNB : British National Bibliography
BPL : Boston Public Library
BPS : Bits Per Second
BS : British Standard
BSA : Bibliographic Society of America
BSI : British Standard Institute
BSO : Broad System of Ordering
BTI : British Technology Index
CA : Chemical Abstracts
CAIN : Cataloguing and Indexing
CALIBER : Convention on Automation of Libraries in Education and Research Institutions
CALIBNET : Calcutta Library Network
CAP : Centralised Acquisition of Periodicals
CAPL : Canadian Association of Public Libraries
CAR : Computer Assisted Retrieval
CARDS : Card Automated Reproduction Demand System
CARIS : Current Agricultural Research Information System
CARISPLAN : Caribbean Information System for Economic and Social Planning
CAS : Current Awareness Service
CASSI : Chemical Abstracts Service Source Index

CBI : Cumulative Book Index
CC : Colon Classification
CARE : Consortium for Academic and Research Ethics
CCC : Classified Catalogue Code
CCF : Common Communication Format (*Net Exam-2010 J*)
CCL : Common Commanded Language
CDP : Custom Developed Programme
CD-ROM : Compact Disc Read Only Memory
CDS/ISIS : Computerised Documentation System/Integrated Sets of Information System
CEAN : Central Electricity Authority Network
CFTRI : Central Food Technological Research Institute
CI : Citation Index
CIC : Coconut Information Centre
CIL : Central Institute of Indian Language
CILIP : Charted Institute of Library and Information Professional
CIP : Cataloguing in Publication
CIRDAP : Centre on Integrated Rural Development for Asia and the Pacific
CLA : Canada Library Association
CLENE : Continuing Library Education Network and Exchanged (USA)
CLIR : Council on Library and Information Resources
CLRI : Central Leather Research Institute (Chennai)
CLS : Certificate in Library Science
CMS: : Content Management System
CMTI : Central Machine Tool Institute (Bangalore)
COBOL : Common Business Oriented Language
CODATA : Committee on Data for Science and Technology
COM : Computer Output Microfilm
COMLA : Commonwealth Library Association
COMPENDEX : Computerised Engineering Index
CPI : Canadian Periodical Index
CPM : Critical Path Method
CPU : Central Processing Unit
CRG : Classification Research Group
CSIR : Council of Scientific & Industrial Research (Delhi)
CSNET : Computer Science Network (USA)
CSIRO : Commonwealth Scientific and Industrial Research Organisation
CTI : Current Technology Index
CU : Control Unit
DAE : Department of Atomic Energy
DARE : Department of Agricultural Research and Education (New Delhi)
DARPNET : Defence Advanced Research Project Network
DAT : Digital Audio Tape
DBMS : Database Management System
DBT : Department of Biotechnology
DC : Dictionary Catalogue
DDC : Dewey Decimal Classification
DELNET : Delhi Library Network (*Net Exam-2010J*)
DESIDOC : Defence Scientific Information and Documentation Centre
DEVINSA : Development Information Network on South Asia
DEVSIS : Development Science Information System
DIN : Document Identification Number
DIS : Development Information System (U.N.)
DLA : Delhi Library Association
DMP : Dot Matrix Printer
DNB : Dictionary of National Biography
DNES : Department of Non-conventional Energy Sources

DOD : Department of Ocean Development (New Delhi)
DOS : Disc Operating System
DRDO : Defence Research and Development Organisation
DRTC : Documentation Research and Training Centre (Bangalore)
DSIR : Department of Scientific and Industrial Research
DST : Department of Science and Technology (New Delhi)
DTP : Desk Top Publishing
DVD : Digital Video Disc
DVR : Digital Video Recorder
EC : Expansive Classification (of C.A. Cutter)
EDSAC : Electronic Delay Storage Automatic Computer
EGA : Extended Graphic Adopter
ENIAC : Electronic Numerical Integration and Calculator
ENVIS : Environment Information System
EPROM : Erasable Programmable Read Only Memory
ERIC : Educational Resource Information Centre
ERNET : Education and Research Network
ETC : European Translation Centre (Holland)
EUNET : European Network (UK)
FID : International Federation for Information and Documentation
FILA : Federation of Indian Library Association. It was founded in December 1966.
FORTRAN : Formula Translator
GD : Geographical Device
GIS : Geographic Information System
GOC : Good Office Committee
HELLIS : Health Literature Library and Information Service
HRD : Human Resource Development
HRM : Human Resource Management
HRP : Human Resource Planning
HTML : Hyper Text Mark Up language
HTTP : Hyper Text Transfer Protocol
IAEA : International Atomic Energy Agency
IALL : International Association of Law Libraries
IASLIC : Indian Association of Special Libraries and Information Centre
IIB : International Institute of Bibliography. It is known as FID.
IBM : International Business Machine
Ibid: : In research paper, to refer to the immediate previous reference the Ibid term is used.
ICA : Information Centre for Aeronautics
ICAR : Indian Council of Agricultural Research
ICCR : Indian Council for Cultural Relation
ICDM : Information Centre for Development Policy Modelling
ICDR : International Centre for Diarrhoeal Diseases Research
ICHR : Indian Council of Historical Research
ICMR : Indian Council of Medical Research (New Delhi)
ICPR : Indian Council of Philosophical Research
ICs : Integrated Circuits
ICSSR : Indian Council for Social Science Research
IDC : International Documentation Centre
IDRC : International Development Research Centre. It was established in 1976.
IDSA : Institute of Defence Studies and Analysis (New Delhi)
IFD : International Federation for Documentation

IFIS : International Food Information Service
IFLA : International Federation of Library Association and Institution (*Net Exam-2003 D*)
ILA : Indian Library Association. It was established on 1933 at Calcutta.
ILL : Inter Library Loan
ILSA : Indian Library Science Abstract
INPADOC : International Patent Documentation Centre (*Net Exam-2002 J*)
INB : Indian National Bibliography
INFLIBNET : Information & Library Network. It was established on 1988.
INFOTERRA : International Referral System for Environmental Information
INIS : International Nuclear Information System. It was started since 1970.
INSAT : Indian National Satellite
INSDOC : Indian National Scientific Documentation Centre (New Delhi)
IPA : International Publishers Association
IR : Information Retrieval
IRPTC : International Register of Potentially Toxic Chemicals
IRS : Information Retrieval System
IRTC : Industrial Toxicology Research Centre
ISA : Indian Standardisation Association
ISBD : International Standard Bibliographic Description
ISBN : International Standard Book Number
ISDN : Integrated Service Digital Network
ISDS : International Serials Data System
ISI : Indian Standard Institution
ISO : International Organisation for Standardisation
ISONET : International Organisation for Standardisation Network
ISRO : Indian Space Research Organisation (Tumba, Trivandrum)
ISSN : International Standard Serial Number
ITIB : Industrial and Technological Information Bank
JANET : Joint Academy Network
JSTOR : Journal Storage
KGEU : Knowledge Generation Exchange and Utilisation
KIPS : Knowledge Information Processing System
KWIC : Key Word In Context
LA : Library Association
LA (UK) : (The) Library Association of the United Kingdom. It was founded on 1877.
LAA : Library Association of Australia
LAMP : Linux Apache.MySQL Perl (*Net Exam-2013 J*)
LAN : Local Area Network
LC : Library of Congress
LCC : Library of Congress Classification
LCSH : Library of Congress Subject Headings
LIBRIS : Library Information System (Stockholm)
LISA : Library and Information Science Abstract (Bi-Monthly of LA) (*Net Exam-2002 D*)
LISC : Library and Information Science
LIST : Library and Information Science Today
LITA : Library and Information Technology Association (Chicago)
LIU : Local Information Unit
LLA : Local Library Authorities
LLC : Logical Link Control
LOCAS : Local Catalogue Service

LOCIS : Library of Congress Information System
LSA : Library Science Abstract
LSI : Large Scale Integration
LUCI : Logical Unit based Cyclic Index
MALA : Madras Library Association
MALIBNET : Madras Library Network
MANs : Metropolitan Area Networks
MAP : Manufacturing Automation Protocol
MARBI : Machine Readable form of Bibliographic Information
MARC : Machine Readable Catalogue
MARC-21 : Machine readable Catalogue 21 Century
MBO : Management by Objective
MEDLARS : Medical Literature Analysis and Retrieval System
MERLIN : Machine Readable Library Information
METS : Metadata Encoding Transmission Standard (*June-2013*)
MICR : Magnetic Ink Character Recorder
MIDLINET : Midwest Region Library Network
MILNET : Military Network
MIS : Management Information System
MISS : Medical Information Science Section (USA)
MLA : Medical Library Association (USA)
MOL : Mail Order Library
MOS : Metal Oxide Semiconductor
MS : Manuscript
MS-DOS : Microsoft Disk Operating System
MSI : Medium Scale Integration
NAAC : National Assessment and Accreditation council (*Net Exam-2010 J*)
NACILA : National Council of Indian Library Association
NACL : National Advisory Commission on Libraries (USA)
NACO : National Coordinated Cataloguing Operations
NAI : National Archives of India
NAL : National Aeronautical Laboratory
NAL : National Agricultural Library (USA)
NAPC : National Programme for Acquisition and Cataloguing
NASSDOC : National Social Science Documentation Centre. It was established on 1970.
NATIS : National Information System
NBT : National Book Trust
NCCP : National Coordinated Cataloguing Programme
NCL : National Central Library
NCL : National Chemical Laboratory (Pune)
NCSI : National Centre for Science Information (Bangalore)
NIC : National Informatics Centre
NICDAP : National Information Centre for Drug and Pharmaceuticals (Lucknow)
NICFOS : National Information Centre for Food Science (Mysore)
NICHEM : National Information Centre for Chemistry and Chemical Technology
NICLAI : National Information Centre for Leather and Allied Industry
NCLIS : National Commission on Libraries and Information Science
NICMAP : National Information Centre for Machine Tools and Allied Products
NICNET : National Informatic Centre Network
NIFOR : National Information Service
NII : National Institute of Immunology (New Delhi)
NILA : North India Library Association

NISCAIR : National Institute of Science Communication and Information Resources
NIP : National Information Policy
NISIET : National Institute of Small Industry Extension Training (Hyderabad)
NISO : National Information Standard Organisation (USA)
NISS : National Social Science Information System (India)
NISSAT : National Information System for Science and Technology
NLM : National Library of Medicine (USA)
NML : National Medical Library (New Delhi)
NTC : National Translation Centre (Chicago)
NTIS : National Technical Information Service (USA)
NUC : National Union Catalog
NUCSSI : National Union Catalogue of Scientific Serials in India
NYSILL : New York State Inter Library Loan Network
NYT : New York Times
OCLC : (The) On-line Computer Library Centre
OCLC : Ohio College Library Centre
OCR : Optical Character Recognition
OECD : Organisation for Economic Cooperation and Development
OLAS : On-line Acquisition System
OPAC : On-line Public Access Catalogue
OR : Operation Research
OSI : Open System Interconnection
PC : Personal Computer
PCM : Pulse Code Modulation *(Net Exam-2012 D)*
PDNs : Public Data Networks
PDF : Portable Document Format
PERT : Programme Evaluation and Review Technique
PIS : Patents Information System (Nagpur) *(Net Exam-2003 J)*
PLANNER : Promotion of Library Automation and Networking in North-Eastern Region
POPIN : Population Information Network (New York)
POPSI : Postulate based Permutated Subject Indexing
POSDCORB : Planning Organising Staffing Directing Co-ordinating Reporting and Budgeting
POTS : Plain Old Telephone System
PPBS : Planning Programming Budgeting System
PPP : Point to Point Protocol
PRECIS : Preserved Context Indexing System
PROM : Programmable Read Only Memory
PST : Permutes Subject Index
PSTN : Public Switched Telephone Network
PTLA : Publishers Trade List Annual
RAILNET : Computer Network for Railways
RAM : Random Access Memory
RAMP : Records and Archives Management Programme
RDC : Rules for Dictionary Catalogue (of C.A. Cutter)
RDA : Resource Description and Access
RFID : Radio Frequency Identification *(Net Exam-2009 D)*
RIC : Regional Information Centre
RLG : Research Libraries Group
RLIN : Research Library Information Network (USA)
RMDC : Regional Mineral Resource Development Centre
ROM : Read Only Memory
RRRLF : Raja Ram Mohan Roy Library Foundation. It was established on 1972.
RT : Related Terms
SAM : Serial Access Memory
SAMARC : South African Machine Readable Cataloguing

SBDN : Satellite Based Data Network
SC : Subject Classification (J.D. Brown)
SCI : Science Citation Index
SDC : System Development Corporation
SDI : Selective Dissemination of Information
SEAMIC : South-East Asian Medical Information Centre
SENDOC : Small Enterprise National Documentation Centre. It was established on 1971.
SHE : Subject Heading for Engineering
SIRNET : Scientific and Industrial Research Network
SLA : Special Libraries Association
SLIP : Serial Line Internet Protocol
SLSH : Sears List of Subject Headings
SMS : Short Message Service
SNA : Systems Network Architecture (IBM)
SONET : Synchronous Optical Network
SPC : Stored Programme Control
SPIN : Special Interest Network
SSDC : Social Science Documentation Centre (now called NESSDOC)
STC : Short Title Catalogue *(Net Exam-2002 D)*
STSI : Science Technology and Social Information
SWALCAP : South-West Academic Libraries Co-operative Automation Project (UK)
TDNs : Terrestrial Data Networks
TELEX : Tele-printer Exchange
TIB : Technology Information Bank
TIFR : Tata Institute of Fundamental Research (Mumbai)
TIPS : Technology Information Pilot System
TIS : Trade Information Service
TLA : Tripura Library Association
TOP : Technical and Office Protocol
TRC : Technology Research Centre
TTL : Transistor-Transistor Logic
UAP : Universal Availability of Publication
UBC : Universal Bibliographic Control
UDC : Universal Decimal Classification
UGC : University Grant Commission
UIN : User Identification Number
UNESCO : United Nation Educational Scientific and Cultural Organisation
UNISIST : United Nations Information System in Science and Technology
UNIVAC : Universal Automatic Computer
URL : Uniform Resource Locator *(Net Exam-2006 J)*
USB : Universal Serial Bus
UTLAS : University of Toronto Library Automation System
VDU : Visual Display Unit
VGA : Video Graphic Adopter
VLOG : Video (web-)log
VLSI : Very Large Scale Integration
VPN : Virtual Private Network
WADEX : Word and Author Index
WAN : Wide Area Network
WAPIS : Water and Power Information System
WLN : Western Library Network
WIPO : World Intellectual Property Organisation *(Net Exam-2006 D)*
WLIC : World Library and Information Congress
WLSP : World List of Scientific Periodicals
WORM : Write Once Read Many
WP : Word Processing
WPI : World Patents Index
WTI : World Translation Index
WWW : World Wide Web
YAS : Young Adult Service
ZBB : Zero Base Budgeting

Chapter 2
Books and Authors/Editors

Who authored/edited the following:

Q. 1. Write the name of editor of the *Encyclopedia of Librarianship* (Bowes and Bowes, London).

Ans. Thomas Landu.

Q. 2. Who enumerate the Principles of "Right Book to the Right Reader Right Time"?

Ans. Drury.

Q. 3. Who said "Best books for the largest number at the least cost."? (*NET Exam.* 1995)

Ans. Melvil Dewey.

Q. 4. The book entitled *National Library of India: A Critical Study* has been written by (*NET Exam.* 1991)

Ans. B.S. Keshavan.

Q. 5. The book entitled *Little Science Big Science* was written by (*NET Exam.* 1991)

Ans. Deric de Solla Price.

Q. 6. Write the name of book written by R.S. Parkhi making a comparative study of Decimal Classification and Colon Classification, published by Asia Publishing House, New York.

Ans. *Decimal Classification and Colon Classification in Perspective.*

Q. 7. Write the author of *Five Laws of Library Science.*

Ans. Dr. S.R. Ranganathan.

Q. 8. Who has written the following book: *University Library: The Organisation, Administration and Functions of Academic Libraries*"?

Ans. Louis Round Wilson and Maurice F. Tauber.

Q. 9. Name the author of *Organisation of Knowledge in Libraries and Subject Approach to Books.*

Ans. H.E. Bliss.

Q. 10. Who wrote *Grammar of Classification*, 4th Ed., 1955?

Ans. W.C. Berwick Sayers.

Q. 11. Write the name of editors of *Library Science Today: Ranganathan Fesstschrift*, Vols. I, II.

Ans. Vol. I by Prof. P.N. Kaula and Vol. II by A.K. Dasgupta.

Q. 12. Who wrote *A History of Library Association 1877-1977?*

Ans. W.A. Munford.

Q. 13. Write the name of editor of *Making of Librarianship in Pakistan, 1987.*

Ans. Sayed Jalaluddin Haider.

Q. 14. Write the name of the book on Classification written by J. Mills which was first published by Chapman and Hall in 1960.

Ans. *A Modern Outline of Library Classification.*

Q. 15. Write the name of the author of *The Eighteen Editions of the Dewey Decimal Classification*, Albany, N.Y.

Ans. J.P. Comaromi.

Q. 16. Who was the author of *Indian Library Literature: An Annotated Bibliography*?

Ans. Ram Gopal Prasar.

Q. 17. Who wrote *Introduction to Cataloguing and Classification of Books*, 2nd Ed., Chicago, ALA, 1943?

Ans. Margaret Mann.

Q. 18. Write the name of author of *Books that Changed the World* 1956, a book that has been translated into 12 languages and appeared under different titles in revised versions.

Ans. Robert Bingham Downs (1903).

Q. 19. Write the name of the author of *The Theory of Book Selection for Public Libraries*.

Ans. L.R. McColvin.

Q. 20. Who wrote the *Rules for Dictionary Catalogue*?

Ans. C.A. Cutter.

Q. 21. Who wrote *Punjab Library Primer*?

Ans. Asa Don Dickinson.

Q. 22. Who was the editor of *List of Subject Headings for Small Libraries*?

Ans. M.E. Sears.

Q. 23. Who was the author of *Principles of Book Classification*?

Ans. E.W. Humle.

Q. 24. Who was the author of *Manual of Library Classification and Shelf Arrangement*?

Ans. J.D. Brown.

Q. 25. Who wrote *Ranganathan: A Pattern Maker*?

Ans. A.P. Srivastava.

Q. 26. Who wrote *Prolegomena to Library Classification*?

Ans. Dr. S.R. Ranganathan.

Q. 27. Who wrote *Memories of Libraries Including a Handbook of Library Economy*?

Ans. Edward Edwards.

Q. 28. Who is the author of *Studies in Coordinate Indexing*?

Ans. Mortimer Taube.

Q. 29 Who is author of *A Librarian Memories: Portraits and Reflection, 1952*?

Ans. E.A. Savage.

Q. 30. Who said "To provide the right book to the right reader at the right time"?

Ans. Drury in 1930.

Q. 31. Write the McColvin Principles about the Theory of Book Selection.

Ans. Books in themselves are nothing. They have no more meaning than the white paper upon which they are printed, until they are made serviceable by demand. The more closely book selection is related to the demand, the greater is resultant and possible service.

Q. 32. Write the principles of Ranganathan about the books selection.

Ans. First three laws of library science are helpful in formulating the principles of document selection.

Q. 33. Who compiled the *Directory of Periodicals Published in India*?

Ans. Susheel Kumar.

Q. 34. Who published the *Library Development Plan : Thirty Years Programme for India Prepared by Ranganathan*?

Ans. University of Delhi in 1950.

Q. 35. Who wrote the *Living with Book*?

Ans. Haines.

Q. 36. Who wrote *Putting Knowledge to Work*?

Ans. Pauline Atherton.

Q.37 Who wrote *Dictionary of Anonymous and Pseudonymous Literature*?

Ans. S. Halkett and J. Laing.

Q. 38. Who wrote *Computer and Common Sense*?

Ans. Mortimer Taub.

Q. 39. Who wrote *Manual of Library Economy*?

Ans. N.R. Look.

Q. 40. Who said "Where is the Wisdom, We Lost in Knowledge"?

Ans. T.S. Eliot.

Q. 41. Who wrote the Foreword to the first edition of *The Five Laws of Library Science*? *(NET 17 NOV II Paper)*

(a) B.I. Palmer
(b) Henry E. Bliss
(c) P.S. Sivaswamy Aiyer
(d) W.C. Berwick Sayers

Q. 42. Arrange the following publications of S.R. Ranganathan in their year of first publication: *(NET 15D II Paper)*

(i) Reference Service
(ii) Colon Classification
(iii) Five Laws of Library Science
(iv) Prolegomena to Library Classification

Codes:

(a) (iii), (i), (iv), (ii) (b) (i), (ii), (iv), (iii)
(c) (iii), (ii), (iv), (i) (d) (ii), (iii), (iv), (iv)

Q. 43. 'Time and Motion' study was enunciated by ________. *(NET 17J III Paper)*

(a) Edward Evans
(b) Frank and Lillian Gilbreth
(c) Harrington Emerson
(d) G. McGregor

Q. 44. Match the following: *(NET 17J III Paper)*

List – I

(A) Maslow, A
(B) Alderfer, C.P.
(C) Frederick Herzberg
(D) David McClelland

List – II

(i) Two factor theory
(ii) Acquired-needs theory
(iii) ERG Theory
(iv) Hierarchy of needs

Codes:	(A)	(B)	(C)	(D)
(a)	(i)	(iii)	(iv)	(ii)
(b)	(ii)	(iv)	(i)	(iii)
(c)	(iv)	(iii)	(i)	(ii)
(d)	(iii)	(ii)	(iv)	(i)

ANSWER SHEET

41. (c) 42. (c) 43. (b) 44. (c)

Chapter 3
Academic Library

SUBJECTIVE QUESTIONS

Q. 1. Write the various committees and commissions appointed by the U.G.C.

Ans. (i) Library Committee (1957): Chairman Dr. S.R. Ranganathan. Regarding Library grant, purchase of books, cultivating reading habits, facilities for inter-library loan, photocopying, reference and documentation service, etc.

(ii) Review Committee on Library Science (1961): Chairman Dr. S.R. Ranganathan. Regarding standard for teaching, curriculum, qualification of the student for each course, guidelines for conducting examination and lay down minimum standard for passing.

(iii) Education Commission (1964-66): Chairman D.S. Kothari—To evaluate our education system as well as the libraries.

(iv) Mehrotra Committee (1983): Chairman R.C. Mehrotra—To consider the revision of pay scale, career/professional development and service condition of teacher in universities and colleges.

(v) Committee on National Network set up for Universities/Libraries (1988): Chairman Prof. Yash Pal. The Chairman of committee suggested measure for networking of libraries and information centre in universities, information centre, colleges.

(vi) Curriculum Development Committee in Library and Information Science (1990-93): Regarding the Curriculum Development of library science. Members are Prof. P.N. Kaula, Prof. S.G. Mahajan, Prof. A.K. Anand, Dr. P.K. Mahapatra, etc.

Q. 2. What are the important programmes of the UGC for developing Academic Libraries?

Ans. Following are the important programmes of the UGC for developing of the academic libraries:

(i) Wheat Loan Educational Exchange Programme (1951-61).
(ii) Book Banks (1963-64).
(iii) Regional Library Centre (1974).
(iv) National Information Centre and Inter University Centre.
(v) Library buildings.

Q. 3. Where was the first one year Postgraduate Diploma course in Library Sc. started (in India)?

Ans. Madras University in 1937.

Q. 4. Write the name of first person in India to receive Ph.D. Degree in Lib.Sc.

Ans. D.B. Krishna Rao, in 1953 from Delhi University.

Q. 5. Write the name of university in India that changed the Diploma course in library science to Bachelor Degree in Lib.Sc.

Ans. Aligarh Muslim University in 1958.

Q. 6. Name the university, which created the professorship in library science for the first time.

Ans. Goming University, 1886.

Q. 7. When was Dr. S.R. Ranganathan appointed as a National Research Professor of Library Science?

Ans. In 1962.

Q. 8. Write the name of Indian institution offering library and information science education for special library.

Ans. DRTC, Bangalore and INSDOC, New Delhi.

Q. 9. Write the name of first Indian university that started M.Lib.Sc. and M.Phil.

Ans. University of Delhi.

Q. 10. Write the name of institution in India that run courses of B.Lib.Sc. for women candidate only.

Ans. S.N.D.T. Women University, Bombay.

Q. 11. Library education in India was started by two Americans in 1911 and 1915 in the States of Baroda and Punjab. Write the names of the persons.

Ans. W.A. Borden and A.D. Dickinson.

Q. 12. Write the name of publishers of *Journal of Education for Librarianship* (*JEL*)?

Ans. State College, Pennsylvania, USA.

Q. 13. Write the number of students and teachers were there in the first school of Library Science established by Melvil Dewey.

Ans.

Part-time teachers	—	7
Students	—	20
It was started in the year	—	1887

Q. 14. Which commission initially recommended 6% of the total college budget for development of libraries?

Ans. Radhakrishnan Commission.

Q. 15. Who was the chairman of the Raj Commission?

Ans. Professor K.N. Raj.

Q. 16. Which commission recommended 10% of the total college budget for development of libraries?

Ans. Kothari Commission.

Q. 17. Write objectives of a primary school library?

Ans. (a) To create a love for book.

(b) To generate interest in using them for learning.

Q. 18. Who was the chairman of Secondary Education Commission (1952-53)?

Ans. Late Dr. Lakshmana Swamy Mudaliar.

Q. 19. Who was the chairman of UGC library committee report "University and College"?

Ans. Dr. S.R. Ranganathan.

Q. 20. When and why the "Indian University Act" was passed?

Ans. The Indian University Act was passed in 1904 with the objectives that university and college libraries should be well equipped and should have reference libraries to provide an opportunity to the student to form habit of independent.

Q. 21. What were the major recommendations of the University Education Commission (1948)?

Ans. The major recommendations of University Education Commission were:

1. Sanction of 6.25% of the total budget of ₹ 40/- per student as the annual grant for library.
2. Special non-recurring grant once in every five years to strength the collection library should follow open access system, adequate and qualified staff. Twelve working hours a day, etc.

Q. 22. List out the major commissions and committees appointed by the U.G.C. for improvement of university libraries in India.

Ans. The major commissions and committees appointed by the UGC for improvement of university libraries are:

1. The Library Committee (1957)—Dr. S.R. Ranganathan.
2. Review Committee on Library (1961)—Dr. S.R. Ranganathan.
3. Education Commission (1964-66)—Prof. D.S. Kothari.
4. Committee on National Network System for University libraries (1988)—Prof. Yash Pal.
5. Curriculum Development Committee in Library & Information Science Continuing since 1990 (Members).

Q. 23. When was the UGC established in India?

Ans. In India, the UGC was established in December 1953 and made a statutory body in November 1956 by Act of the Parliament to maintain the standard of higher education in India.

Q. 24. What is the aim of Library Committee?

Ans. Its aim is to develop institution of higher learning and strengthen library facilities in universities.

Q. 25. When was the Library Committee submitted its report?

Ans. The Library Committee submitted its report in 1959.

Q. 26. Where is the headquarter of INFLIBNET?

Ans. Ahmedabad (Gujarat).

Q. 27. Write the names of four Regional Centres of INFLIBNET.

Ans. 1. J.L. Nehru University, New Delhi (North)
2. Indian Institute of Science, Bangalore (South)
3. Jadavpur University, Calcutta (East)
4. University of Pune (West).

Q. 28. In which Five-year Plan the INFLIBNET was established?

Ans. In Seventh Five-year Plan.

OBJECTIVE QUESTIONS

1. Among the following, which is not an extension activity in School Libraries? (*NET Exam.* 1999/96)
   (a) Story Telling
   (b) Classification of Books
   (c) Display and Exhibition of Books
   (d) Library Orientation Programme
2. GOC helps libraries in determining (*NET Exam.* 2000)
   (a) Foreign exchange rates
   (b) Name of foreign agents and vendors
   (c) Books available in the market
   (d) Which books to buy
3. Who was awarded first Ph.D. in Library Science by an Indian University? (*NET Exam.* 1991)
   (a) S.R. Ranganathan (b) J.S. Sharma
   (c) D.B. Krishna Rao (d) C.P. Shukla
4. INFLIBNET is a programme sponsored by (*NET Exam.* 1996)
   (a) NISSI
   (b) Planning Commission
   (c) Ministry of Electronics
   (d) UGC
5. GOC stands for (*NET Exam.* 1996)
   (a) Government Office Control
   (b) General Office Correspondence
   (c) Good Office Committee
   (d) Good Office Conduct
6. The book entitled *Documentation and its Facets* is edited by
   (a) Amitabha Chatterjee
   (b) Arunkanti Dasgupta
   (c) Bimalendu Guha
   (d) S.R. Ranganathan
7. Which of the following should be the primary objective of College Library? (*NET Exam.* 1996/1998)
   (a) To promote research activities
   (b) To encourage reading habits
   (c) To support teaching programmers of the college
   (d) To provide for the recreational needs of the student
8. Systematic evaluation of the strengths and weaknesses of an employee, with regard to his/her performance in an organisation is called (*NET Exam.* 1998)
   (a) Job evaluation
   (b) Job analysis
   (c) Performance evaluation
   (d) Performance appraisal
9. The query on "use of audio-visuals in teaching Science at Primary School" can be framed as (*NET Exam.* 1998)
   (a) Audio-visual aids and Science and Primary Schools
   (b) Audio-visual aids or Science or Primary Schools
   (c) Audio-visual aids or Science and Primary Schools
   (d) Audio-visual aids and Science or Primary Schools
10. Who among the following was associated as the pioneer in LIS education in India?
    (a) S.R. Ranganathan (b) W.A. Borden
    (c) J.S. Morgan (d) Melvil Dewey
11. Library orientation, bibliographic instruction and user education are related in the following was (*NET Exam.* 1998)

(a) All mean the same thing
(b) User education is wider and encompasses the other two
(c) Library orientation is wider and encompasses the other two
(d) None of the above

12. According to Education Commission, 1964-66 of university ______ budget should be earmark for its library expenditure. (*NET Exam.* 1994)
(a) 10% (b) 8% (c) 6.5% (d) 6%

13. The UGC has recommended _______ of university budget for expenditure on its Library.
(a) 10% (b) 8% (c) 6.5% (d) 6%

14. The College Library budget is approved by
(a) UGC
(b) Executive Council
(c) Principal of the College
(d) Library Committee

15. In imperial research on the effect of user education on Library "Library use" would be considered
(a) An independent variable
(b) A dependent variable
(c) An intervening variable
(d) Not variable at all

16. The UGC Library Committee has suggested per capita expenditure formula for (*NET Exam.* 1996J)
(a) Purchase of books and other reading materials
(b) Salaries of librarians and other staff
(c) Building maintenance
(d) Periodical Subscription

17. Which of the following network is not primary for academic purposes?
(a) ERNEST (b) JANET
(c) NICNET (d) INFLIBNET

18. Among the following, which is not an extension activity in School Libraries?
(a) Display and exhibition of books
(b) Classification of books
(c) Story telling
(d) Library orientation programme

19. Exhibition of books is related to the extension activities of the library.(*NET Exam.* 1996J)
(a) True (b) False

20. In School Library, which of the following materials would you not expect to find?
(a) Audio-visuals (b) Maps
(c) Magazines (d) Research Reports

21. Parry Committee Report (UK) relates to
(a) Public libraries (b) University
(c) National library (d) Special report

22. The Report of the UGC Library Committee chaired by Dr. S.R. Ranganathan (1959) is known as
(a) Research and Reference Libraries
(b) Public & Special Libraries
(c) College and University
(d) University and College Libraries

23. The Report of the Education Commission (1964-66) entitled Education and National Development discussed the role of the libraries.
(a) Primary Education
(b) Higher Education
(c) Secondary Education
(d) None of the above

24. Secondary School Library fulfils the requirements of students covered in the class
(a) 9 to 10 (b) 6 to 12
(c) 6 to 8 (d) 11 and 12

25. Academic Libraries consist of
(a) School, College, University Libraries
(b) Primary, Secondary, Hr. Secondary School Libraries
(c) Research Libraries
(d) College and University Libraries

26. Twenty per cent of total college budget was recommended for the development of the College Library was
(a) Raj Commission
(b) Kothari Commission
(c) Ranganathan Commission
(d) Chattopadhyay Commission

27. UNISIST is a joint programme of (*NET Exam.* 1997)
(a) UNESCO and FID
(b) UNESCO and IFLA
(c) UNESCO and IMF
(d) UNESCO and ICSU

28. In research on motivation among University Library personnel, if the researcher takes every fifth person from each category of staff

(e.g. Jr. Librarian, Asst. Librarian, Deputy Librarian, etc.), it would be (*NET Exam.* 1997)

(a) A Random Sample
(b) A Stratified Sample
(c) The whole population
(d) Not a representative sample

29. Which of the following statements can be considered as advantages of class libraries in a school? (*NET Exam.* 1996D)
(a) They limit the number of books a child to select from
(b) They increase the number of copies required
(c) They do not require cataloguing and classification
(d) They permit a better irrigation of book into teaching

30. Which of the following organisations is holding seminars and conferences in alternate years?
(a) ILA (b) IATLIS (c) ALA (d) IASLIC

31. UNISIST is (*NET Exam.* 1999J)
(a) A network (b) A programme
(d) An agency (d) A software

32. Match the following:

(A) Decision-making	(1) Teachers
(B) To Pursue academic work	(2) Govt. Official
(C) Pursue their vocation	(3) Student
(D) To impart Education	(4) Professional

(a) A(1), B(2), C(3), D(4)
(b) A(4), B(1), C(2), D(3)
(c) A(3), B(4), C(1), D(2)
(d) A(2), B(3), C(1), D(4)

33. Every book its reader is not UNESCO manifesto.
(a) True (b) False

34. Dr. S.R. Ranganathan was appointed honorary Professor of library science in 1947 at Delhi University.
(a) True (b) False

35. First Ph.D. awarded in Library Science given by University of Delhi to Sri S.R. Ranganathan.
(a) True (b) False

36. S.R. Ranganathan was initially a professor of Lib.Sc.
(a) True (b) False

37. First Delhi University started the M.Lib.Sc. and M.Phil. Course.
(a) True (b) False

38. UGC was founded in the year 1953.
(a) True (b) False

39. In a library which of the following position are line position (*Net Exam.* 2001J)
1. Junior Library Assistant
2. Subject Specialist
3. Deputy Librarian
4. System Librarian

Codes:
(a) 1 and 2 (b) 1 and 3
(c) 1 and 4 (d) 2 and 4

40. A pre-print is a/an (*Net Exam.* 2001D)
(a) Article to be presented in a conference
(b) Conference paper to be included in the proceedings
(c) Neither (a) nor (b)
(d) Both (a) and (b)

41. The report of advisory committee for libraries (1958) is known as (*Net Exam.* 2002J)
(a) Kothari Commission Report
(b) Sinha Committee Report
(c) Rangnathan Committee Report
(d) Radha Krishnan Commission Report

42. Invisible colleges are (*Net Exam.* 2001J)
(a) networks of people interested in the same subject
(b) help in communication
(c) Neither (a) nor (b)
(d) Both (a) and (b)

43. Books of doubtful authorship of authority are (*Net Exam.* 2002J)
(a) Rare books (b) Unknown works
(c) Extinct books (d) Apocryphal books

44. Which type of document a book is? (*Net Exam.* 2002J)
(a) Meta document
(b) Macro document
(c) Micro document
(d) Serialised document

45. Among the following, which is not an extension activity in School Library? (*Net Exam.* 2004J, 2001J)
(a) Story telling
(b) Classification of books

(c) Library orientation programme
(d) Display and extension of books

46. "Resource" in terms of Library & Information Science is
(a) it encompasses the print and non-print materials
(b) it is used to designate any or all of the materials, functions services and the expertise of professional and non-professional staff
(c) it implies a thing, a person or an action to which one turn for aid and help in time of need
(d) None of the above

47. Sharing in terms of Library & Information Science is (*Net Exam.* 2004J)
(a) apportioning, allotting or contributing some things that is owned to benefit others
(b) partnership for mutual benefits
(c) Both of above
(d) None of above

48. When a library or information centre provides documents from its own resources or from other sources, it is known as (*Net Exam.* 2004J)
(a) Document Delivery Services
(b) Inter-library Loan
(c) Reprography Service
(d) Reference Service

49. "Book Week" in India celebrated every year in the month of (*Net Exam.* 2003J)
(a) September (b) October
(c) November (d) December

50. Inter University Centre for Astronomy and Astrophysics is located at(*Net Exam.* 2003J)
(a) Pune University, Pune
(b) University of Delhi, Delhi
(c) JNU, Delhi
(d) Devi Ahilya University, Indore

51. A college library differs from a university library in India in which way
(a) it has fewer research materials
(b) it is usually smaller than the University library
(c) Both (a) and (b)
(d) None of the above

52. The resource sharing strategy of a library may not included (*Net Exam.* 2001J)
(a) Joint acquisition
(b) Shared use
(c) Exchange of materials
(d) Restricted access

53. The "specialized services" of a University Library is/are (*Net Exam.* 2002D)
(a) User education and user orientation seminars
(b) Special lectures and demonstration of new services
(c) Exhibition and special displays
(d) All of the above

54. UGC Library Committee suggest how many percentage of Library budget should be spent on book? (*Net Exam.* 2002D)
(a) 10% (b) 20% (c) 25% (d) 30%

55. Match the following (*Net Exam.* 2004J)

Column A	Column B
(A) Radhakrishnan Committee	1. 1979
(B) Mudaliar Commission	2. 1964
(C) Kothari Commission	3. 1952-53
(D) K.S. University Review	4. 1948

Codes:	A	B	C	D
(a)	4	3	2	1
(b)	4	2	3	1
(c)	1	2	3	4
(d)	2	1	3	4

56. Library Technology Reports is a publication of (*Net Exam.* 2004J)
(a) ILA (b) ALA (c) SLA (d) IATLIS

57. NICNET was designed by (*Net Exam.* 2004J)
(a) IIT, New Delhi
(b) National Informatics Centre
(c) NISCAIR
(d) Indian Library Association

58. Academic library consists of (*Net Exam.* 2003D)
1. College libraries 2. University libraries
3. School libraries 4. Research libraries

Codes:
(a) All the four (b) 1 and 2
(c) 2 and 3 (d) Alone 1

59. The concept of "Resource Sharing" started in 1955 because (*Net Exam.* 2003D)
1. Inadequate library budget
2. Increasing cost of books
3. Subscription of periodical

Codes:
(a) 1 and 2 (b) 2 and 3
(c) All the three (d) 1 only

60. Library Resource can be categorized into (*Net Exam.* 2003D)
1. Personnel and Material
2. Function and Services
3. Personnel and Books
4. Staff and Services

Codes:
(a) 1 and 2 (b) 3 and 4
(c) 1 and 3 (d) 2 and 4

61. The Library Cooperation in modern times is helpful for (*Net Exam.* 2003D)
1. Acquiring books
2. Recording books
3. Making books available storing books
4. Existing document profiles are matched with interest profile

Codes:
(a) 1 and 2 (b) 1 and 4
(c) 2 and 3 (d) 1, 2 and 3

62. Which of the following Central Universities does not provide Ph.D degree in Library and Information Science in India (*Net Exam.* 2003D)
(a) JNU, New Delhi
(b) University of Delhi
(c) IGNOU, New Delhi
(d) Jamia Hamdard University, New Delhi

63. Inter-University Consortium for Educational Communication is situated at (*Net Exam.* 2003D)
(a) Poona University, Poona
(b) JNU, New Delhi
(c) Anna University, Chennai
(d) Kota University, Rajasthan

64. Extension services to blind person comes under the purview of which law of Library Science? (*Net Exam.* 2003D)
(a) First and second laws
(b) All the five laws
(c) Third law
(d) Second law and fifth law

65. User studies are conducted in order to know (*Net Exam.* 2003D)
1. information requirements of the user
2. materials requirements of the users
3. financial requirements of the user

Codes:
(a) 1 only (b) 2 only
(c) 3 only (d) 1, 2 and 3

66. In India, the standardization of the conversion rates for buying foreign books is done by (*Net Exam.* 2003D)
(a) Publisher Forum
(b) Library Association
(c) Good Office Committee
(d) Book Seller Organization

67. In a Bibliographic database, the data elements to be specified is/are (*Net Exam.* 2003D)
(1) a numerical identifier called tag
(2) a descriptive name
(3) the maximum length
(4) an indicator for the repeatability of a field

Codes:
(a) 1 and 4 (b) 2 and 3
(c) All the four (d) 2, 3 and 4

68. The main function of the College Library is/are (*Net Exam.* 2004D)
1. Providing adequate and comfortable physical facilities for study
2. Giving student a wider and deeper understanding of various subjects
3. Training of young persons for various professions like law, medicine, engineering and technology

Codes:
(a) All the three (b) 1 and 3
(c) 1 and 2 (d) 1 only

69. **Assertion (A):** Several methods can be devised for assisting librarian to keep abreast of development in his field to maintain efficiency.

Reason (R): Seminars, conferences, workshops can solve the purpose.

Codes:
(a) Both (A) and (R) are true but (R) is not the correct explanation of (A)
(b) Both (A) and (R) are true and (R) is the correct explanation of (A)
(c) (A) is true but (R) is false
(d) (A) is false but (R) is true

70. Match the following: (*Net Exam.* 2005J)
List-I: Types of users of information
I. Student
II. Professionals
III. Government Officials

IV. Teachers

List-II: Purpose of use of information

(A) Decision making
(B) To impart knowledge
(C) To prepare for the course programme
(D) To pursue their respective vocation

Codes:

(a) I-C, II-D, III-A, IV-B
(b) I-D, II-A, III-B, IV-C
(c) I-C, II-C, III-D, IV-A
(d) I-B, II-B, III-C, IV-D

71. Annual convention of INFLIBNET organized to discuss progress of the library automation and library services is known as (*Net Exam.* 2005J)
(a) ISCON (b) NACLIN
(c) CALIBER (d) INFONET

72. **Assertion (A):** Training programme for library and information professionals can be developed on the lines of proportional education and continuing education.

Reason (R): Continuing education programme must take care of information demands of clientele of the parent organization from time to time. (*Net Exam.* 2007J)

Codes:

(a) Both (A) and (R) are true, but (R) is not the correct explanation of (A)
(b) Both (A) and (R) are false
(c) (A) is false and (R) is true
(d) (A) is true and (R) is false

73. CALIBER is sponsored by (*Net Exam.* 2007J)
(a) INFLIBNET (b) DELNET
(c) AGRINET (d) CALIBNET

74. Which of the following is correctly matched? (*Net Exam.* 2004D)
(a) Mehrotra Committee (1983)—Recruitment procedure and revision of pay scale
(b) C.D. Committee (1993)—Revision of eligibility of appointment of librarian in college
(c) Review Committee on LIS (1961)—Salaries of the staff
(d) Punnayya Committee (1994)—Starting of library cess

75. The UGC Library Committee has suggested per capita expenditure formula for (*Net Exam.* 2004D)
(a) Purchase of books and other reading materials
(b) Periodical subscription
(c) Building maintenance
(d) Salaries of all staff

76. Who is the first emeritus fellow professor of Library and Information Science appointed by University Grant Commission? (*Net Exam.* 2004D, 2002D)
(a) S.R. Ranganathan (b) P.N. Kaula
(c) P.B. Mangla (d) B.S. Keshvan

77. Which honour was awarded to Dr. Ranganathan in recognition of his contributions to Librarianship and Library Services? (*Net Exam.* 2004D)
(a) Nobel Prize (b) Padama Bhusan
(c) Padama Shree (d) Gyanpith Award

78. The first person to get Ph.D. in Library and Information Science from University of Delhi in 1957 was (*Net Exam.* 2005D)
(a) D.B. Krishna Rao (b) S. Satyamurthi
(c) M.L. Khanna (d) Dew Dickenson

79. In which university, Dickinson, an American was appointment for the first time as University Librarian? (*Net Exam.* 2005D)
(a) AMU, Aligrah
(b) University of Delhi
(c) BHU, Varanasi
(d) Punjab University, Chandigarh

80. In which of the following organization is/are promoting user education in India? (*Net Exam.* 2005D)
1. NISCAIR, New Delhi 2. DRTC, Banglore
3. BIS, New Delhi 4. IARI, New Delhi
(a) 1 and 2 (b) 1, 2 and 3
(c) 4 only (d) 1 only

81. Who proposed the Information and Library Network (INFLIBNET)? (*Net Exam.* 2005D)
(a) Prof. V.S. Jha (b) Prof. R. Pandey
(c) Prof. Yash Pal (d) Prof. R. Shaw

82. National Commission on Libraries and Information Science (NCLIS) is located at (*Net Exam.* 2005D)
(a) USA (b) UK (c) India (d) UAE

83. Book Bank Scheme of University Grant Commission was introduced in the year (*Net Exam.* 2005D)

(a) 1965-66 (b) 1961-62
(c) 1963-64 (d) 1951-52

84. Directories of Special and Research Libraries in India is published by (*Net Exam.* 2005D)
(a) IASLIC (b) NISCAIR
(c) SENDOC (d) LESTEC

85. How many books/thousand is an accepted practice to write off the lost books in a library? (*Net Exam.* 2005D)
(a) 10 (b) 6 (c) 8 (d) 4

86. Match the following (*Net Exam.* 2005D)
Column A
(A) First School of Librarianship of Dewey
(B) Establishment of UNESCO
(C) Establishment of RRRLF
(D) Inauguration of DRTC
Column B
1. Jan. 5, 1887 2. Nov. 4, 1946
3. May 22, 1972 4. Aug. 18, 1962

Codes:	A	B	C	D
(a)	2	1	4	3
(b)	1	2	4	3
(c)	4	3	2	1
(d)	1	2	3	4

87. Curriculum Development Committee on Library and Information Science has been constituted by (*Net Exam.* 2006J)
(a) University Grant Commission
(b) University of Delhi
(c) Ministry of Science and Technology
(d) National Institute of Scientific Communication and Information Resources

88. Grey Literature means
(a) The literature published by a publisher named as "Grey Publisher"
(b) The literature which is not published and is not available through normal book selling channels
(c) The literature published and made available in Grey Shades
(d) The literature which is published and made available through special publishers

89. Match the following (*Net Exam.* 2006D)
List-I
(A) Kothari Commission
(B) Radhakrishnan Commission
(C) Mehrotra Commission
(D) Fyzee Commission
List-II
(i) Status and pay scale of librarian
(ii) Public Library System
(iii) Library budget as a percentage of organization budget
(iv) Importance of library in Academic Institutions
(v) Special Libraries

Codes:	A	B	C	D
(a)	iii	i	v	ii
(b)	iii	iv	i	ii
(c)	ii	iii	i	v
(d)	iv	iii	ii	i

90. Orientation of library users is a kind of (*Net Exam.* 2006D)
(a) Reference Services
(b) Referral Services
(c) Current Awareness Services
(d) Selective Dissemination of Information Services

91. The first All India Conference of Librarians in 1918 held at (*Net Exam.* 2006J)
(a) Baroda (b) Calcutta
(c) Madras (d) Lahore

92. Match the following (*Net Exam.* 2001J)

List-I	List-II
(A) OCLC	(i) City
(B) INFLIBNET	(ii) International
(C) CALIBNET	(iii) Regional
(D) ASTINFO	(iv) National

Codes:	A	B	C	D
(a)	ii	i	iv	iii
(b)	ii	iv	i	iii
(c)	iii	ii	iv	i
(d)	iii	i	ii	iv

93. **Assertion (A):** Copyright Act safeguards the interest of the author.
Reason (R): This act is essential to maximize the circulation of documents.
Codes:
(a) Both (A) and (R) are true and (R) is the correct explanation
(b) Both (A) and (R) are true but (R) is not the correct explanation
(c) (A) is true (R) is false
(d) (A) is false but (R) is true

94. Match the following: (*Net Exam.* 2007D)

List - I
(A) Fyzee Committee
(B) Knowledge Commission
(C) Mehrotra Committee
(D) Kothari Commission
List - II
(i) Library budget
(ii) Status and pay scale of librarian
(iii) Public libraries
(iv) Knowledge society
(v) Importance of library in academic institutions

Codes:	**A**	**B**	**C**	**D**
(a)	i	iv	iii	v
(b)	iv	ii	v	iii
(c)	v	ii	iv	iii
(d)	iii	iv	ii	i

95. The "Wheat Loan Educational Exchange Programme" was initiated in (*Net Exam.* 2007D)
(a) 1951 (b) 1972 (c) 1981 (d) 1999

96. Who is the Chairman of National Knowledge Commission? (*Net Exam.* 2011D, 2008J, 2008D)
(a) Dr. Sukhadeo Thorat
(b) Dr. M.S. Swaminathan
(c) Dr. Bhalchandra Mungekar
(d) Sam Pitrodaa

97. Match the following: (*Net Exam.* 2008J)

List-I	**List-II**
(A) Library is a people's University	(i) Kothari
(B) Library is a growing organization	(ii) Urquart
(C) Library can be useful to society	(iii) Rangnathan
(D) Library is the heart of the University	(iv) Sayajirao Gaekwad

Codes:	**A**	**B**	**C**	**D**
(a)	iv	iii	ii	i
(b)	iv	i	iii	ii
(c)	ii	iv	iii	i
(d)	iv	ii	i	iii

98. Match the following:

List-I	**List-II**
(A) P. Wassermann	(i) Line of thinking
(B) P. Atherton	(ii) Foundation of education for librarianship
(C) J.H. Shera	(iii) New librarianship
(D) Maurice B. Line	(iv) Putting knowledge work

Codes:	**A**	**B**	**C**	**D**
(a)	iv	iii	ii	i
(b)	iv	i	iii	ii
(c)	ii	iv	iii	i
(d)	iii	iv	ii	i

99. Which university appointed the first full-time university librarian? (*Net Exam.* 2008D)
(a) Delhi University (b) Punjab University
(c) Madras University (d) Calcutta University

100. Who categorized the user studies into the following three categories?
(i) Behaviour studies (ii) User studies
(iii) Information flow studies
(a) Maurice B. Line (b) Menzel
(c) Cronin (d) Voigt

101. Arrange the following in chronological order (*NET Exam.* 2011J)
(i) Fayzee Committee
(ii) K.P. Sinha Committee
(iii) Chattopadhya Committee
(iv) Radhakrishnan Committee
Codes:
(a) i, ii, iii, iv (b) iv, iii, i, ii
(c) i, iv, ii, iii (d) iii, i, ii, iv

102. Resource sharing among libraries was promoted by the factors (*Net Exam.* 2010J)
(a) Price escalation
(b) Information explosion
(c) Both (a) and (b)
(d) None of the above

103. Match the following: (*Net Exam.* 2007J)
List-I
(A) B.S. Kesavan (B) W.C.B. Sayers
(C) C.A. Cutter (D) J.D. Brown
List-II
(i) Cataloguing rules
(ii) National library
(iii) School of librarianship
(iv) List of subject heading
(v) Subject classification

Codes:	**A**	**B**	**C**	**D**
(a)	ii	i	iv	iii
(b)	ii	iv	i	iii
(c)	iii	ii	iv	i
(d)	iii	i	ii	iv

104. Information Literacy Competency Standard for Higher Education is prepared by (*Net Exam.* 2013J)
(a) AASL (b) IFLA (c) SCONUL (d) ACRL

105. Which of the following activities are supported by UGC? (*Net Exam.* 2013J)
(i) Facilitating increased access to information
(ii) Monitoring the implementation of revised curriculum
(iii) Making policies for human resource development
(iv) Funding all academic libraries
Codes:
(a) i and ii are correct
(b) i and iii are correct
(c) ii and iii are correct
(d) i and iv are correct

106. Which committee/commission recommended that Imperial Library be designated as Copyright Library? (*Net Exam.* 2013J)
(a) Fayzee Commission, 1939
(b) Riche Committee, 1926
(c) Satham Committee, 1932
(d) Sadler Committee, 1916

107. Indian National Advisory Board for Libraries was setup in 1966 by (*Net Exam.* 2013J)
(a) Association of Indian Universities
(b) Ministry of Education
(c) Planning Commission
(d) University Grant Commission

108. Which of the following methods are suitable to achieve quality of teaching, learning in LIS? (*Net Exam.* 2013J)
(i) Research-led teaching
(ii) State-of-the-art computer lab
(iii) Problem-based learning
(iv) Introducing the course at degree level
Codes:
(a) ii and iv (b) i, iii and iv
(c) i and iii (d) iii and iv

109. **Assertion (A):** Library Science profession in India enjoys the status at par with medical, legal and management professions.
Reason (R): S.R. Ranganthan's contributions and teachings for Indian librarianship secured a status to the profession.
Codes:
(a) (A) is true, but (R) is false
(b) (A) is false, but (R) is true
(c) Both (A) and (R) are true
(d) Both (A) and (R) are false

110. **Assertion (A):** The encouraging environment of all time, full reading halls with the students in the libraries is diminishing day by day.
Reason (R): All the reading materials is easily available and accessible on Internet to all the students. (*Net Exam.* 2013J)
Codes:
(a) Both (A) and (R) are true
(b) Both (A) and (R) are false
(c) (A) is true, (R) is false
(d) (A) is false, but (R) is true

111. Match the following: (*Net Exam.* 2013J)
List-I
(A) Sinha Committee
(B) Dr. S.R. Ranganathan Committee
(C) Report of Dr. Shaw and Dr. D.B. Krishna Rao
(D) Dr. J. Bhore Committee
List-II
(i) Library Staff Strength
(ii) Central Medical Library
(iii) Libraries at Panchayat, Block, District and State level
(iv) National Agriculture System of Agriculture Libraries

Codes:	A	B	C	D
(a)	iii	i	ii	iv
(b)	iv	iii	ii	i
(c)	iii	i	iv	ii
(d)	i	iii	ii	iv

112. Match the following: (*Net Exam.* 2013J)
List-I
(A) Public Library Extension
(B) Academic Library Management
(C) University Libraries for Developing Countries
(D) Planning Academic and Research Library Building
List-II
(i) K.D. Metcalf (ii) M.A. Gelfand
(iii) L.R. McColvin (iv) M.B. Line

Codes:	A	B	C	D
(a)	iii	iv	ii	i
(b)	iv	ii	i	iii
(c)	iii	i	iv	ii
(d)	ii	iii	i	iv

113. **Assertion (A):** LIS education is not uniform throughout India.

Reason (R): Adoption of UGC model syllabus is not mandatory, local LIS requirements vary. (*Net Exam.* 2012J, iii paper)

Codes:

(a) (A) is true, but (R) is false
(b) (A) is false, but (R) is true
(c) Both (A) and (R) are true
(d) Both (A) and (R) are false

114. **Assertion (A):** Collection of audio materials is less used in Academic Libraries.

Reason (R): People consider these materials intellectually less sound and fit only for recreation purpose. (*Net Exam.* 2012J, iii paper)

Codes:

(a) (A) is false but (R) is true
(b) (A) is true, but (R) is false
(c) (A) is true and (R) is partially true
(d) Both (A) and (R) are false

115. Where the first M.Phil. programme in Library and Information Science was started in India (*Net Exam.* 2012J, iii paper)

(a) University of Madras
(b) University of Delhi
(c) University of Mysore
(d) University of Bombay

116. **Assertion (A):** Maximizing the access to information in higher education is the motto of UGC-INFONET.

Reason (R): The financial grants of UGC-INFONET are not being fully utilized by all University Libraries for the assigned purpose.

Codes:

(a) Both (A) and (R) are false
(b) (A) is true and (R) is partially true
(c) (A) is true and (R) is false
(d) (A) is false and (R) is true

117. Which of the following statements can be considered as advantage of class libraries in a school? (*Net Exam.* 2003J)

(a) They limit the number of books a child to select from
(b) They increase the number of copies required
(c) They do not require cataloguing and classification
(d) They permit a better integration of books into teaching

118. **Assertion (A):** There is a tremendous increase in number of doctoral degree being awarded in library and information science.

Reason (R): Any academician in LIS holding a Ph.D. degree is entitled to supervise research program. (*Net Exam.* 2013J)

Codes:

(a) (A) is true and (R) is partially true
(b) Both (A) and (R) are true
(c) Both (A) and (R) are false
(d) (A) is false and (R) is true

119. **Assertion (A):** No single library connect all the demands of the users.

Reason (R): Resource sharing is the need of the day. (*Net Exam.* 2006J)

Codes:

(a) Both (A) and (R) are false
(b) Both (A) and (R) are correct
(c) (A) is false, but (R) is true
(d) (R) is false, but (A) is true

120. The first library science school in the world was started (*Net Exam.* 2006J)

(i) By Melvil Dewey
(ii) At Columbia University, New York (USA)
(iii) By W.C. Berwick Sayers
(iv) At London University, London (UK)

Codes:

(a) i and ii are correct
(b) i and iv are correct
(c) ii and iii are correct
(d) iii and iv are correct

121. The resource sharing strategy of a library does not include (*Net Exam.* 2002J)

(a) Join acquisition (b) Shared use
(c) Exchange of material (d) Restricted access

122. On the basis of user approach to information, it can be categorized into (*Net Exam.* 2002D)

(a) Potential, Expected, Actual and Beneficiary Users
(b) Potential and Beneficiary Users
(c) Potential, Expected, Technologist and Working Users
(d) Scholars, Researchers and Students

123. One of the methods for conducting user studies is (*Net Exam.* 2002D)

(a) Citation Analysis (b) Per Capita Method
(c) Statistical Method (d) Research Design

124. Indirect methods of user education include (*Net Exam.* 2005D)
   1. Library guides and Documentation list
   2. Display List
   3. Questionnaire and Diary
   4. Computer feedback

   Codes:
   (a) 3 only (b) 4 only
   (c) 1 and 2 (d) 3 and 4

125. Which Britisher approved the Library Science Education firstly in India? (*Net Exam.* 2005D)
   (a) Lord Macaulay (b) Sir Morris Gayer
   (c) Sir Richard Morrison (d) Lord Irwin

126. NALANDA is a database of Libraries, contains (*Net Exam.* 2003J)
   1. Academic Libraries 2. Public Libraries
   3. Special Libraries 4. Parliament Libraries

   Codes:
   (a) 1 and 2 (b) 1, 2 and 3
   (c) 2 and 3 (d) 4 only

127. Arrange the following University Libraries according to the year of their establishment: (*NET-2013D ii paper*)
   (i) Madras University Library
   (ii) Delhi University Library
   (iii) Calcutta University Library
   (iv) Bombay University Library

   Codes:
   (a) (iv) (ii) (iii) (i) (b) (ii) (i) (iv) (iii)
   (c) (i) (iii) (ii) (iv) (d) (iii) (iv) (i) (ii)

128. Who is responsible for development and maintenance of UGC official website? (*NET 17 NOV iii paper*)
   (a) MHRD (b) Do E
   (c) NIC (d) INFLIBNET

129. Which of the following are the open access initiatives of INFLIBNET? (*NET 17 NOV iii paper*)
   (i) Shodhganga (ii) e-Shodh Sindhu
   (iii) Infoport (iv) IndCat

   Codes:
   (a) (i) and (ii) are correct
   (b) (ii) and (iii) are correct
   (c) (iii) and (iv) are correct
   (d) (i) and (iii) are correct

130. Match the following consortiums with their corresponding locations: (*NET 17 NOV iii paper*)

   List – I
   (A) UGC-DAE Consortium
   (B) ERMED-India Consortium
   (C) DeLCON-DBT's E-Library
   (D) e-Shodh Sindhu

   List – II
   (1) Manesar (Gurgaon)
   (2) Gandhinagar (Ahmedabad)
   (3) Indore Consortium
   (4) New Delhi

Codes:	**(A)**	**(B)**	**(C)**	**(D)**
(a)	(3)	(4)	(1)	(2)
(b)	(4)	(3)	(2)	(1)
(c)	(1)	(2)	(3)	(4)
(d)	(2)	(1)	(4)	(3)

131. **Assertion (A):** The copyright system, born and bred for print technology, faces a technological revolution in its environment.

   Reason (R): The old print technology's broadcast model of one to many communication is replaced with many to many global connectivity. (*NET 17 NOV iii paper*)

   Codes:
   (a) (A) is true, but (R) is false.
   (b) (A) is false, but (R) is true.
   (c) Both (A) and (R) are true.
   (d) Both (A) and (R) are false.

132. Identify the resource sharing and document delivery principles as given by IFLA. (*NET 17 NOV iii paper*)
   (i) Each country should accept responsibility for providing access to its own publications to any other country.
   (ii) Supplying libraries should accept requests submitted in hardcopy only.
   (iii) From the moment a library dispatches an item to a requesting library until it returns the supplying library is responsible for any loss or damage incurred.
   (iv) Each country should aim to develop an efficient national resource sharing system.

   Codes:
   (a) (i) and (ii) are correct.
   (b) (ii) and (iii) are correct.
   (c) (i) and (iv) are correct.
   (d) (ii) and (iv) are correct.

133. Which of the following is the first book authored by S.R. Ranganathan? (*NET 16J iii paper*)

(a) Library Manual
(b) Five laws of Library Science
(c) Prolegomena to Library Classification
(d) Colon Classification

134. Which among the following is free Audio Book Site? *(NET 16J iii paper)*
(a) Ebrary (b) Virtua
(c) Google Books (d) Librivox

135. Identify the popular modes of staff development practised in libraries: *(NET 16J iii paper)*
i. Planned rotation
ii. Deputing staff to conferences and seminars
iii. Sponsoring for refresher courses
iv. Making them members of other libraries
Codes:
(a) i, ii, iii are correct.
(b) ii, iii, iv are correct.
(c) i, ii, iv are correct.
(d) i, iii, iv are correct.

136. Arrange the following committees/ commissions in ascending order: *(NET 16J iii paper)*
i. Kothari Commission
ii. Radhakrishnan Commission
iii. K.P. Sinha Committee
iv. Ranganathan Committee
Codes:
(a) i, ii, iv, iii (b) ii, iv, iii, i
(c) iv, ii, i, iii (d) iii, i, ii, iv

137. Match the following:

List – I	List – II
(A) Counter	(1) Article metric
(B) PLoS ALMs	(2) Author metric
(C) ORC ID	(3) All metric
(D) Social Media	(4) Journal metric citations

Codes:	(A)	(B)	(C)	(D)
(a)	(3)	(4)	(1)	(2)
(b)	(4)	(1)	(2)	(3)
(c)	(2)	(4)	(3)	(1)
(d)	(1)	(4)	(2)	(3)

138. From which universities S.R. Ranganathan was awarded D. Litt (Honoris Causa)? *(NET 17 NOV ii paper)*
(i) University of Delhi
(ii) University of Madras
(iii) University of London
(iv) University of Pittsburgh
Codes:
(a) (i) and (ii) are correct
(b) (i) and (iii) are correct
(c) (ii) and (iii) are correct
(d) (i) and (iv) are correct

139. **Assertion (A):** Extending the library's reach through strategic partnership, collaborative relationship is an important goal for any academic library.
Reason (R): Partnerships do not allow participating organisations to yield efficiency. *(NET 17 NOV iii paper)*
Codes:
(a) (A) is true, but (R) is false.
(b) (A) is false, but (R) is true.
(c) Both (A) and (R) are true.
(d) Both (A) and (R) are false

140. Sarda Ranganathan chair in Library Science was announced in 1957 at the centenary celebration of *(NET 15J iii paper)*
(a) University of Delhi
(b) University of Madras
(c) University of Bombay
(d) Banaras Hindu University

141. The arithmetic mean is the most commonly used statistical mean to measure: *(NET 15J iii paper)*
(i) Average
(ii) Central tendency of data
(iii) Sum of data points
(iv) Nature of distribution of data
Codes:
(a) (i) and (iii) are correct
(b) (i) and (ii) are correct
(c) (iii) and (iv) are correct
(d) (ii) and (iv) are correct

142. Arrange the following codes of ethics in the order of their development: *(NET 15J iii paper)*
(i) Librarian's Canons of Ethics, First code of ethics for Librarianship in USA.
(ii) Code of Ethics - ALA.
(iii) Code of Professional Conduct - LA, UK
(iv) Code of Ethics for Librarians and Information workers - IFLA
Codes:
(a) (i), (ii), (iii), (iv) (b) (ii), (i), (iii), (iv)
(c) (iv), (ii), (i), (iii) (d) (iii), (i), (ii), (iv)

143. Arrange in chronological order the following initiatives of the UGC for the Development of academic Libraries in India: *(NET 15J iii paper)*

(i) Sponsor of National Information Centres
(ii) Matching Grants for College Libraries
(iii) Appointment of Library Committee on 'University and College Libraries' (Chairman: S.R. Ranganathan)
(iv) Establishment of Information and Library Network (INFLIBNET)

Codes:
(a) iii, ii, i, iv (b) ii, i, iii, iv
(c) iii, i, ii, iv (d) iv, ii, i, iii

144. The service that helps the students to acquire soft skills, writing skills and job-oriented skills is *(NET 14D ii paper)*
(a) Reader's advisory (b) Career guidance
(c) Referral service (d) User education

145. Which of the following concepts are associated with professional ethics? *(NET 14D ii paper)*
(i) Accountability
(ii) Unique training
(iii) High quality service
(iv) Professional independence

Codes:
(a) (i), (ii), (iii) are correct.
(b) (i), (iii) are correct.
(c) (i), (ii), (iv) are correct.
(d) (iii), (iv) are correct

146. Name the Indian Librarian who was honored with the title of 'Khan Bahadur' in 1935 by the British Government?*(NET 15J ii paper)*
(a) S.R. Ranganathan (b) B.S. Kesavan
(c) K.M. Asadullak (d) K. Issac

147. NALANDA, the digital library is an initiation of: *(NET 15J ii paper)*
(a) DRTC
(b) IISC Bangalore
(c) National Institute of Technology, Calicut
(d) NISCAIR

148. Match the following: *(NET 13D ii paper)*
List – I
A. User Education
B. Conservative, Liberal and Moderate Theory of Reference Service
C. Minimum, Middling and Maximum Theories of Reference Service
D. Guide to Reference Book

List – II
1. James I. Wyer 2. Patricia B. Knapp
3. Eugene P. Sheehy 4. Samuel Rothstein

Codes:	A	B	C	D
(a)	2	1	4	3
(b)	1	2	4	3
(c)	3	2	4	1
(d)	4	3	1	2

149. Match the following: *(NET 13D ii paper)*
List – I
(A) Curriculum Development Committee (P.N. Kaula)
(B) Curriculum Development Committee (C.R. Karrisidappa)
(C) Working Group on Libraries
(D) Library Movement in Baroda

List – II
1. 2001 2. 1992 3. 1910 4. 1964

Codes:	A	B	C	D
(a)	2	1	4	3
(b)	1	2	4	3
(c)	4	2	3	1
(d)	3	4	2	1

150. **Assertion (A):** Majority of University Libraries in India are not fully automated.
Reason (R): University Libraries in India are meddling with automation of circulation activities. *(NET Dec. 2013 iii paper)*

Codes:
(a) (A) is true but (R) is false.
(b) (A) is false but (R) is true.
(c) Both (A) and (R) are true.
(d) Both (A) and (R) are false.

151. **Assertion (A):** Majority of academic libraries in India are lagging behind in switching over as technology-oriented service institutions. *(NET 2014J ii paper)*
Reason (R): The apex academic bodies and library Associations have not taken the lead role to devise standards and policies.

Codes:
(a) (A) is true, (R) is false.
(b) (A) is false, (R) is true.
(c) Both (A) and (R) is true.
(d) Both (A) and (R) are false.

152. Damodaran Committee was appointed in 1971 to review working of *(NET 2014J iii paper)*

(a) Medical College Libraries
(b) National Science Libraries
(c) Agriculture Libraries
(d) Polytechnic Libraries

153. Joseph W. Lippincott Award is presented to the librarians for (*NET 2014J iii paper*)
(a) promoting love for books and reading.
(b) advanced study in the field of children's library.
(c) achievements in classification and cataloguing.
(d) outstanding participation in professional library associations.

154. EUAL stands for (*NET 2014J iii paper*)
(a) E-monitoring library for Academics
(b) End User Logistics Association
(c) Electronic Usage of Library Acquisitions
(d) End User License Agreement

155. WIPO Academy deals with (*NET 2014J iii paper*)
(a) Patent Cooperation Treaty
(b) Courses on Intellectual Property
(c) Trademarks Gateway
(d) All of the above

156. Which Education Commission observed "Nothing can be more damaging to a growing department than to neglect its library or give it a low priority"?
(a) Kothari Education Commission
(b) Radhakrishnan Education Commission
(c) Calcutta University Commission
(d) Mudaliar Commission on Secondary Education

157. Which of the following are direct methods of user study? (*NET 2014J iii paper*)
i. Reading habits ii. Analysis of library records
iii. Service preferencesiv. User needs
Codes:
(a) ii & iii (b) ii & iv
(c) i & iv (d) iii & iv

158. Arrange in sequence the following committees workshop in order of their year of constitution: (*NET 2014J iii paper*)
i. UGC Committee for Development of University and College Libraries (S.R. Ranganathan)
ii. UGC Committee on National Network System for University Libraries (Dr. Yashpal)
iii. UGC Review Committee on Library Science (S.R. Ranganathan)
iv. UGC Workshop on Standards for College Libraries
Codes:
(a) iii, iv, i, ii (b) iii, ii, i, iv
(c) i, iii, iv, ii (d) i, ii, iv, iii

159. **Assertion (A):** UGC has devised performance indicators for the promotion of faculty and librarians.
Reason (R): Performance Appraisal is an important tool for merit rating.
(*NET 14D iii paper*)
Codes:
(a) (A) is true, but (R) is false.
(b) (A) is false, but (R) is true.
(c) Both (A) and (R) are true.
(d) Both (A) and (R) are false.

160. **Assertion (A):** The plagiarism detection software implements a generic detection approach for all types of materials.
Reason (R): There is no difference between text and source code plagiarism.
(*NET 14D iii paper*)
Codes:
(a) (A) is true, but (R) is false.
(b) (A) is false, but (R) is true.
(c) Both (A) and (R) are true.
(d) Both (A) and (R) are false

161. **Assertion (A):** UGC notification (2009) mandates submission of electronic theses and dissertations by the researchers in universities to facilitate open access.
Reason (R): UGC wants to monitor the quality of research through open access.
(*NET 14D iii paper*)
Codes:
(a) (A) is true, but (R) is false.
(b) (A) is false, but (R) is true.
(c) Both (A) and (R) are true.
(d) Both (A) and (R) are false.

162. Arrange the following in chronological order: (*NET 14D iii paper*)
i. Rome convention
ii. WIPO copyright treaty

iii. Universal copyright convention
iv. Berne convention

Codes:
(a) i, iv, iii, ii (b) iv, i, ii, iii
(c) iv, iii, i, ii (d) iii, i, iv, ii

163. Match the following: (*NET 14D iii paper*)

List – I	List – II
A. Simple random	1. Natural order
B. Systematic random	2. Representative
C. Stratified random	3. Equal chance
D. Judgement	4. Sub-groups

Codes:	A	B	C	D
(a)	2	1	3	4
(b)	3	1	4	2
(c)	4	2	1	3
(d)	3	2	4	1

164. Match the following: (*NET 15D iii paper*)

List - I
(A) Readers Advisory Service
(B) Referral Service
(C) Review Service
(D) Digest Service

List - II
(1) Market Survey Report
(2) Preparation of Trend Report
(3) Helping reader in selection of right book
(4) Directing the user to the source of information

Codes:	(A)	(B)	(C)	(D)
(a)	(1)	(3)	(4)	(2)
(b)	(2)	(4)	(1)	(3)
(c)	(4)	(3)	(2)	(1)
(d)	(3)	(4)	(2)	(1)

165. **List - I (Commissions)** (*NET 15D iii paper*)
(A) D.S. Kothari Commission
(B) Radhakrishnan Commission
(C) Calcutta Commission
(D) Truman's Commission

List - II (Opinions)
(1) It is right and proper that university should provide great libraries.
(2) The library is second to instructional staff.
(3) Nothing could be more damaging to a department than neglecting its library.
(4) The library is the heart of university work.

Codes:	(A)	(B)	(C)	(D)
(a)	(1)	(3)	(2)	(4)
(b)	(3)	(4)	(1)	(2)
(c)	(2)	(1)	(4)	(3)
(d)	(4)	(2)	(3)	(1)

166. **Assertion (A):** Increased access to digital documents led to substantial increase in Plagiarism.

Reason (R): Most of the people are ignorant of the procedures in citing the digital documents. (*NET 15D iii paper*)

Codes:
(a) Both (A) and (R) are true.
(b) Both (A) and (R) are false.
(c) (A) is true but (R) is false.
(d) (A) is false, but (R) is true.

167. Which of the following are the examples of Web-based learning and education? (*NET 17J iii paper*)
(i) Answer Tips (ii) Moodle
(iii) Revish (iv) Campus bug

Codes:
(a) (i), (ii) and (iv) are correct.
(b) (i), (ii) and (iii) are correct.
(c) (ii), (iii) and (iv) are correct.
(d) (i), (iii) and (iv) are correct.

168. Who was the teacher of S.R. Ranganathan at London? (*Net 15D ii paper*)
(a) J.D. Brown (b) A. Panizzi
(c) W.B.C. Sayers (d) Melvil Dewey

169. Following are some of the problems with "Difficult Materials" usually faced by the users as advocated by Dr. S.R. Ranganathan (*NET 15D ii paper*)
(i) Books with different numbers.
(ii) Books with different styles and standards.
(iii) Books in various forms of exposition.
(iv) Books with different sizes and colours.

Codes:
(a) (i) and (iii) are correct.
(b) (ii) and (iv) are correct
(c) (iii) and (iv) are correct.
(d) (ii) and (iii) are correct.

170. What is the name of the initiative taken by the UGC to provide a 24×7 online store house of all academic awards issued by different academic institutions all over the country?
(a) National Mission on Education Through Information and Communication Technology (NMEICT)
(b) National Academic Depository (NAD)

(c) HEI Online Registration Portal
(d) Swayam Prabha

171. National Knowledge Commission (2005) had the following members from the library and Information profession
(i) P.B. Mangla
(ii) C.R. Karisiddappa
(iii) Kalpana Das Gupta
(iv) A.R.D. Prasad
Codes:
(a) i, ii, iii are correct
b) i, ii, iv are correct
(c) i, iii, iv are correct
(d) ii, iii, iv are correct

172. Arrange the following Padma Shri award recipients in chronological of their year of the award:
(i) Bellari Shamanna Kesvan
(ii) Shiyali Ramamrita Ranganthan
(iii) Prithvi Nath Kaula
(iv) Iyyanki Venkata Ramanyya
Codes:
(a) (i), (ii), (iii) and, (iv)
(b) (i), (iv), (ii) and, (iii)
(c) (ii), (i), (iv) and, (iii)
(d) (ii), (iv), (i) and, (iii)

173. **Assertion (A):** The curriculum of LIS education in India is mostly unsteady as local LIS requirement varies.
Reason (R): Adoption of UGC model syllabus is not mandatory for the LIS school in India.
Codes:
(a) (A) is true but (R) is false
(b) (A) is false, but (R) is true
(c) both (A) and (R) are true
(d) Both (A) and (R) are false

ANSWER SHEET

1. (b)	2. (a)	3. (c)	4. (d)	5. (c)	6. (d)	7. (c)	8. (d)	9. (a)
10. (b)	11. (b)	12. (a)	13. (c)	14. (c)	15. (a)	16. (a)	17. (c)	18. (b)
19. (a)	20. (d)	21. (b)	22. (d)	23. (b)	24. (a)	25. (a)	26. (a)	27. (d)
28. (b)	29. (d)	30. (d)	31. (b)	32. (b)	33. (a)	34. (a)	35. (b)	36. (b)
37. (a)	38. (a)	39. (d)	40. (d)	41. (b)	42. (d)	43. (d)	44. (b)	45. (b)
46. (b)	47. (c)	48. (a)	49. (c)	50. (a)	51. (c)	52. (a)	53. (d)	54. (a)
55. (a)	56. (b)	57. (b)	58. (b)	59. (c)	60. (a)	61. (d)	62. (d)	63. (c)
64. (a)	65. (a)	66. (c)	67. (c)	68. (a)	69. (a)	70. (a)	71. (c)	72. (d)
73. (a)	74. (a)	75. (a)	76. (b)	77. (c)	78. (a)	79. (d)	80. (a)	81. (c)
82. (a)	83. (c)	84. (a)	85. (d)	86. (d)	87. (a)	88. (b)	89. (b)	90. (a)
91. (a)	92. (b)	93. (c)	94. (d)	95. (a)	96. (d)	97. (a)	98. (d)	99. (c)
100. (b)	101. (c)	102. (c)	103. (c)	104. (d)	105. (b)	106. (b)	107. (b)	108. (c)
109. (b)	110. (c)	111. (c)	112. (a)	113. (c)	114. (c)	115. (b)	116. (b)	117. (d)
118. (a)	119. (b)	120. (a)	121. (d)	122. (a)	123. (a)	124. (c)	125. (b)	126. (b)
127. (d)	128. (a)	129. (d)	130. (a)	131. (c)	132. (c)	133. (b)	134. (d)	135. (a)
136. (b)	137. (b)	138. (d)	139. (a)	140. (b)	141. (b)	142. (a)	143. (a)	144. (b)
145. (b)	146. (c)	147. (c)	148. (a)	149. (a)	150. (c)	151. (c)	152. (d)	153. (d)
154. (d)	155. (b)	156. (a)	157. (c)	158. (c)	159. (c)	160. (d)	161. (a)	162. (c)
163. (b)	164. (d)	165. (b)	166. (a)	167. (a)	168. (c)	169. (d)	170. (b)	171. (c)
172. (c)	173. (c)							

Chapter 4
Bibliography and Reference Service

SUBJECTIVE QUESTIONS

Q. 1. Who used by the Bibliography first?

Ans. The word "Bibliography" was used in the sense of copying for the first time in 1656 by Thomas Blount in his *Academic of Eloquence.*

Q. 2. How do catalogues differ from bibliographies?

Ans.

Bibliography	Catalogue
(i) A bibliography is the key to literary resources in given subject.	(i) A catalogue is the key to a given collection.
(ii) A bibliography only lets the scholars to know the existence of a document.	(ii) A catalogue provides key to the physical access of a document.

Q. 3. How many types of bibliography?

Ans. There are five types of bibliography:
(a) Analytical or Critical (b) Descriptive
(c) Textual (d) Historical
(e) Systematic or Enumerative

Q. 4. Who is known as father of bibliography?

Ans. Conrad Gesner.

Q. 5. Write the periodicity of *British National Bibliography*.

Ans. Weekly.

Q. 6. Where the International Bibliography founded?

Ans. Brussels.

Q. 7. Who is known as father of English Bibliography?

Ans. John Leland.

Q. 8. Write the name of first Bibliography of Italy.

Ans. *La Libraria* in 1550 by Darri.

Q. 9. Write the name of first Bibliography of France.

Ans. *Bibliotheque Francoise* in 1584 by Francois Graude.

Q. 10. Write the name of famous German Bibliographer.

Ans. Elbert was a famous German bibliographer who compiled *Allgemeines bibliographies lexicon* in two volumes in 1821-30.

Q. 11. Define the national bibliography.

Ans. According to librarians' glossary, it is defined as "A bibliography of books produced in the language of one country, irrespective of the country in which published, about the country by the native of the country irrespective of residence and books produced in the country, whatever their language."

Q. 12. In how many languages to be published Indian National Bibliography and what they are?

Ans. 15 languages:
Assamese, Bengali, English, Gujarati, Hindi, Kannada, Malayalam, Marathi, Oriya, Punjabi, Sanskrit, Tamil, Telugu, and Urdu. Later on Sindhi was also published.

Q. 13. How many section in the INB?

Ans. Two sections:
(i) Classified (ii) Alphabetical Index.

Q. 14. How many types of reference service?

Ans. There are two types of reference service:
(i) Short Range Reference Service and
(ii) Long Range Reference Service.

Q. 15. How many types of reference function can be discussed?

Ans. Two types:
(i) Responsive (ii) Anticipatory

Q. 16. Define the Anticipatory Service?

Ans. Information service given in anticipation of demand after a general assessment of need, given to groups not to individuals.

Q. 17. Write the alternative name of dictionaries.

Ans. The alternative names of dictionary are following:

(i) Glossary, (ii) Lexicon, (iii) Thesaurus and (iv) Vocabulary.

Q. 18. Who used the word "Thesaurus" first?

Ans. Peter Mark Roget in 1852.

Q. 19. Write the name of first Encyclopedia.

Ans. *Historia Naturalis.*

Q. 20. Who produced the first Encyclopedia?

Ans. Aristotle and Plato.

Q. 21. When was the first edition of *Encyclopedia of Britannica* published?

Ans. The first edition of *Encyclopedia of Britannica* was published in 1768-71 in three volumes.

Q. 22. How many volumes in *New Encyclopedia of Britannica* is published 15th edition?

Ans. *New Encyclopedia of Britannica* consisting of thirty volumes. It has three parts:

(i) Propaedia - 1 volume
(ii) Micropaedia - 10 volumes
(iii) Macropaedia - 19 volumes

Q. 23. Write the country who started the first regular enumeration.

Ans. The United States in 1790.

Q. 24. Write the periodicity of *National Bibliography of India.*

Ans. Monthly.

Q. 25. Write the name of publishers of books in print.

Ans. R.R. Bowker.

Q. 26. Write the periodicity of *National Bibliography of Hong Kong.*

Ans. Quarterly.

OBJECTIVE QUESTIONS

1. The three broad categories of Biographical Dictionaries are (*NET Exam.* 1999)
(a) General, national and special
(b) International, national and local
(c) General, local and special
(d) General, national and international

2. Bibliography of Bibliographies comes under the category (*NET Exam.* 1999)
(a) Primary (b) Secondary
(c) Tertiary sources (d) None of these

3. The secondary sources of information comprised of (*NET Exam.* 1999)
(a) Textbooks and research monographs
(b) Subject periodicals and encyclopedias
(c) Indexing and abstracting periodicals
(d) Bibliography and patents

4. The origin of the concept of "Literary Warrant" was by (*NET Exam.* 1999)
(a) S.R. Ranganathan (b) Wyndham Humle
(c) E.C. Richardson (d) W.C.B. Sayes

5. The early work on modelling of information communication was based on (*NET Exam.* 1999)
(a) Good and Hatt model
(b) Lasswell model
(c) Shannon and Weaver model
(d) Bradford and Price model

6. The term "Lexicography" is associated with (*NET Exam.* 1999)
(a) Compilation of Encyclopedia
(b) Compilation of Handbooks
(c) Compilation of Dictionaries
(d) None of the above

7. A pre-print is a/an (*NET Exam.* 1999)
(a) Article to be presented in a conference
(b) Conference paper to be included in the proceedings
(c) Neither (a) nor (b)
(d) Both (a) and (b)

8. Xerographic process is categorised under (*NET Exam.* 1999)
(a) Photographic process
(b) Reflex method
(c) Silver halide process
(d) Electro static process

9. The *Study Abroad* is a/an (*NET Exam.* 1999)
(a) Encyclopedia (b) Year book
(c) Directory (d) Hand book

10. The "User Profile" is a (*NET Exam.* 1999)
(a) List of description
(b) List of useful citation
(c) List of users
(d) Statement of user information

11. An abstract which is written for a specific group of users is known as (*NET Exam.* 1999)
   (a) Critical abstract (b) Slanted abstract
   (c) Author abstract (d) Indicative abstract
12. In research design, which is consider as the most important component? (*NET Exam.* 1999)
   (a) Observation (b) Formation of hypothesis
   (c) Case study (d) Review of literature
13. "Books in Print" is a (*NET Exam.* 1997 and 1999)
   (a) National Bibliography
   (b) Trade Bibliography
   (c) Retrospective Bibliography
   (d) Subject Bibliography
14. What is an interview? (*NET Exam.* 1999)
   (a) A tool of research
   (b) A process of research
   (c) A type of research
   (d) A method of representation of data
15. Which of the following is not a secondary source of information? (*NET Exam.* 2000)
   (a) An encyclopedia (b) A textbook
   (c) A biographical dictionary (d) Patents
16. Which of the following reference sources will you consult to locate information on the Pokhran test? (*NET Exam.* 2000)
   (a) *Encyclopedia of Britannica*
   (b) *Asian Recorder*
   (c) *Commonwealth Universities Book*
   (d) *Dictionary of National Biography*
17. Information about Indian research studies on bakery and milling is input to IFIS through (*NET Exam.* 2000)
   (a) The Central Rice Research Institute
   (b) Indian Agriculture Research Institute
   (c) National Institute of Nutrition
   (d) Central Food Technological Research Institute
18. Which of the following is not an example of Current Awareness Service (CAS)? (*NET Exam.* 2000)
   (a) SDI (b) An indexing bulletin
   (c) Current contents (d) A reading list
19. Non-bibliographic data bases contain (*NET Exam.* 2000)
   (a) Numeric Data (b) Textual Data
   (c) Visual Data (d) All of the above
20. Indexing and abstracting sources are available in print, optical and online. Among the three formats, there is usually (*NET Exam.* 2000)
   (a) A difference in price, but not in capability
   (b) No difference in price, but difference in capability
   (c) A difference both in price and in capability
   (d) No difference in price or capability
21. In imperial study on the impact of television viewing on violence, violence would be (*NET Exam.* 2000)
   (a) The dependent variable
   (b) An independent variable
   (c) An intervening variable
   (d) Not a variable at all
22. A big difference between the mean and median is an indication that (*NET Exam.* 2000)
   (a) There is a mistake in the calculation
   (b) The calculation is correct
   (c) There is wide variation in the data
   (d) None of the above
23. Which of the following research methods is useful in a study on measuring the active life of periodicals? (*NET Exam.* 2000)
   (a) Survey (b) Citation analysis
   (c) Interviewed (d) Case study
24. The *Indian National Bibliography* does not include (*NET Exam.* 2000)
   (a) Book published in India in English
   (b) Official report
   (c) Books on India published abroad
   (d) Books published in recognised Indian language
25. The document in any library entitled "The Hindu World" is a/an (*NET Exam.* 1994)
   (a) Directory (b) Encyclopedia
   (c) Year Book (d) Gazetteer
26. Cumulative Book Index covers books published in the English language in (*NET Exam.* 1994)
   (a) U.K. (b) U.S.A.
   (c) India (d) All over the world
27. Periodicity of *Indian National Bibliographies* is (*NET Exam.* 1994)

(a) Weekly (b) Monthly
(c) Quarterly (d) Annually

28. _____ subject is one with a basic subject and one or more isolates. (*NET Exam.* 1994)
(a) Complex (b) Specific
(c) Basic (d) Compound

29. Which of the following is not a tool for collection of data in historical method?
(a) Coin (b) Inscription
(c) Newspapers (d) Observation

30. "Grey literature" means? (*NET Exam.* 1996D)
(a) Literature which contains classified information
(b) Documents which are bound in grey cloth
(c) Literature which is semi-published
(d) Literature which is to be published in future

31. Which of the following cannot be considered as a primary source of information? (*NET Exam.* 1996D)
(a) An article describing original research (b) A textbook
(c) A patent (d) A thesis

32. A "Gazette" gives information about (*NET Exam.* 1997/98)
(a) Places to see (b) Old records
(c) History of places
(d) Official announcement and notification

33. Referral service means referring use to (*NET Exam.* 1996D)
(a) Reference books
(b) Other books in the collection
(c) Sources outside the library
(d) Online search

34. The query on "use of audio-visual aids in teaching science at primary school" can be framed as (*NET Exam.* 1996D)
(a) Audio-visual aids and science and primary school
(b) Audio-visual aids or science or primary school
(c) Audio-visual aids or science and primary school
(d) Audio-visual aids and science or primary school

35. The topic "Statistical methods for Social Science" is an example of (*NET Exam.* 1996D)
(a) Lamination (b) Loose Assemblage
(c) Fission (d) Fusion

36. Which of the following is not a secondary source of information? (*NET Exam.* 1996J)
(a) An encyclopedia (b) A textbook
(c) A statistical digest (d) A thesis

37. Concordance means (*NET Exam.* 1996)
(a) An alphabetic index to a book or an author works
(b) A multi-language dictionary
(c) An explanation of idioms
(d) None of the above

38. To carry out a search on "Poverty in Gujarat and Rajasthan", a search statement would need to be framed as (*NET Exam.* 1996)
(a) Poverty AND (Gujarat AND Rajasthan)
(b) Poverty AND (Gujarat OR Rajasthan)
(c) Poverty OR (Gujarat AND Rajasthan)
(d) Poverty OR (Gujarat OR Rajasthan)

39. *Library Literature* is a/an (*NET Exam.* 1996)
(a) Indexing Journal
(b) Bibliography of Books
(c) Trade Bibliography
(d) Abstracting Journal

40. Universal Bibliographic Control is a programme of (*NET Exam.* 1996/99)
(a) UNISIST (b) FID
(c) IFLA (d) American Library Association

41. Name of the President of Cuba can be found in (*NET Exam.* 1995)
(a) *World of Learning*
(b) *International Who's Who*
(c) *Statements Year Book*
(d) *India—A Reference Annual*

42. Times Literary supplement is most useful for (*NET Exam.* 1995)
(a) Book Reviews
(b) News about Great Britain
(c) Digest of Newspapers
(d) Library holding in U.K.

43. Information about Sahitya Akademi can be found in (*NET Exam.* 1995)
(a) *World of Learning*
(b) *Universities Handbook* (India)
(c) *India—A Reference*
(d) *Dictionary of National Annual Biography* (India)

44. The *Statements Year Book* contains information exclusively on (*NET Exam.* 1998 and 1999)
(a) World sport events
(b) United Nations and its agencies
(c) Nations of the world
(d) American events

45. Which of the following cannot be considered as "Primary source of information"? (*NET Exam.* 1998D)
(a) A periodical article
(b) A hand book
(c) Compiled empirical data
(d) A standard

46. A "gazette" gives information about old records.
(a) True (b) False

47. Which country does not have a national bibliography?
(a) United Kingdom (b) U.S.A.
(c) India (d) Australia

48. When a library of information centre provides documents from its own resources or from other resources, it is known as (*NET Exam.* 1998)
(a) Document delivery service
(b) Inter-library loan
(c) Reprography service
(d) Reference service

49. Which of the following can be considered as a key attribute in a bibliographic database? (*NET Exam.* 1997 and 1998)
(a) ISBN (b) Author
(c) Title (d) Main entry access point

50. Alterting service includes (*NET Exam.* 1998)
(a) Circulation of contents pages of journals
(b) Routing of periodicals
(c) Indexing current materials
(d) All of the above

51. In a library, which of the following positions are line positions? (*NET Exam.* 1998)
(A) Jr. Library Assistant (B) Subject Specialist
(C) Dy. Librarian (D) Systems Librarian
Codes:
(a) A and B (b) A and C
(c) A and D (d) All of these

52 Solo research is an investigation conducted by (*NET Exam.* 1991)
(a) A group of person (b) An individual
(c) An organisation (d) Two persons

53. Historical method of research can be applied (*NET Exam.* 1991)
(a) Only in history (b) Only in literary history
(c) In all subjects (d) None of the above

54. Interview is a (*NET Exam.* 1991)
(a) Tool of research
(b) Method of research
(c) Technique of presentation
(d) Type of research of report

55. Which one is primary source of information? (*NET Exam.* 1991)
(a) State-of-the-art report
(b) Current contents list
(c) Union Catalogue
(d) Manuscript

56. *India: A Reference Annual* is (*NET Exam.* 1991)
(a) An annual bibliography
(b) A gazetteer of India
(c) A directory
(d) A year book

57. Books in print covers books published in (*NET Exam.* 1991)
(a) India (b) Great Britain
(c) U.S.A. (d) Throughout the world

58 "Biblio Metrics" is a study of (*NET Exam.* 1991)
(a) Bibliography
(b) Quantitative analysis of publication
(c) Bibliothrapy
(d) Qualitative analysis of political groups

59. Guide to Indian periodical literature provide an alphabetical subject and ________ index.
(a) publisher (b) name
(c) author (d) title

60. The librarians and scholars are primarily concerned with ______ bibliography.
(a) Historical (b) Critical
(c) Descriptive (d) Enumerative

61. The issues of *Indian National Bibliography* are published
(a) half yearly (b) monthly
(c) quarterly (d) bimonthly

62. Online service is part of

(a) Indian news index
(b) Newspaper index
(c) Index to the times
(d) New York times index

63. *National Biographical Dictionary of India* compiled by Jagdish Saran Sharma is published from _____ in _____ volumes.
(a) Delhi Publication Division, 2
(b) Delhi, ICHR, 4
(c) Delhi Sterling, 1
(d) Calcutta, Institute of Historical Studies, 5

64. *Asian Recorder* consists of three parts, viz. events in all countries of Asia, outside Asia and
(a) Sports events of the third world countries
(b) Sports events in Asia
(c) Sports events covering Asia outside Asia
(d) Sports events of all countries

65. *National Atlas of China* edited by Chi-Yun-Chang is an example of ______ atlas.
(a) international (b) local
(c) national (d) historical

66. *Encyclopedia of Anthropology* edited by David E. Hunter and Philip Whitten is a ______ encyclopedia.
(a) special (b) language
(c) subject (d) general

67. Descriptive bibliography selects only
(a) Secondary (b) Analytical
(c) Tertiary (d) Primary

68. In the classified part of BNB, the entries are arranged according to
(a) DDC 18th edition (b) DDC 19th edition
(c) DDC 17th edition (d) DDC 16th edition

69. "Index to the Times of India" is published ________
(a) 1 (b) 2 (c) 4 (d) 3

70. Documentation services are generally grouped into the following two categories.
(a) Responsive and anticipatory
(b) Documentary and non-documentary
(c) Direct and indirect
(d) Current and retrospective

71. According to Ranganathan, reference service is a ______ service.
(a) specialised (b) personal
(c) technical (d) anticipatory

72. The critical edition of all great works are the example of descriptive bibliography.
(a) True (b) False

73. Dictionary, glossary, lexicon, thesaurus, vocabulary, etc. deal with
(a) Objects (b) Subject
(c) Concept (d) Words and their meaning

74. INB and BNB are example of ________ bibliography.
(a) national (b) universal
(c) trade graphy (d) systematic

75. *Indian National Bibliography* is the publication of
(a) DESIDOC
(b) INSDOC
(c) Central Reference Library
(d) National Library

76. The three important steps involved in the process of rendering reference service. Interview with the user assessment of the nature of query and knowledge of
(a) Arrangement of books
(b) Call No. of the books
(c) Location of books
(d) Reference sources

77. Bartho Lomen Gazetter of Britain comes under the category of ______ gazetteers.
(a) national (b) district
(c) local (d) international

78. *Africa Diary* is a _________ publication.
(a) fortnightly (b) bi-monthly
(c) monthly (d) weekly

79. *India Who's Who* is published by
(a) Survey of India (b) INFA Publication
(c) Publication Division (d) Sahitya Akademi

80. ________ is an annual calendar covering miscellaneous matter such as astronomical events, tables, astrological predications are anecdotes.
(a) Statistical sources
(b) Year book
(c) Almanac
(d) Astronomical directory

81. *Asian Recorder* is published from
(a) London (b) New York
(c) Chennai (d) New Delhi

82. Abstracting and indexing periodicals to the category of _______ publication.

(a) tertiary (b) primary
(c) general (d) secondary

83. *Directory of Economics* compiled by Bannock is an example of ______ dictionary.
(a) bilingual (b) multi-lingual
(c) general (d) subject

84. Essays and general literature index comes under the category of bibliographies guides to
(a) Periodical literature
(b) Specific type of biographical material
(c) Collected biographies
(d) Individuals biographies

85. Years books can be divided into two major groups.
(a) International year books and supplement to subject encyclopedia
(b) Statistical year books and supplement to encyclopedia
(c) National year books and supplement to encyclopedia
(d) General year books and supplement to encyclopedia

86. *British National Bibliography* is a ________ publication.
(a) half-yearly (b) quarterly
(c) weekly (d) annual

87. *Prakashan Samachar* is an example of _________ bibliography.
(a) analytical (b) national
(c) trade (d) universal

88. Reference functions are of two kinds, viz.
(a) Direct and indirect
(b) Responsive and anticipatory
(c) Exhaustive and basic
(d) Primary and secondary

89. Fodors Modern Guides, New York is an example of
(a) Directory of institution
(b) Subject bibliography
(c) Gazetteer
(d) Travel guide

90. The publication "Reference Catalogue of Current literature" has changed its name to ______ in the year ______.
(a) Book Seller, 1974
(b) British Books in Print, 1965
(c) Whitaker Cumulative Book List, 1964
(d) English Catalogue of Books, 1975

91. Systematic bibliography is also known as _________ bibliography.
(a) authentic (b) classified
(c) enumerative (d) descriptive

92. The four categories of subject bibliography are
(I) Subject Index, (II) Bibliographies (III) Bibliographies Reviews, (IV) _______.
(a) Library Bulletin (b) Abstract
(c) Data Charge (d) Analytical Tables

93. American book publishing record is a monthly communication of publisher weekly.
(a) True (b) False

94. Reference catalogue of current literature was founded in 1974 by Melvil Dewey.
(a) True (b) False

95. The Mc Grand Hill dictionary of *Modern Economics* is an example of ______ subject dictionary.
(a) multi volume (b) single volume
(c) unabridged (d) abridged

96. "National sample survey reports" come under the category of ______ source.
(a) general (b) statistical
(c) geographical (d) documentary

97. A/An ______ is the key to a given collection and does not include the records of documents not found in that collection.
(a) index (b) documentation list
(c) bibliography (d) catalogue

98. "Fodors Modern Guides", New York is an example of a travel guide.
(a) True (b) False

99. The international relating to universities and institution of higher education in the world could be located from
(a) *World of Learning*
(b) *Manorama Year Book*
(c) *Webster's Bibliographical*
(d) *Encyclopedia Britannica*

100. According to Ranganathan categorisation of bibliographic agencies, FID comes under the category of ______ Centre.
(a) International General
(b) International Special
(c) National General
(d) National Special

101. *Ulrich International Periodical Directory* is a ______ source of information.
(a) tertiary (b) secondary
(c) primary (d) None of the above

102. The subject bibliography *Advance in Environmental Science and Technology* forms ______ category.
(a) ordinary (b) bibliographical review
(c) abstracts (d) subject index

103. The record relating to the subject bibliographic is maintained by the ______ division.
(a) maintenance (b) technical
(c) reference (d) acquisition

104. New York Times Index, Indian Press Index and Newspaper Index are the examples of indexing service devoted to
(a) Special kind of document
(b) Newspapers
(c) Periodicals
(d) Report literature

105. ERIC database sponsored by the Department of Health, Education and Welfare, Govt. of U.S.A. deals with
(a) Energy (b) Engineering
(c) Ecology (d) Education

106. A physical map is usually referred to
(a) Indicate location of country
(b) Trace details of mineral resources
(c) Show roads, rail road bridges
(d) Delineation of boundaries of different countries

107. According to Sir Walter Greg, bibliography is essentiality
(a) An organised list of books
(b) The science of the transmission of literary document
(c) A list of items possessed by a library
(d) A collection of books

108. When the items in a bibliography are arranged within a section or sub-division using their years of publication, it is known as critical arrangement.
(a) True (b) False

109. The four indexes include in SCI are
(I) Source Index, (II) Citation Index,
(III) Permuted Subject Index and (IV) ______
(a) Corporate Index (b) Index of Publishers
(c) Title Index (d) Keyword Index

110. Gazetteer of India compiled by Central Gazetteers Unit of Government of India (1965-78) in volumes
(a) 5 (b) 4 (c) 3 (d) 2

111. "Caution News Facts" is prepared on the same line as
(a) Asian Recorder
(b) Facts on File
(c) Africa Diary
(d) Keesings' record of world events

112. "Biological Abstract" has four indexes, viz. Basic, Cross and Bio Systems and
(a) Language (b) Publishers
(c) Author (d) Title

113. Subject Guide to Books in Print uses for its subject heading PRECIS.
(a) True (b) False

114. The subject bibliography is most important category of
(a) Analytical bibliography
(b) Descriptive bibliography
(c) Enumerative bibliography
(d) Textual bibliography

115. Science citation index is a publication of
(a) National Resource Energy and Science Authority, Colombo
(b) INSDOC, New Delhi
(c) National Diet Library, Tokyo
(d) Institute of Scientific Information, Philadelphia

116. ______ define bibliography as "a systematic listing of human communication".
(a) Devon (b) Dibdin
(c) Thomson (d) Verner Clapp

117. *Dictionary of National Biography* edited by S.P. Sen is in ______ volumes covering person from ________.
(a) 4, literature (b) 4, education
(c) 3, politics (d) 4, all walks of life

118. "Indian Ephemeris and Nautical Almanac" is a type of _______ almanac.
(a) general (b) informational
(c) astronomical (d) topical

119. The basic purpose of a current national bibliography as enunciated by Dr. S.R. Ranganathan are: (I) Cultural purpose, (II) Educational purpose and (III) _________.

(a) Sociological (b) Scientific
(c) Political (d) Economical

120. Indian Science Abstract (ISA) is a publication of
(a) INSDOC, Delhi (b) INSA
(c) NISSAT (d) Indian Institute of Science

121. British Book News is an example of a __________ bibliography.
(a) subject (b) trade
(c) international (d) national

122. The three important aspects of the treatment of encyclopedia are
(I) Readability, (II) Objectivity and (III) ________
(a) The type of binding
(b) Quality of paper
(c) Style
(d) The printer and publisher

123. *Webster's Bibliographical Dictionary* is an example of
(a) Current national bibliographical source
(b) Current universal bibliographical source
(c) Retrospective bibliographical source
(d) Current-cum-retrospective universal bibliographical source

124. "Public Affairs Information Service Bulletin" is an
(a) Account of current events
(b) Annotated bibliography
(c) Indexing service on public affairs
(d) Abstracting service on public affairs

125. ___________ is the record of systematic enumeration of population, house, business and trade, livestock other important aspect of a nation of one particular time.
(a) Population statistics
(b) Statistical abstract
(c) Statistical report
(d) Census report

126. General dictionary is useful for
(a) Enriching word power
(b) Solving cross word puzzles
(c) Increasing the I.Q.
(d) Increasing the memory

127. ______ bibliography is a systematic list of all the books published all over the world.
(a) Trade (b) Descriptive
(c) Systematic (d) Universal

128. Ranganathan has defined reference service as
(a) Personal assistance (b) Personal aid
(c) Direct personal aid (d) Personal service

129. *Encyclopedia of Americana* consists of
(a) 30 volumes (b) 10 volumes
(c) 35 volumes (d) 38 volumes

130. Census reports come under the category of _________ sources.
(a) general (b) biographical
(c) statistical (d) geographical

131. Kessings record of world events is a ______ service providing contemporary record of national and international current events.
(a) bimonthly (b) weekly
(c) yearly (d) monthly

132. ________ is the Indian biographical source of literature.
(a) *Who's Who of Indian Writers*
(b) *Contemporary Novelists*
(c) *World Authors*
(d) *Contemporary Indian Authors*

133. "Bibliography is the art of recording books and the science of the making of books and their extent records." This definition was propounded by
(a) Van Hassan (b) Esdaile
(c) Verner Clapp (d) S.R. Ranganathan

134. A slib book list is a _________ subject bibliography.
(a) current (b) retrospective
(c) quarterly (d) weekly

135. Whitakers cumulative book list is based on publishers weekly.
(a) True (b) False

136. National Index of Translation is published by
(a) DESIDOC (b) INSDOC
(c) NISSAT (d) NASSDOC

137. Handling of questions of fact-finding nature is known as
(a) Referral service
(b) Ready reference service
(c) Long-range reference service
(d) Responsive service

138. Biography refers to

(a) A written account of person's life
(b) A collection of lives of people arranging in a alphabetical order
(c) A person who writes a biography of another person
(d) A person who is the subject of biography

139. Demographic year book is an annual publication of
(a) Central Statistical Organisation, New Delhi
(b) United Nations, New York
(c) Bureau of the Census, Washington
(d) Statistical Office, London

140. The scope of an encyclopedia covers plan range on
(a) Format (b) Selection
(c) Purpose (d) Consistency

141. "Polygot" is the name generally given to
(a) Multi-lingual dictionaries
(b) Thesaurus
(c) Monolingual dictionaries
(d) Subject dictionaries

142. The most common example of a prescriptive dictionary is
(a) Random House Dictionary
(b) Dr. Samuel Johnson's English Language
(c) Webster's New International Dictionary
(d) Oxford English Dictionary

143. *Tribal Map of India* is published by
(a) Anthropological Survey of India
(b) Survey of India
(c) National Atlas Organisation
(d) Geological Survey of India

144. The three important characteristics of presentation the topics in an encyclopedia is readability, objectivity and
(a) Authority (b) Format
(c) Style (d) Arrangement

145. ________ maps are used for town and country planning.
(a) Physical (b) Political
(c) Topographic (d) Historical

146. The second part Micro Paedia of *New Encyclopedia Britannica* is in ______ Volumes.
(a) 29 (b) 19 (c) 10 (d) 01

147. Special encyclopedias are designed to satisfy the needs of the adults.
(a) True (b) False

148. Match the following:
(A) Dictionary of Clock and Watches by E. Bruton Arco
(B) The Little Oxford Dictionary, New edition 1980
(C) Punctuate it Right by Harry Show
(D) Twenty-two Language Dictionary by H.L. Ouseg
(I) Translating Dictionary
(II) Special Dictionary
(III) Subject Dictionary
(IV) General Language Dictionary
(a) A-II, B-III, C-IV, D-I
(b) A-IV, B-III, C-II, D-I
(c) A-I, B-II, C-IV, D-III
(d) A-III, B-IV, C-II, D-I

149. World of learning is an example of
(a) Statistical source (b) Almanac
(c) Directory (d) Year book

150. The cumulative book index is national scope and coverage.
(a) True (b) False

151. Topographic maps trace information pertaining to
(a) political boundaries of different countries, states and cities, etc.
(b) rail roads, railway bridges, etc.
(c) general information of a place.
(d) details of geologic, soil, forest and other type of development.

152. Name of the president of Royal Society, London can be found in
(a) *World of Learning*
(b) *Commonwealth University Year Book*
(c) *International Who's Who*
(d) *Statements Year Book*

153. The concept of "Technological Gatekeepers" was first propounded by
(a) Allen (b) Diana Carne
(c) De Solla Prince (d) Derek Austin

154. *World of Learning* is a
(a) Journal
(b) Directory
(c) Textbook on education
(d) Bibliography on education

155. "Book in Print" could be categorised as
(a) National bibliography from India
(b) Trade bibliography from India

(c) National bibliography from U.S.A.
(d) Trade bibliography from U.S.A.

156. MESH is the name of
(a) a Bulletin in Medical Sciences
(b) an International Medical Library
(c) a Controlled Vocabulary Device in Medical Sciences
(d) None of the above

157. *Encyclopedia Americana* is published from
(a) New York (b) India
(c) London (d) America

158. *The International Encyclopedia of Social Science* consists of
(a) 18 Volumes (b) 21 Volumes
(c) 33 Volumes (d) 34 Volumes

159. The detail of book comprising Author, Title, Imprint, Collation, Technically are called (*NET Exam.* 1997D)
(a) Record format
(b) Standard record format
(c) Entries for classification
(d) Bibliographic description

160. Size to size reproduction document is called
(a) Reduction (b) Enlargement
(c) Facsimile (d) None of these

161. In an empirical study of the effect of open access on browsing patterns open access is (*NET Exam.* 1997D)
(a) An independent variable
(b) An dependent variable
(c) Not a variable at all
(d) An interviewing variable

162. Dictionary of National Bibliography (DNB) contains biography of prominent people of (*Net Exam.* 1997)
(a) All nations (b) Europeans
(c) Americans (d) Britishers

163. International standard book description does not standardise (*Net Exam.* 1997)
(a) Type of information to be included in the catalogue entry
(b) Order in which the information is to be entry recorded
(c) The point of access
(d) The punctuation mark to be followed

164. Gazetteers give information about (*Net Exam.* 1999)
(a) Geographic location of places
(b) History of places
(c) Social customs and practices
(d) All of the above

165. Which of the following reference sources will you consult to locate information on "Amaritya Sen"?
(a) *Encyclopedia Britannica*
(b) *Facts on File*
(c) *Commonwealth University Year Book*
(d) *Dictionary of National Bibliography*

166. What is the relation between Current Awareness Service (CAS) and Selective Dissemination of Information (SDI)?
(a) SDI is one form of CAS
(b) CAS is one form of SDI
(c) The two services are the same
(d) There is no relation

167. Bibliographic databases
(a) Include indexing and abstracting databases
(b) Are known as secondary sources of information
(c) Are available through vendors
(d) All of the above

168. The following are the examples of information consolidation.
(1) Bibliographies (3) Abstracts
(2) Digests (4) None of the above
Codes:
(a) 1 and 2 (b) 1 and 3
(c) 2 and 3 (d) 1, 2 and 3

169. Identify the country which does not publish its own national bibliography? (*Net Exam.* 1999)
(a) U.K. (b) U.S.A.
(c) India (d) Australia

170. The heading "employment and wages" are both used in retrieval system, the term should (*Net Exam.* 1999)
(a) Be linked by a "see also" reference
(b) Be linked by a "see" reference
(c) By linked by both "see" and "see also" reference
(d) Not be linked

171. Intellectual Property Right (IPR) are recognised by (*Net Exam.* 1999)
(a) Copyright Law (b) Patent Law
(c) Neither (a) nor (b) (d) Both (a) and (b)

172. Match the following:

(A) Arrangement 1. Clear and legible type faces
(B) Authority 2. See and see also reference
(C) Index 3. Reputation of publishers
(D) Typography 4. Alphabetical or classified

(a) A - 4, B - 3, C - 2, D - 1
(b) A - 3, B - 2, C - 4, D - 1
(c) A - 4, B - 1, C - 3, D - 2
(d) A - 3, B - 2, C - 4, D - 1

173. Match the following:

(A) Treatment 1. Current or retrospective
(B) Scope 2. Accuracy, objectivity, reliability
(C) Advances 3. Staff rules
(D) Family health hand books 4. Current trends in development

(a) A - 2, B - 1, C - 4, D - 3
(b) A - 4, B - 3, C - 2, D - 1
(c) A - 3, B - 4, C - 2, D - 1
(d) A - 4, B - 3, C - 1, D - 2

174. Match the following:

(A) Hand books/Manuals 1. Knit to fit
(B) Cooking recipes hand books 2. Staff Car rules
(C) Official hand books 3. Baking book
(D) Recreation and hobbies 4. Established knowledge

(a) A - 4, B - 3, C - 2, D - 1
(b) A - 3, B - 4, C - 2, D - 1
(c) A - 1, B - 2, C - 3, D - 4
(d) A - 2, B - 1, C - 4, D - 3

175. Match the following:

(A) Encyclopedia Britannica 1. Voltaire, Rousseau, contributed articles
(B) Johann Heinrich Alsted 2. 1st Encyclopedia having article written
(C) Pierre Larousse 3. Encyclopedia septem Jomis Distincta
(D) John Hariss 4. 1st edition appeared in three volumes in 1771

(a) A - 4, B - 3, C - 2, D - 1
(b) A - 3, B - 4, C - 1, D - 2
(c) A - 1, B - 4, C - 2, D - 3
(d) A - 2, B - 1, C - 3, D - 4

176. Match the following:

(A) Isidore of seville 1. Etymologies or origins
(B) General dictionary 2. Assist in enriching word power
(C) Special dictionary 3. Helping solving cross word puzzles
(D) Translating dictionary 4. Useful for translators

(a) A - 1, B - 2, C - 3, D - 4
(b) A - 2, B - 3, C - 4, D - 1
(c) A - 4, B - 3, C - 2, D - 1
(d) A - 3, B - 4, C - 1, D - 2

177. Match the following:

(A) General dictionary 1. Recorder and standardiser of a language
(B) Special dictionary 2. Useful aids to Poets
(C) Translating dictionary 3. Useful to learn a new foreign language
(D) Subject dictionary 4. Helpful aid to the scientist

(a) A - 3, B - 4, C - 1, D - 2
(b) A - 2, B - 1, C - 4, D - 3
(c) A - 4, B - 3, C - 2, D - 1
(d) A - 1, B - 2, C - 3, D - 4

178. Who and when produced the first encyclopedia?

(a) Pilny in 77 A.D. (historia naturals in 37 Vols.)
(b) Louis Moreri 75 A.D. (in 1674)
(c) Marcus Terentius
(d) John Harias

179. Match the following.

(A) Random House Encyclopedia 1. Propaedia, Micropaedia and Macropaedia
(B) Encyclopedia Francoise 2. Encyclopedia of Education
(C) Encyclopedia Britannica 3. Collier Encyclopedia Year Book
(D) Special Encyclopedia 4. Colarpedia and Alphapedia
(E) Supplement of Encyclopedia 5. National Encyclopedia

(a) A - 4, B - 5, C - 1, D - 2, E - 3
(b) A - 5, B - 4, C - 3, D - 2, E - 1
(c) A - 5, C - 3, B - 4, D - 1, E - 2
(d) A - 4, B - 3, C - 2, D - 1, E - 5
(e) A - 3, B - 4, C - 5, D - 2, E - 1

180. The concept of 'Reference Service' is given by (*NET Exam.* 2001D)
(a) J.H. Shera (b) A. Strauss
(c) S.R. Ranganathan (d) Samuel Green

181. An abstract which is written for a special group of users is known as (*NET Exam.* 2001D)
(a) Critical abstract (b) Slanted abstract
(c) Author abstract (d) Indicative abstract

182. 'Books in Print' is a (*NET Exam.* 2001D)
(a) National Bibliography
(b) Trade Bibliography
(c) Retrospective Bibliography
(d) Subject Bibliography

183. Descriptive bibliography is primarily concerned with (*NET Exam.* 2002D)
1. Librarians 2. Scholars
3. State Library
Codes:
(a) 1 and 3 (b) 2 only
(c) 1 and 2 (d) 3 only

184. "Subject Guide to Books in Print" selects its subject heading from (*NET Exam.* 2002D)
(a) ALA list (b) POPSI
(c) Chain procedure (d) Sears' list of Subject heading

185. Who started the "Reference Services" in India? (*NET Exam.* 2002D)
(a) Dr. S.R. Ranganathan (b) Prof. P.N. Kaula
(c) W.A. Borden (d) R.R. Bowker

186. Andrew Carnegie was a (*NET Exam.* 2002D, 2002J)
(a) Classificationist (b) Librarian
(c) Information Scientist (d) Philanthropist

187. Translation service comes under the category of (*NET Exam.* 2002J)
(a) Secondary source (b) Primary Source
(c) Reference source (d) Tertiary source

188. PRECISE and POSI are (*NET Exam.* 2002J)
(a) Subject heading lists
(b) Indexing techniques
(c) Cataloguing codes
(d) Classification schemes

189. The index to any Atlas is also known as (*NET Exam.* 2002J)
(a) Index to Atlas (b) Atlas Index
(c) Gazetteer (d) Travel Guides

190. Which country does not have a national bibliography?
(a) United Kingdom (b) United States of America
(c) Australia (d) India

191. Which is the world's largest and most comprehensive bibliographic database? (*NET Exam.* 2002D)
(a) OCLC Access service (b) World Cat
(c) PRECIS (d) First search service

192. Who is a Bibliothecar? (*NET Exam.* 2002D)
(a) Philanthropist
(b) Librarian
(c) Information Scientist
(d) Computer Operator

193. If you want to know the birth place of S.R. Ranganathan, then which source will you choose? (*NET Exam.* 2002D)
(a) *India: A Reference Manual*
(b) *Dictionary of National Biography*
(c) *Indian National Bibliography*
(d) *World of Biography*

194. Which one is a online bibliographic services? (*NET Exam.* 2002D)
(a) DIALOG and NISCAIR
(b) DIALOG and ORBIT
(c) NISSAT and INIs
(d) All of the above

195. First known "Encyclopaedia" was written by (*NET Exam.* 2002D)
(a) Paul Otlet (b) Hippocrates
(c) Aristotle (d) Charak

196. Match the column: (*NET Exam.* 2002D)

Column–A	Column–B
(A) Establishing Knowledge	(i) Family health Handbooks
(B) Baking book	(ii) Handbooks
(C) Where there is no Doctor	(iii) Cooking recipes handbooks
(D) Knit to Fit	(iv) Official handbooks
(E) Staff Car rules	

Codes:	A	B	C	D	E
(a)	(ii)	(iii)	(i)	–	(iv)
(b)	(iii)	(i)	(ii)	(iv)	(v)
(c)	(ii)	(iii)	–	(i)	(iv)
(d)	(i)	(ii)	(iii)	(iv)	–

197. What is the month of publication of "Books in Print Supplement" (Bowker), annual? (*NET Exam.* 2003D)
(a) January (b) April
(c) June (d) December

198. Match the books against their authors: (*NET Exam.* 2012D)
List–I
(A) *Introduction to Modern Information Retrieval* (McGraw Hill)
(B) *Indexing Concepts and Methods* (Academic Press)
(C) *Thesaurus Construction: A Practical Manual* (Aslib)
(D) *Organising Knowledge: An Introduction to Managing Access to Information* (Ashgate)
List–II
(i) H. Borko and C. Benier
(ii) G. Salton and M.J. McGill
(iii) J.E. Rowley and R. Hartley
(iv) J. Aitchison and A. Gilchrist

Codes:	**A**	**B**	**C**	**D**
(a)	(i)	(ii)	(iii)	(iv)
(b)	(ii)	(i)	(iv)	(iii)
(c)	(iv)	(i)	(ii)	(iii)
(d)	(iii)	(i)	(iv)	(ii)

199. Which of the following sources is to present consolidated information available in various forms and to repackage the same in a condensed form for users? (*NET Exam.* 2003D)
(a) Surveys (b) Reviews
(c) Trend reports (d) State-of-the-art reports

200. Identify the correct order of evolution of the following storage order. (*NET Exam.* 2006D)
(a) Paper, Micro card, Magnetic tape, Clay tablet
(b) Clay tablet, Paper, Micro card, Magnetic tape
(c) Micro card, Magnetic tape, Clay tablet, Paper
(d) Magnetic tape, Clay tablet, Paper, Micro card

201. The GMD in a catalogue entry according to AACR-II revised edition is given (*NET Exam.* 2006D)
(a) After the title proper
(b) Before the title
(c) After the statement of responsibility
(d) Before the statement of responsibility

202. Which of the following is considered as key attribute in Bibliographic Database? (*NET Exam.* 2004D)
(a) Main entry access point (b) Title entry
(c) Author entry (d) ISBN

203. World of Learning is a(*NET Exam.* 2004D)
(a) Directory
(b) Annual Bibliography
(c) Dictionary (special)
(d) Trade bulletin

204. Bibliography that deals with the art of writing, printing, illumination and finding, etc. is (*NET Exam.* 2004D)
(a) Historical Bibliography
(b) Textual Bibliography
(c) Title Bibliography
(d) Trade Bibliography

205. In KWIC index, the keyword is derived from (*NET Exam.* 2004D)
(a) the title (b) the abstract
(c) the full text (d) the author

206. For the cataloguing of book, National Library of India uses (*NET Exam.* 2004D)
1. ASCR-I 2. CCC
3. AACR-II 4. AACR-II and CCC
Codes:
(a) 3 only (b) 2 and 1
(c) 2 only (d) 4 only

207. The Universal Bibliographic Control (UBC) programme was sponsored by IFLA in the year (*NET Exam.* 2004D)
(a) 1974 (b) 1931 (c) 1981 (d) 1973

208. Which of the following services in designated to identify the most suitable documents to a specific user? (*NET Exam.* 2004D)
(a) Document Delivery Service
(b) Selective Dissemination of Information
(c) Internal Link Service
(d) Current Awareness Service

209. Which kind of bibliography is a systematic list of all the books published all over the world? (*NET Exam.* 2003J)
(a) Author (b) Universal
(c) Trade (d) Title

210. Boolean Searching is (*NET Exam.* 2003J)

(a) used for computerized database
(b) based on post-coordinate indexing
(c) combined search statement using AND, OR and NOT
(d) all of the above

211. Sear's list was first published in (*NET Exam.* 2003J)
(a) 1937 (b) 1923 (c) 1925 (d) 1927

212. If you want to know the districts of Uttar Pradesh then which of the following source will you find? (*NET Exam.* 2003J)
(a) *India: Manual of Reference*
(b) *District Gazetteer of India*
(c) *Word of Learning*
(d) *Census of India*

213. If a catalogue represents the collection of two or more libraries, then it will be a (*NET Exam.* 2003J)
(a) Union Catalogue (b) UB Catalogue
(c) Bibliographical Catalogue (d) Author Catalogue

214. "Directory of American Research and Technology (DART)" is published by (*NET Exam.* 2003J)
(a) Whitakers (b) Sterling
(c) R.B. Bowker (d) None of these

215. Bibliolus is a (*NET Exam.* 2003D)
(a) National bibliography
(b) Public library
(c) General bibliography
(d) Mobile library

216. What is the relationship between ISBD and Cataloguing Codes? (*NET Exam.* 2004D)
(a) They are not related at all
(b) Cataloguing codes will include bibliographic description
(c) ISBD includes cataloguing rules
(d) ISBD can replace cataloguing codes

217. The record relating to the subject bibliographies is maintained by the (*NET Exam.* 2003J)
(a) Acquisition division (b) Periodical division
(c) Technical division (d) Reference division

218. The important characteristics of presentation of topic in an encyclopaedia is/are (*NET Exam.* 2003J)
1. Ability 2. Objectivity
3. Style 4. Format
(a) 1 and 2 (b) 1 and 4
(c) 1, 2 and 3 (c) All of the above

219. PRECIS has been originated from (*NET Exam.* 2003D)
(a) SLIC (b) KWIC
(c) Uniterm Indexing (d) Chain Procedure

220. "Indian Library Science Abstract" is a publication of (*NET Exam.* 2003D)
(a) IASLIC (b) ILA
(c) NISCAIR (d) National Library

221. The International Standard ISO-2709 is derived from (*NET Exam.* 2004J)
(a) UNIMARC (b) CCF
(c) ANSI (d) MARC-II

222. Among the following Boolean operator which is used for searching? (*NET Exam.* 2004J)
(a) AND (b) NOT
(c) AND and OR (d) OR

223. Citation Analysis helps in (*NET Exam.* 2004J)
(a) Selective Cataloguing
(b) Subject Cataloguing
(c) Descriptive Cataloguing
(d) Identification of Document

224. Kerdex is used to have a control on (*NET Exam.* 2004J)
(a) Periodicals
(b) Books
(c) Maps and globes
(d) Audio, visual programmes.

225. ISDN stands for: (*NET Exam.* 2007J)
(a) International Standard Digital Network
(b) International Standard Distributed Network
(c) Integrated Services Digital Network
(d) Integrated Services Distributed Network

226. Encyclopedia of Library and Information Science is published by (*NET Exam.* 2007J)
(a) H.W. Wilson (b) R.R. Bowker
(c) Marcel Dekker (d) Andrew Deutsch

227. ISBN now consists of (*NET Exam.* 2007J)
(a) 10 digits (b) 13 digits
(c) 15 digits (d) 8 digits

228. INDEST is a (*NET Exam.* 2007J)
(a) Bibliography (b) Consortium
(c) Directory (d) Dictionary

229. Multilingual dictionaries are also known as (*NET Exam.* 2007J)

(a) Report literature
(b) Polygots
(c) Translation dictionaries
(d) All of these

230. Match the following: (*NET Exam.* 2007J)

List-I	List-II
(A) Subject indexing	(i) P.M. Rogget
(B) Keyboard indexing	(ii) H.P. Luhn
(C) Automated indexing	(iii) H. Ohlman
(D) SLIC indexing	(iv) M.E. Sears
	(v) S.L. Mc Nold

Codes:	A	B	C	D
(a)	(iii)	(ii)	(iv)	(ii)
(b)	(iv)	(i)	(ii)	(iii)
(c)	(ii)	(i)	(v)	(iv)
(d)	(v)	(iii)	(iv)	(ii)

231. Routing of periodicals is considered as (*NET Exam.* 2007J)
(a) CAS
(b) SDI
(c) Translation service
(d) Indexing and Abstracting service

232. Which one of the following is not correctly matched? (*NET Exam.* 2006J)
(a) Books in Print–Trade Bibliography
(b) Cumulative Book Index–Books published in English language
(c) British Books in Print–R.R. Bowker
(d) National Bibliography–INB

233. **Assertion (A):** ISBD (S) is concerned with the serial publications. (*NET Exam.* 2007D)
Reason (R): It is not used for the serials which have ceased their publication.
Codes:
(a) (A) is true but (R) is false.
(b) (A) is false but (R) is true
(c) Both (A) and (R) are true
(d) Both (A) and (R) are false.

234. World of Learning is (*NET Exam.* 2007D)
(a) A Bibliography (b) An Abstract
(c) An Encyclopaedia (d) A Directory

235. This literature is not published and not available through normal book selling channels. (*NET Exam.* 2007D)
(a) Grey Literature (b) Text Books
(c) Journals (d) None of the above

236. These documents are not primary sources. (*NET Exam.* 2007D)
(a) Thesis (b) Patents
(c) Conference Papers (d) Reference Books

237. Match of the following: (*NET Exam.* 2007D)

List-I	List-II
(A) Pre-natal Cataloguing	(i) Shared Cataloguing Programme
(B) NPAC	(ii) Library of Congress
(C) CIP	(iii) NUCSSI
(D) Union Catalogue	(iv) S.R. Ranganathan

Codes:	A	B	C	D
(a)	(iii)	(ii)	(i)	(iv)
(b)	(iv)	(i)	(ii)	(iii)
(c)	(i)	(iv)	(iii)	(ii)
(d)	(ii)	(iii)	(i)	(iv)

238. **Assertion (A):** User profile is an essential component of SDI service.
Reason (R): SDI is a personalized current awareness service. (*NET Exam.* 2008J)
Codes:
(a) Both (A) and (R) are true
(b) Both (A) and (R) are false
(c) Both are partially true
(d) (A) is true but (R) is false

239. **Assertion (A):** IFLA's UBC programme encourages the use and exchange of standardized bibliographic description.
Reason (R): Use of standard enables to bring uniformity in bibliographic description and interchange of bibliographic data. (*NET Exam.* 2008D)
Codes:
(a) Both (A) and (R) are false
(b) Both (A) and (R) are true
(c) (R) is true but (A) is false
(d) (A) is true but (R) is false

240. Match the following items give in List-I and List-II (*NET Exam.* 2008DJ)
List-I
(A) Bibliographic description
(B) Short-range reference service
(C) SDI
(D) Uniterm
List-II
(i) Current Awareness Service
(ii) Post Coordinating Indexing
(iii) Abstract
(iv) Ready Refer Source

Codes:	A	B	C	D
(a)	(iii)	(iv)	(i)	(ii)
(b)	(ii)	(i)	(iii)	(iv)
(c)	(iv)	(i)	(ii)	(iii)
(d)	(ii)	(iii)	(iv)	(i)

241. Arrange according to year of establishment. (*NET Exam.* 2008D)
(a) Chemical Abstracts, Biological Abstracts, Science Citation Index, Indian Science Abstracts.
(b) Chemical Abstract, Science Citation Index, Indian Science Abstracts, Biological Abstract.
(c) Biological Abstracts, Chemical Abstracts, Science Citation Index, Indian Science Abstracts.
(d) Chemical Abstracts, Biological Abstracts, Indian Science Abstracts, Science Citation Index.

242. Glossary is a (*NET Exam.* 2008D)
(a) List of technical words with definitions
(b) List of words in a language
(c) List of thematically arranged words
(d) Alphabetical index to passages of work

243. Which of the following is not an example of Current Awareness Service (CAS)? (*NET Exam.* 2008D)
(a) A Reading List
(b) Current Contents
(c) An Indexing Bulletin
(d) Selective Dissemination of Information

244. A gazette gives information about (*NET Exam.* 2008D)
(a) Places of tourist interest
(b) History of places
(c) Official announcement and notification
(d) Old records

245. Number of digits is ISBN now are (*NET Exam.* 2008D, 2007J)
(a) 10 digits (b) 11 digits
(c) 12 digits (d) 13 digits

246. Dublin core is related to: (*NET Exam.* 2008D)
(a) Metadata (b) MARC
(c) ISBD (d) CCF

247. MeSH is the name of a (*NET Exam.* 2008D)
(a) Medical Library
(b) Controlled Vocabulary
(c) Online Database
(d) CSIR Unit

248. Which is the primary source for finding out Indian periodicals in Agriculture? (*NET Exam.* 2008D)
(a) Ulrich International Periodical Directory
(b) Reference Asia
(c) Press in India
(d) INFA Yearbook

249. Who is the Chairman of National Knowledge Commission? (*NET Exam.* 2008D)
(a) Harsha Parekh (b) P.B. Mangla
(c) Kalpana Dasgupta (d) Sam Pitroda

250. Which of the following indexes only paper presented in the conferences? (*NET Exam.* 2008D)
(a) LISA
(b) Current Research Abstracts
(c) Research-in-Progress
(d) ISTP

251. Biological Abstract has indexes. These are (*NET Exam.* 2008D)
1. Basic index 2. Title index
3. Bio-systematic index 4. Author index
(a) All the four (b) 2 & 4
(c) 2 & 3 (d) 1 & 2

252. The quotation "Where is the Wisdom, We Lost in Knowledge..." is by (*NET Exam.* 2009D)
(a) John Keats (b) M.P. Carter
(c) T.S. Eliot (d) Marshall McLuhan

253. **Assertion (A):** An indexing language is an artificial language as it uses controlled vocabulary.
Reason (R): It provides different relationships between terms. (*NET Exam.* 2009D)
(a) Both (A) and (R) are false.
(b) Both (A) and (R) are true.
(c) (A) is true but (R) is false.
(d) (A) is false but (R) is true.

254. The most popular form of current Awareness Service is (*NET Exam.* 2009D)
(a) title announcement
(b) contents list
(c) information bulletin
(d) personal contacts

255. Arrange the following bibliographies according to their data of origin: (*NET Exam.* 2009D)

(i) Indian National Bibliography
(ii) Cumulative Book Index
(iii) Book in Print
(iv) British National Bibliography

Codes:

(a)	(iii)	(iv)	(i)	(ii)
(b)	(ii)	(iii)	(iv)	(i)
(c)	(i)	(ii)	(iii)	(iv)
(d)	(iv)	(ii)	(i)	(iii)

256. Arrange the following secondary publications according to the beginning of their publication in chronological order. (*NET Exam.* 2009J)

(i) Biological Abstracts
(ii) Chemical Abstracts
(iii) LISA
(iv) Index Medicus

Codes:

(a)	(i)	(ii)	(iii)	(iv)
(b)	(i)	(iii)	(ii)	(iv)
(c)	(ii)	(i)	(iii)	(iv)
(d)	(iii)	(i)	(iv)	(ii)

257. **Assertion (A):** Indexing periodical retrieves information, which includes brief summary of the article.

Reason (R): It provides list of articles along with the title, authors and other bibliographic details. (*NET Exam.* 2010J)

Codes:
(a) Both (A) and (R) are true.
(b) Both (A) and (R) are false.
(c) (A) is true, but (R) is false.
(d) (A) is false, but (R) are true.

258. Match the following: (*NET Exam.* 2009D)

List-I
(A) Little Science, Big Science
(B) Documentation
(C) The Third Wave
(D) The Information Society

List-II
(i) S.C. Bradfold (ii) William Martin
(iii) Eric J de Solla Price (iv) Alwin Toffler

Codes:	A	B	C	D
(a)	(i)	(ii)	(iii)	(iv)
(b)	(iii)	(i)	(iv)	(ii)
(c)	(iv)	(iii)	(ii)	(i)
(d)	(ii)	(i)	(iv)	(iii)

259. Match the following: (*NET Exam.* 2009D)

List-I	List-II
(A) Mcfee	(i) DOAJ
(B) Directory	(ii) Antivirus
(C) Personal Web pages	(iii) Vendor on Internet
(D) Amazon.com	(iv) Blogs

Codes:	A	B	C	D
(a)	(ii)	(i)	(iv)	(iii)
(b)	(i)	(iv)	(iii)	(ii)
(c)	(ii)	(iii)	(iv)	(i)
(d)	(iv)	(iii)	(ii)	(i)

260. Which national agency in India is assigning the ISBN? (*NET Exam.* 2009D)
(a) Raja Ram Mohan Roy National Education Resource Centre
(b) Delhi Public Library
(c) Federation of Publishers in India
(d) National Library of India

261. Who propounded "Conservative, moderate and liberal theories of reference service"? (*NET Exam.* 2009D)
(a) William A. Katz (b) S.R. Ranganathan
(c) James I. Wyer (d) R. Emery

262. The input Centre for INIS in India is (*NET Exam.* 2009D)
(a) DRDO (b) DSIR (c) TFIR (d) BARC

263. **Assertion (A):** SDI is a user-oriented current information service.

Reason (R): It is an alerting service directed towards groups.

Codes:
(a) Both (A) and (R) are true.
(b) (A) is true, but (R) is false.
(c) (A) is false, but (R) is true.
(d) Both (A) and (R) are false.

264. Match the following: (*NET Exam.* 2010D)

List-I	List-II
(A) Nadir to Ascending	(i) Hypothesizing
(B) Ascending to Zenith	(ii) Verification
(C) Zenith to Descending	(iii) Deductive
(D) Descending to Nadir	(iv) Empirical

Codes:	A	B	C	D
(a)	(i)	(iii)	(ii)	(iv)
(b)	(ii)	(iv)	(i)	(iii)
(c)	(iii)	(i)	(iv)	(ii)
(d)	(iv)	(i)	(iii)	(ii)

265. Match the following: (*NET Exam.* 2010D)

List-I
(A) Books in Print
(B) Ulrich International Periodical Directory
(C) World of Learning
(D) Who's Who in India
List-II
(i) Bibliography of periodicals
(ii) Trade Bibliography
(iii) Biographical source
(iv) Directory

Codes:	A	B	C	D
(a)	(ii)	(i)	(iv)	(iii)
(b)	(i)	(ii)	(iii)	(iv)
(c)	(iii)	(i)	(iv)	(ii)
(d)	(i)	(iii)	(iv)	(ii)

266. Who had given the 'Minimal and Maximum' theories of reference service? (*NET Exam.* 2009J)
(a) C.M. Winchell (b) S.R. Ranganathan
(c) James I. Wayer (d) S. Rothstein

267. Match the following: (*NET Exam.* 2012D)
List-I
(A) Means of improving operations and services
(B) Preparation of to-do-list
(C) Performance guidelines
(D) Reinforce the spines of books
List-II
(i) Preservation (ii) Standards
(iii) Time management (iv) Evaluation

Codes:	(A)	(B)	(C)	(D)
(a)	(iv)	(iii)	(ii)	(i)
(b)	(iv)	(ii)	(iii)	(i)
(c)	(ii)	(iv)	(iii)	(i)
(d)	(iii)	(ii)	(i)	(iv)

268. Match the following: (*NET Exam.* 2010D)

List-I	List-II
(A) William Martin	(i) Little Science Big Science
(B) Alvin Toffler	(ii) Information Society
(C) Eric J de Solla Price	(iii) Documentation
(D) S.C. Bradford	(iv) The Third Wave

Codes:	A	B	C	D
(a)	(ii)	(iv)	(iii)	(i)
(b)	(iv)	(ii)	(iii)	(i)
(c)	(ii)	(iv)	(i)	(iii)
(d)	(i)	(iv)	(ii)	(iii)

269. The idea of Thesaurofacet was developed by (*NET Exam.* 2011D)
(a) G. Bhattacharya (b) S.R. Ranganathan
(c) Jean Aitchison (d) Derek Austin

270. The Digital Millennium Copyright Act (DMCA) is (*NET Exam.* 2011D)
(a) United States Copyright Law
(b) British Copyright Law
(c) European Copyright Law
(d) Russian Copyright Law

271. Gazetteer of India was first published by (*NET Exam.* 2011D)
(a) Ministry of Education and Social Welfare
(b) Ministry of Information and Broadcasting
(c) Ministry of Home Affairs
(d) Controller of Publications

272. Which of the following has stopped publishing in the print from 2012? (*NET Exam.* 2012D)
(a) Europe World Yearbook
(b) Times of India Directory
(c) New Encyclopedia Britannica
(d) Keesing's Contemporary Archives

273. Which of the following is not providing encyclopedia type of information? (*NET Exam.* 2012D)
(a) Encyclopedia of Associations
(b) Compton's Encyclopedia
(c) World book Encyclopedia
(d) Encyclopedia Americana

274. Name of the President of Sri Lanka can be found in (*NET Exam.* 2012D)
(a) *International Who's Who*
(b) *Statement's Yearbook*
(c) *Who's Who in the World*
(d) *Wilson Biographies*

275. NICRYS is information system for (*NET Exam.* 2012D)
(a) Machine tools (b) Food Science
(c) Crystallography (d) Drugs

276. **Assertion (A):** Encyclopedias are not relevant for finding geographically information.
Reason (R): Encyclopedias are the substitute for all categories of references sources. (*NET Exam.* 2012D)
Codes:
(a) (A) is false but (R) is true.
(b) Both (A) and (R) are true.
(c) Both (A) and (R) are false.
(d) (A) is true but (R) is false.

277. Identify the correct order of the LIS Associations as per their year of establishment. (*NET Exam.* 2012D)
(a) CLA, ALA, SLA, IASLIC
(b) ALA, SLA, CLA, IASLIC
(c) SLA, IASLIC, ALA, CLA
(d) CLA, SLA, IASLIC, ALA

278. Match the following: (*NET Exam.* 2012D)

List-I (Subjects)	List-II (Modes of Formation)
(A) India	(i) Agglomeration
(B) Agriculture of wheat	(ii) Lamination
(C) Biochemistry	(iii) Fusion
(D) Biological Sciences	(iv) Denudation

Codes:	A	B	C	D
(a)	(ii)	(iv)	(iii)	(i)
(b)	(i)	(iii)	(ii)	(iv)
(c)	(iv)	(iii)	(i)	(ii)
(d)	(iv)	(ii)	(iii)	(i)

279. Auto abstracting involves use of computers to (*NET Exam.* 2011J)
(a) structure the content of an abstract
(b) prepare indicative abstract
(c) pickup significant words
(d) arrange words in order

280. *New Encyclopaedia Britannica* is published from (*NET Exam.* 2011J)
(a) London (b) New York
(c) Paris (d) Chicago

281. All Union Institute for Scientific and Technical Information (VINITI) was established in (*NET Exam.* 2011J)
(a) 1952 (b) 1953 (c) 1954 (d) 1956

282. **Assertion (A):** A bibliographic utility is an organization that offers bibliographic services to subscribing libraries.
Reason (R): Library of Congress is a bibliographic utility. (*NET Exam.* 2011J)
Codes:
(a) (A) is true, but (R) is false.
(b) (A) is false, but (R) is true.
(c) Both (A) and (R) are true.
(d) Both (A) and (R) are false.

283. CCF for bibliographic record refers to (*NET Exam.* 2012D)
(i) Data transfer
(ii) Data storage
(iii) Standard tags of data identification
(iv) Formatting of records
Codes:
(a) (i) and (iii) are correct
(b) (i), (ii) and (iv) are correct
(c) (ii) and (iii) are correct
(d) (iii), (i) and (ii) are correct

284. Which of the following are not reference service? (*NET Exam.* 2012D)
(i) Preparation of user profile
(ii) Initiation of freshman
(iii) Compilation of documentation list
(iv) Readers Advisory
Codes:
(a) (i) and (ii) (b) (ii) and (iii)
(c) (i) and (iii) (d) (iii) and (iv)

285. **Assertion (A):** Informative abstracts provide a concise summary of the subject content of an article.
Reason (R): These are title-oriented than finding-oriented. (*NET Exam.* 2012D)
Codes:
(a) Both (A) and (R) are true.
(b) (A) is true but (R) is false
(c) (A) is false but (R) is true.
(d) Both (A) and (R) are false.

286. **Assertion (A):** LIS profession is not considered at par with medical and legal professions.
Reason (R): There is no constitutional body for LIS profession like Medical Council of India (MCI) and Bar Council of India (BCI). (*NET Exam.* 2012D Paper III)
Codes:
(a) Both (A) and (R) are true.
(b) Both (A) and (R) are false.
(c) (A) is true but (R) is false.
(d) (A) is false but (R) is true.

287. Who used the phrase 'control-access directional type sources'?
(a) R.E. Bopp (b) B.C. Wynar
(c) W.A. Katz (d) R. Balay

288. **Assertion (A):** Information Literacy provides training to use maximum resources available in a library. (*NET Exam.* 2011J)
Reason (R): Information Literacy always aims at specific group of users.
Codes:
(a) (A) is false, but (R) is true.
(b) Both (A) and (R) are false.
(c) Both (A) and (R) are true.
(d) (A) is true, but (R) is false.

289. **Assertion (A):** LISA is a primary source of information.

Reason (R): All primary sources provide original information. (*NET Exam.* 2011J)

Codes:

(a) (A) is false, but (R) is true.
(b) (A) is true, but (R) is false.
(c) Both (A) and (R) are false.
(d) Both (A) and (R) are true.

290. Match the following: (*NET Exam.* 2011J)

List-I

(A) Books in Print
(B) World of Learning
(C) Keesing's Record of World Events
(D) Fodor's Guide to India

List-II

(i) Directory (ii) Trade bibliography
(iii) Travel guide (iv) Newspaper digest

Codes:	A	B	C	D
(a)	(ii)	(i)	(iv)	(iii)
(b)	(ii)	(iii)	(i)	(iv)
(c)	(iv)	(i)	(ii)	(iii)
(d)	(iii)	(ii)	(i)	(iv)

291. Match the following: (*NET Exam.* 2012D Paper III)

List-I	**List-II**
(A) Altavista	(i) Subject search engine
(B) Lycos	(ii) Meta search engine
(C) Geoindex	(iii) Regional search engine
(D) Savvysearch	(iv) General search engine

Codes:	A	B	C	D
(a)	(iii)	(ii)	(i)	(iv)
(b)	(iii)	(iv)	(ii)	(i)
(c)	(iv)	(iii)	(i)	(ii)
(d)	(iv)	(i)	(ii)	(iii)

292. Vocabulary in a database is controlled by (*NET Exam.* 2012D Paper III)

(i) Thesaurus files (ii) Import files
(iii) Standard files (iv) Authority files

Codes:

(a) (i) and (ii) are correct
(b) (iii) and (iv) are correct
(c) (i) and (iii) are correct
(d) (ii) and (iii) are correct

293. Match the following: (*NET Exam.* 2013J)

List-I

(A) Systematic Bibliography
(B) Analytical or Critical Bibliography
(C) Historical Bibliography
(D) Documentary Bibliography

List-II

(i) List of macro/micro ideas of articles
(ii) Investigation of physical nature of books
(iii) Listing of items with minimum details
(iv) Concerned with art of writing, printing and binding

Codes:	A	B	C	D
(a)	(i)	(iv)	(iii)	(ii)
(b)	(ii)	(i)	(iv)	(iii)
(c)	(iii)	(ii)	(iv)	(i)
(d)	(ii)	(iv)	(iii)	(i)

294. Match the following queries with their appropriate category of reference source: (*NET Exam.* 2013J)

List-I

(A) Enrolment of students in a university
(B) Weather of Denmark
(C) No. of foreigners visited World Book fair in 2011
(D) No. of hospitals in China

List-II

(i) Yearbook (ii) Statistical source
(iii) Directory (iv) Geographical Source

Codes:	A	B	C	D
(a)	(iv)	(iii)	(i)	(ii)
(b)	(i)	(iii)	(ii)	(iv)
(c)	(ii)	(iv)	(i)	(iii)
(d)	(iii)	(iv)	(i)	(ii)

295. Match the following: (*NET Exam.* 2011D)

List-I	**List-II**
(A) Bibliography	(i) Persons
(B) Yearbook	(ii) Words
(C) Dictionary	(iii) Current information
(D) Biography	(iv) Books

Codes:	A	B	C	D
(a)	(i)	(iii)	(ii)	(iv)
(b)	(ii)	(iii)	(iv)	(i)
(c)	(iv)	(iii)	(ii)	(i)
(d)	(i)	(ii)	(iv)	(iii)

296. **Assertion (A):** Encyclopaedia is the queen of all reference sources. (*NET Exam.* 2011D)

Reason (R): Encyclopaedias are more suitable for finding trend information.

Codes:

(a) Both (A) and (R) are true.
(b) (A) is true, but (R) is false.

(c) (A) is false but (R) is true.
(d) Both (A) and (R) are false.

297. Arrange the following according to their year of publication (*NET Exam.* 2011D)
(i) New Encyclopaedia Britannica
(ii) Encyclopaedia Americana
(iii) Encyclopaedia of Library & Information Science
(iv) McGraw Hill Encyclopaedia of Science & Technology

Codes:

(a)	(ii)	(i)	(iv)	(iii)
(b)	(i)	(ii)	(iv)	(iii)
(c)	(iii)	(i)	(iv)	(ii)
(d)	(iii)	(iv)	(i)	(iii)

298. **Assertion (A):** Systematic and efficient use of statistical tools in research helps in precise interpretation of research results.
Reason (R): Statistical tools cannot give specific explanations of the data. (*NET Exam.* 2013J)
Codes:
(a) Both (A) and (R) are true.
(b) (A) is true and (R) is false.
(c) Both (A) and (R) are false.
(d) (A) is false and (R) is true.

299. Information on Prime Minister of Bangladesh can be found in (*NET Exam.* 2013 J)
(a) *International Who's Who*
(b) *Who's Who in Bangladesh*
(c) *Current Biography*
(d) *Statesman's Yearbook*

300. 'Eradication of Malaria in India 1990-1999'—a report can be categorised under (*NET Exam.* 2013J)
(a) Trend Report (b) Review Report
(c) State of the Art Report (d) Research Report

301. ERIC is sponsored by (*NET Exam.* 2013J)
(a) US National Health Institute
(b) Health and Rehabilitation Services Division, ALA
(c) Department of Health Education & Welfare, Government of USA
(d) Health Science Information Centre, USA

302. Historical/Government records related to an organization are maintained in (*NET Exam.* 2013J)
(i) Achieves (ii) Museums
(iii) Repositories (iv) Government Libraries
Codes:
(a) (i) and (ii) are correct.
(b) (ii) and (iii) are correct.
(c) (i) and (iii) are correct.
(d) (ii) and (iv) are correct.

303. *Who's Who in India*, an irregular publication is published by (*NET Exam.* 2013J)
(a) Business Press, Bombay
(b) Sterling, New Delhi
(c) Tradesman & Men Asia, Delhi
(d) Sahitya Samsad, Calcutta

304. Match the following: (*NET Exam.* 2013J)

List-I	**List-II**
(A) Trade Publisher	(i) UNESCO
(B) Subject book publisher	(ii) American Psychological Society
(C) Government Press	(iii) Harper Collins
(D) Scholarly Publisher	(iv) W.B. Saunders

Codes:	**A**	**B**	**C**	**D**
(a)	(ii)	(iv)	(iii)	(i)
(b)	(iv)	(iii)	(i)	(ii)
(c)	(i)	(iv)	(iii)	(ii)
(d)	(iii)	(iv)	(i)	(ii)

305. Information about Government of India's stand on 'FDI' can be found in (*NET Exam.* 2013J)
(a) Gazetteer of India
(b) Britannica Book of the Year
(c) Statesman's Yearbook
(d) Asian Recorder

306. Who used the word Bibliography first? (*NET Exam.* 2005D)
(a) Melvil Dewey
(b) Peter Phyrr
(c) L.J. de Saint Charles
(d) Dr. Ranganathan

307. The internationally agreed upon number given to a book is called (*NET Exam.* 2005D)
(a) ISBN (b) ISDN (c) ISNR (d) ISSN

308. PRECISE is used in (*NET Exam.* 2005D)
1. BND & IND 2. ISBD
3. ISBN & ISBD
(a) 1 only (b) 2 only
(c) 1 & 3 (d) 1 & 2

309. According to laws of library and information science, Bibliothecar is the (*NET Exam.* 2005D)
(a) Librarian
(b) Translator
(c) Information Scientists
(d) Research Associate

310. Match the following: (*NET Exam.* 2013J)
List-I
(A) Statistical Quality/Process Control (SQC/SPC)
(B) Check Sheets
(C) Pereto Chart
(D) Fish Bone Diagram
List-II
(i) Identify the intensity of each problem in the production process.
(ii) Selected variables checked.
(iii) Identify the relationship between problems and causes.
(iv) Record variables in the production process.

Codes:	A	B	C	D
(a)	(ii)	(iv)	(i)	(iii)
(b)	(iv)	(ii)	(iii)	(i)
(c)	(iii)	(iv)	(i)	(ii)
(d)	(i)	(ii)	(iv)	(iii)

311. **Assertion (A):** Machine translation is not a fully dependable service.
Reason (R): The semantics of language are not fully encoded in algorithms. (*NET Exam.* 2011J)
Codes:
(a) (A) is true, but (R) is false.
(b) Both (A) and (R) are true.
(c) (A) is false, but (R) is true.
(d) Both (A) and (R) are false.

312. Science Abstracts published by (*NET Exam.* 2011J)
(a) INSPEC (Institute of Electrical Engineering)
(b) Institute of Physics, London
(c) American Institute of Physics
(d) PSOJ (Physical Society of Japan)

313. Vocabulary in a database is controlled by (*NET Exam.* 2013J)
(i) Thesaurus files (ii) Dictionary files
(iii) Standard files (iv) Authority files
Codes:
(a) (i) and (ii) are correct.
(b) (iii) and (iv) are correct.
(c) (i) and (iii) are correct.
(d) (i) and (iv) are correct.

314. Limitations of Bibliometrics is/are (*NET Exam.* 2013J)
(i) Analysing research and development trends
(ii) Describing text, not necessarily meaning and context
(iii) Identifying the active areas of research
(iv) Citation bias
Codes:
(a) (ii) and (iv) are correct.
(b) (i) and (iii) are correct.
(c) (i), (ii) and (iv) are correct.
(d) (ii) and (iii) are correct.

315. Walford's *Guide to Reference Material* is published by (*NET Exam.* 2013J)
(a) American Library Association, Chicago
(b) R.R. Bowkar, London
(c) Library Association Publishing, London
(d) Learned Information Ltd., New Jersey

316. Which of the following are 'Inclusive geographical sources'? (*NET Exam.* 2012J)
(i) Maps (ii) Atlases
(iii) Encyclopaedias (iv) Yearbooks
Codes:
(a) (i) and (ii) are correct
(b) (iii) and (iv) are correct
(c) (ii) and (iii) are correct
(d) (ii) and (iv) are correct

317. Match the following: (*NET Exam.* 2012J)

List-I	**List-II**
(A) User orientation	(i) Bibliographic service
(B) Information repackaging	(ii) Reference service
(C) Translation	(iii) Digest series
(D) Indexing	(iv) Support service

Codes:	A	B	C	D
(a)	(i)	(iv)	(iii)	(ii)
(b)	(iii)	(ii)	(i)	(iv)
(c)	(iv)	(i)	(ii)	(iii)
(d)	(ii)	(iii)	(iv)	(i)

318. Arrange the following according to their year of first publication: (*NET Exam.* 2012J)
(i) Encyclopaedia Britannica
(ii) Encyclopaedia Americana
(iii) Encyclopaedia of Library and Information Science
(iv) McGraw-Hill Encyclopaedia of Science and Technology

Codes:

(a)	(iv)	(iii)	(i)	(ii)
(b)	(i)	(ii)	(iv)	(iii)
(c)	(iii)	(i)	(iv)	(ii)
(d)	(ii)	(iv)	(i)	(iii)

319. Arrange the following according to their year of origin: (*NET Exam.* 2012J)
(i) Bradford's Law (ii) Lotka's Law
(iii) Statistical Bibliography (iv) Zipf's Law

Codes:

(a)	(i)	(iii)	(iv)	(ii)
(b)	(i)	(ii)	(iv)	(iii)
(c)	(iv)	(iii)	(i)	(ii)
(d)	(iii)	(ii)	(iv)	(i)

320. "Biotechnology" is formed as a result of (*NET Exam.* 2012J)
(a) Fusion (b) Lamination
(c) Fission (d) Agglomeration

321. Match the following: (*NET Exam.* 2012J)

List-I
(A) Guidance to use RTI Act
(B) Orientation in use of multimedia
(C) Providing user with list of information sources
(D) Directing the user of INFLIBNET to seek needed information

List-II
(i) Documentation service
(ii) Referral service
(iii) Informative Literacy
(iv) Reference service

Codes:	A	B	C	D
(a)	(iii)	(ii)	(i)	(iv)
(b)	(iv)	(ii)	(iii)	(i)
(c)	(ii)	(i)	(iv)	(iii)
(d)	(iv)	(iii)	(i)	(ii)

322. Science Citation Index is published by: (*NET Exam.* 2012J)
(a) Thomson Reuters (b) H.W. Wilson
(c) Whitaker (d) R.R. Bowker

323. Information about scale and projection can be found in (*NET Exam.* 2012J)
(a) Encyclopaedias
(b) Handbooks of Manuals
(c) Geographical sources
(d) Directories

324. Match the following: (*NET Exam.* 2012D)

List-I
(A) Asian Recorder
(B) Union Catalogue of Scientific Serials
(C) Books-in-Print
(D) Social Science Index

List-II
(i) Location of specific volume of journal
(ii) Articles on Green Revolution
(iii) Obituary of Dev Anand
(iv) Availability of books

Codes:	A	B	C	D
(a)	(iv)	(iii)	(i)	(ii)
(b)	(i)	(iv)	(ii)	(iii)
(c)	(iii)	(i)	(iv)	(ii)

325. Arrange the following publications according to their year of origin. (*NET Exam.* 2012D)
(i) Social Science Citation Index
(ii) LISA
(iii) Library Literature and Information Science
(iv) Library Journal

Codes:

(a)	(i)	(iii)	(iv)	(ii)
(b)	(ii)	(iv)	(i)	(iii)
(c)	(iv)	(iii)	(ii)	(i)
(d)	(iii)	(ii)	(iv)	(i)

326. Arrange the following in a chronological order according to their year of establishment: (*NET Exam.* 2012D)
(i) Library of Congress
(ii) NISCAIR
(iii) Delivery of Books Act
(iv) National Library of India

Codes:

(a)	(iii)	(iv)	(ii)	(i)
(b)	(ii)	(iii)	(i)	(iv)
(c)	(i)	(iv)	(iii)	(ii)
(d)	(iv)	(i)	(iii)	(ii)

327. Match the following: (*NET Exam.* 2012D)

List-I
(A) Directory (B) Annuals
(C) Bibliography (D) Newspaper Digest

List-II
(i) Information Please Almanac
(ii) Keesing's Record of World Events
(iii) Encyclopaedia of Associations
(iv) Publishers' Weekly

Codes:	A	B	C	D
(a)	(iii)	(i)	(iv)	(ii)
(b)	(i)	(iii)	(iv)	(ii)
(c)	(iii)	(ii)	(iv)	(i)
(d)	(iv)	(i)	(ii)	(iii)

328. Match the following: (*NET Exam.* 2012D)

List-I
(A) Guiding users to the place of information
(B) Guiding users in the use of information
(C) Alerting users with the latest arrivals
(D) Providing users with summarized information

List-II
(i) Digest (ii) User orientation
(iii) Referral (iv) Current Awareness

Codes:	A	B	C	D
(a)	(iii)	(iv)	(i)	(ii)
(b)	(iii)	(ii)	(iv)	(i)
(c)	(iv)	(i)	(iii)	(ii)
(d)	(ii)	(i)	(iii)	(iv)

329. Which of the following are Trade Bibliographies? (*NET Exam.* 2012D)
(i) Books-in-Print
(ii) Indian Books-in-Print
(iii) Indian National Bibliography
(iv) British National Bibliography

Codes:
(a) (i) and (iii) are correct
(b) (ii) and (iv) are correct
(c) (i) and (ii) are correct
(d) (ii) and (iii) are correct

330. Which of the following is not a part of word treatment in language dictionaries? (*NET Exam.* 2012J)
(a) Gloss (b) Vernacular
(c) Etymology (d) Grammatical information

331. Which reference tool defines Reference service as "...that phase of work which is directly concerned with assistance to readers in securing information and in using the resources of the library in study and research"? (*NET Exam.* 2013J)
(a) Encyclopaedia of Librarianship
(b) Encyclopaedia of Library and Information Science
(c) ALA Glossary of Library Terms
(d) ALA World Encyclopaedia of Library & Information Services

332. A version of KWIC augmented with author/name is called (*NET Exam.* 2012J)
(a) WADEX (b) KWOC
(c) KWAC (d) KWIC

333. Match the following: (*NET Exam.* 2012J)

List-I	List-II
(A) Cole and Eales	(i) Statistical Bibliography
(B) Hume	(ii) Scientometrics
(C) Pritchard	(iii) Statistical Analysis
(D) T. Braun	(iv) Bibliometrics

Codes:	A	B	C	D
(a)	(iv)	(iii)	(ii)	(i)
(b)	(iii)	(i)	(iv)	(ii)
(c)	(ii)	(iii)	(i)	(iv)
(d)	(i)	(iii)	(iv)	(ii)

334. The concept of 'Stopword' list is relevant in the context of (*NET Exam.* 2012J)
(a) Uniform Indexing (b) Citation Indexing
(c) Chain Indexing (d) Keyword Indexing

335. Who of the following is not the author of any reference book? (*NET Exam.* 2012J)
(a) C.M. Winchell (b) William A. Katz
(c) Louis Shores (d) Maurice B. Line

336. Match the following: (*NET Exam.* 2012D)

List-I	List-II
(A) Classification	(i) LISA
(B) Cataloguing	(ii) UDC
(C) Subject Heading	(iii) AACR
(D) Library Science Abstracts	(iv) LCSH

Codes:	A	B	C	D
(a)	(ii)	(i)	(iv)	(iii)
(b)	(ii)	(iii)	(iv)	(i)
(c)	(iv)	(iii)	(i)	(ii)
(d)	(ii)	(iv)	(i)	(iii)

337. **Assertion (A):** Library & Information centres are knowledge/management centres.

Reason (R): Libraries handle tacit knowledge.

Codes:
(a) Both (A) and (R) are true.
(b) (A) is partially true, but (R) is false.
(c) (A) is false, but (R) is true.
(d) Both (A) and (R) are false.

338. Match the following: (*NET Exam.* 2012D)

List-I
(A) *Guide to Use of Books and Libraries*
(B) *If You Want to Evaluate Your Library*
(C) *Cuneiform to Computer: A History of Reference Sources*
(D) *Subject Approach to Information*

List-II
(i) F.W. Lancaster (ii) A.C. Foskelt
(iii) Jean K. Gates (iv) William A. Katz

Codes:	A	B	C	D
(a)	(ii)	(iii)	(iv)	(i)
(b)	(i)	(iv)	(iii)	(ii)
(c)	(iii)	(i)	(iv)	(ii)
(d)	(iv)	(ii)	(i)	(iii)

339. Which of the following are review type services? (*NET Exam.* 2012D)
(i) Current Awareness
(ii) Trend Reports
(iii) News Clippings
(iv) State of the Art Report
Codes:
(a) (i), (ii), (iii) are correct.
(b) (i), (iii), (iv) are correct.
(c) (ii) & (iv) are correct.
(d) (ii) & (iii) are correct.

340. Arrange the following according to their year of origin: (*NET Exam.* 2012D)
(i) Indian National Bibliography
(ii) British National Bibliography
(iii) Cumulative Book Index
(iv) Books in Print
Codes:

(a)	(i)	(iii)	(iv)	(ii)
(b)	(ii)	(i)	(iii)	(iv)
(c)	(iv)	(iii)	(ii)	(i)
(d)	(iii)	(iv)	(ii)	(i)

341. In a thesaurus, under an item "Internal Migration," which of the following lines would you expect to fund? (*NET Exam.* 2001J)
(a) BT Migration
(b) NT Rural-to-Urban Migration
(c) RT International Migration
(d) All of the above

342. Which of the following reference sources will you consult to locate information on the Pokhran test? (*NET Exam.* 2001J)
(a) *Encyclopaedia Britannica*
(b) *Asian Recorder*
(c) *Commonwealth Universities Yearbook*
(d) *Dictionary of National Biography*

343. Which of the following is not an example of Current Awareness Service (CAS)? (*NET Exam.* 2001J)
(a) SDI (b) An Indexing Bulletin
(c) Current Contents (d) A reading List

344. Non-bibliographic Databases contain (*NET Exam.* 2001J)
(a) Numeric Data (b) Textual Data
(c) Visual Data (d) All of the above

345. Indexing and abstracting sources are available in print, optical and online. Among the three formats there is usually(*NET Exam.* 2001J)
(a) a difference in price, but not in capability
(b) no difference in price, but difference in capability
(c) a difference both in price and in capability
(d) no difference in price or capability

346. A document description is not found in a (*NET Exam.* 2001J)
(a) Catalogue entry (b) Citation
(c) Bibliographic entry (d) Class number

347. Which of the following sources with you consult to locate information on "Amartya Sen"? (*NET Exam.* 2002J)
(a) *Facts of File*
(b) *Asian Recorder*
(c) *Dictionary of National Biography*
(d) *Encyclopaedia Britannica*

348. Bibliography deals with the art of writing, printing, illumination and binding, etc. is (*NET Exam.* 2003 J)
(a) Textual bibliography
(b) Historical Bibliography
(c) Title Bibliography
(d) Trade Bibliography

349. Indicate the name of the philosopher who was the exponent of Scientific Method. (*NET Exam.* 2001D)
(a) Aristotle (b) Bacon
(c) Confucious (d) Descrates

350. The Indian National Bibliography does not include (*NET Exam.* 2001J)
(a) Books published in India in English
(b) Official reports
(c) Books on India, published abroad
(d) Books published in recognized Indian language.

351. The three broad categories of Biographical Dictionaries are (*NET Exam.* 2001D)
(a) General, National and Special
(b) International, National and Local
(c) General, Special and Local
(d) General, National and International

352. The term 'Lexicography' is associated with (*NET Exam.* 2001D)

(a) Compilation of Encyclopaedia
(b) Compilation of Handbooks
(c) Compilation of dictionaries
(d) None of the above

353. Andrew Carnegie was a (*NET Exam.* 2001D)
(a) Philanthropist (b) Cataloguer
(c) Network Expert (d) Librarian

354. Bibliography of Bibliographies come under the category
(a) Primary Sources (b) Secondary Sources
(c) Tertiary Sources (d) None of the above
(*NET Exam.* 2001D)

355. The origin of the concept of 'Literary Warrant' was by (*NET Exam.* 2001D)
(a) S.R. Ranganathan (b) Wyndham Hulme
(c) E.C. Richardson (d) W.C.B. Sayers

356. The *Study Abroad* is a/an (*NET Exam.* 2001D)
(a) Encyclopaedia (b) Yearbook
(c) Directory (d) Handbook

357. Which of the following key terms of references assigned to National Knowledge Commission (NKC) constituted in June 2005 under the Chairmanship of Sam Pitroda for preparing a blue print to reform knowledge-related institutions and their infrastructure? (*NET 17J ii paper*)
(i) Build Excellence in Education System and increase India's competitive advantage in the field of knowledge.
(ii) Establishment of one "Knowledge Pool" (KP) in each state capital and to check the drop-out rate of school going children in a acquiring knowledge.
(iii) Promote creation of knowledge in S & T Labs and improve management of institutions engaged in IPR activities.
(iv) Promote knowledge applications in Agriculture and Industry and use of knowledge capabilities in making Government effective, transparent, and accountable.

Codes:
(a) (ii), (iii) and (iv) are correct.
(b) (i), (ii) and (iv) are correct.
(c) (i), (iii) and (iv) are correct.
(d) (i), (ii) and (iii) are correct.

358. Which of the following is a collaborative network of Reference Librarians? (*NET 17 NOV iii paper*)
(a) World Cat (b) eSS
(c) Question Point (d) Global Scholar

359. Resource Description and Access (RDA) is divided into how many sections? (*NET 17 NOV iii paper*)
(a) 9 (b) 10 (c) 11 (d) 12

360. Which of the following indicate the purpose of reference list in a thesis/dissertation? (*NET 17 NOV iii paper*)
(i) Allows author to credit the work of others that directly influenced the present work.
(ii) Gives interested readers the information necessary to identify and retrieve the sources.
(iii) An expansive list that covers works that are consulted.
(iv) Recommends to the interested readers the works that are not cited in the text.

Codes:
(a) (i) and (ii) are correct
(b) (ii) and (iii) are correct
(c) (iii) and (iv) are correct
(d) (ii) and (iv) are correct

361. Identify the document which is published by H.W. Wilson. (*NET 17J iii paper*)
(a) Europa World Yearbook 55th ed. 2014
(b) The International Who's Who 78th ed. 2014
(c) Sears List of Subject Headings 20th ed. 2010
(d) Ulrich's Periodicals Directory 53rd ed. 2015

362. Who, among the following, had visualized the establishment of Village Knowledge Centres (VKCs) in 2.3 lakh Panchayats to empower the villagers with knowledge? (*NET 16J iii paper*)
(a) Jawaharlal Nehru (b) Dr. S.R. Ranganathan
(c) Dr. Abdul Kalam (d) C.V. Raman

363. In 1930, who theorized that reference work may be conservative, moderate and liberal? (*NET 16J iii paper*)
(a) James I. Wyer (b) William A. Katz
(c) S.R. Ranganathan (d) S. Rothestein

364. Which of the following type of publication is/are included in the INB? (*NET 16J iii paper*)

(a) Guides to Textbooks
(b) Maps
(c) The first issue of a periodical
(d) Back volumes of periodicals

365. Indian patents on all areas are published in
(a) India : A reference annual
(b) Indian chemical patent index
(c) Gazette of India, Part-III
(d) None of the above

366. Match the following:
List – I
A. Narrative account of the progress of any given field of study
B. Systematic view of recent
C. Systematic condensation of a written work
D. Short summary of the main of a larger work
List – II
i. Trend Report ii. Review developments
iii. Compendium iv. Digest points

Codes:	A	B	C	D
(a)	ii	i	iii	iv
(b)	iii	iv	ii	i
(c)	iii	i	ii	iv
(d)	iv	i	iii	ii

367. Match the following: *(NET 16J iii paper)*
List – I
A. Abstractor
B. Classifier
C. Reference Librarian
D. Collection Development Manager
List – II
1. Credible Authors and Publishers
2. Strong subject base and command over language
3. Thought contents of documents
4. Inquisitive and good psychologists

Codes:	A	B	C	D
(a)	2	4	1	3
(b)	2	3	4	1
(c)	3	2	4	1
(d)	4	2	3	1

368. Match the following: *(NET 16J iii paper)*
List – I
A. Greenpilot B. Kalasampada
C. Gallica D. SACO
List – II
1. Library of Congress
2. Indira Gandhi National Centre for Arts
3. German National Library of Medicine
4. Bibliotheque Nationale de France

Codes:	A	B	C	D
(a)	1	2	3	4
(b)	2	4	1	3
(c)	3	2	1	4
(d)	3	2	4	1

369. **Assertion (A):** Not all bibliographic records require a uniform title.
Reason (R): Most published works are published only once and are never republished and translated. *(NET 16J iii paper)*
Codes:
(a) Both (A) and (R) are true.
(b) Both (A) and (R) are false.
(c) (A) is true, but (R) is false.
(d) (A) is false, but (R) is true.

370. **Assertion (A):** A controlled vocabulary may take some form of classification scheme. *(NET 16J iii paper)*
Reason (R): In a controlled vocabulary semantically related terms are not linked.
Codes:
(a) Both (A) and (R) are true.
(b) Both (A) and (R) are false.
(c) (A) is true, but (R) is false.
(d) (A) is false, but (R) is true.

371. **Assertion (A):** RDA replaces the General Material Designations (GMD). *(NET 16J iii paper)*
Reason (R): The problem with the GMDs was inconsistent categorization.
Codes:
(a) Both (A) and (R) are true.
(b) (A) is true, but (R) is false.
(c) (A) is false, but (R) is true.
(d) Both (A) and (R) are false.

372. Which of the following are the products of Chemical Abstract services? *(NET 17 NOV iii paper)*
(i) Sci Finder (ii) Sci Val
(iii) Methods Now (iv) Analytical Services
Codes:
(a) (i) and (iii) are correct
(b) (ii) and (iv) are correct
(c) (i), (ii) and (iii) are correct
(d) (ii), (iii) and (iv) are correct

373. Who among the following are associated with established theories of reference service? *(NET 17 NOV iii paper)*

(i) C.M. Winchell (ii) James I. Wyer
(iii) Daniel Brophy (iv) Samuel Rothstein

Codes:
(a) (i) and (ii) are correct
(b) (ii) and (iv) are correct
(c) (iii) and (iv) are correct
(d) (i) and (iii) are correct

374. Controlled vocabularies fall broadly into following categories *(NET 17 NOV iii paper)*
(i) Subject Heading Lists (ii) Thesauri
(iii) Folksonomies (iv) Ontologies

Codes:
(a) (i) and (iii) are correct
(b) (ii), (iii) and (iv) are correct
(c) (i), (ii) and (iv) are correct
(d) (iii) and (iv) are correct

375. 'Embargo' in the context of 'Book Trade' is *(NET 17 NOV iii paper)*
(i) a limitation on access, to older resources by the publishers.
(ii) perpetual ban on the access of the given resources of a publisher.
(iii) a limitation on access to resources placed by publishers.
(iv) a limitation on access to the resources usually to prevent the cancellation of individual subscription.

Codes:
(a) (iii) and (iv) are correct
(b) (i) and (ii) are correct
(c) (i) and (iii) are correct
(d) (i), (iii) and (iv) are correct

376. Match the following: *(NET 17 NOV iii paper)*

List – I	List – II
(A) Political Map	(1) Features of land
(B) Route Map	(2) Roads and bridges, etc.
(C) Physical Map	(3) Limiting territorial boundaries
(D) Thematic Map	(4) Mining, agriculture, etc.

Codes:	(A)	(B)	(C)	(D)
(a)	(4)	(1)	(2)	(3)
(b)	(1)	(2)	(3)	(4)
(c)	(3)	(2)	(1)	(4)
(d)	(2)	(3)	(1)	(4)

377. Match the following mechanisms of information processing with corresponding service as given by S. Seetharama *(NET 17 NOV iii paper)*

List – I	List - II
(A) Announcement	(1) Translation Service
(B) Evaluation	(2) Current Awareness Service
(C) Document access	(3) Indexing Service
(D) Accretion	(4) State-of-the-art report

Codes:	(A)	(B)	(C)	(D)
(a)	(3)	(2)	(4)	(1)
(b)	(2)	(4)	(1)	(3)
(c)	(1)	(3)	(2)	(4)
(d)	(4)	(1)	(3)	(2)

378. Match the following queries with corresponding type of reference service *(NET 17 NOV iii paper)*

List – I
(A) Communication with Library
(B) Reference query through e-mail
(C) Use of e-resources seeking
(D) Webforms

List - II
(1) Asynchronous reference service Staff through VoIP
(2) Online reference service
(3) Virtual Reference Desk answers
(4) Reference interview

Codes:	(A)	(B)	(C)	(D)
(a)	(4)	(3)	(1)	(2)
(b)	(1)	(2)	(4)	(3)
(c)	(3)	(1)	(2)	(4)
(d)	(2)	(4)	(3)	(1)

379. Match the following with corresponding explanation *(NET 17 NOV iii paper)*

List – I
(A) Embargo (B) Big Deal
(C) Front List (D) Standing order

List – II
(1) Publisher's list of new titles
(2) Authorization for regular shipment of new editions of specific products
(3) Publisher's restriction one-resource access
(4) Large bundled e-journal package of single publisher on discounted price

Codes:	(A)	(B)	(C)	(D)
(a)	(3)	(4)	(1)	(2)
(b)	(1)	(4)	(3)	(2)
(c)	(4)	(2)	(1)	(3)
(d)	(2)	(3)	(1)	(4)

380. **Assertion (A):** Avoidance of difficult reference questions are usually an outcome of

momentary panic in the face of a seemingly impenetrable question.

Reason (R): Reference never adhere to few helpful tips such as developing handy-referral systems, both within and outside the reference area, and fail to establish a context for the questions to counter such panic attack. *(NET 17 NOV iii paper)*

Codes:

(a) (A) is true, but (R) is false.
(b) (A) is false, but (R) is true.
(c) Both (A) and (R) are false.
(d) Both (A) and (R) are true.

381. Which of the following statements are wrong with reference to INB? *(NET 17 NOV ii paper)*

(i) Excludes musical scores
(ii) First appeared in 1951
(iii) Classified part follows CC, but DDC numbers assigned at the bottom
(iv) The main entries are in Roman Script

Codes:

(a) (i) and (ii) are correct
(b) (ii) and (iii) are correct
(c) (iii) and (iv) are correct
(d) (i) and (iv) are correct

382. Information about recent floods in Bihar can be found in: *(NET 17 NOV ii paper)*

(i) Asian Recorder
(ii) Data India
(iii) India; a reference annual
(iv) Statistical Abstract, India

Codes:

(a) (i) and (ii) are correct
(b) (i) and (iii) are correct
(c) (i), (ii) and (iii) are correct
(d) (ii), (iii) and (iv) are correct

383. Which of the following questions fall under the category of ready reference service? *(NET 17 NOV ii paper)*

(i) Population of Varanasi
(ii) Height of Qutub Minar
(iii) Concept of Symbiosis
(iv) Collection development in university libraries

Codes:

(a) (i), (ii) and (iv) are correct
(b) (i), (ii) and (iii) are correct
(c) (ii), (iii) and (iv) are correct
(d) (i), (iii) and (iv) are correct

384. Match the following terms with the corresponding authors who coined them:

List – I

(A) Knowledge Economy
(B) Documentation
(C) Informatics
(D) Information Retrieval

List – II

(1) Mikhailov, Chernyi and Gilyarevskii
(2) Calvin Mooers
(3) Paul Otlet
(4) Peter Drucker

Codes:	**(A)**	**(B)**	**(C)**	**(D)**
(a)	(2)	(3)	(4)	(1)
(b)	(1)	(4)	(2)	(3)
(c)	(4)	(3)	(1)	(2)
(d)	(3)	(1)	(2)	(4)

385. Match the following: *(NET 17 NOV ii paper)*

List – I

(A) Bibliography (B) Biography
(C) Statistical Source (D) Newspaper Digest

List – II

(1) Number of people recently died of dengue in Delhi
(2) Number of volumes of a book
(3) Number of siblings of Mahatma Gandhi
(4) Number of primary schools in Mumbai

Codes:	**(A)**	**(B)**	**(C)**	**(D)**
(a)	(4)	(2)	(1)	(3)
(b)	(2)	(1)	(3)	(4)
(c)	(2)	(3)	(4)	(1)
(d)	(3)	(4)	(2)	(1)

386. Which of the following are examples of collaborate virtual reference service? *(NET 15J iii paper)*

(i) Ask A Librarian (ii) Wikis
(iii) Folksonomies (iv) Question Point: 24/7 Reference

Codes:

(a) (ii) and (iii) are correct
(b) (i) and (ii) are correct
(c) (i) and (iv) are correct
(d) (i) and (iii) are correct

387. **Assertion (A):** Keeping one's skills and knowledge current is the ethical obligation of a reference librarian.

Reason (R): It is the responsibility of the reference librarian to satisfy the current information needs of users.

(NET 15J iii paper)

Codes:

(a) Both (A) and (R) are true
(b) (A) is true but (R) is false
(c) (A) is false but (R) is true
(d) Both (A) and (R) are false

388. **Assertion (A):** The controlled vocabulary system is more difficult to search than the natural language system.

Reason (R): A natural language system has the major advantage that it is completely specific. *(NET 15J iii paper)*

Codes:

(a) Both (A) and (R) are true
(b) Both (A) and (R) are false
(c) (A) is true but (R) is false
(d) (A) is false but (R) is true

389. **Assertion (A):** The Anomalous State of Knowledge (ASK) model is based on the understanding that, given such an anomaly the user is probably unable to state precisely what is needed to resolve the lack of information. *(NET 16J ii paper)*

Reason (R): The ASK can be used to formulate an appropriate search strategy.

Codes:

(a) Both (A) and (R) are true
(b) Both (A) and (R) are false
(c) (A) is true but (R) is false
(d) (A) is false but (R) is true

390. 'Bibliographic Coupling' was first advocated by

(a) B.K. Sen (b) S.R. Ranganathan
(c) M.M. Kessler (d) S.C. Bradford

391. Identify parts of social science citation Index. *(NET 15J ii paper)*

(i) Corporate Index
(ii) Permuterm Subject Index
(iii) Source Index
(iv) Title Index

Codes:

(a) (i), (ii) and (iii) are correct.
(b) (ii), (iii) and (iv) are correct.
(c) (iii), (iv) and (i) are correct.
(d) (iv), (i) and (ii) are correct.

392. Match the following: *(NET 15J ii paper)*

List - I

(A) Barack Hussein Obama-II
(B) GDP Growth in last year
(C) Universities in U.K.
(D) Area of Ganjam District

List - II

(1) Gazetteer (2) Who is Who
(3) Year Book (4) World of Learning

Codes:	A	B	C	D
(a)	1	2	3	4
(b)	2	3	4	1
(c)	4	2	1	3
(d)	3	4	2	1

393. **Assertion (A):** There is no need for distinct geographical sources like Gazetteers, maps, atlas, etc.

Reason (R): Some of the general reference sources like encyclopaedias, yearbooks, almanacs also include geographical information. *(NET 15J ii paper)*

Codes:

(a) Both (A) and (R) are true.
(b) Both (A) and (R) are false.
(c) (A) is true but (R) is false.
(d) (A) is false but (R)is true.

394. When the last print version of Encyclopaedia Britannica was published?

(NET 14D ii paper)

(a) 2009 (b) 2010 (c) 2011 (d) 2012

395. The following is a collaborative network of Reference Librarians.

(a) Worldcat (b) INDEST
(c) Question point (d) Global scholar

396. Match the following: *(NET 14D ii paper)*

List – I	List – II
(A) Biographical source	1. Full text sources online
(B) Encyclopaedia	2. ODLIS
(C) Directory	3. Linkedin
(D) Dictionary	4. Liswiki

Codes:	A	B	C	D
(a)	1	2	3	4
(b)	2	3	1	4
(c)	4	2	3	1
(d)	3	4	1	2

397. According to S.R. Ranganathan, the reference service aimed at freshman is called

(NET 15D iii paper)

(a) General Help to General Reader
(b) Short Range Reference Service
(c) Long Range Reference Service
(d) Initiation

398. "Guide for the Preparation and Publication of Abstracts" was published by: *(NET 15D iii paper)*
(a) IFLA (b) FID (c) OCLC (d) UNESCO

399. What type of directory is the "Times of India Directory and Yearbook including Who's Who"? *(NET 15D iii paper)*
(a) General (b) Special
(c) Professional (d) Trade

400. Folksonomy is a: *(NET 15D iii paper)*
(a) System in which users apply public tag to micro documents only.
(b) System in which users apply public tag to online items.
(c) System in which users do not apply public tag to online items.
(d) System in which users apply public tag to only print items.

401. Which of the following types of publications are excluded in INB? *(NET 15D iii paper)*
(i) Maps
(ii) First issue of periodical
(iii) Newspapers
(iv) Books in regional languages

Codes:
(a) (ii) and (iii) are correct
(b) (iii) and (iv) are correct
(c) (i) and (iii) are correct
(d) (iv) and (i) are correct

402. Null hypothesis is based on which of the following assumptions?*(NET 15D iii paper)*
(i) No relationship between the two variables in the total population
(ii) Relationship between the two variables in the total population
(iii) Variables are related after having statistically rejected
(iv) Variables are related before statistical analysis

Codes:
(a) (i) and (iv) are correct
(b) (i) and (iii) are correct
(c) (i) and (ii) are correct
(d) (ii) and (iv) are correct

403. Match the following: *(NET 15D iii paper)*

List – I
(A) Books in print
(B) The stateman's year book
(C) Ulrich's International Periodical Directory
(D) Encarta Encyclopedia

List – II
(1) Prouest (2) Microsoft
(3) Palgrave MacMillan (4) R.R. Bowker

Codes:	**(A)**	**(B)**	**(C)**	**(D)**
(a)	(2)	(4)	(1)	(3)
(b)	(3)	(4)	(1)	(2)
(c)	(1)	(4)	(2)	(3)
(d)	(4)	(3)	(1)	(2)

404. Match the following: *(NET 15D iii paper)*

List – I
(A) Bibliographic service
(B) Alert service
(C) Condensation service
(D) Support service

List – II
(1) E-mail to user with links to latest e-journals
(2) Translated copy of a document
(3) Compilation of audio records by a singer
(4) Abstracting selected and analysed information

Codes:	(A)	(B)	(C)	(D)
(a)	(4)	(1)	(3)	(2)
(b)	(1)	(4)	(2)	(3)
(c)	(3)	(2)	(1)	(4)
(d)	(3)	(1)	(4)	(2)

405. Match the following:*(NET-2013 D ii paper)*

List – I
(A) Books in Print
(B) Social Science: A Bibliography of Doctoral Dissertations
(C) Asian Social Science Bibliography
(D) Cumulative Book Index

List – II
1. National Bibliography
2. Trade Bibliography
3. National & Trade Bibliography
4. Subject Bibliography

Codes:	A	B	C	D
(a)	2	1	4	3
(b)	1	3	2	4
(c)	4	1	2	3
(d)	3	2	1	4

406. Match the following: *(NET-2013D ii paper)*

List – I	List – II
(A) Dictionary	1. Foreign Language
(B) Glossary	2. Synonymous terms
(C) Thesaurus	3. Words, Synonyms
(D) Lexicon	4. Specific subjects

Codes:	A	B	C	D
(a)	3	4	2	1
(b)	4	3	1	2
(c)	1	2	4	3
(d)	2	4	3	1

407. Match the following: *(NET-2013D ii paper)*

List – I	List – II
(A) Current Biography	1. Russia
(B) Index Translationum	2. University of Illinois
(C) VINITI	3. U.S.A.
(D) Library Trends	4. UNESCO

Codes:	A	B	C	D
(a)	3	4	1	2
(b)	4	1	2	3
(c)	1	2	3	4
(d)	2	3	4	1

408. **Assertion (A):** In the study of History, as an academic discipline, a primary source is an artefact, a document, a recording or other source of information that was created during the event or immediately after the event.

Reason (R): Primary sources are considered as original material or evidences about the topic and are fundamental to history.

(NET-2013D ii paper)

Codes:
(a) (A) is true, but (R) is false.
(b) (A) is false, but (R) is true.
(c) Both (A) and (R) are true.
(d) Both (A) and (R) are false.

409. **Assertion (A):** Indian National Bibliography is the most comprehensive source of Indian publications.

Reason (R): National Library of Kolkata is entitled to receive one copy of each Indian publication under Delivery of Book Act.

(NET-2013D ii paper)

Codes:
(a) (A) is true, but (R) is false.
(b) (A) is false, but (R) is true.
(c) Both (A) and (R) are true.
(d) Both (A) and (R) are false.

410. **Assertion (A):** As per the generally accepted principles of construction of statistical tabulation, every table should have a clear, concise and adequate title so as to make the table intelligible without reference to the text and this title should always be placed just below the body of the table.

Reason (R): A statistical table which reflects its title just above the table and supply information about several interrelated characteristics of data makes the table unwield and inconvenient.

(NET-2013D ii paper)

Codes:
(a) Both (A) and (R) are true.
(b) Both (A) and (R) are false.
(c) (A) is true, but (R) is false.
(d) (A) is false, but (R) is true.

411. **Assertion (A):** Reference section in a Library became insignificant.

Reason (R): The Web 2.0 services replaces the reference desk services.

(NET-2013D ii paper)

Codes:
(a) (A) is true, but (R) is false.
(b) Both (A) and (R) are true.
(c) Both (A) and (R) are false.
(d) (A) is false and (R) is true

412. **Assertion (A):** Newspaper Digests are the best sources of information to get current and authentic information like books.

Reason (R): These sources are compiled by going through various newspapers.

(NET-2013D ii paper)

Codes:
(a) Both (A) and (R) are true.
(b) (A) is partially true but (R) is true.
(c) Both (A) and (R) are false.
(d) (A) is true but (R) is partially true.

413. **Assertion (A):** Encyclopaedias have been regarded as the substitute of all categories of reference sources as these provide all types of information.

Reason (R): Encyclopaedias provide comprehensive information on all aspects which otherwise are scattered in different categories of reference sources.

(NET-2013D ii paper)

Codes:
(a) (R) is true but (A) is false.
(b) Both (A) and (R) are true.
(c) (A) is true but (R) is false.
(d) Both (A) and (R) are false

414. Ontology is *(NET 2013D iii paper)*
(a) A Documentation service
(b) An Indexing method
(c) Classification of Internet based documents
(d) Cataloguing of Internet based documents

415. Who are the publishers of 'Year Book on Human Rights'? *(NET-2013D iii paper)*
(a) United Nations
(b) Ministry of Law, Govt. of India
(c) Europa Publishers
(d) R.R. Bowker

416. ASTINFO stands for *(NET 2013D iii paper)*
(a) Asian Scientific and Technological Information Network
(b) Association of Scientific and Technological Information Scientists in Asia
(c) International Network for Exchange of Science and Technology Information
(d) Regional Network for the Exchange of Information and Experience in Science and Technology in Asia and the Pacific

417. IFLA's programme for capacity building of library associations is named as *(NET-2013D iii paper)*
(a) BSLA (b) ALP (c) CLM (d) PAC

418. The measure of certainty or predictability is called as *(NET-2013D iii paper)*
(a) Entropy (b) Feedback
(c) Redundancy (d) Distortion

419. A characteristic in which information tends to leak and the more it leaks, the more we have, is *(NET-2013D iii paper)*
(a) Synergetic characteristics
(b) Diffusive characteristics
(c) Compressible characteristics
(d) Shareable characteristics

420. Arrange the following according to their year of origin: *(NET-2013D iii paper)*
i. Indian National Bibliography
ii. British National Bibliography
iii. Cumulative Book Index
iv. Books in Print

Codes:
(a) i ii iv iii (b) iii iv ii i
(c) ii iii iv i (d) iv i ii iii

421. Arrange the following according to their year of emergence: *(NET 2013D iii paper)*
i. LISA
ii. Dissertation Abstracts International
iii. Indian Science Abstracts
iv. Indian Library & Information Science Abstracts

Codes:
(a) iii iv ii i (b) iv iii i ii
(c) ii i iii iv (d) i ii iii iv

422. Arrange in sequence the medium used for 'Virtual Reference' in the order of their progress. *(NET 2013D iii paper)*
i. Web form ii. Ask a Service
iii. E-mail iv. Social Networking

Codes:
(a) i ii iii iv (b) ii iii iv i
(c) iii i ii iv (d) iv ii i iii

423. Match the following: *(NET 13D iii paper)*
List – I
A. Index Translationum
B. Translation Register Index (TR-I)
C. World Trans Index
D. Commonwealth Index of Unpublished Translations

List – II
1. NISCAIR 2. NTC, Chicago
3. UNESCO 4. ITC, Delft, Netherlands
5. ASLIB

Codes:	A	B	C	D
(a)	2	3	1	4
(b)	3	2	4	5
(c)	5	3	1	2
(d)	4	2	5	3

424. **Assertion (A):** All reference sources provide uptodate information in their respective categories.
Reason (R): As these are compiled from primary sources of information. *(NET 13D iii paper)*

Codes:
(a) Both (A) and (R) are true.
(b) Both (A) and (R) are false.
(c) (A) is false but (R) is partially true.
(d) (A) is true but (R) is false.

425. **Assertion (A):** Online Reference Service can be offered using IMs, SMs, VoIP, Video, Blogs, Websites and host of such other mechanisms.

Reason (R): Majority of academic libraries in India are equipped with required infrastructure. *(NET 2013D iii paper)*

Codes:

(a) Both (A) and (R) are true.
(b) (A) is true, (R) is false.
(c) (A) is false, (R) is true.
(d) Both (A) and (R) are false

426. **Assertion (A):** For providing an effective reference service, best & up to date reference collection is not as important as is the competent reference librarian.

Reason (R): An efficient reference librarian can serve the users more effectively even in the absence of best reference collection. *(NET 2013D iii paper)*

Codes:

(a) (A) is true but (R) is false.
(b) Both (A) and (R) are true.
(c) (A) is false but (R) is true.
(d) Both (A) and (R) are false.

427. Books of Unknown or doubtful authorship is known as: *(NET 2014J II paper)*

(a) Apograph (b) Incunabulla
(c) Apocryphal books (d) Blue Books

428. Arrange the following in the ascending order of their first year of publication *(NET 2014J II paper)*

(i) BNB (ii) INB
(iii) Compendex (iv) Roget's Thesaurus of English words

Codes:

(a) (iv), (iii), (i), (ii) (b) (iii), (ii), (iv), (i)
(c) (ii), (iv), (i), (iii) (d) (i), (iii), (ii), (iv)

429. Arrange the following in the chronological order of their first year of publication: *(NET 2014J II paper)*

(i) Arts and Humanities Index
(ii) Social Science Citation Index
(iii) ISI Web of Science
(iv) Science Citation Index

Codes:

(a) (iv), (ii), (i), (iii) (b) (ii), (iii), (iv), (i)
(c) (iii), (ii), (i), (iv) (d) (iv), (i), (iii), (ii)

430. Match the following: *(NET 2014J II paper)*

List – I

A. Fundamentals of Reference Service
B. Introduction to Reference Works
C. Reference Service
D. Guide to Reference Books

List – II

1. A.J. Walford
2. S.R. Ranganathan
3. F.N. Cheney and W.J. Williams
4. William A. Katz

Codes:	**A**	**B**	**C**	**D**
(a)	2	1	4	3
(b)	3	4	1	2
(c)	4	2	3	1
(d)	3	4	2	1

431. **Assertion (A):** Case situations are seldom comparable and as such the information gathered in case studies is often not comparable.

Reason (R): The subject under case study are usually described in terms of the characteristics exhibited by the subject/case itself. *(NET 2014J II paper)*

Codes:

(a) Both (A) and (R) are true.
(b) Both (A) and (R) are false.
(c) (A) is true, but (R) is false.
(d) (A) is false, but (R) is true.

432. **Assertion (A):** Intellectual Property Rights facilitate free flow of information.

Reason (R): Effective free flow of information is the pre-requisite for knowledge society. *(NET 2014J II paper)*

Codes:

(a) (A) is true, but (R) is false.
(b) (A) is false, but (R) is true.
(c) Both (A) and (R) are true.
(d) Both (A) and (R) are false.

433. **Assertion (A):** The total output of Indian publications is reflected in 'Indian National Bibliography'.

Reason (R): A number of publishers in India are defaulters and do not deposit their publications as per Delivery of Books and Newspapers (Public Libraries) Act. *(NET 2014J II paper)*

Codes:
(a) Both (A) and (R) are true.
(b) Both (A) and (R) are false.
(c) (A) is true, but (R) is false.
(d) (A) is false, but (R) is true.

434. **Assertion (A):** No library is self sufficient in terms of resources even in electronic age.
Reason (R): Resource sharing and consortia initiatives are essential to meet user needs. *(NET 2014J II paper)*
Codes:
(a) (A) is true and (R) is false.
(b) (A) is false and (R) is true.
(c) Both (A) and (R) are true.
(d) Both (A) and (R) are false.

435. **Assertion (A):** Indexing and abstracting services fulfil the 4th Law of Library Science.
Reason (R): These services serve as the substitute to the primary journals. *(NET 2014J II paper)*
Codes:
(a) (A) is true, but (R) is false.
(b) Both (A) & (R) are false.
(c) Both (A) & (R) are true.
(d) (A) is false, but (R) is true.

436. Which of the following source(s) you refer to get information on old name for 'Zaire'? *(NET 2014J iii paper)*
i. Encyclopaedias ii. Yearbooks
iii. Gazetteers iv. Directories
Codes:
(a) (i) and (ii) are correct.
(b) (i), (ii) and (iii) are correct.
(c) (i) and (iii) are correct.
(d) (ii), (iii) and (iv) are correct.

437. Arrange the following according to their year of origin: *(NET 2014J iii paper)*
i. Bowker Annual
ii. Europa World Yearbook
iii. India; a reference annual
iv. Stateman's yearbook
Codes:
(a) iv, i, ii, iii (b) i, ii, iv, iii
(c) iv, iii, i, ii (d) ii, i, iv, iii

438. Arrange the following in the order of development: *(NET 2014J iii paper)*
i. GML ii. Hypermedia
iii. SGML iv. Memex
Codes:
(a) i, ii, iii, iv (b) iv, ii, i, iii
(c) ii, iii, iv, i (d) iii, ii, i, iv

439. Match the following:*(NET 2014J iii paper)*
List – I
A. Behaviour Science
B. Philosophical Studies
C. Ontology
D. Biological Science
List – II
1. Cognitive Process of Information
2. Studies on Epistomology
3. Information Processing in Living Things
4. Study of Nature of Existence

Codes:	A	B	C	D
(a)	4	3	1	2
(b)	3	2	4	1
(c)	2	1	3	4
(d)	1	2	4	3

440. Match the following biographical publications from India with the respective compilers: *(NET 2014J iii paper)*

List – I	List – II
A. India, Who's Who	1. S.P. Sen
B. Who's Who in India	2. J.S. Sharma
C. Dictionary of Indian Biography	3. Business Press, Mumbai
D. National Biographical Dictionary of India	4. INFA Pub., New Delhi

Codes:	A	B	C	D
(a)	3	4	2	1
(b)	1	2	3	4
(c)	2	3	1	4
(d)	4	3	1	2

441. Match the following for locating the information: *(NET 2014J iii paper)*
List – I
A. Information on recent Nobel Prize winners
B. Current developments in Library & Information Science
C. Books on Economic Policies of India
D. Articles on Cloud Computing
List – II
1. Bibliographic Service 2. Indexing Services
3. Trend Sources 4. Digest Services

Codes:	A	B	C	D
(a)	4	3	1	2
(b)	3	1	4	2
(c)	2	3	4	1
(d)	1	2	3	4

442. **Assertion (A):** There is no need for libraries to invest on reference collection.

Reason (R): Web is a treasure of all types of information that can replace reference desk. *(NET 2014J iii paper)*

Codes:

(a) Both (A) and (R) are true.
(b) Both (A) and (R) are false.
(c) (A) is true, but (R) is false.
(d) (A) is false, but (R) is true.

443. **Assertion (A):** All unabridged dictionaries provide word meaning, antonyms, synonyms and places, etc.

Reason (R): All dictionaries provide information on antonyms and homonym, etc. *(NET 2014J iii paper)*

Codes:

(a) (A) is true, but (R) is false.
(b) Both (A) and (R) are true.
(c) (A) is false, but (R) is true.
(d) Both (A) and (R) are false.

444. From which year the Encyclopaedia Britannica ceased its print version? *(NET 2014D iii paper)*

(a) 2009 (b) 2010 (c) 2011 (d) 2012

445. Identify the founders of Wikipedia from the following: *(NET 2014D iii paper)*

i. Michael E. Davis ii. Jimmy Wales
iii. Richard Stallman iv. Larry Sanger

Codes:

(a) ii and iii are correct.
(b) i and ii are correct.
(c) i and iii are correct.
(d) ii and iv are correct.

446. Alerting service is provided *(NET 2014D iii paper)*

i. Before and after the publication of primary source
ii. For specific search formulation by user
iii. For retrieval of information
iv. For individuals as well as groups

Codes:

(a) i and ii are correct.
(b) i and iv are correct.
(c) ii and iii are correct.
(d) iii and iv are correct.

447. **Assertion (A):** Multilingual dictionaries provide equivalent words in three or more languages. *(NET 2014 D iii paper)*

Reason (R): They generally do not define the words but they give equivalent words in one or more foreign languages.

Codes:

(a) Both (A) and (R) are true.
(b) Both (A) and (R) are false.
(c) (A) is true, but (R) is false.
(d) (A) is false, but (R) is true.

448. Which of the following is not a synchronous virtual reference service? *(NET 2013 SEPT iii paper)*

(a) Chat (b) E-mail
(c) Video-conferencing (d) Voice over IP

449. "World directory of sources of Patents" is published by *(NET 2013 SEPT iii paper)*

(a) Bowker-Saur, U.S.A.
(b) WIPO
(c) Patent Information System, India
(d) Derwent, London

450. Arrange the following according to the year of origin: *(NET 2014D iii paper)*

i. Encyclopaedia Britannica
ii. World Book Encyclopaedia
iii. Wikipedia
iv. Encyclopaedia Americana

Codes:

(a) iv, i, ii, iii (b) i, iv, ii, iii
(c) ii, iv, i, iii (d) i, ii, iv, iii

451. Arrange the following according to their date of origin: *(NET 2014D iii paper)*

i. Librametry
ii. Statistical bibliography
iii. Statistical analysis
iv. Bibliometrics

Codes:

(a) i, iii, ii, iv (b) ii, iii, i, iv
(c) iii, i, ii, iv (d) iii, ii, i, iv

452. Match the following: *(NET 2014D iii paper)*

List – I

A. Informing about best books
B. Guidance to use citation manual
C. Providing prints for downloads
D. Providing list of URLs

List – II

1. Support service 2. Bibliography
3. Readers advisory 4. Users education

Codes:	**A**	**B**	**C**	**D**
(a)	2	3	1	4
(b)	3	4	1	2

(c)	4	2	3	1
(d)	2	4	3	1

453. Match the following national organizations with their relevant mission: *(NET 2014D iii paper)*

List – I	List – II
A. National Mission on Libraries	1. Digitization of AYUSH literature
B. National Mission for Manuscripts	2. Nurturing of talent
C. T.K.D.L.	3. Capacity building
D. NME-ICT	4. Connects India's past with present

Codes:	A	B	C	D
(a)	1	2	3	4
(b)	3	4	1	2
(c)	4	3	2	1
(d)	2	1	3	4

454. Which of the following sites are offered by Britannica Library, a product of Encyclopaedia Britannica? *(NET 2017J iii paper)*
   (i) Children (ii) Young Adult
   (iii) Patron (iv) Reference Centre
   Codes:
   (a) (i), (ii) and (iii) are correct.
   (b) (i), (ii) and (iv) are correct.
   (c) (ii), (iii) and (iv) are correct.
   (d) (iv), (iii) and (i) are correct.

455. Identify the key attributes of 'Digest' from the following: *(NET 2017J iii paper)*
   (i) Significant ideas on one document area arranged separately in an unhelpful sequence.
   (ii) A Methodically arranged compendium or summary of literary, historical, legal, scientific or other written matters.
   (iii) Informative in nature and contains brief description of more than one document.
   (iv) Often prepared by a non-subject specialist without understanding and assimilating the contents of documents.
   Codes:
   (a) (i) and (ii) are correct.
   (b) (i) and (iii) are correct.
   (c) (i) and (iv) are correct.
   (d) (ii) and (iii) are correct.

456. Which of the following communication channels are used frequently in Virtual Reference Service? *(NET 2017J iii paper)*
   (i) Bulletin Board (ii) Instant Messaging
   (iii) R.S.S. (iv) Voice-Over-I.P.
   Codes:
   (a) (i) and (ii) are correct
   (b) (ii) and (iii) are correct
   (c) (ii) and (iv) are correct
   (d) (i), (ii) and (iv) are correct

457. Identify the affinitive/associative relationship of the following: *(NET 2017J iii paper)*
   (i) Genus-Species (ii) Translations
   (iii) Genetic (iv) Concurrent
   Codes:
   (a) (i) and (ii) are correct
   (b) (ii) and (iii) are correct
   (c) (iii) and (iv) are correct
   (d) (i) and (iv) are correct

458. Arrange in sequence the evolution of reference service: *(NET 2017J iii paper)*
   (i) Reference work with subject specialization.
   (ii) Aid Reader/Assistance to Reader
   (iii) Long Range Reference Service
   (iv) 'Personal relation between librarians and readers'
   Codes:
   (a) (ii), (iii), (iv), (i) (b) (i), (iii), (ii), (iv)
   (c) (iv), (ii), (i), (iii) (d) (iii), (iv), (ii), (i)

459. What type of information sources are Almanacs? *(NET 2015D ii paper)*
   (a) Ready Reference (b) Dictionary
   (c) Directory (d) Bibliographic

460. **Assertion (A):** Controlled Vocabulary based on Indexing requires intellectual ability to assign keywords to the thought contents of the documents in such a way that these selected terms could effectively represent the contents. *(NET 2015D ii paper)*
   Reason (R): Retrieval Systems based on Natural Language-based Indexing such as Google gives maximum precision.
   Codes:
   (a) Both (A) and (R) are true.
   (b) (A) is true, but (R) is false.
   (c) (A) is false, but (R) is true.
   (d) Both (A) and (R) are false.

461. Anukriti is a *(NET 2018J)*
   (a) Bibliographic India Website
   (b) Indexing India Website
   (c) Translating India Website
   (d) Abstracting India Website

462. Identify the odd one out: (*NET 18J*)
(a) Reference Entry (b) Centred Entry
(c) Analytical Entry (d) Added Entry

463. Vocabulary in a data base is controlled by (*NET 18J*)
(i) Thesaurus File (ii) Import File
(iii) Standard Files (iv) Authority Files
Codes:
(a) i and ii are correct
(b) iii and iv are correct
(c) i and iv are correct
(d) ii and iii are correct

464. Pre-coordinate indexing systems comprise (*NET 18J*)
(i) NEPHIS (ii) SLIC
(iii) Peek a boo (iv) Edge-Notched card
Codes:
(a) i and ii are correct
(b) i and iv are correct
(c) ii and iii are correct
(d) iii and iv are correct

465. Identify the correct statement from the following: (*NET 18J*)
(i) In uniterm indexing system, terms are recorded in numerical file according to the system known as terminal digit posting
(ii) Main activities of TREC are divide into Routing and Tracks
(iii) Recall and precision tend to vary in searching
(iv) False drops in post coordinate indexing system cannot be eliminated
Codes:
(a) i and ii are correct
(b) iii and iv are correct
(c) i and iii are correct
(d) ii and iv are correct

466. Which of the following are review type services? (*NET 18J*)
(i) Current Awareness List
(ii) Trend Reports
(iii) News Clipping
(iv) State of the Art Report
Codes:
(a) (i) and (ii) are correct
(b) (i) and (iv) are correct
(c) (ii), and (iv) are correct
(d) (ii), and (iii) are correct

467. Match the following queries with their appropriate category of reference sources: (*NET 18J*)

List-I	List-II
(A) Enrolment of students in university	(i) Year Book
(B) Weather of Denmark	(ii) Statistical sources
(C) Number of foreigners visited	(iii) Directory of World Book Fair
(D) Number of hospital in Singapore	(iv) Geographical sources

Codes:	(A)	(B)	(C)	(D)
(a)	(i)	(iv)	(iii)	(ii)
(b)	(i)	(iii)	(ii)	(iv)
(c)	(ii)	(iv)	(i)	(iii)
(d)	(iii)	(iv)	(i)	(ii)

468. Match the following: (*NET 18J*)

List-I	List-II
(A) Muktabodha	(i) Research Guide
(B) Net First	(ii) Online citation and reference management tool
(C) Zotero	(iii) Abstracting and indexing databases of OCLC
(D) RG Score	(iv) Digital library of Indology

Codes:	(A)	(B)	(C)	(D)
(a)	(iv)	(iii)	(ii)	(i)
(b)	(iv)	(ii)	(iii)	(i)
(c)	(ii)	(i)	(iv)	(iii)
(d)	(iii)	(ii)	(i)	(iv)

469. Match the following: (*NET 18J*)

List-I (Type of Research)	List-II (Focus)
(A) Ethnographic	(i) Present events
(B) Evaluative	(ii) Social behaviour
(C) Descriptive	(iii) Causation
(D) Experimental	(iv) Judgement about quality

Codes:	(A)	(B)	(C)	(D)
(a)	(ii)	(iv)	(i)	(iii)
(b)	(iv)	(iii)	(ii)	(i)
(c)	(ii)	(iii)	(iv)	(i)
(d)	(iv)	(ii)	(i)	(iii)

470. Match the following: (*NET 18J*)

List-I (Countries)	List-II (Name of the library)
(A) Egypt	(i) Library of Ashurbanipal
(B) Turkey	(ii) Villa of Papyri
(C) Italy	(iii) Library of Pergamum
(D) Iraq	(iv) Royal Library of Alexandria

Codes:	(A)	(B)	(C)	(D)
(a)	(iv)	(ii)	(iii)	(i)
(b)	(iv)	(iii)	(ii)	(i)
(c)	(i)	(iii)	(iv)	(ii)
(d)	(iii)	(ii)	(i)	(iv)

471. Arrange the following according to the year of their first publication: *(NET 18J)*
   (i) bibliotheca Universalis by Konard Gesner
   (ii) Catalogue of the books in the 15th Century by the British Museum
   (iii) The Bibliographic Instructive Rare Books by G.E. Bura
   (iv) Union catalogue of learned periodical Publication in South Asia by S.R. Ranganathan

   Codes:
   (a) i, ii, iv, iii (b) ii, i, iv, iii
   (c) i, iii, ii, iv (d) iv, i, iii, ii

ANSWER SHEET

1. (b) 2. (c) 3. (c) 4. (b) 5. (b) 6. (c) 7. (d) 8. (d) 9. (d)
10. (d) 11. (c) 12. (d) 13. (b) 14. (a) 15. (d) 16. (b) 17. (d) 18. (d)
19. (a) 20. (c) 21. (b) 22. (c) 23. (a) 24. (b) 25. (a) 26. (b) 27. (b)
28. (d) 29. (d) 30. (c) 31. (b) 32. (d) 33. (c) 34. (a) 35. (b) 36. (d)
37. (a) 38. (a) 39. (a) 40. (c) 41. (b) 42. (b) 43. (c) 44. (c) 45. (b)
46. (b) 47. (b) 48. (d) 49. (d) 50. (d) 51. (b) 52. (b) 53. (c) 54. (a)
55. (d) 56. (d) 57. (d) 58. (b) 59. (c) 60. (d) 61. (b) 62. (d) 63. (c)
64. (d) 65. (c) 66. (c) 67. (d) 68. (d) 69. (d) 70. (a) 71. (b) 72. (b)
73. (d) 74. (a) 75. (c) 76. (d) 77. (a) 78. (d) 79. (b) 80. (c) 81. (d)
82. (d) 83. (d) 84. (c) 85. (d) 86. (c) 87. (c) 88. (b) 89. (d) 90. (b)
91. (c) 92. (b) 93. (a) 94. (a) 95. (c) 96. (b) 97. (d) 98. (a) 99. (a)
100. (a) 101. (a) 102. (b) 103. (c) 104. (b) 105. (d) 106. (a) 107. (b) 108. (b)
109. (a) 110. (b) 111. (b) 112. (c) 113. (b) 114. (c) 115. (d) 116. (d) 117. (d)
118. (c) 119. (d) 120. (a) 121. (b) 122. (c) 123. (d) 124. (c) 125. (d) 126. (a)
127. (d) 128. (d) 129. (a) 130. (c) 131. (d) 132. (a) 133. (b) 134. (a) 135. (b)
136. (b) 137. (b) 138. (a) 139. (b) 140. (b) 141. (a) 142. (b) 143. (a) 144. (c)
145. (c) 146. (c) 147. (b) 148. (d) 149. (c) 150. (b) 151. (d) 152. (c) 153. (d)
154. (b) 155. (d) 156. (c) 157. (a) 158. (a) 159. (d) 160. (d) 161. (a) 162. (d)
163. (b) 164. (d) 165. (b) 166. (a) 167. (d) 168. (a) 169. (b) 170. (a) 171. (d)
172. (a) 173. (a) 174. (a) 175. (a) 176. (a) 177. (d) 178. (a) 179. (a) 180. (d)
181. (b) 182. (b) 183. (c) 184. (d) 185. (a) 186. (d) 187. (a) 188. (b) 189. (c)
190. (b) 191. (a) 192. (b) 193. (b) 194. (b) 195. (c) 196. (a) 197. (b) 198. (b)
199. (c) 200. (b) 201. (a) 202. (a) 203. (a) 204. (a) 205. (a) 206. (a) 207. (a)
208. (b) 209. (c) 210. (c) 211. (b) 212. (b) 213. (a) 214. (c) 215. (d) 216. (b)
217. (a) 218. (c) 219. (a) 220. (a) 221. (c) 222. (d) 223. (a) 224. (a) 225. (c)
226. (c) 227. (b) 228. (b) 229. (b) 230. (b) 231. (a) 232. (b) 233. (a) 234. (d)
235. (a) 236. (d) 237. (b) 238. (a) 239. (b) 240. (a) 241. (a) 242. (a) 243. (a)
244. (c) 245. (d) 246. (a) 247. (b) 248. (a) 249. (d) 250. (d) 251. (a) 252. (c)
253. (b) 254. (c) 255. (a) 256. (c) 257. (d) 258. (b) 259. (a) 260. (a) 261. (c)
262. (d) 263. (b) 264. (d) 265. (a) 266. (a) 267. (a) 268. (c) 269. (c) 270. (a)

271. (d) 272. (c) 273. (a) 274. (b) 275. (c) 276. (b) 277. (b) 278. (d) 279. (a)
280. (d) 281. (a) 282. (c) 283. (a) 284. (c) 285. (b) 286. (a) 287. (c) 288. (c)
289. (a) 290. (a) 291. (c) 292. (b) 293. (c) 294. (d) 295. (c) 296. (a) 297. (a)
298. (a) 299. (d) 300. (a) 301. (c) 302. (c) 303. (a) 304. (d) 305. (d) 306. (c)
307. (a) 308. (b) 309. (a) 310. (a) 311. (b) 312. (c) 313. (b) 314. (a) 315. (c)
316. (a) 317. (d) 318. (b) 319. (d) 320. (a) 321. (d) 322. (a) 323. (c) 324. (c)
325. (c) 326. (c) 327. (a) 328. (b) 329. (c) 330. (a) 331. (c) 332. (a) 333. (b)
334. (d) 335. (d) 336. (b) 337. (b) 338. (c) 339. (c) 340. (d) 341. (d) 342. (b)
343. (d) 344. (d) 345. (c) 346. (d) 347. (a) 348. (b) 349. (a) 350. (b) 351. (a)
352. (c) 353. (a) 354. (c) 355. (b) 356. (d) 357. (c) 358. (c) 359. (b) 360. (a)
361. (c) 362. (c) 363. (a) 364. (c) 365. (c) 366. (a) 367. (b) 368. (d) 369. (a)
370. (c) 371. (a) 372. (a) 373. (b) 374. (c) 375. (a) 376. (c) 377. (b) 378. (c)
379. (a) 380. (a) 381. (b) 382. (a) 383. (b) 384. (c) 385. (c) 386. (c) 387. (a)
388. (d) 389. (c) 390. (c) 391. (a) 392. (b) 393. (d) 394. (b) 395. (c) 396. (d)
397. (d) 398. (d) 399. (a) 400. (b) 401. (c) 402. (b) 403. (d) 404. (d) 405. (a)
406. (a) 407. (a) 408. (c) 409. (b) 410. (b) 411. (d) 412. (b) 413. (c) 414. (c)
415. (a) 416. (d) 417. (a) 418. (c) 419. (b) 420. (b) 421. (c) 422. (c) 423. (b)
424. (c) 425. (b) 426. (b) 427. (c) 428. (a) 429. (a) 430. (d) 431. (b) 432. (b)
433. (d) 434. (c) 435. (a) 436. (c) 437. (a) 438. (b) 439. (d) 440. (d) 441. (a)
442. (b) 443. (a) 444. (d) 445. (d) 446. (b) 447. (a) 448. (b) 449. (b) 450. (b)
451. (d) 452. (b) 453. (b) 454. (b) 455. (d) 456. (c) 457. (c) 458. (c) 459. (a)
460. (b) 461. (c) 462. (b) 463. (c) 464. (a) 465. (c) 466. (c) 467. (d) 468. (a)
469. (a) 470. (b) 471. (c)

Chapter 5
Catalogue and Cataloguing

SUBJECTIVE QUESTIONS

Q. 1. From which Greek word the word catalogue had been derived?

Ans. Kata Loges.

Q. 2. Define the library catalogue.

Ans. A library catalogue may be defined as a list of documents and other materials organised in systematic order, available in library.

Q. 3. Who invented the dictionary catalogue?

Ans. Charles Ami Cutter in 1876.

Q. 4. What is the difference between library catalogue and bibliography?

Ans. A library catalogue is a list of reading and reference material acquired by a library. Whereas a bibliography is an organised list of reading materials of a particular author or at a particular subject or a particular geographical region.

Q. 5. What is thickness of library catalogue card?

Ans. 0.025 cms.

Q. 6. Name four important cataloguing codes.

Ans. The four important cataloguing codes are

(1) Anglo-American Cataloguing Rules of 1908.
(2) American Library Association Cataloguing Rules of 1949.
(3) Anglo-American Cataloguing Rules, edition 2, 1978.
(4) Classified catalogue code of Dr. S.R. Ranganathan in 1934.

Q. 7. What is unit card?

Ans. A unit card is a basic catalogue card, in the form of main entry, which when duplicate may be used as a unit for all other entries, for that work in a catalogue by addition of the appropriate heading—(AACR–1).

Q. 8. What is the standard size of a basic catalogue card?

Ans. 5″ × 3″ (12.5 cm × 7.5 cm).

Q. 9. List our different types of inner forms of a library catalogue.

(i) Alphabetic Author Name Title Subject Dictionary
(ii) Classified Subject part Alphabetical Index
(iii) Alphabetical-Classed Subject part Alphabetical Index

Q. 10. Differentiate between author catalogue and name catalogue.

Ans. Author catalogue list only the name of authors whereas a name catalogue lists works on an author, name series, place name occurring in names.

Q. 11. Define the classified catalogue.

Ans. A classified catalogue is a form of subject catalogue, in which the entries are arranged by the class number, which represents the subject of documents, according to the classification scheme chosen for a library.

Q. 12. Who developed PRECIS and where it was adopted for the first time?

Ans. Derek Austin in 1970. Adopted in the *British National Bibliography* in 1977.

Q. 13. Define collaborator.

Ans. A person who associates with another person or other persons to produce a work.

Q. 14. List the types of entries in classified catalogue.

Ans. In Ranganathan's classified catalogue we find the following entries:

(a) Main Entry (b) Cross Reference Entry.

Q. 15. How many parts are there in Ranganathan classified catalogue?

Ans. Ranganathan's classified catalogue consists of two parts, namely:

The classified part and the alphabetical part.

Q. 16. List the type of entries in a dictionary catalogue.

Ans. The type of entries in dictionary catalogue are:

(a) Main Entry (b) Collaborator Entry
(c) Book Index Entry (d) Subject Entry
(e) Title Entry (f) Cross Reference Entry.

Q. 17. Write the eight parts of main entry.

Ans. The eight parts of the main entry:

(a) Heading (b) Body of the entry
(c) Physical description (d) Series
(e) Note (f) Standard number and terms of responsibility
(g) Tracing (h) Call number.

Q. 18. List the six sections of main entry of classified catalogue.

Ans. The six sections of main entry of a classified catalogue are:

(i) Leading section
(ii) Heading section
(iii) Title section
(iv) Note section
(v) Accession number
(vi) Tracing section.

Q. 19. What is another name of added entries?

Ans. Secondary entries.

Q. 20. Who used the term Pre-natal cataloguing for the first time?

Ans. Dr. S.R. Ranganathan.

Q. 21. Write another name for the "Normative Principles" of Cataloguing given by Dr. S.R. Ranganathan.

Ans. Cannons of Cataloguing.

Q. 22. List the prominent ALA rules for filing.

Ans. The Prominent ALA rules for filing related to:

(a) Word by word (b) Articles
(c) Initials (d) Abbreviations
(e) Sign and symbols (f) Numerals
(g) Order entries under the same word (h) Author arrangement
(i) Subject arrangement (j) Cross reference
(k) Alphabetical arrangement for English and foreign word entries, according to order of the English alphabet.

Q. 23. List a few areas of library co-operation.

Ans. A few areas of library co-operation are:

(a) Acquisition
(b) Technical processing
(c) Inter library lending
(d) Preparation of bibliographies
(e) Compilation of union catalogues directories, etc.
(f) Information service line translation, reprography, etc.

Q. 24. Write two types of library network.

Ans. (i) Networks in which the participating libraries form a centralised agency.

(ii) Networks in which the participating libraries serve each other.

Q. 25. Write the full expansion of NPAC.

Ans. National Programme of Acquisition and Cataloguing.

Q. 26. List the centralised cataloguing service offered by institution.

Ans. Centralised cataloguing service offered by following institutions:

(a) Library of Congress
(b) British National Bibliography Division of the British Library.

Q. 27. State the cataloguing rule for intergovernmental corporate bodies.

Ans. The name of an intergovernmental body should be entered in the English form, it is given on the items issued by it.

Q. 28. Write the expanded form of PRECIS.

Ans. Preserved Context Index System.

Q. 29. Write the expanded form of LCSH.

Ans. Library of Congress list of Subject Heading.

Q. 30. Write the expanded form of POPSI.

Ans. Postulate-based Permuted Subject Indexing.

Q. 31. When the LCSH was organised?

Ans. In 1897.

Q. 32. Write the expanded form of SLSH.

Ans. Sears List of Subject Heading.

Q. 33. When the SLSH was published first?

Ans. In 1923.

Q. 34. Who designed the POPSI?

Ans. Ganesh Bhattacharya of DRTC, Bangalore.

Q. 35. How many parts are there in AACR-2?

Ans. They are: Part I, Description, Pt. II, Headings or Access points—their determination.

Q. 36. How many levels of description in AACR-2 are there?

Ans. There are three levels of description in AACR-2.

Q. 37. What is call number?

Ans. Class number and book number together are known as the call number.

Q. 38. What is the chief source of information for book?

Ans. The title page is the chief source of information for a book.

Q. 39. Which project are called MARC I and MARC II?

Ans. The library of Congress started in 1966 a pilot projects for a machine-readable cataloguing data, MARC I and stopped it in 1968. This was followed by permanent subscription service called MARC II.

Q. 40. Write the two number entries of classified catalogue.

Ans. Main Entry and Cross Reference Entry.

Q. 41. Define the running title of a book.

Ans. The brief title which is repeated on the top of each verso.

Q. 42. Write the expanded form of FLECC.

Ans. 'Federal Libraries' Experiment in Co-operative Catalogue.

Q. 43. Write two types of Limited Cataloguing.

Ans. (i) Selective Cataloguing.
(ii) Simplified Cataloguing.

Q. 44. Write the expanded form of UBC.

Ans. Universal Bibliographic Control.

Q. 45. Write the name of document brought out by the Indian Standard Institutes, New Delhi for preparation of catalogue code.

Ans. 'Practice for layout of library catalogue' (1st Revision), New Delhi, ISI, 1967.

Q. 46. What is a Tell-Tale title of document?

Ans. A title that discloses the subject of a document.

Q. 47. What are the broad categories of corporate bodies recognised by CCC?

Ans. Government, conferences and institution.

Q. 48. How many entries are in CCC?

Ans. Main entry, cross reference entry, class index entry, book index entry and cross reference index entry.

Q. 49. Write the other name for Cross Reference Entry of a classified catalogue.

Ans. Subject analytical.

Q. 50. Which page is known as the half title page?

Ans. The recto of leaf usually preceding the title leaf containing half title of the document (CCC).

Q. 51. Who is known as a father of Dictionary Catalogue?

Ans. C.A. Cutter.

Q. 52. Write the dimensions of the books.

Ans. According to AACR-2 rule of the dimension about the books are following:

(a) Give the height of the item in centimeters, to the next whole centimeter up (e.g. it is an item measures 17.2 centimeters, give 18 cm). Measure the height of the binding if volume is bound otherwise, measure the height of the item itself. If the item measures less than 10 centimeters, give the height in millimeters. (Rule 2.5 D1)

(b) If the width of the volume is eighty less than half the height or greater than the height, give the height × width
20 × 8 cm
20 × 3.2 cm. (Rule 2.5 D2)

(c) If the volume in a multipart item differs in size smallest or smaller and the largest or larger size, separated by a hyphen.
24-28 cm. (Rule 2.5 D3)

(d) Give the height and the width single sheet, if such a sheet is designed to be folded when issued, the dimension of the sheet when folded:

48 × 30 cm folded to 24 × 15 cm.

If the sheet is designed to be read in pages when folded, describe it as one folded sheet and give the number of imposed pages and the height of the sheet when folded:

1 folded sheet (8p); 18 cm. (Rule 2.5 D4)

(e) If the item consists of separate physical units of varying height bound together, give the height of the binding only. (Rule 2.5 D5)

(*Source* AACR-2)

Q. 53. When the MARC project was completed?

Ans. In 1967.

Q. 54. What is Unit card?

Ans. A unit card is a basic catalogue card in the form of main entry. Which when duplicated may be used as a unit for all other entries for that work in a catalogue by addition of the appropriate heading (AACRI).

OBJECTIVE QUESTIONS

1. __________ link in chain procedure is usually a part of class number, which is not likely to be looked up by a reader.
   (a) Missing (b) False
   (c) Sought (d) Unsought
2. The two indexing model, viz. LCSH and SLSH are of __________ type.
   (a) descriptive (b) alphabetical
   (c) enumerative (d) classified
3. In PRECIS, the index entries and reference are brought together and merged according to word-by-word arrangement.
   (a) True (b) False
4. In chain procedure, class index entry is derived from __________.
   (a) Book No. (b) Collection No.
   (c) Class No. (d) Call No.
5. SLSH is widely used in small type of libraries.
   (a) True (b) False
6. LCSH can serve to index only macro level documents.
   (a) True (b) False
7. Filling of entries in SLSH follows the ______.
   (a) CCC rules for filling
   (b) ALA filling rules, 1980
   (c) Word by word arrangement
   (d) Letter by letter arrangement
8. In LCSH complex heading display phase relation of subject concept.
   (a) True (b) False
9. Four types of cross reference are used in LCSH, viz. see, see also, general and special hierarchical.
   (a) True (b) False
10. The three guiding principles of the Sears list of subject heading are specific and direct entry, common usage and terms of approach.
    (a) True (b) False
11. LCSH originated at the Library of Congress in the year
    (a) 1970 (b) 1923 (c) 1984 (d) 1897
12. The method of deriving subject heading through chain procedure is designed by
    (a) Bhattacharya (b) Derek Austen
    (c) Minie Eari Sears (d) S.R. Ranganathan
13. If the catalogue represents the collection available in a number of libraries, it is termed as
    (a) Dictionary catalogue
    (b) Classified catalogue
    (c) Union catalogue
    (d) Library catalogue
14. __________ references are provided, when there are entries in a catalogue under both Referred firm and Referred-to-headings.
    (a) See (b) See also
    (c) See and see also (d) Explanatory
15. The unit card principle is associated with __________ form of a catalogue. (*NET Exam.* 1999D)
    (a) register (b) card
    (c) sheaf (d) printed
16. Cataloguing in publication is called "Prenatal Cataloguing" by
    (a) Rider (b) Bliss
    (c) Ranganathan (d) Sayers
17. __________ is the only cataloguing code which provides rules for subject entries.
    (a) ALA code (b) CCC
    (c) AACR-II (d) Vatican code

18. __________ form of catalogue is portable, flexible and compact.
    (a) Sheaf or loose leaf (b) Book
    (c) Card (d) Register
19. The two parts of classified catalogues are
    (a) Classified part and Name index
    (b) Classified part and Author index
    (c) Classified part and Alphabetical
    (d) None of the above
20. The three major computers produced physical forms of library catalogues are
    (a) Printed, card and micro fiche
    (b) Register, card and micro form
    (c) Register, sheaf, card
    (d) Printed, card and micro form
21. Match the following aspects of cataloguing with the years given below:
    (A) CCC (1) 1949
    (B) AACR-II (2) 1908
    (C) ALA Code (3) 1978
    (D) AACR-I (4) 1934
    (a) A – 1, B – 2, C – 3, D – 4
    (b) A – 4, B – 3, C – 1, D – 2
    (c) A – 3, B – 4, C – 1, D – 2
    (d) A – 3, B – 1, C – 2, D – 4
22. Bound register form of library catalogue is still used in
    (a) Modern libraries (b) Special libraries
    (c) Big libraries (d) Small libraries
23. British Museum code is prepared by __________ in the year __________.
    (a) Ranganathan, 1934
    (b) British Library Association, 1949
    (c) Cutter, 1903
    (d) Panizzi, 1841
24. Alphabetical-classified and Alphabetic-classed forms of the catalogue are
    (a) Older forms (b) Modern forms
    (c) Inner forms (d) Outer forms
25. Trade catalogues are useful in library for
    (a) Retrieving the documents successful
    (b) Building up its collection
    (c) Providing subject approach to the catalogue
    (d) Arranging books on the shelf
26. Machine readable cataloguing (MARC) was launched in the year __________ by __________.
    (a) 1986, INSDOC
    (b) 1976, National Library of India
    (c) 1966, Library of Congress
    (d) 1960, British Library
27. Unit card unit record system, the main and added entries carry
    (a) Brief description
    (b) Detailed description
    (c) Different description
    (d) Same description
28. Author catalogue is used for university, research and special libraries to meet effectively subject approach of specialises.
    (a) True (b) False
29. A library catalogue is a list of
    (a) Periodical acquired by a library
    (b) Library furniture
    (c) Books and all other types of materials of a library
    (d) Non-book materials of a library
30. The directing wards "for documents in this class and its subdivisions see the classified part of the catalogue under the class number" are used in
    (a) Class Index Entry
    (b) Cross Reference Entry
    (c) Cross Reference Index Entry
    (d) Main Entry
31. Free indexing language is commonly used in indexing system.
    (a) True (b) False
32. According to CCC, the safest course to determine the choice of heading is to rely on the canon of
    (a) Context (b) Prepotency
    (c) Individualisation (d) Ascertainably
33. The pseudonym of the author Eric Arthur Blair is
    (a) A.E. (b) Mark Twain
    (c) George Orwell (d) George Eliot
34. British museum General catalogue of printed book is a
    (a) Name (b) Subject (c) Author (d) Title
35. According to AACR-II, __________ entry is an entry form of an item for which a comprehensive has been made.

(a) cross reference (b) title
(c) main (d) analytical

36. The six sections of main entry according to CCC are leading, heading, title, note, acc. no. and
(a) Physical description section
(b) Subject heading section
(c) Tracing section
(d) ISBN, ISSNNO section

37. Subject heading and Thesauri are two types of _______ indexing languages.
(a) natural (b) free
(c) controlled (d) their official names only

38. In AACR-II, societies are entered directly under
(a) The Subordinate body
(b) The best known name
(c) The name
(d) Their official names only

39. In AACR-II, the dimensions of the item are recorded in
(a) Series area (b) Note area
(c) Tracing (d) Physical description area

40. Subject analytical entry in CCC is known as
(a) Cross reference entry (b) References
(d) Alternate name entry (d) Cross reference index entry

41. Books in print and Who's Who is Indian writers _______ of information of works of Indian authors.
(a) ready reference source
(b) primary source
(c) chief source
(d) secondary source

42. CCC puts societies academic and religious bodies under
(a) Others (b) Agencies
(c) Institutions (d) Subordinate bodies

43. The eight parts of the main entry according to AACR-II are heading, body of the entry, physical description, series, note, standard no., tracing and call no.
(a) True (b) False

44. In author catalogue, books are entered under
(a) Surnames only
(b) Personal names only
(c) Corporate name only
(d) Both personal and corporate name only

45. According AACR-II, the name of international and inter-governmental body should be entered in the
(a) Predominant form only
(b) Brief form only
(c) English form only
(d) Official language only

46. ___________ is a compilation of words and phrases showing system, hierarchical and other relations to provide a standard vocabulary for information storage and retrieval systems.
(a) Vocabulary (b) Subject Heading List
(c) Dictionary (d) Thesaurus

47. Pseudonym is ___________ name.
(a) first (b) corporate
(c) fictitious (d) real

48. Most of the sacred books and many old and medieval texts are ___________ works.
(a) composite (b) anonymous
(c) multicolumn (d) pseudonyms

49. According to CCC, in a class index entry of a political publication the directing words are emitted for
(a) All the class index entries
(b) Specific class index entry
(c) Optional class index entry
(d) Generic class index entry

50. A ___________ is inserted between the name of the sponsor and the title proper of the periodical in CCC.
(a) comma (b) dash
(c) colon (d) semi colon

51. In CCC, the rendering of the name of the author G. Bhattacharya will be
(a) Bhattacharya, (G)
(b) BHATTACHARYA (G)
(c) G. BHATTACHARYA
(d) Bhattacharya, G.

52. In CCC, if the head of the government is the author, then the heading would be
(a) The designation of the head
(b) The name of the territory
(c) The name of the head
(d) The name of the office of the head

53. The first edition of AACR was revised in
(a) 1979 (b) 1967 (c) 1978 (d) 1908

54. In the edition statement, according to AACR-2 the editions are to be written in
(a) Indo-Arabic numeral (b) Roman
(c) Figures (d) Words

55. The book, *Anglo-American Cataloguing Rules*, Edition 2 has two parts, namely
(a) Description, Determination of headings
(b) Rule parts, Description part
(c) Rule part, Practical part
(d) Alphabetical, Classified.

56. The rendering of the name Pranab Kumar Mukharjee in AACR-2 would be
(a) Mukharjee, Pranab Kumar
(b) Mukharjee, P K
(c) Mukharjee, (Pranab Kumar)
(d) Pranab Kumar, Mukharjee

57. In AACR-2, when relevant information is taken from outside the main sources, it is written
(a) In circular brackets (b) In italics
(c) In bold (d) In square brackets

58. In AACR-2, the individual title of different volumes are to be recorded in the notes area as points.
(a) True (b) False

59. Common usage, uniformity in heading specific entry and _______ are the principles involves in determining subject headings.
(a) special references (b) scatter references
(c) cross references (d) specific references

60. In AACR-2 in the case of books written by three authors, the main entry will be made under
(a) First name (b) Second name
(c) Third name (d) All of these

61. UNESCO, WHO, FAO, ILO, etc. are the example of
(a) Commission (b) Committees
(c) Government bodies (d) Institution

62. In case there are four authors and none are attributed principal responsibility hence, the main entry is to be prepared by ___________ in AACR-2.
(a) collaborator of the book
(b) series of the book
(c) title of the book
(d) first author of the book

63. In AACR-2, the series area in the main entry is after the
(a) Edition area
(b) Material details area
(c) Physical description area
(d) Publication distribution area

64. According to AACR-2, in the tracing section of the main entry card, first we record
(a) Subject entry (b) Series entry
(c) Author entry (d) Title entry

65. In most of the cases, the main entry is a/an ___________entry in AACR-2. In some cases, it is a title entry.
(a) analytical (b) author
(c) collaborator (d) series

66. If there are more books under the same series there is no need to prepare author card. In the same card other books can be shown. This is called ___________ in CCC.
(a) pseudo series
(b) consolidation of series
(c) rendering of series
(d) multiplicity of series

67. If the book is not having any author but contains the name of collaborator, the heading section contains ______ in CCC.
(a) name of the collaborator
(b) name of the publishers
(c) title information
(d) series information

68. If all the volumes of the books, which have been published, are not possessed by the library, it is called
(a) Half set (b) Broken set
(c) Incomplete set (d) Complete set

69. The document, annual report of Reserve Bank of India is an example of
(a) Institution as author
(b) Government as author
(c) Committee as author
(d) Conference as author

70. When articles by different authors are published under one title, that book is known as ___________ in CCC.
(a) ordinary composite book
(b) festschrift
(c) composite book
(d) artificial composite book

71. For a periodical publication, three kinds of class index entries are prepared, viz. ______ in CCC.
(a) specific, generic, optional
(b) special, generic, optional
(c) Specific, general, optional
(d) Special, general, optional

72. If the title page contains the names of two authors, the heading section contains
(a) Name of the first author only
(b) Name of the second author only
(c) Both the names
(d) Both the names with the conjunction 'and' connecting them

73. In CCC, the name of the series in the book index entry is rendered in caps in
(a) Note section (b) Title section
(c) Second section (d) Leading section

74. In CCC, in case of pseudonymous works it the title page contains pseudonym, and the real name in subordinate manner then the heading section contains the pseudonym of the author and the real name of the author added thereafter and
(a) Enclosed in circular brackets
(b) In the next line
(c) Without brackets
(d) Enclosed in square brackets

75. Pseudo series is the creation of
(a) AACR-2 (b) Author
(c) CC Code (d) Publisher

76. In CCC, the name of the series in the main entry is rendered in
(a) Title section (b) Note section
(c) Heading section (d) Second section

77. The main entry of simple periodical publication consists of Leading, Heading, Series, Holding, Tracing and
(a) Directing section
(b) Index number section
(c) Periodicity section
(d) Second section

78. A person who collects matter from the books of various persons or one who selects and puts together from the work of one person is called author.
(a) True (b) False

79. In AACR-2, the entry element for government is the geographical name of country.
(a) True (b) False

80. Cross-reference entry is also called ______ entry in CCC.
(a) class index (b) title analytical
(c) class number (d) subject analytical

81. In the main entry of CCC, the leading section is made up of the ______ of the document.
(a) accession number (b) title
(c) class number (d) call number

82. In the case of commissions and committees, the name of the chairman of the commission or committee is written in the __________ area in AACR-2.
(a) Heading (b) Notes
(c) GMD (d) Physical description

83. Indian Council of Historical Research is a government agency. According to AACR-2, in such cases the main entry is made under
(a) The name of the director
(b) The geographical name
(c) The name of the organisation
(d) The government

84. In AACR-2, in case of sacred scriptures, the heading part of the main entry is the subtitle.
(a) True (b) False

85. In CCC, the class index entries are prepared for the __________ only.
(a) unsought links (b) sought links
(c) false links (d) missing links

86. The classified part of the CCC consists of main entry and
(a) Book Index Entry
(b) Class Index Entry
(c) Cross Reference Entry
(d) Cross Reference Index Entry

87. In CCC, tracing is done on the __________ of the main entry card.
(a) lower portion of the front side
(b) front side
(c) back side
(d) right portion of the front side

88. According to AACR-2, Vedas, Upanishads and Bhagavad-Gita are the example of
(a) Uniform title (b) Corporate bodies
(c) Composite works (d) Multi-volume works

89. In AACR-2, in case of sacred scriptures the heading part of the main entry is the
(a) Parallel title (b) Subtitle
(c) Uniform title (d) Collective title

90. In AACR-2, the serial publications are entered under the
(a) Name of the publishers
(b) Name of the editor
(c) Title
(d) Name of the sponsor

91. The word catalogue has been derived from the ___________ expression kata logos.
(a) French (b) Spanish
(c) Greece (d) Latin

92. The 2nd edition of Anglo-American cataloguing Rules was published in
(a) 1941 (b) 1978 (c) 1908 (d) 1935

93. Who has developed SLIC?
(a) S.R. Ranganathan (b) J.R. Sharp
(c) C.A. Cutter (d) Derek Austin

94. The opposite of Tell-Tale title is
(a) Story telling book
(b) Short title of the book
(c) Fanciful title
(d) Title that discusses the subject of the work

95. How to write size according to AACR-2 on a catalogue card of a book, height of which is 17.2 cm?
(a) 18 cm (b) 17 cm
(c) 17.2 cm (d) 18.2 cm

96. The revised version of the MARC is known as (*NET Exam.* 1998D)
(a) MARC-III (b) MARC-II
(c) MARC-I (d) None of the above

97. Standard size of the Catalogue card is (*NET Exam.* 1998D)
(a) 12.7 cm × 7.5 cm (b) 12.5 cm × 7.5 cm
(c) 10.0 cm × 5.0 cm (d) 5.0 cm × 3.0 cm

98. Tell-Tale title means (*NET Exam.* 1998D)
(a) Story telling book
(b) Title that discusses the subject of the work
(c) Fanciful title
(d) Big title

99. KWIC Indexing was devised by (*NET Exam.* 1998D)
(a) Derek Austin (b) C.W. Cleverdon
(c) H.P. Luhan (d) Melvil Dewey

100. Union catalogue is a form of (*NET Exam.* 1998D)
(a) Centralised Catalogue
(b) Limited Catalogue
(c) Co-operative Catalogue
(d) Descriptive Catalogue

101. Hierarchical relation in a thesaurus is a relation between (*NET Exam.* 1998D)
(a) BT and RT (b) RT and BT
(c) NT and RT (d) BT and NT

102. According to AACR-II, University Grant Commission (India) will be rendered as (*NET Exam.* 1995D)
(a) India, University Grant Commission
(b) India, Ministry of Education, University Grant Commission
(c) India, University (Grant Commission)
(d) University Grant Commission, India

103. Work of unknown authorship is called (*NET Exam.* 1995D)
(a) Pseudonymous work
(b) Anonymous work
(c) Factious work
(d) None of the above

104. Pre-Natal Cataloguing stands for (*NET Exam.* 1995D)
(a) Selective cataloguing
(b) Descriptive cataloguing
(c) Cataloguing in publication
(d) Comparative cataloguing

105. Citation Analysis helps in (*NET Exam.* 1995D)
(a) Subject indexing
(b) Identification of core documents
(c) Descriptive cataloguing
(d) Selective cataloguing

106. Which of the following are the core content of ISI web of knowledge? (*NET Exam.* 2013D)
(i) Current Contents (ii) ISI proceedings
(iii) Derwent Information Index (iv) AGRICOLA

Codes:

(a)	(i)	(iv)	(iii)
(b)	(i)	(ii)	(iii)
(c)	(ii)	(iii)	(iv)
(d)	(i)	(ii)	(iv)

107. The author associated with PRECIS is (*NET Exam.* 1995D)

(a) F.W. Lancaster (b) D.J. Foskett
(c) Derek Austin (d) Pauline Atherton

108. Thesaurus for indexing stands for (*NET Exam.* 1995D)
(a) Controlled vocabulary
(b) Dictionary of name
(c) A dictionary of works
(d) Name of a language dictionary

109. Which of the canons of cataloguing mentioned below prescribed that the information for choice and rendering should be taken from title and its overflow pages? (*NET Exam.* 1994)
(a) Canon of Individualisation
(b) Canon of Currency
(c) Canon of Pre-potence
(d) Canon of Ascertain ability

110. In CCC, subject analytical entries are known as (*NET Exam.* 1994)
(a) Cross Reference entries
(b) Cross Reference Index entry
(c) Class Index entry
(d) Book Index entry

111. Which of the following codes does not allow to finding out information from outside the title or overflow pages in determining the choice of heading? (*NET Exam.* 1994)
(a) CCC (b) AACR-I
(c) Rules for Dictionary Catalogue
(d) Vatican Code

112. International conference on cataloging principles was held in the year (*NET Exam.* 1994, 1997J)
(a) 1949 (b) 1952 (c) 1961 (d) 1969

113. According to AARC-II, when there are four authors and no one is principal author and one editor, the entry will be prepared under (*NET Exam.* 1994)
(a) Under the editor
(b) Under the first author
(c) Under all the authors
(d) Under the title

114. For recording of subscription and receipt of periodicals Ranganathan suggested (*NET Exam.* 1994)
(a) Ledger system (b) Two-Card system
(c) Three-Card system (d) None of these

115. OPAC stands for (*NET Exam.* 1994)
(a) Online Public Access Catalogue
(b) Online Processing of Automated Catalogue
(c) Online Processing of Analogue Computer
(d) None of the above

116. PRECIS was designed by (*NET Exam.* 1994, 1995)
(a) S.R. Ranganathan (b) Derek Austin
(c) D.J. Foskett (d) F.W. Lancaster

117. POPSI is (*NET Exam.* 1994, 1995)
(a) A scheme of library classification
(b) A computer system
(c) An indexing system of subject entries
(d) A catalogue code

118. Canons of cataloguing were first formulated by (*NET Exam.* 1995J)
(a) Seymour Lubetzky (b) Charles A. Cutter
(c) S.R. Ranganathan (d) Anthony Panizzi

119. According to CCC (Ed. 5), Ministry of Education, Government of West Bengal will be rendered as (*NET Exam.* 1995J)
(a) West Bengal, Ministry of Education
(b) West Bengal, Education (Ministry of .....)
(c) WEST BENGAL, EDUCATION (Ministry of ....)
(d) Ministry of Education of (West Bengal)

120. British Museum Catalogue code was formulated by (*NET Exam.* 1995)
(a) S. Lubetzky (b) C.A. Cutter
(c) Anthony Panizzi (d) C.C. Jewelt

121. ISBN consists of (*NET Exam.* 1995)
(a) 8 digits (b) 14 digits
(c) 10 digits (d) 12 digits

122. Which of the following is a pseudonymous name? (*NET Exam.* 1995)
(a) Suryakant Tripathi 'Nirala'
(b) George Orwell
(c) Prem Chand
(d) Mahadevi Verma

123. Controlled vocabulary in indexing is called (*NET Exam.* 1995)
(a) A thesaurus
(b) A language dictionary
(c) A dictionary of synonyms
(d) A list of subject heading

124. Three-card system is used for (*NET Exam.* 1995J)

(a) Cataloguing of books
(b) Acquisition and control of periodicals
(c) Shelf-list
(d) Circulation of books

125. Shelf-list in a library used for (*NET Exam.* 1995)
(a) Stock verification
(b) Shelving of books
(c) Acquisition of books
(d) Selection of books

126. What is the relationship between ISBD and catalogue code? (*NET Exam.* 2000)
(a) They are not related to all
(b) Cataloguing codes will include bibliographic description
(c) ISBD includes cataloguing rules
(d) ISBD can replace cataloguing codes

127. Which of the following is not a part of the MARC record structure?(*NET Exam.* 2000)
(a) Leader (b) Directory
(c) Recorded terminator (d) Check digit

128. Which of the following organisations was joined with Library Association to form CILIP in 2002?
(a) Institute of Bibliography
(b) Institute of Information Scientists
(c) Institute of Documentation
(d) Institute of Librarianship

129. In thesaurus, under an item "Internet Migration" which of the following lines would you expect to find? (*NET Exam.* 2000)
(a) BT Migration
(b) NT rural to urban
(c) RT International Migration
(d) All of the above

130. Who had founded Documentation Inc. to explore new methods of information indexing and retrieval?
(a) S.C. Bradford (b) Jennifer Rowley
(c) Mortimer Taube (d) S.R. Ranganathan

131. A document description is not found in a (*NET Exam.* 2000)
(a) Catalogue entry (b) Citation
(c) Bibliographic entry (d) Class number

132. According to AACR-II, the heading of main entry for conference proceeding edited by an individual is prepared under (*NET Exam.* 2000)
(a) Name of editor
(b) Place of conference
(c) Title of the volume
(d) Name of the conference

133. A Boolean query using only AND and NOT is
(a) Fuzzy query (b) Conjunctive query
(c) Routing query (d) Probabilistic query

134. Which of the following are the main role operators of PRECIS? (*NET Exam.* 2013D)
(i) Key System (ii) Action
(iii) Performer of action (iv) Form of Document
Codes:
(a) (i), (ii) and (iii) (b) (ii), (i) and (iv)
(c) (i), (iii) and (iv) (d) (ii), (iii) and (i)

135. Which of the following are called 'path finders' to the literature?
(i) Bibliography (ii) Catalogue
(iii) Shelf List (iv) Indices and Abstracts
Codes:
(a) (i) & (ii) are correct
(b) (i), (ii) & (iv) are correct
(c) (i) & (iv) are correct
(d) (ii) & (iii) are correct

136. Bibliography of Bibliographies comes under the category (*NET Exam.* 1999D)
(a) Primary sources (b) Secondary sources
(c) Tertiary sources (d) None of the above

137. Which of the following associations have sponsored the Text Encoding Initiatives (TEI)?
(i) ACL (ii) ACRL (iii) ALLC (iv) ACH
Codes:
(a) (i), (ii) and (iii) are correct
(b) (ii), (iii) and (iv) are correct
(c) (i), (iv) and (ii) are correct
(d) (i), (iii) and (iv) are correct

138. Which indexing system uses a single term and an accession number of the document as an indicator of reference?(*NET Exam.* 1999D)
(a) NEPHIS (b) Relative Index
(c) KWIC (d) PRECIS

139. The unit card principle is associated with (*NET Exam.* 1999)
(a) Sheaf Catalogue (b) Card Catalogue
(c) Printed Catalogue (d) Machine Readable Catalogue

140. National Index of Translation is published by (*NET Exam.* 1999)
(a) NASSDOC (b) DESIDOC
(c) SENDOC (d) INSDOC

141. Which of the following cannot be considered as thesaurus? (*NET Exam.* 1999)
(a) MESH (b) TEST
(c) LCSH (d) None of the above

142. Periodical publication 'Indian Science Abstracts' is brought out by (*NET Exam.* 1999)
(a) DBSI – DOC (b) INSA
(c) INSDOC (d) NISSAT

143. POPSI, PRECIS, Chain procedure and SLIC are the example of (*NET Exam.* 1999)
(a) Indexing system
(b) Classification system
(c) Cataloguing codes
(d) Abstracting procedure

144. In KWIC indexes, the keyword appears
(a) At the beginning of each entry
(b) At a highlighted word
(c) At the centre of the line
(d) At the end of the entry

145. According to AACR-II, if a book has been edited by four persons the main entry should be made under first editor.
(a) True (b) False

146. According to AACR-II, the heading for IX All India Library conference will be
(a) IX All India Library conference
(b) All India Library conference (9th)
(c) Ninth All India Library conference
(d) All India Library conference

147. In study undertaken to find out how users approach the library catalogue, all those who use the catalogue on a particular day are interviewed. This would be considered as (*NET Exam.* 1998J)
(a) A random sample
(b) A stratified sample
(c) The whole population
(d) Not a representative sample

148. Post-co-ordinate indexes over course difficulties created by (*NET Exam.* 1998J)
(a) Fixed citation order
(b) Synonymous terms
(c) Time taken in searching
(d) Anonymous terms

149. It is sometimes stated that in computerised catalogue, cataloguing rules and classification codes serve no purpose. Do you agree that in a computerised catalogue (*NET Exam.* 1998)
(a) Cataloguing rules are not necessary
(b) Classification serves no purpose
(c) Both are required
(d) Neither is required

150. Which of the following statements about a thesaurus is correct? (*NET Exam.* 1998)
(a) A thesaurus helps the indexes, not the term
(b) A thesaurus includes descriptors and lead terms
(c) A thesaurus links only broader to narrower terms
(d) A thesaurus-based indexing system has an uncontrolled vocabulary

151. Which of the following is a union catalogue? (*NET Exam.* 1996J)
(a) Ulrich's International Periodicals Directory
(b) New serials Titles
(c) NUCSSI
(d) Press in India

152. The originator of 'Science Citation Index' is (*NET Exam.* 1996J)
(a) Eugene Garfield (b) Farradane
(c) H.P. Luhn (d) Berwick Sayers

153. In which of the following types of indexes are access points not derived automatically? (*NET Exam.* 1996J)
(a) KWIC (b) Citation Indexing
(c) KWOC (d) POPSI

154. According to AACR-II, if a book has been written by four authors, main entry should be made under (*NET Exam.* 1996J)
(a) First author (b) All author
(c) Title (d) First three authors

155. Shelf-list cards (i) Duplicate the arrangement of the shelves (ii) are used in stock verification (iii) represent each volume on the shelf. Which of the phrases is correct? (*NET Exam.* 1996)
Codes:
(a) (i) and (ii) (b) (i) and (iii)
(c) (ii) and (iii) (d) All of these

156. The "Pre-natal cataloguing" was used for the first time by (*NET Exam.* 1996D)
(a) S.R. Ranganathan (b) C.A. Cutter
(c) A.C. Foskett (d) E.J. Coates

157. Who developed PRECIS? (*NET Exam.* 1996D)
(a) Derek Langridge (b) Derek de Solla Price
(c) Eric de Grolier (d) Derek Austin

158. According to AACR-II, if a book has been edited by four persons the main entry should be made under (*NET Exam.* 1996)
(a) The first editor (b) Editor
(c) Title (d) The first three editors

159. ASTINFO stands for (*NET Exam.* 2013D)
(a) Asian Scientific and Technological Information Network
(b) Association of Scientific and Technological Information Scientists in Asia
(c) International Network for Exchange of Science and Technology Information
(d) Regional Network for the Exchange of Information and Experience in Science and Technology in Asia and the Pacific

160. Rules for Dictionary Catalogue was devised by (*NET Exam.* 1996, 1998D)
(a) Anthony Panizzi (b) C.A. Cutter
(c) C.C. Jewet (d) S. Lubetzky

161. Which of the following words of Dr. S.R. Ranganathan undertook a comparative study of five cataloguing codes? (*NET Exam.* 1991)
(a) Theory of library catalogue
(b) Library catalogue; fundamentals and procedures
(c) Headings and canons
(d) Cataloguing practices

162. How to write size according to AACR-II on a catalogue card of a book, the height of which is 20.5 cm and width is 32 cm? (*NET Exam.* 1991)
(a) 20 cm (b) 21 cm
(c) 20 × 32 cm (d) 21 × 32 cm

163. The code that recognises the concept of principal author is (*NET Exam.* 1991)
(a) CCC (b) ACCR-I and II
(c) R.D.C. (d) Vatican Code

164. The first international cataloguing code entitled A.A. Code was devised by ALA and the Library Association in the year (*NET Exam.* 1991)
(a) 1901 (b) 1908 (c) 1939 (d) 1949

165. BNB is at present deriving subject index entries according to (*NET Exam.* 1991)
(a) Chain Indexing (b) PRECIS
(c) KWIC (d) POPSI

166. Authority file is used in (*NET Exam.* 1991)
(a) Reference Division
(b) Acquisition Division
(c) Technical Division
(d) Maintenance Division

167. The terms NT and BT are used in (*NET Exam.* 1995D)
(a) Chain indexing (b) KWIC
(c) Thesaurus (d) POPSI

168. Atom Index is brought out by (*NET Exam.* 1997J)
(a) INIS (b) AGRIS
(c) BARC (d) Dept. of Nuclear Science

169. Which of the following is union catalogue? (*NET Exam.* 1997J)
(a) Ulrich Periodical Directory
(b) New Serials Titles
(c) Press in India
(d) NUCSSI

170. Entries in Indian science abstracts are arranged according to (*NET Exam.* 1997J)
(a) DDC (b) UDC (c) LC (d) CC

171. Chief source of information for cataloguing a monograph is (*NET Exam.* 1997J)
(a) Contents Page (b) Title Page
(c) Half-title Page (d) Preface

172. In a retrieval system the coordination of concepts done by the searcher at the search stage is known as
(a) Pre-Coordinate (b) Post Coordinate
(c) Under Coordinate (d) Over Coordinate

173. Union Catalogue are
(a) Primary sources (b) Secondary sources
(c) Tertiary sources (d) None of the above

174. Which of the following is not the feature of an information retrieval system? (*NET Exam.* 1997D)
(a) Relevance (b) Recall
(c) Precision (d) Perception

175. According to the AACR-II when the title page of a book contains names of four authors and the third name is printed in a bold letter the heading of the main entry will be under

(a) The first author (b) The second author
(c) The third author (d) The title

176. Which of the following pairs is wrong? (*NET Exam.* 1999J)
(a) Eugene Garfield-Citation Indexing
(b) H.P. Lohan-KWIC Indexing
(c) S.R. Ranganathan-Chain Indexing
(d) Derek Austin-POPSI

177. Among the different Boolean operations OR is used (*NET Exam.* 1999D)
(a) To widen the search
(b) To narrow the search
(c) To end the search
(d) To begin the search

178. Which of the following is not an abstracting services? (*NET Exam.* 1999J)
(a) ERIC (b) LISA
(c) Medline (d) Excerpta Medica

179. Post coordinate index overcome difficulties created by? (*NET Exam.* 1999J)
(a) Fixed citation order
(b) Synonymous terms
(c) Time delays
(d) Inconsistencies

180. According to AACR-II, the heading of main entry for an encyclopedia is prepared under
(a) Name of editor (b) Name of the Publishers
(c) Title (d) Place of Publication

181. The paper entitled "The Crisis in Cataloguing" published in *Library Quarterly* (Vol. 11, Oct. 1941) was authored by
(a) Seymour Lubetzky (b) Michael Gorman
(c) Andrew Osborn (d) David J. Haykin

182. The code based on ICCP is (*NET Exam.* 1999J)
(a) CCC (b) AACRII
(c) AACRII-R (d) AACRI

183. Boolean searching (*NET Exam.* 1999J)
(a) Is used on computerised database
(b) Is based on Post Coordinate indexing
(c) Combines search statements using "AND", "OR" and "NOT"
(d) All of the above

184. The number of methods of "Analysis" proposed in AACR2R (1988) is
(a) three (b) four (c) five (d) six

185. Which of the following combinations is wrong?

(a)	PRECIS	Dreck Austin	BNB
(b)	KWIC	H.P. Luhan	Chemical Titles
(c)	Citation indexing	Eugene Garfield	SCI
(d)	Relational indexing	E.J. Coates	Biological Abstracts

186. Which one of the following search devices will lead to an increase in the Recall output?
(a) Boolean 'AND' (b) Boolean 'NOT'
(c) Proximity operators (d) Truncation

187. The citation indexes are now available online as
(a) Web of Science (b) JCCC
(c) Scopus (d) FBSCO

188. KWIC indexing technique is based (*NET Exam.* 1996J)
(a) Title (b) Citation
(c) Abstracts (d) Full text

189. MESH is an example of (*NET Exam.* 1996J)
(a) Classification scheme (b) Thesaurus
(c) Abstract's Journal (d) Classification

190. National Union catalogue of scientific serials in India is published by (*NET Exam.* 1996J)
(a) National Library (Calcutta)
(b) National Reference Library
(c) INSDOC
(d) Delhi Public Library

191. Citation Analysis can be used to identify (*NET Exam.* 1998J)
(a) less used periodicals
(b) half line of periodicals
(c) journal with the highest impact factor
(d) All of the above

192. Acc. No. is a part of the call number of book.
(a) True (b) False

193. Who wrote "Catalogue is a list of books which is arranged on some definite plan"?
(a) S.R. Ranganathan (b) C.A. Cutter
(c) Margaret Mann (d) W.C.B. Sayers

194. Dictionary catalogue consists of all types of entries in one alphabetical order.
(a) True (b) False

195. Match the following:
(A) Fanciful Title (1) specific entry giving maximum information about the whole of a document

(B) Main Entry (2) Collection
(C) Publication area for one work (3) Record of the heading under which an item is represented in the catalogue
(D) Tracing (4) That does not disclose the subject of the work

(a)	A – 4	B – 1	C – 2	D – 3
(b)	A – 3	B – 2	C – 3	D – 4
(c)	A – 2	B – 3	C – 1	D – 4
(d)	A – 1	B – 4	C – 4	D – 3

196. Match the following:
(A) Reference Manual (1) LC
(B) UNIMARC (2) UNESCO
(C) CCF (3) IFLA
(D) MARC (4) UNISIST

(a)	A – 4	B – 3	C – 2	D – 1
(b)	A – 3	B – 2	C – 1	D – 4
(c)	A – 2	B – 4	C – 3	D – 3
(d)	A – 3	B – 1	C – 4	D – 2

197. Ranganathan first used Pre-natal Catalogue.
(a) True (b) False

198. Match the following:
(A) AACR-2 (1) 1934
(B) Vatican Code (2) 1908
(C) A.A. Code (3) 1931
(D) Classified Catalogue code (4) 1978

(a)	A – 4	B – 3	C – 2	D – 1
(b)	A – 1	B – 2	C – 4	D – 3
(c)	A – 2	B – 4	C – 3	D – 1
(d)	A – 1	B – 2	C – 3	D – 4

199. Match the following:

List I	List II
(A) 1938	(1) CIS Programme
(B) 1743	(2) CIP Programme
(C) 1958	(3) Chain Procedure
(D) 1971	(4) Printed Catalogue

(a)	A – 3	B – 4	C – 1	D – 2
(b)	A – 4	B – 3	C – 2	D – 1
(c)	A – 2	B – 3	C – 4	D – 1
(d)	A – 1	B – 2	C – 3	D – 4

200. MESH is example of Thesaurus.
(a) True (b) False

201. S.R. Ranganathan developed the chain indexing.
(a) True (b) False

202. **Statement (A):** An informative abstract is necessarily longer. (*NET Exam.* 1997D)
Statement (B): An informative abstract is always more useful.
(a) Statements (A) and (B) both are correct
(b) Statement (A) is incorrect but (B) is correct
(c) Statements (A) and (B) both are incorrect
(d) Statement (A) is correct but (B) is incorrect

203. If a selected play of Shakespeare have been translated by A.D. Patil and compiled with notes by S.M. Shah, the main entry in AACR-II will be made under (*NET Exam.* 1997D)
(a) Shakespeare William
(b) Patel A.D.
(c) Shah S.M.
(d) Selected plays of Shakespeare

204. In KWIC indexes the keyword is (*NET Exam.* 1997J)
(a) Derived from the title
(b) Taken from abstract
(c) Selected from the full text
(d) Assigned by the author

205. PRECIS is used by (*NET Exam.* 1999J)
(a) Indian National Bibliography
(b) British National Bibliography
(c) CC for its index
(d) None of the above

206. In a thesaurus, under the term "Domestic violence" which of the following lines would you expected to find?
(a) B.T. Violence (b) N.T. Child Abuse
(c) R.T. Dowry (d) All of the above

207. In a study undertaken to find out how uses approach the library catalogue, all those who use the catalogue on a particular day are interviewed? Would this be considered as (*NET Exam.* 1996J)
(a) Not of a representative sample
(b) A stratified sample
(c) The whole population
(d) A random sample

208. Indian National Bibliography is arranged under two parts. General Publication and ________ Publications.
(a) Private (b) Electronic
(c) Governmental (d) Non-book

209. Which of the following combinations is wrong? (*NET Exam.* 2001J)
(a) PRECIS-Dreck Austin-BNB
(b) KWIC-H P luhan-Chemical Titles

(c) Citatio Indexing-Eugene Garfield SCI
(d) Relational Indexing-E J Coates Biological Abstracts

210. Citation Indexing was first developed in the field of (*NET Exam.* 2001J, 2003J)
(a) Science (b) Mathematics
(c) Law (d) Social Science

211. Among the different Boolean operators "AND" is used (*NET Exam.* 2001J)
(a) to widen search (b) to narrow search
(c) to begin the search (d) to end the search

212. Which of the following names are associated with Post-Coordinate Indexing? (*NET Exam.* 2001J)
(a) Taube, Mooers, Batten
(b) Taube, Austin, Coates
(c) Taube, Austin, Garfield
(d) Mooers, Taube, Garfield

213. The subject headings "Money" and "Inflation" are both used in a retrieval system. The two term should (*NET Exam.* 2001J)
(a) not be linked
(b) be linked by a "see reference"
(c) be linked by both "see" and "see also" reference
(d) be linked by a "see also" reference

214. The ICCP did not lead to (*NET Exam.* 2001J)
(a) arrangement on the need for uniformity and standard
(b) a definition of main entry
(c) a recognition of corporate authorship
(d) the development of MARC format

215. In KWIC index the keyword appears (*NET Exam.* 2001J)
(a) at the beginning of each entry
(b) at the centre of the line
(c) as the highlighted word
(d) at the end of the line

216. Analytical entry is prepared for (*NET Exam.* 2001D)
(a) Alternative title (b) Full document
(c) Part of a document (d) None of these

217. "Canons for Characteristics" are part of (*NET Exam.* 2001D)
(a) Verbal plan (b) Notational plan
(c) Idea plan (d) Structural plan

218. Phoenix schedules are part of (*NET Exam.* 2001D)
(a) DDC (b) BC (c) UDC (d) LCC

219. The Unit Card Principle is associated with (*NET Exam.* 2001D)
(a) Sheaf Catalogue
(b) Card Catalogue
(c) Printed Catalogue
(d) Machine Readable Catalogue

220. The principle for facet sequence given by Ranganathan is (*NET Exam.* 2001D)
(a) Wall Picture Principle
(b) Law of Parsimony
(c) Local Variation
(d) Spatial Contiguity

221. POPSI, PRECIS, Chain procedure and SLIC are the example of (*NET Exam.* 2001D)
(a) Indexing system
(b) Classification system
(c) Cataloguing codes
(d) abstracting procedures

222. Prenatal cataloguing is synonyms with (*NET Exam.* 2001D)
(a) Classified Catalogue
(b) Cataloguing in publication
(c) Subject cataloguing
(d) All of the above

223. In KWIC index, the keyword is (*NET Exam.* 2002D)
(a) derived from the title
(b) selected from the full text
(c) taken from the full text
(d) assigned by the author

224. If two citations are cited together, it is known as (*NET Exam.* 2006J)
(a) Double citation (b) Twin citation
(c) Co-citation (d) Controlled citation

225. Who would be credited for designing thesaurus? (*NET Exam.* 2002D)
(a) Morle Roget (b) M. Tabue
(c) Helen Broun (d) E. Garfield

226. The cost of cataloguing a single book is (*NET Exam.* 2002J)
(a) Unit Cost (b) Entry Cost
(c) Profit Cost (d) Unrestricted Cost

227. Monthly catalogue published by controller of publication division, provides information on the current publication of (*NET Exam.* 2002D)

(a) Personnel Department
(b) Government of India
(c) Medical Council of India
(d) Indian Library Association

228. Post co-ordinate index overcome difficulties created by (*NET Exam.* 2002J)
(a) fixed citation order
(b) synonyms terms
(c) time taken in searching
(d) inconsistency

229. Which is a computer held catalogue which can be searched by a user sitting at a remote terminal? (*NET Exam.* 2004J)
(a) OPAC (b) COM (c) MARC (d) CCF

230. International Standard Book Description does not standardise (*NET Exam.* 2003J)
(a) the point of access
(b) type of information to be included in the catalogue entry
(c) the punctuation marks to be followed
(d) order in which the information is to be recorded

231. Chemical abstract uses which of the following for standardization purpose? (*NET Exam.* 2003J)
(a) ISSN (b) CODEN (c) ISBN (d) PASCAL

232. A link in pseudo chain mode of digit group forming part of a book number is (*NET Exam.* 2003J)
(a) sought link (b) pseudo link
(c) pseudo chain (d) tracing

233. The "Subject Reference Code" (SRC) is related to (*NET Exam.* 2003J)
(a) Library of Congress Classification
(b) Universal Decimal Classification
(c) Broad System of Classification
(d) Bibliographic Classification

234. In classified part of INB, the entries are arranged according to (*NET Exam.* 2003J)
(a) CC 6th & 7th edition
(b) DDC 16th edition
(c) DDC 19th edition
(d) UDC 3rd Abridge edition

235. NT and BT are used in which of the following category? (*NET Exam.* 2003J)
(a) PRECIS (b) Thesaurus
(c) POPSI (d) Chain Indexing

236. Under which types of service, the compilation of Bibliographies, Retrospective Search, Document Back up, Reference Services and Translation service come (*NET Exam.* 2003D)
(a) Anticipatory Services
(b) Responsive services
(c) Referral Services
(d) Telecommunication Services

237. In thesaurus under an item "Internal Migration" which of the following lines would you except to find (*NET Exam.* 2003D)
(a) BT Migration
(b) RT International Migration
(c) NT Rural to Urban
(d) All the above

238. Literature search is essentially a process of (*NET Exam.* 2003D)
(a) Information Bureau
(b) Information Retrieval
(c) Ready Reference Service
(d) Current Awareness Service

239. When computerised data is reproduced on microfilm without first being produced in paper form. It is (*NET Exam.* 2005D)
(a) MARC (b) Microchip
(c) COM (d) Microform

240. Identify the chronological order of the following catalogue: (*NET Exam.* 2003D)
Codes:
(i) AACR II (ii) CCC
(iii) AA Code (iv) ALA Code
Codes:

(a)	iii	iv	i	ii
(b)	ii	iv	iii	i
(c)	iii	ii	iv	i
(d)	iv	i	ii	iii

241. "Asian Recorder" consists of three parts, namely Event in all countries of Asia, Asia outside Asia and (*NET Exam.* 2003D)
(a) Sports Events of Asia
(b) Sports Events of all countries
(c) Sports of third world countries
(d) None of the above

242. Which of the following is a translator program? (*NET Exam.* 2003D)
(a) Assembler (b) Interpreter
(c) Complier (d) All the above

243. "Natural Science" can be formed by which of the following modes? (*NET Exam.* 2003D)
(a) Cluster (b) Lamination
(c) Agglomeration (d) Loose assemblage

244. According to the principle of equitable allocation, how many percentage of publication grant is allowed for periodicals? (*NET Exam.* 2003D)
(a) 50% (b) 60% (c) 70% (d) 80%

245. Match the following: (*NET Exam.* 2003D)

Column A (Books)	Column B (Year)
(A) 2nd edition of cataloguing practice	1. 1951
(B) 1st edition of CCF	2. 1976
(C) Drafting of BSO	3. 1971
(D) A A Code of Cataloguing (ALA)	4. 1908

Codes:	A	B	C	D
(a)	1	2	3	4
(b)	2	1	3	4
(c)	4	3	2	1
(d)	4	2	3	1

246. Pre-natal cataloguing means (*NET Exam.* 2006D)
(a) Simplified Cataloguing
(b) Prepublication Cataloguing
(c) Selective Cataloguing
(d) Shared Cataloguing

247. Notification to the user for receipt of new arrival or documents in the library comes under the (*NET Exam.* 2005D)
(a) Reference service (b) Inter-library loan
(c) CAS (d) SDI service

248. The major functions required of an automation cataloguing system are (*NET Exam.* 2003J)
1. Database creation 2. Search
3. Retrieval
Codes:
(a) 2 only (b) 1 and 2
(c) 3 only (d) 1, 2 and 3

249. British Union Catalogue of Periodicals (BUCOP) is a record of periodicals of the— from 17th. Century to present day, in British libraries (*NET Exam.* 2003J)
(a) India (b) Great Britain
(c) World (d) USA, UK

250. OCLC is (*NET Exam.* 2006J)
(i) Online Computer Library centre
(ii) At Dublin (Ohio)
(iii) At New York
(iv) Ohio College Library centre
Codes:
(a) i and ii are correct
(b) i and iii are correct
(c) iii and iv are correct
(d) ii and iv are correct

251. Pre-coordinating indexing system is followed in: (*NET Exam.* 2006J)
(i) Chain Indexing (ii) POPSI
(iii) UNITERM (iv) PRECIS
Codes:
(a) i and iv are correct
(b) i, ii and iii are correct
(c) i, ii and iv are correct
(d) ii and iv are correct

252. **Assertion (A):** Library catalogue meet most of the approaches of the users.
Reason (R): Catalogue include all the details of the document. (*NET Exam.* 2006J)
Codes:
(a) Both (A) and (R) are true
(b) (A) is true but (R) are false
(c) Both are partially true
(d) (R) is true, and (A) is false

253. The donation from Andrew Carnegie were mainly meant for the (*NET Exam.* 2003D)
(a) purchase of books
(b) construction of library building
(c) furniture of the library
(d) salaries of the semi-professional staff

254. In how many parts the CC-6 can be divided? (*NET Exam.* 2003D)
(a) 6 (b) 4 (c) 3 (d) 2

255. Arrange the physical forms of catalogue in the chronological sequences: (*NET Exam.* 2006D)
(a) Register, Sheaf Catalogue, Card Catalogue, OPAC
(b) Sheaf Catalogue, Register, Card Catalogue, OPAC
(c) Card Catalogue, Sheaf Catalogue, Register, OPAC
(d) Sheaf Catalogue, Card Catalogue, Register, OPAC

256. OCLC Project, MARC Project are the example of (*NET Exam.* 2007J)
(a) Co-operative storage materials
(b) Co-operative Acquisition of materials
(c) Co-operative processing materials
(d) Co-operative sharing materials

257. Which one is published by UPLA? (*NET Exam.* 2004J)
(a) GRATHLOKAM (b) GRANTHANA
(c) UPLANEWS (d) GRANTHALAYEE

258. Who was the first librarian to use the phrase reference interviews? (*NET Exam.* 2004J)
(a) Margaret Hutchins (b) H.E. Bliss
(c) S.R. Ranganathan (d) B.S. Keshvan

259. Notification to user for receipt of new arrival of documents in the library comes under the category (*NET Exam.* 2004D)
(a) Reference Service
(b) Inter-library loan
(c) Current Awareness Service
(d) Selective Dissemination of Information

260. The catalogue codes were developed in the order as (*NET Exam.* 2006J)
(a) Anglo American Code (Joint code), Rules for Dictionary Catalogue, ALA rules for author and title entries, AACRI
(b) Rules for Dictionary Catalogue, ALA rules for author and title entries, AACRI, Anglo American Code (Joint code)
(c) Rules for Dictionary Catalogue, Anglo American Code (Joint code), ALA rules for author and title entries, AACRI
(d) ALA rules for author and title entries, AACRI, Rules for Dictionary Catalogue, Anglo American Code (Joint code)

261. Arrange the contributors in management in the proper chronological order (*NET Exam.* 2006J)
(i) Peter Drucker (ii) Henry Gantt
(iii) Ishikawa (iv) Juran
(a) Peter Drucker, Henry Gantt, Juran, Ishikawa
(b) Henry Gantt, Peter Drucker, Juran, Ishikawa
(c) Henry Gantt, Juran, Ishikawa, Peter Drucker
(d) Ishikawa, Henry Gantt, Juran, Peter Drucker

262. Arrange the following in the chronological sequences
(i) CCF (ii) Metadata
(iii) ISBD (iv) MARC Code
Codes:
(a) iv, iii, i, ii (b) iii, iv, i, ii
(c) i, iii, iv, ii (d) iii, i, iv, ii

263. Match the following (*NET Exam.* 2006J)

List-I	**List-II**
(A) CCF	(i) OCLC
(B) UNIMARC	(ii) American Library Association
(C) DUBLIN CORE	(iii) Library of Congress
(D) USMARC	(iv) UNESCO
	(v) IFLA

Codes:	**A**	**B**	**C**	**D**
(a)	v	iv	i	iii
(b)	iv	v	i	iii
(c)	iii	v	iv	ii
(d)	ii	iv	v	i

264. Match the following: (*NET Exam.* 2006J)
List-I (Contributor)
(A) Public Library Manifesto (B) POPSI
(C) UDC (D) MARC
List-II (Organization)
(i) INSPEC (ii) National Library Medicine
(iii) AGRIS (iv) INIS

Codes:	**A**	**B**	**C**	**D**
(a)	i	ii	iii	iv
(b)	ii	i	iii	iv
(c)	iii	i	iv	ii
(d)	i	ii	iii	iv

265. Match the following:
List-I
(A) Origin of a word
(B) Synonyms of a word
(C) how to install a gadget
(D) Address of Oxford University
List-II
(i) World of Learning (ii) Dictionary of Etymology
(iii) Encyclopedia (iv) Manual
(v) Thesaurus

Codes:	**A**	**B**	**C**	**D**
(a)	ii	v	v	iii
(b)	v	iii	iv	i
(c)	v	iv	i	iii
(d)	ii	v	iv	i

266. Which of the following would be the correct chronological sequence? (*NET Exam.* 2006D)
(a) Bibliometrics, Informetrics, Librametry, Webometrics
(b) Librametry, Bibliometrics, Informetrics, Webometrics
(c) Librametry, Informetrics, Bibliometrics, Webometrics
(d) Bibliometrics, Informetrics, Webometrics, Librametry

267. Identify the odd one (*NET Exam.* 2006D)
(a) LISA (b) Psychological Abstracts
(c) Index Medicus (d) World of Learning

268. **Assertion (A):** Reference services is the hub of all library activities. (*NET Exam.* 2006D)
Reason (R): It is provided in the shortest possible time.
Codes:
(a) (A) is true, but (R) is false
(b) (R) is true, but (A) is false
(c) Both (A) and (R) are true, but (R) is not the right explanation of (A)
(d) Both (A) and (R) are true, and (R) is the right explanation

269. The principles of literary warrant was propounded by (*NET exam.* 2006D)
(a) S.R. Ranganathan (b) W. Humle
(c) Melvil Dewey (d) Derek De Sola Price

270. Arrange the following catalogue codes according to the year of publication. (*NET Exam.* 2007J)
(i) Classified Catalogue Code (ii) AA code
(iii) AACR II (iv) RDC

Codes:	A	B	C	D
(a)	i	iii	ii	iv
(b)	iv	ii	i	iii
(c)	ii	iii	i	iv
(d)	i	iv	iii	ii

271. Match the following: (*NET Exam.* 2007J)
List-I
(A) Biological Abstract
(B) Statesman Yearbook
(C) Indian Science Abstract
(D) Cumulative Book List
List-II
(i) H.W. Wilson
(ii) NISCAIR
(iii) Institute of Scientific Information
(iv) UN Statistical Office

Codes:	A	B	C	D
(a)	i	iii	iv	ii
(b)	iii	iv	ii	iii
(c)	iv	ii	iii	i
(d)	ii	i	i	iv

272. Match the following: (*NET Exam.* 2008J)

List-I	List-II
(A) BLAISE	(i) Library of Congress
(B) MARC project	(ii) INS DOC
(C) Union Catalogue Project	(iii) Intel
(D) Microchip	(iv) British Library

Codes:	A	B	C	D
(a)	iii	ii	iv	ii
(b)	i	ii	iii	iv
(c)	iv	i	iii	ii
(d)	ii	iii	i	iv

273. **Assertion (A):** Operators using 'AND', 'OR' and 'NOT' are mostly used in online IR.
Reason (R): User interfaces cannot transform the natural language input into Boolean search Query Codes. (*NET Exam.* 2008J)
Codes:
(a) Both (A) and (R) are true
(b) (A) is true but (R) is false
(c) (R) is true but (A) is false
(d) Both (A) and (R) are false

274. **Assertion (A):** AACR-2 like CCC can satisfy all approaches of the users.
Reason (R): Both AACR-2 and CCC are comprehensive cataloguing code.
Codes:
(a) (A) is true but (R) is false
(b) (R) is true but (A) is false
(c) Both (A) and (R) are true
(d) Both (A) and (R) are false

275. Which of the following does not fall into the category of pre-coordinating indexing?
(a) Chain indexing
(b) Uniform indexing
(c) LCSH
(d) Sears list of subject headings

276. Arrange the following in the chronological sequence of their development (*Net Exam.* 2010J)
(i) ISBD (ii) CCF (iii) FRBR (iv) MARC

Codes:
(a) i, ii, iv, iii (b) iv, i, ii, iii
(c) iii, ii, iv, i (d) i, iv, ii, iii

277. A type of indexing where terms are coordinated prior to searching (*NET Exam.* 2010J)
(a) Post-coordinating indexing
(b) Pre-coordinating indexing
(c) Uniterm indexing
(d) None of the above

278. Bibliographical coupling is related to (*NET Exam.* 2010J)
(a) Bibliographical studies
(b) Bibliographic compilation
(c) Modes of subject formation
(d) Vocabulary control

279. ISBN consists of (*NET Exam.* 2010J)
(a) 6 digits (b) 8 digits
(c) 13 digits (d) 15 digits

280. The Boolean operator 'AND' is related to (*NET Exam.* 2010J)
(a) Productive (b) additive
(c) Logical difference (d) None of these

281. Match the following: (*NET Exam.* 2010J)
List-I
(a) International Conference of Cataloguing Principles
(b) International Meeting of Cataloguing Expert
(c) International Symposium of Bibliographic Exchange Format
(d) First CCF Users Meeting
List-II
(i) 1969 (ii) 1961 (iii) 1990 (iv) 1978

Codes:	**A**	**B**	**C**	**D**
(a)	ii	i	iv	iii
(b)	iii	ii	iv	i
(c)	iv	iii	i	ii
(d)	iii	i	iv	ii

282. **Assertion (A):** An indexing language is much more than a list index that are acceptable to users.
Reason (R): An indexing language helps users discriminate between terms and reduces ambiguity in the language.
Codes:
(a) Both (A) and (R) are true and (R) is not the correct explanation
(b) Both (A) and (R) are true and (R) is the correct explanation
(c) (A) is false, but (R) is true
(d) (A) is true, but (R) is false

283. Match the following: (*NET Exam.* 2010J)

List-I	**List-II**
(A) Keyword Indexing	(i) J.R. Sharp
(B) Citation Indexing	(ii) H.P. Luhan
(C) Uniterm Indexing	(iii) E. Garfield
(D) SLIC Indexing	(iv) M. Taube

Codes:	**A**	**B**	**C**	**D**
(a)	ii	iii	iv	i
(b)	iii	iv	i	ii
(c)	iv	i	iii	ii
(d)	i	iii	ii	iv

284. Indexing system in which the coordination of terms is dine at the search stage was first introduced by (*NET Exam.* 2010D)
(a) S.R. Ranganathan (b) Derek Austin
(c) Morfiner Taube (d) H.P. Luhn

285. The basic structure of MARC communications format include leader, record directory and one of the following (*NET Exam.* 2002J)
(a) ISBN (b) Tag
(c) Field Length (d) Variable field

286. ISBN changed from 10 digits to 13 digits (*NET Exam.* 2010D)
(a) January 2007 (b) January 2008
(c) January 2006 (d) January 2005

287. **Assertion (A):** Web OPAC is a computerised library catalogue available to the patrons online. (*NET Exam.* 2010D)
Reason (R): It can be searched by the users within the four walls of the library only.
Codes:
(a) (A) is true but (R) is false
(b) (A) is false but (R) is true
(c) Both (A) and (R) are true
(d) Both (A) and (R) are false

288. 260 tag in MARC format marks (*NET Exam.* 2010D)
(a) The edition
(b) The publication information
(c) The physical description
(d) A topical subject heading

289. **Assertion (A):** ISBDs were devised by UNESCO. (*NET Exam.* 2010D)

Reason (R): They are the standards for all types of bibliographic activities.

Codes:

(a) (A) is false but (R) is true
(b) (A) is true but (R) is false
(c) Both (A) and (R) are true
(d) Both (A) and (R) are false

290. Arrange the following according to their development (*NET Exam.* 2010D)

(i) CCC (ii) ISBD
(iii) CCF (iv) MARC II

Codes:

(a) i, iv, ii iii (b) i, ii, iv, iii
(c) i, iv, iii, ii (d) iv, ii, iii, i

291. Arrange the following chronologically according to their development (*NET Exam.* 2010D)

(i) Punch Card (ii) Floppy Disc
(iii) Magnetic Disc (iv) Optical Disc

Codes:

(a)	ii	iii	i	iv
(b)	i	iii	ii	iv
(c)	i	ii	iii	iv
(d)	iv	i	ii	iii

292. Arrange the following according to the year of publication: (*NET Exam.* 2008J)

(a) Encyclopaedia Britannica, Encyclopaedia Americana Encyclopaedia of Library & Information Science, McGraw-Hill Encyclopaedia of Science & Technology
(b) Encyclopaedia Britannica, Encyclopaedia of Library & Information Science, McGraw-Hill Encyclopaedia of Science & Technology, Encyclopaedia Americana
(c) Encyclopaedia Britannica, Encyclopaedia Americana, McGraw-Hill Encyclopaedia of Science & Technology Encyclopaedia of Library & Information Science
(d) Encyclopaedia Britannica, McGraw-Hill Encyclopaedia of Science & Technology, Encyclopaedia Americana Encyclopaedia of Library & Information Science

293. Arrange different codes according to year of origin: (*NET Exam.* 2008J)

(a) Anthony Pannizi code, cutter's rules for dictionary catalogue, classified catalogue code, Anglo American cat. Rules-II
(b) Anthony Pannizi code, classified catalogue code, cutter's rules of dictionary catalogue, Anglo American cat. Rules-II
(c) Anthony Pannizi code, Anglo American cat. Rules-II, classified catalogue code, cutter's rules for dictionary catalogue
(d) Anthony Pannizi code, cutter's rules of dictionary catalogue Anglo American cat. Rules-II, classified catalogue code

294. Subject indexing systems were developed in order as (*NET Exam.* 2008J)

(a) Chain indexing, Systematic indexing, PRECIS, COMPASS
(b) Systematic indexing, Chain indexing, PRECIS
(c) Systematic indexing, PRECIS, Chain indexing, COMPASS 1
(d) Systematic indexing, COMPASS, Chain indexing, PRECIS

295. **Assertion (A):** PRECIS is not based upon any particular system of classification. (*NET Exam.* 2008D)

Reason (R): PRECIS is not built around any theoretical ideas in classification.

Codes:

(a) (A) is true but (R) is false
(b) (A) is false but (R) is true
(c) Both (A) and (R) are true
(d) Both (A) and are (R) false

296. Arrange the following standards according to the year of their introduction. (*NET Exam.* 2008D)

(a) ISBN, ICCP, CCF, ISDS
(b) CCF, ICCP, ISBN, ISDS
(c) ICCP, ISBN, ISDS, CCF
(d) ISDS, ISBN, ICCP, CCF

297. What is the relationship between ISBD and cataloguing codes? (*NET Exam.* 2001J)

(a) They are not related at all
(b) Cataloguing codes will include bibliographic description
(c) ISBD includes cataloguing rules
(d) ISBD can replace cataloguing codes

298. The term 'bibliographics' was first used by (*NET Exam.* 2011J)

(a) S.R. Ranganathan (b) Alan Pritchard
(c) Allen Kent (d) A.C. Foskett

299. Union list is the record of (*NET Exam.* 2011J)

(a) Library members living in a union territory
(b) Periodical available in a group of libraries

(c) Library unions located in a union territory
(d) List of members of a library union

300. An increase in the level of specificity of indexing results in increase in (*NET Exam.* 2011J)
(a) Recall (b) Precision
(c) Noise (d) Both recall and precision

301. Arrange the following in chronological order: (*NET Exam.* 2011J)
(i) ISBD (ii) MARC
(iii) CCF (iv) Resource Description and Access (RDA)

Codes:
(a) ii, i, iii, iv (b) i, iv, iii, ii
(c) iii, iv, i, ii (d) ii, iv, i, iii

302. Match the following: (*NET Exam.* 2012D)

List-I	**List-II**
(A) Bradford	(i) Citation indexing
(B) Lotka	(ii) Distribution of articles published in periodicals
(C) Zipf	(iii) Scientific productivity of author
(D) Garfield	(iv) Frequency of word occurrence in a text

Codes:	A	B	C	D
(a)	iv	i	iii	ii
(b)	ii	iii	iv	i
(c)	iii	iv	i	ii
(d)	iv	iii	ii	i

303. According to AACR-II, the heading of the main entry for conference proceeding edited by an individual is prepared under (*NET Exam.* 2001J)
(a) name of editor
(b) place of conference
(c) title of the volume
(d) name of the conference

304. Match the following: (*NET Exam.* 2010D)

List-I	**List-II**
(A) AACR-I	(i) 1978
(B) AACR II	(ii) 1967
(C) ALA code	(iii) 1934
(D) CCC	(iv) 1949

Codes:	A	B	C	D
(a)	iv	ii	iii	i
(b)	ii	i	iii	iv
(c)	i	iii	iv	ii
(d)	ii	i	iv	iii

305. Match the following: (*NET Exam.* 2010D)

List-I	**List-II**
(A) E.J. Coates	(i) KWIC
(B) H.P. Luhan	(ii) Things, Property, Material, Action
(C) Derek Austin	(iii) Concrete and process
(D) J. Kaiser	(iv) PRECIS

Codes:	A	B	C	D
(a)	i	ii	iii	iv
(b)	ii	i	iv	iii
(c)	iii	ii	i	iv
(d)	iv	i	ii	iii

306. Who is the author of *Subject Catalogue*? (*NET Exam.* 2011J)
(a) E.J. Coates (b) J. Kaiser
(c) C.A. Cutter (d) J.W. Metcalf

307. The principle of local variation is mainly applicable in (*NET Exam.* 2011J)
(a) Cataloguing (b) Reference services
(c) Circulation (d) Acquisition

308. As specified by AACR-II(R), the source of information for machine readable data file is (*NET Exam.* 2012D)
(a) Internal user label (b) Title page
(c) Colophon (d) Title frame

309. Read the following example and indicate the name of the indexing system used; 'Remuneration of teachers in French University'. The indexing heading are set as the following two lines: (*NET Exam.* 2012D)

France University?? Teachers? Remuneration
Universities? France Teachers? Remuneration
(a) Chain procedure (b) POPSI
(c) PRECIS (d) KWIC

310. **Assertion (A):** The array of classes 11, 12, 13 and the array of classes 31, 32, 33 are said to be collateral arrays.

Reason (R): They are derived from the original universe 'O'. (*NET Exam.* 2012D)

Codes:
(a) (A) is false, (R) is true
(b) (A) is true, (R) is false
(c) Both (A) and (R) are true
(d) Both (A) and (R) are false

311. SCOPUS is a/an (*NET Exam.* 2011D)
(a) Indexing Database
(b) Numerical Database

(c) Full Text Database
(d) Abstract and Citation Database

312. Arrange the following bibliographical standards according their year of development: (*NET Exam.* 2011D)
(i) ISBD (ii) MARC
(iii) Dublin Core (iv) RDF
(a) i, iii, ii, iv (b) ii, i, iv, iii
(b) iii, ii, iv, i (d) iv, iii, i, ii

313. Arrange the following according to their year of emergence (*Net Exam.* 2011D)
(i) RDC (ii) ALA Code
(iii) FRBR (iv) AACRI
Codes:
(a) i, ii, iii, iv (b) iv, i, ii, iii
(c) i, ii, iv, iii (d) i, iv, ii, iii

314. Who is the author of *Systemic Indexing*? (*NET Exam.* 2011D)
(a) E.J. Coates (b) J. Kaiser
(c) C.A. Cutter (d) J.W. Metcalf

315. Which of the model is not based on the analysis of the subject?(*NET Exam.* 2011D)
(a) Citation Indexing (b) PRECIS
(c) Chain Indexing (d) Uniterm Indexing

316. Match the following: (*NET Exam.* 2013J)
List-I
(A) Key to given collection
(B) Key to literary sources on a subject
(C) Representation of subject
(D) Condensation of document
List-II
(i) Abstract (ii) Index
(iii) Catalogue (iv) Bibliography

Codes:	A	B	C	D
(a)	iii	iv	ii	i
(b)	ii	iii	iv	i
(c)	i	ii	iii	iv
(d)	iv	i	ii	iii

317. Arrange the following according to year of publication (*NET Exam.* 2013J)
(i) Colon Classification
(ii) Prolegomena to Classification
(iii) Five Laws of Library Science
(iv) Classified Catalogue Code
Codes:
(a) iii, iv, i, ii (b) iv, ii, i, iii
(c) iii, i, iv, ii (d) i, ii, iv, iii

318. Match the following: (*NET Exam.* 2013J)

List-I	**List-II**
(A) Resource Description	(i) MARC
(B) Resource Discovery	(ii) ISO 10160/10161
(C) Resource Exchange	(iii) Dublin Core
(D) Interlibrary Loan	(iv) Z 39.50

Codes:	A	B	C	D
(a)	ii	i	iv	iii
(b)	iv	ii	i	iii
(c)	iii	iv	ii	i
(d)	iii	iv	i	ii

319. Match the following: (*NET Exam.* 2013J)

List-I	**List-II**
(A) Indian Cultural heritage	(i) TKDL
(B) Race & Brittle	(ii) IGNCA
(C) Traditional knowledge	(iii) C-DAC
(D) Mobile Digital Library	(iv) National Library

Codes:	A	B	C	D
(a)	i	iv	iii	ii
(b)	iv	iii	ii	i
(c)	ii	iv	i	iii
(d)	iii	ii	iv	i

320. How do we render the name, Bernardo Augustine De Voto? (*NET Exam.* 2013J)
(a) Voto, Bernardo, Augustine De
(b) De Voto, Augustine De
(c) Bernardo Augustine, De Voto
(d) De Voto, Bernardo Augustine

321. In MARC 21, subject access fields are (*NET Exam.* 2012D)
(a) 3xx (b) 4xx (c) 5xx (d) 6xx

322. **Assertion (A):** An indexing language is an artificial language and it uses controlled vocabulary. (*NET Exam.* 2012D)
Reason (R): Controlled vocabulary provides relation between and among terms.
Codes:
(a) Both (A) and (R) are true
(b) (A) is true, but (R) is false
(c) (A) is false, but (R) is true
(d) Both (A) and (R) are false

323. Which of the following is not the prerequisite for National Information Policy? (*NET Exam.* 2012D)
(a) Legislative Framework
(b) Production of National Bibliography
(c) Advisory and Administrative Body
(d) ICT infrastructure facilities

324. **Assertion (A):** "Name Authority File" should be used in library. (*NET Exam.* 2012J)

Reason (R): All works of an author should be collocated.

Codes:

(a) (A) is true, but (R) is false
(b) Both (A) and (R) true and (R) is the correct explanation of (A)
(c) (A) is false, but (R) is true
(d) Both (A) and (R) are false

325. **Assertion (A):** Abstracting services facilities literature review. (*NET Exam.* 2012J)

Reason (R): Literature review summaries major findings of various studies.

Codes:

(a) (A) is true, but (R) is false
(b) (A) is false, but (R) is true
(c) Both (A) and (R) is true
(d) Both (A) and (R) are false

326. Which of the following are not styles of citation? (*NET Exam.* 2012J)

(i) Anglo American Cataloguing Rules
(ii) MLA Handbook for Writers of Research Papers
(iii) Chicago Manual of Style
(iv) Little Science Big Science

Codes:

(a) i, and ii are correct
(b) iii, and iv are correct
(c) i, and iv are correct
(d) ii, and iii are correct

327. Match the following: (*NET Exam.* 2012J)

List-I

(A) Obligation of the State
(B) Shelf arrangement Catalogue
(C) Open Access & Shelf Arrangement
(D) Library location/hours

List-II

(i) First Law (ii) Second Law
(iii) Third Law (iv) Fourth Law

Codes:	A	B	C	D
(a)	ii	iv	iii	i
(b)	iv	iii	ii	i
(c)	i	iii	iv	ii
(d)	iii	ii	i	iv

328. Name the technique used for searching sorted data in a database. (*NET Exam.* 2013J)

(a) Boolean Operator (b) Inverting file
(c) Indexing (d) Binary

329. The process of establishing headings and providing 'Cross references' is called (*NET Exam.* 2013J)

(a) Access point
(b) Headings
(c) Authority control
(d) Bibliographic Records

330. Match the following: (*NET Exam.* 2012J)

List-I	**List-II**
(A) C.A. Cutter	(i) Selective Listing
(B) Kaiser	(ii) Thing-paramaterial-action
(C) J.R. Sharp	(iii) Concrete and process
(D) D.J. Coates	(iv) Syndetic cataloguing

Codes:	A	B	C	D
(a)	iv	i	ii	iii
(b)	iv	iii	i	ii
(c)	iii	iv	ii	i
(d)	ii	iii	iv	i

331. Which section of AACR-II (R) deals with serial publications? (*NET Exam.* 2012J iii paper)

(a) Part-A, Section-3 (b) Part-B, Section-3
(c) Part-A, Section-12 (d) Part –B, Section-12

332. In cataloguing the square brackets [ ] are used (*NET Exam.* 2012J)

(a) to enclose information taken from outside
(b) to enclose the details of printed/ manufacturer
(c) to enclose series statements
(d) to enclose statement of accompanying material

333. Roget's International Thesaurus is a (*NET Exam.* 2012J)

(a) Classified List of Words
(b) Book of Synonyms
(c) List of Standard Terms
(d) List of Scientific Terms

334. Rules for dictionary catalogue was devised by (*NET Exam.* 2008D)

(a) Panizzi (b) C.C. Jewet
(c) S. Lubetzky (d) C.A. Cutter

335. Identify the sequence of the 'title' and 'statement of responsibility' area from the following: (*NET 17 J ii paper*)

(i) Title proper
(ii) Parallel title
(iii) General Material Designation (GMD)
(iv) Statement of responsibility

Codes:
(a) (i), (iii), (ii) and (iv)
(b) (iii), (ii), (i) and (iv)
(c) (iv), (iii), (ii) and (i)
(d) (ii), (i), (iii) and (iv)

336. Match the following Main Entry fields with their corresponding tag as are given numbers in MARC 21: *(NET 17J ii paper)*

List – I	List – II
A. 100	1. Main Entry – Uniform Title
B. 110	2. Main Entry – Meeting Name
C. 111	3. Main Entry – Personal Name
D. 130	4. Main Entry – Corporate Name

Codes:	A	B	C	D
(a)	3	4	2	1
(b)	4	3	2	1
(c)	1	3	4	2
(d)	2	4	1	3

337. **Assertion (A):** Electronic indexing and abstracting services are not advantageous over print.

Reason (R): Electronic indexes work on much the same principles as print. *(NET 17J ii paper)*

Codes:
(a) (A) is true, but (R) is false.
(b) (A) is false, but (R) is true.
(c) Both (A) and (R) are false.
(d) Both (A) and (R) are true.

338. Which of the following does not come under the domain of Descriptive bibliometrics (Descriptive Studies)? *(NOV 2017 iii paper)*
(a) Geographical Distribution of Documents
(b) Nature of Information Conveyed
(c) Subject Distribution
(d) Medium of Communication

339. Arrange year-wise development of the following indexing systems: *(NOV 2017 iii paper)*
(i) Relational Indexing by J.E.L. Farradane
(ii) Chain Indexing by S.R. Ranganathan
(iii) Subject Indexing by J.E. Coates
(iv) PRECIS by Derek Austin

Codes:
(a) (ii), (i), (iii), (iv) (b) (i), (ii), (iii), (iv)
(c) (iii), (iv), (ii), (i) (d) (iv), (iii), (i), (ii)

340. Arrange, from among the following, the areas of access-points in their proper sequence as given in ISBD. *(NOV 2017 iii paper)*
(i) Notes (ii) Series
(iii) Edition (iv) Material Specific details

Codes:
(a) (i), (ii), (iii), (iv) (b) (iii), (iv), (ii), (i)
(c) (ii), (iii), (iv), (i) (d) (iv), (iii), (ii), (i)

341. Match the following leading Abstracting and Indexing tools/Databases with their corresponding Publishers/Content Providers: *(NOV 2017 iii paper)*

List – I	List – II
(A) LISA	(1) NISCAIR
(B) ILSA	(2) EBSCO
(C) LISTA	(3) IASLIC
(D) Indian Science Abstracts	(4) ProQuest

Codes:	(A)	(B)	(C)	(D)
(a)	(4)	(3)	(2)	(1)
(b)	(1)	(2)	(3)	(4)
(c)	(2)	(4)	(1)	(3)
(d)	(3)	(1)	(4)	(2)

342. **Assertion (A):** The content-based indexing techniques enable identification of wanted persons in photographs of crowds.

Reason (R): The content-based indexing system uses all sorts of characteristics of the image to guess what it is about. *(NOV 2017 iii paper)*

Codes:
(a) (A) is true but (R) is false.
(b) (A) is false but (R) are true.
(c) Both (A) and (R) are false.
(d) Both (A) and (R) are true.

343. Chapter – 9 of AACR-2 has changed its name in AACR 2R 2002. Identify the changed name. *(NET 16J iii paper)*
(a) Computer Files
(b) Electronic Resources
(c) Machine Readable Data Files
(d) Computer Resources

344. 760 tag in MARC format marks *(NET 16J iii paper)*
(a) the Edition
(b) the Publication Information
(c) Main Series Entry
(d) A Topical Subject Heading

345. In thesaurus SN (Scope Note) provides (*NET 16J iii paper*)

i. related terms
ii. restriction in usage of description
iii. brief descriptions of sense or framework in which the terms should be used
iv. clarification of ambiguity

Codes:

(a) i, ii and iii are correct.
(b) i, ii and iv are correct.
(c) ii, iii and iv are correct.
(d) i, iii and iv are correct.

346. Arrange the following steps of index construction in proper order: (*NET 16J iii paper*)

i. Index scoring
ii. Item selection
iii. Index validation
iv. Examination of empirical relationships

Codes:

(a) i, ii, iii, iv (b) i, iii, iv, ii
(c) ii, iv, i, iii (d) ii, i, iii, iv

347. **Assertion (A):** Dictionary catalogue is very easy to consult.

Reason (R): Dictionary catalogue consists of author and title entries only. (*NET 16J iii paper*)

Codes:

(a) (A) is false, but (R) is true.
(b) (A) is true, but (R) is false.
(c) Both (A) and (R) are true.
(d) Both (A) and (R) are false.

348. **Assertion (A):** Authority work deals with formulation and recording of authorised access points.

Reason (R): Without authority control, the burden is placed on user. (*NET 16J iii paper*)

Codes:

(a) Both (A) and (R) are true.
(b) Both (A) and (R) are false.
(c) (A) is true, but (R) is false.
(d) (A) is false, but (R) is true.

349. p, q, r in the schema of operators in PRECIS belong to (*NET 17N iii paper*)

(a) Core elements
(b) Extra-core concepts
(c) Dependent elements
(d) Special classes of action

350. The MARC Field 264 has different second indicator values to indicate separate data elements in RDA. Match these second indicator values with the respective data elements: (*NET 17N iii paper*)

List – I	List – II
(A) –0	(1) Distribution statement
(B) –1	(2) Publication statement
(C) –2	(3) Manufacture statement
(D) –3	(4) Production statement

Codes:	(A)	(B)	(C)	(D)
(a)	(4)	(2)	(1)	(3)
(b)	(3)	(2)	(4)	(1)
(c)	(2)	(4)	(3)	(1)
(d)	(1)	(2)	(3)	(4)

351. Match the following NISO (National Information Standard Organisation) standards with their corresponding descriptions applicable to Libraries: (*NET 17N iii paper*)

List – I	List – II
(A) Z 39.41	(1) Dublin core Metadata Element set
(B) Z 39.63	(2) Syntax for Digital Object Identifier (DOI)
(C) Z 39.84	(3) Inter library loan data elements
(D) Z 39.85	(4) Printed information on spines

Codes:	(A)	(B)	(C)	(D)
(a)	(1)	(2)	(3)	(4)
(b)	(3)	(2)	(4)	(1)
(c)	(4)	(3)	(2)	(1)
(d)	(2)	(1)	(3)	(4)

352. A cross reference that gives an indexer complete control over the cross references of an index is known as (*NET 14D ii paper*)

(a) see also cross reference
(b) check also cross reference
(c) see cross reference
(d) inverted cross reference

353. Identify content management software from the following: (*NET 14D ii paper*)

(i) Evergreen (ii) Drupal
(iii) Joomla (iv) New Genlib

Codes:

(a) (i) and (ii) are correct.
(b) (ii) and (iii) are correct.
(c) (iii) and (iv) are correct.
(d) (i) and (iv) are correct.

354. Identify open source softwares for library management. *(NET 14D ii paper)*
(i) New Genlib (ii) SOUL
(iii) LIBSYS (iv) KOHA
Codes:
(a) (i) and (ii) are correct.
(b) (ii) and (iii) are correct.
(c) (iii) and (iv) are correct.
(d) (i) and (iv) are correct.

355. **Assertion (A):** Abstracts are precise representation of the content of a document.
Reason (R): Researcher have time constraints to go through the original articles. *(NET 14D ii paper)*
Codes:
(a) (A) is true, but (R) is false
(b) Both (A) and (R) are true.
(c) (A) is false, but (R) is true.
(d) Both (A) and (R) are false.

356. Which of the search strategy is useful to increase recall output? *(NET 16J ii paper)*
(a) Proximity operators
(b) Boolean operators 'NOT'
(c) Truncation
(d) Boolean operators 'AND'

357. Chapter 12 of AACR-2 has changed its name in AACR-2R, 2002. Identify the changed name. *(NET 16J ii paper)*
(a) Integrated Resources
(b) Continuing Resources
(c) Periodical Resources
(d) Online Resources

358. Arrange the following indexing journals according to the year of their first publication: *(NET 16J ii paper)*
i. Engineering Index, New York
ii. Humanities Index, New York
iii. Index Medicus, Bethesda
iv. Agrindex, Rome
Codes:
(a) iv, iii, i and ii (b) iii, ii, iv and i
(c) i, iii, ii and iv (d) iii, i, ii and iv

359. Who developed the theory of Information Supply and Indexing based on five axioms (doctorines) such as—definability; order; sufficient degree of order; predictability; and Fidelity? *(NET 15J iii paper)*
(a) Robert Fugmann (b) William Cooper
(c) E. Garfield (d) Calvin Mooers

360. Boolean Logic was propounded by *(NET 15J iii paper)*
(a) P.K. Boole (b) G.R. Boole
(c) K.S. Boole (d) George Boole

361. The 'Other Title Information' in statement of Responsibility Area in AACR II is preceded by a: *(NET 15J iii paper)*
(a) Semicolon (b) Hyphen
(c) Dash (d) Colon

362. According to AACR-2 the source from which the title proper is taken is known as: *(NET 15J iii paper)*
(a) Chief Source of Information
(b) Preferred Source of Information
(c) Prescribed Source of Information
(d) Referred Source of Information

363. The search in a Boolean query may be expanded by the following methods *(NET 15J iii paper)*
(i) Using thesaurus or list of related terms
(ii) Stemming or reduction of a word to its root form
(iii) Using literals
(iv) Specifying number of terms
Codes:
(a) (i) and (iv) are correct
(b) (ii) and (iii) are correct
(c) (iii) and (iv) are correct
(d) (i) and (ii) are correct

364. Identify the correct sequence of entities in Group 1 of Functional Requirements of Bibliographic Records (FRBR). RDA 0.2 version: *(NET 15J iii paper)*
(a) Expression, Works, Items, Manifestation
(b) Works, Items, Expression, Manifestation
(c) Works, Expression, Manifestation, Item
(d) Works, Expression, Item, Manifestation

365. Match the following MARC 21 elements with corresponding tags *(NET 15J iii paper)*

List - I	**List - II**
(A) Personal Main Entry	(1) 700
(B) Personal Subject Heading	(2) 245
(C) Personal Added Entry	(3) 100
(D) Bibliographic Title	(4) 600

Codes:	**(A)**	**(B)**	**(C)**	**(D)**
(a)	(1)	(4)	(2)	(3)
(b)	(2)	(1)	(3)	(4)
(c)	(3)	(4)	(1)	(2)
(d)	(4)	(2)	(3)	(1)

366. Match the following: *(NET 15J iii paper)*

List - I	List - II
(A) Physical Description	(1) 3 XX
(B) Main Entry Level	(2) 1 XX
(C) Control Fields	(3) 70 X to 75 X
(D) Added Entry	(4) 00 X

Codes:	**(A)**	**(B)**	**(C)**	**(D)**
(a)	(1)	(2)	(4)	(3)
(b)	(2)	(3)	(1)	(4)
(c)	(3)	(4)	(2)	(1)
(d)	(4)	(3)	(1)	(2)

367. **Assertion (A):** Web-OPAC is a computerized library catalogue available to the readers on-line. *(NET 15J iii paper)*

Reason (R): It can be searched by the users within the four walls of the library only.

Codes:
(a) (A) is true but (R) is false
(b) (A) is false but (R) is true
(c) Both (A) and (R) are true
(d) Both (A) and (R) are false

368. Pre co-ordinate Indexing system perceives: *(NET 13D ii paper)*
(i) Syntax (ii) Semantic
(iii) Context (iv) Relation

Codes:
(a) (i) and (iv) are correct
(b) (i), (ii) and (iii) are correct
(c) (ii), (iii) and (iv) are correct
(d) (ii) and (iv) are correct

369. An indispensable function of Thesaurus is to *(NET 13D ii paper)*
(i) Knowledge Classification
(ii) Grouping the words together according to similarity of meaning
(iii) Representation of Relationship between concepts
(iv) Knowledge Engineering

Codes:
(a) (i) and (ii) are correct.
(b) (ii) and (iii) are correct.
(c) (iii) and (iv) are correct.
(d) (i) and (iv) are correct

370. Which of the following are the components of Search Engine? *(NET 13D ii paper)*
(i) Spider (ii) TCP/IP
(iii) Search Mechanism (iv) Index

Codes:
(a) (iv), (i) and (ii) (b) (iii), (ii) and (i)
(c) (i), (iii) and (iv) (d) (ii), (iv) and (iii)

371. What is the correct sequence of the following sections of the main entry as per classified catalogue code (CCC)? *(NET 13D ii paper)*
(i) Note Section (ii) Leading Section
(iii) Heading Section (iv) Title Section

Codes:
(a) (i) (iv) (iii) (ii) (b) (ii) (iii) (iv) (i)
(c) (iii) (iv) (ii) (i) (d) (iv) (i) (iii) (ii)

372. Arrange the following indexing sources according to the year of their first publication: *(NET 13D ii paper)*
(i) Biological Abstracts
(ii) Chemical Abstracts
(iii) Index Medicus
(iv) Poole's Index to Periodical Literature

Codes:
(a) (i) (ii) (iii) (iv) (b) (iv) (iii) (ii) (i)
(c) (iv) (ii) (i) (iii) (d) (i) (iv) (iii) (ii)

373. Which of the following are the main role operators of PRECIS? *(NET 13D ii paper)*
(i) Key System (ii) Action
(iii) Performer of action (iv) Form of Document

Codes:
(a) (i), (ii) and (iii) (b) (ii), (i) and (iv)
(c) (i), (iii) and (iv) (d) (ii), (iii) and (i)

374. Arrange the following according to their levels *(NET 13D iii paper)*
i. Canons of Cataloguing
ii. Laws of Library Science
iii. General Normative Principles
iv. Principles of Cataloguing

Codes:
(a) ii iv i iii (b) i iii ii iv
(c) iv i iii ii (d) iii ii i iv

375. What is the relationship between ISBD and cataloguing codes? *(NET 14J iii paper)*
(a) They are not related to each other
(b) ISBD includes cataloguing rules
(c) ISBD can replace cataloguing rules
(d) Anglo-American codes include bibliographic description

376. Who first used the phrase 'Bibliographical Control'? *(NET 14J iii paper)*

(a) Paul Otlet (b) Henry La Fontaine
(c) Luther Evans (d) Conrad Gessner

377. LIPHIS (Linked Phrase Indexing System) was developed by *(NET 2014J iii paper)*
(a) T.C. Craven (b) J. Farradane
(c) J.C.R. Yeats (d) P. Ekern

378. Which of the following gives complete control over the cross references of an index to the Indexer? *(NET 2014J iii paper)*
(a) See also cross reference
(b) Check also cross reference
(c) See cross reference
(d) Inverted cross reference

379. What type of bibliography is 'Indian National Bibliography'? *(NET 2014J iii paper)*
(a) Enumerative (b) Analytical
(c) Descriptive (d) Textual

380. Which of the following are the characteristic features of Post-coordinate indexing system? *(NET 2014J iii paper)*
i. Index terms are pre-determined
ii. Coordination of terms done by users
iii. No fixed citation order
iv. Multiple entries prepared for each document

Codes:
(a) i and ii are correct.
(b) ii and iii are correct.
(c) i and iii are correct.
(d) ii and iv are correct.

381. Match the following MARC 21 tags with respective fields: *(NET 2014J iii paper)*

List – I	List – II
A. 020	1. Publication and Distribution
B. 100	2. Series Statement
C. 260	3. ISBN
D. 440	4. Personal name

Codes:	A	B	C	D
(a)	1	2	3	4
(b)	2	4	3	1
(c)	3	2	4	1
(d)	3	4	1	2

382. **Assertion (A):** PANDEX is an indexing system which sometimes allows changing the lead term to a standard form in order to provide better collocation of terms.

Reason (R): It facilitates the first input string to be truncated after 18 characters and second after 11 characters. *(NET 2014J iii paper)*

Codes:
(a) Both (A) and (R) are true.
(b) Both (A) and (R) are false.
(c) (A) is false, but (R) is true.
(d) (A) is true (R) is false.

383. 'Indian Citation Index' (ICI) is developed by *(NET 14D iii paper)*
(a) Informatics India (b) Veeru's technologies
(c) DELNET (d) Knowledge Foundation

384. The class index entries which are derived from the class number of a document are based upon: *(NET 14D iii paper)*
(a) Unsought links (b) Missing links
(c) False links (d) Sought links

385. **Assertion (A):** Wikis have provided everybody an opportunity for authoring, editing and publishing. *(NET 14D iii paper)*

Reason (R): Web has provided very generic rules for creation, maintenance and development of Wikis.

Codes:
(a) (A) is true, but (R) is false.
(b) (A) is false, but (R) is true.
(c) Both (A) and (R) are true.
(d) Both (A) and (R) are false.

386. **Assertion (A):** Precision ratio is a measure of the efficiency of an indexing system.

Reason (R): Presence of relevant terms increases the precision ratio. *(NET 14D iii paper)*

Codes:
(a) (A) is true, but (R) is false.
(b) Both (A) and (R) are true, but (R) is not the correct explanation of (A).
(c) Both (A) and (R) are true and (R) is the correct explanation of (A).
(d) (A) is false, but (R) is true.

387. Arrange the following according to their publication year: *(NET 14D iii paper)*
i. Sears' list of subject headings ii. Panizzi code
iii. AACR-I iv. CCC

Codes:

(a) iv, ii, iii, i (b) i, iii, ii, iv
(c) ii, i, iv, iii (d) iii, iv, i, ii

388. Match the following: *(NET 15J ii paper)*

List - I		**List - II**	
(A)	Iliad	(B)	QuestionPoint
(C)	WebJunction	(D)	WorldCat

(1) "Collective collection" of world libraries
(2) Cost effective training and staff development programme
(3) High quality reference service
(4) Interlibrary loan operation

Codes:	**(A)**	**(B)**	**(C)**	**(D)**
(a)	(4)	(3)	(2)	(1)
(b)	(3)	(2)	(1)	(4)
(c)	(2)	(1)	(4)	(3)
(d)	(1)	(4)	(3)	(2)

389. **Assertion (A):** Boolean Logical lows a user to logically relate multiple concepts together to define what information is needed.

Reason (R): If the operators (AND, OR, NOT) are interpreted in their normal interpretation, they act too restrictive or too general. *(NET 15J ii paper)*

Codes:

(a) Both (A) and (R) are true.
(b) Both (A) and (R) are false.
(c) (A) is true and (R) is false.
(d) (A) is false and (R) is true.

390. **Assertion (A):** While using OPAC user need to have some understanding of inverted files and search strategies. *(NET 15J ii paper)*

Reason (R): Online catalogues place the responsibility for a search strategy on the user.

Codes:

(a) (A) is true but (R) is false.
(b) Both (A) and (R) are true.
(c) Both (A) and (R) are false.
(d) (A) is false, but(R) is true.

391. Ministry of Education, Government of Delhi will be rendered according to Classified Catalogue Code (CCC) as *(NET 15D iii paper)*

(a) Ministry of Education (Delhi)
(b) Delhi, (Education (Ministry of -)
(c) Delhi, Ministry of Education
(d) DELHI, EDUCATION (Ministry of -)

392. Arrange the following Catalogue Codes according to their first publication year: *(NET 15D iii paper)*

(a) CCC, AA code, ALA code, AACR-I
(b) ALA code, CCC, AA code, AACR-I
(c) AA code, ALA code, CCC, AACR-I
(d) AACR-I, CCC, AA code, ALA code

393. **Assertion (A):** AACR-2 instructs that no information should be added to catalogue from other than the title page.

Reason (R): The main source of cataloguing information is the "Title Page" and the "Verso of the title page" *(NET 15D iii paper)*

Codes:

(a) Both (A) and (R) are true.
(b) (A) is true but (R) is false.
(c) (A) is false but (R) is true.
(d) Both (A) and (R) are false.

394. The 'Letter by Letter' Method of alphabetization in Dictionary catalogue is known as *(NET 17 NOV ii paper)*

(a) Nothing before something
(b) Something before nothing
(c) All through
(d) Something after more

395. Match the following indexing/abstracting publications with the corresponding institution. *(NET 17 NOV ii paper)*

List – I

(A) Indian Citation Index
(B) INSPEL (Retrospective, 1970)
(C) Med Ind
(D) Indian Animal Science

List – II

(1) ICMR
(2) ICAR
(3) Diva Enterprises, Delhi
(4) NASSDOC Abstracts

Codes:	**(A)**	**(B)**	**(C)**	**(D)**
(a)	(2)	(3)	(4)	(1)
(b)	(3)	(4)	(1)	(2)
(c)	(1)	(2)	(3)	(4)
(d)	(4)	(1)	(2)	(3)

396. Match the following NISO (National Information Standard Organisation) standards with their corresponding descriptions applicable to Libraries:

List – I	List - II
(A) Z39.2	(1) Guidelines for Abstracts
(B) Z39.4	(2) ISSN
(C) Z39.9	(3) Guidelines for Indexes and Related Information Retrieval Devices
(D) Z39.14	(4) Information for interchange format

Codes:	(A)	(B)	(C)	(D)
(a)	(4)	(3)	(2)	(1)
(b)	(1)	(2)	(3)	(4)
(c)	(2)	(4)	(3)	(1)
(d)	(3)	(1)	(2)	(4)

397. According to AACR 2R who will be considered for the access point of the Main Entry for the document entitled Adventures of Tom Sawyer by Mark Twain; rewritten for young readers by Felix Sutton. *(NET 17J iii paper)*

(a) Sawyer, Tom (b) Twain, Mark
(c) Mark Twain (d) Sutton, Felix

398. Arrange the following bibliographic utilities according to their year of origin: *(NET 17J iii paper)*

(i) Ohio College Library Center
(ii) Washington Library Network
(iii) UTLAS
(iv) RLIN

Codes:

(a) (i), (ii), (iii), (iv) (b) (i), (iii), (iv), (ii)
(c) (i), (ii), (iv), (iii) (d) (i), (iv), (iii), (ii)

399. Match the following: *(NET 17J iii paper)*

List – I

(A) The Crisis in Cataloguing
(B) Headings and Canons: Comparative Study of Five Catalogue Codes
(C) Our Enduring Values: Librarianship in the 21st century
(D) Readings in library Cataloguing

List – II

(1) Michael Gorman
(2) Raymond Knox Olding
(3) Andrew D. Osborn
(4) S.R. Ranganathan

Codes:	(A)	(B)	(C)	(D)
(a)	(3)	(4)	(1)	(2)
(b)	(1)	(4)	(2)	(3)
(c)	(2)	(1)	(3)	(4)
(d)	(3)	(4)	(2)	(1)

400. **Assertion (A):** In RDA the 'rule of 3', to provide upto three authors, is now the main instruction. *(NET 17J iii paper)*

Reason (R): RDA does not encourage access to the names of persons and corporate bodies important to the users.

Codes:

(a) (A) is true, but (R) is false.
(b) (A) is false, but (R) is true.
(c) Both (A) and (R) are true.
(d) Both (A) and (R) are false.

401. The Class Index entries which are derived from the class number of a document in classified catalogue are based upon *(NET 15D ii paper)*

(a) Unsought Links (b) Missing Links
(c) False Links (d) Sought Links

402. In Classified Catalogue Code of Ranganathan the conflict of authorship includes: *(NET 15D iii paper)*

(i) Person versus Person
(ii) Person versus Corporate body
(iii) Government versus Institution
(iv) Person versus Publisher

Codes:

(a) i, ii, and, iii are correct
(b) i, ii and iv are correct
(c) ii, iii and iv are correct
(d) iv, iii and i are correct

403. Match the following *(NET 15D iii paper)*

List - I	List - II
(A) Browne	(1) OCLC
(B) SWOT analysis	(2) Digital Library Software
(C) WorldCat	(3) Charging System
(D) Greenstone	(4) Management Practice

Codes:	(A)	(B)	(C)	(D)
(a)	(4)	(1)	(3)	(2)
(b)	(1)	(2)	(4)	(3)
(c)	(iii)	(4)	(1)	(2)
(d)	(2)	(1)	(3)	(4)

404. Match the following: *(NET 15D iii paper)*

List - I	List - II
(A) Statistical Analysis	(1) Pitcharard
(B) Statistical Bibliography	(2) S.R. Ranganathan
(C) Librametry	(3) E.W. Hume
(D) Bibliometrics	(4) Francil Cole

Codes:	(A)	(B)	(C)	(D)
(a)	(4)	(3)	(2)	(1)
(b)	(3)	(4)	(1)	(2)
(c)	(1)	(2)	(3)	(4)
(d)	(2)	(3)	(1)	(4)

405. Which of the following Sections constitute the parts of main entry according to CCC (Ed. 5)

(i) Leading Section (ii) Title Section
(iii) Format Section (iv) Note Section

Codes:

(a) i, ii, and iii are correct
(b) i, ii, and iv are correct
(c) ii, iii, and iv are correct
(d) i, iii, and iv are correct

ANSWER SHEET

1. (d)	2. (c)	3. (b)	4. (c)	5. (a)	6. (b)	7. (b)	8. (b)	9. (b)
10. (b)	11. (d)	12. (d)	13. (c)	14. (b)	15. (b)	16. (c)	17. (b)	18. (a)
19. (c)	20. (d)	21. (b)	22. (d)	23. (d)	24. (c)	25. (b)	26. (c)	27. (d)
28. (b)	29. (c)	30. (a)	31. (b)	32. (d)	33. (c)	34. (c)	35. (d)	36. (c)
37. (c)	38. (c)	39. (d)	40. (d)	41. (c)	42. (c)	43. (a)	44. (b)	45. (c)
46. (d)	47. (c)	48. (b)	49. (a)	50. (a)	51. (a)	52. (b)	53. (c)	54. (a)
55. (a)	56. (a)	57. (d)	58. (b)	59. (c)	60. (a)	61. (d)	62. (c)	63. (c)
64. (a)	65. (b)	66. (b)	67. (a)	68. (c)	69. (a)	70. (a)	71. (a)	72. (a)
73. (a)	74. (a)	75. (c)	76. (b)	77. (c)	78. (b)	79. (b)	80. (d)	81. (d)
82. (b)	83. (c)	84. (b)	85. (b)	86. (c)	87. (c)	88. (a)	89. (c)	90. (c)
91. (c)	92. (b)	93. (b)	94. (c)	95. (a)	96. (b)	97. (b)	98. (b)	99. (c)
100. (c)	101. (d)	102. (a)	103. (b)	104. (c)	105. (b)	106. (b)	107. (c)	108. (a)
109. (d)	110. (a)	111. (d)	112. (c)	113. (d)	114. (c)	115. (a)	116. (b)	117. (c)
118. (c)	119. (c)	120. (c)	121. (c)	122. (c)	123. (a)	124. (b)	125. (a)	126. (b)
127. (d)	128. (b)	129. (d)	130. (d)	131. (d)	132. (d)	133. (b)	134. (a)	135. (c)
136. (c)	137. (c)	138. (c)	139. (b)	140. (d)	141. (c)	142. (c)	143. (a)	144. (a)
145. (b)	146. (d)	147. (a)	148. (a)	149. (c)	150. (b)	151. (c)	152. (a)	153. (d)
154. (c)	155. (c)	156. (a)	157. (d)	158. (c)	159. (d)	160. (b)	161. (a)	162. (d)
163. (b)	164. (d)	165. (b)	166. (c)	167. (c)	168. (a)	169. (d)	170. (b)	171. (b)
172. (b)	173. (c)	174. (d)	175. (c)	176. (d)	177. (a)	178. (a)	179. (a)	180. (c)
181. (c)	182. (d)	183. (d)	184. (c)	185. (d)	186. (d)	187. (a)	188. (a)	189. (b)
190. (c)	191. (d)	192. (b)	193. (b)	194. (a)	195. (a)	196. (a)	197. (a)	198. (a)
199. (a)	200. (a)	201. (a)	202. (b)	203. (a)	204. (a)	205. (b)	206. (d)	207. (d)
208. (c)	209. (d)	210. (c)	211. (a)	212. (a)	213. (d)	214. (d)	215. (a)	216. (c)
217. (c)	218. (a)	219. (c)	220. (a)	221. (a)	222. (b)	223. (a)	224. (c)	225. (a)
226. (a)	227. (b)	228. (a)	229. (a)	230. (a)	231. (b)	232. (a)	233. (a)	234. (b)
235. (b)	236. (a)	237. (d)	238. (a)	239. (d)	240. (c)	241. (b)	242. (d)	243. (c)
244. (c)	245. (a)	246. (b)	247. (c)	248. (d)	249. (c)	250. (a)	251. (c)	252. (a)
253. (b)	254. (c)	255. (a)	256. (c)	257. (c)	258. (a)	259. (c)	260. (c)	261. (a)
262. (a)	263. (b)	264. (c)	265. (d)	266. (b)	267. (d)	268. (c)	269. (b)	270. (b)
271. (b)	272. (c)	273. (c)	274. (c)	275. (b)	276. (b)	277. (b)	278. (a)	279. (c)
280. (b)	281. (a)	282. (b)	283. (a)	284. (c)	285. (c)	286. (a)	287. (a)	288. (b)
289. (a)	290. (a)	291. (c)	292. (c)	293. (a)	294. (b)	295. (a)	296. (c)	297. (b)

298. (b)	299. (b)	300. (b)	301. (a)	302. (b)	303. (d)	304. (d)	305. (b)	306. (a)
307. (a)	308. (a)	309. (c)	310. (b)	311. (d)	312. (None)	313. (a)	314. (b)	315. (c)
316. (a)	317. (c)	318. (d)	319. (c)	320. (d)	321. (d)	322. (a)	323. (b)	324. (b)
325. (c)	326. (c)	327. (a)	328. (d)	329. (c)	330. (b)	331. (c)	332. (a)	333. (a)
334. (d)	335. (a)	336. (a)	337. (b)	338. (b)	339. (a)	340. (b)	341. (a)	342. (d)
343. (b)	344. (c)	345. (c)	346. (c)	347. (b)	348. (a)	349. (c)	350. (a)	351. (c)
352. (d)	353. (b)	354. (d)	355. (b)	356. (c)	357. (b)	358. (d)	359. (a)	360. (d)
361. (d)	362. (a)	363. (d)	364. (c)	365. (c)	366. (a)	367. (a)	368. (c)	369. (b)
370. (c)	371. (b)	372. (b)	373. (a)	374. (d)	375. (d)	376. (c)	377. (a)	378. (d)
379. (a)	380. (b)	381. (d)	382. (d)	383. (d)	384. (d)	385. (c)	386. (b)	387. (c)
388. (a)	389. (a)	390. (b)	391. (d)	392. (c)	393. (c)	394. (c)	395. (b)	396. (a)
397. (d)	398. (c)	399. (b)	400. (d)	401. (d)	402. (a)	403. (c)	404. (a)	405. (b)

Chapter 6
Classification

SUBJECTIVE QUESTIONS

Q. 1. Who invented the Library of Congress Classification Scheme?

Ans. Under the direction of J.C.M. Hanson and Charles Martel different groups of specialists developed the individual classes.

Q. 2. Who has used the decimal fraction notation for arrangement of books on shelves for the first time?

Ans. Melvil Dewey.

Q. 3. Write the Latin word from which the term "Classification" is derived.

Ans. Classis.

Q. 4. Write the name of college when Melvil Dewey first worked as a student library assistant.

Ans. Amherst College.

Q. 5. Write the name of recent general classification scheme that was published by FID in 1978.

Ans. Broad System of Ordering (BSO).

Q. 6. Write the early scheme of knowledge classification that is based on the principle of Dichotomy and Primitive Human Instinct.

Ans. Immanuel Kant's Classification (1781).

Q. 7. Who was the classificationist that made a systematic attempt to formulate a theory classification as early as 1901?

Ans. E.C. Richardson.

Q. 8. Who enunciated the colon classification? And when was it first published?

Ans. Dr. S.R. Ranganathan in 1933.

Q. 9. When was the first edition of *DDC* published and in how many pages?

Ans. In 1876, 42 pages.

Q. 10. Write the name of the scheme of classification devised by H.E. Bliss.

Ans. Bibliographic classification in 1940-53 in four volumes.

Q. 11. Who defined notation as shorthand sign?

Ans. E.C. Richardson.

Q. 12. The 7th edition of C.C. differs from the 6th edition. How?

Ans. In 7th edition of C.C. there are no levels for space [S] and time [T] Categories.

Q. 13. Who edited the DDC edition from 16th to 19th?

Ans. Benjamin A. Custer.

Q. 14. Write the name of edition of colon classification the Greek letter delta was used for first time.

Ans. 2nd edition of CC (1939).

Q. 15. Write the Sequence of Fundamental Categories when they are arranged according to their order of decreasing concreteness.

Ans. [P] [M] [E] [S] [T].

Q. 16. Write the steps that are involved in classifying a document according to S.R. Ranganathan and what are they?

Ans. Total nine steps.

Step 0 – Raw title; Step 1 – Expressive title; Step 2 – Title in Kernal terms; Step 3 – Analysed title; Step 4 – Transformed title; Step 5 – Title in Standard terms; Step 6 – Title into focal number; Step 7 – Classes Number; Step 8 – Verification by reverse translation.

Q. 17. Write the name of the scheme of classification and its deviser wherein "Categorical tables" are provided.

Ans. Subject classification J.D. Brown.

Q. 18. Write the name of person which has given the concepts of Public and Private times.

Ans. Dr. S.R. Ranganathan.

Q. 19. Write about Phoenix schedule.

Ans. A completely new development of the schedule for specific subject.

Q. 20. Write the four kinds of mnemonics recognised by Dr. S.R. Ranganathan.

Ans. Alphabetical (Verbal) mnemonics, scheduled mnemonics, systematic mnemonics and seminal mnemonics.

Q. 21. Write the French abbreviation of the Universal decimal Classification. Who initiated this scheme and where?

Ans. Henri La Fontaine and Paul Otlet. At International Conference of Librarians held at Brussels in 1895.

Q. 22. Write the indicator digit for space in UDC.

Ans. Circular brackets ().

Q. 23. Write the symbols used in UDC for representing the common Auxiliaries of race and nationality.

Ans. (= ......)

Q. 24. Write the new common schedule of isolates that has been added to the 7th edition of colon classifications.

Ans. Common Matter Property Isolates.

Q. 25. Where and when was the classification society of India established?

Ans. At Varanasi in 1983.

Q. 26. In which basis for the formation of cutter book numbers?

Ans. Surname of the author.

Q. 27. How many Auxiliary tables are given in DDC (18th edition)?

Ans. Seven.

Q. 28. How many Auxiliary tables are given in DDC (20th edition)?

Ans. Seven.

Q. 29. Write the name of classification wherein the "Floating tables are obtained".

Ans. Library of Congress Classification.

Q. 30. A marker of a scheme of classification is 'Classifier' according to H.E. Bliss.

Ans. Classificationist.

Q. 31. What is the full name of Hindi version of DDC? Who was editor?

Ans. "Selective Hindi Dewey Decimal Classification and Relative Index" 1977. Translated and Edited by Prabhu Narayan Gaur.

Q. 32. Write the name of the bibliography brought out by the classification society of England.

Ans. CLASS.

Q. 33. Write the name of title under which the DDC was published for the first time in 1876.

Ans. A classification and subject index, for cataloguing and arranging the books and pamphlets of a library.

Q. 34. Write the edition of DDC in which the Area Table Listing space isolates was mentioned for the first time.

Ans. 17th ed. of DDC (1965).

Q. 35. Write the name of person who edited the DDC seven time.

Ans. Evelyn Mary Seymour (edited 4th editions between 1891-1919).

Q. 36. What is the new heading given for table 2 under the 20th ed. of DDC?

Ans. T2: Geographic areas, historical periods and persons.

Q. 37. What is the new heading given for class 070 under the 20th ed. of DDC?

Ans. Documentary media, educational media, news media, journalism publishing.

Q. 38. Who is known as a father of modern Library Classification?

Ans. Melvil Dewey.

Q. 39. Define the call number.

Ans. The ordinal number which determines the places of a document on the shelves in a library. The number consists of class number, book number and collection number.

Q. 40. Define the accession number.

Ans. The number given to a book from the accession register, serially in the order of receipt.

Q. 41. Define the shelf list.

Ans. A list of books in a library the entries being brief and in card form arranged in the same classified sequence as the books on the shelves.

Q. 42. Who was the first librarian of Hartford Theological Seminary, USA?

Ans. E.C. Richardson.

Q. 43. Who enunciated the five fundamental categories and what they are?

Ans. Dr. S.R. Ranganathan.

PMEST — Time, Space, Energy, Matter and Personality.

Q. 44. Who used the canons in first time?

Ans. W.C. Sayers.

Q. 45. Where is the first International Conference on Bibliography was held?

Ans. In 1895 at Brussels.

Q. 46. Write the other name of "Auxiliary Tables" in CC.

Ans. Common isolates.

Q. 47. In CC (6th edition), how many types of Auxiliary table?

Ans. Two types:

1. Anteriorising Common Isolates (ACI)
2. Posteriorising Common Isolates (PCI).

Q. 48. When was seventh edition of CC published?

Ans. In 1987.

Q. 49. Who enunciated the shorthand sign?

Ans. Richardson.

Q. 50. Define the notation.

Ans. A notation is an ordered series of symbols representing terms. In a library classification scheme, the terms are ordered into classes and their subdivision. The symbols comprising a notation, therefore, stand in the place of classes and their subdivision to mechanise the process of sorting and replacement.

Q. 51. How many types of notation and what they are?

Ans. Two types:

(a) Pure (b) Mixed Notation.

Q. 52. How many types of Canon?

Ans. There are two types of canons:

(i) Canon of decreasing extension.
(ii) Canon of modulation.

Q. 53. Define the book number.

Ans. The book number of a book individualises it among the books having the same class number.

Q. 54. How many pages in the first edition of DDC?

Ans. Only 42 pages.

Q. 55. Define Pre-Coordinate System.

Ans. A system that coordinates or combines terms to form a subject heading or facet to form a number in anticipation of demand. All classification schemes are, therefore, pre-coordinate system.

Q. 56. Who enunciated the UDC and when?

Ans. Paul Otlet and Henri La Fontaine in 1895.

Q. 57. When was the CC (1st edition) published?

Ans. In 1933.

Q. 58. How many class numbers according to CC?

Ans. According to CC, class number are of three types; they are:

1. Basic Class Number
2. Compound Class Number
3. Complex Class Number.

Q. 59. Write the name of the three important personalities that worked for development of UDC.

Ans. Paul Otlet, Henri La Fontaine and Frits Donker Duyvis.

Q. 60. Who enunciated the subject classification?

Ans. J.D. Brown in 1906.

OBJECTIVE QUESTIONS

1. In colon classification digit "2" in space isolate stands for (*NET Exam.* 1998D)
   (a) World (b) Mother Country
   (c) India (d) Favoured Country
2. In CC the anteriorising common isolates are represented by (*NET Exam.* 1998D)
   (a) Roman capitals
   (b) Indo-Arabic numerals
   (c) Roman Small and Indo-Arabic numerals
   (d) None of these

3. Three great achievements in U.S.A. were noticed, i.e. enunciation of DDC classification scheme, formation of American Library Association and the publication of first journal of the librarianship in the year
   (a) 1857 (b) 1859 (c) 1876 (d) 1901
4. PMEST order is applied within (*NET Exam.* 1998J)
   (a) Main classes (b) Canonical classes
   (c) Basic classes (d) The entire field of knowledge
5. In colon classification parenthesis () is used to indicate (*NET Exam.* 1998J)
   (a) Subject Device
   (b) Chronological Device
   (c) Geographical Device
   (d) Classic Device
6. The Seven auxiliary tables of DDC form (*NET Exam.* 1991)
   (a) Enumerative features
   (b) Synthetic features
   (c) Analytical features
   (d) Descriptive features
7. In C.C. the title 'Medical Jurisprudence' can be classified and sharpened with the help of
   (a) Subject Device (b) Alphabetical Device
   (c) Classic Device (d) Enumerative Device
8. Enumerative classification means
   (a) Classification with mixed notation
   (b) Classification scheme providing readymade class number for all subjects of past, present and anticipatable future
   (c) Universal classification
   (d) Numeric classification scheme
9. P-notes are issued for revision of (*NET Exam.* 1996)
   (a) DDC (b) BC (c) UDC (d) LC
10. In a classification scheme for persons, the following groups are created on the basis of age: Infants, Children Adolescents and Adults, Age represents (*NET Exam.* 1996)
    (a) An array (b) A fact
    (c) A chain (d) None of these
11. **Statement A:** All faceted scheme of classification need not to be analytico-synthetic.

    Statement B: All analytico-synthetic schemes are faceted. (*NET Exam.* 1996)

    Codes:
    (a) Both Statements are correct
    (b) Only Statement A is correct
    (c) Only Statement B is correct
    (d) Both Statements are incorrect
12. In CC, the principle that helps in the identification of personality category is (*NET Exam.* 2000)
    (a) Cow-Calf Principle
    (b) Whole-organ Principle
    (c) Neti-neti Principle
    (d) Later-in-time Principle
13. In DDC Phoenix schedules represent (*NET Exam.* 2000)
    (a) Classes which are slightly modified
    (b) Classes which are completely changed
    (c) Classes to be modified in future
    (d) Classes not to be modified
14. The table of standard subdivision helps a classification scheme (*NET Exam.* 2000)
    (a) To ensure consistency
    (b) To add Mnemonic value
    (c) Both (a) and (b)
    (d) None of the above
15. In UDC the inter-relationship between the two subjects is denoted by
    (a) Ampersand followed by Roman Smalls
    (b) A colon
    (c) Double colon
    (d) Hyphen
16. Which series of the following class numbers belong to First, Second and Third summaries of DDC consecutively? (*NET Exam.* 1999D)
    (a) 110, 345, 000 (b) 300, 624, 310
    (c) 560, 400, 120 (d) 800, 320, 624
17. Phoenix schedules are part of (*NET Exam.* 1999D)
    (a) DDC (b) BC (c) UDC (d) LCC
18. Colon classification (Ed-7) is (*NET Exam.* 1995)
    (a) An enumerative scheme
    (b) An almost faceted scheme
    (c) A rigidly faceted scheme
    (d) A freely faceted scheme
19. Table 3 in DDC 19th edition stands for (*NET Exam.* 1995)
    (a) Standard Subdivision
    (b) Language Division

(c) Groups of persons
(d) Literature Subdivision

20. In class number 22;46:51.44 the digits 46 represent (*NET Exam.* 1995)
(a) Personality (b) Energy
(c) Matter (d) Space

21. The index given in the DDC is called (*NET Exam.* 1995)
(a) An Analytical Index
(b) Relative Index
(c) Subject Index
(d) Coordinate Index

22. Colon Classification was first published in the year (*NET Exam.* 1995D)
(a) 1933 (b) 939 (c) 1941 (d) 1944

23. The table in DDC, which provides for Racial, Ethnic, National Groups is (*NET Exam.* 1995)
(a) Table–2 (b) Table–7
(c) Table–3 (d) Table–5

24. How many editions of DDC are published till now?
(a) 22 (b) 18 (c) 20 (d) 19

25. The digits 'J64' in the class number 0111, 2J64, 51 represent (*NET Exam.* 1995)
(a) Personality (b) Energy
(c) Matter (d) Time

26. How many tables are there in 19th edition of DDC? (*NET Exam.* 1995)
(a) Four (b) Six (c) Seven (d) Eight

27. How many tables are there in 21st edition of DDC? (*Central School Exam.*)
(a) Five (b) Sixth (c) Seven (d) Eight

28. How many tables are there in 20th edition of DDC? (*C.S. Exam.*)
(a) Four (b) Seven (c) Eight (d) Six

29. Principle of Osmosis has been propounded by (*NET Exam.* 1995)
(a) Melvil Dewey
(b) S.R. Ranganathan
(c) W.C. Berwick Sayers
(d) C.A. Cutter

30. LISA (Library & Information Science Abstracts) is arranged according to
(a) DDC
(b) Colon Classification
(c) UDC
(d) A special scheme of classification

31. First Edition of DDC was published in
(a) 1876 (b) 1873 (c) 1870 (d) 1886

32. In UDC the common isolates are called (*NET Exam.* 1994)
(a) Standard subdivision
(b) Auxiliary subdivision
(c) Form division
(d) Viewpoints

33. In UDC the sign (—) dash is used to indicate all types of phase and facet relation (*NET Exam.* 1994)
(a) Colon (b) Dot
(c) Comma (d) Semicolon

34. The concept of common isolates was first formulated by (*NET Exam.* 1994)
(a) Melvil Dewey (b) S.R. Ranganathan
(c) J.D. Brown (d) H.E. Bliss

35. The Headquarters of IFLA is located at (*NET Exam.* 1994)
(a) The Hague (b) Paris
(c) Washington DC (d) New York

36. In a classification scheme the groups special libraries, medical libraries, hospital libraries, represent (*NET Exam.* 1991J)
(a) A facet (b) An array
(c) A chain (d) A characteristic

37. B.S.O. is
(a) Classification scheme
(b) A cataloguing code
(c) A thesaurus
(d) An exchange format

38. What is the edition of CC in which the fundamental categories were introduced for the first time? (*NET Exam.* 1996J)
(a) Second (b) Third
(c) Fourth (d) Sixth

39. The principle for facet sequence given by Ranganathan is (*NET Exam.* 1991)
(a) Wall-Picture principle (b) Law of parsimony
(c) Local variation (d) Spatial contiguity

40. Mnemonics means
(a) Economics of classification
(b) Aid to memory
(c) Ethnics of classification
(d) None of the above

41. "Canon of Recall Value" was developed by
(a) Charles Ammi Cutter
(b) B.S. Kesavan

(c) G. Bhattacharya
(d) Ranganathan

42. Phase relation may have to be shown at the (*NET Exam.* 1996D)
(a) Subject level (b) Facet level
(c) Array level (d) All of the above

43. Hospitality in chain can be secured by these two devices.
(a) Gap and fractional devices
(b) Sector and new digit devices
(c) Emptying digit and empty digit devices
(d) Alphabetical and mnemonic devices

44. In academic special and to a large extent in public libraries the majority of readers approach document on the basis of
(a) Language approach (b) Author approach
(c) Title approach (d) Subject approach

45. Table 2 of DDC deals with (*C.S. Exam.*)
(a) Languages (b) Standard Subdivision
(c) Person (d) Area

46. The personality facet in the main class history is taken from
(a) The main class religion
(b) The annexure page
(c) Schedule itself
(d) Space isolate table

47. Ranganathan defines ______________ as "that division of knowledge whose extension and intension are equal to these of its thought content".
(a) specific subject
(b) basic subject
(c) library classification
(d) artificial language

48. In colon classification the indicator digits h, t, j and a are used for _____ kind of phase.
(a) tool (b) bias
(c) general (d) influencing

49. Collection is termed as ____________ by S.R. Ranganathan.
(a) subordination (b) parallel sequence
(c) filiatory sequence (d) consensus

50. _________ was the first Classificationist to use simple Indo-Arabic Numerals (0-9) as ordinal numbers for systematic listing of subject in his classification scheme.
(a) Melvil Dewey (b) S.R. Ranganathan
(c) J.D. Brown (d) G.O. Kelly

51. The basic plan of DDC is divided into ________ division.
(a) ten (b) three (c) nine (d) eight

52. In case of two areas present in a subject, both are used and joined by __________ in building the class number.
(a) 00 (b) 099 (c) 09 (d) 0

53. In DDC the notations of tables 3 and 4 are applicable only to their respective main classes
(a) Philosophy and related disciplines
(b) Arts and Literature
(c) Literature and Languages
(d) Philosophy and Religion

54. Classification Research Group (UK) came into
(a) 1955 (b) 1950 (c) 1952 (d) 1954

55. The four major devices used in CC are chronological geographical subject and devices
(a) Alphabetical (b) Empty digit
(c) Gap (d) Decimal fraction

56. How many volumes in 20th edition of DDC?
(a) 4 (b) 3 (c) 5 (d) 6

57. Tick the class number for the title lecture method of teaching university student
(a) TR:3:97 (b) T4:397
(c) T4, 3:97 (d) T43:97

58. "Specific subject of that division of knowledge whose extension and intention are equal to those of its thought content" was defined by
(a) Sayers (b) Dewey
(c) Bliss (d) Ranganathan

59. The dynamic theory of library classification was developed by
(a) Brown (b) Ranganathan
(c) Sayers (d) Bliss

60. The call number of a document consists of three elements, viz. class number, book number and _________ number.
(a) accession (b) collection
(c) facet (d) isolated

61. In DDC the notations of tables 3 and 4 are applicable only to their respective main class
(a) Language and law
(b) Literature and language
(c) Literature and history
(d) None of the above

62. The 19th edition of DDC was published in
(a) 1989 (b) 1988 (c) 1979 (d) 1980

63. The 19th edition volume 3 is devoted to
(a) Schedule (b) Table
(c) Relative index (d) None of the above

64. Ranganathan formulated four principles, viz. whole-organ, cow-calf, wall picture, and act and action actor tool principles of ________ sequence.
(a) literary warrant (b) parallel
(c) facet (d) helpful

65. Gap device and decimal fraction device are used for extra pollution in chain.
(a) True (b) False

66. The three summaries provided at the end of volume __________ illustrate the division of universe of knowledge in DDC.
(a) 111 (b) 11
(c) 1 (d) All of the above

67. The canon of ________ Mnemonics states that "a scheme of classification should use one and the same digit to devote seminally equivalent concepts in whatever subject they may occur".
(a) seminal (b) scheduled
(c) systematic (d) All of the above

68. According to S.R. Ranganathan, ________ category is the central core of a subject.
(a) place (b) personality
(c) matter (d) energy

69. Subject arrangement of documents is also known as
(a) Classified alphabetical sequence
(b) Alphabetical sequence
(c) Filiatory sequence
(d) Literary warrant

70. Facet analysis synthesis is the two predominate future of
(a) DDC (b) CC (c) BC (d) UDC

71. In UDC the class 4 Linguistics was cancelled in 1963 and merged in class
(a) 3 Social science (b) 7 Arts
(c) 8 Literature (d) Sayers

72. Notation is defined as "Shorthand" signed by
(a) Ranganathan (b) Bliss
(c) Richardson (d) Sayers

73. The notation in UDC consists of Indo-Arabic numerals, Roman alphabet, punctuation marks and
(a) Mathematical signs (b) Pictorial signs
(c) Greek letters (d) All of the above

74. A range of numbers beginning with a somatically rich digit, with one empty digit, or with two empty digits and so is called sector.
(a) True (b) False

75. A symbol connecting two facets is known as connector
(a) True (b) False

76. UDC is a faceted scheme of classification
(a) True (b) False

77. The isolates under canonical class "H8", i.e. 'cosmic Hypotheses' are not enumerated, they can be individualised by_____ device.
(a) gap (b) enumerative
(c) chronological (d) subject

78. In the class number 0111, 3N05, 31 for the title "Mulk Raj Anand—Morning face comma 31" is _______ of personality facet.
(a) fourth round (b) third level
(c) fourth level (d) third round

79. An array is set of co-ordinate class.
(a) True (b) False

80. Subject "Drug Habit" comes under the main class
(a) Agriculture (b) Psychology
(c) Sociology (d) Medicine

81. The number in square brackets in DDC means
(a) Can be attached to any number
(b) Can be used only with tables
(c) No more in use
(d) Can be used in 19th edition of DDC

82. In colon classification class number for a system is derived by the __________ device.
(a) subject (b) chronological
(c) alphabetical (d) geographical

83. In 6th ed. of CC common isolates are of two types, namely
(a) Personality CI and Energy CI
(b) Space CI and Time CI
(c) ACI and PCI
(d) Special CI and General CI

84. _______ of a book individualises it among the books having the same class number.
   (a) Book number (b) Decimal Fraction device
   (c) Call number (d) Year number

85. How many steps were involved in CC?
   (a) 9 (b) 8 (c) 7 (d) 6

86. In which year 21st edition was published?
   (a) 1996 (b) 1991 (c) 1995 (d) 1994

87. _____________ symbols used in library classification for arrangement of documents of the basis of subject treatment in them.
   (a) Accession number (b) Characteristics
   (c) Artificial language (d) None of these

88. Notation is one the special features of library classification distinguishing it from knowledge classification.
   (a) True (b) False

89. Under class number 398.47 you will find a note, it is of __________ type note.
   (a) inclusion (b) class in
   (c) class here (d) class elsewhere

90. Author number in main class literature is got by subject device.
   (a) True (b) False

91. Colon classification scheme is devised by _________ in the year __________.
   (a) Neelameghan, 1952
   (b) Bhattacharya, 1940
   (c) Ranganathan, 1933
   (d) Melvil Dewey, 1876

92. The standard subdivisions always consist at least of two digits of which the first is ______.
   (a) Indo-Arabic numerals 1-9
   (b) Zero
   (c) Roman cap
   (d) Roman small

93. Common isolates were first identified and used by
   (a) Ranganathan (b) H.E. Bliss
   (c) G. Bhattacharya (d) Dewey

94. Match the following and tick the right answer:

(A) J.D. Brown	1. Bibliographic classification
(B) H.E. Bliss	2. Colon classification
(C) S.R. Ranganathan	3. Subject classification
(D) Otlet & Fontaine	4. Universal Decimal classification

   (a) A-1, B-4, C-2, D-3
   (b) A-4, B-2, C-3, D-1
   (c) A-2, B-3, C-1, D-4
   (d) A-3, B-1, C-2, D-4

95. If the fundamental category manifests itself more than once in one and in the same specific subject the sequence of the energy isolates is fixed on a general principal of
   (a) Actual-Action, Actor-Tool Principle
   (b) Cow and Calf Principle
   (c) Wall Picture Principle
   (d) Whole-organ Principle

96. In colon classification the title "A general study of public and special libraries" represents phase relation of
   (a) Bias type (b) Basic classes
   (c) General type (d) Influence type

97. An array is a set of
   (a) Coordinate classes (b) Basic classes
   (c) Chain of classes (d) Subordinate class

98. The number used in DDC to denote subjects have only
   (a) First value (b) Semantic value
   (c) Cardinal value (d) Ordinal value

99. The abbreviation r.e.n. used in the Index shows the table No.
   (a) 1 (b) 5 (c) 6 (d) 7

100. The three important qualities of a good notation are: (i) Correlative and subsidiary, (ii) Simple and brief, and (iii) _________.
   (a) Scientific (b) Systematic
   (c) Synthetic features (d) None of these

101. __________ is a set of coordinate classes of subdivision.
   (a) Postulate (b) Array
   (c) Chain (d) Mnemonic

102. In UDC the hyphen series denote aspect studies activities, processes, operation, plant and equipment.
   (a) True (b) False

103. In UDC the facet indicators used for common auxiliaries are as follows: colon, square brackets and
   (a) Dash (b) Double colon
   (c) Semicolon (d) Comma

104. In UDC common isolates are called
   (a) Common Subdivision
   (b) Auxiliary Subdivision

(c) Standard Subdivision
(d) None of the above

105. According to S.R. Ranganathan there are three planes of works: Ideas, verbal and _________ plane.
(a) scientific (b) conceptual
(c) notational (d) None of the above

106. In CC the volume number in book number is individualised by
(a) Colon (b) Comma
(c) Dot (d) Semicolon

107. In scheme of colon classification the undersized book is denoted by _________ the call number.
(a) underline (b) encircle and underline
(c) over line (d) encircle

108 Auxiliary table are known as _________ in CC.
(a) Special Auxiliaries
(b) Common Auxiliaries
(c) Common Isolates
(d) None of the above

109. In which volume has used for index and manual of 21st edition of DDC?
(a) Vol-IV (b) Vol-I
(c) Vol-II (d) Vol-III

110. Who is editor of DDC 21st edition?
(a) Joan Mitchell (b) G. Bhattacharya
(c) Melvil Dewey (d) B.S. Kesavan

111. DRTC is not a promoting research in the field of library classification.
(a) True (b) False

112. Table 4 is exclusively meant for the main class _________ and is to be confined with the base number __________.
(a) 800, 820 – 890 (b) 800, 810 – 880
(c) 400, 420 – 490 (d) 400, 410 – 480

113. If the class number for a document involves two standard subdivisions then
(a) Only one is used on preferential basis
(b) Second one is used
(c) Both are used
(d) First one is used

114. How many kinds of notation are there?
(a) 5 (b) 2 (c) 3 (d) 4

115. Class number 551, SM, 2, 951 are example of
(a) Mixed Notation (b) Group Notation
(c) Pure Notation (d) Faceted Notation

116. The concept of facet analysis and mental categories is dealing with
(a) Five laws of Library Science (b) Canons
(c) Mnemonics (d) Postulates

117. In the seventh edition of colon classification the connecting symbol for phase relation is
(a) Comma (,) (b) Dot (.)
(c) Ampersand (&) (d) Zero (0)

118. To inform the users of DDC, the developments regarding the scheme DDC, the bulletin __________ is published at interval.
(a) additions notes and decisions
(b) bulletin of DDC
(c) extension and corrections of DDC
(d) periodical of DDC

119. The first summary in DDC is also called
(a) Main Sub-section (b) Section
(c) Division (d) Ten main classes

120. In DDC schemes have the three-figure notation in essential.
(a) True (b) False

121. The class no. for the title "Ayurvedic treatment of 'Diarrhea' is LB, 25:452:6" where LB stands for
(a) Common isolate (b) Special facet
(c) Basic facet (d) System facet

122. According E.W. Hulme, all classification could arranged into two groups, viz. Mechanical and Philosophic.
(a) True (b) False

123. The subject biography comes under in 920 in DDC 19th Edition.
(a) True (b) False

124. The use of Principle of bottom-upwards can be seen in the main classes botany and science and in the scheme of colon classification.
(a) True (b) False

125. The three postulates of facet sequence of Ranganathan are (i) Postulate of concreteness, (ii) Postulate of round, and (iii) Postulate of level.
(a) True (b) False

126. The fundamental category ___________ constitutes any action, physical or mental involving all kinds of entities, animate

or inanimate, concrete of conceptual, intellectual or intuitive.
(a) personality (b) matter property
(c) matter material (d) Energy

127. Library classification helps to arrange documents in a systematic order, which is most convenient to the readers and the library staff. It brings related subjects in close proximity, called ______ by Henry Bliss.
(a) collocation
(b) parallel sequence
(c) subject arrangement
(d) artificial arrangement

128. In the main class Economic the isolate 9A to 9Q under '9 personnel management' represent
(a) Concrete sector
(b) Least concrete sector
(c) Still more concrete sector
(d) More concrete sector

129. In the main class literature foci in P2 stands for
(a) Work (b) Form
(c) Author (d) Language

130. The main class "C" physics further divided into
(a) Canonical class (b) Generic class
(c) Compound (d) Host class

131. Common isolate M is applicable
(a) Before time facet (b) After time facet
(c) After space facet (d) Before space facet

132. The problem facet is common for the main class Biology, Botany and
(a) Zoology (b) Geology
(c) Animal Husbandry (d) Agriculture

133. ________ are Principles of classification, used in this sense first by Sayers.
(a) Mnemonics (b) Chain
(c) Array (d) Canons

134. The various plants and animal groups are arranged according to principle of literary warrant in the schemes.
(a) True (b) False

135. The system of ordinal numbers representing classes in a scheme of library classification is called
(a) Isolate number (b) Notation
(c) Facet formula (d) Fundamental categories

136. UDC is devised by
(a) Ranganathan
(b) Fremont Rider
(c) Paul Otlet and La Fontaine
(d) Melvil Dewey

137. Phase analysis and synthesis have been developed to accommodate ________ subject in the scheme of classification.
(a) general (b) complex
(c) compound (d) basic

138. According to S.R. Ranganathan the two canons for chain are as
(a) Canon of helpful sequence and consistent sequence
(b) Canon of decreasing extension and increasing intention
(c) Canon of decreasing extension and modulation
(d) Canon of exhaustiveness and exclusiveness

139. To break the monotony of lengthy numbers and to aid memory a ________ is used after three digits DDC.
(a) comma (b) dot
(c) colon (d) semi-colon

140. In DDC language, form, author, period from the basis of classification of documents in
(a) Literature (b) History
(c) Law (d) Social Science

141. In the schedule of political science the notation for (P2) and (E) cum (2P) are taken from the main class
(a) Sociology (b) History
(c) Economics (d) Law

142. Semi-colon is used in the book number to present
(a) Volume number (b) Supplement number
(c) Copy number (d) Accession number

143. __________ in his book entitled *Library Classification Evolution of a Dynamic Theory* identified two stages of development of library classification.
(a) R.S. Parkhi (b) S.R. Ranganathan
(c) E.C. Richardson (d) J.D. Brown

144. The structure of DDC is based on the schemes devised by
(a) Bliss
(b) Paul Otlet and Henri La Fontaine

(c) Ranganathan
(d) Bacon and Harris

145. In DDC __________ is not enumerated in its schedules.
(a) basic isolates (b) common isolates
(c) special isolates (d) facet isolates

146. A system of ordinal numbers used to represent the classes in the scheme of classification is called
(a) Notational system (b) Mnemonic
(c) Homonym (d) Synonym

147. _______ isolates are the control focus of any subject.
(a) Matter (b) Personality
(c) Special (d) Basic

148. Compound subject is one with a _______ and one or more isolate ideas.
(a) facet (b) complex subject
(c) basic subject (d) Specific subject

149. ________ means analysis of a subject into its facets obtained on the basis of systematic application of a set of characteristics.
(a) Facet analysis (b) Facet synthesis
(c) Facet sequence (d) Specific subject

150. In CC Anteriorising to closed common isolates (ACI) are of three types, which are applicable before space facet, after space facet and
(a) After energy facet
(b) After personality facet
(c) Before time facet
(d) After time facet

151. ____________ is the first set of division obtained on the basis of the application of characteristics of a class.
(a) Idea (b) Array (c) Isolate (d) Facet

152. DDC is an
(a) Almost enumerative classification
(b) Almost faceted classification
(c) Rigidly faceted classification
(d) Enumerative classification

153. Ranganathan has postulated five fundamental categories as
(a) Part, Process, Action, Places, Time
(b) Personality, Matter, Energy, Space, Time
(c) Entities, Materials, Operation, Space, Time
(d) Product, Process, Action, Space, Time

154. According to Ranganathan School of thought there are two groups of matter
(a) Matter Property, Matter Process
(b) Matter Material, Matter Method
(c) Matter Material, Matter Property
(d) Matter Property, Matter Method

155. In Dewey Decimal classification facet analysis is used
(a) Directly (b) Partially explicitly
(c) Explicitly (d) Implicitly

156. In UDC the common isolates are called
(a) Viewpoint Number
(b) Form Division
(c) Auxiliary Subdivision
(d) Standard Subdivision

157. Ranganathan has enunciated three postulates for facet sequence as
(a) Postulate of fundamental categories, Basic facet and Round & Levels.
(b) Postulate of concreteness, Round, Level.
(c) Postulate of fundamental categories, Basic Facet, Isolate Facet.
(d) None of these

158. According to colon classification the title "Psychology of Doctors" is an example of
(a) Inter Facet phase relation
(b) Inter subject relation
(c) Inter subject phase relation of comparison type
(d) Inter array phase relation

159. The credit of introducing the concept of common isolates goes to
(a) Sayers (b) Paul Otlet and La Fontaine
(c) Melvil Dewey (d) Ranganathan

160. In the 7th edition of colon classification, in the subject 'Electronic calculator' the enumeration of programming language is done according to the principle of _________ sequence.
(a) later in time (b) latter in evolution
(c) alphabetical (d) decreasing quantity

161. Collection number in call number is to indicate the collection in which that book placed in library. The collection numbering scheme be formulated and maintained by the
(a) Maintenance section
(b) Technical section

(c) Acquisition section
(d) Reference section

162. The class number for the title 'Biography of C.V. Raman' is CW M88. Where W stands for the term works.
(a) True (b) False

163. Classification is a mental process by which things or ideas are assembled according to their likeness. The likeness, which exists in the Universe of things and in ideas, is called _______ in classification.
(a) Division (b) Characteristic
(c) Notation (d) Isolate

164. The _________ facts can occur only in the last round among the facets of a specific subject.
(a) Space and Time (b) Time and Energy
(c) Time and Matter (d) Space and Personality

165. "Mathematics for Economics" is an example of _______ type of phase relation.
(a) influence (b) tool
(c) bias (d) general

166. In _____ phase relation two isolate ideas of the same facet interest form complex subject.
(a) intra-facet (b) intra-array
(c) inter-subject (d) None of the above

167. Hospitality in chain can be secured by the two devices mainly
(a) Emptying digit and empty-emptying digit device
(b) Facet and enumeration device
(c) Sector and new digit device
(d) Gap and Decimal Fraction Device

168. The add to instructions appearing throughout the DDC schedule is an example of
(a) Scheduled Mnemonics
(b) Seminal Mnemonics
(c) Systematic Mnemonics
(d) Alphabetical Mnemonics

169. Encyclopedias, Dictionaries, Periodicals and so on are referred to as
(a) Viewpoints
(b) Standard Subdivisions
(c) Outer forms of presentation
(d) Inner forms of presentation

170. Complex subject is formed by a combination of
(a) One basic subject with two isolate ideas
(b) One basic subject with two isolates within one and the same array of isolate ideas
(c) Two or more subjects basic or compound
(d) One basic subject and one or more isolate ideas

171. PMEST order is applied with in
(a) Main classes
(b) Canonical classification
(c) Basic classes
(d) the entire fields of knowledge

172. BSO is a (*NET Exam.* 1997J)
(a) Classification Scheme
(b) Cataloguing Code
(c) Treasures
(d) Exchange Format

173. In colon classification the symbol semicolon (;) indicates the fundamental category
(a) Personality (b) Matter
(c) Energy (d) Space

174. Dichotomy means division into
(a) Two (b) Five (c) Ten (d) Many

175. In which kind of relation the title "psychology for teacher" is a (*NET Exam.* 1997J)
(a) General (b) Bias
(c) Influence (d) Comparison

176. In UDC the symbol colon (:) is used for
(a) Extension (b) Addition
(c) Relation (d) Coordination

177. In DDC the universes of knowledge is first divided into
(a) 10 main divisions
(b) 100 divisions
(c) 1000 sections
(d) 10,000 subdivisions

178. Cutters three-figure table in divided three sequence, i.e.
(a) Language Number, Book Number, Acc. No.
(b) Class Number, Book Number, Author Number
(c) Roman Capital, Years Number, Language Numbers
(d) Consonants, Values and Alphabets

179. Name the principles of classification, which emphasis that two facets belonging to the same subjects are not to be separated even though they are distinct from each other and

separable but should be kept together in the same round? (*NET Exam.* 1997D)
(a) Whole-organ Principle
(b) Cow-calf Principle
(c) Wall picture Principle
(d) None of the above

180. Mathematics for engineering is the example of (*NET Exam.* 1997D)
(a) Tool phase relation
(b) Comparison phase relation
(c) Difference phase relation
(d) Bias phase relation

181. Two kinds of auxiliaries in UDC are (*NET Exam.* 1997D)
(a) Form and Language
(b) Anterior and Posterior
(c) Space and Time
(d) Common and special

182. Match the following standard subdivisions from DDC:

List-I	List-II
(A) Philosophy & Theory	(i) 07
(B) Serial Publications	(ii) 05
(C) Collections	(iii) 01
(D) Study and Teaching	(iv) 08

Codes:	A	B	C	D
(a)	i	ii	iv	iii
(b)	iii	iv	ii	i
(c)	iii	ii	iv	i
(d)	ii	iv	i	iii

183. In Dewey decimal classification, tables of precedence are provided so that these can be
(a) Alternate ways of arrangement
(b) Consistency
(c) Addition of Standard-Subdivision
(d) All of the above

184. In UDC the symbol-05 (Hyphen naught five) denotes the common auxiliaries of
(a) Places (b) Materials
(c) Form (d) Persons

185. Match the following:

(A) Ranganathan	(1) Principles of Book classification
(B) Sayers	(2) Classification theoretical and Practical
(C) Richardson	(3) Colon Classification
(D) Hulme	(4) Prolegomena to Lib. classification

(a)	A – 4	B – 3	C – 2	D – 1
(b)	A – 3	B – 2	C – 4	D – 1
(c)	A – 2	B – 4	C – 3	D – 1
(d)	A – 3	B – 2	C – 1	D – 4

186. Accession number is a part of book number.
(a) True (b) False

187. Bliss devise the three steps of classification.
(a) True (b) False

188. Match the following:

(A) H.E. Bliss	(1) Bibliographic classification
(B) S.R. Ranganathan	(2) UDC
(C) Paul Otlet	(3) DDC
(D) Dewey	(4) Colon classification

(a)	A – 1	B – 4	C – 2	D – 3
(b)	A – 2	B – 3	C – 4	D – 2
(c)	A – 3	B – 2	C – 3	D – 1
(d)	A – 4	B – 1	C – 1	D – 4

189. Match the following:

(A) DDC	(1) 1933
(B) Expensive classification	(2) 1876
(C) Colon classification	(3) 1905
(D) UDC	(4) 1879

(a)	A – 3	B – 2	C – 3	D – 4
(b)	A – 2	B – 4	C – 1	D – 3
(c)	A – 4	B – 3	C – 2	D – 1
(d)	A – 1	B – 1	C – 4	D – 2

190. Dewey Decimal classification is related to Enumerative.
(a) True (b) False

191. First edition of DDC was published in 1876.
(a) True (b) False

192. Match the following:

(A) Language Table	(1) Space isolates
(B) Add 000 – 999	(2) Common isolates
(C) Area Table	(3) Subject devices
(D) Standard Subdivision	(4) Language isolates

(a)	A – 2	B – 1	C – 4	D – 1
(b)	A – 1	B – 4	C – 2	D – 3
(c)	A – 3	B – 2	C – 2	D – 4
(d)	A – 4	B – 3	C – 1	D – 2

193. Match the following:

(A) Characteristic	(1) Principles of division
(B) Class	(2) Class consisting of one and only one entity
(C) Array	(3) Class derived on the basis of single characteristic

(D) Attribute (4) Property, quality, or quantitative measure of entity

(a) A – 4 B – 3 C – 1 D – 2
(b) A – 3 B – 2 C – 1 D – 4
(c) A – 2 B – 4 C – 3 D – 1
(d) A – 1 B – 1 C – 4 D – 3

194. Match the following:

(A) Second level matter (1) M2
(B) Second round personality (2) 2P
(C) Second round & third level personality (3) 2P3
(D) Second level personality (4) P2

(a) A – 1 B – 2 C – 3 D – 4
(b) A – 2 B – 3 C – 4 D – 1
(c) A – 3 B – 4 C – 2 D – 1
(d) A – 4 B – 1 C – 2 D – 3

195. Match the following:

List I	List II
(A) Multiple class	(1) Grouping of entities sharing the same characteristics
(B) Characteristics	(2) Component of facet
(C) Isolate	(3) Principle of division
(D) Unitary class	(4) Class consisting of more than one entity

(a) A – 4 B – 3 C – 2 D – 1
(b) A – 2 B – 4 C – 3 D – 1
(c) A – 3 B – 1 C – 2 D – 4
(d) A – 1 B – 2 C – 3 D – 4

196. Match the following:

List I	List II
(A) Physics	(1) V
(B) Political Science	(2) U
(C) Geography	(3) W
(D) History	(4) C

(a) A – 4 B – 3 C – 2 D – 1
(b) A – 3 B – 2 C – 4 D – 1
(c) A – 2 B – 1 C – 3 D – 4
(d) A – 1 B – 2 C – 3 D – 4

197. Wall Picture Principle is one of the Principles of (*NET Exam.* 1997J)

(a) Helpful Sequence
(b) Alphabetical Sequence
(c) Classified Alphabetical Sequence
(d) Facet Sequence

198. The concept of 'Empty Digit' facilitates

(a) Hospitality in chain
(b) Interpolation in Array
(c) Extrapolation in Army
(d) Interpolation of Army

(*NET Exam.* 1995J)

199. Canons for characteristic are part of (*NET Exam.* 1999D)

(a) Verbal Part (b) Notational Plane
(c) Idea Plane (d) Structure Plane

200. Match the following: (*NET Exam.* 2004D)

Column I	Column II
(A) WCB Sayers	1. Grammar of Classification
(B) Library of Congress	2. Cataloguing in Publication
(C) ILA	3. Journal of Librarianship

Codes:	**A**	**B**	**C**
(a)	2	3	1
(b)	1	2	3
(c)	3	2	1
(d)	1	3	2

201. Match the following: (*NET Exam.* 2005D)

Column I	Column II
(A) Total National Symbol in CC-7	1. 14
(B) Father of Library movement of UK	2. Edward Edwards
(C) Set up of RRRLF	3. 1972
	4. 1974

Codes:	**A**	**B**	**C**
(a)	1	2	3
(b)	3	2	1
(c)	1	3	4
(d)	4	3	1

202. Fujio is called Dewey of (*NET Exam.* 2005D)

(a) Nepal (b) Kenya (c) Russia (d) Japan

203. Which statement is/are correct: (*NET Exam.* 2005D)

1. The first Grammar of Classification is WCB Sayers
2. Subject Classification by J.D. Broun is an example of freely faceted classification.
3. Colon Classification is an excellent example of enumerative classification.

(a) 1, 2 & 3 (b) 1 & 2
(c) 2 & 3 (d) 3 only

204. The decision to make or not to make an entry under a term is governed by the (*NET Exam.* 2006J)

(a) Canon of Ascertainability
(b) Canon of Prepotence
(c) Canon of Sought Heading
(d) Canon of context

205. **Assertion (A):** Classification as a tool for organization of knowledge will continue to persist.

Reason (R): In the age of e-documents classification is redundant.

(*NET Exam.* 2006J)

Codes:
(a) Both (A) and (R) true
(b) (A) is correct and (R) is false
(c) (R) is correct (A) is false
(d) Both (A) and (R) are false

206. Which is not correctly matched? (*NET Exam.* 2004D)
(a) Personality → , (Comma)
(b) Matter → . (Dot)
(c) Energy → : (colon)
(d) Time → . (dot)

207. Which is the correct sequence of the following in the chronological order of publication? (*NET Exam.* 2006J)
(a) 14th edition of DDC, 1st edition of CC, rider International Classification, Board System of Ordering
(b) 1st edition of CC, 14th Edition of DDC, Broad System of Ordering, rider's International classification
(c) Riders International classification, 1st edition of CC, Broad System of ordering, 14th Edition of DDC
(d) 1st edition of CC, Riders International Classification, 14th Edition of DDC, Broad System of Ordering

208. Select the right sequence of contribution of classification in the chronological order (*NET Exam.* 2006J)
(a) Francis Bacon, W.T. Harris, Melvil Dewey, J.D. Brown
(b) W.T. Harris, Francis Bacon, Melvil Dewey, J.D. Brown
(c) Francis Bacon, Melvil Dewey, J.D. Brown., W.T. Harris
(d) Francis Bacon, J.D. Brown, W.T. Harris, Melvil Dewey

209. Match the following:

List-I	List-II
(A) Classarus	(i) Jean Aitchison
(B) Relative Index	(ii) J.L. Ferradane
(C) Thesauro facet	(iii) S.R. Ranganathan
(D) Relational Indexing	(iv) G. Bhattacharya
	(v) Melvil Dewey structure

Codes:	A	B	C	D
(a)	iii	i	ii	v
(b)	iv	v	i	ii
(c)	ii	v	i	iii
(d)	iii	ii	i	iv

210. "Prevention of Cholera in India" generates the following index terms according to modified 'Chain Indexing', arrange them in correct order (*NET Exam.* 20012J, 2006J)
(i) India (ii) Cholera (iii) Disease
(iv) Treatment (v) Medicine

Codes:

(a)	iii	iv	i	ii	v
(b)	ii	i	iii	iv	v
(c)	iv	iii	ii	v	i
(d)	i	iii	iv	v	ii

211. Match the following: (*NET Exam.* 2006D)

List-I	List-II
(A) Subject classification	(i) J. Aitchinson
(B) Thesauro facet	(ii) C.A. Cutter
(C) Classified Catalogue Code	(iii) J.D. Brown
(D) Rule of Dictionary Catalogue	(iv) S.R.Ranganathan

Codes:	A	B	C	D
(a)	iii	i	iv	ii
(b)	ii	iii	i	iv
(c)	iv	ii	iii	i
(d)	i	ii	iii	iv

212. In CC, the principle that helps in the identification of personality is (*NET Exam.* 2001J)
(a) Cow calf principle
(b) Whole Organ Principle
(c) Neti-neti principle
(d) Later in time principle

213. In DDC Phoenix schedule represent (*NET Exam.* 2001J)
(a) Classes which are slightly modified
(b) Classes which are completely changed

(c) Classes to be modified in the future
(d) Classes not to modified

214. The table of standard subdivision helps a classification scheme. (*NET Exam.* 2001J)
(a) to ensure consistency
(b) to add mnemonic value
(c) both the above
(d) None of the above

215. In UDC the inter-relationship between the two subjects detonated by (*NET Exam.* 2001J)
(a) Ampersand followed by Roman smalls
(b) A Colon
(c) Double colon
(d) Hyphen

216. Which series of the following class numbers belong to first, second and third summaries of DDC consecutively? (*NET Exam.* 2001D)
(a) 110,345,000 (b) 300,624,310
(c) 560,400,120 (d) 800,320,624

217. Relationship among concept form of component of subject may be (*NET Exam.* 2001D)
(a) Hierarchical relationship
(b) Non-hierarchical relationship
(c) Associative relationship
(d) Both (a) and (b)

218. Which number does not that the number is used for fixing the position of an entry in a sequence? (*NET Exam.* 2002D)
(a) Ordinal number (b) Cardinal number
(c) Substance number (d) All of the above

219. Match the following: (*NET Exam.* 2007J)

List-I	List-II
(A) Pre-scientific period	(i) pre-1927
(B) Scientific period	(ii) pre-1880
(C) Human relations	(iii) 1880-1927
(D) Synthesis	(iv) 1927-50
	(v) 1950-2007

Codes:	A	B	C	D
(a)	i	iii	iv	v
(b)	ii	iii	iv	v
(c)	iii	iv	v	ii
(d)	ii	iii	v	iv

220. Which of the following postulate state that any of the fundamental categories; Personality and Matter may manifest more than once in one and the same round within a subject and similarity with Space and Time in last round? (*NET Exam.* 2002D)
(a) Level postulates
(b) Level-cluster postulates
(c) Concreteness postulates
(d) First facet postulate

221. Isolates such as winter, night, country, millennia, etc. are the manifestations of (*NET Exam.* 2002D)
(a) personality fundamental category
(b) matter fundamental category
(c) space fundamental category
(d) time fundamental category

222. The subject that has a basic facet and one or more isolate facet (*NET Exam.* 2002D)
(a) Complex (b) Specific
(c) Basic (d) Compound

223. In classification, the group infant, children, _______, adult represent an ARRAY. (*NET Exam.* 2002J)
(a) girl (b) women
(c) boys (d) adolescent

224. How many quadrants, the spiral of scientific (*NET Exam.* 2002J)
(a) 5 (b) 4 (c) 10 (d) 2

225. Relationship among concept from of component of subject may be categorized as (*NET Exam.* 2003J)
1. Hierarchical relationship
2. Specific relationship
3. Non-hierarchical relationship
4. General relationship

(a) 1 & 2 (b) 2 & 4
(c) 1 & 3 (d) 3 & 4

226. What is the sequential order of PMEST?
(a) Of modulation
(b) Of extension
(c) Of increasing concreteness
(d) Of decreasing concreteness

227. Which series or the following class numbers belong to first, second, and third summaries of DDC consecutively?
(a) 110, 345, 000 (b) 300, 624, 310
(c) 560, 400, 120 (d) 400, 420, 324

228. **Assertion (A):** Dewey Decimal Classification is popularly used in libraries with large collection.
Reason (R): It being regularly updated. (*NET Exam.* 2007J)

Codes:
(a) (A) is true but (R) is false
(b) (A) is false but (R) is true
(c) Both (A) and (R) are false
(d) Both (A) and (R) are true

229. "God chosen me as an instrument, the honors done to me should act as an incentive to the younger generation to devote their lives whole heartedly to library science and service". Whose quotation is this?
(a) B.S. Kesavan (b) Melvil Dewey
(c) S.R. Ranganathan (d) W.C.B. Sayers

230. Library is living system "takes a new matter cast on old matter change in size and takes new shapes and term". Whose quotation is this? (*NET Exam.* 2007J)
(a) B.S. Kesavan (b) Melvil Dewey
(c) S.R. Ranganathan (d) W.C.B. Sayers

231. "Choice of books is an unending work". Whose quotation is this? (*NET Exam.* 2008J)
(a) Melvil Dewey (b) W.C.B. Sayers
(c) C.A. Cutter (d) H.E. Bliss

232. Match the following:

List-I	List-II
(A) UDC	(i) H.E. Bliss
(B) DDC	(ii) C.A. Cutter
(C) Expensive classification	(iii) Otlat and La Fontane
(D) Bibliographic classification	(iv) M. Dewey

Codes:	A	B	C	D
(a)	iii	i	ii	iv
(b)	iii	iv	ii	i
(c)	iii	ii	iv	i
(d)	i	ii	iii	iv

233. Arrange the following books in order of their publication. (*NET Exam.* 2009D)
(i) Classified Catalogue Code
(ii) Prolegomena to Library Classification
(iii) Five Laws of Library Science
(vi) Colon classification
Codes:
(a) i, iv, iii, ii (b) iii, ii, iv, i
(c) iii, iv, i, ii (d) iv, i, ii, iii

234. The provision phase relations in DDC was made available from (*NET Exam.* 2009D)
(a) 14th edition (b) 2nd edition
(c) 7th edition (d) 11th edition

235. Arrange the following schemes of classification according to their year of origin (*NET Exam.* 2009D)
(i) Colon Classification
(ii) Expansive Classification
(iii) Universal Decimal Classification
(iv) Dewey decimal Classification
Codes:
(a) ii, iii, iv, i (b) iii, iv, i, ii
(c) iv, ii, iii, i (d) i, ii, iv, iii

236. Real Time Access refers to (*NET Exam.* 2010J)
(a) Access in advance
(b) Access after some time
(c) Access when searched for
(d) None of the above

237. Match the following (*NET Exam.* 2012D)

List-I	List-II
(A) B.S. Kesavan	(i) School of librarianship
(B) Paul Otlet	(ii) National Library of India
(C) W.C.B. Sayers	(iii) UDC
(D) M. Taube	(iv) Uniterm indexing.

Codes:	A	B	C	D
(a)	ii	iii	i	iv
(b)	iii	ii	i	iv
(c)	ii	iii	iv	i
(d)	iv	ii	iii	i

238. Match the following (*NET Exam.* 2010J)

(a) C.A. Cutter	(i) Bibliographic Classification
(b) H.E. Bliss	(ii) Expansive Classification
(c) J.D. Brown	(iii) Universal Classification
(d) Paul Otlet and Henry La Fontaine	(iv) Subject Classification

Codes:	A	B	C	D
(a)	ii	i	iv	iii
(b)	iv	i	ii	iii
(c)	i	iii	iv	ii
(d)	iii	iv	ii	i

239. Arrange the following schemes of classification according to their year of publication: (*NET Exam.* 2010J)
(i) CC (ii) DDC (iii) LC (iv) UDC

Codes:
(a) ii, i, iii, iv (b) ii, iii, iv, i
(c) i, ii, iv, iii (d) iv, iii, ii, i

240. **Assertion (A):** Dewey Decimal is an enumerative scheme of classification.
Reason (R): The scheme has developed several devices and is no more an enumerative scheme of classification. (*NET Exam.* 2010J)
Codes:
(a) (A) is true but (R) is false.
(b) (A) is not true, but (R) is true.
(c) Both (A) and (R) are true.
(d) Both (A) and (R) are false.

241. Dewey Decimal Classification (DDC) is now looked after by (*NET Exam.* 2010J)
(a) UNESCO (b) CILIP
(c) OCLC (d) ALA

242. Arrange the following according to their year of first publication: (*NET exam.* 2012D)
(i) Bliss Classification
(ii) Dewey Decimal Classification
(iii) Library of Congress Classification
(iv) Universal Decimal Classification
Codes:
(a) i, ii, iii, iv (b) i, iii, ii, iv
(c) iii, i, iv, ii (d) ii, iv, i, iii

243. Match the following: (*NET Exam.* 2010D)
List-I
(A) Elements of Library Classification
(B) Little Science Big science
(C) Documentation
(D) Subject Approach to Information
List-II
(i) D.J. de Solla Price (ii) S.R. Ranganathan
(iii) D.J. Foskett (iv) S.C. Bradford

Codes:	A	B	C	D
(a)	ii	i	iv	iii
(b)	iii	ii	i	iv
(c)	iv	ii	iii	i
(d)	i	ii	iii	iv

244. Arrange the following chronologically according to their year of birth (*NET Exam.* 2010D)
(i) S.R. Ranganathan (ii) Melvil Dewey
(iii) C.A. Cutter (iv) B.S. Kesavan
Codes:
(a) ii, i, iv, iii (b) i, iii, iv, ii
(c) iii, ii, i, iv (d) iv, i, ii, iii

245. The spiral of scientific methods involves the following steps in correct sequence (*NET Exam.* 2010D)
(i) Zenith (ii) ascendant
(iii) Nadir (iv) Descendant
Codes:
(a) i, iii, ii, iv (b) ii, iii, i, iv
(c) iii, ii, i, iv (d) i, iv, iii, ii

246. **Assertion (A):** Classification and indexing have always been of central intellectual interest in IR.
Reason (R): Conceptual analysis of the content of the queries and documentation are essentials input to an IR system. (*NET Exam.* 2010D)
Codes:
(a) (A) is true and (R) is false
(b) (R) is true but (A) is false
(c) Both (A) and (R) are true
(d) Both (A) and (R) are partially true

247. Match the following: (*NET Exam.* 2008D)

List-I	**List-II**
(A) Melvil Dewey	(i) Belgium
(B) Berwick Sayers	(ii) USA
(C) B.S. Kesavan	(iii) Britain
(D) Paul Otlet	(iv) India

Codes:	A	B	C	D
(a)	ii	iv	i	iii
(b)	iv	iii	i	ii
(c)	ii	iii	iv	i
(d)	ii	i	iii	iv

248. Arrange the following classification schemes in order to (*NET Exam.* 2008D)
(a) UDC, Expansive Classification, DDC, CC
(b) Expansive Classification, UDC, CC, DDC
(c) DDC, CC, Expansive Classification, UDC
(d) DDC, Expansive Classification, UDC, CC

249. Match the following: (*NET Exam.* 2008D)

List-I	**List-II**
(A) UBC	(i) FID
(B) UDC	(ii) IFLA
(C) MARC	(iii) ASTINFO
(D) Document Supply system	(iv) Library of Congress

Codes:	A	B	C	D
(a)	ii	iv	i	iii
(b)	ii	i	iv	iii
(c)	i	ii	iii	iv
(d)	iii	ii	iv	i

250. Match the following items given in List-I and List-II: (*NET Exam.* 2008D)

List-I	List-II
(A) DDC 19th edition	(i) John Camaroni
(B) DDC 20th edition	(ii) Melvil Dewey
(C) DDC 21st edition	(iii) John Mitchell
(D) DDC 22nd edition	(iv) Benjamib Custer

Codes:	A	B	C	D
(a)	ii	iv	iii	i
(b)	ii	i	iv	iii
(c)	ii	iv	i	iii
(d)	iv	iii	ii	i

251. **Assertion (A):** In Colon Classification, 2 represents mother country and 44 represents India. A given library in India can use 2 or 44 for India.

Reason (R): The above is in conformity with Canon of Homonym. (*NET Exam.* 2011J)

Codes:

(a) Both (A) and (R) are true and (R) is the correct explanation of (A)
(b) Both (A) and (R) are true but (R) is not a correct explanation of (A)
(c) (A) is true, but (R) is false
(d) (A) is false, but (R) is true

252. In "Spiral of scientific Methods" zenith marks (*NET Exam.* 2011J)

(a) Facts (b) Empirical Laws
(c) Fundamental Laws (d) Deduced Law

253. **Assertion (A):** In library classification, an empty digit helps in interpolation between two consecutive ordinal numbers.

Reason (R): An empty digit is a digit with ordinal value but no semantic value. (*NET Exam.* 2011J)

Codes:

(a) Both (A) and (R) are true and (R) is the correct explanation of (A)
(b) Both (A) and (R) are true, but (R) is not a correct explanation (A)
(c) (A) is true, but (R) is false
(d) (A) is false, but (R) is true

254. Arrange the following classification schemes according to their year of first publication. (*NET Exam.* 2011J)

(i) DDC (ii) CC (iii) UDC (iv) LC

Codes:

(a) i, iv, iii, ii (b) i, iv, ii, iii
(c) i, ii, iii, iv (d) ii, i, iv, iii

255. What will be the correct sequence of books in the shelves the following class numbers?

(i) 2:51 (ii) 232 (iii) 2;46 (iv) 2'N65

Codes:

(a) i, ii, iii, iv (b) ii, i, iii, iv
(c) iv, i, iii, ii (d) iii, iv, ii, i

256. Arrange the following subjects in ascending order according to their DDC number. (*NET Exam.* 2011J)

(i) Horticulture (ii) Public Administration
(iii) Metaphysics (iv) Botany

Codes:

(a) i, iv, iii, ii (b) iii, ii, iv, i
(c) ii, iii, i, iv (d) iv, ii, i, iii

257. Match the following: (*NET Exam.* 2011J)

List-I	List-II
(A) C.A. Cutter	(i) Bibliographic Classification
(B) J.D. Brown	(ii) Expensive Classification
(C) S.R. Ranganatha	(iii) Subject Classification
(D) H.E. Bliss	(iv) Colon classification

Codes:	A	B	C	D
(a)	ii	iii	iv	i
(b)	i	ii	iii	iv
(c)	iv	i	ii	iii
(d)	iii	ii	iv	i

258. Match the following: (*NET Exam.* 2012D)

List-I	List-II
(A) Chain Indexing	(i) Derek Austin
(B) Relational Indexing	(ii) S.R. Ranganathan
(C) Subject Indexing	(iii) J.E.L. Farradane
(D) PRECIS	(iv) E.J. Coats

Codes:	A	B	C	D
(a)	i	ii	iv	iii
(b)	ii	iii	iv	i
(c)	i	ii	iii	iv
(d)	ii	iv	i	ii

259. Research in automatic classification for information retrieval of term or cluster of terms is called (*NET Exam.* 2012D)

(a) Evaluation theory
(b) Theory of clumps
(c) Time binding theory
(d) Dynamic theory

260. Match the following: (*NET Exam.* 2012D)

List-I

(A) Collateral classes
(B) Multiple classes

(C) Chain of classes
(D) Co-ordinate classes

List-II
(i) Class comprising two or more entities
(ii) Classes of the same order but not belonging to one in the same order
(iii) A subject fixed with others in the universal of subject
(iv) A sequence of classes made up of any given class and in universe

Codes:	A	B	C	D
(a)	ii	iv	i	iii
(b)	i	iii	ii	iv
(c)	ii	i	iv	iii
(d)	i	iv	ii	iii

261. What will be correct sequence of books in the shelves bearing the following class numbers (*NET Exam.* 2011D)
(i) 2:8'N4 (ii) 2:8a (iii) 2:81 (iv) 2:81a
Codes:
(a) i, iii, ii, iv (b) i, ii, iv, iii
(c) iii, i, iv, ii (d) ii, i, iv, iii

262. Arrange the following in order as given in Colon classification (*NET Exam.* 2011D)
(i) Δ (ii) X (iii) Σ (iv) 4
Codes:
(a) i, iii, ii, iv (b) iv, i, iii, ii
(c) iii, i, iv, ii (d) i, iv, ii, iii

263. Arrange the following in ascending order according to DDC numbers: (*NET Exam.* 2011D)
(i) Rajput painting (ii) Ophthalmology
(iii) Microeconomics (iv) Elections
Codes:
(a) iv, iii, ii, i (b) iv, i, ii, iii
(c) iii, i, iv, ii (d) i, iv, ii, iii

264. Which one is not a canon (as given by Ranganathan) (*NET Exam.* 2009J)
(a) Canon of Comprehensiveness
(b) Canon of Consistence
(c) Canon of Context
(d) Canon of Currency

265. **Assertion (A):** In Library classification, an empty digit helps in interpolation between two consecutive ordinal numbers.
Reason (R): An empty digit is a digit with ordinal value but no semantic value. (*NET Exam.* 2009J)
Codes:
(a) Both (A) and (R) are true
(b) Both (A) and (R) are true and (R) is not a correct explanation.
(c) (A) is true (R) is false
(d) (A) is false but (R) is true

266. **Assertion (A):** In Colon Classification '2' represents mother country and '44' represents India. A given library in India can use '2' or '44' for India. But the rules allow for a choice.
Reason (R): The above is a case of violation of Canon of Homonyms. (*NET Exam.* 2009J)
Codes:
(a) Both (A) and (R) are true and (R) is the correct explanations
(b) Both (A) and (R) are true and (R) is not the correct explanations
(c) (A) is true but (R) is false
(d) (A) is false but (R) is true

267. Match the following: (*NET Exam.* 2009J)

List-I	**List-II**
(A) DDC	(i) 1933
(B) CC	(ii) 1876
(C) Rider's International Classification	(iii) 1905
(D) UDC	(iv) 1961

Codes:	A	B	C	D
(a)	ii	iv	i	iii
(b)	i	iii	ii	iv
(c)	ii	i	iv	iii
(d)	ii	i	iv	iii

268. Phoenix schedules are part of
(a) DDC (b) BC (c) UDC (d) LCC

269. Arrange the following according to their yea of first publication. (*NET Exam.* 2011D)
(i) Colon Classification
(ii) Prolegomena to Library Classification
(iii) Five Laws of Library Science
(iv) Classified Catalogue Code
Codes:
(a) i, ii, iv, iii (b) iv, i, ii, iii
(c) iii, i, iv, ii (d) i, iv, ii, iii

270. The Dewey Decimal Classification divides human knowledge into
(a) 10 basic categories
(b) 100 basic categories

(c) 1000 basic categories
(d) 10000 basic categories

271. **Assertion (A):** CC and UDC are more most suitable classification schemes for special libraries.

Reason (R): Most of the special libraries are using either CC or UDC for collection organization.

Codes:
(a) Both (A) and (R) are true and (R) is the correct explanation of (A)
(b) Both (A) and (R) are true, but (R) is not the correct explanation of (A)
(c) (A) is false but (R) is true
(d) (A) is true, but (R) is false

272. In PRECIS, role operator Zero (0) is allocated for (*NET Exam.* 2011D)
(a) Action (b) Object
(c) Agent (d) Location

273. Match the following DDC numbers: (*NET Exam.* 2013J)

List-I	List-II
(A) Education	(i) 770
(B) Medicine	(ii) 370
(C) Photography	(iii) 610
(D) Astronomy	(iv) 520

Codes:	A	B	C	D
(a)	iii	i	iv	ii
(b)	ii	iii	i	iv
(c)	i	iv	iii	ii
(d)	iv	ii	i	iii

274. "Control, Disease, Malaria, Brain" indicates that it is (*NET Exam.* 2013J)
(a) Raw title (b) Expressive title
(c) Kernal title (d) Transformed title

275. **Assertion (A):** Digitization has proved to be possible for every format and medium held by library.

Reason (R): All libraries are making their text and visual collections digitized.

Codes:
(a) (A) is true, but (R) is false
(b) (A) is false, but (R) is true
(c) Both (A) and (R) are true
(d) Both (A) and (R) are false

Read the passage given below, and answer the questions based on your understanding of the passage. (Question Nos. 276-280)
(*NET Exam.* 2011D)

One of the problems with automatic classification techniques is that they normally involve processing the whole collection in response to every request; this is inefficient, because we know in advance that a substantial part of the collection will not be relevant to the request. One of the major objectives of an information retrieval system is to allow the user to discard with the minimum of effort any items not relevant to an enquiry. Classification schemes set out to achieve this by grouping items according to specified characteristics; provided that our specification meets the user's needs, this grouping will be helpful, but if it does not, our organization of information may prove to be a positive hindrance instead of a help. There has been a substantial amount of research into computer techniques which would achieve the same end, by reducing the size of the collection to be searched in response to any given request. The classical Aristotelian definition of classification states that a class consists of a set of objects having a given characteristic in common, possession of that characteristic, being a necessary and sufficient condition for class membership. A document may be described by a number of terms, derived or assigned, and that we expect to retrieve in answer to a request a set of documents which match the request closely but rarely exactly. This arises because the terms used to describe documents fall into a number of classes, and we can never be exhaustive in our characterization. In other words, we hope to retrieve a set of documents which maximizes the match between the query and the description of the classes into which the desired documents fall, without expecting the match to be exact in classical terms. Aristotelian classification assumes a single essential element; documentary classification assumes that related document will share a number of elements, without necessarily having all of those specified in a particular query.

276. One of the problems of automatic classification is that
(a) It does not process the whole collection to answer a query.
(b) It processes the part collection to answer a query.
(c) It processes the whole collection to answer a query.

(d) The substantial part of the processed collection will be relevant.

277. One of the major objectives of an IR system is
(a) To help the user to express their actual need.
(b) To help the user to discard irrelevant items with the minimum effort.
(c) To help the user not to discard irrelevant items with the minimum effort.
(d) To help the user to maximize their effort to locate an irrelevant item.

278. What does the research in computer techniques aim at?
(a) To increase the size of the collection to be searched not in response to any given request.
(b) To increase the size of the collection to be searched in response to any given request.
(c) To reduce the size of the collection to be searched in response to any given request.
(d) To reduce the size of the collection to be searched not in response to any given request.

279. Aristotelian definition of classification states that
(a) No class should have common characteristics.
(b) A class should consist of a set of common terms.
(c) A class should consist of related common characteristics.
(d) A class should consist. of a set of objects having a given characteristic in common.

280. Documentary classification assumes that
(a) A single element is essential.
(b) Related documents will share a number of elements having all those specified in a particular query.
(c) Related documents will share a number of elements, without necessarily having all those specified in a particular query.
(d) Documents should have a number of elements.

281. What kind of arrangement is followed in LISA (*NET Exam.* 2013J)
(a) Alphabetical (b) Chronological
(c) Classified (d) Geographical

282. **Assertion (A):** Gap device is a non-scientific solution to the problem of growing universe.

Reason (R): A classificationist cannot forecast the areas/subjects wherein some new ones may emerge. (*NET Exam.* 2013J)

Codes:
(a) (A) and (R) are true
(b) (A) is true, but (R) is false
(c) (A) is false and (R) is true
(d) Both (A) and (R) are false

283. **Assertion (A):** Colon Classification is popular in online catalogue.

Reason (R): Traditional classification system are used in online searching advantageously. (*NET Exam.* 2013J)

Codes:
(a) (A) is true, but (R) is false
(b) Both (A) and (R) are true, but (R) is not the correct explanation of (A)
(c) (A) is false, but (R) is true
(d) Both (A) and (R) are true

284. The primary differences between knowledge classification and library classification are (*NET Exam.* 2013J)
(i) Knowledge classification arranges knowledge itself.
(ii) Library classification arrange the expression of knowledge in the form of documents.
(iii) Knowledge classification is the basis of library classification.
(iv) Knowledge classification follows system of numbers, called notation.

Codes:
(a) (i) and (ii) are correct
(b) (ii) and (iii) are correct
(c) (i), (ii) and (iv) are correct
(d) (i), (ii) and (iii) are correct

285. What are the four entities of FRBR model? (*NET Exam.* 2013J)
(a) Personality, matter, energy, space
(b) Books, form, availability, type
(c) Work, expression, manifestation, item
(d) Discipline, entity, action, personality

286. **Assertion (A):** Colon Classification is an enumerative classification scheme.

Reason (R): Colon classification has adopted analytic-synthetic approach for the construction of class number. (*NET Exam.* 2012J Paper iii)

Codes:
(a) (A) is false, but (R) is true
(b) (A) is true, but (R) is false
(c) Both (A) and (R) are true
(d) Both (A) and (R) are false

287. When two or more basic subjects having same relational approach form a specific subject, the relation is termed as (*NET Exam.* 2012J Paper iii)
(a) Speciater relation (b) Co-ordinate relation
(c) Phase relation (d) Hierarchical relation

288. Scalar chain shows (*NET Exam.* 2012J)
(a) Authority structure
(b) Scale of performance of staff
(c) Chain for locating racks
(d) A link in the chain

289. Arrange the following according to their year of origin; (*NET Exam.* 2012J)
(i) Broad System of ordering
(ii) Classification in online System
(iii) Automated Keyword Classification
(v) Classification of research Group
Codes:
(a) iv, iii, i, ii (b) i, ii, iv, iii
(c) iii, i, ii, iv (d) ii, iv, iii, ii

290. Match the following (*NET Exam.* 2012J)

List-I	**List-II**
(A) Law of parsimony	(i) Classification
(B) Principles of Osmosis	(ii) F.W. Lancaster
(C) Paperless society	(iii) Overall economy
(D) APUPA pattern	(iv) Reclassification

Codes:	**A**	**B**	**C**	**D**
(a)	ii	i	iv	iii
(b)	iv	ii	i	iii
(c)	iii	iv	ii	i
(d)	i	iii	ii	iv

291. The order of significance of "Thing, Material and Action" among various components of a compound subject was expand by (*NET Exam.* 2012J)
(a) J. Kaiser (b) E.J. Coates
(c) J.R. Sharp (d) J.E.L. Farradane

292. **Assertion (A):** Classification plays a significant role in online retrieval.
Reason (R): Classification played an important role in annual system. (*NET Exam.* 2012J)
Codes:
(a) (A) is true, but (R) is false
(b) Both (A) and (R) are false
(c) Both (A) and (R) are true
(d) (A) is false, but (R) is true

293. In CC '1' is used for Unity, God, World, First in evolution etc. as a (*NET 17J II Paper*)
(a) Seminal mnemonic
(b) Schedule mnemonic
(c) Alphabetical mnemonic
(d) Syntactical mnemonic

294. The number of successive characteristics forming the basis of its derivation from the Universe of Knowledge is known as: (*NET 17J ii paper*)
(a) Order of an array (b) Order of a class
(c) Open array (d) Collateral array

295. What is the third part of colon classification? (*NET 17J iii paper*)
(a) Schedules (b) Rules
(c) Classic and sacred books (d) Index

296. Subject entry which refers from the name of a class to its class number is known as (*NET 17J ii paper*)
(a) Class Index Entry
(b) Consolidated Entry
(c) Cross Reference Entry
(d) Subject Analytical Entry

297. Which of the following are 'Special Auxiliary Subdivisions' of UDC? (*NET 17J ii paper*)
(i) Apostrophe (ii) Sub-grouping
(iii) Colon (iv) Point-naught
Codes:
(a) (i) and (iv) are correct.
(b) (i) and (ii) are correct.
(c) (ii) and (iii) are correct.
(d) (iii) and (iv) are correct

298. Match the following (*NET 13 SEPT iii paper*)

List – I	**List – II**
A. Intra-Facet Relation	i. S:5210t3
B. Intra-Array Phase Relation	ii. Q 20 m4
C. Intra-Facet Phase Relation	iii. SO b2
D. Inter-Subject Phase Relation	iv. X.440j56

Codes:	**A**	**B**	**C**	**D**
(a)	iv	i	ii	iii
(b)	iv	ii	iii	i
(c)	ii	iii	i	iv
(d)	i	iv	iii	ii

299. Arrange in sequence the following subject classes according to their occurrence in the schedules of DDC, 21st Ed. *(NET 17 NOV iii paper)*
(i) Food Technology
(ii) Public Finance
(iii) General Encyclopaedias
(iv) Bibliographies
Codes:
(a) (iv), (ii), (iii), (i) (b) (iv), (iii), (ii), (i)
(c) (iii), (ii), (i), (iv) (d) (iii), (i), (ii), (iv)

300. **Assertion (A):** Traditional Knowledge Resource Classification (TKRC) is an innovative structured classification system useful for the systematic arrangement, dissemination and retrieval of all subjects.
Reason (R): It is structured, based on International Patent Classification. *(NET 17 NOV iii paper)*
Codes:
(a) (A) is true, but (R) is false.
(b) Both (A) and (R) are true.
(c) (A) is false, but (R) is true.
(d) Both (A) and (R) are false.

301. Arrange the following classification schemes according to their chronological sequence: *(NET 16J iii paper)*
i. Subject classification
ii. Expansive classification
iii. Broad system of ordering
iv. Bibliographic classification
Codes:
(a) i, ii, iii and iv (b) ii, i, iv and iii
(c) iii, i, ii and iv (d) iv, iii, ii and i

302. Identify the symbol of 'Spiritual Experience and Mysticism' as given by CC *(NET 17 NOV ii paper)*
(a) Δ (b) Σ (c) 4 (d) MZA

303. Which of the following is indicated in the third digit of DDC Third Summary? *(NET 17 NOV ii paper)*
(a) Schedule (b) Class
(c) Section (d) Division

304. Identify the basic parts of Colon Classification *(NET 17 NOV ii paper)*
(i) Rules
(ii) Schedule of classification
(iii) Schedule of classics and sacred books
(iv) Geographical schedule
Codes:
(a) (i), (ii) and (iv) are correct
(b) (i), (ii) and (iii) are correct
(c) (ii), (iii) and (iv) are correct
(d) (i), (iii) and (iv) are correct

305. Which of the following are the Canons for characteristics as enunciated by S.R. Ranganathan? *(NET 17 NOV ii paper)*
(i) Canon of relevance
(ii) Canon of Permanance
(iii) Canon of differentiation
(iv) Canon of Interpetation in Chain
Codes:
(a) (ii), (iii), (iv) are correct
(b) (i), (ii), (iii) are correct
(c) (i), (iii), (iv) are correct
(d) (i), (ii), (iv) are correct

306. Match the fundamental categories with corresponding examples: *(NET 17 NOV ii paper)*

List – I	List – II
(a) Asia	(1) Matter
(b) Book Selection	(2) Personality
(c) Microfilms	(3) Energy
(d) University Libraries	(4) Space

Codes:	(A)	(B)	(C)	(D)
(a)	(4)	(3)	(1)	(2)
(b)	(3)	(2)	(4)	(1)
(c)	(2)	(3)	(1)	(4)
(d)	(1)	(4)	(2)	(3)

307. Match the following ACI symbols (CC 6th edition) with their corresponding Isolates *(NET 17 NOV ii paper)*

List – I	List - II
(A) p	(1) Conference
(B) k	(2) Encyclopedia
(C) w	(3) Biography
(D) n	(4) Serials

Codes:	(A)	(B)	(C)	(D)
(a)	(2)	(4)	(3)	(1)
(b)	(1)	(2)	(3)	(4)
(c)	(2)	(1)	(3)	(4)
(d)	(4)	(3)	(2)	(1)

308. **Assertion (A):** Science rests itself upon a series of postulates or assumptions which are themselves fundamentally unproved and unprovable.
Reason (R): One can only assert that these postulates are true, can believe them, but

cannot prove them as they deal with the validity of human knowledge.

(*NET 17 NOV ii paper*)

Codes:

(a) (A) is true, but (R) is false.
(b) (A) is false, but (R) is true.
(c) Both (A) and (R) are true.
(d) Both (A) and (R) are false.

309. In Ranganathan's terminology 'Latent Facet' is a (*NET 16J ii paper*)
(a) Facet added at the end
(b) Hidden Facet
(c) Important Facet
(d) Current of all Facets

310. Identify the correct statements associated with Universal Decimal Classification Scheme (UDC) (*NET 16J ii paper*)
i. It is faceted classification scheme.
ii. Paul Otlet and Henry La Fontaine are associated with it.
iii. It has relative index.
iv. It uses pure notation.
Codes:
(a) i, ii are correct. (b) ii, iii are correct.
(c) iii, iv are correct. (d) i, iv are correct.

311. PMEST in colon classification of S.R. Ranganathan is (*NET 16J ii paper*)
i. Decreasing order of concreteness
ii. Decreasing order of association
iii. Decreasing order of classification
iv. Decreasing order of fundamental categories
(a) i, ii are correct (b) i, iv are correct
(c) i, iii are correct (d) ii, iv are correct

312. Match the following: (*NET 16J ii paper*)

List – I	**List – II**
A. Subject Classification	1. J. Aitchison
B. Thesaurofacet	2. S.R. Ranganathan
C. Classaurus	3. J.D. Brown
D. APUPA	4. G. Bhattacharya

Codes:	**A**	**B**	**C**	**D**
(a)	4	3	2	1
(b)	1	2	3	4
(c)	3	1	4	2
(d)	2	4	1	3

313. **Assertion (A):** Chain procedure is a systematic and almost mechanical method of deriving subject headings.
Reason (R): It does not always operate well only with a faceted scheme of classification.
Codes:
(a) (A) is true, but (R) is false.
(b) (A) is false, but (R) is true.
(c) Both (A) and (R) are false.
(d) Both (A) and (R) are true.

314. The term 'Partial Comprehension' in the Theory of Classification is known as (*NET 15J iii paper*)
(a) Denudation (b) Fission
(c) Lamination (d) Agglomeration kind-I

315. Which of the following are the salient features of UDC-IME? (*NET 15J ii paper*)
(i) Minimum three digits in a class number
(ii) Main Class 4 is vacant
(iii) Notation is independent of any Language or scripts
(iv) More suitable to micro-documents
Codes:
(a) (i), (ii) and (iii) are correct.
(b) (i), (ii) and (iv) are correct.
(c) (ii), (iii) and (iv) are correct.
(d) (i), (iii) and iv) are correct.

316. **Assertion (A):** To increase the specificity, we need to accept long notations.
Reason (R): An important quality of notation is brevity. (*NET 14D ii paper*)
Codes:
(a) Both (A) and (R) are true and (R) is the correct explanation of (A).
(b) (A) is false, but (R) is true.
(c) (A) is true, but (R) is false.
(d) Both (A) and (R) are true, but (R) is not the correct explanation of (A).

317. What is intercalation in UDC? (*NET 15D iii paper*)
(a) Prefix of auxiliary (b) Suffix of auxiliary
(c) Infix of auxiliary (d) Super-impose

318. The first order of division of classes in DDC is based on (*NET 15D iii paper*)
(a) Jewett's system of classification
(b) System of Paris Book Sellers
(c) The Fixed Location System
(d) Francis Bacon's three fountains of learning

319. Which of the following are the synthetic features of 'Dewey Decimal classification'? (*NET 15D iii paper*)

(i) Relative Index (ii) Enumeration of Schedules
(iii) Tables (iv) Add to Instruction

Codes:
(a) (i) and (ii) are correct
(b) (ii) and (iii) are correct
(c) (iii) and (iv) are correct
(d) (i), (iii) and (iv) are correct

320. Which of the following are the Special Auxiliaries of Universal Decimal Classification (Medium Edition 1993)? *(NET 15D iii paper)*
(i) Point of view .00
(ii) Materials -03
(iii) Point-not series .0/.9
(iv) Hyphen series -1/-9

Codes:
(a) (i) and (iv) are correct
(b) (i) and (iii) are correct
(c) (iii) and (iv) are correct
(d) (ii) and (iv) are correct

321. According to S.R. Ranganathan the steps in classifying documents include the following analysis of the title. Arrange the steps in the sequential order: *(NET 15D iii paper)*
(i) Expressive title (ii) Kernel title
(iii) Analysed title (iv) Transformed title

Codes:
(a) (i), (ii), (iii) and (iv)
(b) (ii), (iii), (iv) and (i)
(c) (iii), (iv), (i) and (ii)
(d) (iv), (i), (ii) and (iii)

322. **Assertion (A):** An example for an array of geographical divisions can be Asia, India, Bihar, Patna.

Reason (R): An Array is a series of coordinate sub-divisions which are obtained by dividing a class or division according to a single characteristics.

Codes:
(a) Both (A) and (R) are true.
(b) Both (A) and (R) are false.
(c) (A) is true but (R) is false.
(d) (A) is false but (R) is true.

323. In colon classification which indicator has been used for indicating interpolation? *(NET 13D ii paper)*
(a) Comma (b) Hyphen
(c) Asterisk (d) Ampersand

324. In colon classification, which mnemonic is displayed in the use of digit '4' as for pathology, disease, transport, hybrid etc.? *(NET 13D iii paper)*
(a) Seminal (b) Systematic
(c) Scheduled (d) Alphabetical

325. **Assertion (A):** The hierarchy based classification schemes have a major role in the organization of the web.

Reason (R): The 'hotlists' retrieved by robots based search engines use the technique of relevance of subject descriptors. *(NET 13D iii paper)*

Codes:
(a) (A) is true, but (R) is false.
(b) (A) is false, but (R) is true.
(c) Both (A) and (R) are correct.
(d) Both (A) and (R) are wrong.

326. In which scheme of classification, special auxiliaries denote locally recurrent characteristics? *(NET 14J ii paper)*
(a) Dewey Decimal Classification
(b) Universal Decimal Classification
(c) Bibliographic Classification
(d) Colon Classification

327. **Assertion (A):** All classification schemes adopt 'phase relations'.

Reason (R): Subject formation by loose assemblage leads to complex subjects and isolates. *(NET 14J ii paper)*

Codes:
(a) (A) is true, but (R) is false.
(b) Both (A) and (R) are true.
(c) Both (A) and (R) are false.
(d) (A) is false, but (R) is true.

328. Match the following: *(NET 16J ii paper)*

List – I (AACR-II)
A. The size of the document
B. Statement of Responsibility
C. Between place and the name of the publishers
D. Accompanying material

List – II (Connecting Symbols)
1. Colon 2. Plus
3. Semicolon 4. Diagonal slash

Codes:	A	B	C	D
(a)	1	3	4	2
(b)	2	4	3	1

(c)	4	3	1	2
(d)	3	4	1	2

329. 'Cannon of Reticence' is a canon for: *(NET 17 NOV ii paper)*
   (a) Idea Plane
   (b) Verbal Plane
   (c) Notational Plane
   (d) Both Idea and Notational Planes

330. Which of the following does not belong to the set of canons for the characteristics? *(NET 14D iii paper)*
   (a) Canon of Differentiation
   (b) Canon of Ascertainability
   (c) Canon of Currency
   (d) Canon of Relevance

331. Seymour Lubetzky and Mary Piggot are associated with which of the following? *(NET 14D iii paper)*
   (a) Classification (b) Cataloguing
   (c) Indexing (d) Management

332. **Assertion (A):** The objective of "Cross Ref" is to improve access to published scholarly works through collaborative technologies.
   Reason (R): "Cross Ref" is a non-profit membership association founded and directed by publishers. *(NET 14D iii paper)*
   Codes:
   (a) Both (A) and (R) are true.
   (b) Both (A) and (R) are true, but (R) is not the correct explanation.
   (c) (A) is true, but (R) is false.
   (d) (A) is false, but (R) is true.

333. Hierarchical relationship among concepts indicates *(NET 14D iii paper)*
   i. Genus-species relationship
   ii. Equivalence relationship
   iii. Whole-part relationship
   iv. Associate relationship
   Codes:
   (a) ii and iv are correct.
   (b) iii and ii are correct.
   (c) i and iii are correct.
   (d) iv and i are correct.

334. The 'Principle of Facet Sequence' includes *(NET 14D iii paper)*
   i. Cow-calf principle
   ii. Wall-picture principle
   iii. Whole organ principle
   iv. Principle of osmosis
   Codes:
   (a) i, ii and iv are correct.
   (b) i, ii and iii are correct.
   (c) i, iii and iv are correct.
   (d) ii and iv are correct.

335. Arrange the following in correct classified order as per C.C. *(NET 14D iii paper)*
   i. A ii. 2:5 iii. 2a iv. 234
   Codes:
   (a) iii, i, iv, ii (b) i, iii, ii, iv
   (c) iii, ii, iv, i (d) ii, i, iii, iv

336. Arrange the sequence of the following steps followed in classifying a document according to colon classification: *(NET 14D iii paper)*
   i. Title with standard facet terms
   ii. Analyzed title
   iii. Kernel title
   iv. Transformed title
   Codes:
   (a) ii, iv, i, iii (b) i, ii, iii, iv
   (c) iii, ii, iv, i (d) iv, iii, ii, i

337. According to S.R. Ranganathan the canons for chain are *(NET 17J iii paper)*
   (a) Canon of Ascertainability
   (b) Canon of Recall Value
   (c) Canon of array and filitary sequence
   (d) Canon of decreasing extension and modulation

338. In Colon Classification (6th edition) 'LB' denotes *(NET 17J iii paper)*
   (a) Special (b) System
   (c) Canonical Class (d) Rounds

339. Arrange the following class numbers according to Colon Classification, 6th edition *(NET 17J iii paper)*
   (i) 2 (ii) 2 Ob T (iii) 2 ´N (iv) 2k
   Codes:
   (a) (iv), (i), (ii) and (iii)
   (b) (i), (ii), (iv) and (iii)
   (c) (ii), (i), (iii) and (iv)
   (d) (iii), (ii), (i) and (iv)

340. Match the following symbols/signs used in UDC standard edition: *(NET 17J iii paper)*

Signs/Symbols	**Meaning**
(A) → → Double arrow	(1) Examples of combination
(B) □ Diamond	(2) Including
(C) ~ Square	(3) See also

(D) – Approximately equal to (4) subdivide as

Codes:	(A)	(B)	(C)	(D)
(a)	(3)	(1)	(2)	(4)
(b)	(1)	(2)	(3)	(4)
(c)	(2)	(1)	(4)	(3)
(d)	(4)	(3)	(2)	(1)

341. Which of the following are 'Special Auxiliary Subdivisions' of UDC? *(NET 17J ii paper)*
(i) Apostrophe (ii) Sub-grouping
(iii) Colon (iv) Point-naught
Codes:
(a) (i) and (iv) are correct.
(b) (i) and (ii) are correct.
(c) (ii) and (iii) are correct.
(d) (iii) and (iv) are correct.

342. Who has been referred as 'First Grammarian of library classification'? *(NET 16J iii paper)*
(a) S.R. Ranganathan (b) E.W. Hulme
(c) Melvil Dewey (d) W.C.B. Sayers

343. Match the following: *(NET 15D ii paper)*

List-I	List-II
(A) Rules for Dictionary Catalogue	(1) S.R. Ranganathan
(B) PMEST	(2) Kaiser
(C) Systematic Indexing	(3) Cutter
(D) Nested Phrase Indexing System	(4) T.C. Carven

Codes:	(A)	(B)	(C)	(D)
(a)	(3)	(1)	(2)	(4)
(b)	(3)	(1)	(4)	(2)
(c)	(2)	(1)	(3)	(4)
(d)	(1)	(3)	(2)	(4)

344. Match the following *(NET 15D ii paper)*
List-I
(A) Nadir to Ascendant
(B) Ascendant to Zenith
(C) Zenith to Descendant
(D) Descendant to Nadir
List-II
(1) Verification phase (2) Deductive phase
(3) Hypothesising phase (4) Empirical phase

Codes:	(A)	(B)	(C)	(D)
(a)	(3)	(2)	(1)	(4)
(b)	(4)	(3)	(2)	(1)
(c)	(2)	(1)	(4)	(3)
(d)	(1)	(4)	(3)	(2)

345. Who among the following devised the 'Critical Path Method'? *(NET 17J iii paper)*
(i) Morgan R. Walker (ii) Clank Sedore
(iii) Blake William (iv) James E. Kelley
Codes:
(a) (i) and (ii) are correct.
(b) (i) and (iv) are correct.
(c) (ii) and (iii) are correct.
(d) (iii) and (iv) are correct.

346. Match the following. *(NET 13D iii paper)*

List – I	List – II
A. FRBR	1. Paul Otlet
B. POPSI	2. IFLA
C. UDC	3. G. Bhattacharya
D. www	4. Tim Berners-Lee

Codes	A	B	C	D
(a)	2	1	3	4
(b)	2	3	1	4
(c)	2	4	1	3
(d)	4	2	3	1

347. **Assertion (A):** UDC is more suitable for special libraries compared to DDC scheme of classification.

Reason (R): UDC can better accommodate new complex subjects compared to DDC. *(NET 15D iii paper)*

Codes:
(a) Both (A) and (R) are true.
(b) Both (A) and (R) are false.
(c) (A) is true but (R) is false.
(d) (A) is false but (R) is true.

348. **Assertion (A):** In DDC only 'Add to' device provides an opportunity to expand a given number.

Reason (R): DDC is a purely enumerative scheme of classification without synthetic features. *(NET 15D iii paper)*

Codes:
(a) (A) is false, but (R) is true.
(b) (A) is true and (R) is false.
(c) Both (A) and (R) are true.
(d) Both (A) and (R) are false.

349. Arrange the following connecting symbols of CC-6th ed. according to their increasing ordinal value: *(NET 17 NOV iii paper)*
(i)) (arrester) (ii) ← (backward arrow)
(iii) → (forward arrow) (iv) 0 (zero)
Codes:
(a) (i), (iii), (iv), (i) (b) (i), (ii), (iii), (iv)
(c) (iii), (iv), (ii), (i) (d) (iv), (i), (iii), (ii)

350. 'Cannon of Reticence' is a canon for: *(NET 17 NOV II paper)*
(a) Idea Plane
(b) Verbal Plane
(c) Notational Plane
(d) Both Idea and Notational Planes

351. What will be the correct filling order of the following documents classified according to Colon Classification (6th. Reprint edition) *(NET 18J)*
(i) 23.44 Academic library system in India
(ii) 23;43:51.44 Classification of books in academic libraries in India
(iii) 23:62 Lending services in academic libraries
(iv) 23n4451,N82 Journal of academic libraries (Published from New Delhi since 1982)
Codes:
(a) ii, iii, i, iv (b) iv, ii, iii, i
(c) ii, iii, iv, i (d) iv, i, iii, ii

352. Match the following titles with their class numbers according to CC 6th. Edition. *(NET 18J)*

List-I	List-II
(A) Smallpox	(i) L293:46
(B) Fever	(ii) L:414
(C) Diabetics	(iii) L35:4261
(D) Malaria	(iv) L:4231

Codes:	(A)	(B)	(C)	(D)
(a)	(i)	(iv)	(ii)	(iii)
(b)	(iv)	(ii)	(i)	(iii)
(c)	(ii)	(iii)	(i)	(iv)
(d)	(iii)	(iv)	(i)	(ii)

353. **Assertion (A):** principle of canonical sequence is mainly followed to arrange the array of subjects in classification scheme.
Reason (R): This principle sets the proviso that when subjects in an array of subjects are traditionally referred to in a specific sequence, it will be convenient of conform to this traditional sequence. *(NET 18J)*
Codes:
(a) Both (A) and (R) are true
(b) (A) is false, but (R) is true
(c) Both (A) and (R) are false
(d) (A) is true but (R) is false

354. Match the following number of Anteriorising common isolate (Applicable before space fact) of colon classification (6th. Reprint edition) with their correct terms *(NET 18J)*

List-I (Number)	List-II (Term)
(A) Y1	(i) Synopsis
(B) Y3	(ii) Case Study
(C) Y7	(iii) Digest
(D) Y8	(iv) Program of instruction

Codes:	(A)	(B)	(C)	(D)
(a)	(iv)	(i)	(ii)	(iii)
(b)	(iv)	(ii)	(iii)	(i)
(c)	(i)	(ii)	(iv)	(iii)
(d)	(i)	(ii)	(iii)	(iv)

355. Find out the correct sequence of the following forms of Main Class Literature according to Colon Classification (sixth reprint edition) *(NET 18J)*
(a) Poetry, Fiction, Campu, Oration
(b) Poetry, Fiction, Oration, Campu
(c) Poetry, Oration, Fiction, Campu
(d) Fiction, Poetry, Campu, Oration

356. According to Ranganathan classified catalogue code (5th edition), in which among the following cases the initial article to be omitted? *(NET 18J)*
(i) In rendering the name of conference
(ii) In rendering the name of government
(iii) In rendering the name of series
(iv) In rendering the name of an institution
Codes:
(a) i and ii are correct
(b) ii and iv are correct
(c) i, iii and iv are correct
(d) ii, iii and iv are correct

357. Match the following MARC fields with their corresponding descriptions: *(NET 18J)*

List-I	List-II
(A) 020	(i) Electronic Location and Access
(B) 250	(ii) Edition Statement
(C) 440	(iii) Series
(D) 856	(iv) ISBN

Codes:	(A)	(B)	(C)	(D)
(a)	(i)	(ii)	(iii)	(iv)
(b)	(iv)	(ii)	(iii)	(i)
(c)	(iv)	(iii)	(ii)	(ii)
(d)	(ii)	(i)	(iv)	(iii)

358. Arrange the following laws of Library Science enunciated by S R Ranganathan in a sequence as recorded by L S Connaway and I M Faniel for OCLC project *(NET 18J)*

(i) Library as a growing organism
(ii) Save the time of the readers
(iii) Book are for use
(iv) Every book its reader

Codes:
(a) (ii), (iii), (iv), (i) (b) (iii), (iv), (i), (ii)
(c) (i), (ii), (iii), (iv) (d) (iii), (i), (ii), (iii)

ANSWER SHEET

1. (b)	2. (c)	3. (c)	4. (a)	5. (a)	6. (b)	7. (a)	8. (b)	9. (c)
10. (a)	11. (a)	12. (d)	13. (b)	14. (c)	15. (b)	16. (d)	17. (a)	18. (d)
19. (d)	20. (c)	21. (b)	22. (a)	23. (d)	24. (a)	25. (d)	26. (c)	27. (c)
28. (b)	29. (b)	30. (d)	31. (a)	32. (b)	33. (c)	34. (a)	35. (a)	36. (c)
37. (a)	38. (b)	39. (a)	40. (b)	41. (d)	42. (d)	43. (a)	44. (d)	45. (d)
46. (d)	47. (a)	48. (c)	49. (c)	50. (a)	51. (a)	52. (d)	53. (c)	54. (c)
55. (a)	56. (a)	57. (b)	58. (d)	59. (b)	60. (b)	61. (b)	62. (c)	63. (c)
64. (c)	65. (a)	66. (c)	67. (a)	68. (b)	69. (c)	70. (b)	71. (c)	72. (c)
73. (a)	74. (a)	75. (b)	76. (b)	77. (c)	78. (c)	79. (a)	80. (c)	81. (c)
82. (b)	83. (c)	84. (a)	85. (b)	86. (a)	87. (c)	88. (b)	89. (a)	90. (b)
91. (c)	92. (b)	93. (d)	94. (d)	95. (c)	96. (c)	97. (a)	98. (d)	99. (b)
100. (c)	101. (b)	102. (b)	103. (b)	104. (b)	105. (c)	106. (c)	107. (a)	108. (c)
109. (a)	110. (a)	111. (a)	112. (c)	113. (a)	114. (b)	115. (a)	116. (d)	117. (c)
118. (a)	119. (d)	120. (a)	121. (d)	122. (a)	123. (a)	124. (a)	125. (a)	126. (d)
127. (a)	128. (d)	129. (b)	130. (a)	131. (d)	132. (a)	133. (d)	134. (a)	135. (b)
136. (c)	137. (b)	138. (c)	139. (b)	140. (a)	141. (b)	142. (c)	143. (a)	144. (d)
145. (d)	146. (a)	147. (b)	148. (c)	149. (a)	150. (d)	151. (b)	152. (d)	153. (b)
154. (c)	155. (d)	156. (c)	157. (b)	158. (a)	159. (c)	160. (c)	161. (a)	162. (b)
163. (b)	164. (a)	165. (c)	166. (c)	167. (d)	168. (a)	169. (c)	170. (c)	171. (a)
172. (a)	173. (b)	174. (a)	175. (b)	176. (c)	177. (a)	178. (d)	179. (b)	180. (d)
181. (d)	182. (c)	183. (d)	184. (d)	185. (a)	186. (b)	187. (a)	188. (a)	189. (b)
190. (a)	191. (a)	192. (d)	193. (a)	194. (a)	195. (a)	196. (a)	197. (d)	198. (b)
199. (c)	200. (b)	201. (a)	202. (d)	203. (b)	204. (a)	205. (b)	206. (b)	207. (d)
208. (a)	209. (b)	210. (d)	211. (a)	212. (d)	213. (b)	214. (c)	215. (b)	216. (d)
217. (d)	218. (a)	219. (b)	220. (d)	221. (d)	222. (a)	223. (d)	224. (b)	225. (c)
226. (d)	227. (d)	228. (b)	229. (c)	230. (c)	231. (c)	232. (b)	233. (c)	234. (d)
235. (c)	236. (c)	237. (a)	238. (a)	239. (b)	240. (a)	241. (c)	242. (a)	243. (a)
244. (c)	245. (c)	246. (c)	247. (c)	248. (d)	249. (b)	250. (d)	251. (b)	252. (c)
253. (a)	254. (a)	255. (d)	256. (b)	257. (a)	258. (b)	259. (b)	260. (c)	261. (b)
262. (a)	263. (a)	264. (a)	265. (b)	266. (a)	267. (d)	268. (a)	269. (c)	270. (a)
271. (b)	272. (a)	273. (b)	274. (c)	275. (a)	276. (c)	277. (b)	278. (c)	279. (d)
280. (c)	281. (c)	282. (a)	283. (c)	284. (d)	285. (c)	286. (a)	287. (c)	288. (a)
289. (a)	290. (c)	291. (b)	292. (d)	293.(a)	294. (b)	295. (c)	296. (a)	297. (a)
298. (a)	299. (b)	300. (c)	301. (b)	302. (a)	303.(c)	304.(b)	305.(b)	306. (a)
307. (b)	308. (c)	309. (b)	310. (a)	311. (b)	312. (c)	313. (a)	314. (d)	315. (c)
316. (d)	317. (c)	318. (d)	319. (c)	320. (c)	321. (a)	322. (d)	323. (c)	324. (a)
325. (a)	326. (b)	327. (d)	328. (d)	329. (b)	330. (c)	331. (b)	332. (a)	333. (c)
334. (b)	335. (c)	336. (c)	337. (d)	338. (b)	339. (a)	340. (a)	341. (a)	342. (d)
343. (a)	344. (b)	345. (b)	346. (b)	347. (a)	348. (b)	349. (b)	350. (b)	351. (d)
352. (b)	353. (a)	354. (a)	355. (b)	356. (c)	357. (b)	358. (a)		

Chapter 7
Information Science and Research Methodology

SUBJECTIVE QUESTIONS

Q. 1. Write the four different phases through which the SDI system function.

Ans. (a) Modification (b) Feedback
(c) Notification (d) Selection

Q. 2. Write three prominent and different types of output units of a computer system?

Ans. (a) COM (Computer Output Microfilm)
(b) VDT (Visual Display Terminal)
(c) Line Printers/Letter Quality Printer.

Q. 3. Write the name of journal that publishes synopses of Ph.D. those accepted by the Indian Universities in Social Science.

Ans. *ICSSR Journal of Indian Dissertation Abstracts* since 1973.

Q. 4. Write the name of person responsible for development of POPSI in India?

Ans. Prof. G. Bhattacharya.

Q. 5. Write the alternative name for post co-ordinate index.

Ans. Manipulative index.

Q. 6. Write the different categories into which books could be divided according to S.R. Ranganathan.

Ans. Conventional, neo-conventional, non-conventional and meta documents.

Q. 7. Write the five conventional methods used for conducting information need surveys.

Ans. Questionnaire method; Interview method; Diary method; Observation by self-method and Operation research study.

Q. 8. Who invented the term 'Informatics'?

Ans. Mikhailov, Cherny and Gilyarevaskii.

Q. 9. Write the alternative names from the current awareness list.

Ans. 'Title-Announcement service or a Title-journal.'

Q. 10. Write the name of the places where the regional Centres of National Social Science Documentation Centre (NASSDOC), New Delhi is setup.

Ans. Hyderabad, Mumbai, New Delhi, Shillong, Kolkata and Chandigarh.

Q. 11. What is the document storage system of SENDOC called?

Ans. T R A I L S
T stands for trade literature.
R stands for report literature.
A stands for area literature.
I stands for institutional literature.
L stands for library literature.
S stands for secondary literature.

Q. 12. When was the first issue of 'Asian Recorder' came out?

Ans. January 1955.

Q. 13. Write the name of four important sectoral information centres of NISSAT setup in India.

Ans. (1) National Information Centre for Machine Tool and Allied Products (at CMTI, Bangalore).
(2) National Information Centre for Food Science and Technology (at CFTRI, Mysore).
(3) National Information Centre in Leather and Allied Industries (at CLRI, Chennai).
(4) National Information Centre for Drug and Pharmaceuticals (at CDRI, Lucknow).

Q. 14. What is LUCI? Explain it.

Ans. Logical Unit-based Cyclic Index. It is a different vision of chain indexing system.

Q. 15. Name the largest thesaurus published so far what part does it contains?

Ans. Thesaurus of Engineering and Scientific Terms (TEST), first published in 1967—Alphabetical part, Hierarchical index, Permuted index and subject category index.

Q. 16. Write the name of organisation in India that has been acting as the national input Centre for AGRIS system.

Ans. Indian Council of Agricultural Research (ICAR).

Q. 17. Write the name of the computer-based data bank having a complete control over the world periodical publications.

Ans. International Serials Data System (ISDS).

Q. 18. In which country the idea of Standard Book Number (SBN) was developed and when?

Ans. In Great Britain, in 1967.

Q. 19. Write the name of two periodical publications brought out by the Russian Science Information Centre of INSDOC.

Ans. Contents List of Soviet Scientific Periodicals (monthly). Russian Scientific and Technical Publication: An Accession List (bi-monthly).

Q. 20. Write the name of originator of Science Citation Index (SCI).

Ans. Eugene Garfield.

Q. 21. Give periodicity of science citation index year of first publication and its important parts.

Ans. Quarterly—first publication in 1964. Citation Index, Source Index and Permuted Subject Index.

Q. 22. Write the name of current source of information to know about the latest theses accepted by the Indian universities.

Ans. *University News* (weekly published by AIU) special number of *Indian Dissertation Abstracts* (Quarterly).

Q. 23. Write the name of two indirect methods of conducting information need surveys.

Ans. Analysis of library record and the citation analysis.

Q. 24. Write the full expansion of KWIC. And who developed it?

Ans. Key Word In Context. It is developed by H.P. Luhn.

Q. 25. Write the name of four types of information requirements of a user in the field of information science.

Ans. (a) Current approach
(b) Everyday approach
(c) Exhaustive approach
(d) Catching up approach

Q. 26. Write the name of popular magazine brought out by DESIDOC twice in year.

Ans. *Popular Science and Technology.*

Q. 27. Write the name of organisation in U.K. that is maintaining the Commonwealth Index of Unpublished Translations.

Ans. ASLIB.

Q. 28. Who devised the Zato system of Post Co-ordinate Indexing?

Ans. Calvin Mooers.

Q. 29. According to Ranganathan call "review of progress" related to a particular field by different name. What is it?

Ans. Narrative bibliography.

Q. 30. Write the name of two international agencies that jointly worked at beginning for the establishment of UNISIST a world science information system.

Ans. UNESCO and ICSU (International Council of Scientific Unions).

Q. 31. Who invented the term 'Information Retrieval'? And when?

Ans. Calvin Mooers, in 1950.

Q. 32. Write the name of institute in India that provides technical and other related information service for person interested in starting small-scale industries.

Ans. Small Enterprises National Documentation Centre (SENDOC), Hyderabad.

Q. 33. What is the Soviet equivalent of the term 'Information Science' uses the USA?

Ans. Informatics.

Q. 34. Write the name of three factors involved in the preparation of documentation list.

Ans. Coverage of literature, case of approach and speed.

Q. 35. Write the name of four important personalities that have made lasting contribution to the indexing theory and practice.

Ans. J. Kaiser, J.E.L. Faradizes, E.J. Coats and S.R. Ranganathan.

Q. 36. Write the year that was designated as the Information Technology Year.

Ans. 1972.

Q. 37. When was NISSAT established and what is the full name of NISSAT?

Ans. On 13 May 1977. Full form is National Information System for Science and Technology.

Q. 38. What do you mean by the term 'Sensitive Paper'?

Ans. A type of paper, which is treated with lights sensitive chemical for photographic purpose.

Q. 39. Define the Data.

Ans. The term 'Data' (plural form of datum but by usage construed as singular) refers to an individual fact, statistics or a piece of information or a group or a body of facts, statistics or the like.

Q. 40. Write the three categories of documents with their different types.

Ans. **Primary Sources:** A source will be considered as a primary source in case it carries newly generated information, original work of research, or new interpretation of already known facts. The document is the first and often the only published record of original research. The information contained in primary sources is generally scattered and unorganised. Take for example, the case of swine flu, a new disease for human beings. Ever since the first case was reported in Mexico in April 2009, a lot of research work is going on in the world to find out a vaccine to contain it, medicines to cure those who are already affected, etc. The literature on this is being published in the world in hundreds of sources and scores of languages. Hence, it is highly scattered and unorganised. Another fact is that literature that appears in the primary sources takes time to get assimilated in the universe of knowledge, since results of experiments are double-checked, all findings, new explanations; new ideas, etc. are deliberated upon by peers. When their opinion is favourable, then only these find a chance to enter into the universe of knowledge

Secondary Sources: A source which is more or less completely dependent on primary sources for its existence is a secondary source. Information in secondary sources is organised and arranged according to a definite plan. Indexing and abstracting periodicals are one of the examples of secondary sources. Indexing periodical, indexes the contents of periodicals or some other type of publications usually on regular basis, whereas abstracting periodical along with the contents also gives the abstract. The abstract can be indicative or informative. Indexing and abstracting periodicals may be either general in nature or on a specific theme. In any abstracting and indexing periodical you will notice that articles of the same topic have all been put together, and of related topics close by. They are no more scattered. Even if the articles are in different languages you will find the abstracts in the same language. In a way it is overcoming the language barrier. As the bibliographical details of the primary sources are usually given in the secondary sources, these sources act as a key to primary sources. In a review article, also a secondary source, the entire information on a particular topic for a certain period is first collected, then digested and finally a report is written wherein the entire matter is organised coherently. Here the entire phenomenon of scattering is done away with and the whole matter gets well-organised.

Tertiary Sources: A source that is entirely dependent on secondary sources or primary and secondary sources for its existence is a tertiary source. Sources like 'guides to reference sources' and 'bibliography of bibliographies' are examples of tertiary sources. These sources act as key to primary sources as well as secondary sources. Some authors have considered directories, yearbooks, etc. also as tertiary sources as they help the searcher in using primary and secondary sources.

There are sources, like directory of on-going research projects, which are placed under tertiary sources. For such publications data is directly gathered from scientists (primary sources), as such they deserve to be placed under primary sources. Why such publications have been placed under tertiary sources is not quite clear.

Primary Sources

- Periodicals (solely devoted to report original work)
- Research Reports
- Conference Proceedings
- Reports of Scientific Expeditions
- Official Publications
- Patents
- Standards
- Trade Literature
- Theses and Dissertations
- Laboratory Notebooks
- Diaries
- Memoranda
- Internal Research Reports
- Minutes of Meetings
- Company Files
- Correspondence
- Personal Files, etc.

Secondary Sources

- Periodicals (non-primary) – Abstracting Services – Indexing Services – Reviews of Progress
- Reference Books, e.g., – Encyclopaedias – Dictionaries – Handbooks – Tables – Formularies
- Treatises
- Monographs, and
- Textbooks

Tertiary Sources

- Yearbooks
- Directories

Bibliographies (List of Books, Location Lists of Periodicals, Lists of Indexing and Abstracting Services)

- Guides to 'The Literature'
- Lists of Research in Progress
- Guides to Sources of Information
- Guides to Libraries
- Guides to Organisations

Q. 41. Define the Primary documents, Secondary documents and Tertiary documents.

Ans. Primary information is newly generated information, and therefore, the documents, which record and disseminate it are called primary documents.

Secondary information is derived from primary information and the documents in which they are recorded are known as secondary document.

Tertiary documents are those that record information about secondary documents.

Q. 42. How many types of information service?

Ans. The eight types of information services are:

(a) Reference service
(b) Current Awareness Service (CAS)
(c) Selective Dissemination of Information Service (SDI)
(d) Literature Searching service
(e) Indexing and Abstracting service
(f) Reprography service
(g) Document Delivery service
(h) Translation service

Q. 43. How many types of bibliographical services?

Ans. There are basically four types of bibliographical services:

(a) Current Awareness Service (CAS).
(b) Selective Dissemination of Information (SDI).
(c) Indexing and Abstracting Service.
(d) Literature Searching Service.

Q. 44. How many types of Documentation and Information Centres?

Ans. The three types of Documentation and Information Centres are:

(a) By ownership
(b) By specialised interest.
(c) By levels, i.e. those institutions that operate at the global, regional, national, or local levels.

Q. 45. How many types of functional phases of SDI system?

Ans. The four types of functional phase of SDI are:
(a) Selection (b) Notification
(c) Feedback (d) Modification

Q. 46. Define the Referral Centre.

Ans. An organisation for directing researchers for information and data to appropriate sources such as libraries, information evaluation centres documents, and documentation centres and individuals. A referral centre does not supply data or documents.

Q. 47. Write some names of the famous consultancy organisation in India.

Ans. Some of the famous consultancy organisations in India are:
(i) Water & Power Consultancy Service (India) Ltd.
(ii) Tata Consultancy Service.
(iii) Engineers India Ltd.
(iv) Tata Consultancy Engineers.
(v) M.M. Suri and Associates.
(vi) M.N. Dastur and Co. Pvt. Ltd.
(vii) National Industrial Development Corp. Ltd.
(viii) Fact Engineering and Design Organisation.

Q. 48. Define Trade Catalogue.

Ans. It is an inventory describing the products, which a firm produce or deals in.

Q. 49. Write the names of some organisations who are involved in the translation activities in India.

Ans. (i) The National Council of Educational Research and Training (NCERT) and National Book Trust, are both engaged in translation of textbooks into various Indian languages.
(ii) State Council of Educational Research and Training, performs translations into bilingual form, from English to the state language of vice-versa.
(iii) The Indian Council of Cultural Relation, Delhi does literary translations to projects Indian culture and Indian national personalities and leaders.
(iv) The Central Hindi Directorate, Hindi Akademi and Sahitya Akademi do translation work.
(v) The Central Institute of English and Foreign Languages, Hyderabad, and the Institute of Asian Studies, Chennai perform translation activities.

OBJECTIVE QUESTIONS

1. UNESCO information programme is known as (*NET Exam.* 2000)
(a) NATIS (b) GIP (c) UAP (d) UBC

2. SENDOC is the national documentation centre for (*NET Exam.* 2000)
(a) Science and Environment
(b) Sociology and Economic
(c) Sri Lanka
(d) Small Scale Enterprises

3. The following is not an example of re-packaging of information. (*NET Exam.* 2000)
(a) Trend reports (b) Catalogue
(c) Summary (d) Digest

4. The relationship between the terms "Ship" and "Boats" is (*NET Exam.* 2000)
(a) Syntactic relationship
(b) Semantic relationship
(c) Both (a) and (b)
(d) Neither (a) nor (b)

5. The term 'Exponential Growth' is referred to (*NET Exam.* 1999D)
(a) Linear Growth
(b) Geometrical Progression
(c) Arithmetical Progression
(d) Normal Frequency Distribution

6. NICDROM is a sectoral information centre relating to (*NET Exam.* 1999D)
(a) Drug research
(b) Organisational Management
(c) CD-ROM
(d) Bibliometrics

7. The first commercial online system to be introduced was (*NET Exam.* 1999)
(a) DIALOG (b) BRS
(c) ORBIT (d) OCLC

8. The term 'Information Retrieval' was coined by
(a) H.P. Luhn (b) Calvin N. Mooers
(c) Mortimer Taube (d) Derek Austin

9. Mode of formation of subject oceanography is (*NET Exam.* 1991D)

(a) Distillation (b) Cluster
(c) Agglomeration (d) Loose assemblage

10. Which of the following institutes in India provides technical and other related Information service to Small Scale industry? (*NET Exam.* 1998)
(a) DESIDOC (b) INSDOC
(c) NISSAT (d) SENDOC

11. Atom Index is brought out by (*NET Exam.* 1998)
(a) INIS (b) AGRIS
(c) BARC (d) Dept. of Nuclear Science

12. If you are asked to arrange the concept of information, knowledge and data in ascending order of complexing. Which of the following sequence is correct? (*NET Exam.* 1998, 1996D)
(a) Data-information-knowledge.
(b) Knowledge-information-data.
(c) Information-data-knowledge.
(d) Information-knowledge-data.

13. An individual who connects an internal colleague with an external sources of information is a (*NET Exam.* 1998)
(a) Information Broker
(b) Information Intermediary
(c) Information Consultant
(d) Technological Gatekeeper

14. The PGI is framed out of merging (*NET Exam.* 1998D)
(a) UNESCO and UNISIST
(b) UNISIST and NATIS
(c) UNISIST and IFLA
(d) UNISIST and FID

15. Hypothesis is a (*NET Exam.* 1998D)
(a) Law (b) Postulate
(c) Theory (d) Speculation

16. Origin of INSPEC is traced to (*NET Exam.* 1998)
(a) Science Citation Index (USA)
(b) Electronics Abstracts (UK)
(c) Engineering Index (USA)
(d) Physic Abstracts (UK)

17. An on-line information system comes under the category of (*NET Exam.* 1998)
(a) Data base vendor
(b) Data base producer
(c) Data base generator
(d) Data consultant

18. Which of the following services is not offered by INSDOC? (*NET Exam.* 1998D)
(a) Document delivery
(b) Abstracting and indexing services
(c) Translation service
(d) On-line information retrieval

19. Which among the following is not a NISSAT sector centre?
(a) NICHEM (b) NICNET
(c) NICMAP (d) NICTAS

20. MEDLINE on CD-ROM is published by (*NET Exam.* 1998D)
(a) UMI (b) Silver platter
(c) Cambridge Scientific (d) NLM (USA)

21. Diffusion of innovation and its acceptance normally allows
(a) Logistic curve (b) S-shape curve
(c) Linear curve (d) Frequency polygon

22. The universal availability of publication is a programme launched by (*NET Exam.* 1998D)
(a) IFLA (b) UNESCO
(c) UN (d) FID

23. Inductive Logic proceeds from (*NET Exam.* 1998D)
(a) Particular to general
(b) Particular to Particular
(c) General to Particular
(d) General to General

24. Laswell model is more known as (*NET Exam.* 1998D)
(a) Information Transfer Model
(b) Communication Model
(c) Mathematical Model
(d) Telecommunication Model

25. The NISSAT's sectoral information centre on Drugs is located at (*NET Exam.* 1994D)
(a) New Delhi (b) Mumbai
(c) Bangalore (d) Lucknow

26. Providing latest information to research Scholars/Scientists and others on their Research work is through
(a) C.A.S. (b) Classification
(c) Both (a) and (b) (d) None of the above

27. Which of the following is the full form of INFLIBNET?

(a) Information and Library Network
(b) Information Library Network
(c) International Federation of Library Network
(d) International Film Network

28. National Science Library of India is located at (*NET Exam.* 1994D)
(a) Indian Institute of Science, Bangalore
(b) The National Library, Kolkata
(c) INSDOC, New Delhi
(d) BARC, Mumbai

29. NASSDOC is an organ of (*NET Exam.* 1994D)
(a) INSDOC (b) Dept. of Science and Technology
(c) DESIDOC (d) ICSSR

30. The Library and Information Division of ICAR is the national centre for all _______ activities. (*NET Exam.* 1994D)
(a) AGRIS (b) INIS (c) FID (d) IFLA

31. National Index of Translations is Published by (*NET Exam.* 1994D)
(a) The National Library, Kolkata
(b) NASSDOC
(c) DESIDOC
(d) INSDOC

32. Which type of research aims at immediate results? (*NET Exam.* 1994D)
(a) Fundamental (b) Applied
(c) Pure (d) Standard Research

33. Ascendant is one of the ______ on the spirals of science method. (*NET Exam.* 1994D)
(a) quadrants (b) cardinal Points
(c) vertices (d) angles

34. The subject Biochemistry is the result of which mode of formation of subject? (*NET Exam.* 1994D)
(a) Denudation (b) Distillation
(c) Fusion (d) Fission

35. IBM stands for (*NET Exam.* 1994D)
(a) Indian Bureau of Mines
(b) Indian Board of Management of Library Automation
(c) International Board of Machine Operation
(d) International Business Machine Corporation

36. Complex subjects are formed by (*NET Exam.* 1995J)
(a) Fission (b) Lamination
(c) Loose Assemblage (d) Distillation

37. Recall and relevance are the forms used in (*NET Exam.* 1995J)
(a) Reference service
(b) Information service
(c) Library management
(d) Book selection

38. Fusion is (*NET Exam.* 1995)
(a) A mode of thinking
(b) A mode of formation of subjects
(c) A notational system
(d) A mode of book selection

39. SDI stands for (*NET Exam.* 1995D)
(a) Special Documentation for Information
(b) Selective Documentation of Information
(c) Special Documentation Institute
(d) Selective Dissemination of Information

40. ASLIB is now known as (*NET Exam.* 1995D)
(a) Association for Information Management
(b) Association of Special Libraries
(c) Association of Special Libraries and Information Bureau
(d) American Special Library Board

41. INB is a (*NET Exam.* 1995)
(a) Primary source of information
(b) Secondary source of information
(c) Tertiary source of information
(d) None of the above

42. CCF stands for (*NET Exam.* 1995D)
(a) Colon Classification Fields
(b) Common Communication Format
(c) Classified Catalogue Format
(d) Common Classification Features

43. BLAISE is the information network in (*NET Exam.* 1995D)
(a) Bangladesh (b) Brazil
(c) UK (d) Latin America

44. The concept "Term Truncation" is used in (*NET Exam.* 1995)
(a) Thesaurus construction
(b) Subject heading list
(c) Search formulation
(d) Citation analysis

45. The logical operators AND, OR and NOT were devised by (*NET Exam.* 1995)

(a) Charles Babbage (b) Herman Hollerith
(c) George Boole (d) Vannevar Bush

46. RLIN stands for (*NET Exam.* 1995D)
(a) Retrieval of Library and Information News
(b) Research Linked Information Network
(c) Research Library and Information Network
(d) Retrieval in Library and Information

47. INFROSS is one of the major users studies conducted in (*NET Exam.* 1995)
(a) India (b) USA (c) Germany (d) UK

48. "Optical Fiber" is used in (*NET Exam.* 1995)
(a) Telecommunication
(b) Computerised Cataloguing
(c) Automatic Classification
(d) Reference and Information Service

49. INSDOC is a part of (*NET Exam.* 1995)
(a) Council of Scientific and Industrial Research (CSIR)
(b) National Science Library
(c) Department of Electronics (Govt. of India)
(d) NISSAT

50. Transborder data flow means (*NET Exam.* 1996)
(a) Exchange of documents between countries
(b) Free flow of books between countries
(c) Exchange of electronic information between countries
(d) None of the above

51. National Translation Service in India is located at
(a) NISSAT (b) INSDOC
(c) DESIDOC (d) NASSDOC

52. The concept of S.D.I. was introduced by (*NET Exam.* 1996)
(a) H.P. Luhn (b) S.R. Ranganathan
(c) D.J. Foskett (d) None of the above

53. Bio-Technology is an example of how knowledge grows by (*NET Exam.* 1999J, 1996J)
(a) Fusion (b) Lamination
(c) Fission (d) Loosemblage

54. INIS is an example of (*NET Exam.* 1996)
(a) Distributed input and centralised output
(b) Centralised input and output
(c) Centralised input and distributed output
(d) Distributed input and output

55. Cranfield studies are an example of (*NET Exam.* 1996)
(a) Survey research
(b) Experimental research
(c) Historical research
(d) Case study

56. Data become ______________ when it is proposed, interpreted and presented in an organised or logical form to facilitate a better comprehension of the concerned topic issue.
(a) statistics (b) information
(c) topics (d) facts

57. Information gets generated as a result of the different types of
(a) Events
(b) Human activities
(c) Research and development
(d) Business and activities

58. BARC is an Indian input centre for the
(a) INIS (b) ENVIS
(c) AGRIS (d) NISSAL

59. Growth of information beyond a manageable limits is
(a) Explosion of information
(b) Increased growth
(c) Decline growth
(d) Exponential growth

60. Fixing of the toner particles in the image can be done by
(a) Electric charge (b) Press
(c) Heat (d) Chemicals

61. Match the following:

(A) Words/phrases, meaning and usage, synonyms etc.	(1) Who's who bibliographic dictionary
(B) Technical terms	(2) Bibliographic index abstracts
(C) Related to literature	(3) Technical dictionaries
(D) Related to person	(4) Language dictionaries

(a)	A-4	B-2	C-3	D-1
(b)	A-4	B-3	C-2	D-1
(c)	A-3	B-4	C-1	D-2
(d)	A-2	B-3	C-4	D-1

62. Spirit duplication method is also known as

(a) Heterography (b) Electrofax
(c) Diazographic Process (d) Xerography

63. The chemical abstracts service (CAS) was started by the American Chemical Society.
(a) True (b) False

64. Tertiary documents are those that record information about ________ documents.
(a) government (b) reference
(c) secondary (d) primary

65. The study of reproduction of graphic materials in whatever form they are, is known as graphic reproduction.
(a) True (b) False

66. Reader-printer in the library uses tapes for reading and printing.
(a) True (b) False

67. DIALOG information service are for
(a) Index search
(b) Abstract search
(c) Reference search
(d) On-line computer search

68. Match the following:

(A) Background information Subject	1. Who who's Biographical dictionaries
(B) Facts about country	2. Geographical Dictionary Atlas, Maps, etc.
(C) Places	3. Statesman Year book
(D) Person	4. Encyclopedias

(a)	A-4	B-3	C-2	D-1
(b)	A-3	B-2	C-4	D-1
(c)	A-2	B-4	C-3	D-2
(d)	A-1	B-2	C-3	D-4

69. Microfilm cameras are basically of two types, planetary and
(a) Optical (b) Photoconductor
(c) Rotary (d) Ordinary

70. Information can be categorised into three types statistical descriptive and
(a) Analytical or Interpretive (b) Tabulate
(c) Systematic (d) Logical

71. PIS stands for
(a) Physics information system
(b) Patent information system
(c) Petrochemical information system
(d) Police information system

72. Directories come under the category of ________ documents.
(a) tertiary (b) secondary
(c) primary (d) government

73. The Indian science abstract is published by
(a) INSDOC
(b) National Science Library
(c) Department of Science and Technology
(d) NISSAT

74. Proper and complete recording of published information is known as
(a) Bibliographical Record
(b) Information Record
(c) Bibliographical Control
(d) Information Control

75. ________ is a material carrier of information.
(a) Graph (b) Number
(c) Machine readable form (d) Text

76. Index Medicus was established during
(a) 1940 (b) 1879 (c) 1800 (d) 1910

77. Microfilm is used for reducing the ________ size of the original documents.
(a) 70% (b) 60% (c) 98% (d) 50%

78. Diazonium is a ________ is a substance.
(a) magnetic sensitive (b) photo sensitive
(c) electric sensitive (d) heat sensitive

79. LISA in library stands for
(a) Literature Indexing Science Abstracts
(b) Library and Information Science Abstracts
(c) Librarian Information Scientist Association
(d) Library and Information Science Association

80. Documents produced in limited quantities and are not for wider circulation are called
(a) Secret documents (b) Published documents
(c) Formal documents (d) Informal documents

81. 35 mm Roll film is used for recording large size of documents such as newspaper, maps, engineering, drawing, etc.
(a) True (b) False

82. Knowledge consists of ________ body of information.
(a) connected (b) disconnected
(c) organised (d) unorganised

83. Four important national level information centres are

(a) NICFOS (b) NISSAT
(c) NICMAP (d) SENDOC

84. Match the following:

(A) Subject Dictionary	(1) Help in enriching word power		
(B) Translating Dictionary	(2) Useful for translators		
(C) Special Dictionary	(3) Help in solving cross word Puzzles		
(D) General Dictionary	(4) Beneficial to the student of management		

(a) A – 4 B – 2 C – 3 D – 1
(b) A – 3 B – 1 C – 4 D – 2
(c) A – 2 B – 4 C – 2 D – 1
(d) A – 1 B – 2 C – 3 D – 4

85. CAS stands for
(a) Content Analysis Service
(b) Current Awareness Service
(c) Computer Application Service
(d) Chemical Abstract Service

86. In case of Electro fax copies bond paper is used.
(a) True (b) False

87. Facts are raw information.
(a) True (b) False

88. Information or knowledge that is packed in documents broadly group under categories
(a) Teaching (b) Three
(c) One (d) Two

89. _________ is essentially and information related activity.
(a) Teaching (b) Research
(c) Education (d) Study

90. Translation of documents come under the category of tertiary documents.
(a) True (b) False

91. The computer database available for on-line searching in the field of Engineering is current technology index.
(a) True (b) False

92. Match the following:

(A) Paul Otlet	(1) Documentation
(B) John Harriss	(2) First Encyclopedia having articles written by subject specialist
(C) Europa Publication	(3) Word of learning
(D) Encyclopedia Britannica	(4) First edition only three volumes

(a) A – 1 B – 3 C – 4 D – 2
(b) A – 1 B – 2 C – 3 D – 4
(c) A – 2 B – 3 C – 4 D – 1
(d) A – 4 B – 3 C – 2 D – 1

93. Documents which themselves contain the desired information in a concise form are called
(a) Primary type (b) Reference type
(c) Survey type (d) Bibliographical type

94. Information is made up of
(a) Symbolic elements (b) Microform
(c) Number (d) Paper-Print

95. Guide to literature belong to the category of
(a) Tertiary documents
(b) Primary documents
(c) Travel documents
(d) Secondary document

96. Atlases are the collection of
(a) Pictures (b) Pictures and graphs
(c) News digest (d) Maps

97. Logical operator in search was named after
(a) George Boole (b) Alfred Venn
(c) Dunne Venn (d) John Venn

98. Referral centres suggest sources likely to satisfy clients.
(a) True (b) False

99. The documents which are published on a continuing basis are known as
(a) Serial Publication (b) Reports Publication
(c) Series Publication (d) Journal Publication

100. The exponential growth of information is popularly known as
(a) Information explosion
(b) Exponential information
(c) Exponential growth
(d) Information growth

101. Match the following:

(A) CAS	(1) Notification of new arrival
(B) Computerised SDI	(2) H.P. Luhn
(C) Initiation service	(3) To intimate new user regarding Lib. Sc.
(D) Reference service	(4) Personnel assistance to user

(a) A – 1 B – 2 C – 4 D – 3
(b) A – 4 B – 3 C – 2 D – 1

(c) A – 3 B – 4 C – 2 D – 1
(d) A – 1 B – 2 C – 3 D – 4

102. Display of new arrival sources in the library is classified a circulation service.
(a) True (b) False

103. _________ Literature constitutes a major category of primary literature.
(a) Bibliographical (b) Encyclopedia
(c) Journal (d) Book

104. Literature search could be equated with
(a) Ready reference service
(b) Reference service
(c) Indexing and abstracting service
(d) Long-range reference service

105. The four functional phases of SDI system are Selection, Notification, Feedback and
(a) Filling (b) Modification
(c) Recording (d) Circulation

106. Computer is an important link in the information transfer chain which links are the source of information to the ultimate users.
(a) True (b) False

107. Inter-library loan is one function of ______ service.
(a) literature searching (b) document delivery
(c) current awareness (d) reference

108. Research is a creative work undertaken on a systematic basis in order to increase the stock of
(a) Branches of knowledge
(b) Knowledge of data
(c) Knowledge of information
(d) Knowledge

109. Match the following:

(A) Books	(1) Secondary
(B) Reviews	(2) Conventional
(C) Directories	(3) Primary
(D) Conference proceedings	(4) Tertiary

(a) A – 1 B – 2 C – 3 D – 4
(b) A – 2 B – 3 C – 4 D – 1
(c) A – 4 B – 3 C – 2 D – 1
(d) A – 3 B – 1 C – 4 D – 2

110. Secondary documents are created to facilitate access to information contents of
(a) Government (b) Reference
(c) Tertiary (d) Primary

111. Selective Dissemination of Information (SDI) is a type of
(a) Referral service
(b) Indexing and Abstracting service
(c) Content Analysis service
(d) Current Awareness service

112. ________ was established as a project of the S & T plan of the Fifth Five-year plan.
(a) ENVIS (b) NISSAT
(c) NIC (d) INSDOC

113. Dissemination of publication containing copies of contents page of journals is known as
(a) Content Analysis
(b) Current content service
(c) Content by Journal Service
(d) Current contents

114. Diaz process is extensively used for making copies of painting.
(a) True (b) False

115. Large scale of information worldwide resulted in the
(a) Research and development
(b) Trade practices
(c) Information Society
(d) Technological events

116. Knowledge is _______ form of information.
(a) statistical (b) raw
(c) organised (d) unorganised

117. Match the following:

(A) Primary documents	(1) Bibliography of bibliographies, Directories, Literature guide, Directories.
(B) Tertiary documents	(2) Indexing, News digest, Reviews.
(C) Secondary documents	(3) Journals, Reports, Theses.

(a) A – 3 B – 1 A – 2
(b) A – 2 B – 3 A – 1
(c) A – 3 B – 2 A – 1

118. Reserve Bank of India notification on exchange control is _____ type of information.
(a) textual (b) descriptive and Textual
(c) data (d) factual

119. According to sources of generation, information can be grouped as
(a) News, information and knowledge
(b) Published, published and non-print
(c) Manuscript, print and non-print
(d) Primary, secondary and tertiary

120. Document like "Books of reading" which reproduce papers already published referred as
(a) Survey document
(b) Tertiary document
(c) Secondary document
(d) Primary document

121. Roster of Indian scientific and technical translator is maintained by
(a) DRDO (b) CSIR
(c) INSDOC (d) DESIDOC

122. Fundamental phases of SDI includes
(a) User profile and document database
(b) Selection, notification, feedback and modification
(c) Document profile and user profile
(d) Selection, notification and feedback

123. ___________ service includes supply of photocopy of documents.
(a) Reprography (b) Document delivery
(c) Literature (d) Reference

124. Match the following:
(A) Data (1) Yarn
(B) Information (2) Cloth
(C) Knowledge (3) Cotton

(a)	A – 3	B – 1	C – 2
(b)	A – 2	B – 3	C – 1
(c)	A – 3	B – 2	C – 1

125. ________ is the period of time between two closely related events.
(a) Time-Lag (b) Exponential growth
(c) Growth (d) Development

126. ___________ is a survey of the primary literature in a specific field.
(a) Bibliography (b) Abstract
(c) Index (d) Review

127. ___________ is a bibliographic type goes to secondary publication.
(a) Textbooks (b) Current awareness serials
(c) Literature guides (d) Library accession list

128. Secondary documents are created to facilitate access to information contents of primary document.
(a) True (b) False

129. MEDLARS stands for
(a) Medical Literature Analysis Retrieval Service
(b) Medical Literature and Retrieval System
(c) Medical Analysis Research System
(d) Medical Literature and Retrieval Service

130. For India INSDOC has published a directory, which gives details about the translators and the translation centre for Science and Technology. The title of the directory is
(a) Translators for Science and Technology
(b) Science and Technical Translation Service
(c) Roster of Indian Scientific and Technical Translators
(d) Directory of Indian Scientific and Technical Translators

131. Match the following:
(A) Media (1) Carries that disseminate information or knowledge
(B) Recipient (2) Carries message or content of information
(C) Source (3) Person who receive and use information
(D) Channel (4) Mode of communicating message through signals, symbols, text, etc.

(a)	A – 2	B – 3	C – 4	D – 1
(b)	A – 3	B – 2	C – 1	D – 4
(c)	A – 4	B – 3	C – 2	D – 1
(d)	A – 2	B – 4	C – 3	D – 1

132. In 1970s INSDOC established its information dissemination centre at
(a) IIT, Mumbai (b) IIT, Chennai
(c) IIT, Delhi (c) IIT, Kanpur

133. The selection phase of SDI service, matches document characteristics with database.
(a) True (b) False

134. The term Selective Dissemination of Information (SDI) was coined by
(a) Alfred J. Lotka
(b) F.W. Lancaster
(c) Hans Peter Luhn
(d) Dr. S.R. Ranganathan

135. SENDOC stands for
(a) Small Enterprises National Documentation Centre
(b) Science and Engineering Documentation Centre
(c) Science and Engineering National Documentation Centre
(d) Small Enterprises Documentation Centre

136. Govt. officials need information for
(a) Communication (b) Meetings
(c) Reviewing (d) Decision-making

137. Translation of documents comes under the category of ________ documents.
(a) reference (b) tertiary
(c) secondary (d) primary

138. Match the following:

(A) Rogers	(1) Humanistic theory		
(B) Sears	(2) Reinforcement theory		
(C) Berlyne	(3) Curiosity and exploration		
(D) Weiner	(4) Attribution and personal causation theory		

(a)	A – 1	B – 2	C – 3	D – 4
(b)	A – 4	B – 3	C – 2	D – 1
(c)	A – 3	B – 4	C – 1	D – 2
(d)	A – 4	B – 3	C – 2	D – 1

139. Routing of journals comes under the category of __________ service.
(a) current awareness service
(b) circulation
(c) inter library loan
(d) reference

140. ENVIS is an acronym for
(a) Environmental Institutional Security
(b) Environmental Information Service
(c) Environmental Information System
(d) Engineering Vital Information Sector

141. Research in progress bulletins belongs to
(a) Chemical abstracts service
(b) Computer application services
(c) SDI
(d) CAS

142. The BARC is identified as national input centre for (*NET Exam.* 1999D)
(a) AGRIS (b) INIS
(c) DEVSIS (d) SPINES

143. The production of mental reflection and imagination is known as (*NET Exam.* 1997D)
(a) Information (b) Idea
(c) Data (d) Knowledge

144. The device that enables the computers to communicate over telephone lines is
(a) NETWORK (b) ON-LINE
(c) MODEM (d) None of the above
(*NET Exam.* 1997J)

145. The detail of a book comprising author, title imprint collation technically is called
(a) Record format
(b) Standard record format
(c) Entries for classification
(d) Bibliographic description

146. IATLIS is an organisation of (*NET Exam.* 1997J)
(a) Academic Libraries
(b) Teachers of Library and Information Science
(c) Special Libraries
(d) School Libraries

147. Which of the following is not a secondary source of information (*NET Exam.* 1997J)
(a) An abstracting journal
(b) A handbook
(c) A statistical digest
(d) A patent

148. Directing user to the right source of information is called (*NET Exam.* 1997J)
(a) Current awareness service
(b) Digest service
(c) Data service
(d) Referral service

149. Intellectual Property rights are recognised as (*NET Exam.* 1997J)
(a) Copyright (b) Patent
(c) Neither (a) nor (b) (d) Both (a) and (b)

150. Among the following, which is not a NISSAT sectoral centre (*NET Exam.* 1997J)
(a) National Chemical Laboratory
(b) National Informatics Centre
(c) Control Drug Research Institute
(d) ATIRA

151. Four cell design is used in (*NET Exam.* 1999J)
(a) Survey (b) Experiments
(c) Case Studies (d) Historical Research

152 In a research report/paper to refer to an earlier but not immediately preceding reference, to the following term is used. (*NET Exam.* 1997)
(a) Op. cit. (b) Loc. cit.
(c) Ibid. (d) None of the above

153. Hypothesis is a (*NET Exam.* 1997J)
(a) Generalisation (b) Law
(c) Theory (d) Theory of tested

154. Growth of information beyond manageable limit is known is (*NET Exam.* 1997D)
   (a) Information growth
   (b) Informational explosion
   (c) Exponential growth
   (d) Information explosion

155. GISTNIC is a part of (*NET Exam.* 1997J, 1997D)
   (a) SIRNET (b) INFLIBNET
   (c) DELNET (d) NICNET

156. The most suitable method for making copies from double-sided document is reflex method. (*NET Exam.* 1997D)
   (a) True (b) False

157. ASLIB Cranfield research project was mainly concerned with (*NET Exam.* 1997D)
   (a) Classification and cataloguing
   (b) Information retrieve
   (c) Evaluation of Indexing system
   (d) Selecting Dissemination of information

158. Research Design gives the
   (a) Blueprint of the research activity
   (b) Procedure of research activity
   (c) Techniques of research
   (d) Procedures of designing tools

159. The four-cell design is used in
   (a) Surveys (b) Experiments
   (c) Case studies (d) Historical research

160. Redundancy of information is (*NET Exam.* 1997D)
   (a) Unnecessary and should be eliminated
   (b) Unnecessary but cannot be avoided
   (c) Necessary and sometime useful
   (d) Necessary and always desirable

161. In research on information need of chartered accountants a questionnaire is sent to every fifth member on the official register of chartered accountant, would this be (*NET Exam.* 1997D, 1996J)
   (a) Random sample
   (b) A stratified sample
   (c) The whole population
   (d) Not a representative sample

162. In providing SDI (*NET Exam.* 1997D)
   (a) Incoming documents profiles are method with readers interest
   (b) Readers interest profiles are created and matched with existing documents profiles
   (c) Both (a) and (b)
   (d) Neither (a) nor (b)

163. ISO 2709 exchange format specifics (*NET Exam.* 1999J)
   (a) A three part record structure
   (b) The tags to be used
   (c) The size of the magnetic tape
   (d) The cataloguing code to be followed

164. The India input centre for INIS is (*NET Exam.* 1999J)
   (a) Tata Institute of Fundamental Research
   (b) Bhabha Atomic Research Centre
   (c) Raman Research Institute
   (d) Indian Institute of Science

165. The research design of study should not include (*NET Exam.* 1999J)
   (a) Findings (b) Hypothesis
   (c) Methodology (d) Scope

166. Mean, Median and Mode are (*NET Exam.* 1999J)
   (a) Measures of control tendency
   (b) Measures of deviation
   (c) Ways of sampling
   (d) None of the above

167. In a research study the review of literature will not help in (*NET Exam.* 1999J)
   (a) Providing an overview of what has been
   (b) Indicating possible methodologies to be used
   (c) Selecting a sample
   (d) Identifying possible variables

168. Which of the following networks is not involved in content provision?
   (a) MEDLARS (b) OCLC
   (c) 1-NET (d) INIS

169. Bar code technology is useful for (*NET Exam.* 1999J)
   (a) Circulation (b) Acquisition
   (d) Stock taking (d) All of the above

170. CD-ROM is (*NET Exam.* 1999J)
   (a) A map-storage device
   (b) A preservation tool
   (c) A publication medium
   (d) All of the above

171. E-mail mainly uses (*NET Exam.* 1999J)
   (a) Computer network
   (b) Postal network
   (c) Television network
   (d) Telephone network

172. According to the Shannon-weaver model of communication which of the following cannot be considered as a source? (*NET Exam.* 1999J)
(a) Research Scientist
(b) Government Agencies
(c) Learned Societies
(d) Computer Networks

173. A special library has handbooks, patents, research reports, manuals, and technical digest. Which of the above are primary sources? (*NET Exam.* 1996D)
(a) Manuals (b) Technical Digits
(c) Handbooks (d) Patents and research reports

174. Which of the following cannot be considered as a primary source of information? (*NET Exam.* 1996D)
(a) An article describing
(b) A textbook original research
(c) A patent
(d) A thesis

175. Universal availability of publication (UAP) is a programme of
(a) UNESCO (b) IFLA
(c) FID (d) British Library

176. Among the following which is not a NISSAT sectoral centre? (*NET Exam.* 1996D)
(a) National Chemical Laboratory
(b) National Informatics Centre
(c) Central Drug Research Institute
(d) Ahmedabad Textiles Industries Research

177. SENDOC is a documentation centre on (*NET Exam.* 1996D)
(a) Steel Enterprises
(b) Stock exchange
(c) Small-scale industries
(d) Sugar industry

178. Which of the following cannot be required as multimedia (*NET Exam.* 2000D)
(a) A tape slide Programme
(b) A CD-ROM with text and visuals
(c) Microfilm
(d) A Web Page

179. A hypothesis that is tested for its rejection is
(a) Alternative Hypothesis
(b) Statistical inference
(b) Observation
(d) Null hypothesis

180. A system contains (*NET Exam.* 1991D)
(a) Parts
(b) Inter-related parts having a purpose
(c) A composite of items
(d) None of the above

181. Tree of Porphyry is a schematic representation of
(a) Deca choromy (b) Dichotomy
(c) Polychotomy (d) None of the above

182. AGRIS is mainly sponsored by (*NET Exam.* 1991D)
(a) UNESCO and IFLA
(b) UNISIST and IFLA
(c) UNISIST and FAO
(d) UNO and CAB

183. 'Half line' of information implies
(a) Information is useful only that halt the time
(b) As information ages, it is useless
(c) The life of information is reduced
(d) Dead information in not used

184. Which of the following statements about systems analysis is correct? (*NET Exam.* 1998D)
(a) System analysis identifies the flow of work
(b) System analysis is work necessary only if the library is to be computerised
(c) System analysis can only be done by an outside consultant
(d) All of the above

185. In a research paper, to refer to the immediate previous reference the following term is used: (*NET Exam.* 1998D)
(a) Op. cit. (b) Ibid.
(c) Loc. cit. (d) None of the above

186. Which among the following is not a 'Modes' of formation of subjects? (*NET Exam.* 1998D)
(a) Collection (b) Fusion
(c) Fission (d) Agglomeration

187. Define research
(a) A method to obtain solution of the problems
(b) A descriptive method to obtain solution of the problem
(c) A systematic method to obtain solution of the problem
(d) Systematic method to obtain tentative solution of the problem

188. Define aim of research
(a) To discover laws
(b) To discover rules of research
(c) To discover laws and theories
(d) To discover laws, theories and principles

189. Mean for research
(a) Searching nothing
(b) Searching facts
(c) Searching data
(d) Searching facet and their meaning

190. Analysis of data is second step of Research Methodology.
(a) True (b) False

191. Research is a creative work undertaken in order to increase the stock of
(a) Data
(b) Information
(c) Information & Knowledge
(d) Knowledge

192. Deductive logic is related in spiral to scientific method with
(a) Nadir (b) Zenix
(c) Zenith (d) None of the these

193. How many research methods are in number?
(a) Four (b) Three (c) Two (d) One

194. Write the main type of research.
(a) Question arise (b) Observational
(c) Practical (d) Statistical

195. Scientific method of research can be used in all described lines.
(a) True (b) False

196. What is an interview?
(a) Type of research (b) Method of research
(c) A tool of research (d) None of the above

197. The 4 cell design is used in
(a) Surveys (b) Case Studies
(c) Experiments (d) Historical Research

198. Formulation of fundamental law is
(a) Pure research
(b) Applied research
(c) Developmental research
(d) Research design

199. The headquarters of FID is located as (*NET Exam.* 1995D)
(a) New York (b) London
(c) The Hague (d) Berlin

200. Future-oriented research is
(a) Historical (b) Experimental
(c) Survey (d) None of the above

201. Which of the following is not a secondary source of information?
(a) An encyclopaedia
(b) A textbook
(c) A biographical dictionary
(d) Patents

202. Information about Indian research studies on bakery and million is input to IFIS through
(a) Central Rice Research Institute
(b) Indian Agricultural Research Institute
(c) National Institute of Nutrition
(d) Central Food Technological Research Institute

203. In an empirical study on the impact of television viewing on violence, violence would be
(a) the dependent variable
(b) an independent variable
(c) an intervening variable
(d) not a variable at all

204. A big difference between the mean and median is an indication that (*NET Exam.* 2001J)
(a) there is a mistake in the calculation
(b) the calculation is correct
(c) there is a wide variation in the data
(d) None of the above

205. In a communication model noise refers to (*NET Exam.* 2001J)
(a) loudness of signal
(b) lack of understanding between sender and receiver
(c) any disturbance which affects the transmission
(d) irrelevant information

206. SENDOC is the national documentation centre for (*NET Exam.* 2001J)
(a) Science and Environment
(b) Sociology and Economics
(c) Sri Lanka
(d) Small Scale Enterprise

207. The following is not an example of re-packaging of information. (*NET Exam.* 2001J)
(a) Trend report (b) Catalogue
(c) Summary (d) Digest

208. INSDOC has been merged with NISCOM and is now known as (*NET Exam.* 2001J)
(a) DELNET (b) NISCAIR
(c) DESIDOC (d) NASSDOC

209. The relationship between the terms "Ship" and "Boats" is (*NET Exam.* 2001J)
(a) syntactic relationship
(b) semantic relationship
(c) both (a) and (b)
(d) Neither (a) nor (b)

210. Which of the following cannot be regarded as 'multimedia'? (*NET Exam.* 2001J)
(a) A tape-slide programme
(b) A CD-ROM with text and visuals
(c) Microfilm
(d) A web page

211. A hypothesis that is tested for its rejection is (*NET Exam.* 2001D)
(a) Alternative hypothesis
(b) Statistical inference
(c) Observation
(d) Null hypothesis

212. The BARC is identified a national input centre for (*NET Exam.* 2001D)
(a) AGRIS (b) INIS
(c) DEVSIS (d) SPINES

213. The secondary sources of information comprised of (*NET Exam.* 2001D)
(a) Textbooks and Research Monographs
(b) Subject Periodicals and Encyclopaedias
(c) Indexing and Abstracting Periodicals
(d) Bibliography and Patents

214. The early work on modeling of information communication was based on (*NET Exam.* 2001D)
(a) Goode and Hatt model
(b) Lasswell model
(c) Shannon and weaver model
(d) Bradford and Price model

215. The logical steps involved in scientific investigation are (*NET Exam.* 2001D)
(a) identification of the problem
(b) Formulation of the hypothesis
(c) Collection of data
(d) All the above

216. Xerographic process is categorised under (*NET Exam.* 2001D)
(a) Photographic process
(b) Reflex method
(c) Silver halide process
(d) Electrostatic process

217. "Universal Bibliographical Control" is a programme of (*NET Exam.* 2001D)
(a) FID (b) IFLA
(c) UNISIST (d) ALA

218. "National Index of Translations" is published by (*NET Exam.* 2001D)
(a) NASSDOC (b) DESIDOC
(c) SENDOC (d) NISCAIR

219. In research design which is considered as the most important components? (*NET Exam.* 2001D)
(a) Observation
(b) Formatting of Hypothesis
(c) Case Study
(d) Review of literature

220. 'NICDROM' is a sectorial information centre relating to (*NET Exam.* 2001D)
(a) Drug research
(b) Organisational Management
(c) CD-ROM
(d) Bibliometrics

221. Periodical publication 'Indian Science Abstracts' is brought out by (*NET Exam.* 2001D)
(a) DESIDOC (b) INSA
(c) NISCAIR (d) NISSAT

222. The first commercial on-line system to be introduced was (*NET Exam.* 2001D)
(a) DIALOG (b) BRS
(c) ORBIT (d) OCLC

223. What is an interview? (*NET Exam.* 2001D)
(a) A tool of research
(b) A process of research
(c) A type of research
(d) A method of presentation

224. Which of the following is not a functional phase of Selective Dissemination of Information? (*NET Exam.* 2002D)
(a) Selection (b) Notification
(c) Feedback (d) Classification

225. Arrange the following according to their year of establishment: (*NET Exam.* 2012J)
(i) NIC (ii) DESIDOC
(iii) NISCAIR (iv) NASSDOC
Codes:
(a) (i), (iii), (ii), (iv) (b) (iii), (i), (iv), (ii)
(c) (iv), (i), (iii), (ii) (d) (ii), (iv), (i), (iii)

226. In a 'search engine', which of the following device is automatically log on web pages and index their content? (*NET Exam.* 2001J)
 (a) Crowler (b) Spiders
 (c) Indexer (d) Invented file searcher

227. When the power is switch on the file which automatically executed is? (*NET Exam.* 2002D)
 (a) DOS.EXE (b) SYSTEM.EXE
 (c) BOOT.EXE (d) AUTOEXEC.BAT

228. Which of the following agency used computer for the first time in India? (*NET Exam.* 2002D)
 (a) DRTC, Bangalore
 (b) National Library, Kolkata
 (c) NISCAIR, New Delhi
 (d) Indian Statistical Institute

229. National Information System for Science and Technology (NISSAT) does not work for (*NET Exam.* 2002D)
 (a) Sponsoring DELNET and MYLIBNET
 (b) Library education and Training
 (c) The Development of National Information System
 (d) Raja Ram Mohan Library Foundation

230. MEDLARS is a programme of (*NET Exam.* 2002D)
 (a) IFLA (b) FID
 (c) LA-UK (d) National Medical Library, USA

231. The commonly used transmission media is (*NET Exam.* 2002D)
 (a) Microwave transmission
 (b) Satellite transmission
 (c) Coaxial cables
 (d) Circuit switching

232. The single network in which the voice of data can be carried over a single network is (*NET Exam.* 2002D)
 (a) Open System Interconnection (OSI)
 (b) Integrated Services Digital Network (ISDN)
 (c) E-mail Service Providers (ESP)
 (d) Gateway Internet Access Service (GIAS)

233. Which is not a software developed by DELNET? (*NET Exam.* 2002D)
 (a) DELSIS (b) DELSERCH
 (c) DEL-DOS (d) DELIIS

234. Which one is not a objective of National Information System for Science and Technology (NISSAT)?(*NET Exam.* 2002D)
 (a) Development of National Information Services.
 (b) Promotion of existing Information System & Services
 (c) Use of existing infrastructural facilities
 (d) Promotion of National and International Cooperation in Information

235. Which source provides information on the process and materials involved in the manufacture of a product? (*NET Exam.* 2002D)
 (a) Patents (b) Trade literature
 (c) Specifications (d) Standards

236. Which of the following statements are true? (*NET Exam.* 2002J)
 1. Information system is a growing organization.
 2. Save the time of user, information are for use.
 3. The basic component of a library according to Vth law of library science is documents and information are for use.
 4. Resource sharing is essential feature of any school library.
 (a) 3 & 4 (b) 1 & 2
 (c) 2 & 3 (d) 1 & 4

237. ISBD uses (*NET Exam.* 2002J)
 (a) BNB (b) PRECIS
 (c) ISAC (d) All of these

238. Centre for Research on User studies (CRUS) was established by (*NET Exam.* 2002J)
 (a) ASLIB (b) Library of Congress
 (c) NISCAIR (d) British Library

239. The layer which identify destination of data is (*NET Exam.* 2002J)
 (a) MAC (b) Physical layer
 (c) Parallel layer (d) TCP/IP

240. Optical fibre is used in (*NET Exam.* 2002J)
 (a) Telecommunication
 (b) Computerised Cataloguing
 (c) Automated Classification
 (d) Reference and Information Services

241. Library attached with Forest Research Institute, Dehradun, fall under the category of (*NET Exam.* 2002J)
 (a) Public library (b) Academic libraries
 (c) Special library (d) Business libraries

242. Which is a wrong statement? (*NET Exam.* 2002J)

(a) OCLC is Online Computer Library Centre
(b) NICNET is designed by National Informatics Centre
(c) Library of Congress does not have Rare Book division
(d) Xerography is dry copying process

243. Large scale use of information has converted the present knowledge society into (*NET Exam.* 2003J)
(a) Information age
(b) Information society
(c) Information explosion
(d) Both (a) and (b)

244. Match of Columns (*NET Exam.* 2003J)

Column A

A. Study of acquisition, handling & communication of information
B. Author's right to claim ownership of a created work
C. Information stored on computer files, and accessible via a remote terminal and telecommunication link

Column B

1. Documentation
2. Intellectual Property right
3. Database
4. Copyright

Codes:	A	B	C
(a)	1	4	3
(b)	1	2	3
(c)	4	3	1
(d)	4	3	1

245. The Diazo process is extensively used for making copies of (*NET Exam.* 2003J)
(a) microfilm (b) microfiche
(c) micro documents (d) All of these

246. Medical Jurisprudence is found by which modes of formation of subject. (*NET Exam.* 2003J)
1. Fusion 2. Cluster
3. Lamination 4. Fission
(a) All the four (b) 4 only
(c) 1 and 4 (d) 2, 3 and 4

247. Which of the following associations sponsored AGRIS? (*NET Exam.* 2003J)
(a) ICAR (PUSA) (b) IARI
(c) FAO (d) UNICEF

248. When some existing exchange control regulations are amended, the notifications are published regularly in Reserve Bank of India Bulletin. It is an example of the (*NET Exam.* 2003J)
(a) Data (b) Information
(c) Knowledge (d) News

249. Which is an International Storage and Retrieval System for Nuclear Science and Technology? (*NET Exam.* 2003J)
(a) AGRIS (b) INIS
(c) NVCCSI (d) NISCAIR

250. IASLIC is co-operating with (*NET Exam.* 2003J)
(a) NISSAT (b) UNISIST
(c) INIS (d) AGRIS

251. To provide Selective Dissemination of Information (*NET Exam.* 2003J)
(a) existing document profile are matched with interest profile
(b) existing user profile is matched with incoming document profile
(c) proper feedback mechanism is operationalise
(d) All of the above

252. Which of the following is a term used for working assumption of a solution to a problem? (*NET Exam.* 2010J)
(a) Research (b) Hypothesis
(c) Bibliography (d) Thesis

253. A search term in context of Selective Dissemination of Information service can be (*NET Exam.* 2003D)
(a) a single depositor
(b) word from a Thesaurus
(c) references in articles
(d) a single word, a sequence of words in a string, an author name, the name of an institution, or the title of a journal, a subject heading and a classification code

254. The most suitable method for making copies from double scaled documents is (*NET Exam.* 2003D)
(a) Reflex method
(b) Silver method process
(c) Electro photography
(d) Electrofax

255. In an Information & Retrieval System, co-ordination of concept done by the searcher at the search stage is (*NET Exam.* 2003D)

(a) Pre-coordinate (b) Post-coordinate
(c) Under-coordinate (d) Over-coordinate

256. Bibliography on "India in 2000 A.D." is a publication of (*NET Exam.* 2003D)
(a) NASSDOC (b) DESIDOC
(c) NISCAIR (d) RRRLF

257. Match the following: (*NET Exam.* 2003D)
Column A
(A) A packaged carrier of information and knowledge.
(B) A recorded message, irrespective of physical form or content.
(C) Organised information irrespective of physical form.
Column B
1. Data 2. Book
3. Information 4. Knowledge

Codes:	**A**	**B**	**C**
(a)	4	3	1
(b)	2	3	4
(c)	2	3	1
(d)	3	1	4

258. Which type of needs of the users are satisfied by Documentation Centres, Information Analysis Centres, Databanks, Media Resource Centres etc.?
(a) Recreational needs
(b) Social needs
(c) Information needs
(d) Special needs

259. How many sectorial centres of NISSAT are there? (*NET Exam.* 2004J)
(a) 10 (b) 20 (c) 4 (d) 6

260. Xerography is (*NET Exam.* 2004J)
(a) Dry copying process
(b) Wet copying process
(c) Diazo-graphic process
(d) None of these

261. Relational DBMS are so-called because (*NET Exam.* 2004J)
(a) The data they can manipulate is stored as relation in form of tables in which information arranged in rows and columns.
(b) They can work with more than one file at a time.
(c) They indicate relation between differentiation.
(d) They are command driven entities.

262. Which international association promote international contact among Library Associations and Librarians? (*NET Exam.* 2004J)
(a) International Federation of Library Association and Institution (IFLA).
(b) International Federation of Documentation (IFD)
(c) Raja Ram Mohan Rai Library Foundation (RRRLF)
(d) International Librarians Association Geneva

263. The HR function/s of Library and Information Unit is/are (*NET Exam.* 2005D)
1. Customer satisfaction and RD.
2. Quality of products and services.
3. Personnel planning and productivity.
(a) 1 & 2 (b) 3 only
(c) 1, 2 & 3 (d) None of these

264. Which association organized the seminar on Users and Library and Information Services? (*NET Exam.* 2005D)
(a) NISCAIR (b) IASLIC
(c) ISAC (d) ICCR

265. Which of the following statements are correct? (*NET Exam.* 2005D)
1. B.S.O. was drafted in the year 1971.
2. Computer Aided Subject System (COMPASS) was introduced for ABPR.
3. The machine readable cataloguing was firstly started in India by NISCAIR.
(a) 1 & 3 are correct (b) 3 & 2 are correct
(c) 1, 2 & 3 are correct (d) None of above

266. The synonymous relationship between the terms is known as (*NET Exam.* 2005D)
(a) Hierarchical relationship
(b) Genus-Species relationship
(c) Associate relationship
(d) Equivalence relationship

267. The large-scale growth in the organized body on information and continuous addition of output of current research activities characterize the phenomenon (*NET Exam.* 2005D)
(a) Explosion of books
(b) Explosion of research
(c) Explosion of organized body
(d) Information explosion

268. Granthalaya, the library software is designed by (*NET Exam.* 2005D)

(a) NISCAIR (b) DRTC
(c) INFLIBNET (d) AVNIS

269. Isak Collijn was a Swedish National Librarian and was the president of (*NET Exam.* 2004D)
(a) ALA (b) IFLA
(c) FID (d) UNESCO

270. The PGI is framed out of merging (*NET Exam.* 2004D)
(a) UNISIST, FID (b) UNISIST, UNESCO
(c) UNISIST, IFLA (d) UNISIST, ALA

271. Which of the following institutes in India provides technical and other related information services to small scale industry? (*NET Exam.* 2004D)
(a) SENDOC (b) NISCAIR
(c) NISSAT (d) ILA

272. The official agency assigning ISSN in India is (*NET Exam.* 2004D)
(a) NISCAIR (b) DELNET
(c) INFLIBNET (d) MEDLARS

273. The four functional phase of SDI system are selection, notification, feedback and (*NET Exam.* 2004D)
(a) Modification (b) Arrangement
(c) Classification (d) Users' education

274. Barcode Technology is useful for (*NET Exam.* 2004D)
1. Circulation 2. Acquisition
3. Stock Taking 4. Weeding out
(a) 1, 2 & 3 (b) 1 & 2
(c) 3 & 4 (d) 2, 3 & 4

275. ERIC database sponsored by the Department of Health Education and Welfare, Federal Government of USA deals with (*NET Exam.* 2004D)
(a) Economics (b) Ethics
(c) Energy (d) Education

276. Match the following: (*NET Exam.* 2004D)

Column A (Software)	**Column B (Responsible Institutions)**
(A) Suchika	1. NISCAIR
(B) Granthalaya	2. DESIDOC
(C) CODEN	3. ASTM
	4. LASTEC

Codes:	**A**	**B**	**C**
(a)	2	1	3
(b)	2	3	1
(c)	1	2	3
(d)	1	3	2

277. Third step of POPSI is (*NET Exam.* 2004D)
(a) Short display
(b) Display of Component
(c) Selection of Approach term
(d) Display of Subject Index term

278. The headquarters of National Informatics Centre (NIC) is situated at (*NET Exam.* 2004D)
(a) New Delhi (b) Kolkata
(c) Bangalore (d) Hyderabad

279. ASLIB was started in the year (*NET Exam.* 2004D)
(a) 1924 (b) 1915 (c) 1933 (d) 1955

280. An electronic mail discussion forum for providers and users of information service in India called LISFORUM has set at NCSI in the year (*NET Exam.* 2004D)
(a) 1995 (b) 2002 (c) 2005 (d) 1987

281. The information centres which are highly specialized types of information institutions that emerged to provide critical, analytical and evaluated support service to institutions involved in high level are (*NET Exam.* 2004D)
(a) Information Analysis Centres
(b) Referral Centres
(c) Documentation Centres
(d) Mission-oriented Information Centres

282. Information and knowledge are the central instrument of change in (*NET Exam.* 2004D)
(a) Industrial Society
(b) Agricultural Society
(c) Information Society
(d) All of the above

283. Knowledge is an organized body or (*NET Exam.* 2004D)
(a) Facts (b) Data
(c) Information (d) Intelligence

284. Universal Availability of Publications (UAP) is a programme of (*NET Exam.* 2004D)
(a) UNESCO (b) FID
(c) IFLA (d) UNO

285. Indian Library Association has created a database of libraries. Name it. (*NET Exam.* 2005D)

(a) OASIS (b) IWIS
(c) SOUL (d) NALANDA

286. Primary Sources of Information are (*NET Exam.* 2005D)
(a) Materials which are most authentic and original and usually take the form of a journal article, report or a patent.
(b) The original information is selected, modified and rearranged in a suitable format for the purpose of easy location by users.
(c) Information that is a distillation and collection of basic sources of information.
(d) Any of the above.

287. Match the column (*NET Exam.* 2005D)

Column A (Books)	Column B (Publishers)
(A) *Standard World Over*	1. BIS
(B) *Universities Handbook, India*	2. AIU
(C) *World Tables*	3. WTO
(D) *Facts on File*	4. CAS

Codes:	A	B	C	D
(a)	3	2	1	4
(b)	1	2	3	4
(c)	4	1	3	2
(d)	1	4	3	2

288. Information Gatekeepers come under (*NET Exam.* 2005D)
(a) Human resources
(b) Documentary sources
(c) Institutional sources
(d) Neo-conventional sources

289. National Institution of Scientific Communication and Information Resources (NISCAIR) merged into NISCOM in the year (*NET Exam.* 2005D)
(a) 2005 (b) 2003 (c) 1992 (d) 2002

290. Which of the following includes experts of computer hardware and software specialists involved in many aspects of system, design, maintenance and similar other services? (*NET Exam.* 2005D)
(a) Information Retrievers
(b) Information Recorder
(c) Information Scientists
(d) All of above

291. The presentation of information in a non-sequential style and pattern is (*NET Exam.* 2005D)
(a) Hypermedia (b) Hypertext
(c) Multimedia (d) HTML

292. Which among the following is considered as an informal channel of Information Communication? (*NET Exam.* 2006J)
(a) Journals (b) Textbooks
(c) Invisible Colleges (d) Technical Reports

293. The term "Bandwidth" refers to (*NET Exam.* 2006J)
(a) The amount of data that can be sent through communication media
(b) The amount of data in a multimedia file
(c) The speed of transmission of data
(d) Number of bands available in a computer

294. ADONIS is a (*NET Exam.* 2006J)
(i) Bibliographic database only
(ii) Numerical database only
(iii) Full text database
(iv) None of the above
(a) (i) and (ii) are correct
(b) (ii) and (iii) are correct
(c) (iii) is correct
(d) (iv) is correct

295. Primary sources include(*NET Exam.* 2006J)
(i) Thesis (ii) Patent
(iii) Abstracting Periodical
(iv) Periodical article
(a) (i), (ii) and (iii) are correct
(b) (i), (iii) and (iv) are correct
(c) (i), (ii) and (iv) are correct
(d) (ii), (iii) and (iv) are correct

296. Hypothesis is a (*NET Exam.* 2006J)
(i) Solution to the problems
(ii) Statements of assumption
(iii) Statement to be tested
(iv) Fact
(a) (i) and (iii) are correct
(b) (ii) and (iii) are correct
(c) (i) and (ii) are correct
(d) (i) and (iv) are correct

297. Shannon and Weaver are associated with (*NET Exam.* 2006J)
(i) Mathematical theory of communication
(ii) Models of communication
(iii) Theories of Management
(iv) Library software packages
(a) (i) and (ii) are correct
(b) (i) and (iii) are correct
(c) (ii) and (iii) are correct
(d) (ii) and (iv) are correct

298. **Assertion (A):** Information can be obtained from several sources other than the libraries.

Reason (R): Library Science is narrower in scope than information science.

(*NET Exam.* 2006J)

Codes:

(a) (A) is false and (R) are true
(b) (R) is false and (A) is true
(c) Both (A) and (R) are false
(d) Both (A) and (R) are true

299. Select the right chronological sequence of information systems, as per their year of establishment.

(*NET Exam.* 2006J)

(a) INIS, AGRIS, NISSAT, Patent Information System (India)
(b) AGRIS, NISSAT, INIS, Patent Information System (India)
(c) Patent Information System (India), INIS, AGRIS, NISSAT
(d) NISSAT, AGRIS, INIS, Patent Information System (India)

300. Match the following: (*NET Exam.* 2006J)

List-I	List-II
(A) Soul	(i) DESIDOC
(B) WINISIS	(ii) ALGORITHM
(C) SANJAY	(iii) Informatics (India)
(D) SLIM	(iv) UNESCO
	(v) DRTC

Codes:	A	B	C	D
(a)	iv	v	i	ii
(b)	v	iii	iv	i
(c)	iv	v	ii	iii
(d)	v	iv	i	ii

301. Match the following: (*NET Exam.* 2006J)

List-I	List-II
(A) Translation Service	(i) BLDSC
(B) Information repackaging Service	(ii) DELNET
(C) Document Delivery Service	(iii) ITC
(D) Library Networking	(iv) Information Analysis Centre
	(v) DRTC

Codes:	A	B	C	D
(a)	(ii)	(iv)	(i)	(iii)
(b)	(iii)	(iv)	(i)	(ii)
(c)	(v)	(iv)	(ii)	(i)
(d)	(iii)	(v)	(iv)	(ii)

302. Match the following: (*NET Exam.* 2006J)

List-I (Publication)	List-II (Institution/System)
(A) AGRINDEX	(i) INSPEC
(B) ATOMINDEXt	(ii) National Library of Medicine
(C) Physics Index	(iii) AGRIS
(D) Index MEDICUS	(iv) INIS

Codes:	A	B	C	D
(a)	(iv)	(i)	(iii)	(ii)
(b)	(i)	(iii)	(iv)	(ii)
(c)	(iii)	(iv)	(i)	(ii)
(d)	(i)	(ii)	(iii)	(iv)

303. Match the following:

(*NET Exam.* 2006D)

List-I (Medium/Connectivity)	List-II (Type)
(A) Fax	(i) Optical Storage
(B) CD-ROM	(ii) Magnetic Storage
(C) Floppy Disc	(iii) Switching System
(D) Circuit	(iv) Image Transmission

Codes:	A	B	C	D
(a)	(iv)	(i)	(ii)	(iii)
(b)	(ii)	(i)	(iii)	(iv)
(c)	(i)	(ii)	(iii)	(iv)
(d)	(iii)	(ii)	(i)	(iv)

304. Match the following: (*NET Exam.* 2006D)

List-I	List-II
(A) IFLA	(i) Science Citation Index
(B) UNESCO	(ii) First Search
(C) OCLC	(iii) Patent Information
(D) ISI	(iv) Public Library Manifesto
	(v) Universal Availability of Publications

Codes:	A	B	C	D
(a)	(iii)	(iv)	(ii)	(i)
(b)	(iv)	(v)	(iii)	(iv)
(c)	(v)	(iv)	(ii)	(i)
(d)	(v)	(i)	(iv)	(ii)

305. Technological Gatekeeper is

(*NET Exam.* 2006D)

(i) An informal channel
(ii) A term coined by T.J. Allen
(iii) A formal channel
(iv) A term coined by Derek De J. Solla Price

(a) (i) and (ii) are correct
(b) (i) and (iii) are correct
(c) (ii) and (iii) are correct
(d) (iii) and (iv) are correct

306. Which of the following is not correctly matched? (*NET Exam.* 2006D)
(a) DELNET–Telecommunication Network
(b) Digital Library–Print Material
(c) Thesaurus–List of Descriptors
(d) ISBN–Serial Number

307. Informal Communication among knowledgeable persons is known as (*NET Exam.* 2006D)
(a) Invisible College
(b) Information Gatekeeper
(c) Communication Gatekeeper
(d) Knowledge Management

308. Which of the following are produced by Institute of Scientific Information: (*NET Exam.* 2006D)
(i) Science Citation Index (ii) Current Contents
(iii) Index Medicus (iv) Atom Index
(a) (i), (ii) and (iii) (b) (i) and (ii)
(c) (ii) and (iii) (d) (i) and (iv)

309. If the size of the study population is very small, the following sampling method will give better results: (*NET Exam.* 2006D)
(a) Purposive (b) Stratified
(c) Random (d) Census

310. Which of the following search devices will lead to an increase in the Recall output? (*NET Exam.* 2006D)
(a) Boolean 'And' (b) Boolean 'Not'
(c) Proximity Operators (d) Truncation

311. **Assertion (A):** Systems analysis identifies the flow of work. (*NET Exam.* 2006D)
Reason (R): Systems analysis is not necessary if the library is to be automated.
Codes:
(a) Both (A) and (R) are correct
(b) Both (A) and (R) are false
(c) (A) is true and (R) is false
(d) (R) is true and (A) is false

312. Match the following
Column A
(A) National Information centre for Drugs and Pharmaceuticals (NICDAP)
(B) National Information Centre for Crystallogrphy (NICRYS)
(C) National Information Centre for Food Science and Technology (NICFOS)
Column B
(i) Lucknow (ii) University of Chennai
(iii) Mysore (iv) Karnal

Codes:	A	B	C
(a)	1	2	3
(b)	3	2	1
(c)	2	4	3
(d)	1	3	2

313. Match the following: (*NET Exam.* 2006D)

List-I (Terms)	**List-II (Forms of Communication)**
(A) Invisible College	(i) Physical Carrier
(B) Noise	(ii) Formal Carrier
(C) Medium	(iii) Barrier
(D) Document	(iv) Informal Channel

Codes:	A	B	C	D
(a)	(i)	(ii)	(iii)	(ii)
(b)	(i)	(iii)	(iv)	(ii)
(c)	(iii)	(iv)	(i)	(ii)
(d)	(i)	(ii)	(iii)	(iv)

314. Match the following: (*NET Exam.* 2006D)

List-I (Research Methods)	**List-II (Type)**
(A) Content Analysis	(i) Data Collection Tool
(B) Questionnaire	(ii) Qualitative Methods of Analysis
(C) Observation	(iii) Methods of Research
(D) Case Study	(iv) Direct Method

Codes:	A	B	C	D
(a)	(i)	(iv)	(iii)	(ii)
(b)	(ii)	(i)	(iv)	(iii)
(c)	(iii)	(ii)	(i)	(iv)
(d)	(iv)	(iii)	(ii)	(i)

315. The term 'Precision' to measure the performance of Information Retrieval, terms was suggested by (*NET Exam.* 2006D)
(a) S.R. Ranganathan (b) F.W. Lancaster
(c) Cyril Cleverdon (d) H.P. Luhn

Read the passage given below, and answer the question based on your understanding of the passage. (Q. No. 316-320)

To meet the challenge of change, much thought is currently being given to information studies, curricula and the requirement of a more broad-based education for the information scientist of the present. A developing country like India cannot afford to neglect these aspects of manpower training which is crucial to the success of development efforts. In the context of proliferation of literature, the information professional can hardly keep track of the information requirements of his clientele, unless he is well versed in modern information handling methods. Manpower for our libraries and information centres is presently drawn from library schools run by the universities and two specialized information science programmes offered by the DRTC and NISCAIR. Certain studies have revealed that "professionals trained by special institutes are far better in the information fields than their colleagues, the products of the University Departments". It is pertinent at this point to design and formulate curricula in respect of the various levels of training to be imparted. Any consideration of the system of training to be meted out has to be at par with the present set up, function and purpose of the existing information centres.

316. Nowadays much though is given for (*NET Exam.* 2007J)
   (a) Curriculum requirements
   (b) Broad based education
   (c) Information scientists
   (d) All the above

317. India cannot afford to neglect the aspects of manpower training because (*NET Exam.* 2007J)
   (a) of proliferation of library schools
   (b) of in-sufficient provision of library schools
   (c) they are crucial to the success of development
   (d) they are not crucial for the success of development

318. Specialized information science education institutes produce better professionals as (*NET Exam.* 2007J)
   (a) Library schools fail to produce good professionals
   (b) Library schools are unable to meet the demands of the society
   (c) They have better curricula and infrastructure
   (d) They do not have good curricula

319. LIS education is now pertinent to (*NET Exam.* 2007J)
   (a) Design curricula
   (b) Follow existing curricula
   (c) Have status quo in curricula
   (d) Reduce the curricula

320. Training for librarianship must be at par (*NET Exam.* 2007J)
   (a) with the old set up
   (b) with the future set up
   (c) with the present set up
   (d) with the previous set up

321. **Assertion (A):** Libraries of tomorrow will become more information service-oriented centres.

   Reason (R): They would require more powerful tools for storage and retrieval of information. (*NET Exam.* 2007J)

   Codes:
   (a) Both (A) and (R) are true and (R) is the correct explanation of (A)
   (b) Both (A) and (R) are true but (R) is not the correct explanation of (A)
   (c) (A) is true but (R) is false
   (d) (A) is false but (R) is true

322. **Assertion (A):** Research is a total process consisting of a series of steps.

   Reason (R): Sometimes, several steps are carried out simultaneously. (*NET Exam.* 2007J)

   Codes:
   (a) Both (A) and (R) are true
   (b) Both (A) and (R) are false
   (c) (A) is true and (R) is false
   (d) (R) is true and (A) is false

323. Match the following: (*NET Exam.* 2007J)

List-I	List-II
(A) NISCAIR	(i) MINISIS
(B) DESIDOC	(ii) Libsys
(C) IDRC	(iii) Granthalaya
	(iv) Sanjay
(D) INFOTEK	(v) SLIM

Codes:	A	B	C	D
(a)	(ii)	(v)	(iii)	(iv)
(b)	(i)	(ii)	(v)	(iv)
(c)	(iii)	(ii)	(i)	(v)
(d)	(iii)	(v)	(i)	(ii)

324. Match the following:

List-I	List-II
(A) INIS	(i) 1950
(B) AGRIS	(ii) 1970
(C) INPADOC	(iii) 1972
(D) OCLC	(iv) 1974
	(v) 1967

Codes:	A	B	C	D
(a)	(ii)	(iii)	(v)	(iv)
(b)	(ii)	(i)	(iv)	(v)
(c)	(iii)	(iv)	(ii)	(i)
(d)	(i)	(iv)	(iii)	(ii)

325. Arrange the following according to the preferred order of sources for information. (*NET Exam.* 2007J)

(i) Colophon (ii) Outside the issue
(iii) Title Page (iv) Preface

Codes:

(a)	(i)	(ii)	(iii)	(i)
(b)	(ii)	(iii)	(i)	(iii)
(c)	(iii)	(i)	(iv)	(ii)
(d)	(iii)	(i)	(iv)	(ii)

326. "Search strategy is the mirror in the dark". Whose quotation is this? (*NET Exam.* 2007J)
(a) Kartz (b) Ranganathan
(c) Bliss (d) Cutter

327. **Assertion (A):** Historical, Descriptive and Experimental Methods are scientific methods. (*NET Exam.* 2007J)
Reason (R): A scientific method is one that adopt a logical and systematic procedure.
Codes:
(a) (A) is true but (R) is false
(b) Both (A) and (R) are true
(c) (A) is false but (R) is true
(d) Both (A) and (R) are true, but (R) is not the correct explanation

328. One of the following has designed models of communication. (*NET Exam.* 2007J)
(a) Shannon and Weaver
(b) Ranganathan and Neelmeghan
(c) Losswell and Gerbher
(d) Blake and Mouton

329. Fundamental facts of research are available in:
(a) Primary sources (b) Secondary sources
(c) Tertiary sources (d) None of the above
(*NET Exam.* 2007J)

330. The following is the search engine for scientific information only.
(*NET Exam.* 2007J)
(a) Google (b) SCIRUS
(c) Yahoo (d) Alta Vista

331. Identify the correct chronological order in which they were set up.(*NET Exam.* 2007J)
(a) ILA, IASLIC, APLA, IATLIS
(b) APLA, ILA, IASLIC, IATLIS
(c) IASLIC, ILA, IATLIS, APLA
(d) IATLIS, IASLIC, ILA, APLA

332. A statement that is to be tested in research is called: (*NET Exam.* 2007J)
(a) Problem (b) Assumption
(c) Hypothesis (d) All the above

333. OAI stand for (*NET Exam.* 2007J)
(a) Open Access Initiatives
(b) Open Archives Initiatives
(c) On-line Archives Initiatives
(d) On-line Access Initiatives

334. Match the following: (*NET Exam.* 2007J)

List-I	**List-II**
(A) Search Engine	(i) PASCAL
(B) Browser	(ii) UNIX
(C) Operating System	(iii) Yahoo
(D) Programming Language	(iv) Netscape
	(v) HTTP

Codes:	**A**	**B**	**C**	**D**
(a)	(i)	(iv)	(v)	(ii)
(b)	(iv)	(iii)	(ii)	(i)
(c)	(iii)	(iv)	(ii)	(i)
(d)	(iv)	(ii)	(i)	(v)

335. Headquarters of IFLA is located in
(*NET Exam.* 2007D)
(a) Paris (b) Washington
(c) London (d) The Hague

336. NACLIN is sponsored by
(*NET Exam.* 2007D)
(a) INFLIBNET (b) DELNET
(c) AGRINET (d) CALIBNET

337. SCOPUS is a (*NET Exam.* 2007D)
(a) Full Text Database
(b) Abstracts and Citation Database
(c) Numerical Database
(d) None of the above

338. Handling of information in the sense of production is called (*NET Exam.* 2007D)
(a) Information Marketing
(b) Information Industry
(c) Information Production
(d) Information Revolution

339. The term "Information Science" came into existence in this year (*NET Exam.* 2007D)
(a) 1988 (b) 1959 (c) 1961 (d) 1975

340. **Assertion (A):** Information Literacy is necessary for the users.

Reason (R): It promotes the use of libraries and information centres.
(*NET Exam.* 2007D)

Codes:
(a) Both (A) and (R) are true
(b) Both (A) and (R) are false
(c) (A) is true but (R) is false
(d) (A) is false but (R) is true

341. Identify the correct chronological order in which the following networks were launched. (*NET Exam.* 2007D)

(i) NICNET (ii) ERNET
(iii) DELNET (iv) INDONET

Codes:

(a)	(iii)	(i)	(ii)	(iv)
(b)	(iv)	(iii)	(i)	(iii)
(c)	(ii)	(i)	(iii)	(iv)
(d)	(i)	(ii)	(iv)	(ii)

342. **Assertion (A):** In survey research, the commonly used techniques for gathering data are questionnaire, the interview and the observational techniques.

Reason (R): These are least effective for collecting data about perceptions, beliefs, attitudes, etc. of persons.
(*NET Exam.* 2007D)

Codes:
(a) (A) is true and (R) is false
(b) (A) is false and (R) is true
(c) Both (A) and (R) are true
(d) Both (A) and (R) is false

343. Opaque paper is a (*NET Exam.* 2008J)
(a) Ultra-white paper
(b) Ultra-white thin paper
(c) Transparent paper
(d) Non-Transparent paper

344. Which is the correct logical sequence of the following: (*NET Exam.* 2008J)
(a) Information, knowledge, data, wisdom
(b) Knowledge, Information, wisdom, data
(c) Data, Knowledge, Information, wisdom
(d) Data, Information, Knowledge, wisdom

345. **Assertion (A):** Consortia cannot provide an effective strategy to increase the buying power of individual libraries.

Reason (R): Consortia arrangement saves the funds of the libraries in developing their information sources: (*NET Exam.* 2008J)

Codes:
(a) (A) is false but (R) is true
(b) (A) is true but (R) is false
(c) Both (A) and (R) are false
(d) Both (A) and (R) are true

Read the passage given below, and answer the questions based on your understanding of the passage. (Q. No. 346-350)

Information is a resource whose generation consumes time and money and whose use conserves time and money. The industrial environment in India is making a quantum jump in the field of technology absorption and innovation. New companies, both in the public and private sector, have been started in the past two years and most of the monopoly business is coming to an end. In other words, the industrial environment is becoming more and more competitive. Information is one of the major resources which will help the company win a competitive edge. Electronics industry is both an important and competitive industry. It has grown 514% from 1970, with an average growth rate of 15% per annum. It is hoped that by 1990 the computer industry would be a ₹ 665 crore sector. There are more than 100 companies in India now manufacturing computers. The survival in this industry by a company largely depends on its openness to adopt new technologies, introduce state-of-the-art products, new marketing strategies, etc. For this the company needs information on the technology, environment and competition. The types of information generally sought by a company include economic information, legal information, information on personnel relations, public relations, technology trends, market trends, etc.

346. Industrial environment in India is making a quantum jump because
(*NET Exam.* 2007D)
(a) Information is a resource whose generation consumes time
(b) Information is a resource whose generation is money
(c) Information is a resource that consumes money and time
(d) Information absorptions and innovation in the field of the technology

347. Monopoly in business is coming to an end because of a: (*NET Exam.* 2007D)
(a) Information (b) Money flow
(c) Competitiveness (d) Lack of information

348. Information is a major resource which (*NET Exam.* 2007D)
(a) helps company to lose money
(b) helps company to achieve popularity
(c) helps company to have an edge in competition
(d) helps company to gain better manpower

349. Electronics industry is both an important and competent industry as it (*NET Exam.* 2007D)
(a) is growing at the rate of fifteen percent
(b) is growing at the rate of five hundred percent
(c) is growing at the rate of fourteen percent
(d) is not growing at all

350. The types of information usually sought by companies are (*NET Exam.* 2007D)
(a) economics and legal information
(b) information on personnel relation
(c) information on technology and market trends
(d) All the above

351. Match the following: (*NET Exam.* 2007D)
List-I
(A) Simplex (B) Half Duplex
(C) Full Duplex (D) Asynchronous
List-II
(i) Communication channel is used in both the direction but only in one direction a at time
(ii) Communication channel is used in one direction
(iii) Bits of information are transmitted continuously transmission
(iv) The communication channel is used in both the directions at the same time
(v) Information is sent at random intervals with start and stop bits for each batch of information

Codes:	**A**	**B**	**C**	**D**
(a)	(ii)	(i)	(iv)	(v)
(b)	(i)	(iv)	(iii)	(ii)
(c)	(v)	(ii)	(i)	(iii)
(d)	(i)	(iii)	(iv)	(ii)

352. Match the following: (*NET Exam.* 2007D)
List-I
(A) INIS (b) AGRIS
(C) MEDLINE (D) INSPEC
List-II
(i) Institute of Electrical Engineering, UK
(ii) International Atomic Energy Agency, Vienna
(iii) Agricultural Organization of UN, Rome
(iv) National Library of Medicine, USA

Codes:	**A**	**B**	**C**	**D**
(a)	(iii)	(ii)	(i)	(iv)
(b)	(ii)	(iii)	(iv)	(i)
(c)	(iv)	(ii)	(iii)	(i)
(d)	(ii)	(i)	(iii)	(iv)

353. Arrange the following research steps according to the sequence of their occurrence: (*NET Exam.* 2007D)
(i) Formulation of hypothesis of research
(ii) Designing of data and analysis plan
(iii) Selection of data gathering method
(iv) Report writing

Codes:

(a)	(iii)	(ii)	(i)	(iv)
(b)	(i)	(iii)	(ii)	(iv)
(c)	(iii)	(i)	(iv)	(ii)
(d)	(ii)	(iv)	(i)	(iii)

354. **Assertion (A):** Information is a resource whose generation consumes time and money.
Reason (R): Information is a resource where we consume time and money.
Codes:
(a) Both (A) and (R) are true but (R) is not the right explanation of (A)
(b) Both (A) and (R) are true and (R) is the right explanation of (A)
(c) (A) is true but (R) is false
(d) (A) is false but (R) is true

355. DESIDOC is documentation centre for (*NET Exam.* 2008J)
(a) Indigenous Knowledge
(b) Defence Science
(c) Rural Development
(d) Khadi & Village Industries

356. Arrange the following Act according to year of enactment: (*NET Exam.* 2008J)
(a) Copyright Act, The Patent Act, Information Tech. Act. IPR Act
(b) The Patent Act, Copyright Act, Information Tech. IPR Act

(c) Copyright Act, IPR Act, The Patent Act, Information Tech. Act
(d) Copyright Act, The Patent Act, IPR Act, Information Tech. Act

357. Fair use is a term most relevant to (*NET Exam.* 2008J)
(a) Intellectual Property Rights
(b) Books borrowed for home reading
(c) Copy right
(d) Use of reference books

358. Cranfield Studies are an example of (*NET Exam.* 2008J)
(a) Survey Research
(b) Experimental Research
(c) Historical Research
(d) Case Study

359. Which of the following is a public domain database? (*NET Exam.* 2008J)
(a) INIS (b) AGRIS
(c) Chemical Abstracts (d) MEDLINE

360. Which of the following is not associated with communication system? (*NET Exam.* 2008J)
(a) Receiver (b) Sender
(c) Channel (d) Entropy

361. **Assertion (A):** Document transfer and information transfer are not the same.
Reason (R): Assimilation of the content of the document by the user constitutes information transfer. (*NET Exam.* 2008J)
Codes:
(a) (A) is true and (R) is false
(b) (R) is true but (A) is false
(c) Both (A) and (R) are true
(d) Both (A) and (R) are false

362. Questionnaire is a (*NET Exam.* 2008J)
(a) Research method
(b) Measurement technique
(c) Tool for data collection
(d) All the above

363. Arrange the following associations in the order of year of establishment. (*NET Exam.* 2008J)
(a) SIS, IASLIC, IATLIS, ILA
(b) IASLIC, ILA, SIS, IATLIS
(c) ILA, SIS, IASLIC, IATLIS
(d) ILA, IASLIC, IATLIS, SIS

364. Dublin core is (*NET Exam.* 2008J)
(a) A set of core activities of a National Library
(b) Collection of metadata elements
(c) Network for the city of Dublin
(d) Revised version of MARC

365. Mean, Median and mode are (*NET Exam.* 2008J)
(a) Measures of deviation
(b) Ways of sampling
(c) Measures of control tendency
(d) None of the above

366. NISCAIRE is a part of (*NET Exam.* 2008J)
(a) DST (b) ISRO (c) DSIR (d) CSIR

367. Use of Microfilming is considerably reduced due to (*NET Exam.* 2008J)
(a) High cost involved in it.
(b) Need for use microfilm reader.
(c) Availability of better Technology in the form of digitization.
(d) All of the above.

368. Match the following: (*NET Exam.* 2008J)

List-I	List-II
(A) Conventional	(i) Patents
(B) Neo-conventional	(ii) Printed books
(C) Non-conventional	(iii) Satellite imageries
(D) Meta documents	(iv) Audio-visual material

Codes:	A	B	C	D
(a)	(i)	(ii)	(iii)	(iv)
(b)	(ii)	(i)	(iv)	(iii)
(c)	(iv)	(i)	(iii)	(ii)
(d)	(iii)	(ii)	(i)	(iv)

369. There are a few basic factors which may be applied in winning the hearts of the readers. They are
(a) Psychological factor, environmental factor, social factor
(b) Self-factor, psychological factor, service factor
(c) Service factor, philosophical factor, self-factor
(d) Technological factor, service factor, self-factor.

370. Linear model of communication is knowledge based on Aristotle's model of communication was proposed by (*NET Exam.* 2010D)
(a) Juger Hebarman
(b) A.J. Wells
(c) C.E. Shannon & W. Weaver
(d) G. Gerbner

371. When a source referred to once in the footnote is referred to again and between them no other reference (i.e. citation) intervenes, then the footnote uses the abbreviation (*NET Exam.* 2010D)
(a) Ibid. (b) Id.
(c) Op. cit. (d) None of these

372. Study carrels are exclusive areas meant to
(a) Students (b) Public
(c) Women (d) Researchers

373. UNIMARC was developed under the umbrella of (*NET Exam.* 2010D)
(a) OCLC (b) IFLA
(c) UNESCO (d) None of the above

374. FRBR is developed by(*NET Exam.* 2012D)
(a) LC (b) UNESCO (c) IFLA (d) FID

375. Match the following: (*NET Exam.* 2010J)
List-I
(A) The Right to Information Act of India
(B) Universal Declaration of Human Rights
(C) Information Technology Act (India)
(D) Digital Millennium Act
List-II
(i) 2000 (ii) 2005 (iii) 1948 (iv) 1998

Codes:	A	B	C	D
(a)	(i)	(ii)	(iii)	(iv)
(b)	(ii)	(iii)	(i)	(iv)
(c)	(iii)	(ii)	(iv)	(i)
(d)	(iv)	(iii)	(ii)	(i)

376. **Assertion (A):** Median is simply the middle value when the data have been arranged in ascending or descending order.
Reason (R): Median refers to the middle value in a distribution. (*NET Exam.* 2010J)
Codes:
(a) Both (A) and (R) are true.
(b) (A) is true, but (R) is false.
(c) (A) is false, but (R) is true.
(d) Both (A) and (R) are false.

377. Match the following: (*NET Exam.* 2010J)

List-I	List-II
(A) CLRI	(i) Hyderabad
(B) SENDOC	(ii) New Delhi
(C) NASSDOC	(iii) Mumbai
(D) BARC	(iv) Chennai

Codes:	A	B	C	D
(a)	(ii)	(i)	(iv)	(iii)
(b)	(iv)	(iii)	(i)	(ii)
(c)	(iv)	(i)	(ii)	(iii)
(d)	(iii)	(i)	(iv)	(ii)

Read the passage given below, and answer the questions based on your understanding of the passage. (Q. No. 378-382)

Invention is the creation of an idea that can be translated to practice. It is also the process of bringing new technology into being. Invention is goal directed, the process is orderly, and it is essentially an intellectual process. An inventor is generally not a big reservoir of existing knowledge or of past failures. A substantial part of a scientist's time is spent in collecting facts. The greater a scientist's familiarity with the great scientific works, the grater will be his own power of invention. Ingenuity is the younger brother of imagination. Theoretical creation is an intermediate step between invention and discovery. A scientist, who is familiar with a number of methods attached to a problem, is most likely to solve the greatest number of problems.

Invention is the basic ingredient of innovation. Innovation is of two kinds, i.e., in product and service. It is a slow process. Innovations which started several years ago may bear fruit now innovation involves the bringing of an invention into commercial use. In some cases, invention and innovation merge into one another. Invention and innovation have been the foundations of industrial development in most advanced countries. Innovation brings about competition and competition brings about efficiency. Of the total innovation process, research is only a part. Research may invent, but invention can only be utilized by the complicated and complex process of innovation. Innovation is more often the result of recognizing and adapting an idea than of invention a new one. Utilization of technical information including research outputs can results in an industrial innovation.

Innovators achieve success, but not imitations. In the past, innovation came from individual scientists. Individual inventors were responsible for innovation. In modern industry it is rarely the case, teams of scientists are really responsible for inventions and innovations. Success in invention and innovation depends not only on originality and imagination but also on knowing what and how to invent and innovate.

378. What is an invention? (*NET Exam.* 2010J)
(a) It is the idea that has the characteristics of application.
(b) A theoretical idea regardless of application
(c) A discovery that does not lead to new technology
(d) A process bereft of use

379. An invention involves: (*NET Exam.* 2010J)
(a) Collection and application of past data.
(b) Simply an effort to explore past knowledge.
(c) Redefining knowledge of the past.
(d) Exploiting past knowledge and newly collected facts.

380. Industrial development and competitive environment are possible when (*NET Exam.* 2010J)
(a) Invention follows innovation
(b) Invention leads to innovation
(c) Invention prevents innovation
(d) Invention has little practical use

381. Invention is carried out at present (*NET Exam.* 2010J)
(a) by an individual researcher with little originality and imagination.
(b) by an individual researcher with high level imagination.
(c) by a group of researchers with adequate originality and imagination.
(d) by industrials to achieve success in business.

382. What is innovation? (*NET Exam.* 2010J)
(a) Innovation is a theoretical process.
(b) Innovation conceals invention.
(c) Innovation is a process of application of invention.
(d) Innovation provides data for invention.

383. Match the following: (*NET Exam.* 2010J)

List-I	List-II
(A) NSSDOC	(i) Defence Science
(B) DEVSIS	(ii) Social Sciences
(C) INIS	(iii) Development Science
(D) DESIDOC	(iv) Nuclear Science

Codes:	A	B	C	D
(a)	(iv)	(ii)	(i)	(iii)
(b)	(ii)	(iii)	(iv)	(i)
(c)	(i)	(ii)	(iii)	(iv)
(d)	(iii)	(ii)	(i)	(iv)

384. Arrange the structure of the research report in correct order: (*NET Exam.* 2010J)
(i) Table of contents (ii) Appendices
(iii) Text (iv) Title page

Codes:

(a)	(iii)	(i)	(iv)	(ii)
(b)	(i)	(ii)	(iii)	(iv)
(c)	(ii)	(iii)	(iv)	(i)
(d)	(iv)	(i)	(iii)	(ii)

385. **Assertion (A):** Data base is a collection of interrelated data stored together. (*NET Exam.* 2010J)

Reason (R): It is an organized, integrated collection of data.

Codes:
(a) Both (A) and (R) are false.
(b) (A) is false, but (R) is true.
(c) Both (A) and (R) are true.
(d) (A) is true, but (R) is false.

386. Which is not a near synonym term to information? (*NET Exam.* 2010J)
(a) Ideas (b) Data (c) Catalogue (d) Facts

387. Who expressed knowledge in a simple mathematical equation k(s) + 1 = k (s +s)? (*NET Exam.* 2010J)
(a) Fritz Machlup (b) B.C. Brooks
(c) N.J. Belkin (d) C.E. Shannon

388. Which Bibliometrics Law describes the frequency of publication by authors in a given field? (*NET Exam.* 2010D)
(a) Lotka's Law (b) Zipf's Law
(c) Bradford's Law (d) None of these

389. WorldCat is maintained by (*NET Exam.* 2010D)
(a) Library of Congress
(b) Online Computer Library Center
(c) American Library Association
(d) None of the above

390. **Assertion (A):** Use of microfilming is becoming obsolete day by day.

Reason (R): ICT has developed digital technologies, which are quick, cheap and easy to handle. (*NET Exam.* 2010D)

Codes:
(a) Both (A) and (R) are true but (R) is not a correct explanation.
(b) Both (A) and (R) are false.

(c) (A) is true but (R) is false.
(d) Both (A) and (R) are true and (R) is the correct explanation of (A).

391. **Assertion (A):** A sample is the representation of a whole.

Reason (R): The sample is subjected to observation and analysis. (*NET Exam.* 2010D)

Codes:
(a) (A) is false but (R) is true.
(b) (A) is true but (R) is false.
(c) Both (A) and (R) are false.
(d) Both (A) and (R) are false.

392. **Assertion (A):** Loose Assemblage is the process of linking together different.

Reason (R): This mode was formerly known as subject bundle. (*NET Exam.* 2010D)

Codes:
(a) (A) is false but (R) is true.
(b) (A) is true but (R) is false.
(c) Both (A) and (R) are true.
(d) Both (A) and (R) are false.

393. **Assertion (A):** Electronic access to information is becoming easy day by day.

Reason (R): The printed materials pouring out of the world presses do not show any decline. (*NET Exam.* 2010D)

Codes:
(a) Both (A) and (R) are true but (R) is not a correct explanation of (A).
(b) (A) is true but (R) is false.
(c) (A) is false but (R) is true.
(d) Both (A) and (R) are false.

394. **Assertion (A):** Primary source is one in which information is original.

Reason (R): Secondary sources repack the original information. (*NET Exam.* 2010D)

Codes:
(a) Both (A) and (R) are true.
(b) (A) is true but (R) is false.
(c) (A) is false but (R) is true.
(d) Both (A) and (R) are false.

395. **Assertion (A):** Libraries are changing in the wake of emerging ICT environment.

Reason (R): Libraries are adopting new competencies to operate services in the environment of information super highways. (*NET Exam.* 2010D)

Codes:
(a) Both (A) and (R) are true.
(b) (A) is true but (R) is false.
(c) (A) is false but (R) is true.
(d) Both (A) and (R) are false.

396. Arrange the following softwares according to their development: (*NET Exam.* 2010D)

(i) E-Print (ii) D-space
(iii) Greenstone (iv) Koha

Codes:

(a)	(iv)	(iii)	(i)	(ii)
(b)	(iii)	(ii)	(i)	(iv)
(c)	(ii)	(i)	(iii)	(iv)
(d)	(i)	(iv)	(iii)	(ii)

397. Match the following: (*NET Exam.* 2010D)

List-I	**List-II**
(A) NTC	(i) UK
(B) ITC	(ii) India
(C) BLDSC	(iii) Netherlands
(D) NISCAIR	(iv) USA

Codes:	**A**	**B**	**C**	**D**
(a)	(iv)	(iii)	(i)	(ii)
(b)	(ii)	(i)	(iv)	(iii)
(c)	(i)	(iii)	(ii)	(iv)
(d)	(i)	(ii)	(iii)	(iv)

398. **Assertion (A):** Knowledge is growing exponentially. (*NET Exam.* 2012D)

Reason (R): Number of researchers have increased.

Codes:
(a) Both (A) and (R) are true.
(b) Both (A) and (R) are false.
(c) (A) is false but (R) is true.
(d) (A) is true but (R) is false.

399. The simple Dublin Core Metadata Element Set (DCMES) consists of (*NET Exam.* 2009D)

(a) 10 elements (b) 15 elements
(c) 14 elements (d) 18 elements

Read the passage below and answer the question based on understanding of the passage (Q. No. 400-404)

Communication media have evolved along with technological transformations and progress. Man's inborn need to communicate led to the first medium for the global transmission of information—the printing press, followed by the rotary printing press. But the need for information has always been in continuous growth, so that inventions such as telegraph had to be adopted for information transmission by waves. Indeed, the radio was one of the societies great technological and democratizing advances. But there is no doubt that television has succeeded in making McLuhan's idea of existence of a television tribe a great reality. Large companies, which control access to information by methods that are close to being a monopoly wage fierce battles in order to control mass media, specially television.

The "fourth power" collects, disseminate and preserve a great quantity of information. This information is thematically diverse and exists in a wide variety of formate and media.

In order to control such an important business asset, almost all television broadcasters have set a documentation service that is responsible for satisfying journalist information needs and for the maintenance of the firms intellectual and cultural heritage.

Documentation centres are just the visible aspects of a great documentation web involving different classes of documents, varied media and the diverse requirements of end users. The computerization of documentation structures is a reality that is sustained by a constant exchange of information between document a lists and communication scientists, aimed at enabling the preservation of information and access to this information by means of a standard set of parameters.

The thematic descriptors must describe, viewed and referred content in the audiovisual documents with precision. Thematic identification has a special importance since it is the usual method of accessing information. For these fields, different television companies use different proprietary ad hoe tools, with thesauri being the formula employed to control vocabulary. There have also been experiments aimed at developing effective tools based on faceted classifications. The fact that audio-visual information has to be analysed from two different perspectives in order to understand the challenges offered by this kind of document should be considered. The visual and the sonorous sometimes are complementary, and consequently must be studied and analysed by the information manager. Sound and visual tracks do often collaborate to create a joint informative message, but it is also very common the case where both contribute to create quite different meanings.

400. The first medium for global transmission of information was (*NET Exam.* 2011D)
   (a) Radio (b) Printing Press
   (c) Television (d) Telegraph

401. The intellectual and cultural heritage of television broadcasting firms is maintained by (*NET Exam.* 2011D)
   (a) Communication media
   (b) Journalists
   (c) Television
   (d) Setting up a documentation service

402. A standard set of parameters is needed for (*NET Exam.* 2011J)
   (a) Establishing documentation centres
   (b) Meeting diverse requirements of users
   (c) Preservation and access to information
   (d) Exchange of documents

403. For organizing information, television companies use tools such as (*NET Exam.* 2011J)
   (a) Thesauri
   (b) Faceted classification
   (c) None-faceted classification
   (d) Thematic descriptions

404. Audio-visual information has to be analysed for (*NET Exam.* 2011J)
   (a) Information management
   (b) Understanding the challenges offered by such documents
   (c) Collaborating sound and visual tracks
   (d) Locating information from different places

405. The term "Hypertext" was coined by (*NET Exam.* 2008D)
   (a) Vannevar Bush (b) John Brown
   (c) M.C. Kith (d) Ted Nelson

406. The term 'Information Retrieval' was coined by (*NET Exam.* 2008D)
   (a) H.P Luhn (b) Calvin Mooers
   (c) Mortimer Taube (d) Derek Austin

407. **Assertion (A):** Action research is a form of interpretive research to study human actions and social practices for immediate application.

   Reason (R): Action research is an applied research, which is focused on the solution to local problems, not to develop any theory for general application. (*NET Exam.* 2008D)

Codes:

(a) (A) is true and (R) is false
(b) (R) is true but (A) is false
(c) Both (A) and (R) are false
(d) Both (A) and (R) are true

408. **Assertion (A):** Information systems support promotion of research, development and innovation relating to the national development of a country.

Reason (R): Information is the basic input to the development. (*NET Exam.* 2008D)

Codes:

(a) Both (A) and (R) are true and (R) is not the correct explanation
(b) Both (A) and (R) are true and (R) is the correct explanation
(c) (A) is true but (R) is false
(d) (A) is false but (R) is true

409. The correct sequence of information flow is (*NET Exam.* 2008D)

(a) Massage > Source > Channel > Receiver
(b) Source > Message > Channel > Receiver
(c) Message > Channel > Source > Receiver
(d) Message > Channel > Receiver > Source

410. Match the following: (*NET Exam.* 2008D)

List-I	List-II
(A) Bradford's Law	(i) Author's production
(B) Lotkas' law	(ii) Citation indexing
(C) Eugene Garfield	(iii) Word frequency
(D) Zipf's Law	(iv) Scattering

Codes:	A	B	C	D
(a)	(i)	(ii)	(iv)	(iii)
(b)	(iii)	(iv)	(ii)	(i)
(c)	(iv)	(ii)	(i)	(iii)
(d)	(iv)	(i)	(ii)	(iii)

411. Match the following items give in List-I and List-II: (*NET Exam.* 2008D)

List-I	List-II
(A) Informatique	(i) English
(B) Informatik	(ii) Italian
(C) Informatica	(iii) French
(D) Informatics	(iv) German

Codes:	A	B	C	D
(a)	(iii)	(iv)	(ii)	(i)
(b)	(ii)	(i)	(iv)	(iii)
(c)	(iv)	(iii)	(i)	(ii)
(d)	(iii)	(i)	(ii)	(iv)

412. Match the following: (*NET Exam.* 2008D)

List-I (Types of document/inf. Centre)

(A) Mission Oriented
(B) Social Science Oriented
(C) Science Subject Oriented
(D) Material Oriented

List-II (institution)

(i) Patent information System (ii) DESIDOC
(iii) NISSAT (iv) NASSDOC

Codes:	A	B	C	D
(a)	(iii)	(iv)	(ii)	(i)
(b)	(iv)	(iii)	(ii)	(i)
(c)	(i)	(ii)	(iii)	(iv)
(d)	(ii)	(iii)	(iv)	(i)

413. Recall and Precision ratios are use in the evaluation of (*NET Exam.* 2008D)

(a) Reference service
(b) Information retrieval
(c) Bibliographic service
(d) Document delivery service

414. **Assertion (A):** Any change in the environment of the subject cannot affect the state of the subject.

Reason (R): A subject can be viewed as a system consisting of a set of interacting component ideas. (*NET Exam.* 2008D)

Codes:

(a) (A) is true and (R) is false
(b) (R) is true but (A) is false
(c) Both (A) and (R) are true
(d) Both (A) and (R) are false

415. Match the following: (*NET Exam.* 2008D)

List-I	List-II
(A) SHE	(i) Nuclear Energy
(B) MESH	(ii) Education
(C) ERIC	(iii) Medicine
(D) INIS	(iv) Engineering

Codes:	A	B	C	D
(a)	(i)	(iii)	(ii)	(iv)
(b)	(iv)	(iii)	(ii)	(i)
(c)	(ii)	(iii)	(i)	(iv)
(d)	(i)	(ii)	(iii)	(iv)

416. Match the following: (*NET Exam.* 2009D)

List-I	List-II
(A) Web Navigation Element	(i) Telecommunication
(B) Shift + Tab	(ii) SQL
(C) ANSI Standard	(iii) Hyperlink
(D) TELNET	(iv) Select the previous link

Codes:	A	B	C	D
(a)	(i)	(ii)	(iii)	(iv)
(b)	(iv)	(iii)	(ii)	(i)
(c)	(iii)	(iv)	(ii)	(i)
(d)	(ii)	(iii)	(i)	(iv)

417. CONPOLIS (India) was set up in the year (*NET Exam.* 2009D)
(a) 1985 (b) 1986 (c) 1987 (d) 1988

418. Entropy is a measure of (*NET Exam.* 2009D)
(a) Degree of relevance of information
(b) Quantity of irrelevant information
(c) Degree of uncertainty in information
(d) Degree of certainty information

419. A research design is (*NET Exam.* 2009D)
(a) A series of guide posts
(b) A series of sampling
(c) A hypothetical statement
(d) A controller of variance

420. In a questionnaire, questionnaire on age, income and gender are the examples of (*NET Exam.* 2009D)
(a) Dependent variables
(b) Intervening variables
(c) Independent variables
(d) Manipulation variables

421. Z39.50 is a standard for (*NET Exam.* 2012D)
(a) Communication Formats
(b) Search and Retrieval Services
(c) Cataloguing Web Resources
(d) Library Management Services

422. Which of the factor is not helping in limiting the external validity? (*NET Exam.* 2012D)
(a) Reactive effect
(b) Ecological validity
(c) Interaction between selection bias of experimental variables
(d) Ecological effect

423. National Knowledge Network is to be implemented by (*NET Exam.* 2012D)
(a) National Knowledge Commission
(b) Information and Library Network
(c) National Information Centre
(d) Department of Information Technology

424. The stages in the product life cycle curve are (*NET Exam.* 2012D)
(a) Introduction, Growth, Maturity, Decline
(b) Introduction, Growth, Maturity, Profit
(c) Growth, Maturity, Profit, Decline
(d) Introduction, Growth, Maturity, Saturation

425. Association of College and Research Libraries (ACRL) (USA) is a (*NET Exam.* 2012D)
(a) Division of American Library Association
(b) Independent Association for Academic & Research Libraries
(c) Division of Special Libraries Association (USA)
(d) Division of IFLA

426. Which of the following are the problems of present information environment? (*NET Exam.* 2012D)
(i) Information indiscipline
(ii) Information literacy
(iii) Information overload
(iv) Information technology

Codes:
(a) (i), (iii) are correct
(b) (i) and (iv) are correct
(c) (ii) and (iv) are correct
(d) (i) and (ii) are correct

427. Arrange the following is correct order: (*NET Exam.* 2011D)
(i) Deductive phase (ii) Empirical phase
(iii) Verification phase (iv) Hypothesizing phase

Codes:

(a)	(i)	(iv)	(iii)	(ii)
(b)	(ii)	(i)	(i)	(iv)
(c)	(iv)	(ii)	(iv)	(i)
(d)	(ii)	(iv)	(i)	(iii)

428. Arrange the following according to their year of enactment: (*NET Exam.* 2011D)
(i) Information Technology Act
(ii) Copyright Act
(iii) RTI Act
(iv) Digital Millennium Copyright Act

Codes:

(a)	(i)	(iii)	(iv)	(ii)
(b)	(ii)	(iv)	(i)	(iii)
(c)	(iii)	(i)	(iv)	(ii)
(d)	(i)	(iv)	(ii)	(iii)

429. Match the following: (*NET Exam.* 2011D)

List-I	**(List-II)**
(A) Ibid.	(i) in the work cited
(B) Op. cit.	(ii) same as above

(C) Loc. cit. (iii) in the same pages
(D) Vide (iv) see

Codes:	A	B	C	D
(a)	(ii)	(i)	(iii)	(iv)
(b)	(iii)	(ii)	(iv)	(i)
(c)	(iv)	(i)	(ii)	(iii)
(d)	(i)	(ii)	(iv)	(iii)

430. The Principle of Canonical Sequence is one of the principles of (*NET Exam.* 2011D)
(a) Facet Sequence
(b) Fundamental Categories
(c) Helpful Sequence
(d) Basic laws

431. **Assertion (A):** Information Society is one where all citizens are educated.
Reason (R): Society of which more than 50% population is involved in information activities. (*NET Exam.* 2012D)
Codes:
(a) Both (A) and (R) are true and (R) is the correct explanation of (A).
(b) Both (A) and (R) are true, but (R) is not the correct explanation of (A).
(c) Both (A) and (R) are false.
(d) (A) is false but (R) is true.

432. Match the following: (*NET Exam.* 2012D)
List-I
(A) Information contribution to the GNP of national
(B) Information that changes human activity
(C) Information that establishes interaction between
(D) Information that forms a modern society
List-II
(i) Social information
(ii) Technological information
(iii) Economic government and people
(iv) Political information

Codes:	A	B	C	D
(a)	(iii)	(i)	(iv)	(ii)
(b)	(i)	(iii)	(iv)	(ii)
(c)	(iv)	(ii)	(i)	(iii)
(d)	(ii)	(iii)	(iv)	(i)

433. Match the following: (*NET Exam.* 2012D)
List-I
(A) Communication Barrier
(B) Communication Medium
(C) Communication Model
(D) Interactive Communication
List-II
(i) Radio (ii) Shannon & Weaver
(iii) Video-conferencing (iv) Noise

Codes:	A	B	C	D
(a)	(i)	(ii)	(iii)	(iv)
(b)	(iv)	(i)	(ii)	(iii)
(c)	(ii)	(iii)	(iv)	(i)
(d)	(iii)	(ii)	(i)	(iv)

434. Identify the odd one: (*NET Exam.* 2011D)
(a) Louis Shores (b) William A. Katz
(c) Samuel Rothstein (d) Michael Gorman

435. INFROSS is an important study frequently quoted in (*NET Exam.* 2011D)
(a) Historical Research (b) Survey Research
(c) Experiment Research (d) Case Study

436. Match the following: (*NET Exam.* 2011D)

List-I	List-II
(A) CDS/ISIS	(i) INSDOC
(B) Sanjay	(ii) CMC
(C) Granthalya	(iii) UNSECO
(D) Maitrayee	(iv) DESIDOC

Codes:	A	B	C	D
(a)	(i)	(iii)	(ii)	(iv)
(b)	(ii)	(iii)	(iv)	(i)
(c)	(iv)	(i)	(ii)	(iii)
(d)	(iii)	(iv)	(i)	(ii)

437. **Assertion (A):** Historical research cannot be regarded scientific as it lacks replication and reliability.
Reason (R): Historical research is truly scientific as it is based on criticism. (*NET Exam.* 2011D)
Codes:
(a) Both (A) and (R) are true.
(b) (A) is true, but (R) is false.
(c) (A) is false but (R) is true.
(d) Both (A) and (R) are false.

438. **Assertion (A):** All research results lead to propounding of new laws, theories and principles.
Reason (R): Laws, Principles and Theories are the result of Scientific Research. (*NET Exam.* 2011D)
Codes:
(a) Both (A) and (R) are true and (R) is the correct explanation of (A).
(b) Both (A) and (R) are true, but (R) is not the correct explanation of (A).

(c) (A) is false but (R) is true.
(d) Both (A) and (R) are false.

439. **Assertion (A):** Hypotheses are essential in all types of research.

Reason (R): Research can be conducted without hypotheses. (*NET Exam.* 2011D)

Codes:
(a) Both (A) and (R) are true and (R) is the correct explanation of (A).
(b) Both (A) and (R) are true, but (R) is not the correct explanation of (A).
(c) (A) is false but (R) is true.
(d) Both (A) and (R) are false.

440. **Assertion (A):** Primary sources provide most authentic information for research.

Reason (R): Primary sources are highly unorganized as far as access is concerned. (*NET Exam.* 2011D)

Codes:
(a) Both (A) and (R) are true and (R) is the correct explanation of (A).
(b) Both (A) and (R) are true, but (R) is not the correct explanation of (A).
(c) (A) is false but (R) is true.
(d) Both (A) and (R) are false.

441. **Assertion (A):** Information Science has emerged from Information Technology.

Reason (R): Information Science has emerged with the agglomeration of many subjects, including information technology. (*NET Exam.* 2011D)

Codes:
(a) Both (A) and (R) are true and (R) is the correct explanation of (A).
(b) Both (A) and (R) are true, but (R) is not the correct explanation of (A).
(c) (A) is false but (R) is true.
(d) Both (A) and (R) are false.

442. NACLIN is sponsored by (*NET Exam.* 2011D)
(a) INFLIBNET (b) MALIBNET
(c) DELNET (d) NICNET

443. Arrange the following steps in research in the sequence of their occurrence: (*NET Exam.* 2011D)
(i) Report writing (ii) Research design
(iii) Collection of data (iv) Analysis of data

Codes:

(a)	(iii)	(iv)	(ii)	(i)
(b)	(i)	(iii)	(iv)	(ii)
(c)	(ii)	(iii)	(iv)	(i)
(d)	(iv)	(ii)	(iii)	(i)

444. Arrange the following in a logical sequence: (*NET Exam.* 2011J)
(i) Formulation of a hypothesis
(ii) Data analysis
(iii) Selection of sample
(iv) Report writing

Codes:

(a)	(i)	(ii)	(iii)	(iv)
(b)	(iv)	(ii)	(i)	(iii)
(c)	(ii)	(i)	(iv)	(iii)
(d)	(i)	(iii)	(ii)	(iv)

445. Identify the correct order as per year of establishment (*NET Exam.* 2011J)
(i) ASLIB (ii) IATLIS (iii) SLA (iv) ALA

Codes:

(a)	(iv)	(iii)	(i)	(ii)
(b)	(iv)	(ii)	(i)	(iii)
(c)	(ii)	(i)	(iv)	(iii)
(d)	(i)	(ii)	(iii)	(iv)

446. **Assertion (A):** Like social scientists, the natural scientists can also collect data by conducting experiments, interviewing/ observing people and reviewing literature.

Reason (R): Social scientists cannot be as objective as can be natural scientists.

Codes:
(a) (A) is true, but (R) is false.
(b) (A) is false, but (R) is true.
(c) Both (A) and (R) are true.
(d) Both (A) and (R) are false.

447. 'Half-life' in Information Science relates to (*NET Exam.* 2011J)
(a) Rate of obsolescence
(b) Rate of growth
(c) Degree of scatter
(d) Information explosion

448. In spiral of scientific method, the span of Zenith to descendent is (*NET Exam.* 2012D)
(a) Empirical phase (b) Hypothesizing phase
(c) Deductive phase (d) Verification phase

449. Semantic differential scale is concerned with (*NET Exam.* 2012D)

(a) Pool of items
(b) Selection from two opposite positions
(c) Five point scale
(d) Selection from a check list

450. Which one of the following is not a recommendation of National Knowledge Commission (India)? (*NET Exam.* 2012D)
(a) Preparation of a National Census of Library.
(b) Encourage greater community participation in library management.
(c) Raja Rammohun Roy library foundation at act as the National co-ordination agency.
(d) Facilitate donation and maintenance of private collection.

451. Which of the following variables cannot be expressed in quantitative terms? (*NET Exam.* 2012D)
(a) Socio-economic status
(b) Marital status
(c) Numerical Aptitude
(d) Professional Attitude

452. The national convention regularly organized by DELNET is known as (*NET Exam.* 2012D)
(a) CALIBER (b) ICDL
(c) NACLIN (d) DELNETCON

453. Who defined "to be information literate, a person must be able to recognize when information is needed and have the ability to locate, evaluate and use effectively the needed information"? (*NET Exam.* 2012D)
(a) SLA (b) ALA (c) IFLA (d) CILIP

454. Which of the following are not partners of National Programme on Technology Enhanced Learning (NPTEL)? (*NET Exam.* 2012D)
(i) IIT Madras (ii) IIT Delhi
(iii) IIIT Bangalore (iv) NIT Rourkela
Codes:
(a) (iii) and (iv) (b) (i) and (iv)
(c) (ii) and (iii) (d) (i) and (ii)

455. **Assertion (A):** Federated search technique is an integral component of an information portal. (*NET Exam.* 2012D)
Reason (R): 'Content Index' contains content that is find by the search server.
Codes:
(a) Both (A) and (R) are true.
(b) Both (A) and (R) are false.
(c) (A) is true but (R) is false.
(d) (A) is false but (R) is true.

456. **Assertion (A):** E-publication have added enormous quantity of literature but adversely affected the quality of literature.
Reason (R): Present decade has accepted E-publication as channels of fast communication. (*NET Exam.* 2012D)
Codes:
(a) (A) is true (R) is false.
(b) (A) is false, but (R) is correct.
(c) Both (A) and (R) are false.
(d) Both (A) and (R) are true.

457. Match the following: (*NET Exam.* 2012D)

List-I	List-II
(A) Mean	(i) Most frequently occurring value
(B) Mode	(ii) Average
(C) Median	(iii) Measure of dispersion
(D) Standard Deviation	(iv) Middle Value

Codes:	A	B	C	D
(a)	(iii)	(iv)	(i)	(ii)
(b)	(ii)	(i)	(iv)	(iii)
(c)	(iv)	(iii)	(i)	(ii)
(d)	(ii)	(iii)	(iv)	(i)

458. Match the following: (*NET Exam.* 2012D)

List-I	List-II
(A) Pen drive	(i) Communication device
(B) i-Pad	(ii) Web Server device
(C) Wifi Modem	(iii) Storage device
(D) Cloud computing	(iv) Computing device

Codes:	A	B	C	D
(a)	(i)	(iii)	(ii)	(iv)
(b)	(iii)	(iv)	(i)	(ii)
(c)	(iv)	(iii)	(ii)	(i)
(d)	(iii)	(ii)	(i)	(iv)

459. **Assertion (A):** In conducting research, Social Sciences are not considered at par with natural sciences.
Reason (R): Research in Social Sciences can't be performed so rigorously as can be in Natural Sciences. (*NET Exam.* 2013J)

Codes:
(a) Both (A) and (R) are true.
(b) Both (A) and (R) are false.
(c) (A) is true, but (R) is false.
(d) (A) is false, but (R) is true.

460. Sector Device is an extension of
(a) Gap Device (b) Empty Device
(c) Octave Device (d) Group Notation Device

461. The 12 rules for relational database were given by (*NET Exam.* 2013J)
(a) E.F. Codd (b) Charles Babbage
(c) James Weyer (d) Tim Berners-Lee

462. Which of the following are prohibited under copyright? (*NET Exam.* 2013J)
(i) Downloading a document, printing multiple copies
(ii) Placing a copyright protected document on web-server
(iii) Downloading a document and save it in folder
(iv) Downloading a document with license to use and E-mailing it

Codes:
(a) (i), (iii) and (iv) are correct.
(b) (i), (ii) and (iii) are correct.
(c) (iii), (iv) and (ii) are correct.
(d) (i), (ii) and (iv) are correct.

463. **Assertion (A):** Research starts in mind first and then in laboratories.
Reason (R): Systematically conducted research leads to generalization. (*NET Exam.* 2013J)
Codes:
(a) (A) is true, but (R) is false.
(b) (A) is false, but (R) is true.
(c) Both (A) and (R) are true.
(d) Both (A) and (R) are false.

464. A graphical representation using symbols to represent operations, data, flow, etc. is (*NET Exam.* 2013J)
(a) Logical Chart (b) Flow Chart
(c) System Flow Chart (d) Network Chart

465. A technique displaying graphic information on screen, pixel by pixel with bits held in main memory is (*NET Exam.* 2013J)
(a) Bit handling (b) Bit mapping
(c) Bit pattern (d) Bit matrix

466. Match the following: (*NET Exam.* 2013J)
List-I
(A) Papyrus (B) Handmade paper
(C) Clay tablets (D) Vellum/Parchment
List-II
(i) Assyria & Babylonia (ii) Egypt
(iii) Medieval Europe (iv) China

Codes:	A	B	C	D
(a)	(ii)	(iv)	(i)	(iii)
(b)	(iv)	(ii)	(iii)	(i)
(c)	(iii)	(iv)	(i)	(ii)
(d)	(iii)	(ii)	(iv)	(i)

467. **Assertion (A):** Micrographic services have lost acceptance for preservation and dissemination of archival material.
Reason (R): ICT has brought in cost effective alternative and replaced micrographic services. (*NET Exam.* 2013J)
Codes:
(a) (A) is true and (R) is partially true.
(b) Both (A) and (R) are false.
(c) (A) is true, (R) is false.
(d) (A) is false, (R) is true.

468. The process of surrogation, repackaging and compaction of the primary literature that results in creation of secondary journals, is (*NET Exam.* 2013J)
(a) Newsletter
(b) Abstracting and Indexing Periodical
(c) House Journals
(d) Electronic Journal

469. When the population is heterogenous, which of the following methods give better results? (*NET Exam.* 2013J)
(a) Purposive Sampling
(b) Quota Sampling
(c) Random Sampling
(d) Stratified Random Sampling

470. Match the following: (*NET Exam.* 2013J)
List-I
(A) Amenable to further algebraic treatment
(B) Estimated without knowing value of extreme items
(C) Mathematically and logically incorrect
(D) The dispersion does not cover all items of a series
List-II
(i) Mean Deviation (ii) Median
(iii) Inter-quartile deviation (iv) Arithmetic means

Codes:	A	B	C	D
(a)	(iv)	(ii)	(i)	(iii)
(b)	(iii)	(ii)	(i)	(iv)
(c)	(ii)	(iv)	(iii)	(i)
(d)	(i)	(iii)	(iv)	(ii)

471. **Assertion (A):** The information seeking behaviour research at the current times is on the social and cultural context of human interaction with information.

Reason (R): Attempt is being made to interpret social and cultural experiences of individuals with respect to their information seeking and searching experiences. (*NET Exam.* 2013J)

Codes:
(a) (A) is true and (R) is false.
(b) Both (A) and (R) are false.
(c) (A) is false and (R) is true.
(d) Both (A) and (R) are true.

472. Which is not a reprographic service? (*NET Exam.* 2013J)
(a) Micro Copying (b) Blue Printing
(c) Paper Printing (d) Thermo Copying

473. **Assertion (A):** Institutions generate information through research and development activities.

Reason (R): All such generated information forms the grey literature. (*NET Exam.* 2013J)

Codes:
(a) Both (A) and (R) are true.
(b) Both (A) and (R) are false.
(c) (A) is true, (R) is partially true.
(d) (A) is false, (R) is true.

474. Match the following: (*NET Exam.* 2013J)

List-I
(A) Carol Kuhlthau (B) David Ellis
(C) M.J. Belkin (D) Marchionini

List-II
(i) 8 stages
(ii) ISB is a 6 stage process
(iii) ISB is of 8 key activities
(iv) ISB is 4 dimension characteristic

Codes:	A	B	C	D
(a)	(ii)	(iii)	(iv)	(i)
(b)	(ii)	(iii)	(i)	(iv)
(c)	(iii)	(i)	(iv)	(ii)
(d)	(iv)	(ii)	(i)	(iii)

475. Whose model of communication of knowledge suggests that communication as an open system may be regarded as subjective, selective, variable and yet unpredictable? (*NET Exam.* 2013J)
(a) G. Gerbner (b) Juger Habermas
(c) E. Shannon and Weaver (d) M. Foucault

476. "Anomalous State of Knowledge (ASK) Model", one of the user-centered models of information retrieval was proposed by (*NET Exam.* 2013J)
(a) P. Ingwersen (b) T. Saracevic
(c) J.N. Belkin (d) Ellis

477. Digitization of various cultural resources is possible through (*NET Exam.* 2013J)
(i) Scanners (ii) Digital cameras
(iii) Video cameras (iv) Smart and Mobile phones

Codes:
(a) (i), (ii) are correct.
(b) (iv), (iii) are correct.
(c) (iii), (iv) are correct.
(d) (i), (ii), (iii) and (iv) are correct.

478. Match the following: (*NET Exam.* 2013J)

List-I	List-II
(A) INFLIBNET	(i) Digital Library
(B) INDESTAICTE	(ii) Resource aggregator
(C) DELNET	(iii) E-consortia
(D) e-Gyankosh	(iv) Organisation

Codes:	A	B	C	D
(a)	(i)	(ii)	(iii)	(iv)
(b)	(iv)	(iii)	(ii)	(i)
(c)	(iii)	(ii)	(i)	(iv)
(d)	(ii)	(iii)	(iv)	(i)

479. **Assertion (A):** Technical writing standards, style manuals and citation standards are very essential in structuring the research report.

Reason (R): Value will get enhanced by standardizing the structure of research report. (*NET Exam.* 2013J)

Codes:
(a) (A) is true and (R) is partially true.
(b) Both (A) and (R) are true.
(c) Both (A) and (R) are false.
(d) (A) is true and (R) is false.

480. Match the following: (*NET Exam.* 2013J)

List-I
(A) Finding solution to the problem of pilferage in libraries

(B) Implementation of cloud computing services in special
(C) A study of mathematician turned librarian
(D) Use of e-resources in Central Universities of India

List-II

(i) Historical Research
(ii) Action Research libraries
(iii) Experimental Research
(iv) Survey Research

Codes:	A	B	C	D
(a)	(ii)	(iii)	(i)	(iv)
(b)	(iii)	(ii)	(iv)	(i)
(c)	(iv)	(i)	(ii)	(iii)
(d)	(i)	(iv)	(iii)	(ii)

481. **Assertion (A):** The effective reprographic service in libraries indirectly demotivates the user of tearing/theft of reading material. (*NET Exam.* 2013J)

Reason (R): The user gets the photocopy of reading materials free of cost.

Codes:
(a) (A) is false and (R) is true.
(b) Both (A) and (R) are true.
(c) (A) is true and (R) is false.
(d) Both (A) and (R) are false.

482. Which of the following is not database object? (*NET Exam.* 2013J)

(a) Tables (b) Queries
(c) Relationships (d) Reports

483. Research is conducted to: (*NET Exam.* 2012J)

(i) Generate new knowledge
(ii) Develop a theory
(iii) Develop communication skills
(iv) Re-interpret existing knowledge

Codes:
(a) (i), (iii) and (ii) are correct
(b) (iii), (ii) and (i) are correct
(c) (i), (ii) and (iv) are correct
(d) (i), (iii) and (iv) are correct

484. Redundancy of information is (*NET Exam.* 2012J)

(a) Unnecessary and should be eliminated
(b) Unnecessary but cannot be avoided
(c) Necessary and sometimes useful
(d) Necessary and always desirable

485. **Assertion (A):** Though information is considered as a commodity, libraries are not sound in finances.

Reason (R): All types of libraries have failed in promoting information as a commodity. (*NET Exam.* 2012J)

Codes:
(a) (A) is true, but (R) is false.
(b) (A) is false, but (R) is true.
(c) Both (A) and (R) are true.
(d) Both (A) and (R) are false.

486. Match the following: (*NET Exam.* 2012J)

List-I

(A) Small set of dependent activities that form longest path of activity network
(B) Delighting the customer by fully meeting their needs
(C) Interconnecting networks depicting tasks duration and dependency
(D) Making better forecasts, judgment and advice

List-II

(i) PERT (ii) CPM (iii) Delphi (iv) TQM

Codes:	A	B	C	D
(a)	(i)	(iii)	(ii)	(iv)
(b)	(ii)	(iv)	(i)	(iii)
(c)	(iii)	(iv)	(ii)	(i)
(d)	(iv)	(ii)	(i)	(iii)

487. **Assertion (A):** INFLIBNET provides document delivery service to all types of libraries in India.

Reason (R): Modern technologies made it possible for electronic transmission of required documents. (*NET Exam.* 2012J)

Codes:
(a) Both (A) and (R) are correct.
(b) (A) is wrong, but (R) is correct.
(c) Both (A) and (R) are wrong.
(d) (A) is correct and (R) is wrong.

488. Identify the odd one out. (*NET Exam.* 2012J)

(a) ANSI (b) BIS (c) BSI (d) ESPN

489. **Assertion (A):** LIS Education in India achieved a landmark of 100 years but quality is compromised.

Reason (R): Unplanned proliferation of LIS schools and open learning programmes. (*NET Exam.* 2012J)

Codes:
(a) Both (A) and (R) are true.
(b) Both (A) are (R) are false.
(c) (A) is false (R) is true.
(d) (A) is true (R) is false.

490. Match the following: (*NET Exam.* 2011D, 2012J)

	List-I		List-II
(A)	Ibid.	(i)	see
(B)	Loc. cit.	(ii)	previously cited
(C)	Op. cit.	(iii)	same reference cited immediately above
(D)	Vide	(iv)	the same place cited

Codes:	A	B	C	D
(a)	(i)	(ii)	(iii)	(iv)
(b)	(ii)	(i)	(iv)	(iii)
(c)	(iii)	(iv)	(ii)	(i)
(d)	(iv)	(iii)	(i)	(ii)

491. BIOS contain (*NET Exam.* 2012J)
(i) Operating System Program
(ii) Bootstrap Program
(iii) Application System Program
(iv) Convert Character to Code Program
Codes:
(a) (i) and (ii) are correct
(b) (ii) and (iii) are correct
(c) (iii) and (iv) are correct
(d) (ii) and (iv) are correct

492. Jubilee Project is associated with what (*NET Exam.* 2012J)
(a) Evaluation of electronic information services
(b) Public library survey
(c) Strategic management of libraries
(d) Scale development

493. In the information transfer cycles, Internet is acting as (*NET Exam.* 2012J)
(i) Primary Publisher (ii) Secondary Publisher
(iii) Tertiary Publisher (iv) Primary Distributor
Codes:
(a) (i), (iii) and (iv) are correct.
(b) (i), (ii) and (iv) are correct.
(c) (ii), (iii) and (iv) are correct.
(d) (i), (ii) and (iii) are correct.

494. In the process of reasoning when we start with a specific statement, and conclude to a general statement, it is called (*NET Exam.* 2012J)
(a) Deductive Reasoning
(b) Inductive Reasoning
(c) Abnormal Reasoning
(d) Transcendental Reasoning

495. Inference Engine is a part of which information system? (*NET Exam.* 2012J)
(a) Management information System
(b) Decision Support System
(c) Expert System
(d) Open System

496. In 1974, Zurkowski used for the first time which of the following term? (*NET Exam.* 2012J)
(a) Digital Literacy (b) Media Literacy
(c) Computer Literacy (d) Information Literacy

497. Solomon Four group design is related to (*NET Exam.* 2012J)
(a) Field studies
(b) Pretest-post test control group design
(c) Data Analysis Model
(d) Statistical Technique

498. Virus is a software which can (*NET Exam.* 2012J)
(a) Manipulate data (b) Replicate itself
(c) Damage computer (d) All the above

499. Which of the following is not related to case study approach in a research design? (*NET Exam.* 2012J)
(a) In-depth Study
(b) Study of one/limited cases
(c) General study
(d) Little concern about generalization to a large population

500. State-of-the-art report generally highlights (*NET Exam.* 2012J)
(a) General Aspects
(b) Technical Aspects
(c) Administrative Aspects
(d) All of the above

501. Even though 'Xerography' is a photocopying method, but it is called(*NET Exam.* 2012J)
(a) Diazographic (b) Thermographic
(c) Electrofax (d) Electrostatic

502. Most foreign investment is being made in the are of (*NET Exam.* 2012D)
(a) Microbiology and life sciences.
(b) Computer science and automotive design
(c) Physical sciences and planting.
(d) Grafting and biology.

503. "Facts on File" can be grouped under (*NET Exam.* 2012D)

(a) Primary sources (b) Secondary source
(c) Tertiary source (d) None of the above

504. Arrange the following IFLA programmes according to their year of commencement. (*NET Exam.* 2012D)

(i) UBC (ii) UAP
(iii) ISBD (iv) International MARC Office

Codes:

(a)	(i)	(iv)	(iii)	(ii)
(b)	(ii)	(iv)	(i)	(iii)
(c)	(iv)	(i)	(ii)	(iii)
(d)	(iii)	(i)	(ii)	(iv)

505. Which of the following are library networks? (*NET Exam.* 2012D)

(i) Internet (ii) DELNET
(iii) NICNET (iv) OCLC

Codes:

(a) (i) and (ii) are correct
(b) (ii) and (iv) are correct
(c) (i) and (iii) are correct
(d) (i) and (iv) are correct

506. The basic characteristics of a system are (*NET Exam.* 2012D)

(i) Interrelated components
(ii) Independent and can stand alone
(iii) Arranged in hierarchical order
(iv) Inputs, processes, outputs and feedback

Codes:

(a) (i), (ii), (iii) are correct
(b) (i), (ii), (iv) are correct
(c) (ii), (iii), (iv) are correct
(d) (i), (iii), (iv) are correct

507. The chi-square technique is used to compare the observed data with that of (*NET Exam.* 2012D)

(a) Collected raw data (b) Expected data
(c) Analysed data (d) Graphical data

508. Match the following: (*NET Exam.* 2012D)

List-I

(A) File transfer protocol
(B) Multimedia
(C) Bandwidth
(D) Electronic Notice Board

List-II

(i) Data transmission capacity
(ii) Integration of text, colour sound and animation
(iii) Bulletin Board
(iv) Internet

Codes:	A	B	C	D
(a)	(iv)	(ii)	(i)	(iii)
(b)	(i)	(iii)	(ii)	(iv)
(c)	(ii)	(i)	(iv)	(iii)
(d)	(i)	(iv)	(ii)	(iii)

509. Foreign companies are outsourcing R&D programmes to India because (*NET Exam.* 2012D)

(a) Quality of research is quite high in India.
(b) Outsourcing is cost effective for foreign companies
(c) There is scarcity of skilled manpower in those countries.
(d) None of the above.

510. Which of the following are not the elements of DOI system? (*NET Exam.* 2012D)

(i) Policies (ii) Subjects
(iii) Description (iv) Resolution

Codes:

(a) (i), (ii) and (iii) are correct
(b) (i), (iii) and (iv) are correct
(c) (i), (ii) and (iv) are correct
(d) (ii), (iii) and (iv) are correct

511. **Assertion (A):** Information Literacy is a basic skill essential for work environment in 21st century.

Reason (R): Information literacy helps to train the users to make use of ICT. (*NET Exam.* 2012D)

Codes:

(a) Both (A) and (R) are true.
(b) Both (A) and (R) are false.
(c) (A) is true, but (R) is false.
(d) (A) is false, but (R) is true.

512. Arrange the following in order of their year of establishment: (*NET Exam.* 2012D)

(i) INIS (ii) AGRIS
(iii) MEDLARS (iv) UNESCO

Codes:

(a)	(iii)	(i)	(iv)	(ii)
(b)	(ii)	(iv)	(i)	(iii)
(c)	(iv)	(iii)	(ii)	(i)
(d)	(i)	(ii)	(iv)	(iii)

513. **Assertion (A):** Primary sources provide most authentic information for research.

Reason (R): Primary sources are highly unorganized. (*NET Exam.* 2012J)

Codes:
(a) (A) is false, but (R) is true
(b) (A) is true, but (R) is false
(c) Both (A) and (R) are correct and (R) is the correct explanation of (A)
(d) Both (A) and (R) are correct, but (R) is not the correct explanation of (A)

514. **Assertion (A):** System analysis identifies the flow of work.

Reason (R): System analysis is not necessary if the library is automated. (*NET Exam.* 2012J)

Codes:
(a) (A) is false, but (R) is true.
(b) (A) is true, but (R) is false.
(c) Both (A) and (R) are false
(d) Both (A) and (R) are true.

515. Match the following: (*NET Exam.* 2012D)

List-I	List-II
(A) OCLC	(i) Bio-Med
(B) INFLIBNET	(ii) Web-Dewey
(C) IISC	(iii) N-List
(D) NLM	(iv) Digital Library of India

Codes:	A	B	C	D
(a)	(ii)	(iii)	(iv)	(i)
(b)	(iii)	(i)	(ii)	(iv)
(c)	(iv)	(ii)	(iii)	(i)
(d)	(i)	(iii)	(iv)	(ii)

516. According to Machlup, the difference between information and knowledge is (*NET Exam.* 2012D)
(a) Information increases with use, whereas knowledge is constant.
(b) Information is stimulatory, whereas knowledge is practical.
(c) Information is shareable, whereas knowledge is one's property.
(d) Information is piecemeal, fragmented, particular, whereas knowledge is structure, coherent and universal.

517. **Assertion (A):** Random samples are not representative of the whole population.

Reason (R): Random numbers are used in forming a random sample. (*NET Exam.* 2012D)

Codes:
(a) (A) is true, but (R) is false.
(b) (A) is false, but (R) is true.
(c) Both (A) and (R) are true.
(d) Both (A) and (R) are false.

518. The general image file formats are: (*NET Exam.* 2012D)
(i) TIFF (ii) JPEG (iii) MPEG (iv) PNG

Codes:
(a) (i), (ii) and (iii) are correct.
(b) (i), (iii) and (iv) are correct.
(c) (i), (ii) and (iv) are correct.
(d) (ii), (iii) and (iv) are correct.

519. Match the following: (*NET Exam.* 2012J)

List-I
(A) Vidyanidhi (B) TKDL
(C) DOAJ (D) E-Prints @ IISc

List-II
(i) Institutional Repository
(ii) Electronic Theses & Dissertations
(iii) Digital Library of Journals
(iv) Digital Archive

Codes:	A	B	C	D
(a)	(ii)	(iv)	(iii)	(i)
(b)	(iii)	(ii)	(i)	(iv)
(c)	(iv)	(iii)	(ii)	(i)
(d)	(i)	(ii)	(iv)	(iii)

520. The significance of the year 2011 for LIS education in India is (*NET Exam.* 2012J)
(a) Golden Jubilee year
(b) Platinum Jubilee year
(c) Diamond Jubilee year
(d) Centenary year

521. Arrange the following according to their year of enactment in India: (*NET Exam.* 2012J)
(i) Freedom of Information Act
(ii) Right to Information Act
(iii) Copyright Act (Revised)
(iv) Information Technology Act

Codes:				
(a)	(iv)	(iii)	(ii)	(i)
(b)	(ii)	(iv)	(iii)	(iv)
(c)	(i)	(i)	(iv)	(ii)
(d)	(iii)	(ii)	(i)	(iv)

522. Which of the following tests can be employed for hypothesis testing? (*NET Exam.* 2012J)
(a) F-test (b) Chi-square test
(c) t-test (d) All of the above

523. What are the major driving forces behind an 'Information society'? (*NET Exam.* 2012J)
(i) RTI (ii) I.CT. (iii) Internet (iv) I.T. ACT

Codes:
(a) (ii) & (i) are correct
(b) (ii) & (iv) are correct
(c) (i) & (iv) are correct
(d) (ii) & (iii) are correct

524. Arrange the following associations according to their year of establishment: (*NET Exam.* 2012J)
(i) IASLIC (ii) ASLIB (iii) ALA (iv) SLA
Codes:

(a)	(iv)	(ii)	(iii)	(i)
(b)	(ii)	(iii)	(iv)	(i)
(c)	(iii)	(iv)	(ii)	(i)
(d)	(i)	(iv)	(ii)	(iii)

525. Digital Reference Service can be offered through (*NET Exam.* 2012J)
(a) FAX (b) OPAC
(c) Ask your librarian (d) Consortia

Read the passage given below, and answer the questions based on your understanding of the passage. (Q. No. 526-530)

Rolland Munro describes accountability as an informal giving that is part of everyday conversation, as well as more formal transactions generally involving some sort of documentary artifact (what we archivists refer to as a "record"). He notes that the authors move "between accounts as stories, explanations and reasons for conduct on the one hand and accounts as coded representations, records, often in the form of numbers, on the other hand". Each of these modes mediates the other in what he refers to as "accountability relationships". "Distributions of materials and devices are as much as effect of the giving and calling for accounts, as they are integral to the business of producing and consuming accounts". Records are both intermediaries in the accountability process and evidence of it.

In our daily language we often refer to accountability as something that must be achieved, rather than a something that is done informally yet continuously. The difference here is between viewing accountability as a thing represented by an artifact such as a record, and thinking about accountability as a process in which people and records must interact to achieve accountability. In this latter view, the focus on accountability becomes an analysis of the methods people use to engage in accountability relations.

526. Rolland Munro described accountability as (*NET Exam.* 2009D)
(a) Classified documentary artifacts
(b) Formal artifacts only
(c) Unpublished and published documents
(d) Informal, formal and documentary records

527. The phrase 'record keeping' is associated with (*NET Exam.* 2009D)
(a) Computer programmers
(b) Archivists
(c) Chartered Accountants
(d) Office Managers

528. What integral components Munro has identified for accounting in the business? (*NET Exam.* 2009D)
(a) Records and Codes
(b) Documentary archives
(c) Materials and devices
(d) Legal Regulations

529. In general usage accountability means (*NET Exam.* 2009D)
(a) Sometimes done informally
(b) Something achieved
(c) Something done continuously
(d) All of the above

530. Accountability, which is represented by an artifact, includes (*NET Exam.* 2009D)
(a) Process, Records, People
(b) Theory, Practice, Records
(c) Theory, Practice, People
(d) People, Records, Accounts

531. Which of the following are the features of Operations Research? (*NET 17J iii paper*)
(i) Aid in decision making
(ii) Handles decision tables
(iii) Optimization of Performance
(iv) Used as motivational technique
Codes:
(a) (i), (ii) are correct
(b) (i), (iii) are correct
(c) (ii), (iv) are correct
(d) (iii), (iv) are correct

532. Which of the following can be used to measure the research output of an individual? (*NET 17j ii paper*)
(i) h-index (ii) benchmark
(iii) g-index (iv) Bookmarks

Codes:
(a) (i) and (ii) are correct.
(b) (ii) and (iii) are correct.
(c) (i) and (iii) are correct.
(d) (iii) and (iv) are correct.

533. Match the following: (*NET 17J ii paper*)

List – I	List – II
A. Sample	1. Height, weight
B. Variable	2. Cluster
C. Range	3. Square root of variance
D. Standard deviation	4. Difference in score distribution

Codes:	A	B	C	D
(a)	3	2	1	4
(b)	2	1	4	3
(c)	1	3	2	4
(d)	4	2	1	3

534. Match the following: (*NET 17J ii paper*)
List – I
A. Basic Research B. Applied Research
C. Action Research D. Survey Research
List – II
1. Problem of gaps in periodical collection in J.N.U. Library
2. Use of measurement technique in Library Science
3. Use of Library in public schools in Delhi
4. Five laws of Library

Codes:	A	B	C	D
(a)	4	2	1	3
(b)	2	4	1	3
(c)	3	2	4	1
(d)	1	2	3	4

535. Match the following: (*NET 17J ii paper*)

List – I	List – II
A. Web of Science	1. Chemical Abstract Service (CAS)
B. Web Junction	2. Elsevier
C. Scopus	3. OCLC
D. SciFinder	4. Thomas Reuters

Codes:	A	B	C	D
(a)	2	3	1	4
(b)	4	1	3	2
(c)	3	4	2	1
(d)	4	3	2	1

536. Which sampling method is not suitable, if unit members are homogenous?
(*NET 17 Nov iii paper*)
(a) Simple random (b) Cluster
(c) Stratified (d) Systematic

537. Match the following statements with corresponding research process:
(*NET 17 Nov iii paper*)
List - I
(A) What is the role of MOOCs in imparting LIS education?
(B) EDUCAUSE (2013) "Selective institutions can be democratized via MOOCs".
(C) MOOCs programmes will replace distance Learning in LIS
(D) Though MOOCs is advantageous, majority respondents preferred distance learning
List - II
(1) Hypothesis
(2) Analytical statement
(3) Formulation of the problem
(4) Literature study

Codes:	(A)	(B)	(C)	(D)
(a)	(3)	(4)	(1)	(2)
(b)	(2)	(3)	(4)	(1)
(c)	(4)	(2)	(3)	(1)
(d)	(1)	(2)	(4)	(3)

538. **Assertion (A):** The fundamental need of a hypothesis is to guide sound research.
Reason (R): Without hypothesis, research is focused and do not become a random empirical wandering. (*NET 17 Nov. iii paper*)
Codes:
(a) (A) is true, but (R) is false.
(b) (A) is false, but (R) is true.
(c) Both (A) and (R) are true.
(d) Both (A) and (R) are false.

539. Match the following: (*NET 16J iii paper*)
List – I
A. Qualitative research
B. Quantitative research
C. Longitudinal research
D. Comparative research
List – II
1. Studies different units or culture or social groups
2. Describes reality as experienced by groups, communities, individuals, etc.
3. Employs measurement and statistical analysis
4. Study of the problem or phenomenon over a period of time

Codes:	A	B	C	D
(a)	1	4	3	2
(b)	2	3	4	1

(c)	3	2	1	4
(d)	4	1	2	3

540. **Assertion (A):** Online survey tools such as Survey Monkey and Question Pro have made data collection, analysis and result extraction much easier and simpler.

Reason (R): Though these tools are being used widely without any doubt in recent time, but social research cannot rely always on the results from an online survey because of their inherent limitations. *(NET 16J iii paper)*

Codes:
(a) Both (A) and (R) are true.
(b) Both (A) and (R) are false.
(c) (A) is true, but (R) is false.
(d) (R) is true, but (A) is false

541. **Assertion (A):** Technical writing, style manuals and citation standards are essential in structuring the research report.

Reason (R): The quality of research can be achieved only by standardizing the structure of a research report. *(NET 16 J iii paper)*

Codes:
(a) (A) is true and (R) is false.
(b) (A) is false and (R) is true.
(c) Both (A) and (R) are true.
(d) Both (A) and (R) are false.

542. Research Methodology involving the construction of theory through analysis of data is known as *(NET 16J ii paper)*
(a) Sampling Theory (b) Grounded Theory
(c) Ideal Theory (d) Basic Theory

543. In which of the following studies, a researcher is required to examine some specific subpopulation, as they change time? *(NET 16J ii paper)*
(a) Trend Study (b) Cohort Study
(c) Cross Sectional Study (d) Panel Studies

544. Deliberate Sampling is known as *(NET 16J ii paper)*

i. Purposive Sampling
ii. Sequential Sampling
iii. Probability Sampling
iv. Non-probability Sampling

Codes:
(a) i and iv are correct
(b) i and iii are correct
(c) i, ii and iv are correct
(d) ii, iii and iv are correct

545. According to APA Style Manual, a section at the end of a paper that includes information that is too detailed for the text of the paper itself and would "burden the reader" or be "distracting" or "in appropriate" is called: *(NET 17 NOV iii paper)*
(a) Appendix (b) Bibliography
(c) References (d) Tables

546. Ex post Facto study is a type of: *(NET 17 NOV ii paper)*
(a) Diagnostic design
(b) Quasi-experimental design
(c) Descriptive design
(d) Historical design

547. Match the following research methods with their corresponding explanation: *(NET 17 NOV ii paper)*

List – I
(A) Formalized research
(B) Conceptual research
(C) Descriptive research
(D) Fundamental research

List – II
(1) Interpretation of abstract ideas
(2) Survey and fact finding enquiries
(3) Formulation of theory
(4) Substantial structure and hypothesis to be tested

Codes:	**(A)**	**(B)**	**(C)**	**(D)**
(a)	(1)	(2)	(3)	(4)
(b)	(2)	(3)	(4)	(1)
(c)	(3)	(4)	(1)	(2)
(d)	(4)	(1)	(2)	(3)

548. **Assertion (A):** Participatory action research follows the conventional model of pure research in which members of the communities under study are treated as passive subjects.

Reason (R): In participatory action research no member of the communities under study participate throughout the research process. *(NET 17 NOV ii paper)*

Codes:
(a) (A) is true, but (R) is false.
(b) (A) is false, but (R) is true.
(c) Both (A) and (R) are true.
(d) Both (A) and (R) are false.

549. **Assertion (A):** The mean is a measure of dispersion. *(NET 17 NOV ii paper)*
Reason (R): The mean is based on every observation and is representative of the whole population.
Codes:
(a) (A) is true, but (R) is false.
(b) Both (A) and (R) are true.
(c) (A) is false, but (R) is true.
(d) Both (A) and (R) are false.

550. In a questionnaire, an item that directs participants to different follow-up questions depending on their response is called *(NET 15J iii paper)*
(a) Contingency question (b) Response set
(c) Secondary question (d) Filter question

551. Arrange the following steps given in sample design in proper sequence *(NET 15J iii paper)*
(i) Source List (ii) Size of the sample
(iii) Sampling unit (iv) Parameters of Interest
Codes:
(a) (iii), (i), (ii), (iv) (b) (iv), (ii), (iii), (i)
(c) (ii), (iv), (i), (iii) (d) (i), (iii), (iv), (ii)

552. Which of the following are characteristics of a review? *(NET 14 D ii paper)*
(i) Analyses research topic
(ii) Indicates inter-relation of ideas
(iii) Presents an integrated picture of development and program
(iv) Provides only current information
Codes:
(a) (ii), (iii), (iv) are correct.
(b) (i), (iii), (iv) are correct.
(c) (i), (ii), (iii) are correct.
(d) (i), (ii), (iv) are correct

553. **Assertion (A):** In a particular study, we may reject the alternative hypothesis.
Reason (R): In the same study the null hypothesis is not rejected. *(NET 15J ii paper)*
Codes:
(a) (A) is true, but (R) is false.
(b) (A) is false, but (R) is true.
(c) Both (A) and (R) are true and (R) is the correct explanation of (A).
(d) Both (A) and (R) are true, but (R) is not the correct explanation of (A)

554. Which of the following sampling techniques offer an 'equal probability selection method'? *(NET 15J ii paper)*
(i) Simple random sampling
(ii) Quota sampling
(iii) Purposive sampling
(iv) Proportional stratified sampling
Codes:
(a) (i) and (ii) are correct.
(b) (ii) and (iii) are correct.
(c) (i) and (iii) are correct.
(d) (i) and (iv) are correct.

555. **Assertion (A):** Median is simply the middle value when the data have been arranged in an ascending or descending order.
Reason (R): Median refers to the middle value in a distribution. *(NET 15J ii paper)*
Codes:
(a) (A) is true, but (R) is false.
(b) (A) is false, but (R)is true.
(c) Both (A) and (R) are false.
(d) Both (A) and (R) are true.

556. **Assertion (A):** Questionnaire is often used in surveys as the primary data collection tool.
Reason (R): Questionnaires prevent personal contact with respondents.*(NET 15J ii paper)*
Codes:
(a) Both (A) and (R) are true.
(b) Both (A) and (R) are false.
(c) (A) is true but (R) is false.
(d) (A) is false but (R) is true.

557. **Assertion (A):** When the data is skewed, the arithmetic mean calculate dismisleading.
Reason (R): Even when the data is skewed, the arithmetic mean gives some valuable information but needs to be interpreted in right manner. *(NET 15J ii paper)*
Codes:
(a) (A) is true, but (R) is false.
(b) Both (A) and (R) are true.
(c) Both (A) and (R) are false.
(d) (A) is false, but (R) is true.

558. When an author has not registered his/her work under copyright but legally proceeded over dispute of ownership. What is the validity of ownership? *(NET 15D iii paper)*

(a) No ownership without Registration
(b) It may not be legally tenable
(c) Ownership is automatic
(d) Both (a) and (b) are correct

559. A copyright law usually aims at the following features: *(NET 15D ii paper)*
(i) Stimulate creative authorship
(ii) Public availability of intellectual works
(iii) Freedom of access to information
(iv) Profit making by publishers
Codes:
(a) (i) and (ii) are correct
(b) (i) and (iii) are correct
(c) (ii) and (iv) are correct
(d) (i), (ii) and (iii) are correct

560. Which of the following is not an example of non-random sampling? *(NET 15D ii paper)*
(a) Snowball Sampling
(b) Convenience Sampling
(c) Quota and Purposive Sampling
(d) Census

561. Arrange in sequence the following steps involved in testing a hypothesis according to C.R. Kothari. *(NET 15D ii paper)*
(i) Selecting random sample and computing appropriate value
(ii) Calculating and comparing the probability
(iii) Selecting significant level
(iv) Making formal statement
Codes:
(a) (ii), (iii), (iv) and (i)
(b) (i), (ii), (iii) and (iv)
(c) (iii), (i), (ii) and (iv)
(d) (iv), (iii), (i) and (ii)

562. Arrange the following Acts according to the year of their respective enactments: *(NET 15D iii paper)*
(i) Digital Millennium Copyright Act
(ii) Right to Information Act (India)
(iii) Information Technology Act (India)
(iv) Indian Copyright Act
Codes:
(a) (iv), (i), (iii) and (ii)
(b) (iv), (ii), (iii) and (i)
(c) (i), (iv), (ii) and (iii)
(d) (ii), (iii), (i) and (iv)

563. Match the following: *(Net 15D iii paper)*
List - I
(A) Descriptive research (B) Applied research
(C) Empirical research (D) Analytical research
List - II
(1) Critical evaluation of available facts or information
(2) Surveys and fact finding enquiries
(3) Relies on experience or observation alone
(4) Finding a solution to an immediate social problem

Codes:	**(A)**	**(B)**	**(C)**	**(D)**
(a)	(2)	(3)	(4)	(1)
(b)	(2)	(4)	(3)	(1)
(c)	(1)	(2)	(4)	(3)
(d)	(1)	(4)	(3)	(2)

564. Match the following *(NET 15D iii paper)*
List - I
(A) Day book system (B) Ledger system
(C) One card (D) Two card system
List - II
(1) Each per book
(2) Browne system
(3) Note down transactions
(4) One page per borrower

Codes:	**(A)**	**(B)**	**(C)**	**(D)**
(a)	(2)	(3)	(4)	(1)
(b)	(3)	(4)	(1)	(2)
(c)	(4)	(1)	(2)	(3)
(d)	(1)	(2)	(3)	(4)

565. **Assertion (A):** Impact factor is the only method for evaluating the performance of an individual researcher.
Reason (R): Impact factor helps Libraries in their Journal subscription. *(NET 15D iii paper)*
Codes:
(a) (A) is true and (R) is false.
(b) (A) is false but (R) is true.
(c) Both (A) and (R) are false.
(d) Both (A) and (R) are true.

566. Which of the following citation style manuals are from the same publisher? *(NET 2013D ii paper)*
(i) A.P.A. (ii) Turabian
(iii) Chicago (iv) M.L.A.
Codes:
(a) (i) and (ii) are correct.
(b) (ii) and (iii) are correct.

(c) (iii) and (iv) are correct.
(d) (ii) and (iv) are correct

567. Which of the following are the basic components of expert system? (*NET-2013 D*)
(i) User interface (ii) Knowledge base
(iii) Inference Mechanism (iv) Schema
Codes:
(a) (i), (ii) and (iii) (b) (ii), (iii) and (iv)
(c) (iii), (iv) and (i) (d) (iv), (iii) and (ii)

568. When the permission of copyright owner is not needed? (*NET-2013 D*)
(i) Criticism or review
(ii) Translation
(iii) Research purpose
(iv) Photocopy for sale
Codes:
(a) (i) and (iii) are correct.
(b) (i) and (iv) are correct.
(c) (iii) and (iv) are correct.
(d) (ii) and (iii) are correct.

569. **Assertion (A):** Chi-square is an important non-parametric test which does not require rigid assumptions in respect of the type of population being studied.
Reason (R): Since χ^2 is a nonparametric test, it requires only the degrees of freedom (implicitly, the size of the population) for using the test. (*NET-2013D ii paper*)
Codes:
(a) (A) is true, but (R) is false.
(b) Both (A) and (R) are true.
(c) (A) is false but (R) is true.
(d) Both (A) and (R) are false.

570. Identify the methods used for plagiarism detection: (*DEC 2013 iii paper*)
(i) Term occurrence analysis
(ii) API Testing
(iii) Citation-based plagiarism detection
(iv) Local similarity assessment
Codes:
(a) (i), (ii) and (iv) are correct.
(b) (i), (iii) and (iv) are correct.
(c) (ii), (iii) and (iv) are correct.
(d) (i), (ii) and (iii) are correct

571. The sources of hypothesis, as enunciated by P.V. Young are: (*DEC 2013 iii paper*)
(i) Genealogy (ii) Culture
(iii) Experiment (iv) Analogy
Codes:
(a) (i), (ii) and (iii) are correct
(b) (i), (iii) and (iv) are correct
(c) (i), (ii) and (iv) are correct
(d) (ii), (iii) and (iv) are correct

572. Match the following: (*DEC 2013 iii paper*)
List – I
A. Survey of requirements
B. Determining cost efficiency and effectiveness
C. Review of the programs and their goals
D. Complete change over basics of system
List – II
1. Design phase 2. Installation phase
3. Analysis phase 4. Evaluation phase

Codes:	**A**	**B**	**C**	**D**
(a)	1	2	3	4
(b)	2	3	4	1
(c)	3	4	1	2
(d)	4	1	2	3

573. Match the following: (*DEC 2013 iii paper*)

List – I	**List – II**
A. Nadir to Ascending	1. Hypothesizing
B. Ascending to Zenith	2. Verification
C. Zenith to Descending	3. Deductive
D. Descending to Nadir	4. Empirical

Codes:	**A**	**B**	**C**	**D**
(a)	1	3	2	4
(b)	2	4	1	3
(c)	3	1	4	2
(d)	4	1	3	2

574. Match the following: (*DEC 2013 iii paper*)
List – I
A. Social Microscope
B. Fundamental Research
C. Ex-post facto research
D. Multi stage random sampling
List – II
1. Cluster Technique
2. No control over variance
3. Case study method
4. Knowledge for knowledge sake

Codes:	**A**	**B**	**C**	**D**
(a)	1	2	3	4
(b)	3	4	2	1
(c)	2	3	1	4
(d)	4	1	2	4

575. **Assertion (A):** Mean, median and mode are the simple techniques to get exact averages for data analysis in research.

Reason (R): These are the well accepted statistical techniques of research for data analysis of historical data.

(DEC 2013 iii paper)

Codes:

(a) (A) is false, but (R) is true.
(b) Both (A) and (R) are true.
(c) (A) is true but (R) is false.
(d) Both (A) and (R) are false.

576. Which one of the following is not the feature of H-index? *(NET 13 SEPT iii paper)*
(a) Mathematically simple index
(b) Applied to any level of aggregation
(c) Publication that are hardly ever cited don't influence it.
(d) Sensitive to performance change.

577. The term 'Literary warrant' for book classification was introduced by *(NET JUNE 2014 ii)*
(a) W.C.B. Sayers (b) Wyndham Hulme
(c) J.D. Brown (d) H.E. Bliss

578. Which of the following are nonprobability sampling? *(NET JUNE 2014 ii)*
(i) Quota sampling (ii) Judgement Sampling
(iii) Cluster Sampling (iv) Multi-stage sampling
Codes:
(a) (i) and (iv) are correct.
(b) (ii) and (iii) are correct.
(c) (i) and (ii) are correct.
(d) (iii) and (iv) are correct

579. Arrange the following processes of research in order: *(NET JUNE 2014 ii)*
(i) Theory Building
(ii) Reflecting and Integrating of Idea
(iii) Research Design
iv) Review of Literature
Codes:
(a) (iv), (iii), (ii), (i) (b) (iii), (i), (iv), (ii)
(c) (ii), (iv), (iii), (i) (d) (i), (ii), (iv), (iii)

580. **Assertion (A):** Mail survey, a data collection technique in which questionnaires are mailed to potential respondents, who in then fill and return at their convenience become obsolete.

Reason (R): Survey-Monkey, the free online survey tool has totally replaced the traditional Mail survey. *(NET JUNE 2014 ii)*

Codes:
(a) (A) is true, but (R) is false.
(b) (A) is false, but (R) is true.
(c) Both (A) and (R) are true.
(d) Both (A) and (R) are false.

581. **Assertion (A):** Interviewing is essential to supplement the research data collected through questionnaire.

Reason (R): Interview is the most suitable technique to collect data as all respondents cooperate more during interview.

(NET JUNE 2014 ii)

Codes:
(a) (A) is false, but (R) is true.
(b) Both (A) and (R) are true.
(c) Both (A) and (R) are false.
(d) (A) is true, but (R) is false.

582. Which form of reasoning is the process of drawing a specific conclusion from a set of premises?

(NET JUNE 2014 iii paper)

(a) Rationalism (b) Deductive reasoning
(c) Inductive reasoning (d) Probabilistic

583. Which of the following are the steps in operational research process?

(NET JUNE 2014 iii paper)

i. Construction of mathematical model
ii. Deriving solution from the model.
iii. Graphic representation of work on a time scale.
iv. Developing network diagram showing interrelationships.

Codes:
(a) i and ii are correct.
(b) ii and iii are correct.
(c) iii and iv are correct.
(d) iv and i are correct

584. Which of the following are statistical programming software?

(NET JUNE 2014 iii paper)

i. GAUSS ii. SAS iii. SPSS iv. SLIM
Codes:
(a) i, iii and iv (b) i, ii and iii
(c) i, ii and iv (d) ii, iii and iv

585. Match the following tools used in Total Quality Management

(NET JUNE 2014 iii paper)

List – I
A. Statistical Quality Control B. Check Sheets
C. Pareto Charts D. Fishbone diagram

List – II
1. Conformance and Maintain sticks
2. To identify relationship between problem and cause
3. Checking variables
4. To identify intensity of problem

Codes:	A	B	C	D
(a)	2	1	4	3
(b)	3	1	4	2
(c)	1	3	2	4
(d)	4	1	3	2

586. Match the following: *(NET JUNE 2014 iii paper)*

List – I (Hypothesis)
A. Null B. Working (Directional)
C. Explanatory D. Descriptive

List – II (Characteristics)
1. Statement of expectations
2. Relational propositions
3. No relation between variables
4. Existence of variables

Codes:	A	B	C	D
(a)	1	4	2	3
(b)	3	4	2	1
(c)	3	2	1	4
(d)	3	1	2	4

587. Match the following: *(NET JUNE 2014 iii paper)*

List – I
A. Theory of Hygiene & Motivation
B. Maturity Theory
C. Expectancy Theory
D. Analysis Theory

List – II
1. Likert 2. Vroom and Lawler
3. Herzberg 4. Argyris

Codes:	A	B	C	D
(a)	2	3	4	1
(b)	3	4	2	1
(c)	2	1	3	4
(d)	4	1	2	3

588. What are the approaches to plagiarism check of academic publications? *(NET 14D iii paper)*

i. String matching ii. Bag of words analysis
iii. Citation analysis iv. Parse trees

Codes:
(a) ii, iv are correct. (b) i, ii, iii are correct.
(c) i, iv are correct. (d) i, iii, iv are correct.

589. **Assertion (A):** Bibliometric study is the popular area of research on which maximum number of Ph.D. degree have been awarded in India.

Reason (R): Bibliometric study adds to the extension of fundamental research. *(NET 14D iii paper)*

Codes:
(a) Both (A) and (R) are true.
(b) (A) is true, but (R) is false.
(c) Both (A) and (R) are false.
(d) (R) is true, but (A) is false.

590. **Assertion (A):** According to National Knowledge Commission, 'the library and information services sector in India has not kept pace with the paradigmatic changes taking place in society'.

Reason (R): There is no proportionate growth in library resources. *(NET 14D iii paper)*

Codes:
(a) Both (A) and (R) are true.
(b) (A) is true, but (R) is false.
(c) Both (A) and (R) are false.
(d) (A) is false, but (R) is true.

591. Match the following: *(NET 14D iii paper)*

List – I	List – II
A. Infringement	1. Unauthorized use of I.P
B. Enforcement	2. Criminal penalties
C. Mis-appropriation	3. Breach of trade secret
D. Counterfeit	4. Intentional forgery

Codes:	A	B	C	D
(a)	2	3	4	1
(b)	1	2	3	4
(c)	3	4	1	2
(d)	4	1	3	2

592. Match the following: *(NET 14D iii paper)*

List – I
A. Barren Hypothesis
B. Idiographic Hypothesis
C. Nomothetic Hypothesis
D. Crude Hypothesis

List – II
1. Indian men marry at 26-28 years age
2. Seema will top this year
3. Loss of limbs
4. Quality of collection

Codes:	A	B	C	D
(a)	4	3	1	2
(b)	3	2	4	1

(c)	2	1	3	4
(d)	1	4	2	3

593. Match the following: (*NET 14D iii paper*)

List – I

A. Multiple choice questions
B. Loaded questions
C. Contingency questions
D. Open ended questions

List – II

1. Personal opinion of interviewer
2. No sets of answers
3. Alternative answers
4. Sub-group of respondents

Codes:	A	B	C	D
(a)	1	4	3	2
(b)	4	2	3	1
(c)	3	1	4	2
(d)	2	3	1	4

594. Match the following: (*NET 14D iii paper*)

List – I	List – II
A. Mean	1. Σ (O–E)2/ E
B. Degree of freedom (df)	2. n + 1/ 2
C. Median	3. (r – 1) (c – 1)
D. Chi-square (χ2)	4. Σx/ n

Codes:	A	B	C	D
(a)	2	4	1	3
(b)	3	2	1	4
(c)	4	3	2	1
(d)	1	2	4	3

595. Which of the following is a measure of dispersion? (*NET 17J iii paper*)
(a) Geometric mean (b) Median
(c) Mode (d) Root Mean Square Deviation

596. If 'r' is a rank of a word and 'f' is its frequency then rf = c, where 'c' is a constant. Which law is this? (*NET 17J iii paper*)
(a) Bradford's law (b) Lotka's law
(c) Narain's law (d) Zipf's law

597. Which of the following rights are granted for 'Literary works' according to Copyright Law of India? (*NET 17J iii paper*)
(i) To make translation
(ii) To use in reporting current events
(iii) To make any adaptation
(iv) To use for the purpose of research

Codes:
(a) (i) and (iii) are correct.
(b) (i) and (ii) are correct.
(c) (ii) and (iii) are correct.
(d) (ii) and (iv) are correct.

598. Which of the following are types of random samples? (*NET 17J iii paper*)
(i) Cluster sampling
(ii) Purposive sampling
(iii) Stratified sampling
(iv) Systematic sampling

Codes:
(a) (i), (iii) and (iv) are correct.
(b) (ii), (iii) and (iv) are correct.
(c) (i), (ii) and (iii) are correct.
(d) (i), (ii) and (iv) are correct.

599. Identify the criteria for evaluation of qualitative research: (*NET 17J iii paper*)
(i) Objectivity (ii) Reliability
(iii) Divisibility (iv) Validity

Codes:
(a) (i), (ii) and (iv) are correct.
(b) (ii), (iii) and (iv) are correct.
(c) (i), (iii) and (iv) are correct.
(d) (i), (ii) and (iii) are correct.

600. Match the following: (*NET 17J iii paper*)

List – I

(A) Systematic Sample (B) Stratified Sample
(C) Cluster Sample (D) Quota Sample

List – II

(1) Population specified by traits, discretionary and inexpensive
(2) Scattered population
(3) Heterogeneous population
(4) Too large population

Codes:	(A)	(B)	(C)	(D)
(a)	(4)	(3)	(2)	(1)
(b)	(1)	(2)	(3)	(4)
(c)	(3)	(1)	(4)	(2)
(d)	(2)	(4)	(1)	(3)

601. Match the following: (*NET 17J iii paper*)

List – I	List – II
(A) Ibid	(1) See
(B) Loc. Cit.	(2) Previously used reference
(C) Op. Cit.	(3) Same reference cited immediately above
(D) Vide	(4) Same page cited (in the place cited)

Codes:	(A)	(B)	(C)	(D)
(a)	(3)	(4)	(2)	(1)
(b)	(d)	(2)	(1)	(3)
(c)	(2)	(1)	(3)	(4)
(d)	(1)	(3)	(4)	(2)

602. Match the following:

List – I

(A) Nominal Scale (B) Ordinal Scale
(C) Ratio Scale (D) Differential Scale

List – II

(1) Places events in order and exhibits their relation
(2) Classifies Objects/Observations
(3) Involves Judges to rank items into categories
(4) Represents the actual amount of variable —theoretically unobtainable

Codes:	**(A)**	**(B)**	**(C)**	**(D)**
(a)	(2)	(1)	(4)	(3)
(b)	(1)	(2)	(3)	(4)
(c)	(3)	(1)	(4)	(2)
(d)	(4)	(3)	(2)	(1)

603. The seven basic statistical tools for quality control was advocated by *(NET 15D ii paper)*

(a) Joseph Juran (b) Phillip Kotler
(c) Kaoru Ishikawa (d) C.A. Cutter

604. Which of the following are uses of work analysis? *(NET D15 ii paper)*

(i) Simplifying the procedures
(ii) Line of authority
(iii) Improvement in various processes
(iv) Unity of Command

Codes:

(a) (ii), (iv) are correct.
(b) (i), (ii), (iii) are correct.
(c) (i), (iv) are correct.
(d) (i), (iii) are correct.

605. **Assertion (A):** The Product of the relative frequency of occurrence of a word and its rank is equal to a constant.

Reason (R): The above statement is known as Bradford's Law of scattering.

Codes:

(a) (A) is false, but (R) is true.
(b) (A) is true, but (R) is false.
(c) Both (A) and (R) are true.
(d) Both (A) and (R) are false.

606. Research methods based on the consensus opinions of panel of experts and judgements is knowns as

(a) Historical methods
(b) Case study methods
(c) Delphi Methods
(d) Interview methods

607. Wikipedia owned by the non profit "Wikipedia Foundation" was launched on January 15, 2001 by *(NET 18J)*

(a) Jimmy Wells and Larry Sanger
(b) Jimmy Wells and Vincent J Aceto
(c) Larry Sanger and W. Kathy
(d) William A. Ford and W. Kathy

608. Which of the following research methods are used in a study of scattering of periodicals? *(NET 18J)*

(i) Bio bibliometric study
(ii) Bibliometric study
(iii) Citation analysis study
(iv) Altmetric study

Codes:

(a) (i) and (iv) are correct
(b) (ii) and (iii) are correct
(c) (i), and (iii) are correct
(d) (i), (ii), and (iii) are correct

609. Match the following search engines with their corresponding subjects/or scientific research discovery information they offer *(NET 18J)*

List-I	**List-II**
(a) Vadlo	(i) Web resources including Twitter and job posting
(b) Mamma	(ii) Life science literature
(c) Athenus	(iii) World known living Languages
(d) Ethnologue	(iv) Science and Engineering

Codes:	**(A)**	**(B)**	**(C)**	**(D)**
(a)	(i)	(iii)	(iv)	(ii)
(b)	(iii)	(iv)	(ii)	(i)
(c)	(ii)	(iv)	(iii)	(i)
(d)	(ii)	(i)	(iv)	(iii)

610. **Assertion (A):** In technical writing, styles manuals and citation standards are essential in structuring and maintaining uniformity of research report.

Reason (A): The quality of research can be achieved only by standardising the structure of research report, but not by the content. *(NET 18J)*

Codes:

(a) Both (A) and (R) are true
(b) Both (A) and (R) is false
(c) (A) is true but (R) is false
(d) (R) is true but (A) is false

611. **Assertion (A):** In social research, a high proportion of refusals to answer a research always occurs solely due to inadequate interview instruction or poor interview training.

Reason (R): Within the questionnaire or interview, even a substantive number of questions often remain unanswered making difficult for the researcher to state an exact figure and forcing him to restudy the questions carefully as fault might lie upon a poor transition. *(NET 18J)*

Codes:

(a) (A) is true but (R) is false
(b) (A) is false, but (R) is true
(c) both (A) and (R) are true
(d) Both (A) and (R) are false

ANSWER SHEET

1. (b)	2. (d)	3. (b)	4. (a)	5. (b)	6. (a)	7. (b)	8. (b)	9. (b)
10. (d)	11. (a)	12. (a)	13. (d)	14. (b)	15. (d)	16. (d)	17. (a)	18. (d)
19. (b)	20. (d)	21. (a)	22. (a)	23. (a)	24. (b)	25. (d)	26. (a)	27. (a)
28. (c)	29. (d)	30. (a)	31. (d)	32. (b)	33. (a)	34. (c)	35. (d)	36. (c)
37. (b)	38. (b)	39. (d)	40. (a)	41. (b)	42. (b)	43. (c)	44. (a)	45. (c)
46. (c)	47. (d)	48. (a)	49. (a)	50. (d)	51. (b)	52. (a)	53. (a)	54. (d)
55. (b)	56. (b)	57. (b)	58. (a)	59. (a)	60. (c)	61. (b)	62. (a)	63. (a)
64. (c)	65. (b)	66. (b)	67. (d)	68. (a)	69. (c)	70. (a)	71. (b)	72. (a)
73. (a)	74. (c)	75. (c)	76. (b)	77. (c)	78. (c)	79. (b)	80. (d)	81. (a)
82. (c)	83. (b)	84. (a)	85. (b)	86. (b)	87. (a)	88. (b)	89. (b)	90. (b)
91. (b)	92. (b)	93. (b)	94. (a)	95. (a)	96. (d)	97. (d)	98. (b)	99. (a)
100. (a)	101. (d)	102. (b)	103. (c)	104. (d)	105. (b)	106. (a)	107. (b)	108. (c)
109. (a)	110. (d)	111. (d)	112. (b)	113. (c)	114. (b)	115. (c)	116. (c)	117. (a)
118. (b)	119. (d)	120. (d)	121. (c)	122. (b)	123. (a)	124. (a)	125. (a)	126. (d)
127. (b)	128. (a)	129. (a)	130. (c)	131. (a)	132. (b)	133. (b)	134. (c)	135. (a)
136. (d)	137. (c)	138. (a)	139. (a)	140. (c)	141. (d)	142. (b)	143. (b)	144. (c)
145. (d)	146. (b)	147. (d)	148. (d)	149. (d)	150. (b)	151. (b)	152. (c)	153. (a)
154. (d)	155. (d)	156. (a)	157. (c)	158. (a)	159. (b)	160. (b)	161. (b)	162. (c)
163. (d)	164. (b)	165. (a)	166. (a)	167. (c)	168. (b)	169. (d)	170. (a)	171. (a)
172. (d)	173. (d)	174. (b)	175. (b)	176. (b)	177. (c)	178. (d)	179. (d)	180. (b)
181. (b)	182. (c)	183. (b)	184. (a)	185. (b)	186. (a)	187. (d)	188. (d)	189. (d)
190. (b)	191. (c)	192. (c)	193. (b)	194. (b)	195. (a)	196. (c)	197. (c)	198. (a)
199. (c)	200. (b)	201. (b)	202. (d)	203. (c)	204. (c)	205. (b)	206. (d)	207. (b)
208. (b)	209. (b)	210. (a)	211. (c)	212. (b)	213. (c)	214. (b)	215. (d)	216. (d)
217. (b)	218. (d)	219. (b)	220. (a)	221. (c)	222. (a)	223. (a)	224. (d)	225. (d)
226. (d)	227. (d)	228. (d)	229. (d)	230. (d)	231. (b)	232. (b)	233. (d)	234. (c)
235. (b)	236. (b)	237. (b)	238. (d)	239. (a)	240. (a)	241. (c)	242. (c)	243. (d)
244. (a)	245. (c)	246. (b)	247. (c)	248. (b)	249. (b)	250. (a)	251. (d)	252. (b)
253. (d)	254. (a)	255. (b)	256. (a)	257. (b)	258. (c)	259. (a)	260. (a)	261. (a)
262. (a)	263. (c)	264. (b)	265. (c)	266. (d)	267. (a)	268. (a)	269. (a)	270. (b)
271. (a)	272. (a)	273. (a)	274. (a)	275. (d)	276. (a)	277. (a)	278. (a)	279. (a)
280. (a)	281. (a)	282. (c)	283. (c)	284. (c)	285. (d)	286. (a)	287. (b)	288. (b)

289. (d) 290. (a) 291. (c) 292. (c) 293. (c) 294. (c) 295. (c) 296. (b) 297. (a)
298. (d) 299. (c) 300. (a) 301. (b) 302. (c) 303. (a) 304. (c) 305. (a) 306. (d)
307. (a) 308. (b) 309. (a) 310. (d) 311. (c) 312. (a) 313. (d) 314. (b) 315. (b)
316. (d) 317. (c) 318. (c) 319. (a) 320. (c) 321. (a) 322. (b) 323. (d) 324. (b)
325. (c) 326. (a) 327. (c) 328. (a) 329. (a) 330. (b) 331. (a) 332. (a) 333. (a)
334. (c) 335. (d) 336. (b) 337. (b) 338. (b) 339. (b) 340. (a) 341. (c) 342. (a)
343. (d) 344. (d) 345. (a) 346. (d) 347. (c) 348. (b) 349. (b) 350. (d) 351. (c)
352. (b) 353. (b) 354. (c) 355. (b) 356. (d) 357. (c) 358. (b) 359. (b) 360. (d)
361. (a) 362. (c) 363. (d) 364. (b) 365. (c) 366. (d) 367. (d) 368. (b) 369. (d)
370. (c) 371. (a) 372. (d) 373. (b) 374. (c) 375. (b) 376. (a) 377. (c) 378. (a)
379. (d) 380. (a) 381. (d) 382. (d) 383. (b) 384. (d) 385. (c) 386. (c) 387. (b)
388. (a) 389. (b) 390. (d) 391. (b) 392. (d) 393. (a) 394. (a) 395. (a) 396. (b)
397. (a) 398. (a) 399. (b) 400. (b) 401. (c) 402. (c) 403. (a) 404. (b) 405. (d)
406. (b) 407. (d) 408. (b) 409. (b) 410. (d) 411. (a) 412. (a) 413. (b) 414. (b)
415. (b) 416. (c) 417. (a) 418. (c) 419. (a) 420. (c) 421. (b) 422. (d) 423. (c)
424. (a) 425. (a) 426. (a) 427. (d) 428. (b) 429. (b) 430. (c) 431. (a) 432. (a)
433. (b) 434. (b) 435. (a) 436. (d) 437. (b) 438. (c) 439. (c) 440. (b) 441. (b)
442. (c) 443. (c) 444. (d) 445. (a) 446. (c) 447. (a) 448. (c) 449. (b) 450. (c)
451. (d) 452. (c) 453. (b) 454. (a) 455. (c) 456. (d) 457. (b) 458. (b) 459. (a)
460. (c) 461. (a) 462. (d) 463. (c) 464. (b) 465. (b) 466. (a) 467. (a) 468. (b)
469. (d) 470. (a) 471. (d) 472. (c) 473. (c) 474. (a) 475. (a) 476. (c) 477. (d)
478. (b) 479. (a) 480. (a) 481. (c) 482. (c) 483. (c) 484. (a) 485. (a) 486. (b)
487. (b) 488. (d) 489. (a) 490. (c) 491. (d) 492. (a) 493. (b) 494. (b) 495. (c)
496. (d) 497. (b) 498. (d) 499. (c) 500. (b) 501. (d) 502. (b) 503. (b) 504. (d)
505. (b) 506. (d) 507. (b) 508. (a) 509. (b) 510. (b) 511. (c) 512. (None) 513. (d)
514. (b) 515. (a) 516. (d) 517. (b) 518. (c) 519. (a) 520. (d) 521. (b) 522. (d)
523. (d) 524. (c) 525. (c) 526. (d) 527. (b) 528. (c) 529. (b) 530. (a) 531. (b)
532. (c) 533. (b) 534. (a) 535. (d) 536. (b) 537. (a) 538. (a) 539. (b) 540. (a)
541. (a) 542. (b) 543. (b) 544. (a) 545. (a) 546. (b) 547. (d) 548. (d) 549. (c)
550. (a) 551. (a) 552. (c) 553 (c) 554. (d) 555. (d) 556. (c) 557. (b) 558. (c)
559. (a) 560. (d) 561. (d) 562. (a) 563. (b) 564. (b) 565. (b) 566. (b) 567. (a)
568. (a) 569. (b) 570. (b) 571. (c) 572. (c) 573. (d) 574. (b) 575. (c) 576. (d)
577. (b) 578. (c) 579. (a) 580. (d) 581. (d) 582. (b) 583. (a) 584. (b) 585. (b)
586. (d) 587. (b) 588. (b) 589. (b) 590. (a) 591. (b) 592. (b) 593. (c) 594. (c)
595. (d) 596. (d) 597. (a) 598. (a) 599. (a) 600. (a) 601. (a) 602. (a) 603. (c)
604 (d) 605. (b) 606. (c) 607. (a) 608. (b) 609. (d) 610. (c) 611. (b)

Chapter 8

Information Technology and Library Automation

SUBJECTIVE QUESTIONS

Q. 1. In which generation and year high-level language started?

Ans. 3rd generation, 1960.

Q. 2. Write the few names of high-level languages.

Ans. FORTRAN, COBOL, ALGOL.

Q. 3. Write the different types of input devices in a computer.

Ans. (a) Keyboard. (b) Light pen.
(c) Optical scanners. (d) Magnetic scanners.

Q. 4. Write the components of storage technology.

Ans. (a) Archival storage. (b) Backup or secondary storage.
(c) Main memory. (d) Cader memory.
(e) CPU.

Q. 5. Write the different types of output devices in a computer.

Ans. (a) Display screen attached to a terminal.
(b) Printers attached to computers.

Q. 6. Write the names of two principal light sources are used in fiber optic communication system.

Ans. (a) Light emitting diodes.
(b) Injection laser diodes.

Q. 7. Write two major categories of semiconductor memories.

Ans. (a) Read Only Memory (ROM).
(b) Random Access Memory (RAM).

Q. 8. ALU stands for

Ans. Arithmetic Logic Unit.

OBJECTIVE QUESTIONS

1. What is a bug?
   (a) Computer Virus
   (b) Error in computer configuration
   (c) Error in a Programme
   (d) None of these
2. Arithmetic Logical Unit (ALU) in the context of computer e-notes (*NET Exam.* 1991)
   (a) Software (b) Hardware
   (c) Human ware (d) None of the above
3. NICNET is project sponsored by (*NET Exam.* 1991)
   (a) Government of India (b) UNISIST
   (c) Human ware (d) UGC
4. MODEM is (*NET Exam.* 1991)
   (a) A mnemonic device used in classification
   (b) A hardware device that converts from one form to another
   (c) A software developed for commercial use
   (d) None of the above
5. FORTRAN is a (*NET Exam.* 1991)
   (a) High-level language
   (b) Computer hardware
   (c) Software developed for commercial use
   (d) None of the above
6. CD-ROM stands for (*NET Exam.* 1991 and 1994)
   (a) Compact Disc Read Out Memory
   (b) Compact Disc Read Only Memory
   (c) Compact Disc Read On Memory
   (d) Compact Disc Read Omitting Memory
7. INFLIBNET stands for (*NET Exam.* 1991)
   (a) Information Library Network
   (b) International Film Library Network
   (c) International Federation for Library Network
   (d) Information and Library Network
8. The type of International Networks accessible to online vendor are (*NET Exam.* 1999)
   (a) WAN (b) MAN
   (c) LAN (d) None of the above

9. The device that converts digital to analog and analog to digital signals known as (*NET Exam.* 1999)
   (a) Analog computers (b) Modem
   (c) VDU (d) Electro fax
10. Which of the following software is useful for word processing? (*NET Exam.* 1999)
   (a) DBASE (b) LIBSYS
   (c) Word Star (d) CDS/ISIS
11. Electronic telecommunications system joining millions of computer together.
   (a) E-mail (b) Internet
   (c) US Mail (d) UPS
12. ISO-9960 is related with
   (a) Standard for encoding data on CD-ROM
   (b) Standard for computer Hardware
   (c) Standard for Information Processing
   (d) Standard for Networking
13. The international body that coordinates the assignment of unique domain names, protocol address is
   (a) IGF (b) IANA (c) ICANN (d) ISP
14. When you create a worksheet in CDS/ISIS you are defining? (*NET Exam.* 2000)
   (a) The external user view
   (b) The internal file structure
   (c) The conceptual frame
   (d) All of the above
15. Which of the following networks does not have its own Telecommunication infrastructure? (*NET Exam.* 2000)
   (a) NICNET (b) ERNET
   (c) INIS (d) EURONET
16. OPAC stands for (*NET Exam.* 1995, 1997 and 2000)
   (a) Online Public Access Catalogue
   (b) Online Periodicals Access Centre
   (c) Online Patents Access Centre
   (d) None of the above
17. Mini Computer are (*NET Exam.* 1998)
   (a) Very small and can be carried around
   (b) Also known as laptop computers
   (c) Support a large number of terminal
   (d) Same as micro computers
18. The computerised form of engineering index is known as (*NET Exam.* 1998)
   (a) COMPENDEX
   (b) ENGINEERING COMDEX
   (c) Online Engineering Index
   (d) Computerised Engineering
19. In computer terminology an error in an programme is known as (*NET Exam.* 1998)
   (a) BUS (b) Bug (c) Virus (d) Blowback
20. Arrange the following storage device according to increasing capacity: (*NET Exam.* 1998)
   (i) Magnetic Tape (ii) CD-ROM
   (iii) Floppy Disk (iv) Magnetic Disk
   Codes:
   (a) iii, i, iv, ii (b) ii, i, iii, iv
   (c) iv, iii, ii, i (d) i, ii, iii, iv
21. The memory capacity of a computer is measured in (*NET Exam.* 1998)
   (a) Bytes (b) Hertz (c) KBPS (d) Chips
22. Which of the following is also available on CD-ROM? (*NET Exam.* 1996)
   (a) Indian National Bibliography
   (b) National Union Catalogue of Scientific serials in India
   (c) Indian Science Abstract
   (d) Indian Books in Print
23. The following are useful input devices (*NET Exam.* 1996)
   (a) Keyboards, RAM and CD-ROM
   (b) OCR, Light Pens and Keyboards
   (c) CD-ROM's, OCR and Floppy Disk
   (d) Hard Disk, Magnetic Tape and Light Pens
24. The full form of ERNET is (*NET Exam.* 1996)
   (a) Eastern Region Network
   (b) Electronic Research Network
   (c) Education and Research Network
   (d) Economics Research Network
25. In the binary system of numbers 100 represents the decimal number (*NET Exam.* 1996)
   (a) 100 (b) 01 (c) 04 (d) 03
26. COM means (*NET Exam.* 1996 and 1998)
   (a) Computer Output Microform
   (b) Catalogue on Magnetic Tapes
   (c) Computer Output Magnetic Tape
   (d) Catalogue on Microform
27. In relation to computer Basic is (*NET Exam.* 1996)
   (a) Core Memory (b) Hardware
   (c) Model (d) Language

28. The text on computer is normally represented in standard code (*NET Exam.* 1998)
(a) Byte (b) Hexadecimal
(c) Machine Language (d) ASCII

29. In how many sizes the Floppy Disk? (*NET Exam.* 1998)
(a) Three (b) Two
(c) Four (d) None of these

30. A byte normally denotes (*NET Exam.* 1995 and 1998)
(a) String of four bits (b) String of six bits
(c) String of eight bits (d) String of bits

31. Which language is low language in computer terminology? (*NET Exam.* 1998)
(a) LISP (b) COBOL
(c) Machine Language (d) BASIC

32. In computer parlance "Bug" denotes (*NET Exam.* 1995)
(a) Computer Virus
(b) Error in hardware configuration
(c) Error in programming
(d) Non-compatibility between hardware and software

33. DELNET is a (*NET Exam.* 1995)
(a) Wide area network
(b) Local area network
(c) National network
(d) Regional network

34. PC falls in the category of (*NET Exam.* 1995)
(a) Super computer (b) Main frame
(c) Mini computer (d) Micro computer

35. Computer memory is measured in
(a) Bytes (b) Kilobytes
(c) Megabytes (d) All of the above

36. Visual display unit (VDU) in computers is used for (*NET Exam.* 1995)
(a) Input (b) Output
(c) Control (d) Storage

37. UNIX is (*NET Exam.* 1995)
(a) Computer Hardware
(b) Application Software
(c) Operating System
(d) Computer high-level language

38. In the context of computers 'bit' means (*NET Exam.* 1995)
(a) Binary digits
(b) British Information Terminal
(c) Books in trade
(d) Birmingham Institute of Technology

39. CDS/ISIS is operated through which of the following operating system? (*NET Exam.* 1994)
(a) DOS (b) XENIX
(c) UNIX (d) None of these

40. Which option is given in CDS/ISIS for creating a new record? (*NET Exam.* 1994)
(a) C (b) N (c) R (d) S

41. Raw, unevaluated, unprocessed and unorganized facts is
(a) Data (b) Information
(c) Knowledge (d) Wisdom

42. The first machine employing concepts similar to those of computer was the (*NET Exam.* 1994)
(a) MARK I (b) UNIVAC
(c) EDSAC (d) Analytical engine

43. The second generation of computer was based on electronic device known as
(a) Resistance (b) Transistor
(c) IC (d) KIPS

44. Fourth generation of computers used
(a) KIPS (b) Silicon Chips
(c) Pentium (d) 486 Chips

45. Union catalogue of scientific serials was developed by
(a) NASSDOC (b) BARC
(c) INSDOC (d) DESIDOC

46. Components of SDI system are use profile, document profile, computer, software
(a) Hardware
(b) Database
(c) Application programme
(d) User Interface

47. IBM stands for
(a) International Business Management
(b) International Bibliographic Management
(c) International Bibliographic Data Management
(d) International Business Machine

48. In India the focal point for distribution of CDS/ISIS is
(a) CSIR (b) NISSAT
(c) DESIDOC (d) INSDOC

49. CDS/ISIS software package was developed by

(a) UNESCO (b) CSIR
(c) Library of Congress (d) IFLA

50. The component of the MARC format structure include
(a) Record directory and variable fields
(b) Leader and record directory field
(c) Leader, record directory and fixed
(d) Leader, record directory and variable fields

51. In machine format the lowest unit of information is
(a) Database (b) Record
(c) Data element (d) Field

52. LAN computers networking stands for
(a) Line and Network
(b) Local Area Network
(c) Local Automated Nodes
(d) Local Area Nodes

53. The lowest unit of information in computer is
(a) Bit (b) KB (c) Byte (d) Digit

54. Operating system constitutes
(a) Word processing and DBMS
(b) System programme and application programmes
(c) Control programmes and processing programmes
(d) System programmes and high-level programmes

55. _______ is a subdivision of a record that holds on piece of data about transaction.
(a) Array (b) Field
(c) Database (d) File

56. _______ is used for topography and page layout aspects.
(a) Lotus 1-2-3 (b) Ventura
(c) Auto CAD (d) Word star

57. The popular and widely used output device is
(a) Hard disk (b) Tape drive
(c) Floppy disk (d) Visual Display Unit

58. There are two basic types of programmes
(a) Word processing programmes and DBMS programmes
(b) System programmes and application programmes
(c) System programmes and desk top programmes
(d) Assembly programmes and high level programmes

59. _________ is a single, integrated circuit that contain an ALU and CPU.
(a) RAM (b) ROM
(c) Microprocessor (d) IC

60. The first generation of computers developed during
(a) 1970's (b) 1960's (c) 1950's (d) 1940's

61. An analog computer operates ________ by rather than by counting.
(a) measuring (b) cell
(c) electricity (d) magnet

62. Logical operators used in computers were developed by
(a) Alfred Venn (b) George Boole
(c) Charles Babbage (d) Howard Aiken

63. The logical operation AND, OR, NOT are devised by
(a) Leibnitz (b) George Boole
(c) Charles Babbage (d) Vincent Atanasoff

64. High-level language are
(a) Disk space dependent
(b) OS dependent
(c) Machine independent
(d) Machine dependent

65. ______ translates a complete programme into machine.
(a) Compiler (b) Utilities
(c) Assembler (d) Translator

66. A programme that converts the mnemonics and symbols of assembly language into the opcodes and operands of machine language is
(a) Assembler (b) Compiler
(c) Utilities (d) Translator

67. _________ is a device that can convert digital computer signals into analog signals and can reverse the procedure at the other of-line.
(a) FAX (b) LASER printer
(c) MODEM (d) Scanner

68. During 1960 the MARC project was started by
(a) UNESCO (b) British Museum Library
(c) Library of Congress (d) IFLA

69. Compact Disk Read Only Memory, an optical disk can hold __________ pages of printed matter.
    (a) lakhs (b) thousand
    (c) hundred (d) ten
70. Maintenance of Library membership files belongs to __________ area.
    (a) serial (b) cataloguing
    (c) reference (d) circulation
71. COM in Library stand for ______ catalogue.
    (a) computer output microfilm
    (b) on Machine
    (c) compact memory
    (d) communication port
72. Sending of reminders to vendors and publishers belongs to the _________ area.
    (a) cataloguing (b) acquisition
    (c) circulation (d) information retrieval
73. Inter Library loan transactions are recorded in _________ area.
    (a) circulation (b) cataloguing
    (c) acquisition (d) information retrieval
74. Vacuum tubes were utilised as internal components in _____ generation computer.
    (a) first (b) second (c) third (d) fourth
75. The Electro mechanical calculating machine were first developed by _________ in 1890.
    (a) Herman Hollerith (b) George Boole
    (c) Leibnitz (d) Charles Babbage
76. The two categories of computers are
    (a) Mini and Micro computers
    (b) General and Special computers
    (c) Analog and digital
    (d) Super computers and Main frame
77. ENIAC stands for
    (a) Electronic Numerical Integrator and Calculator
    (b) Electrified Numerical Integration and Calculator
    (c) Electronic Number Integrator and Calculator
    (d) Electrical Numerical Integrator and Calculator
78. UNIVAC stands for
    (a) United Automatic Computer
    (b) Universal Automatic Computer
    (c) Useful Aadarsh Computer
    (d) Useful Automatic Computer
79. EDSAC stands for
    (a) Electronic Delay Storage Automatic Computer
    (b) Electrical Delayed Stored Automatic Computer
    (c) Electrified Delayed Store Automatic Computer
    (d) Electrical Delayed Store Automatic Computer
80. _____ is a collection of bibliographic record.
    (a) Format (b) Bibliographic database
    (c) Bibliofield (d) File
81. STAIRS is stand for
    (a) Storage and Information Retrieval System
    (b) Storage Information Retrieved System
    (c) Store Information Retrieval System
    (d) Store and Information Reach System
82. There are _________ basic steps involved in defining the database.
    (a) four (b) five (c) six (d) seven
83. The system programmes of ISIS includes
    (a) ISISDEF, ISISUTL, ISISXCH, ISISPAS
    (b) ISISDEF, ISIS and ISISINV
    (c) ISIS, ISISINV
    (d) ISIS and ISISPRT
84. The CDS/ISIS is written in
    (a) BASIC (b) COBOL
    (c) C language (d) PASCAL
85. UNIX is a
    (a) single user operating system
    (b) multi user operating system
    (c) double user system
    (d) None of the above
86. In which year integrated circuit (IC) has come into effect?
    (a) 1962 (b) 1963 (c) 1950 (d) 1940
87. Word processing package have facility for merging document generally known as
    (a) Shell document (b) Mail merge
    (c) Word Processing (d) Mail Sending
88. Which of the following types of memory is non-volatile?
    (a) ROM (b) PROM
    (c) WORM (d) RAM
89. Electronic mail (E-mail) is delivered through (*NET Exam.* 1997)
    (a) Postman (b) Courier
    (c) Speed Post (d) Computer and Modem

90. Sanjay software is developed by
    (a) CMC Limited (b) INSDOC
    (c) DESIDOC (d) UNESCO
91. Arrange the following storage device according to increasing reading speed:
    (I) CD-ROM (II) Floppy Disk
    (III) Magnetic Disk
    Codes:
    (a) I, II, III (b) III, II, I
    (c) I, III, II (d) II, III, I
92. Micro computers are
    (a) same as mini computers
    (b) also known as laptop computers
    (c) based on micro chip
    (d) first computers to be made
93. Textual matter is represented in computer in a standard code such as
    (a) Byte (b) COBOL
    (c) FORTRAN (d) ASCII
94. The word "bit" not stand for binary digit.
    (a) True (b) False
95. A byte usually represents a character.
    (a) True (b) False
96. Computer was applied first in India in 1937.
    (a) True (b) False
97. System programmes are also referred to as system software.
    (a) True (b) False
98. Micro CDS/ISIS is menu driven package.
    (a) True (b) False
99. UNESCO introduced the CDS/ISIS software.
    (a) True (b) False
100. CDS/ISIS written in PASCAL language.
    (a) True (b) False
101. Checkmate software package is used in serial control in library.
    (a) True (b) False
102. Telecommunication is the transmission of information by electronic means.
    (a) True (b) False
103. Modem is a device to convert the digital information into analogue mode.
    (a) True (b) False
104. ALU is a part of CPU.
    (a) True (b) False
105. Match the following:
    (A) Analytical engine (i) John Newmann
    (B) Automatic calculator (ii) Herman Hollerith
    (C) Punched Card (iii) Howard Aiken
    (D) Stored Computer programme (iv) Charles Babbage

Codes:	A	B	C	D
(a)	iv	iii	ii	i
(b)	i	ii	iii	iv
(c)	iii	iv	ii	i
(d)	ii	i	iv	iii

106. Match the following:
    (A) RAM (i) Output devices used for punching graphs
    (B) ROM (ii) Volatile memory
    (C) Printer (iii) Device used for getting hard copy
    (D) Plotter (iv) Non-volatile memory

Codes:	A	B	C	D
(a)	ii	iv	iii	i
(b)	iv	iii	ii	i
(c)	iii	ii	i	iv
(d)	i	ii	iii	iv

107. Match the following:
    (A) Libsys (i) Software developed by UNESCO
    (B) DBMS (ii) Software that assists the user in accessing and managing the data in database
    (C) Word processor (iii) The component of productivity for working with text
    (D) CDS/ISIS (iv) Library Software

Codes:	A	B	C	D
(a)	iv	ii	iii	i
(b)	i	ii	iii	iv
(c)	iii	i	iv	ii
(d)	ii	iii	i	iv

108. Match the following:
    (A) Keyboard (i) Most common input device
    (B) Computer (ii) Electronic equipment
    (C) Visual display unit (iii) Output device
    (D) Control unit (iv) Nerve centre of computer

Codes:	A	B	C	D
(a)	ii	iii	iv	i
(b)	i	ii	iii	iv

(c)	iii	i	ii	iv
(d)	iv	iii	ii	i

109. Match the following:

(A) Integrated circuit used in	(i) first generation computer
(B) Vacuum tube used in	(ii) second generation computer
(C) Silicon chips used in	(iii) third generation computer
(D) Transistor circuit used in	(iv) fourth generation computer

Codes:	A	B	C	D
(a)	ii	iii	iv	i
(b)	iii	i	iv	ii
(c)	iv	ii	iii	i
(d)	i	iv	ii	iii

110. Berne convention was adopted in the year (*NET Exam.* 2009J)
(a) 1911 (b) 1986 (c) 1900 (d) 1947

111. Which of the following is not a computer programming language? (*NET Exam.* 2001J)
(a) FORTRAN (b) BASIC
(c) COBOL (d) ASCII

112. What are three types of basic languages used in computer programming?
(a) Zero, low and high levels
(b) COBOL, BASIC and PROLOG
(c) FORTRON, PL/I and SNOWBOL
(d) Machine, Assembly and high-level languages

113. In how many ways switching system can be established?
(a) Two (b) Three (c) Five (d) Seven

114. Indicate the beginner of INTERNET from the following choices (*NET Exam.* 2001J)
(a) ARPANET (b) INTRANET
(c) TELNET (d) OCLC

115. The 'User Profile' is a (*NET Exam.* 2001D)
(a) List of descriptors
(b) List of useful citations
(c) List of users
(d) Statement on user information

116. Which of the following types of memory is volatile? (*NET Exam.* 2011D)
(a) ROM (b) RAM
(c) PROM (d) WORM

117. Which one of the following is an example of an operating system? (*NET Exam.* 2001D)
(a) DOS (b) WordStar
(c) dBase (d) LOTUS A-B-C

118. LAN is (*NET Exam.* 2002D)
(a) the public networks
(b) operatable at higher speed than WAN
(c) Both (a) and (b)
(d) None of these

119. The simple Dublin Core Metadata Element Set (DCMES) consists of (*NET Exam.* 2010J)
(a) 15 elements (b) 10 elements
(c) 14 elements (d) 18 elements

120. Password security involves (*NET Exam.* 2002J)
(a) authorization (b) authentication
(c) identification (d) All of these

121. ASCII is (*NET Exam.* 2002J)
(a) APC
(b) A programming language
(c) A company
(d) A computer coding-standard

122. Mouse can be used with (*NET Exam.* 2002J)
(a) CDS/ISIS (b) PRECIS
(c) SOUL (d) All of these

123. The steps involved in defining a database using a CDS/ISIS package are: (*NET Exam.* 2002J)
1. Creating the FDT
2. Creating the field select table (FST)
3. Creating a data entry worksheet
4. Defining display/prints format

Codes:
(a) 2, 3 & 4 (b) 1, 2, 3 & 4
(c) 1, 3 & 4 (d) 1 & 2

124. Which was the first generation of computer? (*NET Exam.* 2002J)
(a) UNIVAC-I (b) UNIAC
(c) Microcomputer (d) Supercomputer

125. System software consists of operating systems and control programmes, translators, utilities and service programmes and (*NET Exam.* 2002J)
(a) ROM
(b) Output devices
(c) Secondary storage
(d) Database Management System (DBMS)

126. Network formed between computers spread in Large Geographical Area is (*NET Exam.* 2003J)
(a) LAN (b) Computer Network
(c) Public Network (d) System Software

127. Which of the following has funded ERNET? (*NET Exam.* 2003D)
(a) UNESCO (b) ICSU
(c) UNICEF (d) IFLA

128. In Computer technology, "C" refers to (*NET Exam.* 2003D)
(a) CPU (b) Console System
(c) UNIX (d) Programming Language

129. A LAN is owned by
(a) the user (b) the ISP provider
(c) the administrator (d) All of these

130. Match the following: (*NET Exam.* 2003D)
Column A
(A) The design pertaining, to a form of artistic, educational or commercial communication in Which more than one medium is used.
(B) A set of procedures and standards grouped into seven layers for the exchange of information between terminals and computers.
(C) The exchange of messages and computer files between computers over a computer network.
Column B
(i) OSI (ii) Multimedia
(iii) E-mail (iv) Fax

Codes:	A	B	C
(a)	(ii)	(i)	(ii)
(b)	(ii)	(iii)	(i)
(c)	(iv)	(iii)	(i)
(d)	(ii)	(iv)	(iii)

131. The program, which forms the interface between the hardware and the user is (*NET Exam.* 2003D)
(a) RAM (b) Application programme
(c) Operating system (d) Interpreter

132. How modules are in CDS/ISIS to perform different functions? (*NET Exam.* 2003D)
(a) 2 (b) 4 (c) 6 (d) 10

133. "TARGET", a natural language search system is released by (*NET Exam.* 2003D)
(a) BRS (b) ORBIT
(c) BLAISE (d) DIALOG

134. Formation of subject headings is performed in PRECIS by (*NET Exam.* 2003D)
(a) LCSH (b) Computer
(c) Duplicator (d) Indexer

135. Data are stored serially in CD-ROM by using (*NET Exam.* 2003D)
(a) Spiral tracks (b) Concentric or Spiral tracks
(c) Concentric tracks (d) None of these

136. Which of the following are the components of Search Engine?
(i) Spider (ii) TCP/IP
(iii) Search Mechanism (iv) Index
Codes:
(a) (iv), (i) and (iii) (b) (iii), (ii) and (i)
(c) (i), (iii) and (iv) (d) (ii), (iv) and (iii)

137. An University providing Open Access to Sanskrit dissertations through Internet.
(a) Jawaharlal Nehru University
(b) Delhi University
(c) Mahatma Gandhi University
(d) University of Madras

138. In CDS/ISIS formatting language, what precedes a tag (*NET Exam.* 2004J)
(a) + (b) V (c) / (d) ^ p

139. The first commercial online information system is (*NET Exam.* 2004J)
(a) OCLC (b) ORBIT
(c) BLAISE (d) DIALOG

140. The type of International networks accessible to online vendor are such as (*NET Exam.* 2004J)
(a) WAN (b) MAN
(c) LAN (d) None of these

141. Which memory is volatile in nature?
(a) Static RAM (b) Dynamic RAM
(c) Secondary memory (d) None of these
(*NET Exam.* 2004J)

142. Micro CDS/ISIS is written in (*NET Exam.* 2004J)
(a) C-Language (b) PASCAL
(c) COBOL (d) PROLOG

143. Security of password in Library Automation involves (*NET Exam.* 2004D)
1. Identification 2. Authentication
3. Authorisation 4. Insertion
Codes:
(a) 2 & 4 (b) 2 & 3
(c) 1, 2, 3 (d) All the four

144. Which is ROM memory? (*NET Exam.* 2004D)
(a) EEPROM (b) PROM
(c) EPROM (d) All of these

145. Match the following: (*NET Exam.* 2004D)

Column A (Programme/Software)	**Column B (Owner/Developer)**
(A) UNIX	(i) Intel
(B) SOUL	(ii) Inflibnet
(C) P-4	(iii) AT & T
	(iv) Ken Thompson & Denis Richie

Codes:	**A**	**B**	**C**
(a)	(ii)	(iii)	(i)
(b)	(iv)	(ii)	(i)
(c)	(i)	(ii)	(iii)
(d)	(iv)	(iii)	(i)

146. The important components of Information Technology is/are (*NET Exam.* 2004D)
1. Computer Technology
2. Communication Technology
3. Printing and Publishing Technology
4. Reprography and Micrography

Codes:
(a) 1 & 2 (b) 1, 2, 3 & 4
(c) 2, 3 & 4 (d) 1 & 3

147. Which of the following are common types of protocols? (*NET Exam.* 2004D)
(i) HTTP (ii) FTP
(iii) Telnet (iv) Gopher

Codes:
(a) (i) and (ii) are correct
(b) (i), (ii) and (iv) are correct
(c) (iii) and (iv) are correct
(d) (i), (ii) and (iii) are correct

148. Who defined Digital Library as Global Virtual Library? (*NET Exam.* 2004D)
(a) Allen Kent (b) C. Wellmen
(c) R.R. Larsen (d) M.K. Grogan

149. Softwares on payroll, inventory, control, education are the example of (*NET Exam.* 2004D)
(a) Operating system (b) Application software
(c) UNIX-system (d) Information services

150. Communication Networks are (*NET Exam.* 2005D)
(a) LAN (b) MAN
(c) WAN (d) All of these

151. **Assertion (A):** Research results lead to propound new laws, theories and principles.

Reason (R): Laws, principles and theories are the result of scientific research. (*NET Exam.* 2009J)

Codes:
(a) Both (A) and (R) are true.
(b) Both (A) and (R) are true but (A) is not a correct explanation.
(c) (A) is false and (R) is true.
(d) (A) is true and (R) is false.

152. The term hypertext was coined by (*NET Exam.* 2009J)
(a) Ted Nelson (b) Charles Babbage
(c) Tim Berner Lee (d) Tay Vaughan

153. Conversion of barcode into electrical signals is done by (*NET Exam.* 2009J)
(a) Scanners (b) CRT
(c) Photo Sensor (d) UNICODE

154. **Assertion (A):** Making information available using GSDL is effective than just putting it on the web.

Reason (R): The information available in digital form can be achieved. (*NET Exam.* 2009J)

Codes:
(a) Both (A) and (R) are true and (R) is the correct explanation.
(b) Both (A) and (R) are true and (R) is not the correct explanation.
(c) (A) is true but (R) is false.
(d) (A) is false but (R) is true.

155. **Assertion (A):** Migration is the primary strategy used by most organization for digital archiving.

Reason (R): Migration preserve the physical presence, content, functionality and context of the digital object. (*NET Exam.* 2009J)

Codes:
(a) Both (A) and (R) are true and (R) is not the correct explanation.
(b) Both (A) and (R) are true and (R) is the correct explanation.
(c) (A) is true but (R) is false.
(d) (A) is false but (R) is true.

156. **Assertion (A):** Present day libraries need to develop social networking tools for their library websites.

Reason (R): It helps to reach out the patrons where they live and provide service at the point of need. (*NET Exam.* 2009J)

Codes:

(a) Both (A) and (R) are true.
(b) Both (A) and (R) are true but (R) is not the correct explanation.
(c) (A) is true but (R) is false.
(d) (A) is false but (R) is true.

157. **Assertion (A):** Library Science has been called science because it has good application of scientific tools and techniques as is applicable in natural science and physical science.

Reason (R): Experimental methods of research has good scope in library science. (*NET Exam.* 2009J)

Codes:

(a) Both (A) and (R) are true is not a correct explanation.
(b) Both (A) and (R) are true.
(c) (A) is false but (R) is true.
(d) (A) is true but (R) is false.

158. **Assertion (A):** Hypothesis are essential in all types of research.

Reason (R): Objectives can fulfil the purpose of hypothesis. (*NET Exam.* 2009J)

Codes:

(a) Both (A) and (R) are true.
(b) (A) is false but (R) is true.
(c) (A) is true and (R) is false.
(d) Both (A) and (R) are false.

159. Arrange the following library automation software according to their date of origin (*NET Exam.* 2009J)

(i) SOUL (ii) KOHA
(iii) New GENLIB (iv) LIBSYS

Codes:

(a)	(iv)	(i)	(ii)	(iii)
(b)	(i)	(iii)	(iv)	(ii)
(c)	(iii)	(ii)	(i)	(iv)
(d)	(i)	(iv)	(ii)	(iii)

160. Which statement/s is/are not correct? (*NET Exam.* 2005D, 2009J)

1. The language used in the Information Technology are JAVA, PASCAL, COBOL, etc.
2. Software on pay roll, inventory control, education are the examples of application software.
3. The internal storage which is never altered in random access memory (RAM).

Codes:

(a) 3 only (b) 1 & 2
(c) 1 only (d) 1, 2 & 3

161. The smallest unit of data in a database is

(a) Record (b) File
(c) Field (d) Table

162. A series of interconnected documents stored on the Internet is called (*NET Exam.* 2006J)

(a) Websites (b) Domain Name
(c) Home Page (d) Web Page

163. Identify the development in following Library Software in correct chronological sequence (*NET Exam.* 2006J)

(a) Sanjaya, Libsys, SLIM, SOUL
(b) SLIM, Libsys, SOUL, Sanjaya
(c) Libsys, Sanjaya, SOUL, SLIM
(d) Sanjaya, SOUL, SLIM, Libsys

164. Select the right sequence of the following devices according to their storage capacity in descending order (*NET Exam.* 2006J)

(a) CD, DVD, Floppy Disc, Punched Card
(b) Floppy Disc, Punched Card, CD, DVD
(c) Punched Card, Floppy Disc, CD, DVD
(d) DVD, CD, Floppy Disc, Punched Card

165. Match the following: (*NET Exam.* 2006D)

List I	**List II**
(A) ERNET	(i) Japan
(B) JANET	(ii) Global
(C) RLIN	(iii) India
(D) OCLC	(iv) United Kingdom
	(v) USA

Codes:	**A**	**B**	**C**	**D**
(a)	(v)	(iv)	(i)	(ii)
(b)	(iv)	(v)	(i)	(ii)
(c)	(iii)	(iv)	(v)	(ii)
(d)	(iii)	(ii)	(iv)	(v)

166. Match the following: (*NET Exam.* 2006D)

List I	**List II**
(A) Email	(i) Bulletin Board
(B) FTP	(ii) Remote Log In
(C) TELNET	(iii) Library Network
(D) USENET	(iv) Moving/Downloading Files
	(v) Exchanging Message

Codes:	**A**	**B**	**C**	**D**
(a)	(iv)	(iii)	(v)	(i)
(b)	(v)	(iv)	(ii)	(i)

(c)	(ii)	(iv)	(i)	(iii)
(d)	(v)	(i)	(iv)	(iii)

167. Match the following: (*NET Exam.* 2006D)

List I	List II
(A) MS-DOS	(i) Multi-User Operating System
(B) UNIX	(ii) DTP Software
(C) Excel	(iii) DBMS
(D) Pagemaker	(iv) Single User Operating System
	(v) Spreadsheet Software

Codes:	A	B	C	D
(a)	(iv)	(v)	(i)	(ii)
(b)	(v)	(i)	(ii)	(iii)
(c)	(iii)	(i)	(ii)	(v)
(d)	(iv)	(i)	(v)	(ii)

168. Match the following: (*NET Exam.* 2006D)

List I	List II
(A) Search Engine	(i) Internet Explorer
(B) Subject Gateway	(ii) Dogpile
(C) Net Browser	(iii) FTP
(D) Meta Search Engine	(iv) SOSIG
	(v) Altavista

Codes:	A	B	C	D
(a)	(iv)	(iii)	(ii)	(i)
(b)	(v)	(iv)	(i)	(ii)
(c)	(v)	(i)	(ii)	(iii)
(d)	(v)	(i)	(iv)	(ii)

Read the passage given below and answer the questions based on your understanding of the passage. (Q. No. 169-173)

Digital devices measure and display discrete quantities. Most clocks for example are analog in nature and have hands that sweep along a continuous scale as do the needles on speedometers Digital clocks, however, display discrete numbers standing for the time. The numbers are either there or they are not, and they click into position virtually instantaneously. In fact, speed and accuracy are distinguishing features of most digital devices, because analog equipment comes in a poor second on both counts. A valid comparison can be made between side rules, which are analog, and pocket calculators, which are digital.

Accepts information in a unitary form, i.e., letters, symbols and numbers. These may represent anything the computer user wishes. All calculations and processing of the incoming data are done on the digital computer. Thus, all the mathematical rules and functions may be applied and the results are printed out in conventional letters, symbols or numbers. Thus, these are general purpose computers suitable for information processing in general.

"Hybrid" computers have been developed to take advantage of the strength of both analog and digital devices. Typically, analog computers will measure physical quantities such as temperature or pressure and then relay the data to digital computers, which, because of their greater speed and accuracy, can perform statistical computations on the data easily. The output is then displayed in a convenient form for the human beings responsible for conducting or monitoring the operation in question.

Because of their unique capabilities for symbol manipulation, digital computers loom for more important in applied information science than the other types, and it is to them that we shall be referring when we speak of computers from now on.

169. The distinguishing features of digital devices are: (*NET Exam.* 2006D)
   (i) Speed (ii) Accuracy
   (iii) Timeliness (iv) Easy to Carry
   Codes:
   (a) (i) and (ii) (b) (ii) and (iv)
   (c) (iv), (iii) and (i) (d) (ii), (iii) and (iv)

170. Digital clocks are analog in nature because (*NET Exam.* 2006D)
   (a) they have two hands
   (b) their hands sweep along a continuous scale
   (c) they show time
   (d) display discrete numbers standing for time

171. Hybrid computers are developed to take advantage of (*NET Exam.* 2006D)
   (a) strength of analog devices
   (b) strength of digital devices
   (c) strength of both analog and digital devices
   (d) strength of none of the above

172. Analog computers measure physical quantities because of (*NET Exam.* 2006D)
   (a) the temperature and accuracy
   (b) their greater speed and accuracy
   (c) the human beings
   (d) the complexities in operations

173. Digital computers assume more importance in applied information science because of (*NET Exam.* 2006D)
(a) the lack of capabilities for symbol manipulation
(b) the capabilities for symbol manipulation
(c) the capabilities for digital manipulation
(d) the lack of capabilities for digital manipulation

174. Arrange the following according to their year of development. (*NET Exam.* 2011D)
(i) Java (ii) Visual Basic
(iii) C++ (iv) COBOL

Codes:

(a)	(i)	(iii)	(iv)	(ii)
(b)	(iv)	(iii)	(ii)	(i)
(c)	(iii)	(i)	(iv)	(ii)
(d)	(i)	(iv)	(ii)	(iii)

175. Formatting a document in computer means (*NET Exam.* 2006D)
(a) Editing the content
(b) Changing the appearance
(c) Adding new content
(d) Changing the font size only

176. Identify the correct order of the evolution of the following storage devices (*NET Exam.* 2006D)
(a) DVD, Magnetic tape, Floppy, CD
(b) CD, DVD, Magnetic tape, Floppy
(c) Floppy, CD, DVD, Magnetic tape
(d) Magnetic tape, Floppy, CD, DVD

177. Which one of the sequences is in ascending order? (*NET Exam.* 2006D)
(a) Bytes, Gigabytes, Megabytes, Terabytes
(b) Bytes, Megabytes, Gigabytes, Terabytes
(c) Bytes, Terabytes, Megabytes, Gigabytes
(d) Megabytes, Bytes, Terabytes, Gigabytes

178. In which of the following network topologies, all the computers are connected to a central computer? (*NET Exam.* 2006D)
(a) Ring (b) Star
(c) Bus (d) Peer to Peer

179. Identify the correct order of evolution of computers (*NET Exam.* 2006D)
(a) PC-XT, PC-AT, Main frame, Micro
(b) PC-AT, PC-XT, Main frame, Micro
(c) Micro, PC-AT, PC-XT, Main frame
(d) Main frame, Micro, PC-AT, PC-XT

180. The chronological sequence of the technology is (*NET Exam.* 2006D)
(a) Telephone, Television, Satellite Communication, Internet
(b) Telephone, Satellite Communication, Television, Internet
(c) Telephone, Television, Internet, Satellite Communication
(d) Telephone, Internet, Television, Satellite Communication

181. **Assertion (A):** Internet is an important tool for the dissemination of information.
Reason (R): Large numbers of open sources are available. (*NET Exam.* 2007J)
Codes:
(a) (A) is true but (R) is false.
(b) (A) is false but (R) is true.
(c) Both (A) and (R) are true.
(d) Both (A) and (R) are false.

182. The unit for measuring the speed of the transmission of the data is called (*NET Exam.* 2007J)
(a) Baud (b) Protocol
(c) HTTP (d) RAM

183. The first page of Website is known as (*NET Exam.* 2007D)
(a) Cover Page (b) Home Page
(c) Title Page (d) Half Title Page

184. Match the following:

List I	List II
(A) SOUL	(i) INFOTEK
(B) LIBSYS	(ii) ALGORITHM
(C) SLIM	(iii) UNESCO
(D) WINISIS	(iv) INFLIBNET
	(v) DESIDOC

Codes:	A	B	C	D
(a)	(iii)	(v)	(iv)	(i)
(b)	(iv)	(i)	(ii)	(iii)
(c)	(v)	(iv)	(i)	(iii)
(d)	(i)	(iii)	(v)	(ii)

185. Binary system of number users only (*NET Exam.* 2007D, 2004J)
(a) Two digits (b) Four digits
(c) Eight digits (d) Six digits

186. "Dublin Core Metadata" consists of (*NET Exam.* 2007D)
(a) 11 elements (b) 13 elements
(c) 10 elements (d) 15 elements

187. Identify the development in the following library softwares in correct chronological sequence. (*NET Exam.* 2007D)
(a) CDS/ISIS, SOUL, Green Stone, D-Space
(b) D-Space, SOUL, CDS/ISIS, Green Stone
(c) Green Stone, CDS/ISIS, D-Space, SOUL
(d) SOUL, D-Space, Green Stone, CDS/ISIS

188. Match the following: (*NET Exam.* 2007D)

List I	List II
(A) Protocol	(i) Java
(B) Language	(ii) Internet Explorer
(C) Browser	(iii) Altavista
(D) Search Engine	(iv) Dos
	(v) HTTP

Codes:	A	B	C	D
(a)	(iv)	(v)	(i)	(iii)
(b)	(v)	(i)	(ii)	(iii)
(c)	(ii)	(iv)	(v)	(i)
(d)	(i)	(v)	(iv)	(ii)

189. The use of CD-ROMs in the library significantly relates to which of the following Law? (*NET Exam.* 2009J)
(a) First Law of Library Science
(b) Second Law of Library Science
(c) Fourth Law of Library Science
(d) Fifth Law of Library Science

190. Centralised Acquisition of Periodical (CAP) is a programme of (*NET Exam.* 2002J)
(a) NISCAIR (b) NASSDOC
(c) LASTEC (d) NISSAT

Read the passage given below, and answer the question based on your understanding of the passage. (Q. No. 191-195)

To survive, thrive and beat the competition in today's brutally competitive world, one has to manage the future. Managing the future means managing the information. In order to manage the information, in order to deliver high quality information to the decision-makers at the right time, in order to automate the process of data collection, collation and refinement, organizations have to make Information Technology (IT) an ally, harness its full potential and use it is the best way possible.

We have seen that in today's competitive business environment, the key resource of every organization is information. If the organization does not have an efficient and effective mechanism that enables it to give the decision-makers the right information at the right time, then the chances of that organization succeeding in the next millennium are very remote.

The three fundamental characteristics of information are accuracy, relevancy and timeliness. The information has to be accurate, it must be relevant for the decision-maker and it must be available to the decision-maker when he needs it. Any organization that has the mechanism to collect, collate, analyse and present high quality information to its employees, thus enabling them to make better decisions, will always be one step ahead of the competition. Today, the time available for an organization to react to the changing market trends is very short. To survive, the organization must always be on its toes, gathering and analyzing the data both internal and external. Any mechanism that will automate this information gathering and analysis process will enhance the chances of the organization to beat the competition.

191. Which factors force organization to use IT to harness information? (*NET Exam.* 2008J)
(a) Explosion of sources of information
(b) Availability of latest information on real time basis
(c) Time, volume and complex nature of information on real time basis
(d) Information needs of users are inter-disciplinary in nature

192. Major obstacle in taking accurate futuristic decisions is (*NET Exam.* 2008J)
(a) Availability of more information
(b) cut-throat completion
(c) ever-changing socio-economic and political situations
(d) globalization

193. Which is the most appropriate tool to make better use of information? (*NET Exam.* 2008J)
(a) Well qualified and experienced information professional
(b) Depth classification and indexing
(c) Experts in domain knowledge
(d) Information technology

194. What is the critical characteristic of information delivery system for making it use effective? (*NET Exam.* 2008J)

(a) Efficient channels of communication system
(b) Ability to develop appropriate information products
(c) Right information, delivered at right time
(d) Developing quality photocopying and fax facility

195. What is the crucial decision for an organization to take to beat the competition? (*NET Exam.* 2008J)
(a) To create a mechanism to access, organize and process information within an organization.
(b) To establish a separate department for acquiring and processing information.
(c) To strengthen the libraries already existing in the organization.
(d) To collaborate with university and national and international information systems.

196. Which of the following are ISDN services? (*NET Exam.* 2012D)
(i) RSS (ii) Teletext
(iii) Voice mail (iv) Video conference
Codes:
(a) (i), (iii) and (iv) are correct
(b) (i), (ii) and (iv) are correct
(c) (ii), (iii) and (iv) are correct
(d) (i), (ii) and (iii) are correct

197. **Assertion (A):** XML, just like HTML is a meta language that is capable of containing extendable elements.
Reason (R): XML develop and deploy new specific mark up, enabling automatic authoring and processing of networked information. (*NET Exam.* 2009D)
Codes:
(a) (A) is false but (R) is true.
(b) Both (A) and (R) are true and (R) is not the correct explanation.
(c) (A) is true but (R) is false.
(d) Both (A) and (R) are true.

198. Arrange the following layers of OSI model in the sequence in which they function: (*NET Exam.* 2009D)
(i) Network Layer (ii) Physical Layer
(iii) Transport Layer (iv) Data Link Layer
Codes:

(a)	(iii)	(iv)	(ii)	(i)
(b)	(iv)	(ii)	(i)	(iii)
(c)	(ii)	(iv)	(i)	(iii)
(d)	(i)	(ii)	(iii)	(iv)

199. Arrange in chronological order the following persons who were associated with computing history:
(i) J. Presper Eckart (ii) John W. Mauchly
(iii) August Ada (iv) Charles Babbage
Codes:

(a)	(iii)	(ii)	(i)	(iv)
(b)	(ii)	(i)	(iii)	(iv)
(c)	(i)	(iv)	(iii)	(ii)
(d)	(iv)	(iii)	(ii)	(i)

200. Arrange the following in chronological sequence:
(i) Digital Millennium Copyright Act
(ii) Right to Information Act (India)
(iii) Information Technology Act (India)
(iv) Indian Copyright Act
Codes:

(a)	(iv)	(i)	(iii)	(ii)
(b)	(iv)	(ii)	(iii)	(i)
(c)	(i)	(iv)	(ii)	(iii)
(d)	(ii)	(iii)	(i)	(iv)

201. The 12 rules for relational database were given by (*NET Exam.* 2009J)
(a) Larvy Page (b) Linus Tolward
(c) J. Bills Gates (d) E.F. Codd

202. Arrange the following chronologically according to their use in computers: (*NET Exam.* 2010J)
(i) Vacuum tube (ii) Microchip
(iii) Integrated circuits (iv) Transistors
Codes:

(a)	(i)	(iii)	(ii)	(iv)
(b)	(i)	(ii)	(iii)	(iv)
(c)	(i)	(iv)	(iii)	(ii)
(d)	(ii)	(iv)	(iii)	(i)

203. Arrange the following in chronological order of their origin: (*NET Exam.* 2007D)
(i) Unix (ii) Ms-Dos
(iii) Linux (iv) Windows
Codes:

(a)	(iv)	(ii)	(iii)	(i)
(b)	(ii)	(i)	(iv)	(iii)
(c)	(i)	(iii)	(iv)	(ii)
(d)	(iii)	(i)	(iv)	(ii)

204. **Assertion (A):** Libraries have no scope for the growth and development in future.

Reason (R): E-resources can be used anywhere anytime. (*NET Exam.* 2007D)

Codes:

(a) Both (A) and (R) are true.
(b) Both (A) and (R) are false.
(c) (A) is false but (R) is true.
(d) (A) is true but (R) is false.

205. Following is not a social bookmarking site.
(a) Digg (b) Delicious
(c) Squidoo (d) Facebook

206. The owner of Internet is (*NET Exam.* 2007D)
(a) American Mathematical Society
(b) Department of Science and Technology, Government of India
(c) British Standard Institute
(d) None of the above

207. Arrange the following according to their increasing storage capacity: (*NET Exam.* 2008D)
(i) Cartridge (ii) CD-ROM
(iii) Floppy disks (iv) DVD

Codes:

(a)	(iii)	(i)	(ii)	(iv)
(b)	(i)	(ii)	(iii)	(iv)
(c)	(iv)	(iii)	(i)	(ii)
(d)	(i)	(iii)	(ii)	(iv)

208. **Assertion (A):** Indian libraries are making optimum use of social networking.

Reason (R): Social networking has wider role in dissemination of information. (*NET Exam.* 2012D)

Codes:

(a) (A) is true but (R) is false.
(b) (A) is false but (R) is true.
(c) (A) and (R) both are true.
(d) (A) and (R) both are false.

209. Match the following: (*NET Exam.* 2008J)

List I

(A) Windows (B) Microprocessor
(C) Word processor (D) Software

List II

(i) A revolving disc on which data is stored
(ii) It is use for processing of text
(iii) Collection of programme for computer system
(iv) A graphical user interface working as DOS

Codes:	A	B	C	D
(a)	(iv)	(i)	(ii)	(iii)
(b)	(iii)	(ii)	(i)	(iv)
(c)	(ii)	(iii)	(iv)	(i)
(d)	(i)	(ii)	(iii)	(iv)

210. One of the following is not an open source software. (*NET Exam.* 2008J)
(a) D space (b) Windows
(c) Green-stone (d) Linux

211. Arrange the following in the order of computer generations:
(i) Integrated circuit (ii) Transistor
(iii) Vacuum Tube (iv) Chip

Codes:

(a)	(iv)	(ii)	(iii)	(i)
(b)	(iii)	(ii)	(iv)	(i)
(c)	(i)	(ii)	(iii)	(iv)
(d)	(iii)	(iv)	(ii)	(i)

212. Match the following: (*NET Exam.* 2008J)

List I	**List II**
(A) Software	(i) Keyboard
(B) Hardware	(ii) CD
(C) Storage Device	(iii) SOUL
(D) I/O Device	(iv) CPU

Codes:	A	B	C	D
(a)	(ii)	(iv)	(iii)	(i)
(b)	(ii)	(iii)	(iv)	(i)
(c)	(iii)	(ii)	(iv)	(i)
(d)	(iii)	(iv)	(ii)	(i)

213. **Assertion (A):** Many projects and initiatives are taken to create digital libraries.

Reason (R): Digital library improves the professional status of librarians. (*NET Exam.* 2008D)

(a) Both (A) and (R) are true.
(b) Both (A) and (R) are false.
(c) (A) is true but (R) is false.
(d) (A) is false but (R) is true.

214. Appropriate communication media for CD-Net is (*NET Exam.* 2008D)
(a) Twisted wires (b) Optical fibre
(c) Co-axial cables (d) Ethernet cables

Read the passage given below and answer the questions based on your understanding of the passage. (Q. No. 215-219)

In the late 1990s the publishing world launched a new system into the information and publishing world called Digital Object Identifiers (DOIs). DOIs are alphanumeric character strings that identify objects in an electronic environment.

DOIs are universal, unique and permanent identification tags for online content that is registered in an online directory. DOIs can cover any form of digital files such as text, image, video, audio or even software. DOIs can also cover many levels of content. For example, it might tag an entire book, a chapter in the book, illustrations, individual sentences, or perhaps the book's index. It is a system that identifies creation endeavours and uniquely marks the content of these items. It is intended to individualize information units on the Web.

DOIs can be placed in a variety of places, such as in the object itself, in an information structure that contains the object, on a Web page that describes the element, in a database or as an entry in an indexing system.

The identifier tags have no intrinsic meaning, as a classification code does. They are content labels, each being unique and without duplicates. The identifiers are stored in directory that allows the lookup of the current Internet address of the copyright owner and where the information now resides. The author, publisher or current owner is responsible for maintaining the response page, which presents data about the information item and the conditions of its use.

The directory of DOIs routes inquiries to the up-to-date sites on the Internet for accessing the content of the object. When addresses change, the directory will route the query to where the content is currently located or to where information is given concerning how to obtain it. Over time, when objects move around or change ownership, the directory keeps tabs on these changes.

Although the major purpose of the DOI system is the management of intellectual property, indexing and abstracting services, as well as document delivery services will find DOIs a useful tool.

215. What are DOIs? (*NET Exam.* 2010D)
   (a) DOIs are numbers which identify object in traditional environment.
   (b) DOIs are identifiers consisting of alphanumeric character strings for printed materials.
   (c) DOIs are alphanumeric character strings for electronic serials.
   (d) DOIs are alphanumeric character strings for electronic sources of information available online.

216. What are the materials covered by DOIs? (*NET Exam.* 2010D)
   (a) DOIs cover books and journals.
   (b) DOIs cover texts, images, audio visual materials in digital form.
   (c) DOIs cover electronically available S&T information.
   (d) DOIs cover digital format in US and Europe only.

217. Do DOIs play any role in grouping of information sources? (*NET Exam.* 2010D)
   (a) DOIs constitute the e-classification scheme to group sources of information.
   (b) DOIs are not class numbers as such as have nothing to do with arrangement.
   (c) DOIs play the dual role of identifying and grouping.
   (d) DOIs are only like traditional class number sin e-form.

218. What is the major purpose of DOI system? (*NET Exam.* 2010D)
   (a) To organize e-resources on the Net.
   (b) To manage intellectual property.
   (c) To provide bibliographic description of digitized resources.
   (d) To control free access to e-resources.

219. How does DOI system operate? (*NET Exam.* 2010D)
   (a) Routes inquiries to designated Document Supply Libraries
   (b) Routes inquiries to up to date sits of digital libraries
   (c) Routes inquiries to national e-resources depositories
   (d) Routes inquiries to relevant sites on the Net

220. **Assertion (A):** Library automation is at a slow pace in Indian Libraries.

   Reason (R): Lack of U.G.C. (India) support lead to this situation. (*NET Exam.* 2009D)
   (a) Both (A) and (R) are true.
   (b) Both (A) and (R) are false.
   (c) (A) is true but (R) is false.
   (d) (A) is false but (R) is true.

221. **Assertion (A):** In contemporary digital environment, IPR become the focal point.

Reason (R): Many fold increase of unfair use of I.P. (*NET Exam.* 2009D)

(a) (A) and (R) are true.
(b) (A) and (R) are false.
(c) (A) is true and (R) is false.
(d) (A) is false and (R) is true.

222. The term 'Cyberspace' was first used by (*NET Exam.* 2009D)

(a) Andrew Pollock (b) William Gibson
(c) John Postal (d) Joe Flower

223. An E-book which does not require an internet connection to access its contents is (*NET Exam.* 2009D)

(a) Web book (b) Palm book
(c) Electronic Ink e-book (d) Digital book

224. The process of configuring the disks into tracks and sectors is called (*NET Exam.* 2009D)

(a) Booting (b) Formatting
(c) Labelling (d) All of the above

225. **Assertion (A):** Measuring the Internet and in particular the web's a difficult task.

Reason (R): Web is considered as a new publishing medium with inadequate editorial process. (*NET Exam.* 2009D)

Codes:

(a) Both (A) and (R) are true and (R) is the correct explanation.
(b) Both (A) and (R) are true and (R) is not the correct explanation.
(c) (A) is true but (R) is false.
(d) (A) is false but (R) is true.

226. Arrange the following according to chronological order: (*NET Exam.* 2010J)

(i) Universal Copyright convention
(ii) Berne Convention
(iii) Indian Copyright Act
(iv) WIPO Copyright Act

Codes:

(a)	(ii)	(iv)	(iii)	(i)
(b)	(iii)	(ii)	(iv)	(i)
(c)	(i)	(iii)	(ii)	(iv)
(d)	(ii)	(i)	(iii)	(iv)

227. World Wide Web was first designed by (*NET Exam.* 2010J)

(a) Charles Babbage (b) F.W. Lancaster
(c) Ted Nelson (d) Tim Berner's Lee

228. **Assertion (A):** Libraries are facing a threat and are bound to disappear soon.

Reason (R): Internet and WWW provide access to Oceans of information Worldwide. (*NET Exam.* 2010J)

Codes:

(a) (A) is true, but (R) is false.
(b) (A) is false, but (R) is true.
(c) Both (A) and (R) are true.
(d) Both (A) and (R) are false.

229. The Network Topology in which nodes are connected to a central hub is known as (*NET Exam.* 2010J)

(a) Ring Topology (b) Bus Topology
(c) Star Topology (d) Mesh Topology

230. Use of integrated circuits was made in (*NET Exam.* 2010J)

(a) First Generation Computers
(b) Second Generation Computers
(c) Third Generation Computers
(d) Fourth Generation Computers.

231. **Assertion (A):** RDF supports the use and exchange of metadata on the web.

Reason (R): Bibliographic standards are the means to create and disseminate secondary information. (*NET Exam.* 2012D)

Codes:

(a) (A) is true, (R) is false.
(b) (A) is false, (R) is true.
(c) Both (A) and (R) are correct.
(d) Both (A) and (R) are false.

232. Match the following: (*NET Exam.* 2012D)

List I	**List II**
(A) Informix	(i) Image software
(B) Omni Page	(ii) Remote login software
(C) TIFF Viewer	(iii) DBMS software
(D) Team Viewer	(iv) OCR software

Codes:	**A**	**B**	**C**	**D**
(a)	(ii)	(i)	(iii)	(iv)
(b)	(iii)	(iv)	(i)	(ii)
(c)	(i)	(ii)	(iii)	(iv)
(d)	(iv)	(iii)	(ii)	(i)

233. Identify the correct order as per increasing data storage capacity (*NET Exam.* 2012D)

(a) CD-ROM, DVD, Cartridge, Blue-ray Disc
(b) DVD, Cartridge, Blue-ray Disc, CD-ROM
(c) Cartridge, CD-ROM, DVD, Blue-ray Disc
(d) Blue-ray Disc, DVD, Cartridge, CD-ROM

234. **Assertion (A):** Online service incur heavy investment at the initial stage.
Reason (R): Online services are costlier than print services. (*NET Exam.* 2011D)
Codes:
(a) Both (A) and (R) are true.
(b) (A) is true, but (R) is false.
(c) (A) is false but (R) is true.
(d) Both (A) and (R) are false.

235. **Assertion (A):** Present decade has accepted E-journals as channels of scholarly communications.
Reason (R): E-publications have added enormous quantity of literature but affected the quality of research. (*NET Exam.* 2011D)
Codes:
(a) Both (A) and (R) are true and (R) is the correct explanation of (A).
(b) Both (A) and (R) are true, but (R) is not the correct explanation of (A).
(c) (A) is true but (R) is false.
(d) Both (A) and (R) are false.

236. Which topology of computer network provides faster server access? (*NET Exam.* 2012D)
(i) BUS Network Topology
(ii) RING Network Topology
(iii) MULTIPLE RING Network Topology
(iv) STAR Network Topology
Codes:
(a) (i) and (ii) are correct.
(b) (i) and (iii) are correct.
(c) (ii) and (iii) are correct.
(d) (ii) and (iv) are correct.

237. In 1974, Zurkowski used for the first time, which of the following term? (*NET Exam.* 2012D)
(a) Digital Literacy (b) Media Literacy
(c) Computer Literacy (d) Information Literacy

238. Planting the virus 'Trojan Horse' in computer network is (*NET Exam.* 2012D)
(i) Hacking (ii) Tampering
(iii) Decryption (iv) Intrusion
Codes:
(a) (i), (iii) and (iv) are correct.
(b) (ii), (iii) and (iv) are correct.
(c) (i), (ii) and (iii) are correct.
(d) (i), (ii) and (iv) are correct.

239. **Assertion (A):** Internet can replace libraries.
Reason (R): Google searches will satisfy the maximum users needs. (*NET Exam.* 2012D)
Codes:
(a) Both (A) and (R) are true.
(b) Both (A) and (R) are false.
(c) (A) is true but (R) is false.
(d) (A) is false but (R) is true.

240. **Assertion (A):** A combination of hypertext and Hypermedia contains text, images, sounds and other information.
Reason (R): Hypermedia information is represented in a linear fashion. (*NET Exam.* 2012D)
Codes:
(a) (A) is true and (R) is false.
(b) Both (A) and (R) are true.
(c) (A) is false and (R) is true.
(d) Both (A) and (R) are false.

241. Computer Memory is measured in (*NET Exam.* 2010J)
(a) Bytes (b) Kilobytes
(c) Megabytes (d) All of the above

242. Which one of the following protocols is used in transferring file over internet? (*NET Exam.* 2010J)
(a) POP (b) FTP (c) SMTP (d) TCP/IP

243. Linux is an example of (*NET Exam.* 2010D)
(a) Application software (b) System software
(c) Library software (d) All of the above

244. Transistors were used in which generation of computers? (*NET Exam.* 2010D)
(a) First generation (b) Second generation
(c) Third generation (d) None of the above

245. How different nodes in a network are connected and how they communicate are determined? (*NET Exam.* 2010D)
(a) By Network Connectivity
(b) By Network Topology
(c) By Network Compatibility
(d) None of the above

246. **Assertion (A):** Internet access provides information in abundance.
Reason (R): Information available on internet always lacks authenticity. (*NET Exam.* 2011J)
Codes:
(a) Both (A) and (R) are true and (R) is the correct explanation of (A).

(b) (A) is false, but (R) is true.
(c) Both (A) and (R) are true, but (R) is not a correct explanation of (A).
(d) (A) is true but (R) is false.

247. What is Dublin Core? (*NET Exam.* 2011J)
(a) Content management tool
(b) E-Library software
(c) Metadata standard
(d) Internet Protocol

248. Arrange the following according to the year of establishments: (*NET Exam.* 2011J)
(i) NICNET (ii) INDONET
(iii) INFLIBNET (iv) MALIBNET
Codes:

(a)	(iv)	(i)	(iii)	(ii)
(b)	(iv)	(ii)	(i)	(iii)
(c)	(ii)	(i)	(iv)	(iii)
(d)	(i)	(iii)	(iv)	(ii)

249. Report on 'the development of digital libraries of the past decade' is categorized as (*NET Exam.* 2012D)
(a) Review Report (b) Trend Report
(c) Research Report (d) State of the art report

250. Metadata Dublin core refers to (*NET Exam.* 2012D)
(a) Data elements in database
(b) Bibliographic elements in database
(c) Field elements in database
(d) Subject elements in database

251. Digital library function incorporate:
(i) Creating and capturing
(ii) Storage and management
(iii) Search and access
(iv) Abstracting and reviewing
Codes:
(a) (i), (ii) and (iii) are correct.
(b) (i), (iii) and (iv) are correct.
(c) (ii), (iii) and (iv) are correct.
(d) (i), (ii) and (iv) are correct.

Read the following passage and answer the questions (Q. No. 252-256).

While Boyd allows that some people consider email or discussion lists to be Social Software, he makes an important distinction between traditional communication software and Social Software. He explains that traditional software places people into groups with a top-down approach; in other words, it assigns membership. However, Social Software takes a bottom-up approach, which enables people to organize themselves into a network based on their preferences. Therefore, with a bottom-up approach, people can sign up for a system and build communities using their personal preferences (Marenzi et al., 2008). In contrast, traditional communication software uses a top-down approach where people are assigned into a specific organization or groups. Social Software is based on supporting individuals who interact socially with people who have similar interests (Marenzi et al., 2008). In addition, users typically enjoy Social Software itself and work with various Social Software applications voluntarily. For example, the authors of social media enjoy content that they have created themselves, content that is copied from other media, and mash-ups that contain a mix of content that could possibly be from several authors (Ahonen and Lietsala, 2007). The popularity of social technologies is attributed to the increase in low-cost tools and the critical mass of millions of people who are now connected to the Internet and to the people's need to fell like part of a community (Avram, 2006). These users tend to rely more on their own personal social networks than on traditional business structures. Vinson (2005) describes additional features of Social Software tools: they allow people to easily participate (by both contributing and reading) in the activities; they provide the opportunity for networking and allow for the self-forming of networks since people are usually both consumers and producers; and each individual can be a member on several networks simultaneously (Avram, 2006).

252. People are assigned into specific organization or groups in (*NET Exam.* 2013J)
(a) Top-down approach
(b) Down-top approach
(c) Top-bottom system approach
(d) Down-top system approach

253. The basic feature(s) of social software is/are (*NET Exam.* 2013J)
(a) Social interaction
(b) Personal interaction
(c) Enjoying social software
(d) (a) and (c) are correct.

254. Authors of social media enjoy of contents (*NET Exam.* 2013J)
   (a) Self created contents
   (b) Contents from magazines
   (c) Contents from many formats
   (d) Contents from many languages

255. The reasons attributed to the popularity of social networking is/are (*NET Exam.* 2013J)
   (a) Messes have started using Internet
   (b) All have free access to Internet.
   (c) All are technology literates.
   (d) Stimulation of on-line communities over the traditional communities.

256. The social software tools allow (*NET Exam.* 2013J)
   (a) Easy participation
   (b) Quick networking
   (c) Consumer networking
   (d) Both (a) and (b)

257. Match the following: (*NET Exam.* 2013J)

List I	List II
(A) Internal Files	(i) WPD
(B) Universal File Format	(ii) OeB
(C) Corel's Word Perfect	(iii) HTML
(D) Microsoft Reader	(iv) RTF

Codes:	**A**	**B**	**C**	**D**
(a)	(i)	(iii)	(ii)	(iv)
(b)	(ii)	(iv)	(iii)	(i)
(c)	(iv)	(ii)	(i)	(iii)
(d)	(iii)	(iv)	(i)	(ii)

258. **Assertion (A):** With the emergence of Internet, there is no need for reference service in this technology-based era.

   Reason (R): Internet has allowed access to every one to seek his/her information from anywhere, any time. (*NET Exam.* 2013J)

   Codes:
   (a) Both (A) and (R) are true.
   (b) Both (A) and (R) are false.
   (c) (A) is false but (R) is partially true.
   (d) (A) is true, but (R) is false.

259. The purposes of Metadata are (*NET Exam.* 2013J)
   (i) Unique identification
   (ii) Authentication of records
   (iii) Shelf arrangement
   (iv) Shows the collection of a library

   Codes:
   (a) (i), (ii) are correct.
   (b) (ii), (iii) are correct.
   (c) (iii), (iv) are correct.
   (d) (iv), (i) are correct.

260. The distinct characteristic(s) of digital objects are (*NET Exam.* 2013J)
   (a) Physical medium
   (b) Logical process
   (c) Conceptual recognition and transaction
   (d) All of the above

261. A network in which the host computer controls different nodes which further control other nodes, is known as (*NET Exam.* 2013J)
   (a) Star Network
   (b) Ring Network
   (c) Hierarchical Network
   (d) Multipoint Network

262. Match the following: (*NET Exam.* 2013J)

List I	List II
(A) Icon	(i) Character strings
(B) Menus	(ii) Select objects on the screen
(C) Dialogue Box	(iii) Bit mapped region
(D) Pointing devices	(iv) Obtain information from the end users.

Codes:	**A**	**B**	**C**	**D**
(a)	(i)	(ii)	(iii)	(iv)
(b)	(iii)	(iv)	(ii)	(i)
(c)	(ii)	(iii)	(iv)	(i)
(d)	(iii)	(i)	(iv)	(ii)

263. BUBL link is a (*NET Exam.* 2009J)
   (a) Database (b) OPAC
   (c) Subject gate way (d) Portal

264. Web form is used in (*NET Exam.* 2013J)
   (a) Synchronous Virtual References Service
   (b) Asynchronous Virtual Reference Service
   (c) Both (a) and (b)
   (d) None of the above

265. "Scitation" is the online host service of (*NET Exam.* 2013J)
   (a) American Institute of Physics
   (b) University of Maryland
   (c) Society for Industrial Research
   (d) Oxford University

266. Match the following: (*NET Exam.* 2013J)

List I	List II
(a) PDFA	(i) High colour depth images
(b) HTML	(ii) Rules for encoding documents electronically

(c) TIFF	(iii) File format for long term			
(d) XML	(iv) Language for web pages			
Codes:	A	B	C	D
(a)	(ii)	(iii)	(i)	(iv)
(b)	(iii)	(iv)	(i)	(ii)
(c)	(i)	(iii)	(ii)	(iv)
(d)	(iv)	(ii)	(iii)	(i)

267. The alternatives and modifications to H-Index are (*NET Exam.* 2013J)
(i) I-index (ii) Pure-h Index
(iii) Scimago Journal Rank (iv) European Impact Factor
Codes:
(a) (i) and (iii) are correct.
(b) (i) and (ii) are correct.
(c) (i) and (iv) are correct.
(d) (ii) and (iii) are correct.

268. An online search in which all aspects of the records in natural language may be used as sought terms is (*NET Exam.* 2013J)
(a) Alphabetical collateral search
(b) Multi-aspect search
(c) Free text searching
(d) Streaming search

269. Relational Database is (*NET Exam.* 2012J)
(a) A work which has some relationship to another work
(b) A symbol representing relationship between two concepts
(c) Manipulation commands which relate records in different fields
(d) All of the above

270. Which of the following are 'Open Source Content Management System': (*NET Exam.* 2012J)
(i) Drupal (ii) Atex
(iii) Joomla (iv) Open Cms
Codes:
(a) (i), (ii) and (iv) are correct
(b) (i), (ii) and (iii) are correct
(c) (ii), (iii) and (iv) are correct
(d) (i), (iii) and (iv) are correct

271. **Assertion (A):** Metadata hold much promise for information retrieval and access in the digital age.
Reason (R): Metadata can save a number of functions including description, resource discovery and management of resources. (*NET Exam.* 2012D)
Codes:
(a) (A) is true, but (R) is false.
(b) (A) is false, but (R) is true.
(c) Both (A) and (R) are true.
(d) Both (A) and (R) are false.

272. Which one of the following is not a switching system? (*NET Exam.* 2012D)
(a) Packet (b) Circuit
(c) Router (d) Message

273. Arrange the following according to their year of origin: (*NET Exam.* 2012D)
(i) UNICODE (ii) XML
(iii) HTML (iv) SGML

Codes:				
(a)	(iv)	(iii)	(i)	(ii)
(b)	(iii)	(iv)	(ii)	(i)
(c)	(ii)	(iv)	(i)	(iii)
(d)	(i)	(ii)	(iii)	(iv)

Read the passage given below, and answer the questions based on your understanding of the passage. (Q. No. 274-278)

The primary concern with the longevity of digital documents is the "viewing problem" (Besser, 2000). Unlike analog or physical information, which tends to exist independent of human involvements, digital information needs constant intervention to survive. History has shown that digital documents are problematic by default. Whereas we can actually look at the Sistine Chapel ceiling, painted 500 years ago, it is difficult if not impossible to simply view documents on 8 in. Floppy disks created in the last 20 years, even if there has been an immediate, proactive role in preserving them. Without concerted effort on the part of archivist and preservationists, digital objects quickly become obsolete or inaccessible due to unforeseen, although anticipated, advances in information technology. The variable media art community currently utilizes four digital preservation strategies, all focused on the end product. The first three methods have technical origins and are based on general digital preservation practices. Related to "the viewing problem", they are: refreshing, the upgrade of storage mechanisms; migration, the premeditated upgrade of file formats; and emulation, which focuses on development of operating systems able to run obsolete media. The fourth options, developed by and for the new media art community, is reinterpretation (Depocas et al., 2003), where the curators attempt to recreate a work given comprehensive documentation of the original artifact. Migration and emulation are the two primary methods in managing the problem of obsolete file formats (Waters and Garrett, 1996). Migration focuses on the files themselves, periodically updating files in new software formats. The second method of preservation is emulation, which can be either at the system or the software level. Systems emulation focuses on developing systems that mimic the hardware used to create or run the original artifact.

274. Why digital objects become inaccessible quickly? (*NET Exam.* 2012J)
(a) Because of unforeseen advancement of technology
(b) It is independent of human intervention
(c) It is independent of any technological advancement
(d) None of the above

275. Reinterpretation is a digital preservation strategy where curator intends to (*NET Exam.* 2012J)
(a) Upgrade file formats
(b) Upgrade storage mechanism
(c) Recreate a work
(d) Upgrade operating system

276. What is the focus of system emulation? (*NET Exam.* 2012J)
(a) Developing systems that mimic hardware
(b) Developing systems that mimic software
(c) Developing systems that mimic file formats
(d) None of the above

277. Which of the following is true about migration preservation strategy? (*NET Exam.* 2012J)
(a) Migration is not related to the viewing problem
(b) Migration is related to the viewing problem
(c) Migration requires comprehensive documentation
(d) Migration does not have a technical origin

278. Refreshing preservation strategy focuses on (*NET Exam.* 2012J)
(a) Comprehensive documentation of original artifact
(b) Development of operating system
(c) Not on viewing problem
(d) Upgradation of storage mechanism

279. Match the following: (*NET Exam.* 2012J)
List I
(A) Hubs (B) Repeater
(C) Bus Topology (D) Switches
List II
(i) A physical layer device used to interconnect the media segments of an extended network.
(ii) A physical layer device that connects multiple computers each via a dedicated cable.
(iii) Multiple bridges known for transfer of data between different parts.
(iv) A straight line data highway that carries network information form one network station to another.

Codes:	**A**	**B**	**C**	**D**
(a)	(iii)	(iv)	(ii)	(i)
(b)	(ii)	(i)	(iv)	(iii)
(c)	(iv)	(i)	(iii)	(ii)
(d)	(i)	(iii)	(ii)	(iv)

280. Major problems of 'Information Communication Technology' are (*NET Exam.* 2012J)
(i) Information overload
(ii) Information insecurity
(iii) Lack of innovative technologies
(iv) Lack of control over communication
Codes:
(a) (ii) and (iv) are correct.
(b) (i) and (iv) are correct.
(c) (i), (ii) and (iv) are correct.
(d) (i), (ii) and (iii) are correct.

281. The factors that influence computer file organization are (*NET Exam.* 2012J)
(i) Speed of access (ii) Storage space
(iii) Fixed length fields (iv) File volatility
Codes:
(a) (i), (ii) and (iii) are correct.
(b) (i), (ii) and (iv) are correct.
(c) (ii), (iii) and (iv) are correct.
(d) (i), (iii) and (iv) are correct.

282. Match the following: (*NET Exam.* 2012J)
List I
(A) Textual representation
(B) Computer language
(C) Network tool
(D) Searching technique

List II

(i) Pascal (ii) Gopher
(iii) Boolean operators (iv) ASCI

Codes:	A	B	C	D
(a)	(iv)	(i)	(ii)	(iii)
(b)	(i)	(iv)	(iii)	(ii)
(c)	(iii)	(ii)	(iv)	(i)
(d)	(ii)	(iv)	(iii)	(i)

283. "Internet Public Library" is being maintained by (*NET Exam.* 2012J)
(a) MIT, Massachusetts
(b) University of Michigan
(c) University of Arizona
(d) Drexel University

284. **Assertion (A):** Netiquette mandates that you do your best to act within the laws of cyberspace and society. (*NET Exam.* 2012J)
Reason (R): Failing to respect other people's privacy is bad Netiquette.
Codes:
(a) Both (A) and (R) are false
(b) Both (A) and (R) are true.
(c) (A) is true, but (R) is false.
(d) (A) is false, but (R) is true.

285. Match the following: (*NET Exam.* 2012J)
List I
(A) DRUPAL (B) Moodle
(C) D space (D) New Gen Lib
List II
(i) Integrated Library Management Software
(ii) Digital Library Software
(iii) Content Management Software
(iv) Learning Management Software

Codes:	A	B	C	D
(a)	(iv)	(iii)	(ii)	(i)
(b)	(ii)	(i)	(iv)	(iii)
(c)	(iii)	(iv)	(ii)	(i)
(d)	(i)	(ii)	(iii)	(iv)

286. Match the following: (*NET Exam.* 2012J)

List I	List II
(A) HTML File	(i) Text Format
(B) PDF File	(ii) Film Format
(C) JPG File	(iii) Web Format
(D) AVI File	(iv) Image Format

Codes:	A	B	C	D
(a)	(i)	(ii)	(iv)	(iii)
(b)	(iii)	(i)	(iv)	(ii)
(c)	(i)	(iv)	(ii)	(iii)
(d)	(iv)	(iii)	(i)	(ii)

287. Match the following: (*NET Exam.* 2012J)

List I	List II
(A) Face Book	(i) Video Networking site
(B) Research Gate	(ii) Social Networking site
(C) Oovoo	(iii) Academic Networking site
(D) Flicker	(iv) Photo Networking site

Codes:	A	B	C	D
(a)	(i)	(iii)	(ii)	(iv)
(b)	(iv)	(i)	(ii)	(iii)
(c)	(ii)	(iii)	(i)	(iv)
(d)	(iii)	(iv)	(i)	(ii)

288. Which set of rules is applicable for exchange of files over Internet? (*NET Exam.* 2013J)
(a) FTP/IP (b) HTTP
(c) HTML (d) HYPERLINK

289. Name of the storage medium (compatible with speed of CPU) for storing instructions or data temporarily during processing. (*NET Exam.* 2013J)
(a) RAM (b) ROM
(c) Cache (d) EPROM

290. The information network that connects Universities and Colleges in United Kingdom (*NET Exam.* 2012J)
(a) JANET (b) SERCNET
(c) OCLC (d) BONET

291. Internet filtering is (*NET Exam.* 2012J)
(a) A form of censorship
(b) Acceptable user policy
(c) Access to inappropriate material
(d) Blocking internet facility

292. "Students' visit to Library is influenced by the availability of Internet". State "Students' visit to library" is which kind of variable? (*NET Exam.* 2012J)
(a) Independent Variable
(b) Intervening Variable
(c) Dependent Variable
(d) Intercept Variable

293. **Assertion (A):** Open Systems Interconnection allows connectivity of ICT components.
Reason (R): Network Printer goes slow if it is OSI compatible. (*NET Exam.* 2012J)
Codes:
(a) Both (A) and (R) are true.
(b) Both (A) and (R) are false.
(c) (A) is false, but (R) is true.
(d) (A) is true, but (R) is false.

294. Which one of the following protocol is used in file transfer over internet? (*NET Exam.* 2012J)
(a) FTP (b) SMTP (c) POP (d) TCP/IP

Read the passage given below, and answer the questions based on your understanding of the passage. (Q. No. 295-299)

With the realization across the world that the global economy is going to be increasingly knowledge-based, science and technology have become the subject of discussion not just in classical ministries but also in ministries as diverse as commerce, industry and finance, and in case of United States, even in the State Department. In India, the Prime Minister has made frequent statements about the need to step up scientific research in the country.

Several large companies, including multinationals are outsourcing R&D programmes to India. This is partly because scientists are cheaper in India dollar for dollar, but also because India has a large pool of trained scientists. Industry data shows that R&D is now the third largest segment in India's export of Information Technology (IT) services. Foreign companies have invested over $1 billion in research operations in India from 1998 to 2003 and another estimated $5 billion are in the pipeline. The United States is the biggest investor followed by Germany, France, Denmark and UK. Japan and China have also begun to invest in research programmes in India. Most foreign investment is being directed to research in computer sciences, pharmaceuticals, molecular chemistry, drug discovery, engineering and automotive design and biotechnology, including plant breeding.

Whereas, flow of foreign investments has enthused research institutions that are targeted for collaboration, there is also cause for concern. Although, India now attracts considerable foreign investment in R&D, it has no system in place for assessing how this investment is affecting the country's technological development. Nor is there any mechanism to monitor the impact of such investment on aspects such as skill development, sectoral capacity building, etc. Do such foreign-funded research programmes benefit only the scientists and technicians in the form of better salaries and perks or do they also produce benefits for the country as a whole?

295. Focus on science and technology has increased because (*NET Exam.* 2012D)
(a) Indian commerce and Finance Ministries are giving great importance to it.
(b) World economy has become knowledge based.
(c) US State Department gives priority on S&T.
(d) Knowledge Commission has identified it as one of the potential area of development.

296. The following group of countries are the biggest investors in research? (*NET Exam.* 2012D)
(a) U.S., Germany, India, Russia
(b) Britain, France, U.S., India
(c) France, Denmark, U.S.A., U.K.
(d) Japan, China, India, Denmark

297. What is the cause of concern regarding foreign investment in research? (*NET Exam.* 2012D)
(a) Scientists and technicians involved in research are not paid well.
(b) There are insufficient institutions that can be targeted for research collaboration.
(c) The benefit of such investments doesn't get transferred to India.
(d) Sufficient methods to assess and evaluate the impact of such investment are not available.

298. Most foreign investment is being made in the area of (*NET Exam.* 2012D)
(a) Microbiology and life science
(b) Computer science and automotive design
(c) Physical science and planting
(d) Grafting and biology

299. Foreign companies are outsourcing R&D programmes to India because (*NET Exam.* 2012D)
(a) Quality of research is quite high in India
(b) Out sourcing is cost effective for foreign companies
(c) There is scarcity of skilled manpower in those countries
(d) None of the above

300. Match the following: (*NET Exam.* 2012D)

	List I		List II
(A)	ISDN	(i)	Web page
(B)	URL	(ii)	Video Conferencing

(C) Firewall	(iii) Internet Standard for Information Transmission			
(D) HTTP	(iv) Protecting unauthorized access Internet			
Codes:	**A**	**B**	**C**	**D**
(a)	(iii)	(iv)	(i)	(ii)
(b)	(iv)	(i)	(iii)	(ii)
(c)	(ii)	(i)	(iv)	(iii)
(d)	(i)	(iii)	(ii)	(iv)

301. The large volumes of high velocity, complex and variable data are termed as (*NET* 2017J *ii paper*)
(a) Big data (b) Linked data
(c) Semantic data (d) Ontology-based data

302. Identify the mode of formation of the subject 'Agriculture of Corn': (*NET* 2017J *ii paper*)
(a) Agglomeration (b) Denudation
(c) Fusion (d) Lamination

303. Sony unveiled the first Blu-ray Disc (BD) prototypes in (*NET* 2017J *ii paper*)
(a) September 1982 (b) August 1985
(c) October 2000 (d) November 2005

304. Who differentiated information and knowledge in the following way?
"Information is piecemeal, fragmented, particular; whereas knowledge is structural, coherent and universal." (*NET* 2017J *ii paper*)
(a) B.C. Brooks and N.J. Belkin
(b) S.G. Faibisoff and D.P. Ely
(c) F. Machlup and U. Mansfield
(d) J.H. Shera

305. Identify from the following the Silver Halide process used in reprography: (*NET* 2017J *ii paper*)
(i) Exposure (ii) Miniature
(iii) Developing (iv) Rinsing
Codes:
(a) (i), (ii) and (iv) are correct.
(b) (ii), (iii) and (iv) are correct.
(c) (i), (iii) and (iv) are correct.
(d) (iv), (ii) and (iii) are correct.

306. Identify the type of 'metadata' held by D space for archiving contents: (*NET* 2017J *ii paper*)
(i) Descriptive (ii) Configured
(iii) Structural (iv) Administrative
Codes:
(a) (i), (ii), (iii) are correct.
(b) (ii), (iii), (iv) are correct.
(c) (i), (ii), (iv) are correct.
(d) (i), (iii), (iv) are correct.

307. A Blog usually provides (*NET* 2017J *ii paper*)
(i) a commentary on a particular subject.
(ii) a personal online diary.
(iii) an online brand advertising of a particular individual or company.
(iv) an exclusive pre-paid publishing tool and non-instructional and non-illustrative resource for the scribes.
Codes:
(a) (i), (iii) and (iv) are correct.
(b) (ii), (iii) and (iv) are correct.
(c) (i), (ii) and (iii) are correct.
(d) (i), (ii) and (iv) are correct.

308. Which of the following are pillars of information literacy according to SCONUL seven pillars of information literacy? (*NET* 2017J *ii paper*)
(i) Find (ii) Gather
(iii) Identify (iv) Manage
Codes:
(a) (i), (ii) and (iii) are correct.
(b) (ii), (iii) and (iv) are correct.
(c) (i), (iii) and (iv) are correct.
(d) (i), (ii) and (iv) are correct

309. Identify from the following, the digital library projects were implemented by C-DAC (Agency) Noida: (*NET* 2017J *ii paper*)
(i) Creation of Vidwan database
(ii) Print your own book – Mobile Digital Library
(iii) Creation of Shodhsindhu
(iv) Creation of Digital Library of Books in President House
Codes:
(a) (i) and (ii) are correct.
(b) (ii) and (iii) are correct.
(c) (iii) and (iv) are correct.
(d) (ii) and (iv) are correct.

310. Match the following States with their corresponding E-Government initiatives: (*NET* 2017J *ii paper*)

List – I	**List – II**
A. Kerala	1. Akshaya
B. M.P. (Dhar)	2. BanglarMukh

C. Maharashtra 3. Gyandoot
D. West Bengal 4. Information Junction

Codes:	A	B	C	D
(a)	1	3	4	2
(b)	2	1	3	4
(c)	4	3	2	1
(d)	3	2	4	1

311. **Assertion (A):** There is a connection between the concept of uncertainty and relevance in IR.

Reason (R): In IR both uncertainty and relevance are totally ruled out as part of query document matching.

(*NET* 2017J *ii paper*)

Codes:

(a) (A) is true, but (R) is false.
(b) (A) is false, but (R) is true.
(c) Both (A) and (R) are true.
(d) Both (A) and (R) are false.

312. **Assertion (A):** The efforts of contemporary libraries in using static A-Z lists (as a part of their ERM system) to facilitate access for users who wanted to limit their searches to e-content has failed to yield results.

Reason (R): Such lists maintained locally are, by necessity, more detailed and elaborate, as increase of titles made the maintenance of such lists more labour intensive and complicated. (*NET* 2017J *ii paper*)

Codes:

(a) (A) is true, but (R) is false.
(b) (A) is false, but (R) is true.
(c) Both (A) and (R) are true.
(d) Both (A) and (R) are false.

313. **Assertion (A):** A collaborative culture is an important condition for knowledge transfer between individuals.

Reason (R): Knowledge transfer do not require individuals to come together to interact, exchange, and share ideas and knowledge with one another.

(*NET* 2017J *ii paper*)

Codes:

(a) (A) is true, but (R) is false.
(b) (A) is false, but (R) is true.
(c) Both (A) and (R) are true.
(d) Both (A) and (R) are false.

314. **Assertion (A):** Right to Information Act in India mandates timely response to citizen requests for information sought.

Reason (R): The basic object of the Right to Information Act is to empower the citizens, promote transparency and accountability.

(*NET* 2017J *ii paper*)

Codes:

(a) (A) is true, but (R) is false
(b) (A) is false, but (R) is true
(c) Both (A) and (R) are true
(d) Both (A) and (R) are false

Read the passage given below and answer the questions based on your understanding of the passage. (Question Nos. 315-319)

(*NET 17J ii paper*)

The idea and phrase "serious leisure' comes from Stebbins' interviewees, who used the word "serious" to underline the extent of their passion for a favourite leisure activity. In this case, the term embodies positive qualities such as importance and sincerity, rather than negative traits such as gravity or anxiety. Whereas casual leisure supplies pleasure, and project-base leisure delivers a temporary reward, serious leisure generates deep and enduring sensations of fulfilment. There are six defining characteristics to all serious leisure. First, there is the occasional need to persevere, as when mountain climbers push through exhaustion to reach a peak. Second, is that of finding a leisure career in the activity, with turning points and a sense of advancement. Third, serious leisure takes significant personal effort based on specially acquired knowledge, training, experience, or skill. In this quality, serious leisure is the opposite of its casual counterpart, which requires no expertise. Fourth, there are eight durable benefits or outcomes to serious leisure: self-actualization, self-enrichment, self-expression, regeneration or renewal of self, feelings of accomplishment, enhancement of self-image, social interaction and belongingness, and lasting physical products of the activity. Fifth, serious leisure participants tend to identify strongly with their chosen pursuits, and may be quick to assert their affiliation. Sixth, a unique ethos, or spirit of the community, exists around each serious leisure activity. There are three main types of serious leisure: amateurism, volunteering, and hobbies. Amateurs operate in the fields of art, science, sport, and entertainment.

315. One of the six defining characteristics of serious leisure is (*NET* 2017J *ii paper*)
(a) amateurism (b) requires no expertise
(c) pleasure (d) spirit of the community

316. One of the three main types of serious leisure is (*NET* 2017J *ii paper*)
(a) hobbies (b) sport
(c) entertainment (d) art

317. Which is not one of the eight durable benefits of serious leisure? (*NET* 2017J *ii paper*)
(a) Self-expression (b) Renewal of self
(c) Social interaction (d) Unique ethos

318. The word 'serious' is the phrase 'serious leisure' expresses the idea of (*NET* 2017J *ii paper*)
(a) gravity (b) anxiety
(c) sincerity (d) pleasure sensations

319. A temporary reward comes from (*NET* 2017J *ii paper*)
(a) casual leisure
(b) project-based leisure
(c) serious leisure
(d) enduring sensations of fulfilment

320. Identify the author of *Essays of an Information Scientist* from among the following (*NET* 2017 *NOV iii paper*)
(a) F.W. Lancaster
(b) Derek J. de Solla Price
(c) Eugene Garfield
(d) B.C. Vickery

321. Who has coined the term 'Information Society' from the following? (*NET* 2017 *NOV iii paper*)
(a) B.C. Brookes (b) Fritz Machlup
(c) B.C. Vickery (d) N.J. Belkin

322. Dance's Helical Spiral communication model is a (*NET* 2017 *NOV iii paper*)
(a) Classical (b) Linear
(c) Non-Linear (d) Multi-dimensional

323. What was the theme of IFLA World Library and Information Congress 2017? (*NET* 2017 *NOV iii paper*)
(a) Connections. Collaboration. Community
(b) Dynamic Libraries: Access, Development and Transformation
(c) Libraries, Citizens, Societies: Confluence for knowledge
(d) Libraries. Solidarity. Society

324. Which of the following organisations have introduced "Dig by"—a new mobile application available as a part of 'World Share Management Service'? (*NET 17 NOV iii paper*)
(a) Library of Congress (b) NISCAIR
(c) OCLC (d) UTLAS

325. Percentage (%) sign is used in an URL to represent: (*NET 17 NOV iii paper*)
(a) Space (b) Date (c) Time (d) Person

326. FRBRoo version 2 is based on: (*NET 17 NOV iii paper*)
(a) FRBR model alone
(b) FRAD model alone
(c) FRBR and FRAD models only
(d) FRBR, FRAD and FRSAD models

327. Which one of the following is not Image format? (*NET 17 NOV iii paper*)
(a) TIFF (b) MPEG (c) JPEG (d) GIF

328. 'Half-life' in the context of literary growth is used to indicate: (*NET 17 NOV iii paper*)
(a) Rate of obsolescence
(b) Rate of growth
(c) Degree of scatter
(d) Information explosion

329. Which of the following are the necessary elements of an information society? (*NET 17 NOV iii paper*)
(i) Confidentiality (ii) Vulnerability
(iii) Integrity (iv) Availability
Codes:
(a) (ii), (iii) and (iv) are correct
(b) (i), (ii) and (iii) are correct
(c) (i), (ii) and (iv) are correct
(d) (i), (iii) and (iv) are correct

330. SWAYAM, the free online education was developed by: (*NET 17 NOV iii paper*)
(i) IIT, Madras (ii) AICTE
(iii) IIM, Ahmedabad (iv) MHRD, Govt. of India
Codes:
(a) (ii) and (iv) are correct
(b) (iii) and (iv) are correct
(c) (i) and (ii) are correct
(d) (i) and (iv) are correct

331. Which of the following roles does a library have in the information transfer cycle? *(NET 2017 NOV iii paper)*
(i) Information organization and control
(ii) Primary distribution
(iii) Secondary Publication
(iv) Secondary distribution
Codes:
(a) (ii) and (iv) are correct
(b) (ii) and (iii) are correct
(c) (i) and (iv) are correct
(d) (i) and (ii) are correct

332. 'Entropy' in the context of 'Information Science' is: *(NET 17 NOV iii paper)*
(i) Measure which cannot be normalised by dividing it by information length.
(ii) Measure of unpredictability of the state or equivalently, of its average information content.
(iii) Average amount of information produced by a probabilistic stochastic source of data.
(iv) Way to measure diversity.
Codes:
(a) (i), (ii) and (iv) are correct
(b) (i), (ii) and (iii) are correct
(c) (i), (iii) and (iv) are correct
(d) (ii), (iii) and (iv) are correct

333. Which of the following are Research Information Management System? *(NET 17 NOV iii paper)*
(i) Pure (ii) Quetext
(iii) Converis (iv) VIVO
Codes:
(a) (i), (ii) and (iv) are correct
(b) (i), (ii) and (iii) are correct
(c) (i), (iii) and (iv) are correct
(d) (ii), (iii) and (iv) are correct

334. Jubilee (JISC User Behaviour in Information Seeking: Longitudinal Evaluation of Electronic Information Services) seeks to: *(NET 17 NOV iii paper)*
(i) Predict, monitor and characterise ISB in relation to EIS (Electronic Information Services).
(ii) Provide illuminative and contextual pictures built up overtime to users and non-users.
(iii) Evaluate materials of rarity in nature.
(iv) Adjudge the quality of hard copies of e-reference tools served to readers in a given library over a period of time.
Codes:
(a) (iii) and (iv) are correct
(b) (i) and (ii) are correct
(c) (ii) and (iii) are correct
(d) (i) and (iv) are correct

335. Arrange the steps of the 8W'S Literacy Model in correct order as given by Annette Lamb: *(NET 17 NOV iii paper)*
(i) Webbing (ii) Wishing
(iii) Wondering (iv) Weaving
Codes:
(a) (iii), (i), (ii) and (iv)
(b) (ii), (i), (iii) and (iv)
(c) (iii), (i), (iv) and (ii)
(d) (iii), (ii), (i) and (iv)

336. Match the following sources with their corresponding functions: *(NET 17 NOV iii paper)*
List – I
(A) Counter (B) Affinity string
(C) Link resolver (D) Journal of citation report
List - II
(1) Tracking e-resources usage statistics
(2) Tracking online usage by user categories
(3) Impact factor
(4) Number of times users' connectivity to a resource

Codes:	(A)	(B)	(C)	(D)
(a)	3	4	1	2
(b)	2	4	3	1
(c)	1	3	4	2
(d)	4	2	1	3

337. Match the following threats to 'information society' with the corresponding concept. *(NET 17 NOV iii paper)*
List – I
(A) Compromises intellectual Property
(B) Deliberate acts of theft
(C) Deliberate acts of information extortion
(D) Deliberate acts of espionage or trespass
List – II
(1) Confiscation of equipment or information
(2) Unauthorized access to data
(3) Piracy
(4) Blackmail of information disclosure.

Codes:	(A)	(B)	(C)	(D)
(a)	3	4	1	2
(b)	4	2	3	1
(c)	1	2	3	4
(d)	3	1	4	2

338. Match the following Online Survey Development Cloud based Software Applications/tools with their corresponding founders: *(NET 17 NOV iii paper)*

List – I

(A) Survey Monkey (B) Type Form
(C) Client Heartbeat (D) Survey Gizmo

List - II

(1) Christian Vanek and Scott McDaniel-(Colorado, USA)
(2) Gordon Tan-Brisbane (Austria)
(3) Robert Munoz and David Okuniev-Barcelona (Spain)
(4) Ryan Finley-Sanmateo, California (USA)

Codes:	**(A)**	**(B)**	**(C)**	**(D)**
(a)	1	2	3	4
(b)	4	3	2	1
(c)	2	4	1	3
(d)	3	1	4	2

339. **Assertion (A):** Librarians usually prefer to provide access to e-content for the users via a proxy server, allowing authorized library users to access content from outside the physical confines of a library.

Reason (R): Proxy-server access is possible without IP-address recognition. *(NET 17 NOV iii paper)*

Codes:
(a) Both (A) and (R) are true.
(b) Both (A) and (R) are false.
(c) (A) is true, but (R) is false.
(d) (A) is false, but (R) is true.

340. **Assertion (A):** 'Web Assembly', a standard that enables applications to run securely in browsers (without the use of Plug-ins) is a people-friendly application in using Web.

Reason (R): A web language transforms the way people use their devices and the web making applications are more accessible to people at ease all over the globe. *(NET 17 NOV iii paper)*

Codes:
(a) (A) is true, but (R) is false.
(b) Both (A) and (R) are true.
(c) (A) is false, but (R) is true.
(d) Both (A) and (R) are false.

341. **Assertion (A):** Grounded Theory methods in Qualitative research start from same set of assumptions as traditional Quantitative research design.

Reason (R): The inductive nature of these Grounded Theory methods allows the key issues emerge rather than force them into pre conceived categories. *(NET 17J iii paper)*

Codes:
(a) (A) is true, but (R) is false.
(b) Both (A) and (R) are true.
(c) Both (A) and (R) are false.
(d) (A) is false, but (R) is true.

342. Which of the following Associations had suggested that, for every 3000 persons there should be one public library and India with 1.2 billion population requires 3,30,000 libraries? *(NET 2016J iii paper)*
(a) IASLIC (b) IFLA (c) ALA (d) ASLIB

343. Which of the following sections of the 'Right to Information Act', 2005 (India) grants exemption from disclosure of information? *(NET 2016J iii paper)*
(a) Section – 5 (b) Section – 6
(c) Section – 8 (d) Section – 11

344. The '12 Rules for Relational Database' were given by *(NET 16J iii paper)*
(a) Edgar F. Codd (b) Larvy Page
(c) J. Bill Gates (d) Linus Tolward

345. LOCKOSS (software), an international community initiative by *(NET 2016 iii paper)*
(a) MIT Library
(b) Stanford University
(c) University of Waikato
(d) University of Southampton

346. Identify the principal findings of Vilfredo Pareto study on application of 'Pareto Chart' in social research. *(NET 2016 iii paper)*
(i) Small percentage of population accounted for a large proportion of wealth.
(ii) 80% of results are due to 20% causes and 80% of the profit of an organisation came from 20% of its products.
(iii) Large percentage of population accounted for a small proportion of wealth.
(iv) 20% of causes are responsible for 80% of quality problems.

Codes:
(a) i, ii and iv are correct.
(b) i, ii and iii are correct.

(c) ii, iii and iv are correct.
(d) i, iii and iv are correct

347. Identify the key features of Emptying Digit from the following: (*NET 16J iii paper*)
i. Helps in interpolation between two consecutive ordinal numbers.
ii. Deprives the preceding digit of its semantic value in a digit group.
iii. Deprives the preceding digit of its semantic value in a digit group but does not retain the ordinal value allotted to it.
iv. When it occurs as an initial digit, then it deems semantically poor digit.
Codes:
(a) i and iii are correct.
(b) i and ii are correct.
(c) i and iv are correct.
(d) ii and iv are correct.

348. Identify the websites for best practices: as viewed by June L. Power: (*NET 16J iii paper*)
i. Library Success
ii. Second Life Library 2.0
iii. LISNews.org
iv. Bloomington Delivery Service
Codes:
(a) i, ii, iv are correct. (b) i, ii, iii are correct.
(c) ii, iii, iv are correct. (d) i, ii, iv are correct.

349. Identify the principles for the implementation of the canon of helpful sequence: (*NET 16J iii paper*)
i. Principle of spatial contiguity
ii. Principle of increasing literary warrant
iii. Principle of modulation
iv. Principle of enumeration
Codes:
(a) i and ii are correct.
(b) i and iii are correct.
(c) ii and iv are correct.
(d) i and iv are correct.

350. A sound marketing plan contains (*NET 16J iii paper*)
i. an analysis of macro-environment
ii. a SWOT analysis
iii. a brief statement of mission
iv. an analysis of advertising
Codes:
(a) i, ii and iii are correct.
(b) i, iii and iv are correct.
(c) ii, iii and iv are correct.
(d) i, ii and iv are correct.

351. LANs are distinguished from other types of Networks by the following characteristics: (*NET 16J iii paper*)
i. Full time connectivity to local service.
ii. Unlimited geographic operation.
iii. Data transfer rate.
iv. Low cost and cabling transmission media.
Codes:
(a) ii, iii, iv are correct.
(b) i, ii, iii are correct.
(c) i, iii, iv are correct.
(d) i, ii, iv are correct.

352. Which of the following are the different layers of UNIX operating system? (*NET 16J iii paper*)
i. Kernel ii. Shell
iii. Format iv. Application
Codes:
(a) i, ii and iv are correct.
(b) ii, iii and iv are correct.
(c) i, iii and iv are correct.
(d) i, ii and iii are correct.

353. Identify the web 3.0 features from the following: (*NET 16J iii paper*)
i. Blogs ii. Folksonomy
iii. Semantic web iv. Net vibes
Codes:
(a) i and ii are correct. (b) iii & iv are correct.
(c) ii & iv are correct. (d) i & iv are correct.

354. Identify the characteristics of Library 1.0: (*NET 16J iii paper*)
i. User tagging
ii. Read only catalogue
iii. Print newsletter mailed out
iv. Information as conversation
Codes:
(a) i and iii are correct.
(b) ii and iv are correct.
(c) ii and iii are correct.
(d) iii and iv are correct.

355. Arrange the following events according to their year of occurrence: (*NET 16J iii paper*)
i. Establishment of Documentation Research and Training Centre
ii. First meeting of Classification Research Group, London

iii. Publication of Broad System of Ordering (BSO)
iv. Formation of FID/CA

Codes:

(a) i, ii, iv, iii (b) iv, ii, iii, i
(c) iv, ii, i, iii (d) iv, iii, i, ii

356. Arrange the following bibliographies according to their first publication: *(NET 16J iii paper)*

i. Indian National Bibliography
ii. British Books in Print (Whitaker)
iii. British National Bibliography
iv. Books in print (Bowker)

Codes:

(a) ii, iv, iii and i (b) ii, iv, i and iii
(c) iv, ii, iii and i (d) iv, iii, i and ii

357. Arrange the following according to their year of establishment: *(NET 16J iii paper)*

i. DESINET ii. JANET
iii. RLIN iv. INDONET

Codes:

(a) ii, iii, iv and i (b) i, iv, iii and ii
(c) iii, ii, i and iv (d) iv, iii, ii and i

358. Arrange the following information encountering (IE) steps that occur during an IE experience as developed by SandaErdelez: *(NET 16J iii paper)*

i. Examining ii. Returning
iii. Slopping iv. Capturing

Codes:

(a) iii, ii, iv and i (b) iii, i, iv and ii
(c) i, iv, iii and ii (d) ii, iii, iv and i

359. Match the following: *(NET 16J iii paper)*

List – I (Extension)	List – II (File Content in dBase)
A. .DBF	1. Database Memo file
B. .DBK	2. Database file
C. .DBO	3. Database backup file
D. .DBT	4. Command and procedure object file

Codes:	A	B	C	D
(a)	2	4	1	3
(b)	2	3	4	1
(c)	4	2	1	3
(d)	1	3	4	2

360. Match the following: *(NET 16J iii paper)*

List – I	List – II
A. IFLA	1. Dublin
B. OCLC	2. Toronto
C. RLIN	3. Palo Alto
D. UTL 0AS	4. The Hague

Codes:	A	B	C	D
(a)	4	1	3	2
(b)	1	2	3	4
(c)	2	1	4	3
(d)	3	4	2	1

361. Match the following: *(NET 16J iii paper)*

List – I	List – II
A. Histogram	1. Signs and symbols
B. Bar Charts	2. Data in Circle
C. Pie Chart	3. Length of the bar
D. Pictogram	4. Frequency distribution

Codes:	A	B	C	D
(a)	4	3	2	1
(b)	3	4	2	1
(c)	1	3	2	4
(d)	2	1	3	4

362. Match the following: *(NET 16J iii paper)*

List – I	List – II
A. Facebook	1. Video Networking site
B. Research Gate	2. Social Networking site
C. Oovoo	3. Academic Networking site
D. Flickr	4. Photo Networking site

Codes:	A	B	C	D
(a)	1	3	2	4
(b)	4	1	2	3
(c)	2	3	1	4
(d)	3	4	1	2

363. Match the following: *(NET 16J iii paper)*

List – I

A. Ezproxy B. Greek the Library
C. Outside the box D. Web junction

List – II

1. A community awareness programme
2. Access and authentication software
3. Online learning place for libraries
4. Library focussed community entertainment initiative

Codes:	A	B	C	D
(a)	2	1	4	3
(b)	2	1	3	4
(c)	4	3	2	1
(d)	3	1	4	2

364. Match the following: *(NET 16J iii paper)*

List – I	List – II
A. Bhuvan 3D	1. Operating System
B. Ubuntu	2. ERMS

C. Urkund 3. Geoportal
D. CORAL 4. Anti-plagiarism software

Codes:	A	B	C	D
(a)	1	4	3	2
(b)	4	2	1	3
(c)	3	1	4	2
(d)	3	4	2	1

365. Match the following: *(NET 16J iii paper)*

List – I (Examples)

A. Relation between Political Science with history
B. Geopolitics
C. Medical Jurisprudence
D. Chemical relation between silver and gold

List – II (Type of Relation)

1. Influencing 2. Intra-array general relation
3. Bias 4. General

Codes:	A	B	C	D
(a)	2	3	4	1
(b)	1	4	2	3
(c)	4	1	3	2
(d)	4	1	2	3

366. Match the following: *(NET 16J iii paper)*

List – I

A. Super-imposition Device
B. Subject Device
C. Systems & Specials
D. Mnemonic Device

List – II

1. Treatment of eye disease in children
2. Use of '1' for Unity, God, World
3. Agricultural countries
4. British – India

Codes:	A	B	C	D
(a)	4	3	1	2
(b)	4	3	2	1
(c)	2	3	1	4
(d)	1	4	2	3

367. **Assertion (A):** In recent time, it is easier to copy and paste the contents from a digital document for which people knowingly avoid to credit the source. Hence, increased access to digital documents has provided a means for increase of plagiarism.

Reason (R): Software-assisted detection tools like iThenticate, Turnitin, etc. now allow vast collections of online documents to be compared to each other making successful detection of plagiarism. *(NET 16J iii paper)*

Codes:
(a) Both (A) and (R) are false.
(b) (A) is true, but (R) is false.
(c) (R) is true, but (A) is false.
(d) Both (A) and (R) are true.

368. **Assertion (A):** Precision is the fraction of the documents retrieved that are relevant to the user's information need.

Reason (R): In practical situations, recall and precision are always inversely related. *(NET 16J iii paper)*

Codes:
(a) (A) is false, but (R) is true.
(b) (A) is true, but (R) is false.
(c) Both (A) and (R) are true.
(d) Both (A) and (R) are false.

369. **Assertion (A):** Google search is considered as the biggest threat to contemporary libraries.

Reason (R): Now-a-days, users taking help from Reference Librarian for factual queries has considerably decreased. *(NET 16J iii paper)*

Codes:
(a) Both (A) and (R) are true.
(b) Both (A) and (R) are false.
(c) (A) is true, but (R) is false.
(d) (A) is false, but (R) is true.

370. **Assertion (A):** There are no problems in a retrieval system in which indexers use natural language terms to describe subject matter. *(NET 16J iii paper)*

Reason (R): The complete text of a document may be stored in a machine readable form.

Codes:
(a) Both (A) and (R) are true.
(b) Both (A) and (R) are false.
(c) (A) is true, but (R) is false.
(d) (A) is false, but (R) is true.

371. **Assertion (A):** There is no distinction between needs and demands for information services.

Reason (R): In many situations, the non-active users of a given information service may greatly outnumber the active users. *(NET 16J iii paper)*

Codes:
(a) Both (A) and (R) are true.
(b) Both (A) and (R) are false.

(c) (A) is true, but (R) is false.
(d) (A) is false, but (R) is true.

372. DELNET was initially supported by: *(NET 17 NOV ii paper)*
(a) RRRLF (b) NISSAT
(c) NIC (d) INSDOC

373. Positive Correlation occurs when: *(NET 17 NOV ii paper)*
(a) Two variables move in opposite direction
(b) Both variables move in a zigzag way
(c) Two variables move in the same direction
(d) Both variables are constant

374. Who proposed Big Six Information Literacy Skills? *(NET 17 NOV ii paper)*
(a) C.D. Ferguson
(b) G. Dunsire
(c) E.A. Fox
(d) M.B. Eisenberg and R.E. Berkowitz

375. The protection of non-personal data in Transborder Data Flow uses which of the following legal instruments? *(NET 17 NOV ii paper)*
(i) Copyright (ii) Patent
(iii) Bandwidth (iv) Trademark
Codes:
(a) (i), (ii) and (iii) are correct
(b) (ii), (iii) and (iv) are correct
(c) (i), (iii) and (iv) are correct
(d) (i), (ii) and (iv) are correct

376. Which of the following are non-parametric tests? *(NET NOV 17 ii paper)*
(i) Anova test (ii) Spearman correlation coefficient
(iii) Z test (iv) Chi-Square test
Codes:
(a) (ii) and (iv) are correct
(b) (ii) and (iii) are correct
(c) (i), (ii) and (iv) are correct
(d) (i), (ii) and (iii) are correct

377. Transborder Data Flow includes (in the definition given by United Nations) movements across national boundaries: *(NET 17 NOV ii paper)*
(i) Machine-readable data for processing, storage or retrieval
(ii) Media products (mass diffusion)
(iii) Machine - readable data or magnetic tapes
(iv) Machine - readable data on discs
Codes:
(a) (i), (ii) and (iii) are correct
(b) (ii), (iii) and (iv) are correct
(c) (i), (iii) and (iv) are correct
(d) (i), (ii) and (iv) are correct

378. Arrange the following steps of digital preservation in their sequential order: *(NET 17 NOV ii paper)*
(i) Refreshing (ii) Encapsulation
(iii) Emulation (iv) Data archiving
Codes:
(a) (iii), (ii), (iv), (i) (b) (iv), (ii), (i), (iii)
(c) (i), (iv), (ii), (iii) (d) (i), (iii), (ii), (iv)

379. Arrange in sequence the following steps followed in Programming: *(NET 17 NOV ii paper)*
(i) Programme Code
(ii) Programme Documentation
(iii) Program Test
(iv) Programme Design
Codes:
(a) (i), (ii), (iii), (iv) (b) (iv), (i), (iii), (ii)
(c) (ii), (iii), (iv), (i) (d) (iv), (iii), (ii), (i)

380. Match the following devices with their mediums/system: *(NET 17 NOV ii paper)*

List - I	List – II
(A) Pen drive	(1) Web server device
(B) I-pad	(2) Communication device
(C) Wi-fi modem	(3) Tablet run on iOS mobile operating system
(D) Cloud computing	(4) Storage device

Codes:	(A)	(B)	(C)	(D)
(a)	(2)	(4)	(1)	(3)
(b)	(4)	(3)	(2)	(1)
(c)	(1)	(4)	(2)	(3)
(d)	(3)	(2)	(1)	(4)

381. Match the following Web tools with their corresponding features: *(NET 17 NOV ii paper)*

List – I	List - II
(A) Web 1.0	(1) People Centric and participative/bi-directional
(B) Web 2.0	(2) Linking and Integrating Global files
(C) Web 3.0	(3) Man-Machine Interaction with critical mass of participation and use of AI
(D) Web 4.0	(4) Static and mono-directional

Codes:	(A)	(B)	(C)	(D)
(a)	(4)	(1)	(2)	(3)
(b)	(1)	(2)	(3)	(4)
(c)	(4)	(3)	(2)	(1)
(d)	(3)	(1)	(4)	(2)

382. **Assertion (A):** Web 2.0 has wholly wiped out the digital divide, particularly with regard to individual ability, access to and engagement with technology.

Reason (R): Use of Web 2.0 in learning and teaching is still in an embryonic state.

(NET 17 NOV ii paper)

Codes:
(a) (A) is true, but (R) is false.
(b) (A) is false, but (R) is true.
(c) Both (A) and (R) are true.
(d) Both (A) and (R) are false.

383. **Assertion (A):** It is not economical to store and read video data from secondary storage devices.

Reason (R): Video data require enormous disk storage as image compression ratio is high. *(NET 17 NOV ii paper)*

Codes:
(a) (A) is true, but (R) is false.
(b) (A) is false, but (R) is true.
(c) Both (A) and (R) are true.
(d) Both (A) and (R) are false.

Read the passage given below and answer the questions based on your understanding of the passage. (Question Nos. 384-388).

(NET 17 NOV ii paper)

The medical community is not homogeneous. We have a wide range of kinds of work and, hence, we have a wide range of kinds of needs for information. Therefore, solutions for better access by investigators to information that they need might not help practicing physicians at all.

Science in medicine and the practice of medicine differ greatly. How they differ was described succinctly by Peter Mere Latham well over a century ago: "Medicine is a strange mixture of speculation and action. We have to cultivate a science and to exercise an art. The calls of science are upon our leisure and our choice; the calls of practice are of daily emergence and necessity". Latham's point is well made, but it is not quite detailed enough for our considerations here. Let me sketch out how the information needs of investigators and physicians differ.

(1) An investigator usually poses one question (or faces one problem) at a time and works on it for a long period. A physician constantly faces a quick succession of problems that call for rapid solutions.
(2) The investigator's problem is usually narrow and readily defined. The problems dealt with by the physician tend to be highly various and fogged by many uncertainties.
(3) An investigator's earnings are not tightly coupled to how he spends time from minute to minute and hour to hour. A physician's earnings are tightly coupled to every day's working hours and how they are spent.

These differences lead to differences in kinds of information needs and searches.

(1) The investigator tends to need an exhaustive search of information sources ("the literature") but at infrequent intervals. The time available for the search is relatively large and can be carried out at relatively low cost in "purchase" and in "time-cost".
(2) The physician needs quick access to valid information of immediate and high utility. The time available for a search is small. The "time-cost" for a search is high. The physician has to work mainly with thoroughly digested concepts and with most of the needed data carried in his head; the brain has a very rapid access time. Additional facts needed for clinical decisions must be accessed very rapidly. Both investigator and physician occasionally have needs like those of the other. The investigator may need quick access to a small and specific piece of technical information; the physician may be willing occasionally to embark on a broad search to deal with a rare problem. Further, both have ongoing needs for general awareness of new developments that may come eventually to have high utility. These differences seem to me to determine how investigators and physicians use or do not use various kinds of information materials and sources. Investigators tend to use reports of specific and individual research

efforts-journal articles. They tend to carry out searches themselves or to assign them to close professional associates. They have time to assess and to digest individual papers. Synoptic information, such as that in review articles, is used mainly for orientation to a new problem.

384. How do Peter Mere Latham differentiate calls of 'Science' (in Medicine) from that of the 'practice' (of medicine)?
(a) The calls of science are upon one's leisure and choice, where as the calls of practice are of daily emergence.
(b) 'Medicine' is a non exotic mixture of certainty, while practice of medicine is an infrequent phenomenon.
(c) Science is not a study of the natural world, where as practice is based on facts learned through a formal study.
(d) Science is not a method of reconciling practical ends with scientific laws, where as 'practice' do not allow repeated exercise to make one proficient.

385. How Lathams differentiates the information needs of Investigators from that of Physicians.
(a) An Investigator unconventionally faces with multiple problems at a single point of time and works on it for a long period, while a physician constantly faces slow-witted succession of problems that hardly warrant rapid solution.
(b) An investigator ordinarily faces one question/problem at a time which is usually narrow and rapidly defined, while a physician constantly faces a quick succession of varied problems fogged by many uncertainties.
(c) Earnings of an Investigator are strictly coupled to how he spends time from minute to minute, whereas a Physician's earnings are not tightly coupled to every day working hours.
(d) Information needs of Investigators are solely academic, where as the needs of Physicians are both academic and utilitarian.

386. Who tends to need quick access to valid Information of immediate and high quality?
(a) An Investigator (b) A Screwball
(c) A Physician (d) A Teacher

387. Why 'time cost' for a search made by a Physician is higher?
(a) Slow access to invalid Information.
(b) Access to information that are distant in need and of less utility.
(c) Exhaustive search of information sources.
(d) Rapid access to high quality information needed for clinical decision.

388. Why the Investigators tend to carry-out searches themselves?
(a) They have time to assess and digest individual papers.
(b) They are unaware of appropriate information sources.
(c) They have no access to information/ literature they need.
(d) They cannot afford time to search, identify, and digest the articles of high quality.

389. Which of the following organization declared 17th May as "World Information Society Day"? *(NET 16J ii paper)*
(a) IFLA
(b) World Summit on the Information Society (WSIS)
(c) World Health Organization (WHO)
(d) UNESCO

390. 'Transactional Model of Communication' was suggested by *(NET 16J ii paper)*
(a) Peter Drucker (b) George Zipf
(c) Dean Barnlund (d) A.C. Kessler

391. Information under section 2(f) of the 'Right to Information Act, 2005' means any material in any form, thus include *(NET 16J ii paper)*
i. Records, Documents, Memos, E-mails, Papers
ii. Opinions, Advices, Press Releases, Circulars, Samples
iii. Orders, Log books, Contracts, Reports
iv. Book Chapters, Journal Articles, Sale Deeds, Reprints, Snapshots of Consort

Codes:
(a) i, iii and iv are correct.
(b) ii, iii and iv are correct.
(c) i, ii and iv are correct.
(d) i, ii and iii are correct.

392. The objectives of Metadata are: *(NET 16J ii paper)*

i. Unique identification
ii. Authentication of records
iii. To eliminate the duplicate record.
iv. To arrange the collection.

Codes:
(a) i and iv are correct.
(b) i and ii are correct.
(c) ii and iv are correct.
(d) i and iii are correct.

393. Identify the following Institutional Archives/ Repositories available free: *(NET 16J ii paper)*
i. Project MUSE ii. Web of Science
iii. e-prints iv. Open DOAR

Codes:
(a) i and ii are correct.
(b) ii and iv are correct.
(c) iii and iv are correct.
(d) i and iii are correct.

394. Identify the Audio File Format for Digital libraries: *(NET 16J ii paper)*
i. .tif ii. .jfif iii. .aif iv. .ra

Codes:
(a) iii and iv are correct.
(b) ii and iv are correct.
(c) i and ii are correct.
(d) ii and iii are correct.

395. The available options for extending Wiki vary depending on the software that runs the site. Identify the correct options available to users using "Media Wiki". *(NET 16J ii paper)*
i. GISWikikWBreadCrumbs
ii. Bibwiki
iii. YouTube Tag and FireStats
iv. pbwikiGS

Codes:
(a) i, ii and iii are correct.
(b) ii, iii and iv are correct.
(c) i, iii and iv are correct.
(d) i, ii and iv are correct

396. Arrange the following Dublin core elements in descending order: *(NET 16J ii paper)*
i. Contributor ii. Identifier
iii. Relation iv. Right

Codes:

(a)	iv	iii	ii	i
(b)	i	iv	ii	iii
(c)	i	ii	iv	iii
(d)	i	ii	iii	iv

397. Match the following: *(NET16J ii paper)*

List – I	List – II
A. Pareto Chart	1. Pictorian representation of stages in a process
B. Fish Bone Diagram	2. Tool of recording variables
C. Flow chart	3. Identifies the intensity of each problem in the production line
D. Check-sheet	4. Identifies the relationship between the defects or problems and their root causes

Codes:	**A**	**B**	**C**	**D**
(a)	1	3	4	2
(b)	4	1	2	3
(c)	3	4	2	1
(d)	3	4	1	2

398. **Assertion (A):** Selection of e-resources requires utmost care and caution in order to make the same user-centric.

Reason (R): Availability of seamless online products in the market coupled with abundant internet resources at no cost made the e-resources redundant. *(NET 16J ii paper)*

Codes:
(a) (A), is false, but (R) is true.
(b) Both (A) and (R) false.
(c) (A) is true, but (R) is false.
(d) Both (A) and (R) true.

399. **Assertion (A):** Results from popular web search engines are usually having high recall, but an indexing database can provide high precision.

Reason (R): Indexing databases use controlled vocabulary which is a carefully selected list of words and phrases which are used to tag units of information (document or work) so that they may be more easily retrieved. *(NET 16J ii paper)*

Codes:
(a) Both (A) and (R) is true.
(b) (A) is true, but (R) is false.
(c) Both (A) and (R) are false.
(d) (R) is true, but (A) is false.

400. **Assertion (A):** Web 2.0 is a good set of economic, social and technological trend

that collectively form the basis of the next generation of the Internet.

Reason (R): More than just the latest technology buzzword, Web 2.0 is a transformative force that is propelling libraries towards a new way to offer services. *(NET 16J ii paper)*

Codes:
(a) (A) is true, but (R) is false.
(b) (A) is false, but (R) is true.
(c) Both (A) and (R) are true.
(d) Both (A) and (R) are false.

401. **Assertion (A):** Consortia subscriptions are not always beneficial to libraries as publishers bundle irrelevant titles to inflate the number of titles for better price during negotiations.

Reason (R): In bundled titles, libraries have not to pay for the titles which are not core to them. *(NET 16J ii paper)*

Codes:
(a) (A) is true, but (R) is false.
(b) (R) is true, but (A) is false.
(c) Both (A) and (R) are true.
(d) Both (A) and (R) are false.

Read the passage given below and answer the questions based on your understanding of the passage (Question Nos. 402-406): *(NET 16J ii paper)*

One of the major features of the World Wide Web is the capability to create links between pages. These links are often viewed as analogues of citations in scientific publications (e.g. ROUSSEAU, 1997; BJORNEBORN & INGWERSEN, 2001; CRONIN, 2001). Links can lead to a different site or may lead to a page in the same site. Links for which the source and the target of the page are within the same site or domain are called self-links. Instead of counting self-links, we count self-citations the number of pages on the site having a link or links pointing to the same site. The difference between self-links and self-citations is that for self-citations a page with several self-links is counted with multiplicity one. The reason for counting self-citations instead of self-links is technical: commercial search engines report the number of pages with self-links and not the number of self-links. The term-citations has been coined by ROUSSEAU (1997). In this paper we develop the measures self-linking and self-linked, which correspond to the classical measures for journals: self-citing and self-cited. We calculate these rates for a number of academic institutions on the Web. Self-links seems to be more problematic than citations (of authors in scientific publications), because self-links are often inserted for navigational purposes.

402. Self-links denote:
(a) Links between two websites.
(b) Links between two authors.
(c) Links between source and the target of the page within the same site or domain.
(d) Links between two articles written by two different authors.

403. Commercial search engines report
(a) the number of pages with self-links
(b) the number of self-links
(c) the number of sites
(d) the total number of total citations

404. Self-linking and self-linked measures calculate their rates for
(a) Number of academic institutions on the web
(b) Number of websites on the web
(c) Number of databases available on a given site
(d) Number of subject gateways on the web

405. Links in domain can lead to
i. different site on www
ii. page in the same site
iii. page in the different sites
iv. all available e-documents

Codes:
(a) i and iii are correct.
(b) i and ii are correct.
(c) ii and iv are correct.
(d) iii and iv are correct.

406. Reason for counting self-citations is
(a) Academic (b) Classificatory
(c) Technical (d) Non-technical

407. **Assertion (A):** While taking 'dumb' page image and producing 'smart' e-text that is added to collection of a digital library, Optical Character Recognition (OCR) does not need any manual intervention.

Reason (R): Optical Character Recognition (OCR) process is entirely automatic. *(NET 15J iii paper)*

Codes:
(a) (A) is true but (R) is false
(b) (A) is false but (R) is true
(c) Both (A) and (R) is true
(d) Both (A) and (R) are false

408. **Assertion (A):** RSS feeds automatically allow to view breaking news content from any number of web sites in single interface.

Reason (R): RSS feeds are not helpful to offer user alert services. *(NET 15J iii paper)*

Codes:
(a) Both (A) and (R) are false
(b) Both (A) and (R) are true
(c) (A) is false, but (R) is true
(d) (A) is true, but (R) is false

409. **Assertion (A):** Word of mouth is one of the promotion techniques which does not require any money to be spent if used for the promotion if LIS products and services.

Reason (R): Word of mouth technique is hardly used in libraries. *(NET 15J iii paper)*

Codes:
(a) Both (A) and (R) are true
(b) Both (A) and (R) are false
(c) (A) is true, but (R) is false
(d) (A) is false, but (R) is true

410. **Assertion (A):** Marketing segmentation helps libraries in achieving their goals and objectives as it is easy to decide which type of library service is needed by which type of user.

Reason (R): Libraries do not do segmentation of their users to apply marketing strategy in promoting LIS products and services. *(NET 15J iii paper)*

Codes:
(a) Both (A) and (R) is true
(b) Both (A) and (R) is false
(c) (A) is true but (R) is false
(d) (R) is true but (A) is false

411. **Assertion (A):** The h-index of a scientist is 10, if 10 of his/her papers have at least 10 citations each.

Reason (R): h-index is the only measure to assess a researcher's output. *(NET 15J iii paper)*

Codes:
(a) (A) is true, but (R) is false
(b) (A) is false but (R) is true
(c) Both (A) and (R) are true
(d) Both (A) and (R) are false

412. **Assertion (A):** One-way ANOVA is a technique used to compare means of three or more samples.

Reason (R): The two group case can be covered by a t-test. *(NET 15J iii paper)*

Codes:
(a) Both (A) and (R) are true
(b) (A) is true but (R) is false
(c) (A) is false but (R) is true
(d) Both (A) and (R) are false

413. **Assertion (A):** Structured Query Language (SQL) is a query language used for accessing and modifying information in a database.

Reason (R): SQL allows precise specification of the value for attributes of terms to be retrieved. *(NET 15J iii paper)*

Codes:
(a) (A) is false and (R) is true
(b) (A) is true and (R) is false
(c) Both (A) and (R) are true
(d) Both (A) and (R) are false

414. **Assertion (A):** LOCKSS is a peer to peer preservation system based on the existence of multiple low cost persistent caches of e-Journals, contents hosted at, different institutions licensed to "own" such content.

Reason (R): Participating institutions cooperate through Membership in the LOCKSSAlliance, which is a collaborative network based on the Commercial software model. *(NET 15J iii paper)*

Codes:
(a) (A) is true, but (R) is false
(b) (A) is false but (R) is true
(c) Both (A) and (R) are true
(d) Both (A) and (R) are false

415. **Assertion (A):** The central ideas guiding Qualitative research are same as those of Quantitative research. *(NET 15J iii paper)*

Reason (R): An essential feature of Qualitative research is the recognition and analysis of different perspectives.

Codes:

(a) Both (A) and (R) are true
(b) Both (A) and (R) are false
(c) (A) is true but (R) is false
(d) (A) is false but (R) is true

416. **Assertion (A):** FRAD defines its users some what more narrowly than FRBR.

Reason (R): Functional Requirement for Authority Data (FRAD) takes the same entitles found in FRBR and extends them to the authority context. *(NET 15J iii paper)*

Codes:

(a) Both (A) and (R) are true
(b) Both (A) and (R) are false
(c) (A) is true and (R) is false
(d) (A) is false and (R) is true

417. **Assertion (A):** The implication of the Recall Precision curve is that if we try to improve Recall, we can only do so at the expense of precision.

Reason (R): Recall precision curve represents the average performance of any given system. *(NET 15J iii paper)*

Codes:

(a) Both (A) and (R) are true.
(c) (A) is true but (R) is false.
(b) Both (A) and (R) are false.
(d) (A) is false but (R) is true.

418. **Assertion (A):** Pre Coordinate systems are basically one - place systems.

Reason (R): Pre Coordinate systems avoid the need for the citation or significance order. *(NET 15J iii paper)*

Codes:

(a) Both (A) and (R) are true
(b) Both (A) and (R) are false
(c) (A) is true but (R) is false
(d) (A) is false but (R) is true

419. **Assertion (A):** If the library is to be automated, system analysis is not needed.

Reason (R): System analysis identifies the flow of work. *(NET 15J iii paper)*

Codes:

(a) Both (A) and (R) are true
(b) (A) is false but (R) is true
(c) Both (A) and (R) are false
(d) (A) is true but (R) is false

420. Match the following: *(NET 15J iii paper)*

List - I	List - II
(A) Folksonomy	(1) Tim Wu
(B) Web log	(2) Thomas Vander Wal
(C) Net Neutrality	(3) Tim Berners Lee
(D) Semantic Web	(4) John Barger

Codes:	(A)	(B)	(C)	(D)
(a)	(1)	(3)	(4)	(2)
(b)	(3)	(2)	(4)	(1)
(c)	(2)	(4)	(1)	(3)
(d)	(4)	(1)	(3)	(2)

421. Match the following: *(NET 15J iii paper)*

List - I	List - II
(A) NATIS	(1) IFLA
(B) NIP/NITS	(2) Dept. of Culture, Govt. of India
(C) CONPOLIS, 1985	(3) UNESCO
(D) National Policy on Library and Information System (India) 1986	(4) Raja Ram Mohan Roy Library Foundation

Codes:	(A)	(B)	(C)	(D)
(a)	(1)	(2)	(3)	(4)
(b)	(2)	(3)	(4)	(1)
(c)	(3)	(1)	(2)	(4)
(d)	(4)	(3)	(2)	(1)

422. Match the following: *(NET 15J iii paper)*

List – I	List – II
(A) Elton Mayo	(1) Scientific School
(B) Henry Fayol	(2) Behavioural School
(C) Abraham Maslow	(3) Classical Style of Management
(D) F.W. Taylor	(4) Human Relations School

Codes:	(A)	(B)	(C)	(D)
(a)	(4)	(3)	(2)	(1)
(b)	(3)	(4)	(1)	(2)
(c)	(2)	(3)	(4)	(1)
(d)	(1)	(4)	(2)	(3)

423. Match the following: *(NET 15J iii paper)*

List – I	List – II
(A) Web page	(1) Navigation
(B) Web server	(2) Internet storage
(C) Web site	(3) HTML Doc.
(D) Web browser	(4) Collection of pages

Codes:	(A)	(B)	(C)	(D)
(a)	(3)	(2)	(4)	(1)
(b)	(3)	(4)	(2)	(1)

(c)	(1)	(3)	(4)	(2)
(d)	(1)	(4)	(2)	(3)

424. The protection of copyright in the care of films, photographs, anonymous, pseudonymous publications and works of governments, the 60 year period is counted from: (*NET 15J iii paper*)
(a) the date of birth of creator
(b) year following the death of creator
(c) the date of publication
(d) as per statement of author

425. International Standard Music Number (ISMN) for print music is promoted, coordinated and supervised by: (*NET 15J iii paper*)
(a) International Agency for ISMN, London
(b) International Standards Agency for Music, Sydney
(c) Standards Agency for Music International, Paris
(d) The International ISMN Agency, Berlin

426. In which year the WIPO Copyright Treaty was adopted? (*NET 15J iii paper*)
(a) 1995 (b) 1996 (c) 1997 (d) 1998

427. Which one of the following data bases has not originated from USA? (*NET 15J iii paper*)
(a) BIOSIS (b) MEDLARS
(c) Chemical Abstracts (d) INSPEC

428. The knowledge to which we have valid, conscious, introspective access under all circumstances is called: (*NET 15J iii paper*)
(a) Explicit knowledge
(b) Semi tacit knowledge
(c) Tacit knowledge
(d) Predictive knowledge

429. Identify the full form of the acronym FAIFE (IFLA). (*NET 15J iii paper*)
(a) Full-text Access to Information for Free Expression
(b) Full-text Access to Internet for Free E-resources
(c) Free Archives on Internet for Free Expression
(d) Freedom of Access to Information and Freedom of Expression

430. SYNTOL stands for: (*NET 15J iii paper*)
(a) Syntactic Term On Line
(b) Syntagmatic Term On Line
(c) Syntagmatic Organisation Language
(d) Syntactic Organising Language

431. In 'Open System Interconnect (OSI) Model' the layer between 'Network' and 'Physical' is: (*NET 15J iii paper*)
(a) Data link (b) Transport
(c) Application (d) Presentation

432. The term indicating a distinct intellectual or artistic creation is: (*NET 15J iii paper*)
(a) Item (b) Title (c) Expression (d) Work

433. Identify the statements which are true about E-Books in an online environment: (*NET 15J iii paper*)
(i) E-books are dependent on equipment to be used
(ii) E-books offer seamless access
(iii) All publishers produce the e-books equivalent of their print books
(iv) E-books allows highlighting of contents.
Codes:
(a) (i), (ii), (iii) are correct
(b) (ii), (iii), (iv) are correct
(c) (i), (iii), (iv) are correct
(d) (i), (ii), (iv) are correct

434. Descriptive technologies required to add meaning to the content of web documents include: (*NET 15J iii paper*)
(i) Resource Description Framework (RDF)
(ii) RFID
(iii) Extensible Markup Language (XML)
(iv) Barcode Technology
Codes:
(a) (ii) and (iii) are correct
(b) (i) and (iii) are correct
(c) (iii) and (iv) are correct
(d) (i) and (ii) are correct

435. Which of the following devices may be used for securing extrapolation in chain? (*NET 15J iii paper*)
(i) Decimal fraction device
(ii) Gap device
(iii) Inversion device
(iv) Isolate indicator device
Codes:
(a) (i) and (ii) are correct
(b) (ii) and (iii) are correct
(c) (iii) and (iv) are correct
(d) (i) and (iii) are correct

436. Which of the following are social book marking services? (*NET 15J iii paper*)

(i) Facebook (ii) Dropbox
(iii) Favorites (iv) Delicious

Codes:

(a) (i) and (ii) are correct
(b) (ii) and (iii) are correct
(c) (i) and (iii) are correct
(d) (ii) and (iv) are correct

437. Web-Junction is: *(NET 15J iii paper)*

(i) a place where Public Library Staff gather to build knowledge, skills and support that they need to power relevant vibrant Libraries;
(ii) on Online Learning Community launched by OLLC in 2003 for Library staff;
(iii) providing free training resources on Library Management technology and services;
(iv) an offline platform that provides hands-on training in web-based applications to LIS students only of USA.

Codes:

(a) (i), (ii) and (iii) are correct
(b) (ii), (iii) and (iv) are correct
(c) (i), (iii) and (iv) are correct
(d) (i), (ii) and (iv) are correct

438. RDA replaces the General Material Designations and the class of materials are to represented by: *(NET 15J iii paper)*

(i) Content type (ii) Carrier type
(iii) Media type (iv) Context type

Codes:

(a) (i), (ii) and (iii) are correct
(b) (ii), (iii) and (iv) are correct
(c) (i), (ii) and (iv) are correct
(d) (i), (iii) and (iv) are correct

439. Which of the following are features of Micro subjects? *(NET 15J iii paper)*

(i) A basic subject with isolate ideas
(ii) Subject of great extension and small intension
(iii) Subject of small extension and greater intension
(iv) Subject usually embodied in the form of an article in a periodical, or a part or chapter or section of a book

Codes:

(a) (i) and (ii) are correct
(b) (iii) and (i) are correct
(c) (iii) and (iv) are correct
(d) (ii) and (iv) are correct

440. Which of the following are the features of "Folksonomy"? *(NET 15J iii paper)*

(i) Keyword indexing
(ii) Collaborative tagging
(iii) Posts in chronological order
(iv) Audio files

Codes:

(a) (i) and (ii) are correct
(b) (i) and (iii) are correct
(c) (ii) and (iv) are correct
(d) (iii) and (iv) are correct

441. Which of the following concepts are related to each other? *(NET 15J iii paper)*

(i) Unity of command
(ii) Factor of planning
(iii) Espirit de crops
(iv) Management by objectives

Codes:

(a) (iii) and (iv) are correct
(b) (i) and (iii) are correct
(c) (ii) and (iv) are correct
(d) (i) and (ii) are correct

442. Which of the following are synchronous communication tools? *(NET 15J iii paper)*

(i) Instant Massaging (ii) Blog
(iii) Video conferencing (iv) Bulletin Board

Codes:

(a) (i) and (ii) are correct
(b) (i) and (iii) are correct
(c) (ii) and (iii) are correct
(d) (ii) and (iv) are correct

443. Net-Neutrality in India: *(NET 15J iii paper)*

(i) is the outcome of the absence of any law governing net-neutrality in India;
(ii) requires that all internet users be treated differently and unfairly by user, content, site platform, application, type of attached equipment or mode of communication;
(iii) is emerged due to reported violation of the net-neutrally principles by the Indian ISPs;
(iv) came to public debate after a mobile Telephony Service Provider in India announced to levy additional charges for making voice calls (VoIP) from its network using apps like, 'whats app', skype, etc.

Codes:

(a) (i), (iii) and (iv) are correct
(b) (ii), (iii) and (iv) are correct
(c) (i), (ii) and (iv) are correct
(d) (i), (ii) and (iii) are correct

444. 'Information Filtering System' is primarily designed for: (*NET 15J iii paper*)
(i) unstructured or semi-structured data;
(ii) delivery of information to people who need it;
(iii) removal and selection of data or an object from an incoming stream for a given profile;
(iv) location and inclusion of data or object in the stream.
Codes:
(a) (i), (ii) and (iii) are correct
(b) (ii), (iii) and (iv) are correct
(c) (i), (iii) and (iv) are correct
(d) (i), (ii) and (iv) are correct

445. Which of the following are access authentication methods for digital collection? (*NET 15J iii paper*)
(i) Shibboleth (ii) Open ID
(iii) Open URL (iv) Counter
Codes:
(a) (i) and (ii) are correct
(b) (i) and (iii) are correct
(c) (ii) and (iii) are correct
(d) (ii) and (iv) are correct

446. Identify the principles of PRECIS: (*NET 15J iii paper*)
(i) Context dependency
(ii) Formalisation
(iii) Modulation
(iv) One-to-one relationship
Codes:
(a) (i) and (ii) are correct
(b) (i) and (iii) are correct
(c) (i) and (iv) are correct
(d) (ii) and (iv) are correct

447. Match the following: (*NET 15J iii paper*)

List - I	**List - II**
(A) Loose Assemblage	(1) Organometallic Chemistry
(B) Agglomeration	(2) Physics for Engineers
(C) Fusion	(3) Indology
(D) Clustering	(4) Natural Sciences

Codes:	**(A)**	**(B)**	**(C)**	**(D)**
(a)	(2)	(4)	(1)	(3)
(b)	(3)	(2)	(1)	(4)
(c)	(1)	(3)	(2)	(4)
(d)	(4)	(1)	(3)	(2)

448. Match the following: (*NET 15J iii paper*)

List – I
(A) Central Tendency
(B) Regression Curve
(C) Refinement of Judgement
(D) Absolute zero point

List – II
(1) Ratio Scale
(2) Delphi Method
(3) Mean
(4) Relationship between two variables

Codes:	**(A)**	**(B)**	**(C)**	**(D)**
(a)	(2)	(3)	(4)	(1)
(b)	(1)	(4)	(3)	(2)
(c)	(4)	(2)	(1)	(3)
(d)	(3)	(4)	(2)	(1)

449. S.M.C.R Communication model was developed by (*NET 15J ii paper*)
(a) David KBerlo (b) Harold Lasswell
(c) W. Schramm (d) Charles Osgood

450. Who suggested the 'Seven Lamps of Conduct' as must for library professional? (*NET 15J ii paper*)
(a) Joint Council of Library Association in India (JOCLAI)
(b) Indian Library Association
(c) S.R. Ranganathan
(d) R.L. Mittal

451. DARE, which is a UNESCO database, provides information for: (*NET 15J ii paper*)
(a) Social Sciences (b) Applied Sciences
(c) Law (d) Pure Sciences

452. Which type of information need can be satisfied with Review and State-of-the-Art Reports? (*NET 15J ii paper*)
(a) Everyday (b) Exhaustive
(c) Current (d) Catching Up

453. The Principle which states that if the facet B in a subject will not be operative without the concept behind A is conceded then B should follow A is, known as: (*NET 15J ii paper*)
(a) Principle of later in time
(b) Principle of gradual evolution
(c) Principle of bottom upwards
(d) Wall – picture principle

454. What is the purpose of cookies? (*NET 15J ii paper*)
(a) Identify Users on the server
(b) Act as buffer store

(c) Connects database
(d) Develops dynamic web pages

455. Identify the correct sequence of user tasks that are supported by the structure of FRBR, RDA, 0.2 version: *(NET 15J ii paper)*
(a) Identify, Select, Obtain, Find
(b) Find, Identify, Select, Obtain
(c) Select, Identify, Find, Obtain
(d) Find, Select, Identify, Obtain

456. Which of the following are formal means of communication? *(NET 15J ii paper)*
(i) Adhoctalks (ii) Reports
(iii) Blogs (iv) Meetings
Codes:
(a) (i), (ii) and (iii) are correct.
(b) (ii) and (iii) are correct.
(c) (ii) and (iv) are correct.
(d) (i), (ii) and (iv) are correct.

457. Which of the following elements are associated with Dervin's Model of Information Seeking Behaviour? *(NET 15J ii paper)*
(i) Situation (ii) Extracting
(iii) Gap (iv) Browsing
Codes:
(a) (i) and (ii) are correct.
(b) (ii) and (iii) are correct.
(c) (i) and (iii) are correct.
(d) (ii) and (iv) are correct.

458. Which of the following advantageous features of Portable Document Format (PDF)? *(NET 15J ii paper)*
(i) More compatibility
(ii) Easy editing
(iii) Supports image format
(iv) Good compression ratio
Codes:
(a) (i) and (ii) are correct.
(b) (ii) and (iii) are correct.
(c) (iii) and (iv) are correct.
(d) (iv) and (i) are correct.

459. Identify the three information activities presented by James Krikelas (1983) as the foundation of his ISB model: *(NET 15J ii paper)*
(i) Information gathering
(ii) Information Seeking
(iii) Information computing
(iv) Information giving
Codes:
(a) (i), (ii) and (iv) are correct.
(b) (ii), (iv) and (i) are correct.
(c) (ii), (iii) and (iv) are correct.
(d) (i), (iii) and (iv) are correct.

460. Arrange the following in the order of their development: *(NET 15J ii paper)*
(i) DOS (ii) MACOS
(iii) LINUX (iv) UBUNTO
Codes:
(a) (i), (ii), (iii), (iv) (b) (ii), (iii), (iv), (i)
(c) (i), (iii), (ii), (iv) (d) (ii), (iv), (i), (iii)

461. Match the following: *(NET 15J ii paper)*

List - I	**List – II**
(A) MySQL	(1) Language
(B) Apache	(2) Server
(C) Perl	(3) User Interface
(D) API	(4) RDBMS

Codes:	**(A)**	**(B)**	**(C)**	**(D)**
(a)	(2)	(4)	(3)	(1)
(b)	(4)	(2)	(1)	(3)
(c)	(1)	(2)	(3)	(4)
(d)	(3)	(1)	(2)	(4)

462. Match the following: *(NET 15J ii paper)*
List - I
(A) Real-time communication (B) Telnet
(C) USENET (D) Listserv
List -II
(1) Bulletin Boards (2) Subscribed Membership
(3) Video conferencing (4) Remote Login

Codes:	**(A)**	**(B)**	**(C)**	**(D)**
(a)	2	3	4	1
(b)	3	4	1	2
(c)	4	2	1	3
(d)	3	1	2	4

463. **Assertion (A):** Computers are tools that can help to create more Knowledge.
Reason(R): Knowledge is mechanical hence developed in computers. *(NET 15J ii paper)*
Codes:
(a) Both (A) and (R) are true.
(b) (A) is true, but (R) is false.
(c) Both (A) and (R) are false.
(d) (A) is false, but (R) is true.

464. **Assertion (A):** Open access publication model involves xero cost. *(NET 15J ii paper)*

Reason (R): Open access increases the visibility of the publication, as they are available to the users for free access.

Codes:

(a) Both (A) and (R) are true.
(b) (A) is true but (R) is false.
(c) (A) is false but (R) is true.
(d) Both (A) and (R) are false.

465. Who introduced the concept of 'knowledge industry'? *(NET 14D ii paper)*
(a) Peter Drucker (b) Fritz Machlup
(c) Marc Porat (d) William Saffady

466. Identify the place where IFLA was first found. *(NET 14D ii paper)*
(a) The Hague, Netherlands
(b) Edinburgh, Scotland
(c) Helsinki, Finland
(d) London

467. Information For All Programme (IFAP) was launched by *(NET 14D ii paper)*
(a) IFLA (b) Library of Congress
(c) OCLC (d) UNESCO

468. DMAIC is the acronym for: *(NET 14D ii paper)*
(a) Define, Measure, Access, Improve and Control
(b) Define, Measure, Analyse, Improve and Control
(c) Describe, Measure, Analyse, Improve and Control
(d) Define, Measure, Access, Instruct and Control

469. The mode of displaying graphic information pixel by pixel with bits in main memory is *(NET 14D ii paper)*
(a) Bit handling (b) Bit mapping
(c) Bit pattern (d) Bit matrix

470. An alerting service in the digital environment is offered through: *(NET 14D ii paper)*
(i) RSS feeds (ii) E-mail
(iii) Blogs (iv) Bulletin Board

Codes:

(a) (i), (iii) are correct.
(b) (ii), (iii), (iv) are correct.
(c) (i), (ii), (iii) are correct.
(d) (i), (ii), (iv) are correct.

471. The important methods of measuring impact factor of any information retrieval system are: *(NET 14D ii paper)*
(i) Expression Rate (ii) Precision Rate
(iii) Recall Rate (iv) Depression Rate

Codes:

(a) (i) and (iii) are correct.
(b) (ii) and (iv) are correct.
(c) (ii) and (iii) are correct.
(d) (iii) and (iv) are correct.

472. **Assertion (A):** The value of information depends on its age and the time it is sold.

Reason (R): Newer information tends to have more value. *(NET 14D ii paper)*

Codes:

(a) Both (A) and (R) are true.
(b) Both (A) and (R) are false.
(c) (A) is false, but (R) is true.
(d) (A) is true, but (R) is false.

473. **Assertion (A):** Knowledge organisation and knowledge management are conceptually one and the same.

Reason (R): Simple Knowledge Organisation System (SKOS) is designed for knowledge management. *(NET 14D ii paper)*

Codes:

(a) (A) is true, but (R) is false.
(b) (R) is true, but (A) is false.
(c) Both (A) and (R) are true.
(d) Both (A) and (R) are false.

474. **Assertion (A):** One of the key lessons of the web 2.0 era is that users can add value.

Reason (R): Web 2.0 serve communities of people and are created and maintained by and for the people. *(NET 14D ii paper)*

Codes:

(a) Both (A) and (R) are true.
(b) Both (A) and (R) are false.
(c) (A) is true and (R) is false.
(d) (R) is true and (A) is false.

475. **Assertion (A):** RSS is considered as an alternative to the current awareness service.

Reason (R): RSS feeds enable us to syndicate data automatically. *(NET 14D ii paper)*

Codes:

(a) Both (A) and (R) are true.
(b) Both (A) and (R) are false.
(c) (A) is false, but (R) is true.
(d) (A) is true, but (R) is false.

476. **Assertion (A):** An electronic library may have both born digital and converted digital documents.

Reason (R): A document stored in Unicode is same as storing the scanned image of the document. *(NET 14D ii paper)*

Codes:

(a) (A) is false, but (R) is true.
(b) (A) is true, but (R) is false.
(c) Both (A) and (R) are true.
(d) Both (A) and (R) are false.

477. Arrange the following in chronological order: *(NET 14D ii paper)*
(i) Right to Information Act (India)
(ii) Information Technology Act (India)
(iii) Indian Copyright Act
(iv) Digital Millennium Copyright Act (US)

Codes:

(a) (i) (ii) (iii) (iv) (b) (iv) (i) (ii) (iii)
(c) (ii) (iii) (iv) (i) (d) (iii) (iv) (ii) (i)

478. Arrange the stages in the preparation of State-of-the-Art Report. *(NET 14D ii paper)*
(i) Consultation with subject expert
(ii) Scope determination
(iii) Appraisal of information
(iv) Identification of the collection

Codes:

(a) (ii) (iv) (iii) (i) (b) (iv) (ii) (iii) (i)
(c) (iii) (i) (iv) (ii) (d) (i) (ii) (iii) (iv)

479. An Application Program Interface (API) language is used for *(2013 Set iii paper)*
(a) Network Management
(b) Graphical user Interface
(c) Relational Interface in Data Base Management
(d) Database Management System

480. Arrange the following web browsers in chronological order: *(NET 14D ii paper)*
(i) Safari (ii) Chrome
(iii) Netscape Navigator (iv) Firefox

Codes:

(a) (iv) (i) (ii) (iii) (b) (i) (ii) (iii) (iv)
(c) (ii) (i) (iv) (iii) (d) (iii) (i) (iv) (ii)

481. Arrange the following in chronological order: *(NET 14D ii paper)*
(i) MEDLINE (ii) Pub-Med
(iii) Index Medicus (iv) MEDLARS

Codes:

(a) (iii) (iv) (i) (ii) (b) (iv) (i) (iii) (ii)
(c) (i) (iii) (ii) (iv) (d) (iii) (ii) (iv) (i)

482. Arrange the following according to their year of origin: *(NET 14D ii paper)*
(i) Statistical Bibliography (ii) Librametery
(iii) Bibliometrics (iv) Webometrics

Codes:

(a) (ii) (iii) (i) (iv) (b) (iii) (ii) (i) (iv)
(c) (i) (ii) (iii) (iv) (d) (ii) (i) (iii) (iv)

483. Match the following electronic applications of information society with relevant service: *(NET 14D ii paper)*

List – I	List – II
A. E-Commerce	1. Saakshat
B. E-Governance	2. Living progress
C. E-Education	3. G2C initiatives
D. E-Health	4. Snap Deal

Codes:	A	B	C	D
(a)	3	4	1	2
(b)	2	3	4	1
(c)	4	3	1	2
(d)	4	2	1	3

484. Match the following: *(NET 14D ii paper)*

List – I	List – II
A. Meta search engine	1. HotBot
B. Web directory	2. Search Engine
C. Subject gateway	3. Galaxy
D. Archie	4. Library Spot

Codes:	A	B	C	D
(a)	1	3	4	2
(b)	3	2	1	4
(c)	2	4	1	3
(d)	1	3	2	4

485. Match the following: *(NET 14D ii paper)*

List – I	List – II
A. Nominal variable	1. Temperature in centigrade
B. Interval variable	2. Students and Faculty
C. Ordinal variable	3. Classification of gender
D. Ratio	4. Grades of students

Codes:	A	B	C	D
(a)	2	3	1	4
(b)	3	1	4	2
(c)	1	4	3	2
(d)	4	2	3	1

486. Match the following: *(NET 14D ii paper)*

List – I	List – II
A. Internet	1. Knowledge navigation
B. Computing	2. Collection of E-resources

C. WWW 3. Tools and Techniques for accessing

D. Digital Library 4. Delivery Mechanism

Codes:	A	B	C	D
(a)	4	1	3	2
(b)	4	3	1	2
(c)	2	1	3	4
(d)	3	4	2	1

Direction: Read the following passage carefully and answer the questions that follows: (487-491)

According to Peter Walsh (2003), knowledge production has historically been based on the expert paradigm in which bodies of knowledge are controlled by groups of experts. The differentiation between interior and exterior, expert and layperson, producer and consumer, creates what Walsh (2003) called "knowledge hegemony" in which control over the creation and distribution of knowledge and information is monopolized in the hands of the few. However, advances in information technology—from the printing press to the World Wide Web—have led to the steady erosion of this hegemony in so far as they have allowed greater numbers of people to participate in knowledge production. The printing press, for example, undermined one of the key elements of the medieval Church's knowledge hegemony: the control of book production and libraries. Mass publishing and the spread of literacy formed the basis the Reformation, the Age of Enlightenment, and the Scientific Revolution. Today, the web is undermining the knowledge hegemony of a number of fields such as journalism, publishing, education, and museums. Echoing sentiments similar to those expressed by Benjamin in his essay "The Work of Art in the Age of Mechanical Reproduction" (1936/1968), Walsh (2003) argued that loss of physical control over art, owing to new technological means of mass production and distribution, undermines the ability of museums to control what types of art are made accessible to the public, the context in which they are seen, and the types of discourses about them that are considered "appropriate". The availability of easy to use digital technologies for reproducing, creating, and distributing content—artistic, literary, informational, or otherwise—has effectively weakened existing knowledge hegemonies by lowering the barriers to participation in knowledge production. Participatory cultures therefore produce a counter-hegemonic effect in so far as they "erode monopolistic positions held by professions, educational institutions, and experts, and they increase the diversity of perspectives on the way the world is and the way it could be".

487. According to Walsh, knowledge production has been historically based on
(a) Participatory culture
(b) Application of technology
(c) Expert paradigm
(d) Collective intelligence

488. In knowledge hegemony control over creation of knowledge and information is
(a) in the printing press
(b) in the world wide web
(c) in the libraries
(d) in the hands of a few

489. The main reason for the erosion of the knowledge hegemony of the medieval church was
(a) the printing press (b) world wide web
(c) the libraries (d) action of a few

490. One of the important factors that helped to usher in the age of enlightenment was
(a) world wide web (b) monopoly of information
(c) spread of literacy (d) control of libraries

491. The diversity of perspective is increased by
(a) knowledge hegemony
(b) digital technology
(c) control of book production
(d) participatory culture

492. Digital collection developed for capturing the intellectual output of a single or multi institution is called as *(NET 15D iii paper)*
(a) Digital Library (b) Digital archive
(c) Digital repository (d) Digital publishing

493. INFLIBNET initiative for 'Integrated e-content ports: Gateway to All Learners' is named as: *(NET 15D iii paper)*
(a) e-PG Pathshala (b) IR@ INFLIBNET
(c) INFOPORT (d) e-Acharya

494. International Literacy Day is celebrated on: *(NET 15D iii paper)*

(a) 8th July (b) 9th August
(c) 8th September (d) 18th September

495. SCONUL stands for: *(NET 15D iii paper)*
(a) The Council of National and University Libraries
(b) Scientific National University Libraries
(c) The Scientific Conference on National and University Libraries
(d) The Standing Conference on National and University Libraries

496. The key factor that enforces uniformity throughout retrieval system is: *(NET 15D iii paper)*
(a) Controlled vocabulary
(b) Search strategy
(c) User profile
(d) Database

497. Which of the following tools index cited references? *(NET 15D iii paper)*
(i) D-Space (ii) SCOPUS
(iii) JCCC (iv) Google Scholar
Codes:
(a) (i) and (iii) are correct
(b) (ii) and (iii) are correct
(c) (i) and (iv) are correct
(d) (ii) and (iv) are correct

498. Arrange the following units of computer memory in an ascending order: *(NET 15D iii paper)*
(i) Zettabyte (ii) Exabyte
(iii) Yottabyte (iv) Petabyte
Codes:
(a) (i), (ii), (iv) and (iii)
(b) (ii), (iii), (i) and (iv)
(c) (iv), (ii), (i) and (iii)
(d) (iii), (i), (ii) and (iv)

499. Match the following: *(NET 15D iii paper)*
List - I
(A) Nominal Data (B) Ordinal Data
(C) Interval Data (D) Ratio
List - II
(1) Level of satisfaction regarding library facilities
(2) Frequency of use of internet by different user groups
(3) Ranking of library services by users
(4) Gender details of library users

Codes:	**(A)**	**(B)**	**(C)**	**(D)**
(a)	(1)	(3)	(2)	(4)
(b)	(4)	(2)	(1)	(3)
(c)	(3)	(2)	(4)	(1)
(d)	(4)	(3)	(1)	(2)

500. **Assertion (A):** POP is the main internet standard for electronic mail transmission.
Reason (R): The Post Office Protocol (POP) is a protocol used by local e-mail clients to retrieve e-mail from a remote server over TCP/IP connection. *(NET 15D iii paper)*
Codes:
(a) Both (A) and (R) are true.
(b) Both (A) and (R) are false.
(c) (A) is true, but (R) is false.
(d) (A) is false, but (R) is true.

501. **Assertion (A):** Institutional Repositories (IRs) no more remain an inaccessible resource for the contemporary researchers as they not only open up their scholarly output to the entire world, but also maximized their visibility and impact of these outputs.
Reason (R): Repositories adhere to an internationally agreed set of technical standards by which they pose the metadata of each item and their contents on the Web and as such are interoperable. *(NET 15D iii paper)*
Codes:
(a) Both (A) and (R) are true.
(b) Both (A) and (R) are false.
(c) (A) is true, but (R) is false.
(d) (A) is false, but (R) is true.

502. Name the scientist who said that Information Science is cluster of many disciplines where in the central core is 'Information'. *(NET-13D ii paper)*
(a) B.C. Brooks (b) Fritz Machlup
(c) Daniel Bell (d) N.J. Belkin

503. Who coined the phrase 'Information Retrieval'? *(NET-13D ii paper)*
(a) Calvin Mooers (b) S.R. Ranganathan
(c) J.D. Brown (d) H.P. Luhn

What is Denudation?
(a) Is dividing classes to decrease the extension.
(b) Is dividing classes to increase the extension.
(c) Is dividing classes to increase intension and decrease extension.
(d) Is dividing classes to decrease intension.

504. The International Body that coordinates the assignment of unique domain names, protocol address is *(NET-13D ii paper)*

(a) IGF (b) IANA (c) ICANN (d) ISP

505. Which of the following are the types factors studies under ANOVA? *(NET-13D ii paper)*
(i) Fixed (ii) Frequency
(iii) Calculated (iv) Random
Codes:
(a) (ii) and (iii) are correct.
(b) (i) and (iv) are correct.
(c) (i) and (iii) are correct.
(d) (ii) and (iv) are correct.

506. Which of the following are the models of communication? *(NET-13D ii paper)*
(i) Economic Theory Model
(ii) Stock Adjustment Model
(iii) Shannon Weaver Model
(iv) Schramm Model
Codes:
(a) (iii) and (iv) are correct.
(b) (ii) and (iii) are correct.
(c) (i) and (ii) are correct.
(d) (ii) and (iv) are correct.

507. Which of the following are criteria for Web evaluation? *(NET-13D ii paper)*
(i) Revision (ii) Response time
(iii) Format (iv) Archiving facility
Codes:
(a) (i) and (ii) are correct.
(b) (ii) and (iv) are correct.
(c) (i) and (iii) are correct.
(d) (ii) and (iii) are correct.

508. Which of the following are Library net works? *(NET-13D ii paper)*
(i) Internet (ii) Indonet
(iii) INFLIBNET (iv) OCLC
Codes:
(a) (i) and (ii) are correct.
(b) (ii) and (iv) are correct.
(c) (iii) and (iv) are correct.
(d) (i) and (iv) are correct.

509. Match the following: *(NET-13D ii paper)*

List – I	List – II
A. Encyclopaedia of Associations	i. Secondary sources
B. Whitaker's Almanac	ii. Primary sources
C. LISA	iii. Directories
D. Economic Times	iv. Yearbooks

Codes:	A	B	C	D
(a)	iii	iv	i	ii
(b)	iv	iii	i	ii
(c)	ii	i	iv	iii
(d)	i	iv	iii	ii

510. **Assertion (A):** According to Horton and Merchant, information is a commodity like other resources.
Reason (R): Information is a tangible commodity. *(NET-13D ii paper)*
Codes:
(a) (A) is true, but (R) is false.
(b) Both (A) and (R) are false.
(c) Both (A) and (R) are true.
(d) (A) is false, (R) is true.

511. **Assertion (A):** Information is commodity.
Reason (R): Commodity is a marketable item produced to satisfy human wants or needs. *(NET-13D ii paper)*
Codes:
(a) (A) is false, and (R) is true.
(b) (R) is false and (A) is true.
(c) Both (A) and (R) are false.
(d) Both (A) and (R) are true.

Read the passage given below and answer the questions based on your understanding of the passage (Question Nos. 512-516): *(NET-13D ii paper)*

According to Wikipedia 'social media' is media designed to be disseminated through social interaction, created using highly accessible and scalable publishing techniques. According to search engine partner, the term social media describes media that is posed by the user and can take many different forms. Some type of social media are forums, message boards, blogs, wikis and podcarts. Social media applications include Google, Facebook and YouTube. In social media, communication takes place through messages, status updates, voice chats etc. or through photos/videos sharing, games, virtual goods etc. Antony Mayfield in his e-book titled *What is Social Media?* has defined social media as online media, which encourages contributions and feedback from everyone who is interested, is open to feedback and participation, is a two-way conversation, allows communities to form quickly and communicate effectively to share common interests and thrive on their connectedness.

The growth of social media is phenomenal. It is being used by all netizens all over the world to a great extent in all areas including business, government, fashion, etc. A research conducted by the Institute for Prospective Technological Studies (IPTS) indicates that high take up of social media application outside formal educational settings provides new opportunities for innovation and modernisation. With this growing trend, political leaders have also realized its importance as an effective tool to spread awareness and to reach out their voters. Democratic presidential candidate Barack Obama used it during the Presidential elections. Since then, social media is being highly used by a number of politicians all over the world. Myspace has more than 7400 discussion groups related to politics. According to a survey by manpower, 29% of the companies in America and 20% of companies worldwide have a social media policy. People even update themselves through micro-blogging on every aspect of human life including the natural and human disasters. In China, Twitter became the first media in the world to break the news of the Wenzhou earthquake. Social media is being used in fashion industry as well to generate interest in a brand through publicity across online communities and websites. India is one of the most culturally, linguistically and genetically diverse regions having more than one billion people. It is ranked third in Asia in terms of the internet users and quite a number of them are using social media. In fact, approximately 60 million to 65 million netizens in India open most of their time on social media/ networking sites.

512. Who defined social media as 'online media' which encourages contributions and feedback from everyone who is interested?
(a) Wikipedia
(b) Institute for Prospective Technological Studies (IPTS)
(c) Myspace
(d) Antony Myfield

513. Who used the social media for conversing during recent Presidential Election in U.S.A.?
(a) Jimmy Carter (b) Barack Obama
(c) George Bush (d) John F. Kennedy

514. In China, which social media became the first media to break the news of earthquake?
(a) Facebook (b) YouTube
(c) Twitter (d) MyZamana

515. In Asia, which country is ranked third in terms of using social media by the people?
(a) China (b) Pakistan
(c) Japan (d) India

516. Which social website has more than 7400 discussion groups relate to politics? *(NET 2013 D)*
(a) Orkut (b) Myspace
(c) Facebook (d) Twitter

517. A Boolean query using only AND and NOT is *(NET 13D iii paper)*
(a) Fuzzy query (b) Conjunctive query
(c) Routing query (d) Probabilistic query

518. Who developed Repertory Grid Technique for assessing how the users view the world from their own perspective? *(NET 13D iii paper)*
(a) A. Delphi (b) Calvin Mooers
(c) J. Belkin (d) George Kelley

519. A chart in which some figures are broken down into its constituent parts is *(NET 13D iii paper)*
(a) Bar chart (b) Column chart
(c) Pie chart (d) Band chart

520. OAISTER is an example of digital libraries architecture based on *(NET 13D iii paper)*
(a) CORBA
(b) Software Agents Architecture
(c) Federated Database System
(d) Metadata Harvesting

521. RSS feed is a tool of *(NET 13D iii paper)*
(a) Web 2.0 (b) Web 1.0
(c) Web 3.0 (d) Graphic Design

522. The use of more words or symbols than are necessary to convey a meaning results in *(NET 13D iii paper)*
(a) Efficiency (b) Accuracy
(c) Redundancy (d) Precision

523. Name the similarity measure in which similarity of a document is adjusted such that the similarity of a document to itself is 1. *(NET 13D iii paper)*
(a) Cosine measure
(b) Distance measure
(c) Swet's measure
(d) Normalised similarity measure

524. Which law states that "An information retrieval system will tend not to be used whenever it is more painful and troublesome for a customer to have information than for him not to have it"? *(NET 13D iii paper)*
(a) Bradford's Law (b) Mooer's Law
(c) Ziff's Law (d) Lotka's Law

525. Which of the following facilitate informal communication on the web? *(NET 13D iii paper)*
(i) Split Screens (ii) Chat
(iii) Wikis (iv) RSS feeds
Codes:
(a) (i) & (iii) are correct
(b) (ii) & (iii) are correct
(c) (iii) & (iv) are correct
(d) (i) & (ii) are correct

526. Which of the following associations have sponsored the Text Encoding Initiatives (TEI)? *(NET 13D iii paper)*
(i) ACL (ii) ACRL (iii) ALLC (iv) ACH
Codes:
(a) (i), (ii) and (iii) are correct
(b) (ii), (iii) and (iv) are correct
(c) (i), (iv) and (ii) are correct
(d) (i), (iii) and (iv) are correct

527. Which of the following are limitations of digital libraries? *(NET 13D iii paper)*
(i) Full text searching
(ii) Operational costs
(iii) Rights management
(iv) Hypertext linking
Codes:
(a) (ii), (iii) and (iv) are correct
(b) (ii) and (iii) are correct
(c) (i), (ii) and (iv) are correct
(d) (i) and (iv) are correct

528. "Women are more in library profession than men." Identify the variable in the statement. *(NET 13D iii paper)*
(i) Men and women are independent variables.
(ii) Men and women are dependent variables.
(iii) Library profession is a dependent variable.
(iv) Library profession is an independent variable.
Codes:
(a) (i) and (iii) are correct
(b) (i) and (iv) are correct
(c) (ii) and (iii) are correct
(d) (ii) and (iv) are correct

529. Systematic sampling is *(NET 13D iii paper)*
(i) A type of probability sampling.
(ii) A type of non-probability sampling.
(iii) In which first unit is selected randomly.
(iv) Selected on the basis of specified characteristics.
Codes:
(a) (i) and (iii) are correct
(b) (i) and (iv) are correct
(c) (iii) and (iv) are correct
(d) (ii) and (iv) are correct

530. Which of the following are the Pillars of SCONUL Seven Pillar Model? *(NET 13D iii paper)*
(i) Recognising information need
(ii) Locating and accessing information
(iii) Using information technology for assessing information need.
(iv) Comparing and evaluating information.
Codes:
(a) (i), (ii) and (iii) are correct
(b) (i), (ii) and (iv) are correct
(c) (ii), (iii) and (iv) are correct
(d) (i) and (iv) are correct

531. Resource Description Framework consists which of the following? *(NET 13D iii paper)*
(i) Subject (ii) Thread
(iii) Predicate (iv) Object
Codes:
(a) (i), (ii) and (iii) (b) (ii), (iii) and (iv)
(c) (iii), (iv) and (i) (d) (iv), (i) and (ii)

532. The correlational coefficient is *(NET 2013 Sept iii paper)*
(a) A strength of relationship between two variables.
(b) A typical relationship between two variables.
(c) A linear relationship between two variables.
(d) Non-linear relationship between two variables.

533. Which of the following web resource for LIS has been compiled by academic librarians of universities of California? *(NET 2013 Sept iii paper)*
(a) Infomine
(b) Internet Public Library

(c) Internet Library for Librarians
(d) Current Informed Librarian

534. Match the following: (*NET 13D iii paper*)

List – I

A. Outdated Information
B. Condensed Information
C. Message
D. Vintage model

List – II

1. Information Diffusion
2. Obsolete Information
3. Compressible Information
4. Understanding

Codes:	A	B	C	D
(a)	4	3	2	1
(b)	1	2	4	3
(c)	3	4	2	1
(d)	2	3	4	1

535. Match the following: (*NET 13D iii paper*)

List – I

(A) Technique for identifying the theme of a document
(B) Prussian Instruction
(C) ISO-9960
(D) Baud

List – II

1. Cataloguing
2. Standard for encoding data on CD-ROM
3. Data Transmission Speed
4. Bibliographic coupling

Codes:	A	B	C	D
(a)	4	1	2	3
(b)	1	2	3	4
(c)	2	3	4	1
(d)	3	2	1	4

536. Match the following: (*NET 13D iii paper*)

List – I

(A) Maurice B. Line (B) David Baker
(C) Peter Brophy (D) K.D. Metcalf

List – II

1. Resource Management in Academic Libraries
2. Planning Academic and Research Library Buildings
3. Academic Library Management
4. The Academic Libraries

Codes:	A	B	C	D
(a)	3	1	4	2
(b)	1	2	3	4
(c)	4	1	2	3
(d)	2	3	1	4

537. Match the following: (*NET 13D iii paper*)

List – I

(A) Digital Library (B) Hybrid Library
(C) Virtual Library (D) Electronic Library

List – II

1. Collections are stored in electronic media formats and accessible via computers
2. Access to electronic information in a variety of remote locations through a local online catalogue or other gateway
3. Provides services in a mixed mode electronic and paper environment
4. Collection of electronic resources that provides direct/indirect access to a systematically organised collection of digital objects

Codes:	A	B	C	D
(a)	4	3	2	1
(b)	1	3	4	2
(c)	3	1	2	4
(d)	2	4	1	3

538. Match the following characteristics of DBMS with respective activity:
(*NET 13D iii paper*)

List – I

A. Reduction of redundancy B. Data sharing
C. Data integrity D. Data security

List – II

1. Encryption
2. Centralized control
3. No. of application programs
4. Accurate and consistent data

Codes:	A	B	C	D
(a)	2	3	4	1
(b)	4	3	2	1
(c)	3	4	1	2
(d)	1	2	4	3

539. Match the following: (*NET 13D iii paper*)

List – I	**List – II**
(A) XML	i. Joe Becker
(B) METS	ii. Defence Organizations
(C) UNICODE	iii. W3C
(D) Cryptography	iv. Library of Congress

Codes:	A	B	C	D
(a)	i	ii	iii	iv
(b)	iii	iv	i	ii

(c)	ii	iii	iv	i
(d)	iv	i	ii	iii

540. Match the following evaluation criteria of print materials: (*NET 13D iii paper*)

List – I	List – II
A. Authority	1. Typography
B. Scope	2. Stated purpose
C. Format	3. Publisher's reputation
D. Arrangement	4. Cross references

Codes:	A	B	C	D
(a)	2	3	1	4
(b)	1	4	2	3
(c)	3	2	1	4
(d)	3	4	2	1

541. Match the following: (*NET 13D iii paper*)

List – I
A. Measure of similarity between two documents
B. Similarity measure based on overlap in terms between two documents
C. Document similarity based solely on the occurrence of words
D. Similarity measure which is based on the city block distance between two documents

List – II
1. Proportion of coefficient association
2. Rectangular distance Coefficient
3. Coefficient of association
4. Lexical Similarity

Codes:	A	B	C	D
(a)	1	3	2	4
(b)	3	1	2	4
(c)	3	1	4	2
(d)	2	3	4	1

542. Match the following authors with their statements on information characteristics: (*NET 13D iii paper*)

List – I
A. Peter Drucker B. Borland Cleveland
C. K.J. McGarry D. Williams

List – II
1. Human and shareable
2. Quantity, Quality, Life
3. Natural and man-made physical resources
4. Resources by analogy with classic resources of labour

Codes:	A	B	C	D
(a)	3	1	4	2
(b)	3	2	1	4
(c)	1	3	4	2
(d)	1	4	2	3

543. **Assertion (A):** With the introduction of Internet, need for reference librarians has been minimised to fulfil the users reference needs. (*NET 13D iii paper*)

Reason (R): FAQ facility on internet is substituting the need for human interface in libraries.

Codes:
(a) Both (A) and (R) are partially true.
(b) Both (A) and (R) are true.
(c) Both (A) and (R) are false.
(d) (A) is true but (R) is false.

544. **Assertion (A):** Approaches to Research is not dependent on Epistemologies. (*NET 13D iii paper*)

Reason (R): Scientific research relies on the application of the scientific method.

Codes:
(a) Both (A) and (R) are true.
(b) Both (A) and (R) are false.
(c) (A) is true and (R) is false.
(d) (R) is true and (A) is false.

545. **Assertion (A):** According to the Third Law of Librarianship given by Michael Gorman, we need to use technology intelligently to enhance service. (*NET 13D iii paper*)

Reason (R): Technology is used to solve problems and improve services and achieve cost effectiveness rather than adopted for its own sake.

Codes:
(a) (A) is true, but (R) is false.
(b) Both (A) and (R) are true, but (R) is not correct explanation of (A).
(c) Both (A) and (R) are false.
(d) Both (A) and (R) are true.

546. **Assertion (A):** Semantic web is an extension of www in which web contents cannot be expressed in natural language.

Reason (R): Semantic web can be easily associated with spider web. (*NET 13D iii paper*)

Codes:
(a) Both (A) and (R) are false.
(b) (A) is true, but (R) is false.

(c) Both (A) and (R) are true.
(d) (A) is false, but (R) is true.

547. **Assertion (A):** BIOS is a set of programs that handles startup operations in a computer such as power on, self tested and low level control for hardware.

Reason (R): The graphical display at the beginning of the program prolongs the life of monitor. *(NET 13D iii paper)*

Codes:
(a) Both (A) and (R) are true.
(b) (A) is false, but (R) is true.
(c) Both (A) and (R) are false.
(d) (A) is true, but (R) is false

548. Under which approach of Wersig Neveling's information theory, information is seen as static relations between physical objects which may be perceived or not? *(NET 14J ii paper)*
(a) The meaning approach
(b) The structural approach
(c) The process approach
(d) The knowledge approach

549. Which information theory focuses on the purpose of communication is, to inform, instruct or motivate the receiver? *(NET 14J ii paper)*
(a) Shannon's Theory (b) Weaver's Theory
(c) Ackoff's Theory (d) Yovits' Theory

550. 'Noise' in Information retrieval is due to *(NET 14J ii paper)*
(a) Precision
(b) Recall
(c) Relevant Information
(d) Redundant Information

551. Which of the following makes a network in-secured? *(NET 14J ii paper)*
(a) Encryption
(b) Network Interface Card (NIC)
(c) Password Capture
(d) Static Keys

552. Whose model of communication of knowledge suggests that communication is an open system? *(NET 14J ii paper)*
(a) G. Garbner (b) Juger Habermas
(c) Shannon & Weaver (d) M. Foucault

553. 'Trans Border Data Flow' means *(NET 14J ii paper)*
(a) Exchange of documents between countries
(b) Free flow of information between countries
(c) Flow of information between countries
(d) Exchange of electronic information between countries

554. Which of the following three types of basic languages are used in computer programming? *(NET 14J ii paper)*
(a) Procedural, Non-procedural and Unconditional
(b) Zero, Low and High levels
(c) Machine, Assembly and High level languages
(d) COBOL, BASIC and C

555. FRBR Model consist of which of the following four entities? *(NET 14J ii paper)*
(a) Personality, Matter, Energy, Space
(b) Work, Expression, Manifestation, Item
(c) Book, Form, Availability, Type
(d) Action, Place, Impact, Category

556. The primary distinction between RDA and AACR is *(NET 14J ii paper)*
(a) Structural (b) Relational
(c) Non-structural (d) Combinational

557. Which of the following are reasons for obsolescence of information? *(NET 14J ii paper)*
(i) Information is considered invalid.
(ii) Information is valid but mostly available online.
(iii) Works are extensively cited.
(iv) Information is valid but inadequate for exploration.

Codes:
(a) (i) and (ii) are correct.
(b) (ii) and (iii) are correct.
(c) (i) and (iv) are correct.
(d) (ii) and (iv) are correct.

558. Which of the following are news summaries? *(NET 14J ii paper)*
(i) Data India
(ii) Times of India Index
(iii) New York Times Index
(iv) Asian Recorder

Codes:
(a) (i), (ii) and (iii) are correct.
(b) (ii) and (iii) are correct.
(c) (ii), (iii) and (iv) are correct.
(d) (i) and (iv) are correct.

559. Which of the following are Web-zine? *(NET 14J ii paper)*
(i) Email Magazine (ii) E-Conference
(iii) Online Bulletin (iv) Electronic News Letter
Codes:
(a) (i), (iii) and (iv) (b) (i), (ii) and (iii)
(c) (ii), (iii) and (iv) (d) (i), (ii) and (iv)

560. Which of the following are not the Models of communication? *(NET 14J ii paper)*
(i) Vintage Model (ii) Lasswell's Model
(iii) Epidemic Model (iv) Garbner's Model
Codes:
(a) (i) & (iv) are correct.
(b) (ii) & (iii) are correct.
(c) (i) & (iii) are correct.
(d) (iii) & (iv) are correct.

561. In reference service, assimilation means: *(NET 14J ii paper)*
(i) Recording the retrieved information
(ii) Sharing reference service experience with colleagues
(iii) Furnishing the exact information
(iv) Acquaintance with reference material
Codes:
(a) (i) and (ii) are correct.
(b) (i) and (iv) are correct.
(c) (ii) and (iii) are correct.
(d) (ii) and (iv) are correct.

562. The notation used to increase the capacity of an array are: *(NET 14J ii paper)*
(i) Empty digit (ii) Emptying digit
(iii) Indicator digit (iv) Speciator
Codes:
(a) (i) and (ii) are correct.
(b) (iii) and (iv) are correct.
(c) (i), (ii) and (iii) are correct.
(d) (i), (ii) and (iv) are correct.

563. 'Library Technology Project (LTP) Reports' are published by ________.
(a) ILA (b) ALA (c) CILIP (d) SLA

564. Rich Text Format (RTF) is concerned with *(NET 14J ii paper)*
(i) Formatting features like Font type, size, etc.
(ii) Transporting text documents across different computers.
(iii) Multimedia formatting.
(iv) Formatting based on binary concept.
Codes:
(a) (ii) and (iii) are correct.
(b) (iii) and (iv) are correct.
(c) (i) and (ii) are correct.
(d) (i) and (iv) are correct

565. Arrange the following ISBDs according to their year of formulation: *(NET 14J ii paper)*
(i) ISBD (PM) (ii) ISBD (CF)
(iii) ISBD (M) (iv) ISBD (S)
Codes:
(a) (iii), (ii), (i), (iv) (b) (iii), (iv), (i), (ii)
(c) (iv), (i), (iii), (ii) (d) (iv), (ii), (iii), (i)

566. Match the following: *(NET 14J ii paper)*

List – I	List – II
A. CILIP	1. 1972
B. ASLIB	2. 2002
C. ALA	3. 1876
D. COMLA	4. 1924

Codes:	A	B	C	D
(a)	2	4	3	1
(b)	4	3	2	1
(c)	3	4	1	2
(d)	2	3	4	1

567. Match the following: *(NET 14J ii paper)*
List – I
A. Phenomenon B. Spectrum
C. Modes D. Diffusion
List – II
1. Physical Media for grouping of Information
2. Facts or Occurrence
3. Transfer Process
4. A broad range of varied but related ideas

Codes:	A	B	C	D
(a)	1	3	4	2
(b)	2	4	1	3
(c)	2	3	4	1
(d)	4	1	3	2

568. Match the following: *(NET 14J ii paper)*
List – I
A. Union Catalogue
B. Pamphlets & Brochures
C. Indexing & Abstracting
D. Memoirs of diaries
List – II
1. Primary sources
2. Unpublished sources
3. Tertiary sources
4. Secondary sources

Codes:	A	B	C	D
(a)	4	3	2	1
(b)	2	4	3	1
(c)	3	1	4	2
(d)	1	2	4	3

569. Match the following: *(NET 14J ii paper)*

List – I

A. Information on important recent happenings of India
B. Total number of foreigners visited in India in 2012
C. Name of Prime Minister of India
D. Postal Address of Anna Hazare

List – II

1. India—A Reference Annual
2. Keesing's Record of World Events
3. Statistical Yearbook
4. Who's Who

Codes:	A	B	C	D
(a)	4	1	2	3
(b)	2	3	1	4
(c)	3	2	1	4
(d)	1	4	3	2

570. Match the following: *(NET 14J ii paper)*

List – I

A. Scaler Chain
B. Espirit de Corps
C. Scientific Management
D. Span of control

List – II

1. Direct dealing with subordinates
2. Production, efficiency and prevention of waste
3. Emphasis on Teamwork
4. Top to Bottom

Codes:	A	B	C	D
(a)	4	3	2	1
(b)	3	4	1	2
(c)	4	2	3	1
(d)	2	3	1	4

571. Match the following: *(NET 14J ii paper)*

List – I

A. Skewness B. Modality
C. F distribution D. Correlation

List – II

1. Numbers of frequently appearing variables
2. Degree of association between two/more variables
3. Structure of distribution
4. Ratio of two Chi square variables

Codes:	A	B	C	D
(a)	1	4	2	3
(b)	3	1	4	2
(c)	4	2	3	1
(d)	2	3	1	4

572. **Assertion (A):** RSS (Rich Site Summary) is considered as an alternate to the SDI Service.

Reason (R): RSS Feeds enable us to syndicate data automatically. *(NET 14J ii paper)*

Codes:

(a) Both (A) and (R) are true.
(b) Both (A) and (R) are false.
(c) (A) is false, but (R) is true.
(d) (A) is true, but (R) is false.

Read the passage given below and answer the questions based on your understanding of the passage (Question Nos. 573-577): *(NET 14J ii paper)*

As the global information landscape increasingly facilitate the sharing, repurposing and dissemination of information, the ways in which students are accustomed to interacting with information resources are also changing. For some new students to universities, their understanding of referencing is based solely on fear (McGowan, 2005) and many are familiar with the basic concept of plagiarism. Some students bring with them the academic process that served them well at school—however, these are not suitable at Universities (Chanock, 2008). Students understand they should not copy words without referencing, but fail to grasp the reasons why; the reasons are not explicit and often cloaked in unfamiliar and impenetrable academic language. Pak's (2003) review of literature proved as a handy summation of the investigations, research, and thinking about plagiarism prior to the implementation of various plagiarism detection software products. There are three main schools of thought in referencing and plagiarism discourse. A punitive approach which focuses on the idea that students often deliberately engage in plagiarism and that the appropriate response is one of punishment (Blum, 2009; Sutherland-Smith, 2010; Bilic-Zulle, et al. 2008). A Restorative Justice approach, however, suggests that plagiarism is in fact an act against a community (in this case, a community of students), and that steps need to be taken to restore a level of balance (Wenzel; et al. 2010; Karp and Conrad, 2005; Karp, 2009; Dickson, et al. 2009). An educational approach that espouses that the best method of reducing plagiarism is to educate and support students. Marking criteria and assessment tasks should be linked to building referencing skills (especially in the first year) and ensure that the students learn these skills in a discipline related context (Jaschik; 2008). The approach of both the University of Southern Queensland (USQ) and Swinburne University of Technology is clearly aligned with the third school of thought. Students lack proper understanding of the purposes of referencing. For them, referencing and citing is linked to just words, not ideas (Jackson, 2006), so referencing is regarded as separate to the writing process, instead of an integral part. To help students develop good writing and referencing practices, it is useful if universities help them understand the research culture of tertiary study. Faculties need to make their referencing rules explicit and lectures should provide useful exemplars within courses.

573. Understanding of new students on Referencing is based on
(a) Plagiarism (b) Fear
(c) Ability to write (d) Insatiable desire to learn

574. An appropriate response to deliberate act of plagiarism according to punitive school of thought is
(a) to debar the student from library use
(b) to orient the student about plagiarism
(c) to award punishment
(d) to make him learn about referencing

575. To restore a 'level of balance' is advocated/reflected in
(a) Deterrent Approach
(b) Reformative Approach
(c) Punitive Approach
(d) Restorative Approach

576. 'Educational approach' which aims at reducing plagiarism should be linked with
(a) Building referencing skills of the students
(b) inculcating reading habits of the students
(c) building students as information literate
(d) ignorance of the students on methods of social research

577. Lack of understanding of students about referencing is linked to their
(a) Ideas (b) Words
(c) Experience (d) Intuition

578. A non-linear model of information seeking behaviour was presented by *(NET 2014J iii paper)*
(a) T.D. Wilson (b) Ellis
(c) Kulthou (d) Allen Foster

579. Which of the following programming language is exclusively used for Artificial Intelligence? *(NET 2014J iii paper)*
(a) C (b) J2EE (c) Prolog (d) JAVA

580. To make a program safe, one should take care of *(NET 2014J iii paper)*
(a) Strong authentication and access controls
(b) Error checking controls
(c) Do risk analysis
(d) Vendor's credibility

581. In CDS/ISIS 'delimiters' means *(NET 2014J iii paper)*
(a) Field address (b) Field repeatability
(c) Field format (d) Subfield indicators

582. A systematic method and process of studying and evaluating whether the expenditure for products, materials, or services is justified by the benefits is *(NET 2014J iii paper)*
(a) Break Even Analysis
(b) Cost-Effective Analysis
(c) System Analysis
(d) Administrative Analysis

583. A situation where a digital resource is no longer readable is called *(NET 2014J iii paper)*
(a) Digital Divide
(b) Digital Representation
(c) Digital Rendering
(d) Digital Obsolescence

584. Which of the following are not the features of ISDN? *(NET 2014J iii paper)*
i. Simultaneous Digital Transmission
ii. Set of communication standards
iii. Creates and combines packets
iv. Program to visit web pages
Codes:
(a) i & ii are correct.
(b) ii & iii are correct.

(c) iii & iv are correct.
(d) i & iv are correct.

585. Which of the following facilitate formal communication on the web? *(NET 2014J iii paper)*

i. Wikis ii. Chat
iii. RSS feeds iv. Split screens

Codes:
(a) i & ii are correct. (b) ii & iii are correct.
(c) i & iii are correct. (d) iii & iv are correct.

586. Semantic Web is based on which of the following: *(NET 2014J iii paper)*

i. RDF ii. Ontologies
iii. URL iv. Cloud seeding

Codes:
(a) i, ii & iii are correct.
(b) ii, iii & iv are correct.
(c) i, iii & iv are correct.
(d) i, ii & iv are correct.

587. Which of the following are not web 2.0 Tools? *(NET 2014J iii paper)*

i. Ontologies ii. Facebook
iii. Intelligent Web iv. RSS Feeds

Codes:
(a) i & ii are correct. (b) i & iii are correct.
(c) ii & iii are correct. (d) iii & iv are correct.

588. Who are associated with the development of OSI Model? *(NET 2014J iii paper)*

i. Charles Buchman ii. ISO
iii. MIT, USA iv. UCLA, California

Codes:
(a) i and iv are correct. (b) i and iii are correct.
(c) i and ii are correct. (d) ii and iii are correct

589. Which of the following are plagiarism detection software? *(NET 2014J iii paper)*

(i) Turnitin (ii) iThenticate
(iii) Tulips (iv) Veri Guide

Codes:
(a) (i) and (ii) (b) (i), (ii) and (iii)
(c) (i), (ii) and (iv) (d) (ii) and (iii)

590. Which of the following methods are adopted for offering information literacy? *(NET 2014J iii paper)*

i. Stand alone course
ii. Integrated with curriculum
iii. Online course
iv. Internship

Codes:
(a) i and ii (b) i, ii and iii
(c) ii and iv (d) i, ii and iv

591. Which of the following organizations are involved in providing translation services in India? *(NET 2014J iii paper)*

i. NISCAIR ii. National Library of India
iii. IASLIC iv. IATLIS

Codes:
(a) ii and iv are correct.
(b) ii and iii are correct.
(c) i and iv are correct.
(d) i and iii are correct.

592. Which of the following are International Referral Centres for Scholarly Information? *(NET 2014J iii paper)*

i. DARE
ii. INFOTERRA
iii. International Referral Network
iv. Information Referral

Codes:
(a) ii & iv are correct. (b) i & iv are correct.
(c) i & ii are correct. (d) ii & iii are correct.

593. Which of the following are the works related to IFLA's Committee on Freedom of Access to Information and Freedom of Expression (FAIFE)? *(NET 2014J iii paper)*

i. Publish reports, participate in national and international conferences and organize workshops.
ii. Monitor the state of intellectual freedom within the library community world-wide and publish newsletters and online news.
iii. Respond to violations of free access to information and freedom of expression and make press releases.
iv. Cross-association activities, to bring participants together.

Codes:
(a) i, iii and iv are correct.
(b) ii, iii and iv are correct.
(c) i, ii and iv are correct.
(d) i, ii and iii are correct.

594. Shannon's model of information theory is criticized for which of the following reasons? *(NET 2014J iii paper)*

i. Concern on semantic issues
ii. Engineering bias

iii. Concern for technical transmission
iv. Emphasis on effectiveness

Codes:
(a) i and ii are correct.
(b) ii and iii are correct.
(c) iii and iv are correct.
(d) i and iii are correct.

595. Arrange the following stages of knowledge representation in order: (*NET 2014J iii paper*)

i. Gather data ii. Knowledge database
iii. Codification iv. Content mapping

Codes:
(a) iv, iii, i, ii (b) iii, i, iv, ii
(c) ii, iv, i, iii (d) i, iii, ii, iv

596. Arrange the following according to their year of emergence: (*NET 2014J iii paper*)

i. ERNET ii. NICNET
iii. C-DOT iv. C-DAC

Codes:
(a) ii, iii, i, iv (b) iii, ii, iv, i
(c) iv, ii, iii, i (d) i, iv, iii, ii

597. Arrange the following steps in Flow Chart in order: (*NET 2014J iii paper*)

i. Modularity
ii. Data Structure
iii. Identifying problems into subproblems
iv. Loops and Termination of loops

Codes:
(a) iii, iv, i, ii (b) iii, ii, iv, i
(c) ii, iii, iv, i (d) iv, ii, i, iii

598. Match the following:(*NET 2014J iii paper*)

List – I
A. Information Literacy Competency Standards for Higher Education
B. Seven Pillars of Information literacy
C. Guidelines on Information Literacy for Life Long Learning
D. Information Literacy Working Group

List – II
1. IFLA 2. CAUL 3. ACRL 4. SCONUL

Codes:	A	B	C	D
(a)	3	4	1	2
(b)	4	2	3	1
(c)	3	1	2	4
(d)	2	3	1	4

599. Match the following theories with the respectively profounders: (*NET 2014J iii paper*)

List – I
A. Cybernetics
B. Human information processing
C. Psychological approach to message transmission
D. General Information System

List – II
1. Charles Osgood (1916)
2. Marshal C. Yovits
3. Nobert Wiener (1894–1964)
4. R.L. Ackoff

Codes:	A	B	C	D
(a)	1	3	2	4
(b)	1	2	4	3
(c)	3	1	4	2
(d)	3	2	1	4

600. Match the following:

List – I
A. N. Grogan B. J. Saha
C. Nilfred Ashworth D. L.J. Strauss

List – II
1. Scientific & Technical Libraries
2. Scientific & technical libraries; an introduction to literature
3. Handbook of special librarianship & information work
4. Special libraries and information services in India & USA

Codes:	A	B	C	D
(a)	2	4	3	1
(b)	1	2	4	3
(c)	2	1	3	4
(d)	4	2	1	3

601. Match the following: (*NET 2014J iii paper*)

List – I	List – II
A. Referral	1. Support
B. SDI	2. Reaching out
C. Extension	3. Directing
D. Reprography	4. Anticipating

Codes:	A	B	C	D
(a)	3	4	2	1
(b)	4	2	3	1
(c)	1	4	2	3
(d)	2	3	1	4

602. Match the following: (*NET 2014J iii paper*)

List – I
A. Similar activities are grouped
B. Grouping activities into divisions
C. Integration of projects into functional system

D. Control and Supervision through hierarchy of positions

List – II

1. Bureaucratic System
2. Functional System
3. Departmentalisation
4. Matrix structure

Codes:	A	B	C	D
(a)	4	1	2	3
(b)	3	2	4	1
(c)	1	2	3	4
(d)	2	3	4	1

603. Match the following: (*NET 2014J iii paper*)

List – I	List – II
A. Virtua	1. Veeru Technologies (KIIKM)
B. Alice	2. Infotech Consultants Pvt. Ltd.
C. Libsys	3. Softlink, Australia
D. New Genlib	4. VTLS, Virginia

Codes:	A	B	C	D
(a)	1	3	2	4
(b)	2	4	1	3
(c)	4	2	3	1
(d)	4	3	2	1

604. Match the following file formats with the creators: (*NET 2014J iii paper*)

List – I	List – II
A. RTF	1. Sun Micro System
B. PDF	2. Aldus
C. TIFF	3. Microsoft
D. AU	4. Adobe

Codes:	A	B	C	D
(a)	4	3	2	1
(b)	3	4	2	1
(c)	2	3	4	1
(d)	1	2	4	3

605. **Assertion (A):** Social networking tools are very effective for marketing of Library products and services.

Reason (R): They help to reach out the patrons anywhere and at any time. (*NET 2014J iii paper*)

Codes:

(a) Both (A) and (R) are true.
(b) Both (A) and (R) are false.
(c) (A) is true, but (R) is false.
(d) (A) is false, but (R) is true.

606. **Assertion (A):** Information Literacy is a technique and skill known by the information literate for utilizing the wide range of information sources and tools.

Reason (R): It discourages the use of libraries and information centres and makes the patron independent in identifying, locating and using information sources without depending upon an intermediary. (*NET 2014J iii paper*)

Codes:

(a) Both (A) and (R) true.
(b) Both (A) and (R) are false.
(c) (A) is true, but (R) is false.
(d) (A) is false, but (R) is true.

607. **Assertion (A):** Inverse document frequency is the logarithm of the reciprocal of the number of documents in a collection that contains a given term.

Reason (R): Inverse document frequency measure is computed from term frequency and inverse document frequency. (*NET 2014J iii paper*)

Codes:

(a) Both (A) and (R) are true.
(b) Both (A) and (R) are false.
(c) (A) is true, but (R) is false.
(d) (A) is false, but (R) is true.

608. **Assertion (A):** Subject gateways are suitable for all types of users for finding their information.

Reason (R): Subject gateways are developed by subject and computer experts. (*NET 2014J iii paper*)

Codes:

(a) (A) is true, but (R) is false.
(b) (A) is false, but (R) is true.
(c) Both (A) & (R) are true.
(d) Both (A) & (R) are false

609. **Assertion (A):** The principle of canonical sequence states when subjects in an array of subjects are traditionally referred to in a specific sequence, it will be convenient to conform to this traditional sequence.

Reason (R): In classification scheme, the principle of canonical sequence is mainly followed to arrange the array of subjects. (*NET 2014J iii paper*)

Codes:
(a) Both (A) and (R) are true.
(b) (A) is false, but (R) is true.
(c) (A) is true, but (R) is false.
(d) Both (A) and (R) are false.

610. **Assertion (A):** SGML is an international standard that describes the relationship between a document's content and its structure.

Reason (R): Its primary purpose is to facilitate the sharing of data across different information systems particularly via Internet. *(NET 2014J iii paper)*

Codes:
(a) Both (A) and (R) are false.
(b) (A) is true, but (R) is false.
(c) Both (A) and (R) are true.
(d) (A) is false, but (R) is true.

611. **Assertion (A):** In the digital environment, the users expect from the library the ability to connect broad range of information resources in a variety of formats with a single point access.

Reason (R): Libraries already have much of what is required in the digital environment. *(NET 2014J iii paper)*

Codes:
(a) (A) is true, but (R) is false.
(b) Both (A) and (R) are true.
(c) Both (A) and (R) are false.
(d) (A) is false, but (R) is true.

612. **Assertion (A):** The diary technique enables the researcher to keep record of information activities of the users for a specified period of time. *(NET 2014J iii paper)*

Reason (R): The diary technique is the most suitable technique of user studies over other techniques.

Codes:
(a) Both (A) and (R) are false.
(b) (A) is true, but (R) is false.
(c) Both (A) and (R) are true.
(d) (A) is false, but (R) is true.

613. Name the characteristics of information in which the more information we have, the more we use, the more it becomes useful. *(NET 14D iii paper)*
(a) Synergetic Characteristics
(b) Diffusive Characteristics
(c) Compressible Characteristics
(d) Shareable Characteristics

614. "Pro Quest" is_______. *(NET 13 SEPT iii paper)*
(a) Traditional Commercial Publisher
(b) Scholarly Society Publisher
(c) Electronic Aggregator
(d) Publisher of Higher Learning Institutions

615. Identify the correct sequence of elements of communication: *(NET 14D iii paper)*
(a) Channel-Decoder-Destination-Encoder-Message-Source
(b) Decoder-Channel-Destination-Message-Source-Encoder
(c) Source-Encoder-Message-Channel-Decoder-Destination
(d) Encoder-Decoder-Source-Message-Channel-Destination

616. Who advocated the seven basic statistical tools for quality control? *(NET 14D iii paper)*
(a) Joseph Juran (b) Phillip Crosby
(c) Kauro Ishikawa (d) C.A. Cutter

617. LOCKSS (Lots of Copies Keep Stuff Safe) project was launched by: *(NET 14D iii paper)*
(a) Mellon Foundation
(b) Stanford University
(c) University of California
(d) OCLC

618. KOHA is written in which of the following language? *(NET 14D iii paper)*
(a) C, C++ (b) Java
(c) Karel++ (d) Pearl

619. Which of the following is an example of URN? *(NET 14D iii paper)*
(a) URL (b) URI (c) DOI (d) ISBN

620. The CIP (India) Project is an initiation of: *(NET 14D iii paper)*
(a) RRRLF (b) Delhi Public Library
(c) NISCAIR (d) National Library of India

621. Identify the types of OCR technology *(NET 14D iii paper)*
i. Matrix matching
ii. Instructional analysis

iii. Feature extraction
iv. Structural analysis

Codes:

(a) i, ii, iv are true. (b) i, ii, iii are true.
(c) ii, iii, iv are true. (d) i, iii, iv are true.

622. Match the following search techniques with their relevant example:(*NET 14D iii paper*)

List – I	List – II
A. Truncation	1. Wom?n
B. Wild cards	2. Comput*
C. Proximity	3. edu AND biochemistry AND antibodies
D. Field searching	4. "content collection"/5

Codes:	A	B	C	D
(a)	2	3	4	1
(b)	4	3	2	1
(c)	1	2	3	4
(d)	2	1	4	3

623. Which of the following are features of flash memory? (*NET 14D iii paper*)
i. Erasable & Programmable Read Only Memory
ii. Non-volatile memory
iii. Temporary storage unit
iv. Dynamic RAM

Codes:

(a) i, ii, iii are correct. (b) i, ii, iv are correct.
(c) i, ii are correct. (d) ii, iv are correct.

624. SQL is based on which of the following? (*NET 14D iii paper*)
i. Query string ii. Relational algebra
iii. Relational calculus iv. Web search queries

Codes:

(a) i, ii are correct. (b) ii, iii are correct.
(c) iii, iv are correct. (d) ii, iv are correct.

625. Identify the technology of digitization. (*NET 14D iii paper*)
i. Bit-depth ii. Resolution
iii. Manipulation iv. Image enhancement

Codes:

(a) ii, iii, iv are correct.
(b) i, iii, iv are correct.
(c) i, ii, iv are correct.
(d) i, ii, iii are correct.

626. Identify the abilities of an information literate person: (*NET 14D iii paper*)
i. the ability to find information
ii. the ability to prepare bibliographic description of information
iii. the ability to use information
iv. the ability to evaluate information

Codes:

(a) i, ii, iii are correct. (b) i, iii, iv are correct.
(c) i, ii, iv are correct. (d) ii, iii, iv are correct.

627. Which of the following are threats to information security? (*NET 14D iii paper*)
i. Personal firewalls ii. Compromise to IPR
iii. Anti-spyware iv. Acts of espionage

Codes:

(a) i, ii, iii are correct. (b) ii, iii are correct.
(c) ii, iv are correct. (d) ii, iii, iv are correct.

628. Identify the compression protocols: (*NET 14 D iii paper*)
i. TIFF ii. JPEG iii. ZIFF iv. LZW

Codes:

(a) i, iii, iv are correct.
(b) i, ii, iv are correct.
(c) ii, iii, iv are correct.
(d) i, ii, iii are correct.

629. **Assertion (A):** Webliographies are bibliographic tools for print and electronic documents.

Reason (R): Webliography denotes an enumerative list of hypertext links surrounding a common subject following standard citation styles. (*NET 14D iii paper*)

Codes:

(a) (A) is true, but (R) is false.
(b) (A) is false, but (R) is true.
(c) Both (A) and (R) are true.
(d) Both (A) and (R) are false.

630. **Assertion (A):** DOI is the identification system for the intellectual property in the digital environment.

Reason (R): DOI is developed by WIPO. (*NET 14D iii paper*)

Codes:

(a) (A) is true, but (R) is false.
(b) Both (A) and (R) are true.
(c) Both (A) and (R) are false.
(d) (R) is true, but (A) is false.

631. **Assertion (A):** A database can be searched with a query language.

Reason (R): A database can store a large amount of data. (*NET 14D iii paper*)

Codes:
(a) Both (A) and (R) are true, but (R) is not the correct explanation of (A).
(b) Both (A) and (R) are true and (R) is the correct explanation of (A).
(c) (A) is true, but (R) is false.
(d) (A) is false, but (R) is true.

632. **Assertion (A):** To increase accessibility to information for differently abled users we need to accept assistive technologies. *(NET 14D iii paper)*
Reason (R): Information for all.
Codes:
(a) Both (A) and (R) are true, but (R) is not the correct explanation of (A).
(b) Both (A) and (R) are true and (R) is the correct explanation of (A).
(c) (A) is true, but (R) is false.
(d) (A) is false, but (R) is true

633. Arrange the following activities in the order as given by Ellis in his model of information seeking behaviour: *(NET 14 D iii paper)*
i. Browsing ii. Monitoring
iii. Extracting iv. Differentiating
Codes:
(a) ii, i, iv, iii (b) i, iv, ii, iii
(c) iii, ii, i, iv (d) ii, i, iii, iv

634. Match the following: *(NET 14 D iii paper)*

List – I	List – II
A. India	1. Agglomeration
B. Agriculture of wheat	2. Fusion
C. Bio-chemistry	3. Denudation
D. Biological sciences	4. Lamination

Codes:	A	B	C	D
(a)	3	4	2	1
(b)	4	2	3	1
(c)	2	3	1	4
(d)	1	2	4	3

635. Match the following: *(NET 14 D iii paper)*

List – I	List – II
A. HTML	1. Interpretation by web browser
B. XML	2. Describes data
C. UNICODE	3. Display data
D. VB Script	4. Platform independent

Codes:	A	B	C	D
(a)	1	3	2	4
(b)	3	4	1	2
(c)	2	4	1	3
(d)	3	2	4	1

636. Match the following: *(NET 14 D iii paper)*
List – I
A. Semantic differential scale B. Thurston scale
C. Interval scale D. Likert scale
List – II
1. Graded structure
2. Opposition positions
3. Group of Judgement
4. Equal units of measurement

Codes:	A	B	C	D
(a)	4	3	1	2
(b)	1	4	3	2
(c)	3	2	1	4
(d)	2	3	4	1

637. Which RFID component is attached to the Book/item for identification? *(NET 17J iii paper)*
(a) Barcode (b) Antenna
(c) Reader (d) Tag

638. What is RJ45? *(NET 17J iii paper)*
(a) A network cable connector
(b) A node
(c) An electronic coupler
(d) A video display unit

639. SIP, the communication protocol for signalling and controlling multimedia communication stands for *(NET 17J iii paper)*
(a) Signalling Information Protocol
(b) Internet Session Protocol
(c) Sound Initiation Protocol
(d) Session Initiation Protocol

640. VIDWAN (INFLIBNET) is *(NET 17J iii paper)*
(a) an open source software
(b) an Association of Intellectuals
(c) a Programming Language
(d) a Database of Experts and a network of Researchers and Scientists at national level

641. Which of the following are the two sections stated in 'IFLA Digital Reference Guidelines'? *(NET 17J iii paper)*
(i) Collaborative Virtual Reference
(ii) The Administration of Digital Reference Service
(iii) The Practice of Digital Reference
(iv) Online Tools for Libraries

Codes:
(a) (i) and (iii) are correct.
(b) (ii) and (iii) are correct.
(c) (ii) and (iv) are correct.
(d) (i) and (iv) are correct.

642. Which of the following are the components of a master database in acquisition system/ module? *(NET 17J iii paper)*
(i) Membership Master
(ii) Vendor Master
(iii) Currency master
(iv) Transaction master
Codes:
(a) (i) and (ii) are correct.
(b) (i), (ii) and (iv) are correct.
(c) (ii), (iii) and (iv) are correct.
(d) (ii) and (iii) are correct

643. Which of the following databases are available for scientific community free of cost? *(NET 17J iii paper)*
(i) Inspec (ii) ERIC
(iii) IEEE Xplore (iv) PubMed
Codes:
(a) (i) and (ii) are correct.
(b) (i) and (iii) are correct.
(c) (ii) and (iv) are correct.
(d) (ii) and (iv) are correct.

644. Which of the following are protocol standards? *(NET 17J iii paper)*
(i) z39.50 (ii) z39.71
(iii) z39.05 (iv) z39.81
Codes:
(a) (i), (ii), (iii) are correct.
(b) (ii), (iii) and (iv) are correct.
(c) (i), (iii) and (iv) are correct.
(d) (i), (ii) and (iv) are correct.

645. Which of the following are the Semantic Web technologies?
(i) SKOS (ii) AJAX
(iii) SPARQL (iv) UTF
Codes:
(a) (i) and (ii) are correct
(b) (i) and (iii) are correct
(c) (i), (ii) and (iii) are correct
(d) (ii), (iii) and (iv) are correct

646. Which of the following are discrete distributions? *(NET 17J iii paper)*
(i) Beta (ii) Exponential
(iii) Geometric (iv) Poisson
Codes:
(a) (i) and (ii) are correct
(b) (ii) and (iii) are correct
(c) (i) and (iii) are correct
(d) (iii) and (iv) are correct

647. TRAILS-9 is
(i) A process or an assessment tool for real time assessment of Information Literacy Skill of the student-learners.
(ii) A tool or process used by the School Librarians to produce evidence of Library's impact on student achievements to share with stake-holders.
(iii) A tool to adjudge the quality of library services offered, but not to demonstrate the value of the Library's contribution.
(iv) A tool funded by ILILE (Institute for Library & Information Literacy Education) based on Ohio-K12 Library Academic Content Standards.
Codes:
(a) (ii), (iii) and (iv) are correct.
(b) (i), (ii) and (iv) are correct.
(c) (i), (iii) and (iv) are correct.
(d) (i), (ii) and (iii) are correct.

648. Which of the following are the sources to lookup for DOI?
(i) Central Search List
(ii) DOI Handbook
(iii) Registration Agencies
(iv) Search results using a search engine
Codes:
(a) (i) and (ii) are correct
(b) (iii) and (iv) are correct
(c) (i) and (iii) are correct
(d) (i) and (iv) are correct

649. Arrange in sequence the following types of activity according to Ellis's model of information-seeking behaviour:
(i) Browsing (ii) Chaining
(iii) Differentiating (iv) Extracting
Codes:
(a) (i), (ii), (iii), (iv) (b) (ii), (i), (iii), (iv)
(c) (iii), (iv), (ii), (i) (d) (iv), (i), (ii), (iii)

650. Arrange in sequence the following components of Tom Wilson's Expanded Model in sequential order of their occurrence:
(i) Information seeking behaviour
(ii) Context of information need

(iii) Passive attention and search
(iv) Intervening variables

Codes:
(a) (ii), (iv), (i), (iii) (b) (i), (ii), (iv), (iii)
(c) (iii), (ii), (iv), (i) (d) (i), (iii), (ii), (iv)

651. Match the following: *(NET 17J iii paper)*

List – I	List – II
(A) David Ellis	(1) Process
(B) James Krikelas	(2) Complex
(C) Tom Wilson	(3) Descriptive
(D) Alan Foster	(4) Cognitive

Codes:	(A)	(B)	(C)	(D)
(a)	(2)	(3)	(4)	(1)
(b)	(4)	(2)	(1)	(3)
(c)	(3)	(1)	(4)	(2)
(d)	(1)	(4)	(3)	(2)

652. Match the following Library Automation Software Products with their corresponding developers: *(NET 17J iii paper)*

List – I	List – II
(A) Genesis G4	(1) Innovative Interfaces
(B) VERSO	(2) ExLibris
(C) Aleph	(3) Auto Graphics
(D) Millennium	(4) Library Resource Management System

Codes:	(A)	(B)	(C)	(D)
(a)	(4)	(3)	(2)	(1)
(b)	(1)	(2)	(3)	(4)
(c)	(3)	(4)	(2)	(1)
(d)	(2)	(1)	(4)	(3)

653. Match the following Gateways with their corresponding subjects: *(NET 17J iii paper)*

List – I	List – II
(A) AHDS	(1) Urban Design
(B) ALTIS	(2) Forestry Food, Veterinary & Agricultural Sciences
(C) NOVAGate	(3) Hospitality, Leisure, Sports & Tourism
(D) RUDI	(4) Arts and Humanities

Codes:	(A)	(B)	(C)	(D)
(a)	(3)	(1)	(4)	(2)
(b)	(2)	(3)	(4)	(1)
(c)	(4)	(3)	(2)	(1)
(d)	(1)	(2)	(3)	(4)

654. Match the following: *(NET 17J iii paper)*

List – I
(A) Meta-analysis (B) Conceptual analysis
(C) Content analysis (D) Bibliometric analysis

List – II
(1) The most theoretical form of desk research, clarify terms, concepts
(2) To assess the extent to which concepts and issues are mentioned or not
(3) Quantitative methods for describing analysis patterns of recorded communication
(4) Quantitative data by statistical analysis

Codes:	(A)	(B)	(C)	(D)
(a)	(2)	(1)	(4)	(3)
(b)	(3)	(2)	(1)	(4)
(c)	(1)	(4)	(3)	(2)
(d)	(4)	(1)	(2)	(3)

655. Match the following:

List – I
(A) Impact Factor (B) SNIP
(C) Immediacy Factor (D) Cited Half Life

List – II
(1) Cited during the current year
(2) Duration of citations to article in a journal
(3) Cited during the recent two years
(4) Citation based on the number of citations in a field

Codes:	(A)	(B)	(C)	(D)
(a)	(3)	(4)	(1)	(2)
(b)	(1)	(3)	(2)	(4)
(c)	(2)	(1)	(4)	(3)
(d)	(4)	(1)	(2)	(3)

656. Match the type of services suitable for the queries given below: *(NET 17J iii paper)*

List – I
(A) Alert Service
(B) Documentation Service
(C) Retrospective Search Service
(D) Reference Service

List – II
(1) Can I have details of Lok Sabha elections 2009?
(2) Who won Wimbledon Singles in 2015?
(3) Let me Know the forthcoming conferences on Green Libraries?
(4) Let me have a comprehensive list of articles published on genome in 2016.

Codes:	(A)	(B)	(C)	(D)
(a)	(2)	(3)	(1)	(4)
(b)	(4)	(2)	(1)	(3)
(c)	(1)	(4)	(2)	(3)
(d)	(3)	(4)	(1)	(2)

657. Match the following: *(NET 17J iii paper)*

List – I

(A) W.A. Katz (B) B. Guha
(C) S. Seetharama (D) S.R. Ranganathan

List – II

(1) Documentation and Information
(2) Introduction to reference work 2 V.
(3) Documentation and its facets
(4) Information Consolidation and repackaging: Framework, Methodology, Planning

Codes:	**(A)**	**(B)**	**(C)**	**(D)**
(a)	(3)	(2)	(4)	(1)
(b)	(1)	(3)	(2)	(4)
(c)	(2)	(1)	(4)	(3)
(d)	(4)	(2)	(1)	(3)

658. Match the following: *(NET 17J iii paper)*

List – I	List – II
(A) Literary Warrant	(1) Melvil Dewey
(B) Alternative Location	(2) H.E. Bliss
(C) Decimal Fraction Notation	(3) S.R.Ranganathan
(D) Seminal Mnemonics	(4) E.W. Hulme

Codes:	**(A)**	**(B)**	**(C)**	**(D)**
(a)	(4)	(2)	(1)	(3)
(b)	(2)	(1)	(3)	(4)
(c)	(1)	(3)	(2)	(4)
(d)	(3)	(2)	(4)	(1)

659. **Assertion (A):** 'Information Economy' which is based on the premise that, information has economic value and as such requires an 'Information Market Place' in which such value can be exchanged, holds no good in the contemporary information age.

Reason (R): Information as a valuable resource occupies a slum dwelling in the town of economics, as this economic reality runs counter to the popular and historic notion that, "information is free".

(NET 17J iii paper)

Codes:

(a) (A) is true, but (R) is false.
(b) (A) is false, but (R) is true.
(c) Both (A) and (R) are true.
(d) Both (A) and (R) are false.

660. **Assertion (A):** Libraries should serve as a local centre of information and knowledge and be a local gateway to national and global knowledge.

Reason (R): Libraries must modernize their collection, services and collaborate with other institutions to develop a community-based information system.

(NET 17J iii paper)

Codes:

(a) (A) is true, but (R) is false.
(b) (A) is false, but (R) is true.
(c) Both (A) and (R) are true.
(d) Both (A) and (R) are false.

661. **Assertion (A):** Some modern users are quite apprehensive about virtual reference service chat.

Reason (R): They fear negative judgements from librarians and advisors arising from the content of the chat transcript.

(NET 17J iii paper)

Codes:

(a) (A) is true, but (R) is false.
(b) (A) is false, but (R) is true.
(c) Both (A) and (R) are true.
(d) Both (A) and (R) are false.

662. **Assertion (A):** In recent years, the explosion of information in electronic format has placed a significant burden on the small public libraries.

Reason (R): E-resources are expensive, both in licensing cost and in the technology needed to support them to which small public libraries can hardly afford.

(NET 17J iii paper)

Codes:

(a) (A) is true, but (R) is false.
(b) (A) is false, but (R) is true.
(c) Both (A) and (R) are true.
(d) Both (A) and (R) are false.

663. **Assertion (A):** In the digital environment, the university libraries in India need not build their reference collection.

Reason (R): 'Question Point' of OCLC provides a complete virtual reference management system for subscription.

(NET 17J iii paper)

Codes:

(a) (A) is true, but (R) is false.
(b) (A) is false, but (R) is true.
(c) Both (A) and (R) are false.
(d) Both (A) and (R) are true.

664. **Assertion (A):** Libraries market their products and services to overcome the problems

of under-utilization of their information resources and services.

Reason (R): Libraries are under-utilized because they do not provide access to electronic resources. *(NET 17J iii paper)*

Codes:

(a) (A) is true, but (R) is false.
(b) (A) is false, but (R) is true.
(c) Both (A) and (R) are true.
(d) Both (A) and (R) are false.

665. **Assertion (A):** Podcasting, once an obscure method of spreading information, has become a recognised medium for distributing audio contents—be it corporate or for personal use.

Reason (R): Podcasts, though similar to radio programs, are primarily audio files which the listeners can play at their convenience, using devices that have become more common than portable broadcast receivers. *(NET 17J iii paper)*

Codes:

(a) (A) is true, but (R) is false.
(b) (A) is false, but (R) is true.
(c) Both (A) and (R) are true.
(d) Both (A) and (R) are false.

666. **Assertion (A):** Open-ended questions are suitable to glean more and candid information from the respondents seeking on a specific aspect.

Reason (R): Open-ended questions provide an opportunity to go beyond the closed option of 'yes' or 'No' as it enables to express one's own ideas more candidly. *(NET 17J iii paper)*

Codes:

(a) Both (A) and (R) are false.
(b) Both (A) and (R) are true.
(c) (A) is false, but (R) is true.
(d) (A) is true, but (R) is false.

667. **Assertion (A):** Most of the LIS professionals in India are yet to recognise fully the significance of Web-based OPAC services.

Reason (R): Although some libraries in India have started to develop their own websites and portals with enhanced features of Web-based OPACs, but none of these libraries are yet to have their library page and lack federated search facilities. *(NET 17J iii paper)*

Codes:

(a) (A) is true, but (R) is false.
(b) (A) is false, but (R) is true.
(c) Both (A) and (R) are true.
(d) Both (A) and (R) are false.

668. Mode of formation of subject 'Oceanography' is *(NET 15D ii paper)*

(a) Distilization (b) Cluster
(c) Agglomeration (d) Loose Assemblage

669. As per Indian Copyright Law, Copyright is granted for (Literary Work): *(NET 15D ii paper)*

(a) Fifty years after the book is published
(b) Fifty years after the death of the author
(c) Sixty years after the book is published
(d) Sixty years after the death of the author

670. Which layer of 'OSI' Model occurs between 'Network' and 'Physical'? *(NET 15D ii paper)*

(a) Data Link (b) Transport
(c) Session (d) Presentation

671. Lotka's Law relates to: *(NET 15D ii paper)*

(a) Scattering of Periodicals
(b) Obsolescence of Literature
(c) Seepage of Information
(d) Scientific Productivity

672. 'Half-life' in Information Science relates to: *(NET 15D ii paper)*

(a) Rate of obsolescence
(b) Rate of growth
(c) Degree of scatter
(d) Information explosion

673. Which of the following is not an essential feature of a e-book? *(NET 15D ii paper)*

(a) Mostly cost effective
(b) Scope for online purchase
(c) Search information at ease
(d) Access at slow pace

674. A database contains 100 records on a particular topic. A search was conducted and 80 records were retrieved. Of the 80 records retrieved, 60 were relevant. What is the recall? *(NET 15D ii paper)*

(a) 60 (b) 75 (c) 45 (d) 80

675. Number Twenty (20) is represented in binary digit as: *(NET 15D ii paper)*

(a) 00111100 (b) 00001010
(c) 0001110 (d) 00010100

676. Which of the following are the level of problems in communication process identified by Warren Weaver? *(NET 15D ii paper)*
(i) Technical (ii) Semantic
(iii) Effective (iv) Interpreter
Codes:
(a) i, iii, iv correct (b) i, ii, iii correct
(c) ii, iii, iv correct (d) i, ii, iv correct

677. Which of the following are special features of geographical sources? *(NET 15D ii paper)*
(i) Scale (ii) revision
(iii) rpm (iv) projection
Codes:
(a) i and iv are correct
(b) i and ii are correct
(c) iii and iv are correct
(d) i and iii are correct

678. Match the following Intellectual Property Rights Acts of India with the year of their enactment: *(NET 15D ii paper)*

List-I	List-II
(A) The Design Act	(1) 1970
(B) The Copyright Act	(2) 1958
(C) The Trade and Merchandise Mark Act	(3) 1911
(D) The Patents Act	(4) 1957

Codes:	(A)	(B)	(C)	(D)
(a)	(3)	(2)	(4)	(1)
(b)	(1)	(4)	(2)	(3)
(c)	(2)	(3)	(1)	(4)
(d)	(3)	(4)	(2)	(1)

679. **Assertion (A):** Buying e-journals are advantageous to library as librarians do not have to follow up the missing issues

Reason (R): Perpetual access takes care of missing issues. *(NET 15D ii paper)*
Codes:
(a) Both (A) and (R) are true
(b) (A) is true but (R) is false
(c) (A) is false , but (R) is true
(d) Both (A) and (R) are false.

Read the passage given below and answer the questions based on your understanding of the passage (Questions No. 680-684). *(NET 15D ii paper)*

The vital role played by information and communication technologies in the development of digital environment revolutionized the way libraries handle information for centuries. The ICTs offer increased efficiency in terms of time, human resources and cost; improved quality of information, greater flexibility and responsiveness, increased access and sharing, enhanced degree of user interaction to specific information, review and modify the needs as per the situation. More specifically the Internet takes firm roots in information storage, processing and dissemination and provides global access. The users prefer the ease of use, portability, affordability and access to a wide range of subjects on the net over the rule bound library environment. However, on the other hand, electronic environment is not rosy, as it appears to be. The major issue is content organization. The information is poorly structured on the web while libraries have successful methods for information processing and retrieval. The content mapping, semantic web and ontology are under experimental stages for the purpose of effective organization and retrieval of web resources. Hence, users are apparently in need of librarians to assist them to access pertinent and precise information. Therefore it is high time for library professionals to remodel themselves and act as aggregators, and know-ledge managers through web based services tailor-made to the user information requirements. In this context, Six Sigma applications have an immense value.

Service is the ability of an organisation to constantly and consistently exceed the customer's expectations. Improving customer service in libraries involves making a commitment to assess users' needs and developing action plans that implement user friendly processes. LICs are implementing the same through user studies or surveys to ascertain the level of user satisfaction, seek their opinions and suggestions and improve their service base based on the findings. However, they are not documenting the policies, processes, procedures and important tools of these programmes. Further, they don't have a mechanism to identify the latent and dormant users and their needs. This shows that there is a necessity to apply proved management techniques like Six Sigma to analyse the current service programmes and to suggest for their improvement. It is a fact that there is vast difference between the desired and perceived information needs of library users. The traditional metrics have limitations and hence adoption of Six Sigma is useful as it measures quality capability.

680. What is the impact of ICTs on Library and Information Centres?
   (a) All libraries are digitized
   (b) Increased manpower
   (c) Improved Finances
   (d) Enhanced information access and sharing

681. What is the user's preference in networked environment?
   (a) Exhaustive information
   (b) Access to diversified information at ease.
   (c) Cost effective information
   (d) Both (a) and (c)

682. Why do the user needs assistance from librarian to access information on the Web?
   (a) Semantically connected
   (b) Ontologically structured
   (c) Poorly structured
   (d) Inaccurate information

683. What is to be done to improve customer service in Library and Information Centres?
   (a) Assess user needs
   (b) User friendly processes
   (c) Strategic policies
   (d) Both (1) and (2)

684. How Six Sigma does lead to quality service in libraries?
   (a) Assess the quality of service.
   (b) Perceives user needs.
   (c) Suggests tools and techniques to organize data.
   (d) Provides tailor made services.

685. The 'Right to Information Bill' was enacted by the Parliament of India on *(NET 16J ii paper)*
   (a) 5th May 2005 (b) 15th June 2005
   (c) 12th October 2005 (d) 22nd June 2005

686. Which of the following are linear models of communication? *(NET 15D iii paper)*
   (i) Dance's Helical model
   (ii) Lasswell model
   (iii) W. Schramm's Interactive model
   (iv) Becker's Mosaic model
   Codes:
   (a) (i) and (iii) are correct
   (b) (iii) and (iv) are correct
   (c) (ii) and (iii) are correct
   (d) (i) and (iv) are correct

687. What is Dynamic HTML? *(NET 15D iii paper)*
   (a) Asynchronous Web Development Technique
   (b) Collection of technologies to create interactive, animated website
   (c) Dynamic Web Page
   (d) Digital Signal Processor

688. Which one is not used as transmission media for voice/data communication? *(NET 15D iii paper)*
   (a) Copper wire (b) Co-axial cables
   (c) Plastic wire (d) Optic wire

689. Which of the following memories has the shortest access time? *(NET 15D iii paper)*
   (a) Optical Memory (b) Magnetic Core Memory
   (c) RAM (d) Cache Memory

690. Page Maker is an example of: *(NET 15D iii paper)*
   (a) Operating System
   (b) Electronic Spread Sheet
   (c) Geometrical Software
   (d) Publishing Software

691. Which of the following are the parts of a URL (Universal Resource Locator)? *(NET 15D iii paper)*
   (i) Protocol (ii) Media Access Control
   (iii) Domain name (iv) Path
   Codes:
   (a) (i), (ii) and (iii) are correct
   (b) (ii), (iii) and (iv) are correct
   (c) (i), (iii) and (iv) are correct
   (d) (ii) and (iii) are correct

692. Which approach of information is not given by Wersig and Neveling? *(NET 13D ii paper)*
   (a) Structural Approach
   (b) Knowledge Approach
   (c) Meaning Approach
   (d) Technique Approach

693. Identify the service that is made available through Web 3.0 Technologies *(NET 15D iii paper)*

(a) Message Board (b) FOAF
(c) Flikr (d) Mashup

694. Match the following: *(NET 17J iii paper)*

List – I	List – II
(A) Instagram	(1) Facebook
(B) Face Time	(2) Apple
(C) Tumbir	(3) Google
(D) Picasa	(4) Yahoo

Codes:	(A)	(B)	(C)	(D)
(a)	(4)	(1)	(3)	(2)
(b)	(1)	(2)	(4)	(3)
(c)	(2)	(4)	(3)	(1)
(d)	(4)	(2)	(1)	(3)

695. Arrange in sequence the following phases of disaster planning according to guidelines/ principles of IFLA: *(NET 17J iii paper)*
(i) Preparedness (ii) Prevention
(iii) Recovery (iv) Response
Codes:
(a) (i), (ii), (iii), (iv) (b) (ii), (i), (iv), (iii)
(c) (iii), (i), (ii), (iv) (d) (iv), (iii), (ii), (i)

696. Identify from the following the features of tacit knowledge: *(NET 17J iii paper)*
(i) Resides in human mind
(ii) Cannot be articulated
(iii) Tangible
(iv) Easily accessible
Codes:
(a) (i) and (iii) are correct.
(b) (ii) and (iii) are correct.
(c) (i) and (ii) are correct.
(d) (iii) and (iv) are correct

697. **Assertion (A):** An information literate generally has the potential to determine the nature and extent of the information needed.
Reason (R): An information literate can define and articulate the need better than an information illiterate. *(NET 17J iii paper)*
Codes:
(a) (A) is true, but (R) is false.
(b) (A) is false, but (R) is true.
(c) Both (A) and (R) are true.
(d) Both (A) and (R) are false.

698. Match the following *(NET 15D ii paper)*

List-I	List-II
(A) Likert type	(1) Test of significance of the difference between variables
(B) Chi-square	(2) Test of Measurement
(C) ANOVA	(3) Summation Scale
(D) Test of Validity	(4) Test of significance

Codes:	(A)	(B)	(C)	(D)
(a)	(2)	(4)	(1)	(3)
(b)	(3)	(4)	(1)	(2)
(c)	(3)	(2)	(4)	(1)
(d)	(3)	(1)	(2)	(4)

699. Arrange the following in chronological order *(NET 15D ii paper)*
(i) ISBD (ii) MARC (iii) CCF (iv) RDA
Codes:
(a) (i), (iii), (iv), (ii) (b) (ii), (i), (iii), (iv)
(c) (iii), (ii), (i), (iv) (d) (iv), (i), (ii), (iii)

700. **Assertion (A):** Most Information Retrieval (IR) systems that used qualitative research techniques explored information seeking and retrieval behaviour of users. *(NET 15D iii paper)*
Reason (R): The qualitative research methods help to explore human behaviour.
Codes:
(a) Both (A) and (R) are false.
(b) (A) is false and (R) is true.
(c) Both (A) and (R) are true.
(d) (A) is true and (R) is false.

701. **Assertion (A):** FRBR is very important development towards global sharing of information.
Reason (R): FRBR outlines the relationship between many different interpretations or expressions. *(NET 15D iii paper)*
Codes:
(a) Both (A) and (R) are false.
(b) Both (A) and (R) are true.
(c) (A) is true but (R) is false.
(d) (A) is false and (R) is true.

702. **Assertion (A):** Information reflects the synergic combination of medium and message.
Reason (R): There is no difference between conduit and content. *(NET 15D iii paper)*
Codes:
(a) Both (A) and (R) are true.
(b) Both (A) and (R) are false.
(c) (A) is true but (R) is false.
(d) (A) is false but (R) is true.

703. **Assertion (A):** The Library users have easy and more access to information in networked environment than in print environment.

Reason (R): There is no distortion from barriers to communication process in networked environment. (*NET 15D iii paper*)

Codes:

(a) Both (A) and (R) are true.
(b) (A) is true but (R) is false.
(c) Both (A) and (R) are false.
(d) (A) is false but (R) is true.

704. Match the following:

List - I	List - II
(A) F. Rider	(1) FRBR
(B) E.J. Coates	(2) Citation Indexing
(C) IFLA	(3) International classification
(D) Eugene Garfield	(4) BTI Indexing

Codes:	(A)	(B)	(C)	(D)
(a)	(3)	(4)	(1)	(2)
(b)	(4)	(1)	(2)	(3)
(c)	(1)	(2)	(3)	(4)
(d)	(2)	(3)	(4)	(1)

705. Match the following:

List - I

(A) Protocols (B) Device Drivers
(C) Node (D) Transmission Media

List - II

(1) Work station
(2) Electronics/Radio Signals
(3) Manages Network Services
(4) Languages that allow computers to communicate

Codes:	(A)	(B)	(C)	(D)
(a)	(4)	(3)	(1)	(2)
(b)	(3)	(4)	(2)	(1)
(c)	(1)	(2)	(4)	(3)
(d)	(2)	(1)	(3)	(4)

706. Match the following:

List - I	List - II
(A) Bus	(1) Nodes connected to hub
(B) Star	(2) Each node connects to every other
(C) Ring	(3) Nodes connected to back bone
(D) Mesh	(4) Each node connected to the next

Codes:	(A)	(B)	(C)	(D)
(a)	(4)	(2)	(3)	(1)
(b)	(3)	(1)	(2)	(4)
(c)	(3)	(1)	(4)	(2)
(d)	(1)	(4)	(2)	(3)

707. Match the following organizations with their contribution to information literacy:

List - I

(A) CILIP (B) SCONUL
(C) ACRL (D) IFLA

List - II

(1) Information Literacy Model of Eight Competencies
(2) Guidelines for Information Literacy for Life Long Learning
(3) Information Literacy Competency Standards for Higher Education
(4) Seven Pillars of Information Literacy

Codes:	(A)	(B)	(C)	(D)
(a)	(3)	(4)	(1)	(2)
(b)	(1)	(4)	(3)	(2)
(c)	(2)	(4)	(1)	(3)
(d)	(2)	(4)	(3)	(1)

708. Match the following Information Seeking Behaviour models with corresponding theories:

List - I

(A) Wilson Model of ISB
(B) Derrin's Model of ISB
(C) Kuhlthous Model of ISB
(D) Marchioninis ISB Model

List - II

(1) Tailored to Electronic Environment—the process consists of eight sub-processes.
(2) Association of feelings, thoughts and actions but not cognitive.
(3) Sense making approach-based on situation, gap and outcome-three key elements.
(4) Three fold view on information seeking context information source

Codes:	(A)	(B)	(C)	(D)
(a)	(4)	(3)	(2)	(1)
(b)	(3)	(2)	(1)	(4)
(c)	(1)	(3)	(4)	(2)
(d)	(2)	(4)	(3)	(1)

709. The term "Information Iceberg"? (*Net 2018 J*)

(a) 1/3 Non-Visible and 2/3 Visible
(b) 1/3 Visible and 2/3 Non-Visible
(c) ¼ Non-Visible and ¾ Visible
(d) ¼ Visible and ¾ Non-Visible

710. Ezproxy is a product of

(a) UTLAS (b) OCLC
(c) RLIN (d) Library of Congress

711. Which of the following is not a classical model of information retrieval?
(a) Boolean (b) Cluster
(c) Probabilistic (d) Vector-space

712. Who criticized the concept of main entry as a relic of outdated technology
(a) Michael Gorman (b) Robert L. Maxwell
(c) Pat Oddy (d) Tom Delsey

713. Ambra an innovative open source of platform (for publishing open access resources articles) is developed by
(a) OCLC (b) DOAJ (c) PLOS (d) WDL

714. The term Weblog was coined by
(a) E. Williams (b) Jack Dorsey
(c) Jorn Barger (d) Peter Merholz

715. Which of the following is not file hosting service?
(a) One Drive (b) Google Drive
(c) Live Drive (d) Xbox Live

716. VuFind is the tool used for
(a) Library Automation
(b) Digital Library System
(c) Library Resource Discovery System
(d) Institutional Repository

717. Which one is correct Binary Number for Decimal 115
(a) 1100011 (b) 1010111
(c) 1111111 (d) 1110011

718. A probability which is not associated with the occurrence of an event is expressed as a number between
(a) +1 and -1 (b) 1 and <1
(c) -1 and 0 (d) 0 and 1

719. Wersig and Neveling gave which of the following approaches for defining information?
(i) The Action approach
(ii) The Message Approach
(iii) The Process Approach
(iv) The Structural Approach
Codes:
(a) i, ii, and iii are correct
(b) ii, iii, iv are correct
(c) i, iii, iv are correct
(d) i, ii, iv are correct

720. Which of the following are the features of Classic IR Model?
(i) documents are represented by index term
(ii) all terms are equally useful
(iii) Index term cannot be weighted
(iv) there is an assumption that terms are mutually independent
Codes:
(a) i and ii are correct
(b) iii and iv are correct
(c) i and iii are correct
(d) i and iv are correct

721. Identify the components of 'LAMP' given below
(i) Linux (ii) Acrobat
(iii) MYSQL (iv) Pearl
Codes:
(a) ii and iii are correct
(b) i and iii are correct
(c) i and iv are correct
(d) ii and iv are correct

722. Identify the features of proprietary software
(i) Continuity and Development
(ii) Ease to use
(iii) Transparency
(iv) Documentation and support
Codes:
(a) i, ii and iv are correct
(b) ii, iii and iv are correct
(c) i, ii and iii are correct
(d) i, iii and iv are correct

723. Information seeking behaviour (ISB) essentially refers to and concerned with
(i) De-recognition of some needs perceived by the user.
(ii) The strategies and actions undertaken to locate discreate knowledge elements.
(iii) The experiment conducted on usefulness of library collection with reference to a non-purposive and conscious need of a particular piece of information.
(iv) Interactive utilization of three basic resources such as people, information system.
Codes:
(a) (i) and (ii) are correct
(b) (iii) and (iv) are correct
(c) (i), and (iii are correct
(d) (ii), and (iv) are correct

724. A virtual library:
(i) presupposes a physical existence
(ii) Collection of resources available on one or more computer systems with a single interface or entry point to the collection
(iii) Does not provide access to entire content of a (digital) library via internet
(iv) Provides user assistance services such as reference, interlibrary loan, etc.
Codes:
(a) (i) and (ii) are correct
(b) (ii) and (iii) are correct
(c) (ii), and (iv) are correct
(d) (i), and (iii) are correct

725. The web address that acts as permanent identifier is _________.
(A) URL (B) DOI (C) PURL (D) UDI

726. Match the following popular social networking sites with their corresponding founders:

List-I	List-II
(A) Blog	(i) Tim Vanderhook and Justin Timberlake
(B) Wikis	(ii) Google
(C) LinkedIn	(iii) World Cunningham
(D) Myspace	(iv) Reid Hoffman and his friends

Codes:	(A)	(B)	(C)	(D)
(a)	(ii)	(iii)	(iv)	(i)
(b)	(i)	(ii)	(iii)	(iv)
(c)	(iv)	(iii)	(ii)	(i)
(d)	(iii)	(i)	(iv)	(ii)

727. Match the following

List-I	List-II
(A) Chester Carlton	(i) e-Book
(B) Brewstu Kable	(ii) Xerox Copier
(C) Michael S. Hart	(iii) NDLTD
(D) Edward Fox	(iv) Internet Archive

Codes:	(A)	(B)	(C)	(D)
(a)	(ii)	(iv)	(i)	(iii)
(b)	(iv)	(iii)	(ii)	(i)
(c)	(iv)	(i)	(iii)	(ii)
(d)	(i)	(ii)	(iii)	(iv)

728. Match the following:
List-I (Term)
(A) Data mart (B) Data silo
(C) Data warehouse (D) Data mining
List-II (Explanation)
(i) Specific analytic technique that examining that large pre-Existing database in order to generate new information.
(ii) System that integrate date from databases across an Entire enterprise, used to guide decisions.
(iii) Is a lower cost scaled-down version of a data warehouse that can be implemented in a much shorter time.
(iv) Stand alone data stores available for specific function.

Codes:	(A)	(B)	(C)	(D)
(a)	(ii)	(iv)	(i)	(iii)
(b)	(i)	(iii)	(iv)	(ii)
(c)	(iv)	(iii)	(i)	(ii)
(d)	(iii)	(iv)	(ii)	(i)

729. Match the following terms with their corresponding descriptor

List-I	List-II
(A) Term list	(i) Ontologies
(B) Categories	(ii) System Software
(C) Relationship list	(iii) Taxonomy
(D) Emulators	(iv) Glossaries

Codes:	(A)	(B)	(C)	(D)
(a)	(ii)	(iii)	(iv)	(i)
(b)	(iii)	(ii)	(i)	(iv)
(c)	(iv)	(i)	(ii)	(iii)
(d)	(iv)	(iii)	(i)	(ii)

730. Match the following communication concepts with corresponding explanations:
List-I
(A) Kinesics communication
(B) Haptics communication
(C) Proxemics communication
(D) Iconic communication
List-II
(i) Use of touch to communication
(ii) Use interpersonal space
(iii) Facial Expression, gestures, eye movement
(iv) Interpretation of symbolism

Codes:	(A)	(B)	(C)	(D)
(a)	(i)	(iii)	(ii)	(iv)
(b)	(iii)	(iv)	(ii)	(i)
(c)	(ii)	(iii)	(i)	(iv)
(d)	(iii)	(i)	(ii)	(iv)

731. Arrange the following Information source according to their first year of publication

(a) Ulrich's International Periodical Directory
(b) Guide of Indian Periodical Literature
(c) Library literature
(d) Indian Science Abstract

Codes:
(a) (i), (iii), (ii), (iv) (b) (ii), (iii), (iv), (i)
(c) (iii), (i), (ii), (iv) (d) (iv), (i), (ii), (iii)

732. Arrange the following entities according to FRBR Model
(i) Item (ii) Expression
(iii) Work (iv) Manifestation

Codes:
(a) iii, ii, iv, i (b) iv, i, ii, iii
(c) iii, iv, i, ii (d) iii, i, ii, iv

733. Which of the following are the features of Vector Space Model IR?
(i) Complex model based on non linear algebra
(ii) Term weights are not binary
(iii) Allows computing a continuous degree of similarity between queries and documents
(iv) Do not allow ranking documents according to their possible relevance

Codes:
(a) i and ii are correct
(b) ii and iii are correct
(c) iii and iv are correct
(d) i and iv are correct

734. Arrange the following work components of WINISIS according to the order of sequence of approach
(i) FST (ii) FDT
(iii) Print format (iv) Worksheet

Codes:
(a) ii, iv, iii, i (b) ii, iii, iv, i
(c) i, ii, iii, iv (d) iv, iii, ii, i

735. Arrange the following according to their year of origin
(i) Myspase (ii) MOSAIC
(iii) Friendster (iv) Blogger

Codes:
(a) ii, iii, i, iv (b) i, iv, iii, ii
(c) ii, iv, iii, i (d) iv, ii, iii, i

736. Arranges the filters as proposed by Robert S. Tylor that may be employed by the librarian to approximate the higher information needs of individuals
(i) Personal characteristics of the inquirer
(ii) Relationship of inquiry description to file organisation
(iii) Objective and motivation
(iv) Determination of the subject

Codes:
(a) iii, i, ii, iv (b) iv, iii, i, ii
(c) i, iii, ii, iv (d) iv, ii, i, iii

737. **Assertion (A):** Information, not data, is the fundamental fuel of the current Big Data Phenomenon

Reason (R): The reason behind the quick expansion of Big Data is the extensive degree to which date are created, shared and utilised in recent times

Codes:
(a) (A) is false but (R) is true
(b) (R) is false but (A) is true
(c) Both (A) and (R) false
(d) Both(A) and (R) true

738. **Assertion (A):** Preprint archives, such as arxiv and SSRN rapidly achieved prominence in the field of scholarly communication.

Reason (R): These archives contain Preprint along with DOI.

Codes:
(a) Both (A) and (R) are true
(b) Both (A) and (R) are false
(c) (A) is false, but (R) are true
(d) (A) is true but (R) is false

739. **Assertion (A):** There has been a demand for data exchange between library catalogues and databases with records of documentary information.

Reason (R): Interoperability leads to information reuse as a requisite to access data, and take into account quality, contents, knowledge, products and services

Codes:
(a) Both (A) and (R) are true
(b) Both (A) and (R) are false
(c) (A) is true, but (R) is false
(d) (A) is false but (R) is true

740. **Assertion (A):** In the Information Retrieval domain, Probabilistic Model is becoming unpopular.

Reason (R): Probabilistic Model fails to provide accurate estimate for the first run probabilities since index terms are not weighted and terms are assumed mutually independent.

Codes:
(a) (A) is true but (R) is false
(b) Both (A) and (R) are true
(c) (A) is false, but (R) is true
(d) both (A) and (R) is false

741. **Assertion (A):** System effectiveness may be evident while evaluating an IR system but cost effectiveness may not be satisfactory

Reason (R): A cost effectiveness study of an IR system is the evaluation in terms of how to satisfy the users information requirements in the most efficient and economical way.

Codes:
(a) (A) is false but (R) are true
(b) (A) is true but (R) is false
(c) both (A) and (R) are true
(d) Both (A) and (R) are false

742. **Assertion (A):** TREC is credited for bringing the concept of the evaluation of IR system.

Reason (R): TREC series of IR experiment has drawn attention of the LIS professionals all over the world for providing an open testing event standard evaluation

Codes:
(a) Both (A) and (R) are false
(b) Both (A) and (R) are true
(c) (A) is false, but (R) is true
(d) (A) is true but (R) is false

743. **Assertion (A):** Netiquette mandates that you do your best to act within the laws of cyberspace and society.

Reason (R): Failing to respect others privacy and impolite way of communication in considered breach of Netiquette.

Codes:
(a) Both (A) and (R) are false
(b) Both (A) and (R) are true
(c) (A) is true, but (R) is false
(d) (A) is false but (R) is true.

744. **Assertion (A):** In recent times, it is easier to copy, and paste the contents from a digital document for which people knowingly avoided to credit the sources. Increases access to digital documents has provided a means for increase of plagiarism.

Reason (R): Software assisted detection tools like iThenticate, Turnitin etc. now allow vast collection of online documents to be compared to each other making successful detection of plagiarism

Codes:
(a) both (A) and (R) are false
(b) (A) true but (R) is false
(c) (R) is true but (A) is false
(d) Both (A) and (R) are true

Read the following passage carefully and answer the question based on your understanding (Q. 745-749)

In the agentic sociocogntive view, people are self-organizing, proactive, self-reflecting, and self-regulating, not just reactive organisms shaped and shepherded by external events. People have the power to influence their own action to produce certain results. The capacity to exercise control over ones thought processes, motivation, affect and action operates through mechanisms of personal agency. Human agency has been conceptualized in at least three different ways as either autonomous agency, mechanically reactive agency or emergent interactive agency. The notion that humans operate as entirely independent agents as few serious advocates, although it is sometimes invoked in caricatures of cognitive theories of human behaviour.

The tools for the exercise of agency are derived, in large part, from experiences but what is created by their generative use is not reducible to those experiences. Human action, being socially situated, is the product of a dynamic interplay of personal and situational influences.

A second approach to the self-system is to construe it as mechanically reactive agency. It is an internal system through which external influences operates mechanistically on action, but individuals exert no motivate, self- reflective, self-reactive, creative or directive influence on the process. The self-system is merely a repository for implanted structures and a conduct for external influences. The more dynamic model operating holistically include multilevel neural networks. However, a diverse mix of parallel distributed neural activity cannot remain fragmented. It requires an integratve system. Given the proactive nature of human functioning, such a system must have agentic capabilities as well as integrative reactive ones. Agentic functions get lodged in a hidden network operating without any consciousness. Consciousness is the very substance of phenomenal and functional mental life. It provides the information base for thinking about events, planning, constricting courses of action and reflecting on the adequacy of in thinking and factions. There is an important difference between being conscious of the experience one is undergoing, and consciously producing given experiences. For example, consciousness of one's heart rate and consciously and intentionally doing things known to elevate one's heart rate illustrate the difference between passive undergoing and agentic doing.

The purposive accessing and deliberative processing of information of fashion efficacious course of action represent the fictional consciousness. Consciousness cannot have reduced to an epiphenomenon of the output of a mental process realized mechanically at nonconscious lower levels. In the connectionist line of theorizing, sensory organs deliver up information through their diverse pathways to the hidden network acting as the cognitive agent that does constructing, planning, motivating and regulating. However, stripped of consciousness and agentic capability of decision and action, people are mere automatons undergoing action devoid of any subjectivity, conscious regulation, phenomenological life, or personal identity.

745. In the agentic socio-cognitive view "human action" is the product of
   (a) A dynamic interplay of personal and situational influence
   (b) personal determinants and mechanisms of human functioning
   (c) Social bespoke and practices
   (d) Schematic processing of experiences and memory representation

746. Why the second approach to the self-system is construed by the author as "mechanically reactive agency"?
   (a) An external system through which internal influences operate mechanically.
   (b) An internal system through which external influence operates mechanically on action having no directive influence exerted by the individuals on process.
   (c) An external system through which external influences operate mechanically on action.
   (d) An external system through which external influences operate in which individuals exert direct influences on the process.

747. According to the agentic view of "Personality" what does the 'self-system 'meant to the author
   (a) A repository for implanted structures and a conduit for internal influences.
   (b) A repository for implanted structures and conduit for external influences.
   (c) An archive for preserving unusual human instincts.
   (d) A pen-stock to restrict the flow of unusual and instant human behaviour

748. What does 'consciousness' conceptually meant to the author?
   (a) A demonstration of physical condition based on situation
   (b) The very substance of phenomenal and functional mental life
   (c) The rigid state of mental condition.
   (d) A spiritual state of mind

749. How does the author differentiate between "passive undergoing" and agentic doing?
   (a) Conscious of the experiences one is undergoing and consciously producing given experiences.
   (b) Conscious of the experiences one is undergoing but fail to use the given experiences.
   (c) Conscious of the past experiences and their wrongful use irrelevant to need.
   (d) Unconscious of the experiences and their non-international

ANSWER SHEET

1. (c)	2. (b)	3. (a)	4. (b)	5. (a)	6. (b)	7. (d)	8. (a)	9. (b)
10. (c)	11. (b)	12. (a)	13. (b)	14. (d)	15. (b)	16. (a)	17. (d)	18. (a)
19. (b)	20. (a)	21. (a)	22. (c)	23. (b)	24. (c)	25. (c)	26. (a)	27. (d)
28. (d)	29. (a)	30. (c)	31. (c)	32. (c)	33. (a)	34. (d)	35. (d)	36. (b)

37. (c) 38. (a) 39. (a) 40. (b) 41. (a) 42. (a) 43. (b) 44. (b) 45. (c)
46. (d) 47. (d) 48. (b) 49. (a) 50. (d) 51. (c) 52. (b) 53. (a) 54. (c)
55. (b) 56. (b) 57. (d) 58. (b) 59. (c) 60. (c) 61. (a) 62. (b) 63. (b)
64. (c) 65. (a) 66. (a) 67. (c) 68. (c) 69. (a) 70. (d) 71. (a) 72. (b)
73. (a) 74. (a) 75. (a) 76. (c) 77. (a) 78. (b) 79. (a) 80. (b) 81. (a)
82. (a) 83. (a) 84. (d) 85. (b) 86. (a) 87. (b) 88. (a) 89. (d) 90. (c)
91. (d) 92. (a) 93. (d) 94. (b) 95. (a) 96. (a) 97. (a) 98. (a) 99. (a)
100. (a) 101. (a) 102. (a) 103. (a) 104. (a) 105. (a) 106. (a) 107. (a) 108. (b)
109. (b) 110. (b) 111. (d) 112. (d) 113. (d) 114. (a) 115. (d) 116. (b) 117. (a)
118. (c) 119. (a) 120. (a) 121. (d) 122. (c) 123. (c) 124. (a) 125. (d) 126. (b)
127. (b) 128. (d) 129. (a) 130. (a) 131. (c) 132. (c) 133. (d) 134. (b) 135. (d)
136. (c) 137. (b) 138. (b) 139. (a) 140. (a) 141. (a) 142. (b) 143. (b) 144. (d)
145. (b) 146. (b) 147. (d) 148. (c) 149. (b) 150. (d) 151. (d) 152. (a) 153. (a)
154. (b) 155. (b) 156. (a) 157. (a) 158. (b) 159. (a) 160. (a) 161. (a) 162. (a)
163. (c) 164. (d) 165. (c) 166. (b) 167. (d) 168. (b) 169. (a) 170. (d) 171. (c)
172. (a) 173. (b) 174. (b) 175. (a) 176. (d) 177. (b) 178. (b) 179. (d) 180. (b)
181. (a) 182. (a) 183. (b) 184. (b) 185. (a) 186. (d) 187. (a) 188. (b) 189. (d)
190. (a) 191. (a) 192. (a) 193. (d) 194. (c) 195. (a) 196. (c) 197. (b) 198. (c)
199. (d) 200. (a) 201. (d) 202. (c) 203. (b) 204. (c) 205. (c) 206. (d) 207. (d)
208. (b) 209. (a) 210. (b) 211. (b) 212. (d) 213. (c) 214. (b) 215. (d) 216. (b)
217. (a) 218. (b) 219. (d) 220. (c) 221. (a) 222. (b) 223. (d) 224. (b) 225. (a)
226. (d) 227. (d) 228. (b) 229. (c) 230. (c) 231. (c) 232. (b) 233. (c) 234. (b)
235. (b) 236. (d) 237. (d) 238. (b) 239. (b) 240. (a) 241. (d) 242. (b) 243. (b)
244. (b) 245. (b) 246. (d) 247. (c) 248. (d) 249. (b) 250. (a) 251. (a) 252. (a)
253. (d) 254. (a) 255. (a) 256. (d) 257. (d) 258. (c) 259. (a) 260. (d) 261. (c)
262. (d) 263. (c) 264. (b) 265. (a) 266. (b) 267. (b) 268. (c) 269. (c) 270. (d)
271. (c) 272. (c) 273. (a) 274. (a) 275. (c) 276. (a) 277. (b) 278. (d) 279. (b)
280. (c) 281. (b) 282. (a) 283. (d) 284. (b) 285. (c) 286. (b) 287. (c) 288. (b)
289. (c) 290. (a) 291. (a) 292. (c) 293. (d) 294. (a) 295. (b) 296. (c) 297. (d)
298. (b) 299. (b) 300. (c) 301. (a) 302. (d) 303. (c) 304. (C) 305. (c) 306. (d)
307. (c) 308. (b) 309. (d) 310. (a) 311. (a) 312 (a) 313. (a) 314. (c) 315. (d)
316. (a) 317. (d) 318. (c) 319. (b) 320. (c) 321. (b) 322. (c) 323. (d) 324. (c)
325. (a) 326. (d) 327. (b) 328. (a) 329. (c) 330. (a) 331. (c) 332. (d) 333. (c)
334. (b) 335. (c) 336. (c) 337. (d) 338. (b) 339. (c) 340. (b) 341. (d) 342. (b)
343. (c) 344. (a) 345. (b) 346. (a) 347. (b) 348. (b) 349. (a) 350. (a) 351. (c)
352. (a) 353. (b) 354. (c) 355. (c) 356. (c) 357. (c) 358. (b) 359. (b) 360. (d)
361. (a) 362. (c) 363. (a) 364. (c) 365. (c) 366. (a) 367. (d) 368. (c) 369. (d)
370. (d) 371. (d) 372. (b) 373. (c) 374. (d) 375. (d) 376. (a) 377. (c) 378. (d)
379. (b) 380. (b) 381. (a) 382. (b) 383. (b) 384. (a) 385. (b) 386. (c) 387. (d)
388. (a) 389. (b) 390. (c) 391. (d) 392.(b) 393. (c) 394. (a) 395. (a) 396. (a)
397. (d) 398. (c) 399. (a) 400. (c) 401. (a) 402. (c) 403. (a) 404. (a) 405. (b)
406. (c) 407. (b) 408. (d) 409. (a) 410. (c) 411. (a) 412. (a) 413. (c) 414. (a)
415. (d) 416. (a) 417. (a) 418. (c) 419. (b) 420. (c) 421. (c) 422. (a) 423. (a)

424. (c)	425. (d)	426. (b)	427. (d)	428. (a)	429. (d)	430. (c)	431. (a)	432. (d)
433. (d)	434. (b)	435. (a)	436. (d)	437. (a)	438. (a)	439. (c)	440. (a)	441. (b)
442. (b)	443. (a)	444. (a)	445. (a)	446. (c)	447. (a)	448. (d)	449. (a)	450. (d)
451. (a)	452. (d)	453. (d)	454. (a)	455. (b)	456. (c)	457. (c)	458. (c)	459. (a)
460. (a)	461. (b)	462. (b)	463. (b)	464. (c)	465. (b)	466. (b)	467. (d)	468. (b)
469. (b)	470. (d)	471. (c)	472. (c)	473. (d)	474. (c)	475. (a)	476. (b)	477 (d)
478. (a)	479. (b)	480. (d)	481. (a)	482. (c)	483. (c)	484. (a)	485. (b)	486. (b)
487. (c)	488. (d)	489. (a)	490. (c)	491. (d)	492. (c)	493. (d)	494. (c)	495. (d)
496. (a)	497. (d)	498. (c)	499. (d)	500. (d)	501. (a)	502. (b)	503. (a)	504. (c)
505. (b)	506. (a)	507. (b)	508. (c)	509. (a)	510. (a)	511. (d)	512. (d)	513. (b)
514. (c)	515. (d)	516. (b)	517. (b)	518. (d)	519. (c)	520. (d)	521. (a)	522. (c)
523. (d)	524. (b)	525. (d)	526. (d)	527. (b)	528. (a)	529. (a)	530. (b)	531. (c)
532. (a)	533. (a)	534. (d)	535. (a)	536. (a)	537. (a)	538. (a)	539. (b)	540. (c)
541. (c)	542. (a)	543. (a)	544. (a)	545. (d)	546. (a)	547. (d)	548. (b)	549. (c)
550. (d)	551. (c)	552. (a)	553. (d)	554. (d)	555. (b)	556. (a)	557. (c)	558. (d)
559. (a)	560. (c)	561. (a)	562. (a)	563. (b)	564. (c)	565. (b)	566. (a)	567. (b)
568. (c)	569. (b)	570. (a)	571. (b)	572. (a)	573. (b)	574. (c)	575. (d)	576. (a)
577. (b)	578. (d)	579. (c)	580. (a)	581. (d)	582. (b)	583. (d)	584. (c)	585. (c)
586. (a)	587. (b)	588. (c)	589. (c)	590. (b)	591. (d)	592. (c)	593. (d)	594. (b)
595. (d)	596. (a)	597. (b)	598. (a)	599. (c)	600. (a)	601. (a)	602. (d)	603. (d)
604. (b)	605. (a)	606. (c)	607. (a)	608. (b)	609. (a)	610. (b)	611. (a)	612. (b)
613. (a)	614. (c)	615. (c)	616. (c)	617. (b)	618. (d)	619. (d)	620. (a)	621. (d)
622. (d)	623. (c)	624.(b)	625. (c)	626. (b)	627. (c)	628. (b)	629. (b)	630. (a)
631. (a)	632. (b)	633. (b)	634. (a)	635. (d)	636. (d)	637. (d)	638. (a)	639. (d)
640. (d)	641. (b)	642. (d)	643. (c)	644. (d)	645. (b)	646. (d)	647. (b)	648. (b)
649. (b)	650. (a)	651. (c)	652. (a)	653. (c)	654. (d)	655. (a)	656. (d)	657. (c)
658. (a)	659. (c)	660. (c)	661. (c)	662. (c)	663. (b)	664. (a)	665. (c)	666. (b)
667. (a)	668. (b)	669. (d)	670. (a)	671. (d)	672. (a)	673. (d)	674. (a)	675. (d)
676. (b)	677. (a)	678. (d)	679. (b)	680. (d)	681. (b)	682. (c)	683. (d)	684. (a)
685. (b)	686. (c)	687. (b)	688. (c)	689. (d)	690. (d)	691. (c)	692. (d)	693. (b)
694. (b)	695. (b)	696. (c)	697. (c)	698. (b)	699. (b)	700. (c)	701. (b)	702. (c)
703. (b)	704. (a)	705. (a)	706. (c)	707. (b)	708. (a)	709. (d)	710. (b)	711. (b)
712. (a)	713. (c)	714. (c)	715. (d)	716. (c)	717. (d)	718. (d)	719. (b)	720. (d)
721. (b)	722. (a)	723. (d)	724. (c)	725. (c)	726. (a)	727. (a)	728. (d)	729. (d)
730. (d)	731. (a)	732. (a)	733. (b)	734. (a)	735. (c)	736. (b)	737. (d)	738. (d)
739. (a)	740. (b)	741. (c)	742. (c)	743. (b)	744. (d)	745. (a)	746. (b)	747. (b)
748. (b)	749. (a)							

Chapter 9
Library Management

SUBJECTIVE QUESTIONS

Q. 1. Write the name of Pioneer of Open Access System (British Libraries).

Ans. James Duff Brown.

Q. 2. Who started Browne Charging System and when?

Ans. Miss Nina E. Browne in 1895.

Q. 3. Who started New York Charging System?

Ans. John Cotton Dana; in the year 1900 in Public Library of New York (USA).

Q. 4. Write three Card System introduced by Dr. S.R. Ranganathan.

Ans. Three Card System introduced by S.R. Ranganathan are:
(i) Register Card (ii) Check Card
(iii) Classified Index Card.

Q. 5. Who introduced the Electrically operated book charging system first?

Ans. The Gaylord Brother introduced the electrically operated book charging system in 1932 first.

Q. 6. Write the modern management used techniques.

Ans. Modern management used techniques are Operation Research, Programme Evaluation and Review Technique (PERT) and Critical Path Method (CPM), System analysis and others for improving quality.

Q. 7. Enumerate the eight principles for creating structural pattern of organisation for a large library.

Ans. The eight principles are:
(i) Span of Management
(ii) Scalar Principle and Vertical Hierarchy
(iii) Unity of Command
(iv) Delegation of authority and responsibility
(v) Line and Staff position
(vi) Functional Authority
(vii) Coordination and integration
(viii) Centralisation and decentralisation.

Q. 8. How many types of periodical display racks are there?

Ans. Pigeon Hole type, Step type, Inclined type.

Q. 9. What is the standard height of the Kardex?

Ans. The standard size of the Kardex is 10 cm × 15 cm, one tray can hold 50 cards.

Q. 10. Write the new name of Indian Standard Institution.

Ans. Bureau of Indian Standards.

Q. 11. Write the standard specification for library furniture and fittings.

Ans. Part-I—Timber IS: 1829 (pt-1)—1961. This covered only times of furniture and was revised in 1978.
"Specification for Library furniture and fittings Part-II Steel IS: 1829 (pt-II)—1977."

Q. 12. In how many parts can government documents be broadly divided?

Ans. (i) Parliamentary documents
(ii) Non-parliamentary documents.

Q. 13. Write the basic principles of book selection of some scholars.

Ans. 1. According to the Drury (1930) "To provide the right book to the right reader at right time."
2. According to the Dewey "The best reading for the largest number and least cost."
3. According to the S.R. Ranganathan "1st three laws of the library science are helpful in formulating the principles of document selection."
4. According to the Mc Colvin "Demand for books should determine the policy of collection building."

Q. 14. How many columns are there in the Accession Register? (*C.S. Exam.* 99)

Ans. 14 columns are there in the Accession Register.

Q. 15. At how many places call no. assigned to a document should be written?

Ans. The call no. assigned to a document should be written legibly at three places on the document: (1) On the verso of the title page; (2) On the date label; and (3) On the book tag.

Q. 16. Which books needs full leather binding?

Ans. Usually reference books such as encyclopedias, dictionaries and atlases, etc. need full leather binding.

Q. 17. Which books need half leather binding?

Ans. Periodicals and magazines need half leather binding.

Q. 18. List different kinds of library bindings.

Ans. (a) Casing and paperback
(b) Reinforced binding
(c) Specialised binding for different categories of documents in the library
(d) Full/half leather binding
(e) Full/half cloth binding
(f) Perfect binding for cheap books
(g) Plastic covering for books.

Q. 19. Explain the financial management in a library.

Ans. Financial management is the study of Principles and Practices involved in financial operation in Library. Its scope includes acquisition, distribution and utilisation of fund, balancing revenue and expenditure, general control and evaluation of financial matters.

Q. 20. State the principles that govern the financial management.

Ans. The principles that govern the financial management are:
(i) Effective control (ii) Simplicity
(iii) Regularity and farsightedness
(iv) Economy and (v) Flexibility.

Q. 21. What are the enemies of the library?

Ans. Fire, human beings, water and vermin.

Q. 22. Write the other name for book end.

Ans. Book Support.

Q. 23. Define the 'subscription books' according to S.R. Ranganathan.

Ans. Books for which advance payment is to be made in full or part before their actual publication.

Q. 24. Write the acronym of POSDCORB.

Ans. Planning, Organisation, Staffing, Directing, Co-ordinating, Reporting and Budgeting.

Q. 25. Write the three methods of preparing a library budget.

Ans. (a) On the basis of expenditure of last year
(b) On the basis of work programme of the library
(c) On the basis of authoritative and standard principles.

Q. 26. What is atmospheric condition for the storing of library materials?

Ans. Temperature between 22°-25° relative humidity between 45% to 55% constitute the most suitable condition for storing of library materials.

Q. 27. What is the Indian standard for reinforced binding of library books?

Ans. IS: 3050-1962.

Q. 28. Which country invented paper?

Ans. China in about 105 A.D.

Q. 29. Write the name of oldest paper manuscript.

Ans. The Mohammedans in 1223-24 A.D.

Q. 30. At least how many pages a book should have?

Ans. As per norms prescribed by UNESCO, a book should have at least 49 pages, 22 to 32 cm height and 1.5 to 9 m of thickness.

Q. 31. Categorise the type of non-book materials available in the library.

Ans. The non-book materials in library:
(i) Visual: Still photographs, slides, etc.
(ii) Moving: Film strips, cine films, videocassettes and discs
(iii) Audio: Sound recording, gramophone record, compact disc, Digital audio technology (DAT), audiotape, audiocassettes.

Q. 32. Categorise different types of film media.

Ans. The different types of media are:
(i) Film Strip (ii) Slides
(iii) Cine films (iv) Micro films

Q. 33. Write the standard code of practice for Binding Indian and British standard.

Ans. Indian standard-code of practice for reinforced binding of library books and periodicals IS: 3050-1965 with amendment in February 1968.

British standards: Created by the British Standard Institute in 1980 with amendments in February 1989.

Q. 34. What is the code of covering?

Ans. Indian Standard IS: 1960-1964 reaffirmed in 1960 "specification for book binding leather."

Q. 35. Who has developed the situational theory of leadership?

Ans. The situational theory of leadership has been developed by Paul Harsey and Kermeth Blanchard.

Q. 36. Who was known as father of Scientific management?

Ans. Frederic Winslow Taylor.

Q. 37. Who is considered as the Father of the Human relation movement?

Ans. Elton Mayo.

Q. 38. What is full form of HRM?

Ans. Human Resource Management.

Q. 39. What is the full form of HRD?

Ans. Human Resource Development.

Q. 40. Define the Total Quality Management.

Ans. This is the style of management in which the best principles and practices of scientific management and participative management are blended appropriately to achieve the success for the organisation.

Q. 41. When was the PERT developed?

Ans. In 1958 by the U.S. Navy Project Office.

Q. 42. Write the monitoring techniques used in management of special libraries.

Ans. (i) Operation Research (OR)
(ii) Management Information System (MIS)
(iii) Management by Objective (MBO)
(iv) Network Analysis

Q. 43. What is DELPHI techniques?

Ans. Delphi techniques helps managers and decision-makers to make better for costs and advice.

Q. 44. What is the aim of Marketing Research?

Ans. The aim of marketing research is to testing, identify and measure the markets.

Q. 45. Write some evaluation techniques applicable in libraries.

Ans. Some evaluation techniques applicable in libraries are:
(i) Performance Evaluation
(ii) Performance Measurement
(iii) Marketing Research
(iv) Cost Effectiveness analysis.

Q. 46. Who had invented the MBO?

Ans. MBO was invented by Peter Drucker in 1954.

Q. 47. What is the ISI standard for steel racks?

Ans.

	Height	Width	Depth
Steel Double faced	2175 mm	1840 mm	460 mm
Steel Single faced	2175 mm	1840 mm	230 mm

OBJECTIVE QUESTIONS

1. __________ is a systematic maintenance of income and expenditure flow on records.
(a) Auditing (b) Accounting
(c) Reporting (d) Budgeting

2. ______ is process of separating cover from text and removing old thread, tapes and glue.
(a) Collation (b) Sewing
(c) Pulling (d) Finishing

3. ______ is the systematic evaluation of an employee's performance in the organisation.
(a) Annual report (b) Confidential report
(c) Self-proposal (d) Performance Appraisal

4. Demand, supply and ________ are the major factors governing collection development.
(a) Reader (b) Space
(c) Personnel (d) Finance

5. Book misplaced on the shelves by readers are restored. This work is referred to as
(a) Shelf Rectification (b) Stock Verification
(c) Shifting of books (d) Shelf

6. Browne charging system is originated from
(a) United States (b) United Kingdom
(c) India (d) China

7. __________ is the strongest leather used in fine binding.

(a) Sheepskin (b) Pigskin
(c) Roan (d) Calf leather

8. N.E. Browne devised the charging system having ________ for each borrower.
(a) Book card (b) Temporary slip
(c) Borrower's card (d) Book pockets

9. The overdue charges collected from the defaulters are put in a box called
(a) Fine box (b) Conscience box
(c) Defaulters box (d) Overdue box

10. University Grant Commission grants, the mainly of three types such as recurring, non recurring and
(a) Annual (b) Permanent
(c) Special (d) Ad-hoc

11. Reserve procedure is also known as
(a) Charged Procedure
(b) Demand Procedure
(c) Borrowed Procedure
(d) Hold Procedure

12. A secret page and chosen and uniformity used in all documents for writing accession number is called confidential page.
(a) True (b) False

13. Is a document of few printed pages usually less than 49 and bounded in paper?
(a) Patent (b) Standard
(c) Report (d) Pamphlet

14. The three card system introduced by Ranganathan are register card, the check card and the
(a) Subject card (b) Classified index card
(c) Author card (d) Title card

15. British national bibliography is published by
(a) The British library
(b) British Museum library
(c) British national library
(d) None of the above

16. Circulation systems are categorised into four groups such as register system, card system, semi-mechanical system and
(a) Mechanical system (b) Manual system
(c) Automated system (d) Ledger system

17. Ranganathan recognise four kinds of documents such as conventional document, new conventional document, non-conventional documents and
(a) Primary document (b) Secondary document
(c) Meta document (d) Physical document

18. The arrangement of entries in the classified part of Indian National Bibliography INB is by
(a) Colon Classification
(b) Dewey Decimal Classification
(c) Universal Decimal Classification
(d) Library of Congress Classification

19. Book review digest (BRD) and book review index (BRI) are two ______ publications.
(a) Indian (b) American
(c) British (d) Russian

20. "The best reading for the largest number of least cost" is the principle propounded by
(a) Mc Colvin (b) M. Dewey
(c) S.R. Ranganathan (d) C.W. Hanson

21. Budget provides information on ________ Resources.
(a) Human (b) Manpower
(c) Material (d) Financial

22. As per the norms prescribed by UNESCO, a book should have at least ________ pages. (*NET Exam.* 91)
(a) 40 (b) 45 (c) 49 (d) 59

23. The micro forms comprise at microfilms, microfiche and
(a) micro document (b) micro print
(c) macro document (d) micro opaque

24. Indian patent office is located at
(a) Delhi (b) Mumbai
(c) Kolkata (d) Bangalore

25. Periodical display racks mainly of three types such as Pigeon Hole type, Step type and
(a) Long type (b) Inclined type
(c) Declined type (d) Vertical type

26. Circulation area includes stock rooms ____________ and catalogues.
(a) charging desk (b) reading room
(c) property counter (d) technical section

27. According to S.R. Ranganathan, the document which are directly recorded by instrument are known as
(a) Macro-document (b) Micro-document
(c) Meta document (d) Technical section

28. ___________ divides documents in three categories: Primary, Secondary, and Tertiary.

(a) Hanson (b) Grogan
(c) Drury (d) Dewey

29. Indian maps are issued by the Survey of India, Dehradun.
(a) True (b) False

30. Computer and ___________ technology have become vital component in scientific management.
(a) Printing (b) Reprography
(c) Publishing (d) Communication

31. ________ Law of library science relates to the size of the building space of a library.
(a) First (b) Fourth (c) Third (d) Fifth

32. S.R. Ranganathan divides management into
(a) five (b) three (c) eight (d) seven

33. The organisation structures vary according to the types of libraries such as national, public, academic and
(a) technical (b) special
(c) general (d) scientific

34. Libraries are generally organised on the basis of their function, viz. collection development, technical processing and
(a) Readers' Services (b) Users' Services
(c) Scholar Services (d) Student Services

35. The visitors or readers generally leave their personal belonging in a __________ before going inside library.
(a) Gate counter (b) Clock room
(c) Store room (d) Property counter

36. The routine jobs of a library are performed by a category of staff
(a) Semi professional (b) Supporting staff
(c) Professional (d) Administrative staff

37. Book selection committee comes under the category of ______________ committees.
(a) Statutory (b) Standing
(c) Ad-hoc (d) Working

38. Co-ordinating is one of the seven elements of
(a) General management
(b) Human resource management
(c) Scientific management
(d) Traditional management

39. Library __________ constituted with the purpose of providing collective advice on all matters of the library.
(a) Committee (b) Commission
(c) Seminar (d) Conference

40. The assessment of the right type of staff to be entrusted with the various activities calls for the use of management technique known as
(a) Job assessment (b) Job analysis
(c) Job description (d) Staff analysis

41. __________ service provides current lists of bibliographical citation with or without abstract on a given topic.
(a) Literature search (b) Document supply
(c) Retrieval (d) Special

42. The main purpose of _______ is to help new entrants to get acquainted with every job routine.
(a) staff manual
(b) work analysis
(c) performance appraisal
(d) confidential report

43. _____ of the university is generally the chair person of the university library committee.
(a) Pro-vice chancellor (b) Vice chancellor
(c) Librarian (d) None of these

44. ________ takes into account the actual amount of expenditure spend on each item.
(a) Proportional method
(b) Per-capita method
(c) Methods of detail
(d) None of the above

45. ____________ department is concerned mainly with selection procurement and accessing of documents.
(a) Acquisition (b) Technical
(c) Finance (d) Circulation

46. Planning, organising, staffing, directing, coordinating, reporting and budgeting are ____________ of management.
(a) principles (b) elements
(c) subsystems (d) None of the above

47. Programme evaluation and review techniques (PERT) and critical path method are used for improving quality in
(a) Modern management (b) Organisation
(c) Budgeting (d) Reporting

48. ______________ involves analysing the entire activities of an organisation into homogenous types of works and jobs.

(a) Planning (b) Budgeting
(c) Organising (d) Reporting

49. Ranganathan has divided management function into __________ components.
(a) seven (b) eight (c) six (d) nine

50. Organisational chart is a __________ Aid in showing the horizontal and vertical division of library.
(a) Visual (b) Direct (c) Indirect (d) Audio

51. With increasing computerisation of library operation and services, all housekeeping operations would invariable be ________ while the service points will be __________.
(a) independent, dependent
(b) dependent, independent
(c) decentralised, centralised
(d) centralised, decentralised

52. Academic, Public and special libraries are organised on the basis of
(a) Clientele (b) Location
(c) Resources (d) None of the above

53. Reader activity area in a library, reading room, microform reading rooms and
(a) Stock room (b) Study carrels
(c) Reference section (d) Reprography section

54. Circulation, reader activity, staff activity and other areas are identified __________ service areas in the library.
(a) common (b) special
(c) open (d) closed

55. Kardex is used to have a control on
(a) Books (b) Periodicals
(c) Audio and Video programmes (d) Map and globes etc.

56. ______ categorised documents as primary, secondary and tertiary.
(a) Devis Groan (b) C.W. Hanson
(c) S.R. Ranganathan (d) Melvil Dewey

57. Government documents are generally divided into two categories
(a) Parliamentary, Non Parliamentary
(b) Report, Research
(c) Published and unpublished
(d) Audio & Video

58. Ranganathan __________ laws of library science govern book selection.
(a) first three (b) first two
(c) fourth and fifth (d) All of the above

59. __________ are built to guide selection policies attempting a more direct method of orienting book and library service to cater the needs of the clientele.
(a) Community profile (b) Library surveys
(c) Users surveys (d) None of these

60. Operations research is a tool of (*NET Exam.* 1995)
(a) Library management
(b) Library classification
(c) Library cataloguing
(d) Reference service

61. Kardex is used for
(a) Abstracting
(b) Book selection
(c) Registration of periodicals
(d) Classification

62. The purpose of the shelf list is to facilitate
(a) Stock verification
(b) Duplication checking
(c) Physical processing
(d) Classification

63. Various registers like patron, Inter library loan, over-dues and fine, suggestions and gate registers are maintained by the circulation department.
(a) True (b) False

64. The checking of books selected, books on order, books received and books in process card tray, is done at the stage of
(a) Scanning (b) Scrutiny
(c) Recording (d) Processing

65. Invitation of tenders or quotations job is done at the
(a) Circulation (b) Order placing work
(c) Pre-order work (d) Technical

66. Jobs like gate registers, property counter, vigilance at entrance and exit gate done by
(a) Circulation (b) Reference
(c) Periodical (d) Technical

67. PRECIS and POPSI are
(a) Cataloguing cards
(b) Classification schemes
(c) Subject heading lists
(d) Indexing techniques

68. Books selection card, budget allocation register and Accession registers are used by

(a) Periodical (b) Circulation
(c) Technical (d) Acquisition

69. The two stages of operation in periodical ordering work are
(a) Ordering work or noting work
(b) Ordering and procurement work
(c) Pre-ordering and order placing work
(d) Ordering and receipt of periodicals

70. In binding process gliding is done
(a) for decoration (b) to protect the books
(c) for finishing (d) for the preparation

71. The systematic subject approach to documents on the shelf can be provided through ___________arrangement.
(a) Classified alphabetical
(b) Alphabetical
(c) Classified
(d) Any other type

72. The ____________ guide containing the concerned class numbers and their verbal headings.
(a) Gauge way (b) Bay
(c) Shelf (d) General

73. The work of paging is an integral part of the _______ function of a closed access library.
(a) acquisition (b) reference
(c) technical (d) circulation

74. Under ________ Shelf arrangement books on a particular subject are split into three main groups normal, oversized, undersized.
(a) Broken order (b) Classified order
(c) Special sequence (d) Block

75. For collection which are in active use, ____________shelving is considered to be more suitable.
(a) Conventional (b) Compact
(c) Block (d) Classified

76. ____________ system is high on accessibility but quite low on economy.
(a) Double rows on fixed shelves
(b) Compact storage
(c) Tower stocks
(d) Conventional shelving

77. Back runs of periodicals and magazines require ________ binding.
(a) leather (b) full leather
(c) half leather (d) cloth

78. Who said "Best books for the largest number at the least cost"?
(a) Helen E. Haines (b) S.R. Ranganathan
(c) Francis Drury (d) Melvil Dewey

79. Periodicity at INB is (*NET Exam.* 1991)
(a) Weekly (b) Monthly
(c) Bi-monthly (d) Quarterly

80. For acquisition of 6000 books in library in a year Dr. S.R. Ranganathan in his staff formula has recommended the following professional staff (*NET Exam.* 1991)
(a) 1 person (b) 2 persons
(c) 3 persons (d) 4 persons

81. Preparation at library budget without considering previous year's budget is known as
(a) Performance Budget (b) PPBS
(c) Zero based Budget (d) Budget in detail

82. Organisational structure is the (*NET Exam.* 1991)
(a) Structure of building
(b) Blueprint of the structure
(c) Structure of the subject
(d) Structure of parent body of an institution

83. First exponent of scientific method was
(a) Aristotle (b) Francis Bacon
(c) H.E. Bliss (d) S.R. Ranganathan

84. PPBS relates to (*NET Exam.* 1995)
(a) Management of Statistics
(b) Book selection
(c) Personnel records
(d) Budgeting

85. "Right books to the right reader at the right time." Principle enumerated by (*NET Exam.* 1995)
(a) S.R. Ranganathan (b) Dewey
(c) Drury (d) Italines

86. PERT is a technique for
(a) Collection of data (b) Job analysis
(c) System analysis (d) Job description

87. The Register card, check, and classified index card are used in (*NET Exam.* 1998)
(a) Three card system (b) Kardex system
(c) Circulation (d) All of them

88. If a new library wants to provide for 10,000 books how many double sided standard size racks are required? (*NET Exam.* 1996, 1998)

(a) 20 (b) 100 (c) 10 (d) 50

89. Fundamental element of management are known as
(a) POSDCORB (b) PSODCORB
(c) POSCDORB (d) POSCORB

90. Kardex system is adopted in libraries for: (*NET Exam.* 1996)
(a) Maintenance of news clippings
(b) Maintenance of record of periodicals subscription
(c) Reeling of Microforms
(d) Cataloguing of books

91. The methods of estimating funds for libraries are proportional method of details and (*NET Exam.* 1994)
(a) Staff formula
(b) Per-capita
(c) On the size of book collection
(d) Cataloguing of books

92. If a new library wants to provide for 10,000 books, how many catalogue cards trays should it plan for? (*NET Exam.* 1996)
(a) 10 (b) 40 (c) 80 (d) 100

93. The method of budgeting which is not concerned with what happened previously but it more concerned with the requirements of the future, is known as (*NET Exam.* 1997, J&D)
(a) Line budget (b) Programme budget
(c) Formula budget (d) Zero-based budget

94. Browne charging system will not show (*NET Exam.* 1996)
(a) When a particular book is to be returned
(b) Which books had been borrowed earlier by a number
(c) The number of books overdue
(d) The number of books issued in a subject

95. The Standard "X" and theory "Y" was conceived by (*NET Exam.* 1998)
(a) Maslow (b) Henry Fayol
(c) Peter F. Drucker (d) Douglas Mc Gregor

96. The concept of scientific management was introduced by (*NET Exam.* 1998)
(a) C.I. Bernard (b) Henry Fayol
(c) Peter F. Drucker (d) R.W. Taylor

97. Long range planning reduces
(a) Confusion (b) Efficiency
(c) Costing (d) Uncertainty

98. MBO concept came into existence in (*NET Exam.* 1999)
(a) 1950's (b) 1960's (c) 1970's (d) 1940's

99. The logical steps involved in scientific investigation are (*NET Exam.* 1999)
(a) Identification of the problem
(b) Formulation of the hypothesis
(c) Collection of the data
(d) All of the above

100. Expenditure on furniture is categorised as (*NET Exam.* 1999)
(a) Capital Expenditure
(b) Recurring Expenditure
(c) Non Plan Expenditure
(d) Contingency Expenditure

101. In the acquisition and control of periodicals Ranganathan devised a system which is denoted as (*NET Exam.* 1999)
(a) Kardex (b) Three card system
(c) Shelf list (d) Check list

102. The basic theory regarding human motivation is propounded by (*NET Exam.* 2000)
(a) Taylor (b) Maslow
(c) Mayo (d) Likest

103. Zero growth libraries contradict the fifth law of library science. The statement is (*NET Exam.* 2000)
(a) True, because no new books are added
(b) True, because the total size of the book stock is steady
(c) False, since the library may grow in other way
(d) False, since there can be no zero growth libraries

104. Delphi technique is related to
(a) Budgeting (b) Statistics
(c) Forecasting (d) Performance

105. The PERT approach is device developed (*NET Exam.* 2000)
(a) Better utilise of time in a series of activities
(b) Allow studies to be made between people and machine
(c) Analyses a workflow to facilitate decision-making
(d) Establish quality control

106. The acronym "POSDCORB" was coined by (*NET Exam.* 2000)

(a) Gulick and Urwick (b) Taylor
(c) Mayo (d) Gilberts

107. Which of the following is not true about the short-range planning? (*NET Exam.* 1998)
(a) It is also known as operational planning.
(b) It is specific and detailed.
(c) It is to be used as a general guide.
(d) It is for a limited period of time.

108. Books for which advance payment is to be made in full or in part, are known as (*NET Exam.* 1998 J)
(a) Subscription books (b) Remainder books
(c) Books by gifts (d) None of the above

109. Zero-based budget is concerned with ________ activities of the organisation. (*NET Exam.* 1994)
(a) past (b) present
(c) future (d) remote future

110. Zero-based budget means (*NET Exam.* 1996)
(a) There will be no increase in expenses or income
(b) There will be no budget
(c) The difference between income and expenditure is zero
(d) All proposals for income and expenditure will need to be justified

111. The library will subscribe to journals through an agent. This is the statement of (*NET Exam.* 1996, 1997)
(a) Objectives (b) Policy
(c) Procedure (d) Mission

112. "Reminders" are (*NET Exam.* 1996)
(a) Funds left over after purchasing books
(b) Books which were not bought last year
(c) Books which are sold by the publisher at a heavy discount
(d) Books which were ordered but not supplied

113. Modular planning of library building means (*NET Exam.* 1996)
(a) The library is built in stages
(b) Models are built before the final building
(c) The space is divided into equal units
(d) Different units are built for different functions

114. PPBS relates to personal management. (*NET Exam.* 1994)
(a) True (b) False

115. Cost benefit analysis means (*NET Exam.* 1991)
(a) Performance evaluation based on cost
(b) Finding out unit cost of library operations
(c) Value for money
(d) Performance evaluation based on benefits in relation to inputs

116. H. Fayol belonged to (*NET Exam.* 1991)
(a) Classical school
(b) Human relation school
(c) Decision-making school
(d) Social systems school

117. The concept of scientific management was introduced by
(a) Henry Fayol (b) C.I. Bernard
(c) Peter Drucker (d) F.W. Taylor

118. The weekly record of book published by R.R. Bowker is weekly list of
(a) British books (b) American books
(c) Indian books (d) Australian books

119. A book is ___________ a document.
(a) micro (b) macro
(c) meta (d) learned

120. While job analysis helps to decide the type and quality of staff of library with reference to its functional requirements, its staff size is to be assessed in terms of analysis of its
(a) Work load (b) Qualification
(c) Function (d) Working capacity

121. ___________ are guides to the library staff, giving description of rules, procedures and methods of performing various activities.
(a) Library manuals (b) Staff manuals
(c) Job description (d) Staff records

122. The method of estimating funds for libraries are per capita, proportional and
(a) Staff formula (b) Per Student method
(c) Method of details (d) Staff record

123. Among the various committees that may function in a library, it is the ___________ that meets regularly as required by statutory regulations.
(a) library committee
(b) library advisory committee
(c) library finance committee
(d) library planning committee

124. The library statistics pertains to library resources, technical service and
(a) User service (b) Library collection
(c) Library finance (d) Library staff

125. The UGC recommended _________ of a university budget for expenditure on its library.
(a) 10% (b) 8% (c) 6.5% (d) 6%

126. The facts in figures relating to such aspects as the sources of information in a library, the procurement of documents, the users, the services, the output of staff, the library income and expenditure, etc. are called
(a) Library statistics (b) Library collection
(c) Library resources (d) Annual report

127. __________ of the library is the survey of the actual work done during the preceding year with a view to inform the authorities and others about the achievement made by the library, the failure and the factors responsible for achievements and failures.
(a) Annual Report (b) Records
(c) Pamphlets (d) Receipts

128. The college library budget is approved by
(a) UGC
(b) Executive council
(c) Library committee
(d) Principal of the college

129. Ranganathan has suggested that per capita expenditure on university and college libraries should be @ rupees 20/- per student and per teacher
(a) 100/- (b) 400/- (c) 300/- (d) 50/-

130. In one card catalogue cabinet can hold about __________ cards.
(a) 1000 (b) 500 (c) 100 (d) 2000

131. In one Kardex cabinet can hold ___________ card.
(a) 100 (b) 50 (c) 1000 (d) 200

132. Write the standard size of the Kardex
(a) 10 cm × 15 cm (b) 15 cm × 18 cm
(c) 25 cm × 35 cm (d) 18 cm × 25 cm

133. Write the standard size of catalogue card cabinet
(a) H-225, W-320, D-510 in mm
(b) H-225, W-335, D-510 in mm
(c) H-135, W-150, D-410 in mm
(d) H-50, W-90, D-200 in mm

134. Who is considered as the father of the human relation movement?
(a) Elton Mayo (b) H. Fayol
(c) C.A. Cutter (d) F.W. Taylor

135. Who has developed the theory of situational leadership?
(a) Paul Harsey (b) Kenneth Blanchard
(c) Both (a) and (b) (d) M. Taylor

136. Who has developed the Path Goal Theory?
(a) Robert House (b) M. Taylor
(c) H. Fayol (d) Paul Harsey

137. Who has considered to be the father of scientific management?
(a) Henry Gantt (b) Frederick Winslow
(c) Maslow (d) H. Fayol

138. Who was the co-researcher of Human relationship school?
(a) F.J. Roehlis Berger and Willian J. Dickson
(b) H.W. Taylor and Henry Gantt
(c) Maslow and H. Fayol
(d) C.A. Cutter and Henry Fayol

139. When was operation research (OR) born?
(a) 1939-45 (b) 1940-45
(c) 1935-40 (d) 1950-55

140. MIS stands for
(a) Management Information System
(b) Management Information Service
(c) Machine Index System
(d) Management Informatics System

141. MBO stands for
(a) Management by Objective
(b) Manager by Operation
(c) Managerial by Objective
(d) Management by Omission

142. A retrieval system retrieves a total 50 documents. Out of these 40 are irrelevant another 10 documents which were relevant and not retrieved. The precision percentage for that query would be (*NET Exam.* 1996)
(a) 40% (b) 20% (c) 60% (d) 80%

143. Who propounded the Principle of MBO? (*NET Exam.* 1998J)
(a) Luther Gullick (b) Henry Fayol
(c) Frederick Taylor (d) Peter Drucker

144. Operational approach is a/an (*NET Exam.* 1998D)
(a) Empirical approach
(b) Historical approach
(c) Integrated approach
(d) Situational approach

145. Indicate the name of Philosopher who was the exponent of scientific method? (*NET Exam.* 1991, 1999D)
(a) Aristotle (b) Bacon
(c) Descarfes (d) Confucius

146. Measurement of performance of service activity in relation to cost is (*NET Exam.* 1997J)
(a) Cost effectiveness (b) Cost accounting
(c) Cost analysis (d) Performance analysis

147. PERT is a technique for (*NET Exam.* 1997J)
(a) Work study (b) Collection of data
(c) System analysis (d) Job description

148. In a questionnaire 'open ended' questions are
(a) The questions are open to interpretation
(b) The answers may be incomplete
(c) The answers may be filled in by the respondent
(d) Those where long answers are required

149. Shelf list Card (*NET Exam.* 1997J)
(a) Replicate the arrangement at the shelves
(b) Are used in stock verification
(c) Represent each volume on the shelf
(d) All of the above

150. Main criticism of scientific and classical schools of management is that they (*NET Exam.* 1997J)
(a) Emphasise the formal aspects of organisation
(b) Neglect individual personality
(c) Do not consider intra-organisational conflicts
(d) All of the above

151. Father of scientific management school is of (*NET Exam.* 1997J)
(a) Taylor (b) Fayol
(c) Maslow (d) Mayo

152. In a research on information needs of Chartered Accountants questionnaire is sent to every fifth member on the official register of chartered accountants would this be (*NET Exam.* 1999J)
(a) A random sample
(b) A stratified sample
(c) The whole population
(d) Not a representative sample

153. If a new library wants to provide for 25,000 books, how many double-sided standard size rack are needed?
(a) 20 (b) 30 (c) 80 (d) 50

154. Which person in the following list is not associated with theories of motivation?
(a) Maslow (b) Herzberg
(c) McGregor (d) Hawthorne

155. In a library which of the following position are staff position (*NET Exam.* 1997D)
(i) Junior Library Assistant
(ii) Subject specialist
(iii) Deputy librarian
(iv) System librarian
Codes:
(a) i & ii (b) i & iii
(c) ii & iv (d) iii & iv

156. The father of classical school management is (*NET Exam.* 1999J)
(a) Taylor (b) Fayol
(c) Maslow (d) Mayo

157. A change in the authority is given to an employee brings about a change in his/her
(a) Status (b) Accountability
(c) Responsibility (d) All of the above

158. An organisational structure is determined by
(i) Span of control (ii) Hierarchy
(iii) Space and location
(a) i and ii (b) ii and iii
(c) i and iii (d) All the factors

159. Ranganathan has divided management into nine components.
(a) True (b) False

160. Kardex system is adopted in libraries for the maintenance of periodicals.
(a) True (b) False

161. Dr. S.R. Ranganathan was the pioneer of Open Access System in British libraries.
(a) True (b) False

162. Match the following:
(A) Walter H. Kaiser (1) Brown Charging System
(B) S.R. Ranganathan (2) Photo Charging System

(C) Ralph R. Shaw		(3) Day Book System	
(D) N.E. Browne		(4) Colour Charging System	

Codes:	A	B	C	D
(a)	4	3	2	1
(b)	3	2	1	4
(c)	2	4	1	3
(d)	1	3	4	2

163. One of the techniques used within the library to train professional staff is (*NET Exam.* 1999J)
   (a) to prescribe job standards
   (b) job rotation
   (c) performance appraisal
   (d) sending the staff to conferences and workshops

164. Old and fragile books can be preserved by (*NET Exam.* 1999J)
   (a) Micro filming (b) Rebinding
   (c) Digitising (d) All of the above

165. 1st exponent of Scientific method was (*NET Exam.* 1991D)
   (a) Aristotle (b) Francis Bacon
   (c) H.E. Bliss (d) S.R. Ranganathan

166. Span of control refers to (*NET Exam.* 1996J)
   (a) The number of subordinates to be supervised
   (b) Exercise the strict control over the staff
   (c) Duration over which is to be exercised
   (d) The area which is to be controlled

167. Correct sequence of Cardinal points in the spiral of Scientific method is Descendant, Zenith, Ascendant, Nadir, Descendent. (*NET Exam.* 1991D)
   (a) True (b) False

168. The term Scientific Management was coined by Ranganathan.
   (a) True (b) False

169. Match the following:

(A) Finance	1. Capital involved in a project
(B) Recurring Expenditure	2. A plan expected spending and income
(C) Budget	3. Expenditure related to ongoing items
(D) Capital budget	4. Indicating expenditure or on non-recurring items

Codes:	A	B	C	D
(a)	1	3	2	4
(b)	2	3	4	1
(c)	3	2	4	1
(d)	4	1	3	2

170. ZBB was introduced in 1970.
   (a) True (b) False

171. The staff formula for university and college libraries in India has been formulated by S.R. Ranganathan.
   (a) True (b) False

172. Kardex system is devised for keeping record of periodicals.
   (a) True (b) False

173. Job description is a factual statement of the duties and responsibilities of a specific job.
   (a) True (b) False

174. Match the following:

(A) Abraham Maslow	1. Participative Management
(B) F.W. Taylor	2. Human Behaviour
(C) H. Fayol	3. Need Theory
(D) D. McGregor	4. Scientific Management

Codes:	A	B	C	D
(a)	3	4	2	1
(b)	2	3	4	1
(c)	4	2	3	1
(d)	3	1	2	4

175. Job description help the organisation: (*NET Exam.* 1997D)
   (i) to select the right person for the right job
   (ii) to give more power to the supervisors and
   (iii) to divide the salary structure
   Codes:
   (a) i and ii (b) ii and iii
   (c) i and iii (d) All of the above

176. Which of the following statements is not true for long-range planning?
   (a) It is specific and detailed
   (b) It is flexible
   (c) It covers a periods of more than 5 years
   (d) It acts as general guide

177. Which person in the following list is not associated with theories of motivation?
   (a) Maslow (b) Herzberg
   (c) McGregor (d) Hawthorne

178. Indian Daily Newspapers carry valuable sources for book selection particularly for libraries (*NET Exam.* 1997D)
(a) Private (b) Special
(c) Academic (d) Public

179. Books for which advance payment is to be made in full or in part are known as
(a) Subscription books (b) Reminder books
(c) Books by gift (d) None of these

180. There are total of 50 relevant documents in a collection in response to a query only 30 documents are retrieved of these, only 10 are relevant. What is the recall percentage?
(a) 20% (b) 33% (c) 40% (d) 60%

181. In a questionnaire 'open ended' questions are
(a) The questions are open to interpretation
(b) The answers may be incomplete
(c) The answers may be filled in by the respondent
(d) Those where long answers are required

182. Reviews which appear in leading Indian Daily Newspapers carry valuable sources for book selection particularly for libraries?
(a) Private (b) Special
(c) Academic Library (d) Public Library

183. The collection is built up by the acquisition department but it is the ______ department that facilitate the use of document collection.
(a) reference (b) periodical
(c) technical (d) All of the above

184. Write the standard size of the Accession Register
(a) 16″ × 13″ (b) 18″ × 15″
(c) 20″ × 17″ (d) 25″ × 21″

185. The PERT approach is a device developed to (*NET Exam.* 2001J)
(a) Better utilize of time in a series of activities
(b) Allow studies to be made between people and machine
(c) Analyse a work flow to facilitate decision-making
(d) Establish quality control

186. The acronym "POSDCORB" was coined by (*NET Exam.* 2004D, 2001J)
(a) Gulick and Urwick (b) Taylor
(c) Mayo (d) Gilbreths

187. GOC helps libraries in determining (*NET Exam.* 2001J)
(a) foreign exchange rates
(b) name of foreign agents and vendors
(c) books available in the market
(d) which books to buy

188. An organizational structure is determined by (*NET Exam.* 2001J)
1. span of control 2. hierarchy
3. space and location
Codes:
(a) 1 and 2 (b) 2 and 3
(c) 1 and 3 (d) All of factors

189. The type of international networks accessible to online vendor are such as (*NET Exam.* 2001D)
(a) WAN (b) MAN
(c) LAN (d) None of these

190. The device that converts digital to analog and analog to digital signals is known as (*NET Exam.* 2001D)
(a) Analog Computers (b) MODEM
(c) VDU (d) Electrofax

191. Which of the following are 'TQM' tools?
(i) Fishbone Diagram (ii) Histogram
(iii) Pie Chart (iv) Run Charts
Codes:
(a) (i), (iii) and (iv) are correct.
(b) (i), (ii), (iii) and (iv) are correct.
(c) (ii), (iii) and (iv) are correct.
(d) (i), (ii) and (iv) are correct.

192. Expenditure on furniture is categorized as (*NET Exam.* 2001D)
(a) Capital expenditure
(b) Recurring expenditure
(c) Non-plan expenditure
(d) Contingency expenditure

193. Which indexing system uses a single term and an accession number of the document as an indicator of reference?(*NET Exam.* 2001D)
(a) NEPHIS (b) Relative Index
(c) KWIC (d) PRECIS

194. Delphi technique is related to (*NET Exam.* 2004J, 2001D)
(a) Budgeting (b) Statistics
(c) Forecasting (d) Performance Evaluation

195. The concept of 'Demand theory of Books Selection' was conceived by
(a) A.C. Fosket (b) John Drury
(c) L.R. McCalvin (d) C.A. Cutter

196. Among the following which is/are the book selection tools? (*NET Exam.* 2001D)
(a) Books in print (b) PTLA
(c) Neither (a) nor (b) (d) Both (a) and (b)

197. Zero-growth libraries are that (*NET Exam.* 2002D)
(a) libraries do not get more space
(b) libraries must not by books
(c) libraries do not get more funds
(d) libraries must weed out as many books as they add

198. The common services of a library is/are (*NET Exam.* 2002J)
1. Reader activity 2. Staff activity
3. Circulation 4. Cataloguing

Codes:
(a) 1, 2 & 3 (b) 1, 3 & 4
(c) 2, 3 & 4 (d) 3 & 4

199. The budget for a College Library is approved by (*NET Exam.* 2002J)
(a) Higher Education Deptt. (b) Library Committee
(c) Executive Council (d) College Union

200. The principle which governs the selection of reading material for a library was given by (*NET Exam.* 2002J)
(a) Drury (b) R.R. Bowker
(c) Ranganathan (d) Grogan

201. The systematic subject approach for documents on shelf can be provided through (*NET Exam.* 2002J)
(a) Block arrangement
(b) Alphabetical arrangement
(c) Classified alphabetical arrangement
(d) Classified arrangement

202. The checking of books selected, books on order, books received and books in process card tray, is done at the stage of (*NET Exam.* 2002J)
(a) Scrutiny (b) Processing
(c) Recording (d) Scanning

203. Organisational charts, Block diagrams, work flow charts etc., portray the managerial strength and functions of (*NET Exam.* 2002J)
(a) Management thought (b) Job analysis
(c) Scientific Management (d) Job planning

204. The theory of "X" and "Y" was conceived by (*NET Exam.* 2002J)
(a) Peter Drucker (b) Henry Fayol
(c) Abraham Maslow (d) Douglas McGregor

205. Match the following: (*NET Exam.* 2009J)
(A) Principles of Management (i) F.W. Taylor
(B) Functions of Management (ii) Abraham Taylor
(C) Theory of Hierarchy of needs (iii) Luther Gullick
(D) System School of Management (iv) Henry Fayol

Codes:	**A**	**B**	**C**	**D**
(a)	(ii)	(iii)	(i)	(iv)
(b)	(ii)	(i)	(iv)	(iii)
(c)	(iv)	(iii)	(ii)	(i)
(d)	(i)	(iv)	(iii)	(ii)

206. Which of the following system improves the planning and control of operations by providing better information for decision-making? (*NET Exam.* 2003J)
(a) System Analysis (SA)
(b) Zero-Based Budgeting System (ZBB)
(c) Management Information System (MIS)
(d) Cost and Benefit System (CAB)

207. The command authority of supervisors over their subordinates in an organizational chart is (*NET Exam.* 2003J)
(a) Line authority
(b) Functional authority
(c) Personnel authority
(d) Simplicity authority

208. Libraries used "Library Overdue Charges" in place of "Library Fine". This satisfies the canon of (*NET Exam.* 2003J)
(a) Recall value (b) Reticence
(c) Prepotence (d) Permanence

209. Empirical Theory of Causation was proposed by (*NET Exam.* 2003J)
(a) David Hume, Stuart Mills
(b) Hitler, Robert Boyle
(c) David Hume, Torricelli
(d) Stuart Mills, Robert Boyle

210. Which section of the library perform Collection Development? (*NET Exam.* 2003J)
(a) Periodical Section (b) Acquisition Section
(c) Circulation Section (d) Technical Section

211. Modular planning of library building means

(*NET Exam.* 2003D)

(a) the library is built in stages
(b) different units are built for different functions
(c) models are built before the final building
(d) the space is constituted into modules

212. New York Charging System is introduced by (*NET Exam.* 2003D)

(a) H.E. Bliss (b) C.A. Cutter
(c) Nina Browne (d) John Cotton Dana

213. The assessment of the right type, of staff to be entrusted with the various activities calls for the use of management technique is

(*NET Exam.* 2003D)

(a) Job description (b) Job assessment
(c) Job analysis (d) Staff analysis

214. Special Library Association was founded in the year. (*NET Exam.* 2004D)

(a) 1908 (b) 1909 (c) 1910 (d) 1933

215. Millian Book Project was initiated by

(*NET Exam.* 2009J)

(a) Pittsburg University
(b) Carnegie Mellon University
(c) MIT, USA
(d) Michigan University

216. There are a total of 40 documents in a connection. In response to a query, only 24 documents are retrieved, out of which only 8 were relevant. What is recall percentage?

(*NET Exam.* 2004D)

(a) 20% (b) 60% (c) 33% (d) 40%

217. Critical Path Method and Programme Evaluation and Review Technique are used for improving the quality of

(*NET Exam.* 2005D)

(a) Modern Management (b) Budgeting
(c) Reporting (d) Principles

218. Which is/are the true statement regarding college. Library finance and budgeting?

(*NET Exam.* 2005D)

1. No college can afford to provide all books needed by students pursuing higher level courses.
2. Raj Commission recommended 20% of the college budget for the maintenance and development of the college library.

Codes:

(a) 1 & 2 both (b) 1 only
(c) 2 only (d) None of these

219. The importance of Hypertext is based on

(*NET Exam.* 2005D)

1. It offers a very powerful way of organizing and accessing information technology.
2. In it, information is extensive.
3. It consists of nodes and chunks of information.

Codes:

(a) All the three (b) 2 only
(c) 1 & 2 (d) 3 only

220. ________ is a process of helping employees in an organization to acquire new skills and competence on a continuing basis.

(a) Total Quality Management
(b) Management Information
(c) Financial Resources Development
(d) Human Resources Management

Read the passage given below, and answer the question based on your understanding of the passage. (Q. No. 221-225)

Stock verification implies the physical check-up of the articles on record. It is a common practice in big business houses and government departments to resort to annual stock-taking in order to assess the profit or loss. They try to find out as to what has been sold out and what has been left behind so that a proper quantity of a particular item may be procured from future sale. There is a practice to differentiate between stock and store articles. More importance is attached to stock articles since these are of permanent value and are likely to remain longer in use whereas the store articles are consumable. An analogous example can be cited by referring to two kinds of leaves, i.e. earned and casual leaves allowed to employees. The former can be cumulated whereas the latter cannot be cumulated since it is consumable and lapsable. Naturally, more importance is attached to the former one. Every employee tries to avail of the casual leave first before he requests for earned leave. The similar distinction is made between stock and store or stationery articles. A typewriter is a stock article while a pencil is a store article since the latter is likely to be used up soon. So little importance is attached to the store or stationery articles. The underlying idea behind this differentiation is the awareness of the sense of property which is a gift of the capitalist economy.

221. "Stock verification is a common practice in the following agencies only". Choose the correct answer to justify it: (*NET Exam.* 2005D)
   (a) libraries, government offices and hospitals
   (b) libraries, government offices and residences
   (c) libraries, government offices and business houses
   (d) government offices, business houses and hotels

222. "Annual stock taking is usually done in order to assess profit and loss". Choose the correct answer to justify it:
   (a) The statement is false
   (b) The statement is true
   (c) The statement is partially true only
   (d) None of the above statements are correct

223. Choose the correct answer from the following:
   (a) Stock articles are consumables
   (b) Stock articles remain no longer in use
   (c) Stock articles are not permanent
   (d) Stock articles are of permanent value

224. Choose the correct answer from the following:
   (a) Casual leaves of employees are not consumable
   (b) Casual leaves are subject to cumulation
   (c) Casual leaves are not subject to cumulation
   (d) Casual leaves are not lapsable

225. Choose the right answer from the following:
   (a) It is a consumable
   (b) Little importance is attached to it
   (c) It is not a stationery article
   (d) It is to be used up soon

226. The guiding principles for planning a new library service setup are the
   (a) ISI standard
   (b) Five laws of Library Science
   (c) Principle of Library evolution
   (d) Principle of Later in Time

227. ZBB was developed by (*NET Exam.* 2009J)
   (a) R.D. Sturat (b) S.R. Ranganathan
   (c) Peter A. Pyhrr (d) C.V. Good

228. A search term in a search profile can be (*NET Exam.* 2004J)
   (a) a descriptor
   (b) any word from a thesaurus
   (c) references in the articles
   (d) None of the these

229. The concept of Scientific Management was introduced by (*NET Exam.* 2004J)
   (a) Henry Fayol (b) F.W. Taylor
   (c) Peter Drucker (d) Wan Edwards

230. What are the basic function of the technical section of a library? (*NET Exam.* 2004J)
   (a) Classification, Cataloguing and Physical processing
   (b) Cataloguing and Filling
   (c) Maximise the availability and use of library materials
   (d) None of these

231. Reviews which appear in Indian leading daily newspaper carry valuable source for book selection particularly for (*NET Exam.* 2004J)
   (a) Public libraries (b) Commercial libraries
   (c) Special libraries (d) Academic libraries

232. PERT was developed by (*NET Exam.* 2009J)
   (a) The Navy special project office
   (b) Booz-allen Hamelton
   (c) Both (a) and (b)
   (d) None of the above

233. The collection is built up by the ________ but it is the technical department that facilitates the use of document collection. (*NET Exam.* 2004J)
   (a) periodical department
   (b) acquisition department
   (c) reference department
   (d) circulation department

234. The Library Statistics usually pertains to library resources, technical services and (*NET Exam.* 2005D)
   (a) Users' services (b) Financial services
   (c) Staff appraisal (d) Revenue services

235. Critical Path Method and Programme Evaluation and Review Technique are used for improving the quality of (*NET Exam.* 2005D)
   (a) Modern Management (b) Staff services
   (c) Budgeting (d) None of these

236. Zero based Budgeting system was propounded by (*NET Exam.* 2009J, 2006J)
   (a) Peter Drucker (b) Edward Evans
   (c) Allen Kent (d) Peter Pyhrr

237. Which of the following factors is not considered in the making of a library budget? (*NET Exam.* 2006J)
(a) The size of the organization
(b) The type of users
(c) The collection
(d) The age of library employees

238. "Span of control" refers to (*NET Exam.* 2006J)
(a) The numbers of subordinates to be supervised
(b) Exercise strict control staff
(c) Duration over which the control is to be exercised
(d) The area which is to be controlled

239. **Assertion (A):** Collection development should be judiciously done.
Reason (R): Almost all libraries have limited resources. (*NET Exam.* 2006J)
Codes:
(a) Both (A) and (R) are true and (R) is the correct explanation.
(b) Both (A) and (R) are true but (R) is not the right explanation.
(c) (A) is true, but (R) is false.
(d) (A) is false, but (R) is true.

240. Match the following: (*NET Exam.* 2006J)

List A	List B
(A) Zip's Law	(i) Impact Factor
(B) Lotkas Law	(ii) Circulation Statistics
(C) Bradford's Law	(iii) Authors Productivity
(D) Eugene Garfield	(iv) Scattering
	(v) Scattering

Codes:	A	B	C	D
(a)	(ii)	(iv)	(v)	(i)
(b)	(v)	(i)	(iv)	(ii)
(c)	(iv)	(iii)	(v)	(i)
(d)	(iii)	(iv)	(v)	(ii)

241. Match the following: (*NET Exam.* 2006D)

List I	List II
(A) Z39.50	(i) Standard for Document Description
(B) ISO 9000	(ii) Standard for Library Building
(C) ISO 2709	(iii) Information Retrieval
(D) ISBD	(iv) Quality Related Standards
	(v) Bibliographic Records Structure

Codes:	A	B	C	D
(a)	(iii)	(iv)	(v)	(i)
(b)	(iv)	(v)	(ii)	(iii)
(c)	(v)	(iv)	(ii)	(i)
(d)	(iv)	(iii)	(v)	(ii)

242. Match the following: (*NET Exam.* 2006D)

List I	List II
(A) Management Service	(i) Fission
(B) Biophysics	(ii) Distillation
(C) Gandhian	(iii) Agglomeration
(D) Life Sciences	(iv) Clustering
	(v) Fusion

Codes:	A	B	C	D
(a)	(ii)	(v)	(iv)	(iii)
(b)	(ii)	(iv)	(i)	(iii)
(c)	(iv)	(v)	(ii)	(i)
(d)	(iii)	(v)	(i)	(ii)

243. Which system is devised by Broune? (*NET Exam.* 2004D)
(a) Book Charging System
(b) Account System
(c) Book Referral System
(d) Circulation System

244. Herzberg's is two factor theory deals with (*NET Exam.* 2004D)
(a) Staff recruitment (b) Leadership
(c) Decision-making (d) Motivation

245. Match the following:

List I	List II
(A) Scientific Management	(i) Espirit de crops
(B) Unity of Command	(ii) Peter Drucker
(C) Management by Objectives	(iii) Factor of Planning
(D) Forecasting	(iv) Efficiency and Waste Prevention

Codes:	A	B	C	D
(a)	(iv)	(i)	(ii)	(iii)
(b)	(i)	(ii)	(iii)	(iv)
(c)	(ii)	(iii)	(i)	(iv)
(d)	(iii)	(i)	(iv)	(ii)

246. Arrange the following in the chronological sequence of their development. (*NET Exam.* 2007J)
(i) Pascal (ii) Cobol
(iii) Fortran (iv) Basic
Codes:

(a)	(i)	(ii)	(iv)	(iii)
(b)	(iii)	(ii)	(iv)	(i)
(c)	(ii)	(iv)	(iii)	(i)
(d)	(iii)	(iv)	(ii)	(i)

247. Peter Pyhrr developed this technique (*NET Exam.* 2007J)
   (a) PPBS
   (b) Line by Line Budget
   (c) Zero Based Budgeting
   (d) Performance Budget

248. POSDCORB coined by:(*NET Exam.* 2007J)
   (a) Fayol (b) Maslow
   (c) Gulic (d) Ranganathan

249. Arrange the following according to the work flow: (*NET Exam.* 2007J)
   (a) Dissemination, Selection, Processing, Acquisition
   (b) Selection, Processing, Acquisition, Dissemination
   (c) Selection, Acquisition, Processing, Dissemination
   (d) Processing, Acquisition, Dissemination, Selection

250. **Assertion (A):** Now-a-days marketing of information products is necessity.

   Reason (R): Information is an important source. (*NET Exam.* 2007J)
   (a) Both (A) and (R) are true
   (b) (A) is true but (R) is false
   (c) (A) is false but (R) is true
   (d) Both (A) and (R) are false

251. Match the following: (*NET Exam.* 2007J)

List I	List II
(A) Blake	(i) Chart Technique
(B) Gantt	(ii) Leadership Style
(C) Maslow	(iii) Maturity Immaturity Theory
(D) McGregor	(iv) Theory X and Y
	(v) Motivation Theory

Codes:	A	B	C	D
(a)	(ii)	(iii)	(v)	(iv)
(b)	(ii)	(i)	(iv)	(v)
(c)	(iii)	(iv)	(ii)	(i)
(d)	(i)	(iv)	(iii)	(ii)

252. **Assertion (A):** Book selection must be done judiciously.

   Reason (R): Resource sharing is the need of the day. (*NET Exam.* 2007J)

   Codes:
   (a) Both (A) and (R) are true and (R) is the correct explanation of (A)
   (b) Both (A) and (R) are false
   (c) Both (A) and (R) are true but (R) is not the correct explanation of (A)
   (d) (A) is false but (R) is true

253. Maslow's theory is related to (*NET Exam.* 2007J)
   (a) Motivation (b) Leadership
   (c) Maturity (d) Scientific Management

254. **Assertion (A):** Evaluation of information is necessary.

   Reason (R): Anybody can write on internet. (*NET Exam.* 2007D)

   Codes:
   (a) Both (A) and (R) are false
   (b) Both (A) and (R) are true
   (c) (A) is true but (R) is false
   (d) (A) is false but (R) is true

255. Match the following: (*NET Exam.* 2007D)

List I	List II
(A) Paul Otlet	(i) List of subject heading
(B) Fermont Rider	(ii) Role operators
(C) George Boole	(iii) National Library
(D) Minie Sears	(iv) International Classification
	(v) Universal Decimal Classification

Codes:	A	B	C	D
(a)	(iii)	(i)	(v)	(iv)
(b)	(v)	(iv)	(ii)	(i)
(c)	(iv)	(v)	(i)	(ii)
(d)	(i)	(iv)	(iii)	(v)

256. Match the following: (*NET Exam.* 2007D)

List I	List II
(A) Taylor	(i) Theory of Motivation
(B) Maslow	(ii) X and Y Theory
(C) McGregor	(iii) Scientific Management
(D) Argyris	(iv) Immaturity/Maturity Theory
	(v) Leadership Style

Codes:	A	B	C	D
(a)	(iii)	(iv)	(ii)	(i)
(b)	(iv)	(i)	(v)	(iii)
(c)	(iii)	(i)	(ii)	(iv)
(d)	(v)	(iv)	(iii)	(i)

257. Arrange the following management developments chronologically: (*NET Exam.* 2007D)
   (i) Synthesis Period (ii) Scientific Period
   (iii) Human Relation (iv) Pre-Scientific Period

Codes:

(a)	(iii)	(i)	(ii)	(iv)
(b)	(iv)	(ii)	(iii)	(i)
(c)	(i)	(iv)	(ii)	(iii)
(d)	(ii)	(i)	(iv)	(iii)

258. Weeding of unuseful book from the library is emphasized by this law of library science. (*NET Exam.* 2007D)
(a) Second (b) Third (c) Fourth (d) Fifth

259. System school of Management is based on the contribution of (*NET Exam.* 2007D)
(a) Taylor (b) Gilberts (c) Fayol (d) Urwick

260. **Assertion (A):** Organization chart can be a useful management tool.
Reason (R): It gives clear picture of the formal lines of communication within the library. (*NET Exam.* 2007D)
Codes:
(a) (A) is true but (R) is false
(b) (A) is false but (R) is true
(c) Both (A) and (R) are true
(d) Both (A) and (R) are false

261. **Assertion (A):** Stock verification is essential in the collection development for libraries.
Reason (R): It is a time consuming process. (*NET Exam.* 2007D)
Codes:
(a) (A) is true but (R) is false
(b) Both (A) and (R) are true but (R) is not the right explanation of (A)
(c) Both (A) and (R) are true and (R) is the right explanation of (A)
(d) Both (A) and (R) are false

262. "The high purpose of Book Selection is to provide the right book to the right reader at the right time". Whose quotation is this? (*NET Exam.* 2007D)
(a) Francis Drury (b) H.E. Bliss
(c) Melvil Dewey (d) C.A. Cutter

263. Match the following: (*NET Exam.* 2007D)

List I	List II
(A) Theory of X & Y	(i) Frederic Taylor
(B) Scientific management	(ii) Ouchi
(C) Need hierarchy	(iii) A. Maslow
(D) Theory Z	(iv) D. Mc Gregor

Codes:	A	B	C	D
(a)	(iii)	(ii)	(i)	(iv)
(b)	(iv)	(iii)	(ii)	(i)
(c)	(ii)	(i)	(iv)	(iii)
(d)	(iv)	(i)	(iii)	(ii)

264. **Assertion (A):** ISO 9000 is a quality framework which calls for documentation to adopt TQM in a Library.
Reason (R): ISO 9000 is a valuable component of TQM. (*NET Exam.* 2007D)
Codes:
(a) (A) is true and (R) is false
(b) (R) is true but (A) is false
(c) Both (A) and (R) are false
(d) Both (A) and (R) are true

265. In which Library Service barcode technology is used (*NET Exam.* 2008J)
(a) Stock verification (b) Library Security
(c) Circulation (d) Reference Service

266. Match the following: (*NET Exam.* 2008J)

List I	List II
(A) Planning	(i) Delegation of authority
(B) Staffing	(ii) Audit
(C) Control	(iii) Promotion
(D) Organising	(iv) Resource management

Codes:	A	B	C	D
(a)	(i)	(ii)	(iii)	(iv)
(b)	(ii)	(iv)	(i)	(iii)
(c)	(iii)	(i)	(ii)	(iv)
(d)	(iv)	(iii)	(ii)	(i)

267. **Assertion (A):** Maximization of the use of documents is the motto of the library.
Reason (R): Maximization of the use of documents in the library satisfies the Fifth Law of Library Science.(*NET Exam.* 2008J)
Codes:
(a) Both (A) and (R) are true
(b) Both (A) and (R) are false
(c) (A) is true but (R) are false
(d) (R) is true but (A) is false

268. **Assertion (A):** As the level of recall increases, precision tends to decrease.
Reason (R): Recall and precision tend to vary inversely. (*NET Exam.* 2008J)
Codes:
(a) Both (A) and (R) are true
(b) (A) is true but (R) is false
(c) Both are partially true
(d) (R) is true but (A) is false

269. **Assertion (A):** Subject gateways offer the users an alternative to 'Vacuum Cleaner' type

of search engines, such as Google, Infoseek, Alta Vista etc. (*NET Exam.* 2009D)

Reason (R): Subject Gateways hold manually created records, rich resource description containing relevant information.

(a) Both (A) and (R) are true.
(b) Both (A) and (R) are true and (R) is not the correct explanation.
(c) (A) is true but (R) is false.
(d) (A) is false but (R) is true.

270. Match the following: (*NET Exam.* 2010D)

List I	List II
(A) Henry Fayol	(i) Hierarchy Needs
(B) F.W. Taylor	(ii) Theory X and Theory Y
(C) Abraham Maslow	(iii) Classical Theory
(D) Douglas Mc Gregor	(iv) Scientific Management

Codes:	A	B	C	D
(a)	(iii)	(iv)	(i)	(ii)
(b)	(i)	(ii)	(iii)	(iv)
(c)	(iv)	(iii)	(ii)	(i)
(d)	(i)	(iv)	(iii)	(ii)

271. Theory X and Theory Y relate to (*NET Exam.* 2010J)

(a) Planning (b) Motivation
(c) Innovation (d) None of the above

272. **Assertion (A):** Demand is the only governing factor in Book selection.

Reason (R): Patrons' requirement govern building library collections. (*NET Exam.* 2010J)

Codes:
(a) (A) is true and (R) is false.
(b) (A) is false and (R) is true.
(c) (A) and (R) both are true.
(d) (A) and (R) both are false.

273. Match the following: (*NET Exam.* 2010J)

List I	List II
(A) Fumigation	(i) Acquisition
(B) Building library collection	(ii) Preservation
(C) Kardex	(iii) Reference service
(D) Information Desk	(iv) Registration of Periodicals

Codes:	A	B	C	D
(a)	(ii)	(iii)	(i)	(iv)
(b)	(ii)	(iii)	(iv)	(i)
(c)	(iii)	(ii)	(i)	(iv)
(d)	(ii)	(i)	(iii)	(iv)

274. Match the following: (*NET Exam.* 2010J)

List I
(A) Father of Scientific Management
(B) Father of Administration
(C) Father of Human Relations School
(D) Father of Corporate Strategy

List II
(i) Henry Fayol (ii) Elton Mayo
(iii) F. Hertzberg (iv) F.W. Taylor

Codes:	A	B	C	D
(a)	(iv)	(ii)	(i)	(iii)
(b)	(iv)	(i)	(ii)	(iii)
(c)	(iii)	(iv)	(ii)	(i)
(d)	(ii)	(iii)	(iv)	(i)

275. **Assertion (A):** Deacidification is a measure to preserve documents in any medium.

Reason (R): Digital preservation needs a different preservation care. (*NET Exam.* 2010J)

Codes:
(a) (A) is false, but (R) is true.
(b) (A) is true, but (R) is false.
(c) Both (A) and (R) are true.
(d) Both (A) and (R) are false.

276. **Assertion (A):** Provision of services outside the library regular service centre or outlet is essential to reach more and more patrons.

Reason (R): Library extension services help libraries to cover larger population of patrons. (*NET Exam.* 2010J)

Codes:
(a) (A) is true but (R) is false.
(b) (A) is false but (R) is true.
(c) Both (A) and (R) are true.
(d) Both (A) and (R) are false.

277. Match the following: (*NET Exam.* 2010D)

List I	List II
(A) Henry Fayol	(i) Hierarchy Needs
(B) F.W. Taylor	(ii) Theory X and Theory Y
(C) Abraham Maslow	(iii) Classical Theory
(D) Douglas McGregor	(iv) Scientific Management

Codes:	A	B	C	D
(a)	(iii)	(iv)	(i)	(ii)
(b)	(i)	(ii)	(iii)	(iv)
(c)	(iv)	(iii)	(ii)	(i)
(d)	(i)	(iv)	(iii)	(ii)

Note: Read the passage given below, and answer the question based on your understanding of the passage. (Q. No. 278-282)

One of the major drawbacks of the legacy systems was that it did not have an integrated approach. There would be an accounting system for the finance department, a production planning system for the manufacturing department, an inventory management system for the stores department, and so on. All these systems would perform in isolation. So if a person wanted some information which had to be derived from any of these two systems, he had to get the necessary reports from both systems and then correlate and combine the data.

But in reality, an organization cannot function as islands of different departments. The production planning data is required for the purchasing department. The purchasing details are required for the finance department and so on. So if all the information islands, which were functioning in isolation, were integrated into a single system, then the impact of the would be dramatic. For example, if the purchase department can see the production planning details, it can make the purchasing schedule, if the finance department can see the details of the purchase as soon as it is entered in the system, it can plan of the cash flow that will be necessary for the purchases.

Because the systems work in isolation, collecting and analyzing the data needed for the functioning departments, as well as getting information about some aspect that is dependent on more than one department, becomes a difficult task. But no business executive or decision-maker can take good decisions with the isolated data that he will get from the various reports produced by each department. Even if he collects the data and produces the information that he requires, he would have lost valuable time that would have been better spent in decision-making for that process.

278. The following system can survive in isolation (*NET Exam.* 2008D)
 (a) Accounting system
 (b) Planning system
 (c) Inventory management system
 (d) No system

279. If anyone wants information from two systems, he must get the information (*NET Exam.* 2008D)
 (a) from each system and correlate
 (b) from one system at a time for correlation
 (c) from two systems and need not correlate
 (d) from a many systems as possible and correlate

280. All the systems must be integrated for (*NET Exam.* 2008D)
 (a) isolation (b) proper planning
 (c) dramatic impact (d) huge profit

281. Collecting and arranging data is (*NET Exam.* 2008D)
 (a) needed for library personnel
 (b) needed for functioning department
 (c) needed for production planning
 (d) needed for purchase department only

282. The executives and managers cannot make good decisions (*NET Exam.* 2008D)
 (a) with the isolated data
 (b) only when they collage the data themselves
 (c) only when they were produced with the required information
 (d) when they have lost valuable time

283. Which of the following is not correct? (*NET Exam.* 2008D)
 (a) Maslow's need analysis is useful for understanding motivation of employees.
 (b) Theory Z is the contribution of Japanese style of Management.
 (c) Money is the most powerful motivating agent.
 (d) Mission of an organization is essentially abstract.

284. 'Best is the enemy of the Good is said by
 (a) Drury (b) Urquart (c) Foskett (d) Shera

285. Match the following items given in List I and List II (*NET Exam.* 2008D)

List I	List II
(A) Nascent Micro thought	(i) Colon classification
(B) Access points	(ii) Motivation
(C) Physiological needs	(iii) Documentation
(D) Analytic-synthetic classification	(iv) AACR II

Codes:	A	B	C	D
(a)	(iii)	(iv)	(ii)	(i)
(b)	(iii)	(ii)	(i)	(iv)

(c)	(ii)	(i)	(iv)	(iii)
(d)	(i)	(ii)	(iii)	(iv)

286. TQM was promulgated by (*NET Exam.* 2008D)
(a) Deming and Juran (b) Maslow
(c) Drucker (d) Taylor

287. Match the following items given in List I and List II. (*NET Exam.* 2008D)
List I
(A) Principles of librarianship
(B) Practical guidelines for classification
(C) Rules for Dictionary cataloguing
(D) Five Laws of library science
List II
(i) Berwick Sayers (ii) S.R. Ranganathan
(iii) D.J. Urquart (iv) C.A. Cutter

Codes:	**A**	**B**	**C**	**D**
(a)	(iii)	(i)	(iv)	(ii)
(b)	(i)	(ii)	(iii)	(iv)
(c)	(iii)	(ii)	(iv)	(i)
(d)	(i)	(iii)	(iv)	(ii)

288. Match the following: (*NET Exam.* 2009D)

List I	**List II**
(A) Theory of Knowledge	(i) Farmington Plan
(B) IS : 1553-1960	(ii) Metadata Format
(C) Resource Sharing	(iii) Library Building
(D) TEI	(iv) Epistomology

Codes:	**A**	**B**	**C**	**D**
(a)	(i)	(iii)	(ii)	(iv)
(b)	(ii)	(iii)	(i)	(iv)
(c)	(iv)	(iii)	(i)	(ii)
(d)	(iii)	(i)	(ii)	(iv)

289. Cost benefit analysis means (*NET Exam.* 2009D)
(a) Value for money
(b) Performance evaluation based on cost
(c) Finding out unit cost
(d) Performance evaluation based on inputs

290. RFID Technology is used in (*NET Exam.* 2009D)
(a) Acquisition (b) Serial Control
(c) Circulation Control (d) OPAC

291. **Assertion (A):** With large collection of documents, recall can be measured properly.
Reason (R): The proper estimation of maximum recall for a query requires detailed knowledge of all the documents in the collection. (*NET Exam.* 2009D)
Codes:
(a) Both (A) and (R) are true.
(b) Both (A) and (R) are true and (R) is not the correct explanation.
(c) (A) is true but (R) is false.
(d) (A) is false but (R) is true.

292. Arrange the following four quadrants of spiral of scientific method in their logical order: (*NET Exam.* 2009D)
(i) Ascendant (ii) Nadir
(iii) Zenith (iv) Descendent

Codes:				
(a)	(iv)	(i)	(iii)	(ii)
(b)	(i)	(iii)	(iv)	(ii)
(c)	(iii)	(ii)	(i)	(iv)
(d)	(ii)	(i)	(iii)	(iv)

293. **Assertion (A):** Para-professional staff supports the professional staff in Library routines.
Reason (R): Para-professional staffs acquire skill by experience. (*NET Exam.* 2009D)
Codes:
(a) (A) is false, but (R) is true.
(b) (A) is true, but (R) is false.
(c) Both (A) and (R) are false.
(d) Both (A) and (R) are true.

294. Arrange the following according to their year of development (*NET Exam.* 2011D)
(i) Zipf's Law (ii) Lotka's Law
(iii) Bradford's Law (iv) Five Laws of Library Science

Codes:				
(a)	(i)	(iii)	(iv)	(ii)
(b)	(iv)	(i)	(ii)	(iii)
(c)	(iii)	(iv)	(ii)	(i)
(d)	(i)	(iv)	(ii)	(iii)

295. Zip's Law deals with (*NET Exam.* 2011D)
(a) Scattering of articles in a subject
(b) Productivity of authors in terms of scientific papers
(c) Frequency of occurrence of words in a text
(d) Law of book selection

296. Which national agency in India is assigning the ISSN? (*NET Exam.* 2011D)
(a) BIS (b) RRRLF
(c) NISCAIR (d) National Library, Kolkata

297. 'Quality Circles' in organization is used in (*NET Exam.* 2012D)

(a) Personnel Estimation
(b) Personnel Evaluation
(c) Management Control
(d) Participative Management

298. Douglas McGregor is known for the (*NET Exam.* 2012D)
(a) Theory X & Theory Y
(b) Two Factor Theory
(c) Management grid
(d) Theory of Leadership

299. **Assertion (A):** Qualitative measures must be made quantifiable in order to be convincing.
Reason (R): Qualitative measures are a necessary complement to quantitative measures. (*NET Exam.* 2012D)
Codes:
(a) (A) is true, (R) is false.
(b) (A) is false, (R) is true.
(c) Both (A) & (R) are true.
(d) Both (A) & (R) are false.

300. **Assertion (A):** TQM promotes the way in which a library is organized and perform its ICT functions. (*NET Exam.* 2012D)
Reason (R): TQM is seen as a hindrance to library and information services.
Codes:
(a) Both (A) and (R) are true.
(b) Both (A) and (R) are false.
(c) (A) is false and (R) is true.
(d) (A) is true and (R) is false.

301. **Assertion (A):** Book selection should be done judiciously. (*NET Exam.* 2012D)
Reason (R): A library should acquire important and latest book selection tools.
Codes:
(a) (A) is true but (R) is false.
(b) (A) is false but (R) is true.
(c) Both (A) & (R) are true, but (R) is not the correct explanation of (A).
(d) Both (A) & (R) are true and (R) is the correct explanation of (A).

302. What is the correct order of SCONUL's "Seven Pillar Model of Information Skills"? (*NET Exam.* 2012D)
(i) Recognise information need
(ii) Construct strategies for locating
(iii) Compare and evaluate
(iv) Locate and access

Codes:

(a)	(i)	(ii)	(iii)	(iv)
(b)	(ii)	(iii)	(iv)	(i)
(c)	(i)	(ii)	(iv)	(iii)
(d)	(ii)	(iii)	(i)	(iv)

303. Match the following:
List I
(A) Osgood and Schramm (B) Berlo
(C) Shannon and Weaver (D) George Gerbner
List II
(i) General Model (ii) Mathematical Model
(iii) Circular Model (iv) S.M.C.R. Model

Codes:	**A**	**B**	**C**	**D**
(a)	(i)	(ii)	(iii)	(iv)
(b)	(ii)	(iii)	(iv)	(i)
(c)	(iii)	(iv)	(ii)	(i)
(d)	(iv)	(i)	(ii)	(iii)

304. **Assertion (A):** Performance measurement is necessary to support decision-making in libraries and information centres.
Reason (R): Right decision at a right time helps libraries and information centres to achieve goals. (*NET Exam.* 2011J)
Codes:
(a) Both (A) and (R) are true and (R) is the correct explanation of (A).
(b) Both (A) and (R) are false.
(c) Both (A) and (R) are true, but (R) is not a correct explanation of (A).
(d) (A) is false, but (R) is true.

305. **Assertion (A):** Collection development must be done judiciously. (*NET Exam.* 2011J)
Reason (R): Demand is the only governing factor in book selection.
Codes:
(a) (A) is true and (R) is false.
(b) Both (A) and (R) are true and (R) is the correct explanation of (A).
(c) (A) is false and (R) is true.
(d) Both (A) and (R) are true, but (R) is not a correct explanation of (A).

306. The physical and chemical treatment of materials to retard their further deterioration refers to (*NET Exam.* 2012D)
(a) Conservation (b) Rescuing
(c) Prevention (d) Restoration

307. ISO 9000 standard denotes the (*NET Exam.* 2012D)

(a) Consistence conformance of a product or service to a given set of standard or expectations
(b) Total customer satisfaction
(c) Representation of stakeholders issues
(d) Detailed list of measuring techniques

308. Which of the following are the scientists' approach according to Melvin J. Voigt (1961)?
(i) Current Approach
(ii) Everyday Approach
(iii) Exhaustive Approach
(iv) 'Catching up' or 'Brushing up' approach.
Codes:
(a) (ii), (iii) and (iv) (b) (i), (iii) and (iv)
(c) (i), (ii) and (iv) (d) (i), (ii) and (iii)

309. In the library hierarchy which level of management is responsible for execution of policies? (*NET Exam.* 2013J)
(a) Middle level (b) Operational level
(c) Top level (d) Lower level

310. ZOTERO is a (*NET Exam.* 2013J)
(a) Content Management System
(b) Reference Management System
(c) Serials Management System
(d) Bibliographic, References Management System

311. Impact factor is devised by (*NET Exam.* 2013J)
(a) Eugene Garfield (b) Alan Pritchard
(c) David Hume (d) Louis Brandeis

312. A skilful method of providing means, mechanism and structural elements to streamline organizational work is known as
(a) Role Analysis (b) Strategic Planning
(c) Work Culture (d) Autonomous Planning (*NET Exam.* 2013J)

313. Financial allocation made to a library for purchase of furniture and equipment usually comes under the budget head (*NET Exam.* 2013J)
(a) Recurring grant (b) Endowments
(c) Non-recurring grant (d) Annual grant

314. Match the following:

List I	List II
(A) Douglas McGregor	(i) Scientific Management School
(B) Abraham Maslow	(ii) Theory of Authority Structure
(C) F.W. Taylor	(iii) Self Actualisation Needs
(D) Max Weber	(iv) Theory X and Theory Y

Codes:	A	B	C	D
(a)	(iv)	(iii)	(i)	(ii)
(b)	(ii)	(iii)	(i)	(iv)
(c)	(iii)	(iv)	(ii)	(i)
(d)	(i)	(iv)	(ii)	(iii)

315. Identify the technique(s) to collect the data regarding the number of persons visited the periodical section of the library at different hours of the day.
(i) Questionnaire (ii) Interview
(iii) Observation (iv) Library records
Codes:
(a) (i) and (ii) are correct.
(b) (ii) and (iii) are correct.
(c) (iii) and (iv) are correct.
(d) (ii) and (iv) are correct.

316. Major elements of a profession are
(i) Philosophy (ii) Body of knowledge
(iii) Publicity (iv) Status
Codes:
(a) (i), (ii), (iv) are correct.
(b) (i), (ii), (iii) are correct.
(c) (ii), (iii), (iv) are correct.
(d) (i), (iii), (iv) are correct.

317. Match the following: (*NET Exam.* 2013J)

List I	List II
(A) Unity of command	(i) Specialization
(B) Unit of direction	(ii) Strength in unity
(C) Esprit de corps	(iii) Orders from only one person
(D) Division of work	(iv) One boss, one plan

Codes:	A	B	C	D
(a)	(iv)	(iii)	(ii)	(i)
(b)	(ii)	(iv)	(iii)	(i)
(c)	(iii)	(iv)	(ii)	(i)
(d)	(i)	(iv)	(iii)	(ii)

318. **Assertion (A):** 'Pay and Use' concept has not been accepted in libraries of India.
Reason (R): Library staff do not possess the essential skills required for product development and promotion. (*NET Exam.* 2013J)
Codes:
(a) Both (A) and (R) are true.
(b) (A) is true, but (R) is false.
(c) (R) is true, but (A) is false.
(d) Both (A) and (R) are false.

319. The professional ethics help to (*NET Exam.* 2013J)
(i) Get the right direction
(ii) Enhance image
(iii) Get more salaries
(iv) Resolve day to day issues
Codes:
(a) (ii) and (iii) are correct.
(b) (i) and (iv) are correct.
(c) (i) and (ii) are correct.
(d) (ii) and (iv) are correct.

320. What is/are not common features between RFID & Barcode Technology?
(i) Read more than one item at a time
(ii) Able to locate specific items on shelves
(iii) Programmable
(iv) Read while item is moving
Codes:
(a) (i), (ii) are correct.
(b) (iii), (iv) are correct.
(c) (ii), (iv) are correct.
(d) All the above are correct.

321. When a librarian has to show the rationale for the purchase of more e-resources, which of the followings will help to support his/her stand?
(i) Collection development policy
(ii) Indent from users
(iii) Book selection tools
(iv) All of the above
Codes:
(a) (i) and (ii) are correct.
(b) (i) and (iii) are correct.
(c) (ii) and (iii) are correct.
(d) (iv) is correct.

322. **Assertion (A):** RFID technology is still not widely installed in Indian Library Environment.
Reason (R): The standardization, application and innovation are constantly changing.
Codes:
(a) Both (A) & (R) are true and (R) is the correct explanation of (A).
(b) Both (A) & (R) are true, but (R) is not the correct explanation of (A).
(c) (A) is true, but (R) is false.
(d) (A) is false, but (R) is true.

323. Match the following:
List I
(A) Classical Models (B) Linear Model
(C) Non-linear Model (D) Multi-dimensional
List II
(i) Ruesch and Bateson's Functional Model
(ii) Aristotle
(iii) Lasswell
(iv) Westley and Mackan's Conceptual Model

Codes:	A	B	C	D
(a)	(ii)	(iii)	(iv)	(i)
(b)	(ii)	(iv)	(i)	(iii)
(c)	(i)	(ii)	(iii)	(iv)
(d)	(iii)	(ii)	(iv)	(i)

324. Starting Chaining, Browsing, Differentiating, Monitoring, Extracting, Verification and Ending are important stages of which information seeking behaviour model?
(a) Dervin's Model (b) Ellis Model
(c) Marchionini Model (d) Kuhlthau Model

325. Which of the following is not a language of DBMS?
(a) DDL (b) DML (c) PASCAL (d) PLI

326. Match the following:

List I	List II
(A) Henri La Fontaine	(i) Expansive Classification
(B) H.E. Bliss	(ii) Bibliographic Classification
(C) C.A. Cutter	(iii) LC
(D) J.C.M. Hanson	(iv) UDC

Codes:	A	B	C	D
(a)	(iv)	(ii)	(i)	(iii)
(b)	(iii)	(ii)	(iv)	(i)
(c)	(ii)	(iv)	(i)	(iii)
(d)	(i)	(iii)	(ii)	(iv)

327. The process of planning, allocating, organizing and evaluating library tasks and activities within the framework of major objectives, mission and policy refers to
(a) Functional Control
(b) Functional Classification
(c) Functional Approach
(d) Functional Authority

328. Work study, standardized tools, selecting and training of workers are the contributions of
(a) Louis Brandeis (b) F.W. Taylor
(c) Henry Fayol (d) Lyndall Urwick

329. The 'Cranefield Test', associated with evaluation of information retrieval system was carried under the direction of

(a) C.W. Cleverdon
(b) G. Salton
(c) D.C. Blair & M.E. Maron
(d) E. Voorhees

330. Which of the following principles are associated with library building planning?
(i) Principle of Uniformity
(ii) Principle of Comfortability
(iii) Principle of Simplicity
(iv) Principle of Continuity
Codes:
(a) (i), (ii) and (iii) are correct.
(b) (ii), (iii) and (iv) are correct.
(c) (i), (ii) and (iv) are correct.
(d) (iii), (iv) and (i) are correct.

331. Andrew Carnegie donated two million pounds for development of (*NET Exam.* 2013J)
(a) Library collection (b) Library Building
(c) Library Furniture (d) Library Staff

332. Who said that information is both a product and process?
(a) S.R. Ranganathan (b) J. Martin
(c) D.J. Foskett (d) S.C. Bradford

333. Radio Frequency Identification is used in library for (*NET Exam.* 2012J)
(i) Circulation of Documents
(ii) Cataloguing of Documents
(iii) Security of Documents
(iv) Acquisition of Documents
Codes:
(a) (i) and (ii) are correct.
(b) (ii) and (iv) are correct.
(c) (iii) and (ii) are correct.
(d) (i) and (iii) are correct.

334. Match the following: (*NET Exam.* 2012J)
List I
(A) Classical School (B) X & Y Theory
(C) Newark Charging System (D) MBO
List II
(i) John cotton Danna (ii) Henry Fayol
(iii) Peter Drucker (iv) Douglas McGregor

Codes:	A	B	C	D
(a)	(i)	(iii)	(iv)	(ii)
(b)	(iii)	(iv)	(i)	(ii)
(c)	(ii)	(iv)	(i)	(iii)
(d)	(iii)	(ii)	(iv)	(i)

335. **Assertion (A):** Marketing of Information products is the need of the day.
Reason (R): Information is a resource which consumes lot of time and money. (*NET Exam.* 2012J)
Codes:
(a) (A) is true, but (R) is false.
(b) (A) is false, but (R) is true.
(c) Both (A) and (R) are true.
(d) Both (A) and (R) are false.

336. **Assertion (A):** Browne charging system is simple and less time consuming.
Reason (R): There is permanent issue record available.
Codes:
(a) (A) is false, but (R) is true.
(b) (A) is true, but (R) is false.
(c) Both (A) and (R) are true.
(d) Both (A) and (R) are false.

337. **Assertion (A):** Introduction of TQM in libraries is not possible.
Reason (R): It requires open, cooperative culture and employees responsiveness for customer satisfaction. (*NET Exam.* 2012J)
Codes:
(a) Both (A) and (R) are true.
(b) (A) is true, but (R) is false.
(c) (A) is false, but (R) is true.
(d) Both (A) and (R) are false.

338. Match the following:
List I
(A) Budget prepared using previous period budget
(B) Budget based on norms and standards
(C) Budget planned integrating number of techniques
(D) Budget prepared identifying current tasks independent of previous year
List II
(i) Formula budgets
(ii) Zero-based budget
(iii) Incremental budget
(iv) Planning programming budgeting system

Codes:	A	B	C	D
(a)	(iii)	(i)	(iv)	(ii)
(b)	(i)	(iii)	(iv)	(ii)
(c)	(iii)	(ii)	(i)	(iv)
(d)	(i)	(ii)	(iii)	(iv)

339. Methods and Techniques of Human Resource Planning includes
(i) Selection and Recruitment
(ii) Induction and Placement
(iii) Quality Management
(iv) Performance Evaluation
Codes:
(a) (i), (iv) and (ii) are correct.
(b) (iv), (iii) and (i) are correct.
(c) (i), (ii) and (iv) are correct.
(d) (iii) and (i) are correct.

340. **Assertion (A):** Modern Integrated Library Management Softwares offer user friendly Graphical User Interfaces (GUI) on the web.
Reason (R): Almost every module of modern Integrated Library Management Software is accessible through the internet.
Codes:
(a) Both (A) and (R) are correct.
(b) (A) is correct, but (R) is wrong.
(c) Both (A) and (R) are wrong.
(d) (A) is wrong, but (R) is correct.

341. Who propounded "Minimum, Middling and Maximum Theories" of reference service?
(a) C.M. Winchell (b) James I. Wyer
(c) Samuel Rothstein (d) D.W. Lewis

342. **Assertion (A):** Many libraries have no written collection development policy and yet have sound collection.
Reason (R): Demand driven collection plays a strong role in having a sound collection.
Codes:
(a) (A) is true, but (R) is false.
(b) (A) is false, but (R) is true.
(c) Both (A) and (R) are true.
(d) Both (A) and (R) are false.

343. The initiation, selection, exploration, formulation, collection and presentation are two stages of which model of information seeking behaviour (*NET Exam.* 2012J)
(a) Ellis Model (b) Krikelas Model
(c) Kuhlthau Model (d) Wilson Model

344. Match the following:
List I
(A) Transaction Processing
(B) Operational Control
(C) Management Control
(D) Strategic Planning

List II
(i) Lower Level Managers
(ii) Clerical Staff
(iii) Top Level Managers
(iv) Middle Level Managers

Codes:	**A**	**B**	**C**	**D**
(a)	(iii)	(ii)	(iv)	(i)
(b)	(ii)	(i)	(iv)	(iii)
(c)	(iv)	(ii)	(iii)	(i)
(d)	(i)	(ii)	(iv)	(iii)

345. Idiographic hypothesis is directed towards predicting the behaviour of (*NET Exam.* 2012J)
(a) An Individual (b) Group of People
(c) Masses (d) People from same school of thought

346. The publisher of "Information Power: Building Partnership for Learning" is (*NET Exam.* 2012J)
(a) AASL (b) AECT (c) ALA (d) ILA

347. 'Segmentation' is associated with (*NET Exam.* 2012J)
(a) Reference Service (b) Market Survey Report
(c) Digest Service (d) Indexing Service

348. Blair and Maron evaluation study on retrieval effectiveness of full text search is called (*NET Exam.* 2012J)
(a) SMART Retrieval Experiment
(b) MEDLARS evaluation study
(c) STAIRS project
(d) Cranefield – II Project

349. Transformation of traditional libraries to hybrid/digital libraries is (*NET Exam.* 2012D)
(a) Crisis Management
(b) Re-engineering
(c) Change Management
(d) Project Management

350. Which of the following are Schools of Management thought? (*NET Exam.* 2012J)
(i) Scientific Management School
(ii) Human Behavioural School
(iii) Classical School
(iv) School of Authority
Codes:
(a) (ii) and (iv) are correct.
(b) (i), (ii) and (iv) are correct.

(c) (iii) and (iv) are correct.
(d) (i), (ii) and (iii) are correct.

351. **Assertion (A):** Training methods through brain storming stimulate idea generation.

Reason (R): Training methods do not provide opportunity to unskilled to become skilled. (*NET Exam.* 2012D)

Codes:
(a) (A) is false but (R) is true.
(b) Both (A) and (R) are false.
(c) Both (A) and (R) are true.
(d) (A) is true but (R) is false.

352. **Assertion (A):** Book selection must be done judiciously.

Reason (R): Resource sharing is the need of the hour.

Codes:
(a) Both (A) and (R) are true, but (R) is not the correct statement of (A).
(b) (A) is false, but (R) is true.
(c) (A) is true, but (R) is false.
(d) Both (A) and (R) are false.

353. Match the following: (*NET Exam.* 2012D)

List - I (Budgetary technique)
(A) Line (B) Formula
(C) PPBS (D) Zero-based

List - II (Limitation of budgetary technique)
(i) Detailed information required
(ii) Time consuming
(iii) Do not permit variation
(iv) Do not suggest future

Codes:	A	B	C	D
(a)	(ii)	(i)	(iv)	(iii)
(b)	(iii)	(ii)	(i)	(iv)
(c)	(iv)	(iii)	(i)	(ii)
(d)	(i)	(iv)	(ii)	(iii)

354. Match the following. (*NET Exam.* 2012D)

List - I
(A) Theory of Command (B) Unity of Motivation
(C) MBO (D) Forecasting

List - II
(i) Factor of planning (ii) Efficiency and waste prevention
(iii) Maslow (iv) Peter Drucker

Codes:	A	B	C	D
(a)	(i)	(ii)	(iii)	(iv)
(b)	(iv)	(i)	(ii)	(iii)
(c)	(ii)	(iii)	(iv)	(i)
(d)	(iii)	(ii)	(iv)	(i)

355. Match the following:

List - I
(A) Thurston scale (B) Semantic Differential Scale
(C) Likert Scale (D) Sociometric scale

List - II
(i) Sharing individual preference in a group
(ii) Group of Judges
(iii) Selection from two opposite position
(iv) Intensity structure.

Codes:	A	B	C	D
(a)	(i)	(iv)	(ii)	(iii)
(b)	(ii)	(iii)	(iv)	(i)
(c)	(iv)	(i)	(iii)	(ii)
(d)	(iii)	(ii)	(iv)	(i)

356. Match the following:

List - I
(A) J. Thompson (B) S. Halkett of J. Laing
(C) William A. Katz (D) K.D. Metcalf

List - II
(i) Basic statistics for Libraries
(ii) Planning of Academic and Research Buildings
(iii) Dictionary of anonymous and pseudonymous literature
(iv) Introduction to reference work

Codes:	A	B	C	D
(a)	(i)	(ii)	(iv)	(iii)
(b)	(i)	(iii)	(iv)	(ii)
(c)	(ii)	(iv)	(i)	(iii)
(d)	(iv)	(ii)	(iii)	(i)

357. Match the following: (*NET Exam.* 2012D)

List - I
(A) Right man at right library
(B) Budget
(C) Journal
(D) Identifying user's views and expectations

List - II
(i) Annual financial statement (ii) Deployment
(iii) TQM (iv) ISSN

Codes:	A	B	C	D
(a)	(iii)	(i)	(ii)	(iv)
(b)	(ii)	(i)	(iv)	(iii)
(c)	(iv)	(ii)	(iii)	(i)
(d)	(i)	(iii)	(iv)	(ii)

358. **Assertion (A):** If changes cannot be adopted to its framework, the organizational equilibrium will be imbalanced.

Reason (R): Organisational works in an environment which is marked by dynamic characteristics. (*NET Exam.* 2012D)

Codes:
(a) (A) is true, but (R) is false.
(b) (A) is false, but (R) are true.
(c) Both (A) and (R) are true.
(d) Both (A) and (R) are false.

359. **Assertion (A):** There is need to continuous evaluation and appreciation of value of libraries.
Reason (R): There is economic pressure on public budget. (*NET Exam.* 2012D)
Codes:
(a) Both (A) and (R) are true.
(b) Both (A) and (R) are false.
(c) (A) is true, but (R) is false.
(d) (A) is false, but (R) is true.

360. ISO 26324 : 2012 is a standard for (*NET 17J ii paper*)
(a) RFID in Libraries (b) DOI
(c) Dublin Core (d) Inter Library Transaction

361. ISO 2108 standard is related to: (*NET 17J ii paper*)
(a) International Standard Serial Number
(b) International Standard Book Number
(c) International Technical Report Number
(d) International Standard for Patents Number

362. The Browne charging system does not include (*NET 17J ii paper*)
(a) Reader's ticket (b) Book card
(c) Date slip (d) Transaction slip

363. Which of the following are the characteristics of not-for-profit organizations according to Edward G. Evans? (*NET 17J ii paper*)
(i) Financial sources derived from outside funding sources rather than from sales of service.
(ii) Have clear indicator of effect i.e. profit or loss.
(iii) Organizations are public rather than private.
(iv) Funding preferences for collaborative projects.
Codes:
(a) (i), (ii) and (iv) are correct.
(b) (i), (iii) and (iv) are correct.
(c) (ii), (iii) and (iv) are correct.
(d) (i), (ii) and (iii) are correct

364. Which of the following are the criteria for defined open standard in W3C (2006)? (*NET 17J ii paper*)
(A) Transparency and Impartiality
(B) Maintenance and Relevance
(C) Availability and Openness
(D) Security and Preservation
Codes:
(a) (A), (B), (D) are correct.
(b) (B), (C), (D) are correct.
(c) (A), (C), (D) are correct.
(d) (A), (B), (C) are correct.

365. Arrange the following according to their year of origin/publication: (*NET 17J ii paper*)
(i) Cause and effect diagram (ii) MBO
(iii) Pareto Principle (iv) POSDCORB
Codes:
(a) (i), (ii), (iii), (iv) (b) (ii), (iii), (iv), (i)
(c) (iii), (iv), (i), (ii) (d) (iv), (i), (ii), (iii)

366. Match the following: (*NET 17J ii paper*)

List – I	List – II
A. ABCD	1. Georgia (USA)
B. KOHA	2. New Zealand
C. Weblis	3. Brazil
D. Evergreen	4. Poland

Codes:	A	B	C	D
(a)	3	2	4	1
(b)	4	2	1	3
(c)	3	4	1	2
(d)	1	2	4	3

367. Match the following: (*NET 17J ii paper*)
List – I
A. Library Finance B. Non-plan Grant
C. Non-Recurring Grant D. Plan Grant
List – II
1. Regular Grant
2. Funds given for building, Infrastructure & Machinery
3. Sources of Income and Expenditure
4. Funds given for project under annual / 5 year plan

Codes:	A	B	C	D
(a)	2	3	1	4
(b)	1	4	3	2
(c)	3	1	2	4
(d)	2	1	4	3

368. Hermeneutics, principle is primarily related with (*NET 17 NOV iii paper*)
(a) Interpretation of texts
(b) Interrelation between data and knowledge
(c) Human experience
(d) Human behaviour

369. Who coined the word "Management theory jungle"? *(NET 17 NOV iii paper)*
(a) Henry Fayol (b) F.W. Taylor
(c) Heinz Weihrich (d) Harold Koontz

370. Which of the following cases require the application of a new ISSN? *(NET 17 NOV iii paper)*
(a) Change in publisher
(b) Change in publication medium and title
(c) Change in location of publication
(d) Change in editorial policy

371. Which of the following are the components of a barcode symbol? *(NET 17 NOV iii paper)*
(i) Antenna (ii) Quiet zone
(iii) Transponder (iv) Start character
Codes:
(a) (i) and (iii) are correct
(b) (ii) and (iii) are correct
(c) (ii) and (iv) are correct
(d) (i) and (iv) are correct

372. Arrange in sequence the Maslow's hierarchy of needs: *(NET 17 NOV iii paper)*
(i) Social (ii) Esteem
(iii) Physiological (iv) Safety
Codes:
(a) (iii), (iv), (i), (ii) (b) (iv), (ii), (i), (iii)
(c) (iv), (i), (iii), (ii) (d) (iii), (i), (ii), (iv)

373. Arrange in sequence the following document titles alphabetically word by word: *(NET 17 NOV iii paper)*
(i) Bookfinder (ii) Bookkeeping made simple
(iii) Book bytes (iv) Books that changed the world
Codes:
(a) (i), (ii), (iii), (iv) (b) (ii), (iii), (iv), (i)
(c) (iii), (i), (ii), (iv) (d) (iii), (iv), (i), (ii)

374. Match the following Office Products with their corresponding Producers/Organisations: *(NET 17 NOV iii paper)*

List – I	List – II
(A) Open Office	(1) IBM
(B) MS-Office	(2) Apache Foundation
(C) Lotus Note	(3) Apple
(D) iWork	(4) Microsoft Corporation

Codes:	(A)	(B)	(C)	(D)
(a)	(1)	(2)	(3)	(4)
(b)	(2)	(4)	(1)	(3)
(c)	(1)	(4)	(3)	(2)
(d)	(4)	(2)	(1)	(3)

375. **Assertion (A):** In collection development, pamphlets do not require frequent review like books and journals.
Reason (R): Pamphlet's information value is likely to be short lived, their physical format is usually flimsy and subject to rapid deterioration. *(NET 17 NOV iii paper)*
Codes:
(a) (A) is true, but (R) is false.
(b) (A) is false, but (R) is true.
(c) Both (A) and (R) are true.
(d) Both (A) and (R) are false

376. **Assertion (A):** In recent years, QR codes have become ubiquitous and may replace the use of bar codes.
Reason (R): QR is a two-dimensional code with large capacity for storage. These codes hold information both horizontally and vertically and can be scanned by users with their smart phones at ease. *(NET 17 NOV iii paper)*
Codes:
(a) (A) is true, but (R) is false.
(b) (A) is false, but (R) is true.
(c) Both (A) and (R) are true.
(d) Both (A) and (R) are false.

377. 'Delphi Technique' was first discussed in a monograph by *(NET 14D ii paper)*
(a) O. Helmer (b) E. Nagel
(c) D.M. Potter (d) J.H. Shera

378. Bench marking, SWOT analysis and Environmental Scanning activities should occur continually and consistently in Library's strategic planning process to ensure that *(NET 16J iii paper)*
(a) the organisation is competitive and enabled to meet future needs as they occur.
(b) not to modify or update mission statements of the organisation periodically.
(c) to keep the library stakeholders under cloud about the forward movement of the organisation.
(d) to de-recognise the faster movement of technology.

379. The term 'Gang Plank' is associated with ______ administrative principle. *(NET 16J iii paper)*
(a) Remuneration (b) Stability of Tenure
(c) Scalar Chain (d) Division of Labour

380. Identify the correct sequence of the facet formula for book number as propounded by S.R. Ranganathan: (*NET 16J iii paper*)

i. Evaluation	ii. Language
iii. Year	iv. Form

Codes:

(a) ii, iv, iii and i	(b) ii, i, iv and iii
(c) ii, iii, iv and i	(d) iv, iii and ii

381. Match the following authors with the subjects they are associated with: (*NET 16J ii paper*)

List – I	List – II
A. Peter Suber	1. Management
B. H.E. Bliss	2. Information Technology
C. Henry Fayol	3. Classification
D. Tim Berners Lee	4. Open Access Movement

Codes:	A	B	C	D
(a)	4	3	1	2
(b)	3	2	1	2
(c)	1	3	4	2
(d)	2	4	3	1

382. Match the following: (*NET 16J ii paper*)

List – I

A. Invenio	B. Moodle
C. Share Point	D. PhpMyAdmin

List – II

1. Course Management System
2. Content Management System
3. Digital Library System
4. Web Database Management

Codes:	A	B	C	D
(a)	3	1	2	4
(b)	4	1	2	3
(c)	2	1	3	4
(d)	4	3	2	1

383. **Assertion (A):** Commercial Library Management Softwares need to be discouraged in libraries to make the contemporary librarians free from the dictate of commercial vendors. (*NET 16J ii paper*)

Reason (R): Open source softwares (OSS) are more flexible and are free from much recurring expenditure and wider user base of OSS helps in problem solving better.

Codes:

(a) Both (A) and (R) are true.
(b) Both (A) and (R) are false.
(c) (A) is true, but (R) is false.
(d) (A) is false, but (R) is true.

384. **Assertion (A):** Total quality in organization usually depends upon the skill and competency of library staff. (*NET 16J ii paper*)

Reason (R): Quality management is an information-based management system where professional education alone helps the employee to take decisions judiciously.

Codes:

(a) (A) is false, but (R) is true.
(b) Both (A) and (R) are true.
(c) (A) is true, but (R) is false.
(d) Both (A) and (R) are false

385. **Assertion (A):** Libraries must have a well-defined collection development policy to make their collection balanced, rational and user-friendly. (*NET 16J ii paper*)

Reason (R): Exponential growth of e-resources, their spiralling cost and decreasing budget of libraries have made consortium based system imminent.

Codes:

(a) Both (A) and (R) are true.
(b) Both (A) and (R) are false.
(c) (A) is true, but (R) is false.
(d) (A) is false, but (R) is true.

386. **Assertion (A):** In Gold Open Access, costs are not transferred to authors.

Reason (R): Gold Open Access journals publish peer-reviewed articles without paid subscription barriers for their readers. (*NET 17 NOV iii paper*)

Codes:

(a) (A) is true, but (R) is false.
(b) (A) is false, but (R) is true.
(c) Both (A) and (R) are true.
(d) Both (A) and (R) are false.

387. International Standard Name Identifier (ISNI) consists of (*NET 17 NOV ii paper*)

(a) 10 digits	(b) 12 digits
(c) 13 digits	(d) 16 digits

388. Which of the following are work analysis techniques according to Edward Evans? (*NET 17 NOV ii paper*)

(i) PERT-CPM
(ii) GANTT-Charts
(iii) Operation research
(iv) Cost-effectiveness

Codes:
(a) (iv) and (ii) are correct
(b) (ii) and (iii) are correct
(c) (i) and (iii) are correct
(d) (iii) and (iv) are correct

389. Arrange the following Open Access Initiatives/Policy Statements according to the year of their adoption/declaration at international level. *(NET 17 NOV ii paper)*
(i) The Coalition of Open Access Policy Institutions (COAPI)
(ii) The Berlin Declaration on Open Access to Knowledge in the Sciences and Humanities (BDOAKS and H)
(iii) The Budapest Open Access Initiatives (BOAI)
(iv) Scholarly Publishing and Academic Resources Coalition (SPARC)
Codes:
(a) (i), (ii), (iii), (iv) (b) (iv), (iii), (ii), (i)
(c) (ii), (i), (iv), (iii) (d) (iii), (iv), (ii), (i)

390. **Assertion (A):** Implementation of TQM in Libraries is quite challenging.
Reason (R): Some of the key essentials, like open and cooperative culture and employees responsiveness for customer's satisfaction, required for successful implementation of TQM, are very much noticed in a library. *(NET 17 NOV ii paper)*
Codes:
(a) (A) is true, but (R) is false.
(b) (A) is false, but (R) is true.
(c) Both (A) and (R) are true.
(d) Both (A) and (R) are false.

391. **Assertion (A):** Access to e-collection of a library via Login and password recognition is mostly used than access via IP-address.
Reason (R): Access via IP-address presents a challenge in controlling the distribution of password to non-affiliates. *(NET 17 NOV ii paper)*
Codes:
(a) (A) is true, and (R) is false
(b) Both (A) and (R) are true
(c) (A) is false and (R) is true
(d) Both (A) and (R) are false

392. **Assertion (A):** Interlibrary loan departments in libraries will be affected in positive ways by the development of Massive Digital Libraries.
Reason (R): Because the increased availability of online resources will considerably reduce the need for sending books through traditional mail resulting in the decrease of the workloads of the inter-library loan departments. *(NET 17 NOV ii paper)*
Codes:
(a) (A) is true, but (R) is false.
(b) Both (A) and (R) are true.
(c) (A) is false, but (R) is true.
(d) Both (A) and (R) are false

393. By which mode 'Management Science' and 'Research Methodology' are formed? *(NET 16J ii paper)*
(a) Agglomeration (b) Fusion
(c) Cluster (d) Distillation

394. 'Prefix' element of ISBN consists of _____ number of digits. *(NET 16J ii paper)*
(a) 3 (b) 5 (c) 4 (d) 2

395. Who defined notation as shorthand sign? *(NET 16J ii paper)*
(a) S.R. Ranganathan (b) Benjamin A. Custer
(c) Immanuel Kant (d) E.C. Richardson

396. Collection development principles are given by: *(NET 16J ii paper)*
i. C.A. Cutter ii. Melvil Dewey
iii. S.R. Ranganathan iv. B.S. Kesavan
Codes:
(a) i, ii are correct. (b) ii, iii are correct.
(c) iii, iv are correct. (d) ii, iv are correct.

397. 'Product life-cycle' is helpful in: *(NET 16J ii paper)*
i. deciding marketing strategies best fitted to particular stages in the development of service activities.
ii. maintaining that all products or services follow distinctive pattern overtime.
iii. dealing with the historical aspect of the product.
iv. dealing with the stages of product life-cycle.
Codes:
(a) i, ii, iv are correct.
(b) i, ii, iii are correct.
(c) ii, iii, iv are correct.
(d) i, iii, iv are correct.

398. Identify the following basic steps as advocated by William Edwards for implementing TQM: *(NET 16J ii paper)*

i. Assessment of organisation's culture and training process for the top management.
ii. Formation of Quality Council.
iii. Dissemination of information through established communication system and integration of TQM tools, techniques and training.
iv. Filtering and censoring Information.

Codes:
(a) ii, iii and iv are correct.
(b) i, ii and iii are correct.
(c) i, iii and iv are correct.
(d) i, ii and iv are correct.

399. Identify the correct elements of 'AIDA' model in Marketing Communication. (*NET 16J ii paper*)
(a) Attraction, Investigation, Direction, Action
(b) Attention, Intuition, Desire, Acquisition
(c) Attention, Interest, Desire, Action
(d) Abstract, Institution, Diversity, Action

400. Arrange the following international standards developed in the broader context of 'Information Organisation' in their respective year of development: (*NET 16J ii paper*)
i. ISO-999 ii. ISO-214
iii. ISO-2788 iv. ISO-5963

Codes:
(a) iii, ii, iv, i (b) i, ii, iii, iv
(c) ii, iii, iv, i (d) iv, iii, ii,i

401. Match the following: (*NET 16J ii paper*)

List – I	**List – II**
A. New Gen Lib	1. 1984
B. LIBSYS	2. 2000
C. Koha	3. 2005
D. Open Biblio	4. 2002

Codes:	**A**	**B**	**C**	**D**
(a)	2	1	3	4
(b)	2	1	4	3
(c)	3	1	2	4
(d)	4	3	2	1

402. Match the following: (*NET 16J ii paper*)

List – I
A. Key to a given collection
B. Key to literary sources on a subject
C. Representation of subject concept
D. Condensation of a document

List – II
1. Abstract 2. Index
3. Catalogue 4. Bibliography

Codes:	**A**	**B**	**C**	**D**
(a)	4	2	3	1
(b)	3	2	1	4
(c)	3	4	2	1
(d)	1	3	2	4

403. Match the following: (*NET 16J ii paper*)

List – I	**List – II**
A. Classical School	1. John Cotton Dana
B. X and Y Theory	2. Henry Fayol
C. Newark Charging System	3. Peter Drucker
D. MBO	4. Douglas McGregor

Codes:	**A**	**B**	**C**	**D**
(a)	1	3	4	2
(b)	3	4	1	2
(c)	2	4	1	3
(d)	3	2	4	1

404. Identify the persons who contributed to the development of TQM. (*NET 16J ii paper*)
i. Philip B. Crosby ii. Kaoru Ishikawa
iii. Joseph Juran iv. Michael Gorman

Codes:
(a) i, ii, iii are correct. (b) ii, iii, iv are correct.
(c) i, iii, iv are correct. (d) i, ii, iv are correct.

405. **Assertion (A):** Management is the efficiency in climbing the ladder of success.

Reason (R): Leadership determines whether the ladder is leaning towards right wall. (*NET 16J ii paper*)

Codes:
(a) (A) is true, but (R) is false.
(b) (A) is false, but (R) is true.
(c) Both (A) and (R) are true.
(d) Both (A) and (R) are false.

406. 'Working Papers' fall under the category of (*NET 15J iii paper*)
(a) Books (b) Monographs
(c) News papers (d) Grey Literature

407. Herzberg's 'two factor theory' deals with: (*NET 15J iii paper*)
(a) Staff recruitment (b) Leadership
(c) Decision making (d) Motivation

408. **Assertion (A):** There is no difference between knowledge management and Information Management.

Reason (R): Knowledge and Information are sometimes used synonymously and inter changeably. (*NET 15J iii paper*)

Codes:
(a) (A) is true, but (R) is false
(b) Both (A) and (R) are true
(c) (A) is false but (R) is true
(d) Both (A) and (R) are false

409. A template is a (*NET 14D ii paper*)
(a) Structured specification
(b) Recursive routine
(c) Assembler program
(d) I/O measure

410. Which of the following are standard TQM tools? (*NET 14D ii paper*)
(i) Pie chart (ii) Zigzag chart
(iii) Fishbone diagram (iv) Pareto chart
Codes:
(a) (i), (iv) are correct.
(b) (ii), (iii), (iv) are correct.
(c) (i), (iii), (iv) are correct.
(d) (iii), (iv) are correct.

411. Which of the following organizations are contributing to the implementation of standards for networked information system? (*NET 14D ii paper*)
(i) CNI (ii) W3C (iii) IANA (iv) IEEE
Codes:
(a) (i) and (iii) are correct.
(b) (ii) and (iv) are correct.
(c) (ii) and (iii) are correct.
(d) (i), (ii) are correct.

412. The principle which states 'that between two or more possible alternatives bearing on a particular phenomenon the one leading to overall economy is to be preferred' is known as (*NET 15J ii paper*)
(a) Law of symmetry
(b) Law of Parsimony
(c) Law of Osmosis
(d) Law of Impartiality

413. The cords associated with genealogy file might reasonably be arranged in a: (*NET 15J ii paper*)
(a) Clustered files (b) Tree-structured files
(c) Hashed files (d) Indexed files

414. "Rank x frequency = constant" formula describes the essence of: (*NET 15Jii paper*)
(a) Impact factor (b) Zipf's Law
(c) Fuzzy query (d) Lotka Law

415. Six Sigma inquality management was developed by: (*NET 15J ii paper*)
(a) Motorola (b) IBM
(c) Honeywell (d) GENPACT

416. In Binary Number System digit '11' is represented by: (*NET 15J ii paper*)
(a) 1010 (b) 00001011
(c) 110011 (d) 00010110

417. Arrange the following elements of ISBN in proper order: (*NET 15J ii paper*)
(i) Check Digit
(ii) Registration Group Element
(iii) Publication Element
(iv) Registrant Element
Codes:
(a) (i), (iii), (ii), (iv) (c) (iii), (i), (iv), (ii)
(c) (iv), (ii), (i), (iii) (d) (ii), (iv), (iii), (i)

418. Which of the following display racks are used to display print periodical publications? (*NET 15J ii paper*)
(i) Kardex (ii) Steptype
(iii) Pigeon koletype (iv) Inclinedtype
Codes:
(a) (i), (ii) and (iii) are correct
(b) (ii), (iii) and (iv) are correct
(c) (i), (iii)and(iv) are correct
(d) (i), (ii) and (iv) are correct

419. Match the following: (*NET 15J ii paper*)
List - I
(A) W. Edward Deming
(B) Elton Mayo and others
(C) Kaoru Ishikawa
(D) Shigeo Shingo
List - II
(1) Quality Control Circles
(2) Statistical Process Control
(3) Hawthorne Studies
(4) Zero defect

Codes:	A	B	C	D
(a)	2	3	1	4
(b)	3	1	4	2
(c)	4	2	3	1
(d)	1	4	3	2

420. Match the following: (*NET 15J ii paper*)
List - I
(A) A pictograph that stands for an individual word
(B) A pictograph that stands for an individual idea
(C) Pictographs drawn or painted on rocks
(D) Pictographs incised or carved on rocks

List - II

(1) Pictographs (2) Petrograms
(3) Ideogram (4) Logogram

Codes:	A	B	C	D
(a)	(3)	(2)	(1)	(4)
(b)	(2)	(3)	(4)	(1)
(c)	(4)	(3)	(2)	(1)
(d)	(1)	(4)	(3)	(2)

421. Match the following: *(NET 15J ii paper)*

List - I

(A) Ecological Theory of Human Information Behaviour
(B) Everyday Life Information Seeking
(C) Information Encountering
(D) Anamalous State of Knowledge (ASK)

List - II

(1) Sanda Erdelez (2) Williamson
(3) Nicholas J. Belkin (4) Reijo Savolainen

Codes:	A	B	C	D
(a)	2	4	1	3
(b)	2	1	3	4
(c)	1	4	2	3
(d)	4	1	3	2

422. Match the following: *(NET 15J ii paper)*

List – I

(A) Nominal scale (B) Ordinal scale
(C) Interval scale (D) Ratio scale

List – II

(1) Temperature measurement
(2) Gender as variable
(3) Ranking of library services
(4) Mass of a body

Codes:	A	B	C	D
(a)	3	4	2	1
(b)	2	3	4	1
(c)	2	3	1	4
(d)	1	4	3	2

423. **Assertion (A):** Users need to have training in accessing to a large number of E-journals through consortia. *(NET 15J ii paper)*

Reason (R): Most of the users are not aware of using Web-resources.

Codes:

(a) (A) is true, but (R) is false.
(c) (A) is false, but (R) is true.
(b) Both (A) and (R) are false.
(d) Both (A) and (R) are true.

424. Which of the following are the elements of marketing mix? *(NET 15D iii paper)*

(i) Selling (ii) Place
(iii) Purchasing (iv) Product

Codes:

(a) (i) and (ii) are correct
(b) (ii) and (iii) are correct
(c) (iii) and (iv) are correct
(d) (ii) and (iv) are correct

425. Which of the following are the management theories related to motivation? *(NET 15D iii paper)*

(i) Maslow Theory of Needs
(ii) Drucker Theory
(iii) McGregor Theory of X and Y
(iv) Fayol Theory

Codes:

(a) (i), (ii) and (iii) are correct
(b) (ii), (iii) and (iv) are correct
(c) (i), (ii) and (iv) are correct
(d) (i), (iii) and (iv) are correct

426. Which of the following are the techniques of Total Quality Management (TQM)? *(NET 15D iii paper)*

(i) Quality circles (ii) Empowerment
(iii) Bureaucratic set up (iv) Participative management

Codes:

(a) (i), (iii) and (iv) are correct
(b) (i), (ii) and (iv) are correct
(c) ii, iii and iv are correct
(d) i, iii and ii are correct

427. Identify the correct sequence of the Abraham Maslow's hierarchy of needs: *(NET 15D iii paper)*

(i) Esteem (ii) Belonging
(iii) Safety (iv) Physiological

Codes:

(a) (ii), (iii), (iv) and (i)
(b) (iii), (ii), (iv) and (i)
(c) (iv), (ii), (iii) and (i)
(d) (iv), (iii), (ii) and (i)

428. **Assertion (A):** A recent feature that have been incorporated to Integrated Library Management Software is self-checking or self-issue of books option in the circulation module using RFID technology.

Reason (R): Application of RFID technology is economically viable and suitable to all types of libraries. *(NET 15D iii paper)*

Codes:

(a) Both (A) and (R) are true.
(b) (A) is false, but (R) is true.
(c) (A) is true, and (R) is false.
(d) Both (A) and (R) are false.

429. Arrange in sequence the steps involved in Browne Charging Procedure: *(NET 15D iii paper)*

(i) Stamping the date slip
(ii) Identification of borrower
(iii) Slipping the book card in reader's ticket
(iv) Arrange cards in juxtaposition

Codes:

(a) (i), (iv), (ii) and (iii)
(b) (ii), (iii), (i) and (iv)
(c) (iii), (ii), (iv) and (i)
(d) (iv), (i), (iii) and (ii)

430. Match the following: *(NET 13D ii paper)*

List – I	List – II
A. McGregor Theory X	1. Less External Control
B. McGregor Theory Y	2. PERT
C. Unity of Command	3. Workers' Participation in Decision Making
D. Time and Cost	4. All Powers in One Person

Codes:	A	B	C	D
(a)	3	1	4	2
(b)	4	1	3	2
(c)	2	4	3	1
(d)	1	3	2	4

431. Match the following: *(NET 2013D ii paper)*

List – I

A. W. Edward Deming
B. Joseph M. Juran
C. Armand V. Feigenbaum
D. Kaoru Ishikava

List – II

1. Quality Control Circles
2. TQM
3. Planning, Control, Improvement
4. Plan, Do, Check, Act (PDCA)

Codes:	A	B	C	D
(a)	2	3	4	1
(b)	4	2	1	3
(c)	3	4	1	2
(d)	4	3	2	1

432. Match the following: *(NET-13D ii paper)*

List – I

A. Herbert Hicks B. F.W. Taylor
C. Henry Fayol D. Colonel L. Urwick

List – II

1. The Elements of Administration
2. The Management of Organisation
3. Scientific Management
4. Administrative Management

Codes:	A	B	C	D
(a)	1	4	2	3
(b)	4	2	3	1
(c)	2	3	4	1
(d)	3	4	1	2

433. **Assertion (A):** Knowledge Management involves a number of assets and value added to them. *(NET 13D ii paper)*

Reason (R): Knowledge Management is the core activity of information transfer.

Codes:

(a) (A) is true, but (R) is false.
(b) (A) is true, but (R) is partially true.
(c) Both (A) and (R) are true.
(d) (A) is partially true but (R) is true.

434. A rubber stamp impressed on the verso of title page giving information concerning the records and processing of each individual book acquired is called *(NET 13D iii paper)*

(a) Book stamp (b) Process stamp
(c) Date stamp (d) Accession stamp

435. Which of the following are the advantages of RFID technology in libraries? *(NET 13D iii paper)*

(i) Tags can be read inside a case.
(ii) Hundred of tags can be read at a time.
(iii) Cheaper than Barcode
(iv) More security and Privacy

Codes:

(a) (i) and (iii) are correct
(b) (i) and (ii) are correct
(c) (ii) and (iii) are correct
(d) (iii) and (iv) are correct

436. Which of the following are called 'path finders' to the literature? *(NET 13D iii paper)*

(i) Bibliography (ii) Catalogue
(iii) Shelf List (iv) Indices and Abstracts

Codes:

(a) (i) & (ii) are correct
(b) (i), (ii) & (iv) are correct

(c) (i) & (iv) are correct
(d) (ii) & (iii) are correct

437. Arrange the following factors of TQM in the order of their implementation: *(NET 13D iii paper)*

i. Development of Human Resource Management
ii. Standardisation of Work process
iii. Improvement in Internal Organisation Management
iv. Quality Management Procedures

Codes:
(a) ii iii i iv (b) iii iv ii i
(c) iv iii ii i (d) ii iv iii i

438. Arrange in order the process of stock rectification and stock verification as suggested by S.R. Ranganathan: *(NET 13D iii paper)*

i. Checking with charged tray
ii. Shelf Rectification
iii. Shelf checking
iv. Deciding the Quota

Codes:
(a) iii i iv ii (b) iv i ii iii
(c) iv ii iii i (d) ii iv i iii

439. Match the following: *(NET 13D iii paper)*

List – I
A. Estimation of future expenditure on the basis of previous year expenditure
B. ₹ 15 per student and ₹ 200/- per teacher
C. 6.5%-10% of university budget for the development of library
D. Activities to be accomplished by the library

List – II
1. Programme 2. Comparison
3. Per capita 4. Proportional

Codes:	A	B	C	D
(a)	2	3	4	1
(b)	1	2	3	4
(c)	3	4	1	2
(d)	4	1	2	3

440. Match the following: *(NET 13D iii paper)*

List – I
A. Identification of user categories
B. Prioriting user groups and services
C. Information seeking behaviour of users
D. Product, price, place, promotion

List – II
1. Market positioning 2. Segmentation
3. Marketing Mix 4. Consumer analysis

Codes:	A	B	C	D
(a)	1	2	3	4
(b)	2	1	4	3
(c)	3	4	1	2
(d)	4	3	2	1

441. **Assertion (A):** Performance Based Budgeting demands that the objectives and goals of agency be clear and performance measures and target to put in place.

Reason (R): The key to success firmly rely upon its clear sense of mission and objectives which the funding agencies have proposed to reach them. *(NET 13D iii paper)*

Codes:
(a) (A) is true, but (R) is false.
(b) (A) is false, but (R) is true.
(c) Both (A) and (R) are true.
(d) Both (A) and (R) are false.

442. Match the following: *(NET 2014J ii paper)*

List – I	List – II
A. Check Card	1. Reader's Ticket
B. Kardex	2. Three Card System
C. Newark System	3. Periodicals
D. Browne System	4. Borrower's Card

Codes:	A	B	C	D
(a)	2	3	4	1
(b)	3	4	1	2
(c)	2	4	3	1
(d)	4	1	2	3

443. Cost recovery and profit making aspects in relation to gathering information, organization, services and usage, etc. refer to *(NET 14J iii paper)*

(a) Economy evaluation
(b) Coverage evaluation
(c) Workforce evaluation
(d) User evaluation

444. The three leadership styles identified by Koontz and others are *(NET 14J iii paper)*

i. Autocratic ii. Democratic
iii. Trait approach iv. Free-reign

Codes:
(a) i, ii and iii are correct.
(b) ii, iii and iv are correct.
(c) iii, iv and i are correct.
(d) i, ii and iv are correct.

445. Match the following: (*NET 14J iii paper*)

List – I	List – II
A. Harrold Koontz	1. MBO
B. Rensis Likert	2. Three leadership styles
C. Peter Drucker	3. Four systems management
D. George Haber	4. Problem solving Vs. Decision making

Codes:	A	B	C	D
(a)	1	2	3	4
(b)	3	4	1	2
(c)	4	3	2	1
(d)	2	3	1	4

446. Match the following: (*NET 14J iii paper*)

List – I

A. Principle of Osmosis
B. Theory of Literary Warrants
C. Public Libraries are stagnating pools of books
D. Firewall

List – II

1. Security
2. Sinha Committee
3. Reclassification
4. Dr. S.R. Ranganathan

Codes:	A	B	C	D
(a)	4	2	3	1
(b)	3	4	2	1
(c)	4	3	1	2
(d)	1	2	4	3

447. Identify the assistive softwares: (*NET 14D iii paper*)

i. Cybrarian
ii. Dragon
iii. Jaws
iv. Librarian

Codes:

(a) i and ii are correct.
(b) i and iii are correct.
(c) ii and iii are correct.
(d) iii and iv are correct.

448. **Assertion (A):** An ISO 2709: 2008 record structure and review format has 'Record Label', 'Directory', 'Data fields' and 'Record Separator'.

Reason (R): ISO 2709 is a subset of MARC. (*NET 14D iii paper*)

Codes:

(a) (A) is true, but (R) is false.
(b) (A) is false, but (R) is true.
(c) Both (A) and (R) are true.
(d) Both (A) and (R) are false.

449. **Assertion (A):** Knowledge Management is an extension of conventional library management.

Reason (R): Knowledge Management deals with elements like content, technology and culture. (*NET 14D iii paper*)

Codes:

(a) (A) is true, but (R) is false.
(b) Both (A) and (R) are true.
(c) (A) is false, but (R) is true.
(d) Both (A) and (R) are false.

450. **Assertion (A):** Traditional Management process differ from the 'Quality Management'.

Reason (R): 'Quality Management' focuses on 'customer' in the management process. (*NET 14D iii paper*)

Codes:

(a) (A) is true, but (R) is false.
(b) (A) is false, but (R) is true.
(c) Both (A) and (R) are false.
(d) Both (A) and (R) are true.

451. **Assertion (A):** Social networking tools are very effective for marketing of library products and services.

Reason (R): It does not help to reach out the patrons anywhere any time. (*NET 14D iii paper*)

Codes:

(a) (A) is true, but (R) is false.
(b) (A) is false, but (R) is true.
(c) Both (A) and (R) are true.
(d) Both (A) and (R) are false.

452. Arrange the following steps in the order of accessioning the book: (*NET 14D iii paper*)

i. Arrange books as per bill
ii. Check books as per order placed
iii. Enter the accession number in the register
iv. Write accession number on back of title page of other relevant pages

Codes:

(a) i, ii, iii, iv
(b) ii, iii, i, iv
(c) iii, i, ii, iv
(d) ii, i, iii, iv

453. Match the following: (*NET 14D iii paper*)

List – I	List – II
A. Market segmentation	1. User behaviour
B. Consumer analysis	2. Market mix
C. Market positioning	3. Category of users
D. Market program	4. Prioritising users

Codes:	A	B	C	D
(a)	1	3	2	4
(b)	3	1	4	2
(c)	2	4	1	3
(d)	4	2	3	1

454. Match the following: (*NET 14D iii paper*)

List – I

A. Standing order B. Blanket order
C. Firm order D. Approval order

List – II

1. For serial publications till cancellation
2. Routine publications on order
3. For publications on recommendation
4. For supply of institutional publications as and when published

Codes:	A	B	C	D
(a)	4	2	1	3
(b)	3	2	1	4
(c)	1	4	2	3
(d)	2	4	1	3

455. Which of the following are the types of validity of measurement?

(*NET 14D iii paper*)

i. Construct ii. Current
iii. Content iv. Predictive

Codes:

(a) i, ii, iii are true. (b) ii, iii, iv are true.
(c) i, iii, iv are true. (d) i, ii, iv are true.

456. Which are not open source library softwares?

(*NET 14D iii paper*)

i. Bibliosys ii. Evergreen
iii. New Genlib iv. Virtua

Codes:

(a) i and ii are correct.
(b) i and iii are correct.
(c) i and iv are correct.
(d) ii and iv are correct.

457. Who propounded the 'theory of human relation'?

(a) Rensis Likert (b) Elton Mayo
(c) Barnard (d) None of the above

458. Identify the budget heads of non-recurring budget:

(i) Periodical subscription
(ii) Maintenance of equipment
(iii) Building extension
(iv) Infrastructure development

Codes:

(a) (i) and (ii) are correct
(b) (ii) and (iii) are correct
(c) (iii) and (iv) are correct
(d) (i), (iii) and (iv) are correct

459. Match the following:

List – I

A. Informing about best books
B. Guidance to use citation manual
C. Providing prints for downloads
D. Providing list of URLs

List – II

1. Support service 2. Bibliography
3. Readers advisory 4. Users education

Codes:	A	B	C	D
(a)	2	3	1	4
(b)	3	4	1	2
(c)	4	2	3	1
(d)	2	4	3	1

460. Which of the following are not Change Management Models?

(*NET 13D iii paper*)

(i) Kurt Lewin's Model (ii) Beer's Model
(iii) Lasswell's Model (iv) Epidemic Model

Codes:

(a) (i) & (iii) are correct.
(b) (ii) & (iii) are correct.
(c) (iii) & (iv) are correct.
(d) (ii) & (iv) are correct.

461. Match the following:

(*NET 14J iii paper*)

List – I	List – II
A. Theory of Hygiene & Motivation	1. Likert
B. Maturity Theory	2. Vroom and Lawler
C. Expectancy Theory	3. Herzberg
D. Analysis Theory	4. Argyris

Codes:	A	B	C	D
(a)	2	3	4	1
(b)	3	4	2	1
(c)	2	1	3	4
(d)	4	1	2	3

462. **Assertion (A):** LIS professionals are ultimately bestowed with the responsibility of building the image of the profession.

Reason (R): The measure of the image is the service they render and not their financial gains. (*NET 15D iii paper*)

Codes:
(a) Both (A) and (R) are true.
(b) Both (A) and (R) are false.
(c) (A) is true but (R) is false.
(d) (A) is false but (R) is true.

463. **Assertion (A):** Application of six sigma in library management is a quality programme that improves customers' experience and lowers costs.

Reason (R): Six phases of sigma are necessary in all library operations. *(NET 17J iii paper)*

Codes:
(a) (A) is true, but (R) is false.
(b) (A) is false, but (R) is true.
(c) Both (A) and (R) are true.
(d) Both (A) and (R) are false.

464. Match the following management concepts with their corresponding propounders:

List – I
(A) Quality Trilogy Process
(B) Quality Management Maturity Grid
(C) 14 points for management
(D) Fishbone diagram

List – II
(1) Philip B. Crosby (2) W. Edwards Deming
(3) J.M. Juran (4) Kaoru Ishikawa

Codes:	**(A)**	**(B)**	**(C)**	**(D)**
(a)	(3)	(1)	(2)	(4)
(b)	(1)	(2)	(3)	(4)
(c)	(4)	(3)	(2)	(1)
(d)	(3)	(2)	(4)	(1)

465. Which of the following does not protect intellectual property? *(NET 13 SEPT iii paper)*
(a) Encryption of data
(b) Digital watermark
(c) Uniquely encoded licences
(d) Plug-ins

466. Arrange the following according to the procedural steps: *(NET 14D iii paper)*
i. Receipt of recommendations
ii. Preparing master card
iii. Checking titles of and bibliographical details
iv. Duplication checking from library catalogue

Codes:
(a) i, ii, iii, iv (b) i, iii, ii, iv
(c) iii, i, iv, ii (d) iv, iii, i, ii

467. **Assertion (A):** Inter-library loan services are still a necessity in the information explosion regime.

Reason (R): None of the libraries are self sufficient with respect to their holding. *(NET D15 ii paper)*

Codes:
(a) Both(A) and (R) true.
(b) (A) is true and (R) is false.
(c) Both(A) and (R) are false.
(d) (A) is false and (R) is true.

468. **Assertion (A):** Open Access Publication Model involves zero cost.

Reason (R): Open Access increases the visibility of the publication, as they are available to the users for free. *(NET 15D ii paper)*

Codes:
(a) Both (A) and (R) are true.
(b) (A) is true, but (R) is false.
(c) (A) is false, but (R) is true.
(d) Both (A) and (R) are false.

469. Match the following *(NET 15D ii paper)*

List-I	**List-II**
(A) Turnitin	(1) Electronic Resource Management Software
(B) Drupal	(2) Usage Statistics Software
(C) CORAL	(3) Anti-plagiarism Software
(D) SUSHI	(4) Content Management Software

Codes:	**(A)**	**(B)**	**(C)**	**(D)**
(a)	(3)	(4)	(2)	(1)
(b)	(2)	(4)	(1)	(3)
(c)	(4)	(3)	(2)	(1)
(d)	(3)	(4)	(1)	(2)

470. Arrange in sequence the evolution of Intel Processors *(NET 15D ii paper)*
(i) Pentium (ii) 8008
(iii) 486 TM CPU (iv) 80286

Codes:
(a) (iv), (ii), (iii), (i) (b) (ii), (iv), (iii), (i)
(c) (iii), (ii), (i), (iv) (d) (i), (iv), (ii), (iii)

471. Arrange in sequence the basic components of MBO system: *(NET 15D ii paper)*
(i) Conducting reviews
(ii) Setting objectives
(iii) Appraising performance
(iv) Developing action plans

Codes:
(a) (ii), (i), (iii) and (iv)
(b) (ii), (iv), (i) and (iii)
(c) (i), (ii), (iv) and (iii)
(d) (iii), (i), (iv) and (ii)

472. Which of the following are Impact Printers? *(NET 15D ii paper)*
(i) Inkjet (ii) Line
(iii) Dot Matrix (iv) Laser
Codes:
(a) (ii), (iii) are correct.
(b) (i), (ii), (iii) are correct
(c) (i), (iv) are correct.
(d) iii, (iv) are correct

473. Which among the following are true about publication element of ISBN?
(i) Variable Length (ii) Upto 5 digits
(iii) Fixed Length (iv) Upto 6 digits
Codes:
(a) (i), (iv) are correct.
(b) (i), (ii), (iv) are correct.
(c) (ii), (iii), (iv) are correct.
(d) (i), (iii) are correct.

474. According to Dr. S.R. Ranganathan 'Library Civics and Hygiene' means:
(i) Library behaviour (ii) Library Layout
(iii) Physique of Book (iv) Care of Book
Codes:
(a) (i), (ii) and (iv) are correct.
(b) (iv), (ii) and (iii) are correct.
(c) (i), (iii) and (iv) are correct.
(d) i, ii and iii are correct.

475. According S R Ranganathan which of the following items are not considered as fugitive materials?
(i) News paper clipping (ii) Books
(iii) Pamphlets (iv) Reports
Codes:
(a) i and iii are correct
(b) ii and iv are correct
(c) i and ii are correct
(d) ii and iii are correct

476. Which of the following are the demerits of MBO System? *(NET 15D ii paper)*
(i) Superior-subordinate relationships
(ii) Over simplification
(iii) More coordination
(iv) All variables are not taken into account
Codes:
(a) (i) and (ii) are correct
(b) (i) and (iv) are correct
(c) (ii) and (iii) are correct
(d) (ii)and (iv) are correct

477. **Assertion (A):** A library needs to generate a satisfied customer base which is supportive of library programmes.
Reason (R): If a library's resources and services are measured upto customer's expectations, then repeat use cannot be ensured. *(NET 17J iii paper)*
Codes:
(a) (A) is true, but (R) is false.
(b) (A) is false, but (R) is true.
(c) Both (A) and (R) are true.
(d) Both (A) and (R) are false.

478. Which of the following theories are related to motivation of employees: *(NET 18J)*
(i) Theory 'Z' of the Japanese style of Management propounded by William Ouchi
(ii) Theory 'X' and Theory 'Y' of Douglas Mc Grgar
(iii) Max Webers Theory of Bureaucratic Management
(iv) Maslow's hierarchy of Need Theory
Codes:
(a) i, ii and iv are correct
(b) ii, iii and iv are correct
(c) i, ii, and iii are correct
(d) i, iii and iv are correct

479. Identify the ways in which the library can benefit from the TQM as stated by Jurow and Barnard: *(NET 18J)*
(i) Breaking down interdepartmental barriers.
(ii) Redefining the beneficiaries of library services as internal customers (Staff) and external customers (patrons)
(iii) More inclined to short term goals and defiant to changes to suit users needs
(iv) Reaching a state of continuous improvement
(a) i, ii and iii are correct
(b) ii, iii and iv are correct
(c) i, iii and iv are correct
(d) i, ii and iv are correct

480. Identify the case that require an application for new ISSN number *(NET 18J)*

(i) Change in the publication medium
(ii) Change in publisher
(iii) Change in frequency of publication
(iv) Change in publication title

Codes:

(a) (i) and (ii) are correct
(b) (iii) and (iv) are correct
(c) (i), and (iv) are correct
(d) (ii), and (iii) are correct

481. Identify the key salient traits of Soft data *(NET 18J)*

(i) human intelligence
(ii) certain and definite
(iii) opinions and contradictions
(iv) no scope for constructive criticisms

Codes:

(a) (i) and (ii) are correct
(b) (iii) and(iv) are correct
(c) (i), and (iii) are correct
(d) (ii), and (iv) are correct

482. Match the following section of Copyright Act 1957 (India) with correct explanation *(NET 18J)*

List - I

(A) Section 35 (B) Section 63
(C) Section 63A (D) Section 64

List - II

(i) Offence of infringement of copyright
(ii) Enhanced penalty on second and subsequent convictions
(iii) Civil remedies for infringement of copyright
(iv) Power of people to seize infringing copies

Codes:	**(A)**	**(B)**	**(C)**	**(D)**
(a)	(iii)	(ii)	(i)	(iv)
(b)	(iii)	(i)	(ii)	(iv)
(c)	(ii)	(iii)	(i)	(iv)
(d)	(ii)	(iv)	(iii)	(i)

483. Match the following domain of application with their corresponding metadata schemes: *(NET 18J)*

List - I	**List - II**
(A) ETD domain	(i) METS
(B) Image domain	(ii) CCO
(C) Cultural objects	(iii) ConCore
(D) Learning objects	(iv) VRA-Core

Codes:	**(A)**	**(B)**	**(C)**	**(D)**
(a)	(i)	(ii)	(iii)	(iv)
(b)	(i)	(ii)	(iv)	(iii)
(c)	(iii)	(ii)	(i)	(iv)
(d)	(i)	(iv)	(ii)	(iii)

484. Match the following *(NET18J)*

List - I	**List - II**
(A) Infomix	(i) Image software
(B) Omni page	(ii) Remote login software
(C) Tiff Viewer	(iii) DBMS software
(D) Team viewer	(iv) OCR software

Codes:	**(A)**	**(B)**	**(C)**	**(D)**
(a)	(ii)	(i)	(iii)	(iv)
(b)	(iii)	(iv)	(i)	(ii)
(c)	(i)	(ii)	(iii)	(iv)
(d)	(iv)	(iii)	(ii)	(i)

485. Arrange the following e books sites according to the chronological order of their origin: *(NET 18J)*

(i) Project Gutenberg (ii) Open library
(iii) Google books (iv) DOAB

Codes:

(a) i, iii, ii, iv (b) ii, i, iii, iv
(c) iii, ii, iv, i (d) iv, iii, i, ii

486. **Assertion (A):** As is true an organisation, effective leadership is crucial for success, as poor managerial leadership may mar the organisational goals.

Reason (R): Patterns of poor managerial leadership create low morale, poor organisational climate, distrust towards supervisors among subordinates, lack of team work and consensus building and shared goals, etc. which are clear indicators of a wrong person attained a managerial leadership position. *(NET 18J)*

Codes:

(a) (A) is true but (R) is false
(b) (A) is false, but (R) is true
(c) both (A) and (R) is true
(d) Both (A) and (R) are false

487. **Assertion (A):** Plagiarism is the wrongful appreciation and stealing and publication of another author language, thought ideas of expression.

Reason (R): Plagiarism is in itself a crime, and thus constitute copyright infringement. *(NET 18J)*

Codes:

(a) (A) is true but (R) is false
(b) (A) is false, but (R) is true
(c) both (A) and (R) are false
(d) Both (A) and (R) are true

488. **Assertion (A):** Serial crisis led to the formation of library consortia around the world.

Reason (R): Serial crisis arises due to the situation in which budget of the library for subscription of journals remains static in spite of rising subscription cost of journals which in turn affect the collection development policy of the libraries. *(NET 18J)*

Codes:

(a) Both (A) and (R) are true
(b) Both (A) and (R) are false
(c) (A) is true but (R) is false
(d) (A) is false, but (R) is true

489. **Assertion (A):** Delphi techniques in Social Science Research do not give weightage to consensus.

Reason (R): Consensus option expressed by the panel of expert is valuable in drawing inferences. *(NET 18J)*

Codes:

(a) (A) is true but (R) is false
(b) (A) is false, but (R) is true
(c) both (A) and (R) are true
(d) Both (A) and (R) are false

490. **Assertion (A):** F.W. Lancaster's cocksure prediction of a paperless society by the end of 20th. Century holds no good.

Reason (R): Transition from print dominance to paperless ascendancy change from scroll to codex and introduction of movable type were not only the few historical shifts but were also hugely significant innovations. In spite of rapid technological changes, the future libraries will still accommodate a very large print collection. However, the propelling vision of and information driven paperless society, though seems inevitable to avoid space staff, and cost crunch may buy more time to become a reality. *(NET 18J)*

Codes:

(a) (A) is true but (R) is false
(b) (A) is false, but (R) is true
(c) both (A) and (R) are true
(d) Both (A) and (R) are false

491. Path-Goal Theory of Leader Effectiveness is developed by *(NET 18J)*

(a) Douglas McGregor (b) William Ouchi
(c) Robert House (d) Abraham Maslow

492. Match the following intellectual property rights concepts with their relevant features: *(NET 18J)*

List - I

(A) Copyright (B) Patents
(C) Trade secrets (D) Trademarks

List - II

(i) Commercial source indicators and distinctive signs
(ii) A treaty between government and inventor
(iii) Economic rights
(iv) Information used in operation of a business invaluable to afford the potential economic utility

Codes:	**(A)**	**(B)**	**(C)**	**(D)**
(a)	(i)	(ii)	(iii)	(iv)
(b)	(iii)	(ii)	(iv)	(i)
(c)	(iv)	(iii)	(ii)	(i)
(d)	(ii)	(iv)	(i)	(iii)

493. The main components of an RFID system include

(a) Handheld Reader, RFID label printer, server and External book return
(b) RFID tags, readers or sensors, Antenna and server
(c) RFID label printer, sensors, antenna and server
(d) RFID tags, server, external book return, sensors

494. World Book and Copyright Day is celebrated on

(a) 22nd August (b) 23rd April
(c) 23rd March (d) 20th March

ANSWER SHEET

1. (b)	2. (c)	3. (b)	4. (d)	5. (a)	6. (a)	7. (b)	8. (c)	9. (b)
10. (d)	11. (d)	12. (b)	13. (d)	14. (b)	15. (a)	16. (c)	17. (c)	18. (b)
19. (b)	20. (b)	21. (d)	22. (c)	23. (d)	24. (c)	25. (b)	26. (a)	27. (c)
28. (b)	29. (a)	30. (d)	31. (d)	32. (c)	33. (b)	34. (b)	35. (d)	36. (a)
37. (b)	38. (c)	39. (a)	40. (b)	41. (a)	42. (a)	43. (b)	44. (c)	45. (a)
46. (b)	47. (a)	48. (c)	49. (b)	50. (a)	51. (d)	52. (a)	53. (b)	54. (a)
55. (b)	56. (a)	57. (a)	58. (a)	59. (a)	60. (a)	61. (c)	62. (a)	63. (a)

64. (b) 65. (c) 66. (a) 67. (d) 68. (d) 69. (c) 70. (b) 71. (c) 72. (b)
73. (d) 74. (c) 75. (a) 76. (d) 77. (c) 78. (d) 79. (b) 80. (a) 81. (b)
82. (d) 83. (c) 84. (d) 85. (c) 86. (c) 87. (a) 88. (a) 89. (a) 90. (b)
91. (b) 92. (a) 93. (d) 94. (d) 95. (d) 96. (d) 97. (d) 98. (a) 99. (d)
100. (b) 101. (b) 102. (b) 103. (d) 104. (c) 105. (c) 106. (a) 107. (c) 108. (a)
109. (c) 110. (d) 111. (b) 112. (d) 113. (c) 114. (b) 115. (a) 116. (a) 117. (d)
118. (b) 119. (b) 120. (a) 121. (b) 122. (c) 123. (b) 124. (a) 125. (c) 126. (a)
127. (a) 128. (d) 129. (c) 130. (a) 131. (b) 132. (a) 133. (a) 134. (a) 135. (c)
136. (a) 137. (b) 138. (a) 139. (a) 140. (a) 141. (a) 142. (b) 143. (d) 144. (c)
145. (b) 146. (a) 147. (c) 148. (d) 149. (d) 150. (d) 151. (a) 152. (b) 153. (c)
154. (c) 155. (b) 156. (b) 157. (d) 158. (a) 159. (b) 160. (a) 161. (b) 162. (a)
163. (b) 164. (d) 165. (b) 166. (a) 167. (a) 168. (b) 169. (a) 170. (a) 171. (a)
172. (a) 173. (a) 174. (a) 175. (c) 176. (c) 177. (c) 178. (b) 179. (b) 180. (c)
181. (d) 182. (b) 183. (c) 184. (a) 185. (a) 186. (a) 187. (a) 188. (a) 189. (a)
190. (b) 191. (d) 192. (b) 193. (c) 194. (d) 195. (b) 196. (d) 197. (d) 198. (a)
199. (b) 200. (a) 201. (d) 202. (a) 203. (c) 204. (d) 205. (c) 206. (c) 207. (c)
208. (b) 209. (a) 210. (b) 211. (d) 212. (d) 213. (c) 214. (b) 215. (b) 216. (b)
217. (a) 218. (a) 219. (a) 220. (a) 221. (c) 222. (a) 223. (d) 224. (c) 225. (c)
226. (b) 227. (c) 228. (a) 229. (b) 230. (a) 231. (a) 232. (a) 233. (b) 234. (a)
235. (a) 236. (d) 237. (d) 238. (a) 239. (b) 240. (c) 241. (a) 242. (a) 243. (a)
244. (d) 245. (a) 246. (b) 247. (c) 248. (c) 249. (c) 250. (a) 251. (b) 252. (c)
253. (a) 254. (b) 255. (b) 256. (c) 257. (b) 258. (d) 259. (d) 260. (c) 261. (b)
262. (a) 263. (d) 264. (d) 265. (c) 266. (d) 267. (c) 268. (a) 269. (b) 270. (a)
271. (b) 272. (b) 273. (d) 274. (b) 275. (a) 276. (c) 277. (a) 278. (d) 279. (a)
280. (c) 281. (b) 282. (a) 283. (c) 284. (b) 285. (a) 286. (a) 287. (a) 288. (c)
289. (b) 290. (c) 291. (c) 292. (d) 293. (d) 294. (b) 295. (c) 296. (c) 297. (d)
298. (a) 299. (c) 300. (d) 301. (c) 302. (c) 303. (c) 304. (c) 305. (d) 306. (a)
307. (a) 308. (d) 309. (a) 310. (d) 311. (a) 312. (b) 313. (c) 314. (a) 315. (c)
316. (a) 317. (a) 318. (a) 319. (c) 320. (d) 321. (a) 322. (b) 323. (a) 324. (b)
325. (c) 326. (a) 327. (c) 328. (b) 329. (a) 330. (b) 331. (b) 332. (b) 333. (d)
334. (c) 335. (c) 336. (b) 337. (c) 338. (a) 339. (c) 340. (a) 341. (c) 342. (c)
343. (c) 344. (b) 345. (a) 346. (c) 347. (b) 348. (c) 349. (c) 350. (d) 351. (d)
352. (a) 353. (c) 354. (d) 355. (b) 356. (b) 357. (b) 358. (c) 359. (a) 360. (b)
361. (b) 362. (d) 363. (b) 364. (d) 365. (c) 366. (a) 367. (c) 368. (a) 369. (d)
370. (b) 371. (c) 372. (a) 373. (c) 374. (b) 375. (b) 376. (b) 377. (a) 378. (a)
379. (c) 380. (a) 381. (a) 382. (a) 383. (a) 384. (c) 385. (a) 386. (b) 387. (d)
388. (a) 389. (b) 390. (a) 391. (d) 392. (b) 393. (d) 394. (a) 395. (d) 396. (b)
397. (a) 398. (b) 399. (c) 400. (a) 401. (c) 402. (c) 403. (c) 404. (a) 405. (c)
406. (d) 407. (d) 408. (c) 409. (a) 410. (c) 411. (d) 412. (b) 413. (b) 414. (b)
415. (a) 416. (b) 417. (d) 418. (b) 419. (a) 420. (c) 421. (a) 422. (c) 423. (d)
424. (d) 425. (a) 426. (b) 427. (d) 428. (c) 429. (b) 430. (a) 431. (d) 432. (c)
433. (b) 434. (d) 435. (b) 436. (c) 437. (d) 438. (b) 439. (a) 440. (b) 441. (c)
442. (a) 443. (a) 444. (d) 445. (d) 446. (b) 447. (c) 448. (a) 449. (c) 450. (d)
451. (a) 452. (d) 453. (b) 454. (c) 455. (c) 456. (c) 457. (b) 458. (c) 459. (b)
460. (c) 461. (b) 462. (a) 463. (a) 464. (a) 465. (d) 466. (b) 467. (a) 468. (c)
469. (d) 470. (b) 471. (b) 472. (a) 473. (a) 474. (c) 475. (b) 476. (d) 477. (a)
478. (a) 479. (d) 480. (c) 481. (c) 482. (b) 483. (d) 484. (b) 485. (a) 486. (c)
487. (d) 488. (a) 489. (b) 490. (b) 491. (c) 492. (b) 493. (b) 494. (b)

Chapter 10
Library and Society

SUBJECTIVE QUESTIONS

Q. 1. What is the aim of Education?

Ans. The aim of Education is (i) to impart knowledge; (ii) to inculcate values; and (iii) to impart vocational skills.

Q. 2. Define the role of library in non-formal education.

Ans. Non-formal education is a process of self-learning self-instructional materials, both the paper-print and audio-visual learning kits are necessary for this process of learning. These materials are collected in libraries, for providing facilities to the student for study in the premises of the library or making them available for home study on loan. Library of distance education centres have, therefore, to organise these services, particularly in smaller towns and rural areas.

Q. 3. In how many categories the books can be broadly divided?

Ans. Books can be broadly divided into three categories:

(i) Books of information
(ii) Books of recreation
(iii) Books of inspiration.

Q. 4. Who had enunciated the five laws of library science?

Ans. The five laws of library science were enunciated in 1928 by the late Dr. S.R. Ranganathan, the then Librarian of the University of Madras.

Q. 5. Write the five laws of library science.

Ans. (i) Books are for use
(ii) Every Reader his book
(iii) Every book its Reader
(iv) Save the time of Reader
(v) Library is a growing organism.

Q. 6. Books for all is similar to which other law.

Ans. Second Law, "Every Reader his book".

Q. 7. Which Law is related to child growth and adult growth?

Ans. Fifth Law of Library Science.

Q. 8. Which date is the red letter day for British Library development?

Ans. August 14, 1850.

Q. 9. In which year Edward-Edward had taken over the charge of librarian of Manchester public library?

Ans. In the year 1850, Edward-Edward had taken over the charge of librarian of Manchester public library.

Q. 10. When was Boston public library established?

Ans. The Boston public library was established in the year 1848 by an act passed by the general court of Massachusetts.

Q. 11. Name some of the reports on the public library set up in U.K.

Ans. Some of the reports submitted by committees appointed to look into the working of the public libraries in England were (i) Adam Report, 1915; (ii) Mitchell Report, 1924; (iii) Kenyon Report, 1927; (iv) Mc Colvin Report, 1841; (v) Robert Report, 1957.

Q. 12. For whom Mercantile libraries were beneficial?

Ans. The Mercantile libraries were set up to foster education and recreational reading among their employees. These libraries were also known as "Mechanics Libraries of apprentices" libraries.

Q. 13. How did philanthropy help in the development of libraries in U.S.A.?

Ans. Several public libraries that came into being first later part of 19th century and in the first quarter of 20th century were established mainly through benevolent donation. The well-known new public library is a creation of individual philanthropists. The other few well-known libraries that were established through donation were Enoch part library at Baltimore, John Crerar Library at Chicago and Hennery Huntington Library at San Marino.

Q. 14. In which five-year plan considerable attention was given to library and information system development?

Ans. In Seventh Five-year Plan.

Q. 15. Write the name of first state where library movement was started?

Ans. Baroda state in 1906.

Q. 16. Where well-developed public library system are there without the support of legislation?

Ans. Gujarat have fairly well-developed public library system without the support of legislation.

Q. 17. Who was the chairman of national policy on library and information system and when it was completed?

Ans. The Department of Culture, Ministry of Human Resource Development, Government of India appointed a committee of senior library scientist and other specialists, under the chairmanship of Prof. D.P. Chattopadhyaya in October 1985 to prepare a draft document on National policy on library and information system. The committee completed its assignment and submitted a draft document to the government on 31 May 1986.

Q. 18. List national policies on the other sectors which have a bearing on library development.

Ans. (a) Education Policy (b) Book Policy
(c) Scientific Policy (d) Technology Policy
(e) Information Policy.

Q. 19. State the three historical phases of growth of the National Library of India.

Ans. The three historical phases of the National Library of India are:

(i) First Phase: 1835-1903—Calcutta Public Libraries
(ii) Second Phase: 1903-47—The Imperial Library
(iii) Third Phase: 1948—The National Library of India.

Q. 20. When the New National Library was declared open to the nation?

Ans. The New National Library was declared open to the nation by Union Minister Maulana Abul Kalam Azad, on 21 February 1953.

Q. 21. Where are the following national libraries of different types situated?

Ans. (i) The National Science Library: At the Indian National Scientific Documentation Centre (INSDOC), New Delhi.
(ii) The National Medical Library: Ministry of Health Services.
(iii) A National Library for the Blinded, the Physically Handicapped: Dehradun.
(iv) Khuda Baksh Library: Patna.
(v) Saraswati Mahal Manuscript Library: Tanjore.

Q. 22. Where is the State Lenin Library situated?

Ans. The State Lenin Library is situated in Moscow (the largest library in Europe).

Q. 23. Write the name of State of India where the Public Libraries Act has been passed.

Ans. Nineteen States of India have put their public library acts into statute book.
(i) Tamil Nadu—1948 (then called Madras Public Library Act)
(ii) Andhra Pradesh—(First to enact was Hyderabad Public Libraries Act, 1956 then Andhra Pradesh Public Libraries Act, 1969)
(iii) Karnataka: (The Mysore Public Libraries Act, 1965)
(iv) Maharashtra (The Maharashtra Public Libraries Act, 1967)
(v) The West Bengal Public Libraries Act, 1979
(vi) Manipur Library Act, 1988
(vii) Kerala Public Library Act, 1989
(viii) Haryana Public Library Act, 1989
(ix) Goa Public Library Act, 1993
(x) Mizoram Public Libraries Act, 1993

(xi) Gujarat Public Libraries Act, 2001
(xii) Orissa Public Libraries Act, 2001
(xiii) Uttarakhand Public Libraries Act, 2005
(xiv) Uttar Pradesh Public Libraries Act, 2005
(xv) Rajasthan Public Libraries Act, 2006
(xvi) Bihar Public Libraries Act, 2007
(xvii) Chhattisgarh Public Libraries Act, 2007
(xviii) Pondicherry Library Act, 2007
(xix) Arunachal Pradesh Public Libraries Act, 2009

Q. 24. What are types of library cooperation?

Ans. There are four types of library cooperation
(i) International level (ii) National level
(iii) Regional level (iv) Local level

Q. 25. List three categories of user education programmes.

Ans. Categories of user education programmes are:
(i) User orientation
(ii) Bibliographic orientation
(iii) Training and use of modern technological gadgets.

Q. 26. Before independence write the general Account of Library Association in India.

Ans. The early Library Associations formed in India are:
(i) Baroda Library Association (1910)
(ii) Andhra Desa Library Association (1914)
(iii) Bengal Library Association (1927)
(iv) Madras Library Association (1927)
(v) Indian Library Association (1933)

Q. 27. How many National Libraries are there in U.K.?

Ans. Three, namely:
(i) The British Library
(ii) The National Library of Scotland
(iii) The National Library of Wales

Q. 28. Who is known as the father of Indian Library movement in India?

Ans. Dr. S.R. Ranganathan.

Q. 29. Who had inaugurated the Delhi Public Library?

Ans. Pandit J.L. Nehru on 27 October 1951.

Q. 30. What is the Indian standards specification number for designing of Library buildings?

Ans. IS: 1553-1960.

Q. 31. Write the name of four libraries, which receive four copies of a single book published anywhere in India under the delivery of books Act of 1954 (Amended in 1956).

Ans. (a) National Library, Kolkata
(b) Central Library, Town Hall, Mumbai
(c) Delhi Public Library, Delhi
(d) Connemara Public Library, Chennai.

Q. 32. Write the components of ISBN? And when did it come into operation?

Ans. (Group identified national, geographical, language convenient group); Publisher identifier and a check digit. Total ten digits from 1969 onwards.

Q. 33. Write the name of some important committee, which has recommended on library matters.

Ans. Pubic Library

Some of the reports submitted by committees appointed to look into the working of the Public Libraries:

(a) Dr. S.R. Ranganathan prepared a Library Development plan; Thirty year programme for India, published as a book in 1950 by the University of Delhi. The blueprint drawn by Dr. S.R. Ranganathan was useful to subsequent exercises of formulating national level plans for library development.

(b) The Report of Advisory of Committee for Libraries, also known as Sinha Committee. The report was submitted to the Government of India in November 1958 and in the following year it was published as an official document. The Report has nine chapters: Historical, Present position, structure of libraries, Auxiliary Services and Library Cooperation, Library Personnel, Training for Librarianship, Libraries and Social Education Library Finance and administration.

The Sinha Committee made the following recommendations:

- Libraries at the Panchayat, Block, District and State level have to constitute with appropriate functions and span of control;

- The Book Bureau and Mitra Mandal have to be set up as auxiliary services; Inter library loan service should be established;
- Training should be provided to the library personnel to upgrade their skills;
- Libraries should interact with other social, education and adult education programmes. The library cess of 6 paise per rupee in the property tax should be collected by the local authorizes for building and maintaining libraries; and equivalent sum must be contributed by the state and central governments;
- Library fund with proper supervision must be set up to administer the finance of libraries at various level.

Overall basic recommendations of the Library Advisory Committee have been sound, the lamentable part is that many of the valuable recommendations have remained unimplemented; as a result, even today, the public library development in the country is lagging behind.

(c) The first well-known committee on regional public libraries, is the Library Development Committee, Bombay 1939-40, headed by Shri A.A.A. Fyzee. The terms of reference of the committee were on setting central and regional libraries only. The committee covered a wider field and put forth a scheme for developing libraries in them Bombay Province in six stages to cover even village bellow a population of 1,000. The financial implications of the committee's proposal would not allow the Government of Bombay to implement all the six stages. Arising out of the recommendations of the Fyzee Committee, one central library, three regional libraries and 15 district libraries.

(d) In Andhra Pradesh, a committee was appointed by the government in February 1976 under the chairmanship of justice Gopal Rao Ekbote to review the working of the Andhra Pradesh Public Libraries Act 1960 and to suggest necessary amendments to the Act. The committee submitted report in 1977. The committee made several worthwhile recommendations on various aspects of public library system, in the light of experience of working of the APPL Act 1960. The Government of Andhra Pradesh have accepted the report of Ekbote Committee but did not appear to have implemented the recommendations faithfully. There was an another committee appointed by the Government of Andhra Pradesh in July 1978, under the chairmanship of Sri Vavilala Gopalakrishnayya, to suggest measure for the improvement of private libraries (aided libraries) and to evolve a system of grant I aid to the private libraries. The committee submitted report in November 1978 wherein, it has suggested norms and procedures for identification, grant in aid, inspection, etc. of private libraries. The government had accepted a majority of the recommendations of this committee in 1982.

(e) In Tamil Nadu also, a library reorganizing committee was appointed in 1974 under the chairmanship Shri V.N. Subharayam. The Committee made some valuable recommendations, following which a separate full time district library system officer for each district has been provided to administer the district library system.

Academic Libraries

(i) Secondary Education Commission (October, 1952-June, 1953) under the chairmanship of Dr. A.L. Mudaliar.

The committee pointed out the sad state of affairs of libraries in schools. The commission had emphasized the habit of general reading by children and advocated the establishment of really good libraries in schools and provision of intelligent and effective library service for this purpose.

(ii) Reports of the University Education Commission (December, 1948—August, 1949) under the chairmanship of Dr. S. Radhakrishnan. He discussed in detail the central position of library in academic system. Committee preferred self-study and library work by way of supplementing class instruction.

(iii) The Report of Education Commission (1964-66) under the chairmanship of D.S. Kothari, entitled, Education and National Development. He discussed about the role of librarian in higher education. The report highlighted the skill to use books and documents independently by the students in the learning process. The Education Commission had offered eleven useful and important suggestions for the improvement of university and college libraries.

The Education Commission had also addressed itself to the role of libraries in adult education and recommended establishment of a network of public libraries for purposes of adult education programmes.

(iii) Another, UGC Committee chaired, by Dr. S.R. Ranganathan, the report was published by the University Grant Commission in 1959 as "University and Colleges Libraries". The committee has recommended all round development about the college and university libraries. The recommendation of library personnel and staff strength had given to library staff, status and salary equivalent to academic staff and ensure the provision of adequate staff for various library operation.

Agricultural Libraries

(i) The council invited Dr. Ralph Shaw of the United States to study the requirements of library and bibliographical services for agricultural research and teaching. Dr. Shaw, with co-authorship of Dr. D.B. Krishna Rao, submitted a report on library and bibliographical service (Published by I.C.A.R. in 1959).

Medical Libraries

Some important recommendation concerning medical libraries in the report of the Health Survey and Development Committee, Vol. 2 under the chairmanship of Dr. J. Bhore was published in 1946.

The committee took note of the existing conditions of medical libraries in India and strongly recommended the establishment of central medical library.

Q. 34. Write the basic elements of communication process.

(a) Information (b) Encoder
(c) Message (d) Communication channels
(e) Noise (f) Decoder
(g) Receiver/Destination.

OBJECTIVE QUESTIONS

1. FID was founded by Paul Otlet and
(a) S.R. Ranganathan (b) Dr. D. Dyyis
(c) Melvil Dewey (d) Henry La Fontaine

2. ____________ is the 1st state enacted Public Library Act in India.
(a) Maharashtra (b) Tamil Nadu
(c) Andhra Pradesh (d) Gujarat

3. ________ was the chairman of NAPLIS Committee appointed in October 1985.
(a) Prof. D.P. Chattopadhyaya
(b) Prof. S.R. Ranganathan
(c) Prof. A. Neelameghan
(d) Prof. K.A. Issac

4. _______ is the national library of the U.K.
(a) British National Library
(b) London Public Library
(c) The British Library
(d) British Library

5. The National Book Policy was prepared in the year
(a) 1982 (b) 1985 (c) 1986 (d) 1990

6. Public Libraries have a responsibility to support
(a) Distance Education
(b) Higher Education
(c) Formal and Non-Formal Education
(d) Continuing Education

7. The implication of third and fourth laws give rise to
   (a) Closed access (b) Limited access
   (c) Open access (d) No access
8. In __________ the 1st general library law was enacted at the national level in USA.
   (a) 1956 (b) 1960 (c) 1965 (d) 1958
9. The Library Association (UK) was founded in the year
   (a) 1072 (b) 1827 (c) 1884 (d) 1877
10. Library of Congress is located in
    (a) Washington (b) Moscow
    (c) New York (d) London
11. In 1906 the 1st public library movement was started from
    (a) Madras State (b) Baroda State
    (c) Calcutta (d) Delhi
12. ____________ was a pioneer in establishing social libraries in U.S.A.
    (a) Col. W. Byrd (b) William Brewster
    (c) Banjamin Franklin (d) D. Clinto
13. ____________ is the another form of subscription library which came into existence in later half the 18th century.
    (a) Resource Centre (b) Book Club
    (c) Study Centre (d) Information Centre
14. National Library, Calcutta come under the Administrative control of
    (a) Deptt. of Education
    (b) Deptt. of Libraries
    (c) Deptt. of Culture
    (d) Deptt. of Official Language
15. The National Science Library belongs to
    (a) Indian Institute of Science Bangalore
    (b) DESIDOC, Delhi
    (c) Information of Knowledge
    (d) None of the above
16. Libraries are repositories of
    (a) Books and Journal
    (b) Print and non-print materials
    (c) Information of Knowledge
    (d) None of the above
17. The three types of computerised library networks are
    (a) Local, National, International
    (b) Line, Hierarchical, Multidimensional
    (c) Local, Regional, National
    (d) Star, Hierarchical, Distributed
18. A Computer Network NICNET was designed by
    (a) National Information Centre
    (b) Delhi University Computer Centre
    (c) Indian Institute of Technology
    (d) All of the above
19. The idea of starting an All India association devoted to the progress of special libraries and information centres was crystallised under the chairmanship of
    (a) Dr. S.R. Ranganathan (b) Dr. Hora
    (c) Viswanathan (d) Chattopadhyaya
20. IFLA was founded in the year
    (a) 1929 (b) 1961 (c) 1971 (d) 1981
21. The oldest and largest library association in the world is
    (a) ALA (b) LA (c) ILA (d) IASLIC
22. IASLIC was founded in ___________ at ___________.
    (a) 1955, Calcutta (b) 1933, Delhi
    (c) 1933, Calcutta (d) 1955, Delhi
23. The acronym FID stands for
    (a) International Federation for Documentation
    (b) Federation for Information and Documentation
    (c) International Federation for Information and Documentation
    (d) None of the above
24. INSDOC through its ___________ project acquires foreign periodicals for about 30 libraries of the CSIR.
    (a) Centralised Acquisition of Foreign Periodicals
    (b) Centralised Acquisition of Periodicals
    (c) Acquisition of Foreign Periodicals
    (d) Foreign Periodical Acquisition
25. _______ and _______ Public Libraries Act do not levy any library cess.
    (a) Maharashtra, Karnataka
    (b) Tamil Nadu, West Bengal
    (c) West Bengal, Maharashtra
    (d) Karnataka, West Bengal
26. Four important techniques used to explore the information needs of users are
    (a) Questionnaire, Interview, Diary, Observation
    (b) Questionnaire, Investigation, Diary, Observation

(c) Questionnaire, Investigation, Report, Observation
(d) Questionnaire, Observation, Investigation, Report

27. Which organisation was joined with 'Library Association' to form CILIP in 2007?
(a) Institute of Bibliography
(b) Institute of Information Scientists
(c) Institute of Documentation
(d) Institute of Librarianship

28. Resource sharing in library comprises sharing of
(a) Materials, Function, Services
(b) Staff, Money, Materials, Services
(c) Documentary, Non-documentary Materials Services
(d) Personnel, Materials, Function, Services

29. The two types of observation methods are
(a) Participants and non-participants
(b) Group and Individual
(c) Close and Open
(d) Direct and Indirect

30. The Report of the Education Commission (1964-66) entitled "Education and National Development" discussed the role of libraries in
(a) Higher Education
(b) Primary Education
(c) Secondary Education
(d) None of the above

31. Under interview method the data is collected through ___________ interview.
(a) Structured and unstructured (b) Direct and indirect
(c) Open and close (d) None of the above

32. The concept of 'Ask Library Anything' was originally initiated by
(a) Indian Library Association
(b) ASLIB
(c) Special Library Association
(d) American Library Association

33. Maharashtra has already enacted a public library act.
(a) True (b) False

34. Library of clay tablets were found in
(a) India (b) Medieval Europe
(c) Egypt (d) Assyria and Babylonia

35. National Library for Blind & Physical Handicapped of India is located at
(a) Tanjore (b) Dehradun
(c) Delhi (d) Chennai

36. Before independence the name of the National Library of India was
(a) Calcutta Public Library
(b) Imperial Library
(c) Asiatic Society Library
(d) Coonnemara Public Library

37. National Information Centre for Textiles and Allied Subjects (NICTAS) was established in _____ at _______.
(a) 1977, Lucknow (b) 1977, Mysore
(c) 1981, Madras (d) 1986, Ahmedabad

38. __________ library play an important role in building well informed, skilled and productive individuals and tries to achieve this in a democratic way.
(a) Public (b) Special
(c) Academic (d) None of the above

39. ________ Committee recommended the establishment of Central Medical Library.
(a) Academic
(b) Sankaran
(c) Health survey & development
(d) All of the above

40. Three broad categories of books are
(a) Books of information, recreation, inspiration
(b) Books on knowledge, information, data
(c) Books for children, Middle age
(d) Books for women and old age

41. The five laws of library science were enunciated by
(a) S.R. Ranganathan (b) C.G. Viswanathan
(c) H.E. Bliss (d) W.B. Sayers

42. The characteristics of library as a growing organism are perceived from the __________ Law of Library Science.
(a) Fifth (b) First (c) Second (d) Third

43. _____________ Five-year plan has given considerable attention to library and information system development in India.
(a) Seventh (b) Sixth
(c) First and Fifth (d) Third

44. You have to keep the message of __________ law of library science while choosing the location planning and designing of library building.
(a) First and Second (b) First and Third
(c) First and Fifth (d) Fourth

45. "Book are for all" is a Varian to _______ law, i.e. _______.
(a) First, book are for use
(b) Third, every book its reader
(c) Fourth, save the time of the reader
(d) Second, every reader his book

46. It is a special responsibility of the library to work for education of the illiterate people in its community
(a) Special (b) School
(c) Public (d) Business

47. The law necessities the use of CD-ROM in modern libraries is
(a) Second law (b) Third law
(c) Fifth law (d) Fourth law

48. The library association (London) was founded in (*NET Exam.* 1995-96)
(a) 1976 (b) 1933 (c) 1877 (d) 1910

49. The first librarian of the national library (Calcutta) was (*NET Exam.* 1995)
(a) B.S. Keshavan (b) Y.M. Mulay
(c) S.R. Ranganathan (d) K.M. Assadullah

50. Arrange the following State Library Acts according to their year of Establishment
(i) Goa (ii) West Bengal
(iii) Orissa (iv) Karnataka

Codes:

(a)	iv	ii	iii	i
(b)	iv	ii	i	iii
(c)	ii	i	iii	iv
(d)	iii	ii	i	iv

51. Which of the following is not a library extension activity? (*NET Exam.* 1991)
(a) Book Exhibition (b) Film Show
(c) Inter Library Loan (d) Lecture and Talk

52. UAP Programme has been sponsored by (*NET Exam.* 1991)
(a) Library Congress (b) The British Library
(c) IFLA (d) INSDOC

53. The Indian library association was founded in the year
(a) 1924 (b) 1933 (c) 1950 (d) 1952

54. Parry Committee report (UK) relates to 1967 (*NET Exam.* 1995)
(a) Public Libraries (b) University Libraries
(c) National Libraries (d) Special Libraries

55. William A. Borden the first librarian in Baroda (*NET Exam.* 1995)
(a) U.K. (b) U.S.A.
(c) France (d) Australia

56. Indian National Bibliography is published by (*NET Exam.* 1995)
(a) National Library, Calcutta
(b) Central Reference Library, Calcutta
(c) INSDOC, New Delhi
(d) NASSDOC, New Delhi

57. The concept of "Paperless Society" was 1st given by Derek Austin.
(a) True (b) False

58. Inductive logic proceeds from (*NET Exam.* 1995)
(a) General to specific (b) General to general
(c) Specific to general (d) Specific to specific

59. Which term was coined by Ranganathan for mobile library?
(a) Moving library (b) Library on wheels
(c) Librachine (d) All of the above

60. Mobile library is a kind of
(a) Independent Library (b) Small Library
(c) Extension Library (d) Public Library

61. How many digits does the ISBN contain and when did it come into operation?
(a) 10 digits from 1969 onwards
(b) 12 digits from 1972 onwards
(c) 08 digits from 1962 onwards
(d) 10 digits from 1962 onwards

62. Who was known as the "Prince of Biographers"?
(a) James Boswell (b) Dr. S.R. Ranganathan
(c) M.L. Dewey (d) John Austin

63. A colophon means
(a) Coloured illustration in book
(b) End pages of an old book giving information
(c) About author publishers etc.
(d) The covers of document

64. What was the book written by James Boswell?
(a) *Life of Samuel Johnson*
(b) *Colon classification*

(c) *Eva Sadden*
(d) *Life of Samuel Johnson*

65. Which country does not have a national bibliography? (*NET Exam.* 1998)
(a) United Kingdom (b) U.S.A.
(c) India (d) Australia

66. Resource sharing has to be implemented because (*NET Exam.* 1998)
(a) There is information explosion
(b) There are financial constraints
(c) Information needs have become more complex
(d) All of the above

67. Which of the following Institute of India provides for the establishment of national library under Article?
(*NET Exam.* 1998)
(a) 63 (b) 67 (c) 26 (d) 62

68. Which of the following is not microform?
(*NET Exam.* 1996)
(a) Microfilm (b) Micro Computer
(c) Microfiche (d) Aperture card

69. The concept of anomalous state of knowledge was proposed by (*NET Exam.* 1996)
(a) Belkin (b) Vickery
(c) Lancaster (d) Ranganathan

70. The Indian Library Association published
(*NET Exam.* 1996)
(a) A Bulletin (b) A Newsletter
(c) Both (a) and (b) (d) Neither (a) nor (b)

71. Which of the following statements about national libraries is expected?
(a) To serve the needs of the legislative body
(b) To function as deposit libraries
(c) To participate in universal bibliographic control
(d) To bring out a national bibliography

72. The library will subscribe to journals through an agent this is a statement of
(a) Objective (b) Policy
(c) Procedure (d) Mission

73. Reminders are
(a) Funds left over after purchasing book
(b) Books which are not brought last year
(c) Books which are sold by publishers at a heavy discount
(d) Books which were ordered but not supplied

74. Five laws of Library Science are a set of norms to good
(a) Library Science (b) Librarianship
(c) Society (d) Libraries

75. Which committee/commission described public libraries as "stagnating pools of books"? (*NET Exam.* 1996)
(a) Ranganathan Committee
(b) Sinha Committee
(c) Fyzee Committee
(d) Kothari Commission

76. The Shannon-Weaver Model of information is criticised for (*NET Exam.* 1996)
(a) Being too Mathematical
(b) Being unidirectional
(c) Being primarily suited to electronic communication
(d) All of the above

77. The National Library, Kolkata receives books on deposit under (*NET Exam.* 1996)
(a) The Registration of Books Act, 1887
(b) The Delivery of Books Act, 1954
(c) The Copy Rights Act, 1985
(d) All of the above

78. Library legislation support the Public Library movement by (*NET Exam.* 1996)
(a) Ensuring that funds are made available
(b) Establishing Local Library Authorities
(c) Making Library service mandatory
(d) All of the above

79. Which of the following materials would you not except to find in a Public Library?
(*NET Exam.* 1996)
(a) Newspapers (b) Audio cassettes
(c) Patents (d) Maps

80. The term Librametry was first used by
(*NET Exam.* 1994)
(a) S.R. Braford (b) J.D. Bernal
(c) S.R. Ranganathan (d) J. Foskett

81. The Advisory Committee for Libraries 1957-58
(*NET Exam.* 1994)
(a) Public Libraries (b) Academic Libraries
(c) National Libraries (d) Special Libraries

82. Ranganathan Committee Report on development of University and College Libraries was published by
(*NET Exam.* 1994)

(a) Sharda Ranganathan Endowment of Library Science
(b) D.R.T.C.
(c) Asia Publishing House
(d) U.G.C.

83. Which of the following Law of Library Science prescribes for the state's responsibility for the Public Library Service? (*NET Exam.* 1994)
(a) First Law (b) Second Law
(c) Third Law (d) Fourth Law

84. Which one of the following does not fall under the purview of library extension? (*NET Exam.* 1994)
(a) Branch Library (b) Mobile Library
(c) Extending Library building (d) Exhibition

85. British National Bibliography is a (*NET Exam.* 1994)
(a) Quarterly Publication
(b) Weekly Publication
(c) Bi-Weekly Publication
(d) Monthly

86. Periodicity at Indian National Bibliography is
(a) Weekly (b) Monthly
(c) Quarterly (d) Annually

87. BLAISE is based on
(a) British Library Automated Information Service
(b) British Legislation Automated Information Scheme
(c) Baroda Library Automated Information Service
(d) None of the Above

88. Which of the following libraries is not receiving books under "Delivery of Books Acts"? (*NET Exam.* 1998)
(a) Coonnemara Public Library, Chennai
(b) Central Secretarial Library, New Delhi
(c) National Library, Calcutta
(d) Delhi Public Library, Delhi

89. Who practically demonstrated the process of microphotography?
(a) James Watt (b) Earl Carison
(c) Benjamin Dance (1939) (d) Johannes Gutenberg

90. The official agency assigning ISBN India is (*NET Exam.* 1998)
(a) INSDOC (b) DESIDOC
(c) National Library (d) National Education Resource Centre under RRRLF

91. Current contents comprise (*NET Exam.* 1998)
(a) Contents pages of books
(b) Book review of world publishers
(c) Original contents pages of currents periodical
(d) None of the above

92. Which of the following types of libraries has a verity of library clientele?
(a) Special library (b) Academic library
(c) School library (d) Public library

93. The original concept of "Library cooperation" is traced to (*NET Exam.* 1998)
(a) Dealer Library plan (b) Formington plan
(c) O.C.L.C. (d) None of these

94. The corollary to second law of library science (*NET Exam.* 1998)
(a) Free Book service (b) Free library service
(c) Books for all (d) Books every where

95. ASLIB was established in
(a) 1912 (b) 1922 (c) 1945 (d) 1924

96. Match the following:
List - I
(A) Special library (B) Public library
(C) National library (D) Academic library
List - II
(i) Provides bibliographical services
(ii) Conservation of knowledge
(iii) Popularisation of Govt. information
(iv) Critical compilation

Codes:	**A**	**B**	**C**	**D**
(a)	i	iii	iv	ii
(b)	ii	iv	i	iii
(c)	iii	iv	i	ii
(d)	iv	iii	i	ii

97. Andrew Carnegie was a
(a) Classificationist (b) Library Scientist
(c) Librarian (d) Philanthropist

98. Among the following which has not been considered as a library of national importance? (*NET Exam.* 1999)

(a) Saraswati Mahal Library
(b) Delhi Public Library
(c) Khuda Baksh Oriental Library
(d) The Rampur Raja Library

99. The concept of demand theory of book selection was conceived by
(a) A.C. Foskett (b) Johan Drury
(c) L.R. McColvin (d) C.A. Cutter

100. Among the following which is/are the book selection tools? (*NET Exam.* 1999)
(a) Books in Print (b) PTLA
(c) Neither (a) Nor (b) (d) Both (a) and (b)

101. LA is the Library Association of
(a) Manipur (b) Andhra Pradesh
(c) Great Britain (d) Canada

102. In communication model, noise refer to (*NET Exam.* 1999)
(a) Loudness of signals
(b) Lack of under established between sender and receiver
(c) Any disturbance which effect the transmission
(d) Irrelevant information

103. Extension services to the blind by a public library is justified by (*NET Exam.* 1996, 2000)
(a) The fourth law of library science
(b) The fifth law of library
(c) The first law of library science
(d) All the laws of library science

104. In a library which of the following positions are line positions:
(i) Junior library Assistant
(ii) Subject Specialist
(iii) Deputy Librarian
(iv) System Librarian
Codes:
(a) (i) and (ii) (b) (ii) and (iii)
(c) (i) and (iii) (d) (ii) and (iv)

105. The resource sharing strategy of a library may not include
(a) Joint acquisition
(b) Shared use
(c) Exchange of materials
(d) Restricted access

106. Which of the following is not a national library? (*NET Exam.* 2000)
(a) Library of Congress
(b) British Library
(c) Bibliotheque Nationale
(d) Smithsonian Institute

107. UNESCO Public Library manifesto was last revised in (*NET Exam.* 2000)
(a) 1990 (b) 1998 (c) 1997 (d) 1994

108. Which of the following information receive as a systematic? (*NET Exam.* 1995)
(a) Source, message, channel, receiver
(b) Source, channel, message, receiver
(c) Source, receiver, channel, message
(d) Source, message, receiver, channel

109. The state which does not have library legislation? (*NET Exam.* 1995, 1999J)
(a) Manipur (b) Goa
(c) Bihar (d) Maharashtra

110. The chairman of the advisory committee for libraries appointed by the Govt. of India in 1957 was (*NET Exam.* 1995)
(a) S.R. Ranganathan (b) K.P. Sinha
(c) B.S. Keshavan (d) S. Basuruddin

111. UAP is a core programme of (*NET Exam.* 1991, 1995)
(a) FID (b) IFLA
(c) The British Library (d) The National Library

112. In which of the five laws, the concept of Child growth and Adult growth has been discussed by S.R. Ranganathan?
(a) Second Law (b) Third Law
(c) Fourth Law (d) Fifth Law

113. In which of the following public libraries Acts, provisions for library cess is not provided? (*NET Exam.* 1991, 1996, 1998)
(a) Andhra Pradesh (b) Maharashtra
(c) Tamil Nadu (d) Karnataka

114. The library association (Great Britain) was founded in
(a) 1876 (b) 1877 (c) 1878 (d) 1879

115. The Raja Ram Mohan Roy Library Foundation was established in the year (*NET Exam.* 1996, C.S. 1999)
(a) 1972 (b) 1975 (c) 1977 (d) 1987

116. The State which does not provide for library cess is (*NET Exam.* 1995)

(a) Tamil Nadu (b) Andhra Pradesh
(c) West Bengal (d) Karnataka

117. The State that enacted library legislation in 1965 is (*NET Exam.* 1995)
(a) Karnataka (b) Haryana
(c) Goa (d) Manipur

118. Library of congress is
(a) National Library of the USA
(b) The Library of Indian Congress
(c) The Library of the Parliament of India
(d) National Library of Australia

119. The name of S.C. Bradford is associated with (*NET Exam.* 1995)
(a) Occurrence of terms in a paragraph
(b) No. of articles written by an author
(c) Law scattering
(d) Citation of article

120. A latest revision of UNESCO manifesto of public library was issued in the year (*NET Exam.* 1998)
(a) 1972 (b) 1990 (c) 1994 (d) 1996

121. The model public library established in India with the UNESCO assistance was (*NET Exam.* 1998)
(a) Coonnemara Public Library
(b) Delhi Public Library
(c) National Library
(d) National Science Library

122. A professional association should primarily (*NET Exam.* 1996)
(a) Function as trade union
(b) Work for the development of its members
(c) Undertake research in professional techniques
(d) Serves as an employment exchange

123. Public libraries are having a research role especially in the field of
(a) Linguistics
(b) Information Science
(c) Audio and Video Media
(d) Social and Humanities

124. ____________ revolution in England has given boost to the library movement.
(a) Industrial (b) Green
(c) Religious (d) Social

125. London Library was founded in the year 1841 by
(a) Allen Ramsay (b) Thomas Bray
(c) Thomas Carlyle (d) George Birbeck

126. August 14, 1850 is a red letter day in the British Library Development because the
(a) Public Libraries Bill received royal assent
(b) BNB was launched
(c) British Library was established
(d) British Museum became an open access library

127. In October 1985 a committee of senior library scientist and other specialists under the chairmanship of _______ prepared a draft document on National Policy on Library and information system.
(a) Dr. Dorothes Parker
(b) Dr. D.S. Kothari
(c) Dr. D.B. Krishna
(d) Dr. D.P. Chattopadhyaya

128. National Union Catalogue (NUC) is compiled, maintained and printed by
(a) State Lenin Library
(b) British Library
(c) Library of Congress
(d) National Library of India, Kolkata

129. When and where was the first book printed in India?
(a) 1556, in Goa (b) 1557, in Goa
(c) 1555, in Delhi (d) 1554, in Delhi

130. Who was the British Public Library pioneer?
(a) James Duff Brown (b) H.E. Bliss
(c) S.R. Ranganathan (d) Melvil Dewey

131. What was the first Library Journal published completely in English in India?
(a) *Indian Library Journal*, 1925
(b) *Indian Library Journal*, 1924
(c) *Library Journal*, 1926
(d) *Indian Library Journal*, 1927

132. Who was the first librarian of the Imperial Library, Kolkata?
(a) John Macfar Lane (b) B.S. Keshavan
(c) Hari Nath Dev (d) P.K. Dutta

133. Who is known as the father of Library Movement in U.K.?
(a) Melvil Dewey (b) H.E. Bliss
(c) Edward-Edward (d) H. Duke

134. When did S.R. Ranganathan used the term "Librametry" for first time?

(a) 1948 (b) 1933 (c) 1929 (d) 1942

135. Second law of library science places obligation on the part of the state not to provide free library service to all.
(a) True (b) False

136. Match the following:
(A) Paul Otlet (1) India
(B) S.R. Ranganathan (2) U.S.A.
(C) Melvil Dewey (3) London
(D) S.C. Bradford (4) Belgium

Codes:	A	B	C	D
(a)	4	1	2	3
(b)	3	2	4	1
(c)	2	3	1	2
(d)	1	2	3	4

137. The implication of third and fourth laws gives rise limited to open access.
(a) True (b) False

138. Five laws of Library Science related to save the time of reader.
(a) True (b) False

139. Tamil Nadu (Chennai) Public Libraries Act was passed in 1956.
(a) True (b) False

140. Match the following:
(A) Kerala Public Library Act (1) 1956
(B) Maharashtra Public Library Act (2) 1965
(C) Karnataka Public Library Act (3) 1989
(D) Andhra Public Library Act (4) 1967

Codes:	A	B	C	D
(a)	3	4	2	1
(b)	2	3	1	4
(c)	1	2	3	4
(d)	4	1	2	3

141. Write the name of State in India, where Public Libraries Act has been passed very recently.
(a) Pondicherry (b) Haryana
(c) Tamil Nadu (d) Bihar

142. Write the name of the State which does not have library legislation?
(a) Karnataka (b) Haryana
(c) Bihar (d) Goa

143. The Library Association (U.K.) was founded in 1876.
(a) True (b) False

144. IFLA was founded in 1876.
(a) True (b) False

145. Match the following:
(A) ALA (1) India
(B) LA (2) U.S.A.
(C) ILA (3) U.K.
(D) IASLIC (4) India

Codes:	A	B	C	D
(a)	2	3	4	1
(b)	4	3	2	1
(c)	4	3	1	2
(d)	1	2	3	4

146. IFLA is member of ILA.
(a) True (b) False

147. The RRRLF is concerned with the promotion of
(a) Public Libraries (b) Special Libraries
(c) Academic Libraries (d) None of these

148. Match the following:
(A) Mudaliar Commission (1) 1964
(B) Kothari Commission (2) 1979
(C) Karnataka State University Review Committee (3) 1952
(D) Radhakrishna Commission (4) 1948

Codes:	A	B	C	D
(a)	3	1	2	4
(b)	2	4	3	1
(c)	4	3	2	1
(d)	1	2	3	4

149. The State Lenin Library is located in Paris.
(a) True (b) False

150. The concept of self-renewal was introduced by (*NET Exam.* 1997J)
(a) Atkinson (b) Dr. Parry
(c) Danton (d) M.B. Line

151. RRRLF is a (*NET Exam.* 1997D)
(a) Library Association
(b) A public library
(c) A public trust for supporting libraries
(d) A government body for supporting public libraries

152. Lotka's Laws is concerned with (*NET Exam.* 1997)
(a) Occurrence of words infests
(b) Distribution of papers in periodicals
(c) Average number of author paper
(d) Average number of papers for author

153. National Library Kolkata, receives books on deposit under (*NET Exam.* 1997)

(a) The Registration of Book Act 1887
(b) The Public Libraries Acts 1955
(c) The Copyright Acts 1985
(d) Delivery of Books and Newspapers Acts 1956

154. A library has following section:
Periodicals section. Audio-Visual section. Braille section. Which of the following criteria have been used for departmentalisation?
(a) Customer (b) Product/Material
(c) Function (d) None of the above

155. Bar Code technology is useful for (*NET Exam.* 1999J)
(a) Circulation (b) Acquisition
(c) Stock taking (d) All of the above

156. In the Fifth Law of Library Science growth refers to (*NET Exam.* 1999J)
(a) Space (b) Books
(c) Staff (d) All of the above

157. Library Legislation support the Public Library Movement by (*NET Exam.* 1997D, 1997J)
(a) Ensuring that funds are available
(b) Establishing Local Library Authorities
(c) Making Library Services Mandatory
(d) All of the above

158. The Resource sharing strategy of a Library may enable (*NET Exam.* 1999J)
(a) Jt. acquisition (b) Shared use
(c) Exchange of materials (d) All of these

159. Which of the following States does not have Public Library Legislation? (*NET Exam.* 1999J)
(a) Karnataka (b) West Bengal
(c) Bihar (d) Andhra Pradesh

160. In an empirical study of the effect of Open Access on borrowing patterns open access is (*NET Exam.* 1997J)
(a) An independent variable
(b) A dependent variable
(c) Not a variable at all
(d) An intervening variable

161. Match the following as per Ranganathan's staff formula recommended for a university library:
List - I
(A) Acquisition Section
(B) Reference Section
(C) Periodical Section
(D) Circulation Section
List - II
(i) 1 person for 1500 readers
(ii) 1 person for 500 titles
(iii) 1 person for 6000 titles
(iv) 1 person for 50 readers

Codes:	(A)	(B)	(C)	(D)
(a)	i	iv	iii	ii
(b)	iii	iv	ii	i
(c)	iv	i	iii	ii
(d)	ii	iii	i	iv

162. The Concept of Resource sharing is considered to overcome(*NET Exam.* 1998D)
(a) Information explosion
(b) Information needs are becoming complex
(c) Financial constraints
(d) All of the above

163. Khuda Baksh Library located at Patna.
(a) True (b) False

164. In which date every year celebrated as librarian day? (*C.S. Exam.*)
(a) 12th Aug. (b) 9th Aug.
(c) 12th Sept. (d) 8th Sept.

165. UNESCO's information programme is known as (*NET Exam.* 2001J)
(a) NATIS (b) GIP (c) UAP (d) UBC

166. The basic theory regarding human motivation is propounded by (*NET Exam.* 2001J)
(a) Taylo (b) Maslow
(c) Mayo (d) Likert

167. Zero growth libraries contradict the fifth law of library science. The statement is (*NET Exam.* 2001J)
(a) true, no new book is added
(b) true, because the total size of the book stock is steady
(c) false, since the library may grow in other ways
(d) false, since there can be no zero growth libraries

168. The National Mission on Libraries, India was established in which year? (*NET Exam.* 2001J)
(a) 2009 (b) 2010 (c) 2011 (d) 2012

169. WIPO is located at (*NET Exam.* 2001J)
(a) New York (b) London
(c) Geneva (d) Paris

170. UNESCO Public Library manifesto was revised in (*NET Exam.* 2001J)
(a) 1990 (b) 1998 (c) 1997 (d) 1994

171. The term "Exponential Growth" is referred to (*NET Exam.* 2001D, 2004J)
(a) Liner Growth
(b) Geometrical Progression
(c) Arithmetical Progression
(d) Normal Frequency Distribution

172. The first model of public libraries act in India was drafted in the year (*NET Exam.* 2001D)
(a) 1940 (b) 1942 (c) 1948 (d) 1950

173. Among the following which has not been considered as a library of national importance? (*NET Exam.* 2001D)
(a) Saraswati Mahal Library
(b) Delhi Public Library
(c) Khuda Baksh Oriental Library
(d) Rampur Raja Library

174. Of the following libraries in India, which one is the oldest library?
(a) Asiatic Society Library, Bombay
(b) Connemara Public Library, Madras
(c) Delhi Public Library, Delhi
(d) National Library of India, Calcutta

175. Management is an example of how knowledge grown by (*NET Exam.* 2002D)
(a) Fusion (b) Distillation
(c) Lamination (d) Loose assemblage

176. Who is known as father of Library Movement in USA? (*NET Exam.* 2002D)
(a) Melvil Dewey (b) W. Sayers
(c) Eric de Grolier (d) Tel Farrade

177. Which is/are not the implication of Fourth Law of library science?
(*NET Exam.* 2002D)
(a) Location of library (b) Staff of library
(c) Cataloguing (d) Both (a) and (b)

178. The Library legislation should take care of (*NET Exam.* 2002D)
1. accessibility of information to all sections of the people and provision of finances and the mouds operandi for expenditure.
2. arrangement of a reporting system of the activities of various public libraries.
3. an establishment of institutional network to provide care and preserve documents.

Codes:
(a) 1 and 2 (b) 2 and 3
(c) 1 and 3 (d) 1, 2 and 3

179. Which states entire technical staff of the public libraries comes under the cadre of "Library Services"? (*NET Exam.* 2002D)
(a) West Bengal (b) New Delhi
(c) Karnataka (d) Maharashtra

180. Commonwealth Library Associations headquarter is located at
(*NET Exam.* 2002D)
(a) Nigeria (b) The Hague
(c) New Delhi (d) New York

181. Which organization was established to provide referral service globally, for all sources of environmental information?
(*NET Exam.* 2002D)
(a) UNEP (b) UNESCO
(c) UNICEF (d) WHO

182. Which has been declared an institution of National importance by Government of India? (*NET Exam.* 2002D)
(a) National Library, Kolkata
(b) Delhi Public Library, New Delhi
(c) Connemara Public Library
(d) Asiatic Society Library, Mumbai

183. Which one is the oldest and largest library association in the world?
(a) ILA (b) IFLA (c) ALA (d) AL-UK
(*NET Exam.* 2002J)

184. IASLIC is mainly association of the world
(*NET Exam.* 2002J)
(a) Academic Libraries
(b) Special Libraries
(c) Public Libraries
(d) Documentation Centre

185. William Allenson Berden was associated with Public Library Movement in
(*NET Exam.* 2002J)
(a) Mumbai (b) Punjab
(c) Kolkata (d) Baroda

186. What is the basic record in the library about each document forming part of its collection?
(a) Accession Catalogue (b) Accession register
(c) Order register (d) Book record file
(*NET Exam.* 2002J)

187. Which of the following material could you not expect to find in a public library? (*NET Exam.* 2002J)
(a) Audio Cassettes (b) Newspapers
(c) Patents (d) Maps

188. Library cess is a source of finance for (*NET Exam.* 2002D)
(a) Public Library (b) Special Library
(c) School Library (d) Digital Library

189. Wadia Committee was set up for (*NET Exam.* 2002J)
(a) University education
(b) Development of library
(c) New techniques in library science training
(d) Satisfactory improving in Academic libraries

190. Ranganathan was the founder of (*NET Exam.* 2002J)
(a) ALA (b) ABGILA
(c) IASLIC (d) AGLIS

191. Which of the following Public Library Act/do/does not charge Levy and library cess? (*NET Exam.* 2002J)
1. New Delhi 2. Maharashtra
3. Haryana 4. West Bengal
Codes:
(a) 1 and 3 (b) 2 and 4
(c) 1 and 4 (d) 2 and 3

192. Which of the following recommended the establishment of Central Medical Library? (*NET Exam.* 2002J)
(a) Academic Council of HRD Ministry
(b) Health Survey and Development Committee
(c) Planning Commission
(d) All of the above

193. Which of the following statements about national libraries is/are correct? (*NET Exam.* 2003J)
(a) They have to bring out a National bibliography
(b) They have to function as depository library
(c) They have to participate in Universal bibliography control
(d) All of the above

194. The first concept of "Library cooperation" put to practice is traced to (*NET Exam.* 2003J)
(a) OCLC (b) Fermington plan
(c) Deler Library Plan (d) None of these

195. Established of Raj Ram Mohan Roy foundation at Kolkata (*NET Exam.* 2003J)
(a) May 22, 1972 (b) May 30, 1972
(c) Nov. 22, 1972 (d) Nov. 30, 1972

196. Who was the chairman of foundation Committee for National Policy for Library and Information Science in 1985? (*NET Exam.* 2003J)
(a) Prof. K.N. Raj
(b) Dr. S.R. Ranganathan
(c) Prof. D.P. Chattopadhyaya
(d) Prof. D. Kaul

197. A latest revision of UNESCO manifesto of public library issued in the year (*NET Exam.* 2003J)
(a) 1992 (b) 1994 (c) 1996 (d) 1998

198. Which of the following laws of Library Science prescribes for the states responsibility for Public Library Services?
(a) First Law (b) Second Law
(c) Third Law (d) Fourth Law

199. Which library is functioning as depository library? (*NET Exam.* 2003J)
(a) Central Reference Library, Calcutta
(b) Mumbai Divisional Library
(c) Asiatic Society Library, Mumbai
(d) Connemara Public Library, Chennai

200. Why 18th November 1983 is famous for? (*Net Exam.* 2003D)
(a) The Delhi Library Association was founded
(b) BNB users group was funded in London
(c) Kolkata Public Library was opened to the public
(d) Establishment of UNESCO

201. The structure and the cadre of the staff for libraries (*NET Exam.* 2003D)
(a) Haryana Public Libraries Act
(b) Karnataka Public Libraries Act
(c) Maharashtra Public Libraries Act
(d) West Bengal Public Libraries Act

202. Which of the following agency serves as a focal point in framing the information policy in India for UNISIST/UNESCO? (*NET Exam.* 2003D, 2002J)
(a) INIS (b) NISCAIR
(c) NISSAT (d) LISA

203. PV Verghese prize is a warded by Indian Library Association for (*NET Exam.* 2003D)

(a) Best library (b) Best book
(c) Best services (d) Best article

204. Library of Congress classification is based upon (*NET Exam.* 2003D)
(a) Collocation (b) APUPA pattern
(c) Users warrant (d) Literary warrant

205. What is the name of authority or committee that is responsible for the choosing of books and the staff (*NET Exam.* 2004J)
(a) Indian Library Association
(b) Library Authority
(c) Ranganathan Committee
(d) Any of these

206. The first "Model Public Libraries Act" in India was drafted in the year (*NET Exam.* 2004J)
(a) 1940 (b) 1942 (c) 1948 (d) 1950

207. In 1948, 'The Imperial Library' of Calcutta was renamed as (*NET Exam.* 2004J)
(a) Central Reference Library
(b) Central Secretarial Library
(c) Asiatic Library
(d) National Library India

208. The National Science Library is the part or (*NET Exam.* 2004J)
(a) NASSDOC (b) UGC
(c) NISCAI (d) LASTEC

209. Haryana Public Library Act was passed in the year (*NET Exam.* 2004J)
(a) 1979 (b) 1988 (c) 1989 (d) 1992

210. Will designed catalogue is an essentiality to (*NET Exam.* 2004J)
(a) First law of library science
(b) Second law of library science
(c) Third law of library science
(d) Fourth law of library science

211. RRLF promotes and helps (*NET Exam.* 2004J)
(a) Special Library (b) Public Library
(c) School Library (d) All of the above

212. ________ is an important record of books, which shows the position of any book on the shelves.
(a) Bay Guide (b) Authority File
(c) Accession List (d) Shelf List

213. Which of the following contains the concerned class numbers and their verbal heading? (*NET Exam.* 2004D)
(a) Shelf (b) General entry
(c) Bay (d) Index

214. Indirect methods of user education includes (*NET Exam.* 2004D)
1. Library Guides 2. Display list
3. Documentation list 4. Questionnaire
Codes:
(a) 1 & 2 (b) 3 & 4
(c) 1, 2 & 3 (d) 2, 3 & 4

215. The European translation centre located at (*NET Exam.* 2004D)
(a) London (b) Vienna
(c) New Delhi (d) Paris

216. Which provide both matching and non-matching grants to public libraries in India? (*NET Exam.* 2004D)
(a) RRRLF (b) ILA
(c) Planning Commission (d) UGC

217. On which date Maulana A.K. Azad National Library of India would open for public? (*NET Exam.* 2005D)
(a) Feb. 1, 1953 (b) Sept. 5, 1953
(c) Aug. 15, 1953 (d) Jan. 26, 1953

218. Which department controls the Public Libraries in Mizoram? (*NET Exam.* 2005D)
(a) Human resources
(b) Education
(c) Science and Technology
(d) Information and Broadcasting

219. The chief technical contributions or Dr. Ranganathan to library science are (*NET Exam.* 2005D)
1. Colon Classification (1933)
2. Five Laws of Library Science (1931)
3. Classification and Indexing Theory
Codes:
(a) 1, 2 & 3 (b) 1 only
(c) 1 & 3 (d) 2 & 3

220. Headquarters of Indian Library Association is moved from Kolkata to New Delhi in the year (*NET Exam.* 2005D)
(a) 1933 (b) 1953 (c) 1964 (d) 1965

221. Which organization was established to provide referral service globally for all sources of environmental information? (*NET Exam.* 2005D)

(a) UNEP (b) UNICEF
(c) UNESCO (d) UNCTAD

222. Match the following: (*NET Exam.* 2006J)

List I

(A) Nehru Memorial Museum Library
(B) Connemara Public Library
(C) Bhandarkar Oriental Research Institute Library
(D) Khuda Baksh Oriental Library

List II

(i) Chennai (ii) Pune (iii) Patna
(iv) Delhi (v) Allahabad

Codes:	**A**	**B**	**C**	**D**
(a)	(iii)	(v)	(iv)	(ii)
(b)	(v)	(iv)	(i)	(ii)
(c)	(v)	(ii)	(i)	(iii)
(d)	(iv)	(i)	(ii)	(iii)

223. The author who defined Reference Service as the "Process of establishing contact between a reader and his documents in a personal way" is (*NET Exam.* 2006D)
(a) W.A. Katz (b) L. Shores
(c) M. Hutchins (d) S.R. Ranganathan

224. Raja Ram Mohan Roy Library Foundation (*NET Exam.* 2006D)
(i) Promotes public libraries
(ii) Located at Mumbai
(iii) Promotes school libraries
(iv) Located at Kolkata

Codes:

(a) i & ii are correct (b) i & iv are correct
(c) i & iii are correct (d) iii & iv are correct

225. The National Library for the visually handicapped is located at (*NET Exam.* 2006D)
(a) Allahabad (b) Indore
(c) Dehradun (d) Nainital

226. Identify the correct chronological order in which the following were establishment? (*NET Exam.* 2006D)
(a) National Library of India (Kolkata), Delhi Public Library, Documentation Research and Training Centre, Raja Ram Mohan Roy Library Foundation
(b) Delhi Public Library, Documentation Research and Training Centre, Raja Ram Mohan Roy Library Foundation, National Library of India
(c) Documentation Research and Training Centre, Raja Ram Mohan Roy Library Foundation, National Library of India (Kolkata), Delhi Public Library
(d) Raja Ram Mohan Roy Library Foundation, National Library of India (Kolkata), Delhi Public Library, Documentation Research and Training Centre

227. **Assertion (A):** Computerisation of Public libraries in India is slow.

Reason (R): Non availability of resources. (*NET Exam.* 2006D)
(a) (A) is true, but (R) is false.
(b) (R) is true, but (A) is false.
(c) Both (A) and (R) are true.
(d) Both (A) and (R) are false.

228. This particular law of library science gives emphasis on the delegation of the government to enact library in their respective states (*NET Exam.* 2007J)
(a) First Law (b) Second Law
(c) Third Law (d) Fourth Law

229. Who has not changed its name? (*NET Exam.* 2007J)
(a) Library Association, UK (b) ALA
(c) ASLIB (d) IFLA

230. "Libraries as Gateways to knowledge" is the title of the document (*NET Exam.* 2007J)
(a) National Library Information Policy, 1986
(b) Information Technology Act, 2000
(c) National Knowledge Commission on Libraries, 2007
(d) None of the above

231. Public Library Law has already been passed in the following states. Identify the correct chronological order in which they were enacted. (*NET Exam.* 2009D)
(i) Uttaranchal (ii) Orissa
(iii) Gujarat (iv) Haryana

Codes:

(a) i, ii, iii, iv (b) iv, ii, i, iii
(c) ii, iii, iv, i (d) iii, ii, i, iv

232. Arrange the following Association according to their year of formation. (*NET Exam.* 2009D, 2010J)
(i) ASLIB (ii) LA (iii) ALA (iv) SLA

Codes:
(a) iii, ii, iv, i (b) ii, iv, i, iii
(c) iii, i, iv, ii (d) iv i, iii, ii

233. **Assertion (A):** Library legislation provides proper governance and management.
Reason (R): It ensures free public library service to all irrespective of caste, creed and sex. (*NET Exam.* 2010J)
Codes:
(a) Both (A) and (R) are true.
(b) Both (A) and (R) are false.
(c) (A) is true, but (R) is false.
(d) (A) is false, but (R) is true.

234. Arrange the following states chronologically according to year of enactment of Library Legislation. (*NET Exam.* 2010J)
(i) Tamil Nadu (ii) U.P.
(iii) Gujarat (iv) Mizoram
Codes:
(a) iv, iii, i, ii (b) ii, iv, iii, i
(c) i, iv, iii, ii (d) i, ii, iv, iii

235. Which of the following professional Association does not exist now? (*NET Exam.* 2010J)
(a) IFLA (b) FID (c) ALA (d) IASLIC

236. The Library Association (UK) is now the component of (*NET Exam.* 2010J)
(a) ASLIB (b) CILIP
(c) ALA (d) None of the above

237. Five Laws of Library Science was first published in (*NET Exam.* 2010D)
(a) 1925 (b) 1930 (c) 1931 (d) 1933

238. Arrange the following States according to the year of enactment of library legislation. (*NET Exam.* 2010D)
(i) Pondicherry (ii) Orissa
(iii) Rajasthan (iv) Karnataka
Codes:
(a) iv, i, iii, ii (b) iv, ii, iii, i
(c) iv, iii, i, ii (d) i, iii, ii, iv

239. National Library for Visual handicapped is situated in (*NET Exam.* 2007D)
(a) Mumbai (b) Mysore
(c) New Delhi (d) Dehradun

240. The latest state which enacted Public Libraries Act is (*NET Exam.* 2007D)
(a) Bihar (b) Uttaranchal
(c) Uttar Pradesh (d) Orissa

241. UNISIST, a project of UNESCO was launched in this year (*NET Exam.* 2007D)
(a) 1994 (b) 1972 (c) 1958 (d) 2001

242. IATLIS is an association of (*NET Exam.* 2008D)
(a) Library Science Faculty
(b) Special Librarians
(c) Librarian of Public Libraries
(d) Librarians of Teachers Training Colleges

243. Match the following: (*NET Exam.* 2008D)
List I
(A) Five Laws of Library Science
(B) Subject approach to Information
(C) Organising Knowledge in Libraries
(D) Information Science in Theory and Practice
List II
(i) C.D. Needham (ii) S.R. Ranganatha
(iii) B.C. Vickery & A. Vickery (iv) A.C. Fisted

Codes:	**A**	**B**	**C**	**D**
(a)	(ii)	(iv)	(i)	(iii)
(b)	(i)	(iii)	(iv)	(ii)
(c)	(iii)	(ii)	(iv)	(i)
(d)	(iv)	(ii)	(iii)	(i)

244. Match the following: (*NET Exam.* 2008J)

List I	**List II**
(A) British Library	(i) Russia
(B) Bibliotheque Nationale	(ii) USA
(C) Lenin Library	(iii) UK
(D) Library of Congress	(iv) France

Codes:	**A**	**B**	**C**	**D**
(a)	(iv)	(iii)	(i)	(ii)
(b)	(i)	(ii)	(iii)	(iv)
(c)	(iii)	(iv)	(i)	(ii)
(d)	(iii)	(iv)	(ii)	(i)

245. Identify the association that has change its original name (*NET Exam.* 2008D)
(a) ILA (b) SLA (c) LA (d) ALA

246. With which agency did UNESCO collaborate to establish UNISIST? (*NET Exam.* 2008D)
(a) ICSU (b) FID (c) IFLA (d) ILA

247. National Library for Blind and Handicapped of India is located at (*NET Exam.* 2008D)
(a) Madras (b) Tanjore
(c) Dehradun (d) Delhi

248. **Assertion (A):** UNESCO championed the cause of public library movement.

Reason (R): UNESCO's concert for public library movement is reflected in its "Public Library Manifesto". *(NET Exam.* 2008D)

Codes:

(a) (A) is true, but (R) is false.
(b) (A) is false, but (R) is true.
(c) Both (A) and (R) are false.
(d) Both (A) and (R) are true.

249. Arrange the following public library acts according to the year of enactment *(NET Exam.* 2008D)

(a) Manipur Public Libraries Act, West Bengal Public Libraries Acts, Kerala Public Libraries Acts, Mizoram Public Libraries Acts
(b) West Bengal Public Libraries Acts, Manipur Public Libraries Acts, Kerala Public Libraries Acts, Mizoram Public Libraries Acts
(c) West Bengal Public Libraries Acts, Kerala Public Libraries Acts, Manipur Public Libraries Acts, Mizoram Public Libraries Acts
(d) West Bengal Public Libraries Acts, Manipur Public Libraries Acts, Mizoram Public Libraries Acts, Kerala Public Libraries Acts.

250. Corollary for Second Law of Library Science is *(NET Exam.* 2012J)

(a) Books for all
(b) Free Books services
(c) Free Library services
(d) Books every where

251. World Intellectual property Organization is related to *(NET Exam.* 2012J)

(a) UNESCO
(b) United Nations
(c) US Organization
(d) International Law Organization

252. **Assertion (A):** There is need for Library Legislation in all States of India. *(NET Exam.* 2012J)

Reason (R): To make Public Library System independent and without political influence.

Codes:

(a) Both (A) and (R) are true.
(b) (A) is true, but (R) is false.
(c) Both (A) and (R) are false.
(d) (A) is false, but (R) is true.

253. Match the following:

List I

(a) Connemara Public Library
(b) Khuda Baksh Oriental Public Library
(c) Asiatic Society Library
(d) National Library India

List II

(i) Patna (ii) Kolkata (iii) Chennai (iv) Mumbai

Codes:	A	B	C	D
(a)	(iv)	(ii)	(i)	(iii)
(b)	(iv)	(i)	(ii)	(iii)
(c)	(iii)	(ii)	(i)	(iv)
(d)	(iii)	(i)	(iv)	(ii)

254. Which libraries are functioning as depository libraries? *(NET Exam.* 2012J)

(i) Delhi Public Library
(ii) Connemara Public Library
(iii) British Council Library
(iv) Central Reference Library

Codes:

(a) i, iii, iv are correct (b) i & iii are correct
(c) i & ii are correct (d) ii & iii are correct

255. Arrange the following association according to the year of establishment. *(NET Exam.* 2008)

(a) ALA, CILIP (LA), Special Library Association, ASLIB
(b) CILIP (LA), ALA, Special Libraries Association, ASLIB
(c) ALA, Special Library Association, CILIP (LA), ASLIB
(d) ASLIB, ALA, CILIP (LA), Special Library Association

256. First time efforts for the development of libraries in India were made *(NET Exam.* 2008D)

(a) S.R. Ranganathan
(b) S. Radhakrishnan
(c) Sayaji Rao Gaekwad I
(d) Sayaji Rao Gaekwad III

257. **Assertion (A):** The development of Institutional Repositories in India is at a slow pace.

Reason (R): This can be attributed to the non-availability of open source software and lack of interest among the LIS professionals. (*NET Exam.* 2009D)

(a) Both (A) and (R) are true.
(b) Both (A) and (R) are false.
(c) (A) is true, but (R) is partially true.
(d) (A) is false, but (R) is true.

258. Arrange the following events of Public Library movement in chronological order

(i) Enactment of Press and Registration, Books Act
(ii) Establishment of the Punjab Library, Lahore
(iii) Constitution of Fyzee Committee
(iv) Declaration of Imperial Library (Calcutta) as National Library India

Codes:

(a)	(i)	(iii)	(iv)	(ii)
(b)	(i)	(ii)	(iii)	(iv)
(c)	(ii)	(iii)	(iv)	(i)
(d)	(iv)	(i)	(iii)	(ii)

259. Arrange the following principles and canons according to their levels as enunciated by S.R. Ranganathan (*NET Exam.* 2009D)

(i) Principles of Cataloguing
(ii) General Normative Principles
(iii) Laws of Library Science
(iv) Canons of Cataloguing

Codes:

(a)	(i)	(iv)	(iii)	(ii)
(b)	(ii)	(iii)	(iv)	(i)
(c)	(ii)	(i)	(iv)	(iii)
(d)	(i)	(iv)	(ii)	(iii)

260. RRRLF falls under the (*NET Exam.* 2012J)

(a) Ministry of Human Resource Development
(b) Ministry of Information and Broadcasting
(c) Ministry of Culture
(d) Ministry of Science and Technology

261. Who was the Chairman of National Policy on Library & Information System (1986) (*NET Exam.* 2012J)

(a) D.N. Banerjee (b) D.P. Chattopadhyaya
(c) Sam Pitroda (d) Kalpana Dasgupta

262. Amendment to Delivery of Books (Public Libraries) and Newspaper Act was enacted in India in the year (*NET Exam.* 2011D&J)

(a) 1952 (b) 1954 (c) 1956 (d) 1962

263. National knowledge Commission was launched under the chairmanship of (*NET Exam.* 2011D&J)

(a) Nandan Nilekani (b) Deepak Nayar
(c) Sam Pitroda (d) Ashok Ganguly

264. Library Legislation refers to the development of (*NET Exam.* 2010D&J)

(a) Academic Library (b) Special Library
(c) Public Library (d) None of the Above

265. Number of states in India which have enacted Public Library Legislation till date is (*NET Exam.* 2011D)

(a) Seven (b) Ten
(c) Thirteen (d) Sixteen

266. IASLIC was found in the year (*NET Exam.* 2010D)

(a) 1955 (b) 1965 (c) 1975 (d) 1985

267. Which publication was not authored by S.R. Ranganathan? (*NET Exam.* 2010D)

(a) *Prolegomena to Library Classification*
(b) *Reference Services*
(c) *Ramanujan: The Man and the Mathematician*
(d) *Living with Books*

268. As per India Copyright Law copyright is granted for (*NET Exam.* 2011J)

(a) Fifty years after the book is published
(b) Fifty years after the death of the author
(c) Sixty years after the book is published
(d) Sixty years after the death of the author

269. Which one is the most important problem being faced by Institutional Repositories for archiving the documents? (*NET Exam.* 2011J)

(a) Availability (b) Rarity
(c) Copyright issues (d) Authors resistance

270. Public Library Manifesto was developed by (*NET Exam.* 2011J)

(a) Delhi Public Library (b) UNESCO
(c) RRRLF (d) IFLA

271. Which of the following is not a virtual library? (*NET Exam.* 2012D)

(a) Without wall
(b) With distributed physical location
(c) Providing integrated and unified remote access to geographically distributed collection
(d) Which does not Exist in Reality

272. Which of the following is not an implication of Fourth Law of Library Science? (*NET Exam.* 2012D)

(a) Classified arrangement
(b) Stock room guides
(c) Issues methods
(d) Rural Library services

273. Raja Ram Mohan Roy Library Foundation (RRRLF) was established by (*NET Exam.* 2012D)
(a) Indian Library Association
(b) Development of Culture, Govt. of India
(c) Govt. of West Bengal
(d) Ministry of Home Affairs, Govt. of India

274. Which state library Public Library Act has the provision to collect library fund through land tax?
(a) Tamil Nadu (b) Karnataka
(c) Andhra Pradesh (d) None of the above

275. Which library is authorized to receive books under "Delivery of Books Act"? (*NET Exam.* 2011J)
(a) National Library
(b) Central Library, Delhi
(c) State Central Library, Mumbai
(d) Parliament Library, Delhi

276. Which one is not a Canon (as given by Ranganathan? (*NET Exam.* 2011J)
(a) Canon of Comprehensiveness
(b) Canon of Consistence
(c) Canon of Context
(d) Canon of Currency

277. Who is the father of library movement of USA? (*NET Exam.* 2011J)
(a) F.W. Lancaster (b) Paul Wasserman
(c) Melvil Dewey (d) Allen Kent

278. **Assertion (A):** According to the fifth law of library science is growing organization.
Reason (R): All the resources of library are supposed to grow. (*NET Exam.* 2011J)
(a) (A) is true, but (R) is false.
(b) (A) is false, but (R) is true.
(c) Both (A) and (R) are false.
(d) Both(A) and (R)are true.

279. Arrange the following Public Library Acts according to their year of enactment (*NET Exam.* 2011J)
(i) Pondicherry (ii) Madras
(iii) Haryana (iv) Orissa

Codes:

(a)	(iv)	(iii)	(i)	(ii)
(b)	(ii)	(iii)	(i)	(iv)
(c)	(ii)	(i)	(iv)	(iii)
(d)	(iii)	(ii)	(i)	(iv)

280. The term "exponential growth" refers to (*NET Exam.* 2011J)
(a) Linear growth
(b) Normal mode of distribution
(c) Geometric progression
(d) Arithmetic progression

281. Which of the following states don't have library legislation? (*NET Exam.* 2013J)
(i) Haryana (ii) Delhi
(iii) J&K (iv) Manipur
Codes:
(a) (i) and (ii) are correct
(b) (ii) and (iii) are correct
(c) (i) and (iv) are correct
(d) (ii) and (iv) are correct

282. Give the sequence, the following in order of their origin (*NET Exam.* 2013J)
(i) National Library
(ii) Calcutta Public Library
(iii) Imperial Public Library Acts
(iv) Imperial Library

Codes:

(a)	(ii)	(iii)	(iv)	(i)
(b)	(i)	(ii)	(iii)	(iv)
(c)	(iii)	(i)	(iv)	(ii)
(d)	(ii)	(iv)	(iii)	(i)

283. **Assertion (A):** In spite of political, economic and technological support, the growth of public library system is lopsided.
Reason (R): The public libraries are totally depending on cess/tax amounts. (*NET Exam.* 2013J)
Codes:
(a) Both (A) and (R) are true.
(b) Both (A) and (R) are false.
(c) (A) is true, but (R) is false.
(d) (A) is false, but (R) is true.

284. Which department of the government of India deals with public libraries?
(a) Department of Archaeology
(b) Department of Culture
(c) Department of Primary Education
(d) Department of Science and Technology

285. Match the following: (*NET Exam.* 2013J)

List I
(A) 1st Law of Library Science
(B) 2nd Law of Library Science
(C) 3rd Law of Library Science
(D) 4th Law of Library Science

List II
(i) Real time access
(ii) Search engine & subject gateways
(iii) Web access to resources
(iv) Open access initiatives

Codes:	A	B	C	D
(a)	(iii)	(iv)	(ii)	(i)
(b)	(iv)	(i)	(ii)	(iii)
(c)	(i)	(iii)	(ii)	(iv)
(d)	(ii)	(iv)	(i)	(iii)

286. Which law of Library Science, restated with emphasis on information as a dynamics, continuum and never ending phenomenon? (*NET Exam.* 2013J)
(a) Fifth Law (b) Fourth Law
(c) Third Law (d) Second Law

287. The first printed works are called (*NET Exam.* 2013J)
(a) Impensis (b) Incunabula
(c) Impression (d) Omprimatur

288. Which of the following functions are analysed by ALA as reference service functions? (*NET Exam.* 2012D)
(i) Consultation function
(ii) Guidance function
(iii) Instruction function
(iv) Bibliographic function

Codes:
(a) i, ii, and iii are correct
(b) ii, iii, and iv are correct
(c) i, ii, and iv are correct
(d) i, iii and iv are correct

289. **Assertion (A):** Dr. S.R. Ranganathan has been called "Father of Library and Information Science" in India.

Reason (R): Library Science education in India was started by Dr. S.R. Ranganathan. (*NET Exam.* 2012D)

Codes:
(a) (A) is false, but (R) is true.
(b) (A) is true, but (R) is false.
(c) Both (A) and (R) are true.
(d) Both (A) and (R) are false.

290. Which is the correct sequence of the national libraries in the order of their year of establishment? (*NET Exam.* 2012D)
(i) British Library (formerly British Museum library)
(ii) Library of Congress (Washington, D.C.)
(iii) Lenin Library (Moscow)
(iv) Bibliotheque Nationale (Paris)

Codes:

(a)	(i)	(ii)	(iii)	(iv)
(b)	(ii)	(iii)	(i)	(iv)
(c)	(iii)	(ii)	(iv)	(i)
(d)	(iv)	(iii)	(ii)	(i)

291. **Assertion (A):** The exclusive rights conferred by intellectual property rights can generally be transferred/licenced to third party.

Reason (R): The creators want to make monetary benefit out of their intellectual product. (*NET Exam.* 2012D)

Codes:
(a) (A) is true, but (R) is false.
(b) (A) is false, but (R) is true.
(c) Both (A) and (R) are true.
(d) Both (A) and (R) are false.

292. Headquarters of UNESCO is (*NET Exam.* 2007J)
(a) Washington (b) Paris
(c) London (d) The Hague

293. Which Association was established in 1876? (*NET Exam.* 2007J)
(a) LA (b) ALA (c) ILA (d) IASLIC

294. Match the following: (*NET Exam.* 2008J)

List I	**List II**
(A) Orissa	(i) 2006
(B) Goa	(ii) 2005
(C) Uttaranchal	(iii) 2001
(D) Uttar Pradesh	(iv) 1994

Codes:	A	B	C	D
(a)	(i)	(ii)	(iii)	(iv)
(b)	(iii)	(iv)	(ii)	(i)
(c)	(iv)	(iii)	(ii)	(i)
(d)	(ii)	(i)	(iii)	(iv)

295. **Assertion (A):** In Fifth Law, the word used in 'organism' not organization.

Reason (R): Libraries grow in collection size human resources, physical facilities and services from time to time. (*NET Exam.* 2010D)

Codes:
(a) Both (A) and (R) are true and (R) is the correct explanation of (A).
(b) Both (A) and (R) are true but (R) is correct explanation of (A).
(c) (A) is true, but (R) is false.
(d) (A) is false, but (R) is true.

296. Identify the chronological order of the following Public Libraries Acts (*NET Exam.* 2007D)
(i) Andhra Pradesh Public Libraries Act
(ii) Karnataka Public Libraries Act
(iii) Haryana Public Libraries Act
(iv) Maharashtra Public Libraries Act

Codes:

(a)	(ii)	(iv)	(iii)	(i)
(b)	(i)	(ii)	(iv)	(iii)
(c)	(iii)	(ii)	(i)	(iv)
(d)	(iv)	(iii)	(i)	(ii)

297. Match the following: (*NET Exam.* 2006J)
List I
(A) Madras Public Library Act
(B) West Bengal Public Library Act
(C) Andhra Pradesh Public Library Act
(D) Karnataka Public Library Act
List II
(i) 1965 (ii) 1960 (iii) 1948 (iv) 1979

Codes:	A	B	C	D
(a)	(iii)	(iv)	(ii)	(i)
(b)	(i)	(ii)	(iii)	(iv)
(c)	(iii)	(ii)	(iv)	(i)
(d)	(ii)	(i)	(iv)	(iii)

298. Match the following: (*NET Exam.* 2004D)
List I
(A) Maharashtra Public Library Act
(B) Gujarat Public Library Act
(C) Orissa Public Library Act
(D) West Bengal Public Library Act
List II
(i) 2004 (ii) 2005 (iii) 1967 (iv) 1988
(v) 1979

Codes:	A	B	C	D
(a)	(i)	(iii)	(ii)	(iv)
(b)	(ii)	(v)	(iv)	(iii)
(c)	(iii)	(i)	(ii)	(v)
(d)	(v)	(ii)	(iv)	(iii)

299. Match the following: (*NET Exam.* 2004D)

List I	List II
(A) Maharashtra	(i) 1967
(B) Tamil Nadu	(ii) 1965
(C) Karnataka	(iii) 1948
(D) Andhra Pradesh	(iv) 1960

Codes:	A	B	C	D
(a)	(i)	(iii)	(ii)	(iv)
(b)	(i)	(ii)	(iii)	(iv)
(c)	(iii)	(ii)	(i)	(iv)
(d)	(ii)	(iii)	(i)	(iv)

300. Arrange the following Laws of Library Science as given by Ranganathan: (*NET Exam.* 2011J)
(i) Save the time of the reader
(ii) Books are for use
(iii) Every book has its reader
(iv) Every reader has his book

Codes:
(a) ii, iv, iii, i (b) iv, ii, i, iii
(c) ii, i, iv, iii (d) iii, ii, i, iv

301. Match the following: (*NET Exam.* 2011J)
List I
(A) Best books for the largest numbers
(B) Library is the heart of all university work
(C) First Ph.D. in Library Science
(D) First Librarian of National Library in India
List II
(i) D.B. Krishna Rao (ii) B.S. Kesavan
(iii) S.R. Ranganathan (iv) Melvil Dewey

Codes:	A	B	C	D
(a)	(i)	(ii)	(iii)	(iv)
(b)	(iv)	(iii)	(ii)	(iv)
(c)	(iii)	(iv)	(i)	(ii)
(d)	(iv)	(iii)	(i)	(ii)

302. Match the following: (*NET Exam.* 2011J)

List I	List II
(A) SENDOC	(i) Social Science
(B) INPADOC	(ii) Science
(C) NASSDOC	(iii) Patents
(D) INSDOC (NISCAIR)	(iv) Small Scale Industries

Codes:	A	B	C	D
(a)	(ii)	(iii)	(iv)	(i)
(b)	(i)	(ii)	(iii)	(iv)
(c)	(iv)	(iii)	(i)	(ii)
(d)	(iii)	(iv)	(i)	(ii)

303. Match the following: (*NET Exam.* 2011J)

List I	List II
(A) Library of Congress	(i) 1952
(B) INSDOC	(ii) 1954
(C) Delivery of Books Act	(iii) 1903
(D) Imperial Library Calcutta	(iv) 1800

Codes:	A	B	C	D
(a)	(ii)	(i)	(iii)	(iv)
(b)	(i)	(iii)	(ii)	(iv)
(c)	(iv)	(i)	(ii)	(iii)
(d)	(i)	(ii)	(iii)	(iv)

304. Match the following: (*NET Exam.* 2012J)

List I	List II
(A) RRRLF	(i) Delhi
(B) Connemara Public Library	(ii) Patna
(C) NISCAIR	(iii) Kolkata
(D) Khuda Baksh Oriental Public Library	(iv) Chennai

Codes:	A	B	C	D
(a)	(iv)	(iii)	(ii)	(i)
(b)	(ii)	(iii)	(iv)	(i)
(c)	(iii)	(iv)	(i)	(ii)
(d)	(iv)	(i)	(ii)	(iii)

305. Which principles are corollary to Wall picture principle? (*NET Exam.* 2012J)
(i) Cow-calf principles
(ii) Principle of later-in-time
(iii) Whole organ principle
(iv) All of the above
Codes:
(a) (i) and (ii) are correct
(b) (ii) and (iii) are correct
(c) (i) and (iii) are correct
(d) (i) and (iv) are correct

306. Match the following: (*NET Exam.* 2011D)

List I	List II
(A) ALA	(i) 1927
(B) ILA	(ii) 1876
(C) ASLIB	(iii) 1933
(D) IFLA	(iv) 1924

Codes:	A	B	C	D
(a)	(ii)	(iii)	(iv)	(i)
(b)	(iv)	(i)	(ii)	(iii)
(c)	(i)	(ii)	(iv)	(iii)
(d)	(iii)	(iv)	(i)	(ii)

307. Match the following: (*NET Exam.* 2011D)
List I
(A) Tamil Nadu Public Library Act
(B) Maharashtra Public Libraries Act
(C) Kerala Public Library Act
(D) Orissa Public Library Act
List II
(i) 1948 (ii) 1989 (iii) 1967 (iv) 2002

Codes:	A	B	C	D
(a)	(i)	(iii)	(ii)	(iv)
(b)	(iii)	(ii)	(iv)	(i)
(c)	(ii)	(iii)	(i)	(iv)
(d)	(i)	(ii)	(iv)	(iii)

308. Arrange the following according to their year of enactment: (*NET Exam.* 2012D)
(i) Tamil Nadu Public Library Act
(ii) Kerala Public Library Act
(iii) Maharashtra Public Library Act
(iv) Orissa Public Library Act
Codes:

(a)	(i)	(iii)	(ii)	(iv)
(b)	(ii)	(iii)	(iv)	(i)
(c)	(ii)	(iii)	(i)	(iv)
(d)	(iv)	(iii)	(ii)	(i)

309. 'Parry Committee' (UK) was set up to advise Code (*NET Exam.* 2012D)
(a) School Libraries (b) Public Libraries
(c) Special Library (d) University Libraries

310. Arrange the following Public Library Acts according to their year of enactment: (*NET Exam.* 2012D)
(i) Uttar Pradesh Public Library Acts
(ii) Arunachal Pradesh Public Library Acts
(iii) Orissa Public Library Acts
(iv) Gujarat Public Library Acts
Codes:

(a)	(iv)	(iii)	(i)	(ii)
(b)	(ii)	(iii)	(i)	(iv)
(c)	(ii)	(i)	(iv)	(iii)
(d)	(iii)	(ii)	(i)	(iv)

311. Number of working days of National Library of India in a year (*NET 17J ii paper*)
(a) 350 days (b) 360 days
(c) 362 days (d) 365 days

312. In which of the following places the zonal offices of RRRLF are located? (*NET 17J ii paper*)
(i) Delhi (ii) Trivandrum
(iii) Mumbai (iv) Hyderabad
Codes:
(a) (i) and (iv) are correct.
(b) (i) and (iii) are correct.
(c) (ii) and (iv) are correct.
(4) (ii) and (iii) are correct

313. Arrange in sequence the following committees in order of that year of commencement:
(i) Library Committee
(ii) Committee on national network system for university libraries
(iii) Review committee on Library Science

(iv) Curriculum Development Committee on Library and Information Science

Codes:

(a) i, ii, iii, iv (b) iii, iv, ii, i
(c) iii, ii, i, iv (d) i, iii, ii, iv

314. Arrange the following Public Libraries Acts' according to their year of enactment: *(NET 17J ii paper)*

(i) Gujarat Public Libraries Act
(ii) Chhattisgarh Public Libraries Act
(iii) Goa Public Libraries Act
(iv) Rajasthan Public Libraries Act

Codes:

(a) (i), (iii), (ii), (iv) (b) (iv), (ii), (i), (iii)
(c) (iii), (i), (iv), (ii) (d) (iv), (ii), (iii), (i)

315. **Assertion (A):** Libraries contribute to capacity building, which is essential to community development.

Reason (R): Library programmes and services can influence a person's desire for life-long learning, which is an important component of capacity building. *(NET 17J iii paper)*

Codes:

(a) (A) is true, but (R) is false
(b) (A) is false, but (R) is true
(c) Both (A) and (R) are true
(d) Both (A) and (R) are false

316. How many Working Groups are constituted under National Mission on Libraries, India? *(NET 17 NOV iii paper)*

(a) Two (b) Three (c) Four (d) Five

317. Which of the following components are essential for National Information Policy? *(NET 17 NOV iii paper)*

(i) Legislation framework
(ii) E-Journal consortium
(iii) Digital repositories
(iv) National bibliography

Codes:

(a) (i) and (ii) are correct
(b) (i) and (iv) are correct
(c) (ii) and (iii) are correct
(d) (ii) and (iv) are correct

318. Which of the following are the activities of National Mission on Libraries? *(NET 17 NOV iii paper)*

(i) CIP Project
(ii) Capacity Building
(iii) Library Assistance Programme
(iv) Setting up of Model Libraries

Codes:

(a) (i) and (iv) are correct
(b) (ii) and (iv) are correct
(c) (ii) and (iii) are correct
(d) (iii) and (iv) are correct

319. Which of the following are related to 'Sugamya Pustakalaya'? *(NET 17 NOV iii paper)*

(i) An online platform that makes accessible the content available to 'print disabled people'.
(ii) Created by Department of Empowerment of persons with disabilities (Divyangjan) Ministry of Social Justice and Empowerment, GOI.
(iii) Powered by TCS Access.
(iv) Maintained by National Association for the Blind (India).

Codes:

(a) (i), (ii) and (iv) are correct
(b) (i), (ii) and (iii) are correct
(c) (ii), (iii) and (iv) are correct
(d) (i), (iii) and (iv) are correct

320. Arrange in sequence the following public libraries according to their year of origin *(NET 17 NOV iii paper)*

(i) Connemara Public Library
(ii) Delhi Public Library
(iii) Calcutta Public Library
(iv) Baroda Central Library

Codes:

(a) (iii), (i), (iv), (ii) (b) (iii), (iv), (ii), (i)
(c) (i), (ii), (iv), (iii) (d) (i), (iv), (ii), (iii)

321. Arrange the following laws/principles from lower to higher level as propounded by S.R. Ranganathan. *(NET 17 NOV iii paper)*

(i) Fundamental Laws (ii) Canons
(iii) Principles (iv) Basic Laws

Codes:

(a) (iii), (ii), (i), (iv) (b) (i), (ii), (iii), (iv)
(c) (ii), (iv), (i), (iii) (d) (iv), (iii), (ii), (i)

322. Match the following with their corresponding year of launching: *(NET 17 NOV iii paper)*

List – I

(A) National Mission on Manuscripts
(B) National Mission on Libraries

(C) National Mission on Monuments and Antiquities
(D) National Knowledge Network

List - II

(1) 2003 (2) 2007 (3) 2012 (4) 2010

Codes:	(A)	(B)	(C)	(D)
(a)	(1)	(3)	(2)	(4)
(b)	(4)	(3)	(2)	(1)
(c)	(3)	(2)	(1)	(4)
(d)	(2)	(4)	(3)	(1)

323. Which law of the Library Science, as enunciated by Dr. Ranganathan, covered the words children, blind and the crippled, artisans, neo-literates, farmers, factory workers, and many more under the ambience of Public Library Service?
(NET 2016J iii paper)
(a) First Law (b) Second Law
(c) Fourth Law (d) Fifth Law

324. The term 'Exponential Growth' refers to
(NET 2016J iii paper)
(a) Linear Grow
(b) Normal mode of distribution
(c) Geometric Progression
(d) Arithmetic Progression

325. The World Digital Library (WDL) is an international collaboration led by
(NET 2016J iii paper)
(a) IFLA, with support of Library of Congress
(b) CILIP, with support of UNESCO
(c) CILIP, with support of IFLA
(d) Library of Congress, with support of UNESCO

326. Which of the following important objectives included in 29 objectives laid down by RRRLF for its operation?
(NET 2016J iii paper)
i. To promote library movement in the country.
ii. To enunciate a national library policy and to work towards its adoption by the central and state governments.
iii. To propagate the adoption of library legislation in the country.
iv. To maintain a database of qualified librarians.

Codes:
(a) i, ii and iii are correct.
(b) ii, iii and iv are correct.
(c) i, iii and iv are correct.
(d) i, ii and iv are correct.

327. Match the following:

List – I
A. Arunachal Pradesh Public Libraries Act
B. Orissa Public Libraries Act
C. West Bengal Public Libraries Act
D. Andhra Pradesh Public Libraries Act

List – II
1. 1960 2. 1979 3. 2009 4. 2001

Codes:	A	B	C	D
(a)	2	1	4	3
(b)	3	2	1	4
(c)	4	3	2	1
(d)	3	4	2	1

328. **Assertion (A):** Maximum use of library resources is the motto of the library.
Reason (R): It satisfies the fifth law of library science. *(NET 16J iii paper)*

Codes:
(a) Both (A) and (R) are true.
(b) Both (A) and (R) are false.
(c) (A) is true, but (R) is false.
(d) (A) is false, but (R) is true.

329. Arrange the following libraries in the chronological sequence of their emergence
(NET 17 NOV ii paper)
(i) Rampur Raza Library, UP
(ii) Asiatic Society Library, Bombay
(iii) Connemara Public Library, Chennai
(iv) Sarasvati Mahal Library, Tanjore

Codes:
(a) (i), (ii), (iii), (iv) (b) (ii), (iii), (iv), (i)
(c) (iii), (iv), (i), (ii) (d) (iv), (iii), (ii), (i)

330. Arrange the following printing technologies according to their emergence:
(NET 17 NOV ii paper)
(i) Movable type
(ii) Dot-Matrix printer
(iii) Woodblock printing
(iv) Screen printing

Codes:
(a) (iv), (iii), (ii) and (i)
(b) (iii), (i), (iv) and (ii)
(c) (iii), (iv), (ii) and (i)
(d) (iv), (i), (ii) and (iii)

331. Who identified the eight central values of librarianship? *(NET 16J ii paper)*

(a) Margaret Mann (b) Michael Gorman
(c) David Hume (d) S.R. Ranganathan

332. Who was the first Director of Raja Ram Mohan Roy Library Foundation? *(NET 16J ii paper)*
(a) B.S. Kesavan (b) D.R. Kalia
(c) B.P. Barua (d) S. Bashruddin

333. Which of the following are associated with UNESCO Programme? *(NET 16J ii paper)*
i. General Information Programme (PGI)
ii. World Scientific Information System (UNISIST)
iii. Universal Availability of Publications (UAP)
iv. International Standard Bibliographic Description (ISBD)
Codes:
(a) i, ii are correct. (b) i, iii are correct.
(c) i, iv are correct. (d) ii, iii are correct.

334. Arrange the following museums according to the year of their establishment *(NET 16J ii paper)*
i. Nehru Memorial Museum and Library, Delhi
ii. National Museum, Delhi
iii. Indian Museum, Calcutta
iv. National Gandhi Museum, Delhi
Codes:
(a) iv, i, iii, ii (b) iii, ii, iv, i
(c) ii, iii, iv, i (d) i, iv, iii, ii

335. Match the following: *(NET 16J ii paper)*

List – I	**List – II**
A. Gujarat Public Libraries Act	1. 1965
B. Chhattisgarh Public Libraries Act	2. 1993
C. Karnataka Public Libraries Act	3. 2009
D. Goa Public Libraries Act	4. 2001

Codes:	**A**	**B**	**C**	**D**
(a)	1	4	3	2
(b)	2	1	4	3
(c)	4	2	3	1
(d)	4	3	1	2

336. Which of the viceroys was associated with the imperial library Act.*(NET 15J iii paper)*
(a) Lord Curzon (b) Lord Minto
(c) Lord Willington (d) Lord Vipin

337. Lok Sabha Secretariat Library Service is called as: *(NET 15J iii paper)*
(a) Lok Sabha Library
(b) Legislators Library Services
(c) LARRDIS
(d) M.P. Library Services

338. The term literary warrant was introduced by: *(NET 15J iii paper)*
(a) W.B. Sayers (b) S.R. Ranganathan
(c) Melvil Dewey (d) E.W. Hulmes

339. Which of the following institutions are established by Dr. S.R. Ranganathan? *(NET 15J iii paper)*
(i) INSDOC, Delhi
(ii) DRTC, Bangalore
(iii) Sarada Ranganathan Endowment, Bangalore
(iv) National Library, Kolkata
Codes:
(a) (i) and (ii) are correct
(b) (ii) and (iv) are correct
(c) (i) and (iii) are correct
(d) (ii) and (iii) are correct

340. Which of the following organizations are associated with the development of public libraries? *(NET 15J iii paper)*
(i) UNESCO (ii) RRRLF
(iii) INFLIB NET (iv) DRTC
Codes:
(a) (i) and (ii) are correct
(b) (i) and (iv) are correct
(c) (iii) and (iv) are correct
(d) (ii) and (iv) are correct

341. Arrange the following landmarks in the Library Movement of India in proper sequence: *(NET 15J iii paper)*
(i) First All India Library Conference (Calcutta)
(ii) First All India Public Library Conference (Madras)
(iii) First Public Library Act Enacted in Madras
(iv) First Library Association in India (Andhra Desa Library Association)
Codes:
(a) (iv), (ii), (i), (iii) are correct
(b) (ii), (iv), (iii), (i) are correct
(c) (iii), (ii) (iv), (i) are correct
(d) (i), (iii), (ii), (iv) are correct

342. Arrange the following libraries according to their year of foundation: *(NET 15J iii paper)*
(i) Bibliotheque Nationale de France
(ii) British Library

(iii) Imperial Library
(iv) Library of Congress
Codes:
(a) (i), (ii), (iii), (iv) (b) (i), (iii), (iv), (ii)
(c) (i), (iii), (ii), (iv) (d) (i), (iv), (iii), (ii)

343. Match the following: *(NET 15J iii paper)*
List – I
(A) *Update* (A magazine)
(B) *Information Outlook* (an online digital magazine)
(C) *Reference and User Service Quarterly (RUSQ)*
(D) *Choice* (A monthly journal)
List – II
(1) Association of College and Research Libraries
(2) American Library Association
(3) Special Library Association (USA)
(4) Chartered Institute of Library and Information Professionals (CILIP)

Codes:	**(A)**	**(B)**	**(C)**	**(D)**
(a)	(2)	(4)	(1)	(3)
(b)	(3)	(2)	(4)	(1)
(c)	(4)	(3)	(2)	(1)
(d)	(3)	(2)	(1)	(4)

344. Skill Development Programme (SDP) for public librarians in India is initiated by *(NET 14D ii paper)*
(a) Ministry of Human Resource Development, Govt. of India
(b) Directorate of Library Services, Govt. of West Bengal
(c) Raja Ram Mohan Roy Library Foundation
(d) Indian Library Association

345. **Assertion (A):** Library legislation is not a pre-requisite for providing free library service.
Reason (R): There are states/union territories that are advanced in public library services without library legislation.
(NET 14D ii paper)
Codes:
(a) (A) is true, but (R) is false.
(b) (A) is false, but (R) is true.
(c) Both (A) and (R) are true.
(d) Both (A) and (R) are false.

346. Papyrus was used as a writing material by *(NET 13 SEPT iii paper)*
(a) Summarians (b) Italians
(c) Egyptians (d) Assyrians

347. Who said, "Public Library is the responsibility of Local and National Authorities. It must be supported by specific legislation and financed by National and Local Governments"?
(a) S.R. Ranganathan
(b) Gopala Rao Ekbote
(c) Sinha Committee
(d) UNESCO Manifesto

348. Match the following: *(NET 14D ii paper)*
List – I
A. Books are for use.
B. Every reader his/her book.
C. Every book its reader.
D. Library is a growing organism.
List – II
1. Adopting to future needs
2. Long operating hours
3. Freedom of access to information & knowledge
4. Reference Desk

Codes:	**A**	**B**	**C**	**D**
(a)	2	3	4	1
(b)	4	1	2	3
(c)	1	2	3	4
(d)	3	4	1	2

349. Which one of the following is the implementing agency for 'capacity building' activity of National Mission on Libraries? *(NET 15D iii paper)*
(a) Delhi Public Library
(b) Raja Ram Mohan Roy Library Foundation
(c) National Library of India
(d) Documentation, Research and Training Centre

350. By 2002, which of the following states have enacted their respective Public Library Acts? *(NET 15D iii paper)*
(i) Haryana (ii) Uttar Pradesh
(iii) Mizoram (iv) Rajasthan
Codes:
(a) (i) and (iii) are correct
(b) (i), (ii) and (iii) are correct
(c) (ii) and (iv) are correct
(d) (iii) and (iv) are correct

351. Arrange in sequence the following repository libraries according to their year of establishment: *(NET 15D iii paper)*
(i) Connemara Public Library, Chennai
(ii) Delhi Public Library, Delhi

(iii) Asiatic Society Library, Mumbai
(iv) Central Reference Library, Kolkata

Codes:

(a) (iv), (i), (iii) and (ii)
(b) (i), (ii), (iii) and (iv)
(c) (ii), (iv), (i) and (iii)
(d) (iii), (i), (ii) and (iv)

352. **Assertion (A):** Five Laws of Library Science are the normative principles that are capable of countering any problem faced by the Librarians.

Reason (R): Normative principles are not only considered to be the correct way of doing something, but also determines norms or standards in day-to-day library practice. *(NET 15D iii paper)*

Codes:

(a) Both (A) and (R) are false.
(b) (A) is true and (R) is false.
(c) (A) is false and (R) is true.
(d) Both (A) and (R) are true.

353. Which committee recommended that imperial library be designated as copyright library? *(NET 13D ii paper)*

(a) Fayzee Committee, 1939
(b) Richey Committee, 1926
(c) Statham Committee, 1932
(d) Sadler Committee, 1916

354. Who was the first Librarian of Imperial Library, Calcutta? *(NET 13D ii paper)*

(a) John MacFarlane (b) Harinath De
(c) B.S. Kesavan (d) S.R. Ranganathan

355. Name the Indian Librarian who was honoured with the title of "Khan Bahadur" in 1935 by the British Government. *(NET 13D ii paper)*

(a) S.R. Ranganathan (b) B.S. Kesavan
(c) K.M. Asadullah (d) D.R. Kalia

356. Which approach of information is not given by Wersig and Neveling? *(NET 13D ii paper)*

(a) Structural Approach
(b) Knowledge Approach
(c) Meaning Approach
(d) Technique Approach

357. International Advisory Committee on Documentation, Libraries and Archives (UNESCO) was established in

(a) 1966 (b) 1967 (c) 1968 (d) 1969

358. Arrange the following library associations according to their year of emergence: *(NET 13D ii paper)*

(i) CILIP (ii) ALA (iii) SLA (iv) ASLIB

Codes:

(a) (iii) (iv) (i) (ii) (b) (iii) (iv) (ii) (i)
(c) (ii) (iii) (iv) (i) (d) (ii) (iv) (i) (iii)

359. Match the following *(NET 13D ii paper)*

List – I	**List–II**
A. Library Advisory Committee	1. 1962
B. Review Committee	2. 1963
C. DRTC	3. 1957
D. Sarada Ranganathan Endowned	4. 1961

Codes:	A	B	C	D
(a)	4	3	2	1
(b)	3	4	1	2
(c)	2	1	3	4
(d)	1	4	3	2

360. Match the following: *(NET 13D ii paper)*

List – I	**List – II**
A. Facts on File	i. Periodical Directory
B. World of Learning	ii. Index
C. Concordance	iii. Newspaper Digest
D. Willing's Press Guide	iv. Directory

Codes:	A	B	C	D
(a)	1	3	4	2
(b)	2	1	3	4
(c)	3	4	2	1
(d)	4	2	1	3

361. In which year Janet (U.K.) was established? *(NET 13 D iii paper)*

(a) 1957 (b) 1983 (c) 1987 (d) 1989

362. Who is the compiler of WebBibliography of Rabindranath Tagore? *(NET 13D iii paper)*

(a) Bengal Library Association
(b) RRRLF
(c) National Library of India
(d) IASLIC

363. Which of the following organizations are associated with the concept of '1000 crore plan to link 9000 libraries in India'? *(NET 13D iii paper)*

(i) National Library of India
(ii) National Mission on Libraries
(iii) INFLIBNET
(iv) RRRLF

Codes:
(a) (ii) and (iii) are correct.
(b) (iii) and (iv) are correct.
(c) (i) and (iv) are correct.
(d) (ii) and (iv) are correct.

364. Which of the following are the core content of ISI web of knowledge? *(NET 13D iii paper)*
(i) Current Contents
(ii) ISI proceedings
(iii) Derwent Information Index
(iv) AGRICOLA
Codes:
(a) (i), (iv) and (iii) (b) (i), (ii) and (iii)
(c) (ii), (iii) and (iv) (d) (i), (ii) and (iv)

365. Which of the following are value added information services? *(NET 13D iii paper)*
(i) Aggregator Service
(ii) Referral Service
(iii) Document Delivery Service
(iv) Research Reports/Market Survey Reports
Codes:
(a) (i) and (iii) are correct
(b) (ii) and (iv) are correct
(c) (ii) and (iii) are correct
(d) (i) and (iv) are correct

366. Who are associated with the digitization of the collection of Rabindra Bhavan, VishavBharati? *(NET 13D iii paper)*
(i) RRRLF (ii) C-DAC
(iii) NIC (iv) National Library of India
Codes:
(a) (i) and (iii) are correct
(b) (i) and (ii) are correct
(c) (ii) and (iv) are correct
(d) (iii) and (iv) are correct

367. Arrange in sequence the following Model Public Library Acts/Bills in India: *(NET 2013D iii paper)*
i. Model Public Library Bill by M.D. Sen Committee
ii. Model Public Library Act by S.R. Ranganathan
iii. Model Public Library Act of ILA
iv. Model Public Library Bill by working group of Planning Commission
Codes:
(a) i, ii, iii, iv (b) ii, i, iv, iii
(c) iii, iv, i, ii (d) iv, iii, ii, i

368. Match the following: *(NET 13D iii paper)*
List – I
A. Saraswati Mahal Library, Tanjavur (1535)
B. Khuda Baksh Oriental Public Library, Patna (1876)
C. Library of Asiatic Society of Bengal (1784)
D. Imperial Library, Calcutta (1901)
List – II
1. Lord Curzon 2. Telugu Nayakas
3. Maulana M.B. Khan 4. Sir G. William Jones

Codes:	A	B	C	D
(a)	3	2	4	1
(b)	2	3	1	4
(c)	2	3	4	1
(d)	3	2	1	4

369. Arrange the following Library Acts according to the year of their enactment: *(NET 14J ii paper)*
(i) Arunachal Pradesh (ii) Bihar
(iii) Lakshadweep (iv) Rajasthan
Codes:
(a) (ii), (iv), (iii), (i) (b) (iv), (i), (ii), (iii)
(c) (ii), (iii), (i), (iv) (d) (iv), (iii), (ii), (i)

370. LIS Gateway is maintained by *(NET 2014J iii paper)*
(a) ILA (b) IASLIC (c) SIS (d) IATLIS

371. Public Library Association (PLA) is a division of *(NET 2014J iii paper)*
(a) ALA (b) ILA (c) IFLA (d) IASLIC

372. Arrange the following Library Acts according to their year of enactment: *(NET 2014J iii paper)*
i. Uttarakhand ii. Orissa
iii. Manipur iv. Goa
Codes:
(a) iv, i, ii, iii (b) i, ii, iii, iv
(c) iii, iv, ii, i (d) ii, iii, i, iv

373. Arrange the following libraries according to their year of origin: *(NET 2014J iii paper)*
i. Asiatic Society Library, Bombay
ii. Connemara Public Library, Madras
iii. Delhi Public Library, Delhi
iv. National Library of India, Calcutta
Codes:
(a) i, ii, iv, iii (b) i, iii, iv, ii
(c) ii, iv, iii, i (d) iv, iii, ii

374. Match the following implications with the respective laws of library science: *(NET 2014J iii paper)*

List – I	List – II
A. Location of the library	1. Second Law
B. Obligation of the State	2. Third Law
C. Publicity	3. Fifth Law
D. Strength of Library Staff	4. First Law

Codes:	A	B	C	D
(a)	4	2	1	3
(b)	4	1	2	3
(c)	2	1	3	4
(d)	2	3	4	1

375. **Assertion (A):** Acceptance of First Law of library Science "Books are for Use" has brought forth far reaching change in the present digital environment.

Reason (R): Online access, open access, virtual reference are the results of this acceptance. *(NET 2014J iii paper)*

Codes:
(a) (A) is true, but (R) is false.
(b) (A) is false, but (R) is true.
(c) Both (A) and (R) are false.
(d) Both (A) and (R) are true

376. Who has recommended the establishment of district, taluka, town and village libraries? *(NET 14D iii paper)*
(a) S.R. Ranganathan
(b) Velaga Venkatappayya
(c) Fyzee Report
(d) Library Advisory Committee

377. Arrange the following in chronological order: *(NET 14D iii paper)*
i. Delivery of Books and Newspapers Act
ii. RTI Act
iii. Imperial Library Act
iv. IT (Amendment) Act

Codes:

(a)	i	iv	ii	iii
(b)	iii	i	ii	iv
(c)	iii	ii	i	iv
(d)	iv	iii	i	ii

378. Which law of Library Science states that information is basic input to human growth and development?
(a) Fourth Law (b) Third Law
(c) Second Law (d) Fifth Law

379. Match the following: *(NET 14D iii paper)*

List – I	List – II
A. ALA	1. 1909
B. CILIP	2. 1933
C. SLA	3. 1876
D. ILA	4. 2002

Codes:	A	B	C	D
(a)	4	2	3	1
(b)	3	4	1	2
(c)	1	2	4	3
(d)	3	4	2	1

380. Match the following: *(NET 14D iii paper)*

List – I	List – II
A. Sayaji Rao Gayakwad	1. Revision of salary scale
B. D.P. Chattopadyaya	2. Library building
C. K.D. Metcalf	3. Public libraries
D. B.S. Kesavan	4. Librarian of national library

Codes:	A	B	C	D
(a)	2	1	3	4
(b)	1	2	3	4
(c)	3	1	2	4
(d)	4	3	1	2

381. Arrange in sequence the following state Public Library Acts according to the year of their enactment. *(NET 15J ii paper)*
(i) West Bengal (ii) Orissa
(iii) Arunachal Pradesh (iv) Karnataka

Codes:
(a) (iv), (i), (ii), (iii) (b) (ii), (i), (iv), (iii)
(c) (iii), (ii), (iv), (i) (d) (iv), (ii), (iii), (i)

382. Arrange the following books by S.R. Ranganathan according to their publication year. *(NET 15J ii paper)*
(i) Colon classification
(ii) Elements of library classification
(iii) Philosophy of library classification
(iv) Prolegomena to library classification

Codes:
(a) (i), (iv), (ii), (iii) (b) (iii), (iv), (ii), (i)
(c) (ii), (iii), (iv), (i) (d) (iv), (iii), (ii), (i)

383. Identify the correct chronological order in which the following were established: *(NET 15J ii paper)*
(a) National Library of India (Kolkata), Delhi Public Library, Documentation Research and Training Centre, Raja Ram Mohan Roy Library Foundation
(b) Delhi Public Library, Documentation Research and Training Centre, Raja Ram Mohan Roy Library Foundation, National Library of India (Kolkata)

(c) Documentation Research and Training Centre, Raja Ram Mohan Roy Library Foundation, Delhi Public Library, National Library of India (Kolkata)
(d) Raja Ram Mohan Roy Library Foundation, National Library of India (Kolkata), Delhi Public Library, Documentation Research and Training Centre

Read the passage given below and answer the questions based on your understanding of the passage (Question nos. 384-388)

(NET 15J ii paper)

In British Columbia (B.C.) there are no public libraries on reserve, and the libraries that do-exist on reserve are generally small, under funded band council collections, and band school libraries. In Ontario, the provincial government contributes to the development of public libraries in First Nations Communities. However in 2001-2002, only 52 of 141 First Nation libraries in Ontario received operating grants, and because the operating grants are based on population size many small communities are under funded. Among First Nations Communities, libraries are not always a priority when there are pressing needs in the areas of rights and title claims, infrastructure, education, and health. A First Nations library worker explains: "We need all our money to fund our land claims. If we don't have land, we don't have community. If we don't have community, we don't need a library."

The Library Services for Saskatckewan's Aboriginal Peoples Committee is composed of Aboriginal and public sector representatives who meet six times a year to advise on the implementation of the recommendations.

Public libraries in urban centers tend not to differentiate between Aboriginal people and the general population. As a consequence urban Aboriginal peoples are often not well served. There are exceptions, such as the Albert Library branch of the Regina Public Library and the Spadina branch of the Toronto Public that work.

384. Which of the following reflects the position of libraries In British Columbia?

(NET 15J ii paper)

(a) There are no libraries on reserve.
(b) Public libraries on reserve are under funded.
(c) Band school libraries exist on reserve.
(d) There are 141 First Nations libraries

385. In Ontario in 2001-2002:

(NET 15J ii paper)

(a) Only 52 first Nations libraries existed
(b) Only 141 first nations libraries received operating grants
(c) Many small communities are underfunded
(d) Majority of First Nations libraries received operating grants

386. Among First Nations Communities

(NET 15J ii paper)

(a) libraries are always priority
(b) some times rights and title claims are pressing needs
(c) there are no pressing needs for education and health
(d) they need a library even when they do not have land

387. Which of the following is true about public libraries in urban centres?

(NET 15J ii paper)

(a) Public libraries in urban centres tend to differentiate between aboriginal people and the general population
(b) Urban aboriginal people are often well served by public library
(c) The Albert library branch of the Regina public library does not work closely with local urban aboriginal communities.
(d) Spadina Branch of the Toronto Public library works closely with local aboriginal communities.

388. Which of the following is not true about the library services for Saskatchewan's Aboriginal Peoples Committee?

(NET 15J ii paper)

(a) It has aboriginal representatives
(b) It has public sector representatives
(c) They meet once a year
(d) They advise on the implementation of the recommendation.

389. ALA's newly labelled Public Awareness Campaign "Libraries Transform" launched by ALA President Sari Feldman aims to focus on:

(NET 15J ii paper)

(i) the critical role of the Public Libraries play in digital age;

(ii) the change of perception that libraries are just quiet places to do research, find book and read;
(iii) transforming the lives of all through education and life-long learning;
(iv) to undermine the role of school, academic and special libraries;

Codes:
(a) (i), (ii) and (iii) are correct
(b) (i), (ii) and (iv) are correct
(c) (ii), (iii) and (iv) are correct
(d) (i), (iii) and (iv) are correct

390. Ratnasagar, Ratnaranjaka and Ratnodadhi Library buildings were the part of *(NET 15D ii paper)*
(a) Vikramashila Learning Centre
(b) Takshashila Learning Centre
(c) Nalanda Learning Centre
(d) Vallabhi Learning Centre

391. Which of the following are not the Working Groups under National Mission on Libraries?
(i) National Census of Libraries, Content Creation and Community Information Centres.
(ii) Setting up of National Virtual Library, Networking and ICT Applications in Libraries.
(iii) Library and Information Science Research, Development and Accreditation.
(iv) Upgradation of the Existing Academic Libraries, University and Research Libraries.

Codes:
(a) (i), (ii) are correct.
(b) (ii), (iii) are correct.
(d) (i), (iv) are correct.
(c) (iii), (iv) are correct.

392. Which of the services are being offered by National Library, Kolkata?
(i) Lending (ii) Bibliographic
(iii) NL connect (iv) Online reference services

Codes:
(a) (i), (ii) are correct.
(b) (i), (iv) are correct.
(c) (ii), (iv) are correct.
(d) (iii), (iv) are correct.

393. Match the following national organizations with their relevant mission *(NET 14D iii paper)*

List – I
A. National Mission on Libraries
B. National Mission for Manuscripts
C. T.K.D.L.
D. NME-ICT

List – II
1. Digitization of AYUSH literature
2. Nurturing of talent
3. Capacity building
4. Connects India's past with present

Codes:	A	B	C	D
(a)	1	2	3	4
(b)	3	4	1	2
(c)	4	3	2	1
(d)	2	1	3	4

394. Arrange the following Public Libraries Acts according to their year of enactment *(NET D15 ii paper)*
(i) Maharashtra Public Libraries Act
(ii) Karnataka Public Libraries Act
(iii) Odisha Public Libraries Act
(iv) Mizoram Public Libraries Act

Codes:
(a) (iii), (i), (ii), (iv) (b) (ii), (i) (iii), (iv)
(c) (i), (ii), (iv), (iii) (d) (ii) (i) (iv) (iii)

395. Arrange the following committees according to their year of Constitution?
(i) Committee on National Network System for University Libraries.
(ii) K.P. Sinha Committee
(iii) Review Committee on Library and Information Science
(iv) D.P. Chattopadhyaya Committee on National Policy of Library and Information Services

Codes:
(a) (ii), (iii), (iv), (i) (b) (iii), (iv), (i), (ii)
(c) (iv), (i), (ii), (iii) (d) (i), (ii), (iii), (iv)

396. Match the following: *(NET 17J iii paper)*

List – I
(A) Crowd Funding (B) Crowd sourcing
(C) Hathi Trust (D) Social and Cultural hubs

List – II
(1) Public assistance through donations
(2) Collaborative milieu of knowledge dissemination
(3) Re-setting priorities due to financial constraints

(4) Collaborative huge collection of digital resources

Codes:	(A)	(B)	(C)	(D)
(a)	(2)	(4)	(1)	(3)
(b)	(1)	(3)	(4)	(2)
(c)	(2)	(3)	(4)	(1)
(d)	(1)	(4)	(2)	(3)

397. **Assertion (A):** Majority of State Public Library Acts enacted from 1990s have provision for Library fund with contributions from State and Central Governments.

Reason (R): Library Cess is inadequate to manage public libraries. (*NET 17J iii paper*)

Codes:
(a) (A) is true, but (R) is false.
(b) (A) is false, but (R) is true.
(c) Both (A) and (R) are false.
(d) Both (A) and (R) are true.

398. The ancient Nalanda learning center had which of the following buildings for libraries?
(i) Ratnasagara (ii) Ratnaranjaka
(iii) Ratangarbha (iv) Ratnamanjari
Codes:
(a) (i) and (ii) are correct
(b) (ii) and (iii) are correct
(c) (iii) and (iv) are correct
(d) (iv) and (i) are correct

399. **Assertion (A):** All public libraries in India are maintained from cess.

Reason (R): UNESCO Manifesto recommended that public libraries should be "maintained wholly from public funds".
Codes:
(a) Both (A) and (R) are true.
(b) Both (A) and (R) are false.
(c) (A) is true but (R) is false.
(d) (A) is false but (R) is true.

400. What the name of the committee responsible for Indian standard related to libraries? (*NET 18J*)
(a) TC46 (b) MSD5 (c) BIS-LIB (d) Z39

401. World Book and Copyright Day is celebrated on
(a) 22nd. August (b) 23rd. April
(c) 23rd March (d) 20th. March

402. "To make at least one in every household e-literate" is thrust are of policy (#7) included in (*NET 18J*)
(a) National Knowledge Commission, 2005
(b) National policy on Information Technology, 2012
(c) National Education Policy, 1992
(d) National Policy on library and Information System, 1986

403. Identify which one of the Five Laws of Library Science that Ranganathan remarked as 'trivial truism in his writing "Library Science and Scientific Method" (*NET 18J*)
(a) First Law (b) Second Law
(c) Third Law (d) Fifth Law

404. Why a library Association should have a code of "Professional Conduct"? (*NET 18J*)
(i) Prescribes standards of behaviour expected for the member
(ii) Sets out standards and duties which a professional is expected to observe
(iii) Standards can be used as a point of reference while dealing with disciplined procedures against members
(iv) Standards help to demean the image of the Association and de-ameliorate funding and ensure better functioning of libraries
Codes:
(a) i, ii and iv are correct
(b) ii, iii and iv are correct
(c) i, ii and iii are correct
(d) i, ii and iv are correct

405. Which of the following states do not have provision of library cess in their respective Public Library Act? (*NET 18J*)
(i) West Bengal (ii) Tamil Nadu
(iii) Kerala (iv) Manipur
Codes:
(a) i and iv are correct
(b) i, ii and iii are correct
(c) ii and iii are correct
(d) ii and iv are correct

406. Match the following (*NET 18J*)
List-I
(a) Dr Zakir Hussain Library
(b) J R D Tata Library
(c) Sayaji Rao Gaekward Library
(d) Vikram Sarabhai Library
List-II
(i) Indian Institute of Science, Banglore
(ii) Jamia Millia Islamia, Delhi
(iii) IIM Ahemdabad
(iv) BHU Varanasi

Codes:	(A)	(B)	(C)	(D)
(a)	(iv)	(iii)	(i)	(ii)
(b)	(ii)	(i)	(iv)	(iii)
(c)	(i)	(ii)	(iii)	(iv)
(d)	(ii)	(iii)	(i)	(iv)

407. Arrange the following library acts according to their year of enactment: *(NET 18J)*
(i) Bihar Public Library Act
(ii) Uttaranchal Public Library Act
(iii) Haryana Public Library Act
(iv) Orrisa Public Library Act

Codes:
(a) (ii), (iv), (i), (iii) (b) (i), (ii), (iii), (iv)
(c) (iv), (iii), (ii), (i) (d) (iii), (iv), (ii), (i)

408. Arrange the name of the following librarian of library of Congress in the chronological order of their period of service in LC
(i) Carla Hayden (ii) John James Beckley
(iii) James H. Billington (iv) George Waterston

Codes:
(a) ii, iv, iii, i (b) i, ii, iii, iv
(c) i, ii, iv, iii (d) ii, i, iv, iii

ANSWER SHEET

1. (d)	2. (b)	3. (a)	4. (c)	5. (c)	6. (c)	7. (c)	8. (a)	9. (d)
10. (a)	11. (b)	12. (c)	13. (b)	14. (b)	15. (b)	16. (c)	17. (d)	18. (a)
19. (b)	20. (a)	21. (a)	22. (a)	23. (c)	24. (b)	25. (c)	26. (a)	27. (b)
28. (c)	29. (a)	30. (a)	31. (a)	32. (d)	33. (a)	34. (d)	35. (b)	36. (b)
37. (d)	38. (a)	39. (c)	40. (a)	41. (a)	42. (a)	43. (a)	44. (c)	45. (d)
46. (c)	47. (d)	48. (c)	49. (a)	50. (b)	51. (d)	52. (c)	53. (b)	54. (b)
55. (b)	56. (b)	57. (a)	58. (c)	59. (c)	60. (c)	61. (a)	62. (a)	63. (b)
64. (d)	65. (b)	66. (d)	67. (d)	68. (b)	69. (a)	70. (c)	71. (a)	72. (b)
73. (d)	74. (b)	75. (b)	76. (d)	77. (b)	78. (d)	79. (c)	80. (c)	81. (a)
82. (d)	83. (b)	84. (c)	85. (b)	86. (b)	87. (a)	88. (b)	89. (c)	90. (d)
91. (c)	92. (d)	93. (d)	94. (c)	95. (d)	96. (c)	97. (d)	98. (b)	99. (c)
100. (d)	101. (c)	102. (b)	103. (b)	104. (d)	105. (d)	106. (d)	107. (d)	108. (a)
109. (c)	110. (b)	111. (b)	112. (d)	113. (b)	114. (b)	115. (a)	116. (c)	117. (a)
118. (a)	119. (c)	120. (c)	121. (b)	122. (b)	123. (d)	124. (c)	125. (c)	126. (a)
127. (d)	128. (c)	129. (a)	130. (a)	131. (b)	132. (a)	133. (c)	134. (a)	135. (b)
136. (a)	137. (b)	138. (b)	139. (b)	140. (a)	141. (a)	142. (c)	143. (b)	144. (b)
145. (a)	146. (b)	147. (a)	148. (a)	149. (b)	150. (d)	151. (d)	152. (c)	153. (d)
154. (b)	155. (d)	156. (d)	157. (d)	158. (d)	159. (c)	160. (a)	161. (b)	162. (d)
163. (a)	164. (a)	165. (c)	166. (b)	167. (d)	168. (d)	169. (c)	170. (d)	171. (b)
172. (c)	173. (a)	174. (a)	175. (b)	176. (a)	177. (d)	178. (d)	179. (c)	180. (a)
181. (a)	182. (a)	183. (c)	184. (b)	185. (d)	186. (b)	187. (c)	188. (a)	189. (c)
190. (b)	191. (b)	192. (b)	193. (d)	194. (b)	195. (a)	196. (c)	197. (b)	198. (b)
199. (c)	200. (b)	201. (b)	202. (c)	203. (d)	204. (d)	205. (b)	206. (c)	207. (d)
208. (b)	209. (c)	210. (c)	211. (b)	212. (d)	213. (a)	214. (c)	215. (d)	216. (a)
217. (a)	218. (b)	219. (c)	220. (c)	221. (a)	222. (d)	223. (a)	224. (b)	225. (c)
226. (a)	227. (a)	228. (b)	229. (b)	230. (c)	231. (b)	232. (a)	233. (a)	234. (c)
235. (b)	236. (b)	237. (c)	238. (b)	239. (d)	240. (a)	241. (b)	242. (a)	243. (a)
244. (c)	245. (c)	246. (a)	247. (c)	248. (d)	249. (b)	250. (a)	251. (b)	252. (b)
253. (d)	254. (c)	255. (a)	256. (d)	257. (c)	258. (a)	259. (b)	260. (c)	261. (b)
262. (c)	263. (c)	264. (c)	265. (d)	266. (a)	267. (d)	268. (d)	269. (c)	270. (b)
271. (b)	272. (d)	273. (b)	274. (d)	275. (b)	276. (a)	277. (c)	278. (d)	279. (b)

280. (c)	281. (b)	282. (d)	283. (c)	284. (b)	285. (a)	286. (a)	287. (b)	288. (b)
289. (b)	290. (a)	291. (c)	292. (b)	293. (b)	294. (b)	295. (a)	296. (b)	297. (a)
298. (c)	299. (a)	300. (a)	301. (d)	302. (c)	303. (c)	304. (c)	305. (c)	306. (a)
307. (a)	308. (a)	309. (d)	310. (a)	311. (c)	312. (b)	313. (d)	314. (c)	315. (c)
316. (c)	317. (b)	318. (b)	319. (b)	320. (a)	321. (a)	322. (a)	323. (b)	324. (c)
325. (d)	326. (a)	327. (d)	328. (c)	329. (a)	330. (b)	331. (b)	332. (c)	333. (a)
334. (b)	335. (d)	336. (a)	337. (c)	338. (d)	339. (d)	340. (a)	341. (a)	342. (d)
343. (c)	344. (c)	345. (c)	346. (c)	347. (d)	348. (a)	349. (b)	350. (a)	351. (d)
352. (d)	353. (b)	354. (a)	355. (c)	356. (d)	357. (b)	358. (c)	359. (b)	360. (c)
361. (b)	362. (b)	363. (d)	364. (b)	365. (d)	366. (b)	367. (b)	368. (c)	369. (d)
370. (a)	371. (a)	372. (c)	373. (a)	374. (b)	375. (d)	376. (c)	377. (b)	378. (b)
379. (b)	380. (c)	381. (a)	382. (a)	383. (a)	384. (c)	385. (c)	386. (b)	387. (d)
388. (c)	389. (a)	390. (c)	391. (c)	392. (a)	393. (b)	394. (d)	395. (a)	396. (b)
397. (d)	398. (a)	399. (d)	400. (b)	401. (b)	402. (b)	403. (a)	404. (c)	405. (a)
406. (b)	407. (d)	408. (a)						

Chapter 11
Periodicals

SUBJECTIVE QUESTIONS

Q. 1. What are the periodicals published from ILA, New Delhi?

Ans. (i) Publication of two edition of directory of Indian Libraries, and it is also starting a quarterly journal entitled 'Library Bulletin'.
(ii) The Association publishes ILA Newsletter (Quarterly).
(iii) ILA Members Directory was published in 1987.

Q. 2. What are the publications of IASLIC (Indian Association of Special Libraries and Information Centre)?

Ans. (i) IASLIC Bulletin (Quarterly).
(ii) IASLIC Newsletter (Monthly).
(iii) Indian Library Science Abstract (Annual).

Q. 3. What are the publications of Library Association (LA) UK?

Ans. (i) Library Association Record (Monthly).
(ii) Journal of Librarianship (Quarterly).
(iii) British Humanities Index (Quarterly).
(iv) Applied Social Science Index and Abstracts (Bi-Weekly).
(v) Current Technology Index (Monthly).
(vi) Library and Information Science Abstract (Bi-Monthly).
(vii) Current Research in Library and Information Science (three issues).

Q. 4. What are the publications of ASLIB?

Ans. (i) ASLIB Proceedings (Monthly).
(ii) ASLIB Booklist (Monthly).
(iii) Index to Theses (Annual).
(iv) Net link (3 issues).
(v) Technical Translation Bulletin (3 issues).
(vi) ASLIB Information (Monthly).
(vii) Journal of Documentation (Quarterly).
(viii) ASLIB Newsletter (Monthly).
(ix) Programme: News of Computers in Libraries (Quarterly).
(x) Forthcoming International Scientific and Technical Conference (Quarterly).

Q. 5. What are publications of FID?

Ans. (i) FID News Bulletin (Monthly).
(ii) International Forum on Information Documentation (Quarterly).
(iii) R&D Projects in Documentation and Librarianship (Bi-Monthly).
(iv) Extension and Correction to the UDC (Annual) and FID Directory (Bi-Annual).

Q. 6. What are the publications of IFLA (International Federation of Library Association and Institution)?

Ans. (i) IFLA Journal (Quarterly).
(ii) International Cataloguing (Quarterly).
(iii) IFLA Annual and IFLA Directory (Annual).

Q. 7. What are the publications of INSDOC, New Delhi (Indian National Scientific Documentation Centre)?

Ans. (i) Annals of Library Science and Documentation (Quarterly).
(ii) Indian Science Abstracts (Semi-Monthly).
(iii) Content List of Soviet Scientific Periodicals (Monthly).
(iv) National Index of Translations (Monthly).
(v) Accession List of Russian Scientific publication (Bi-Monthly).
(vi) Natural Resources Survey and Exploration Vasundhara (Quarterly).
(vii) Agricultural Sciences Kalpataru (Quarterly).
(viii) Russian Scientific and Technical Publication and Accession List (Bi-Monthly).

Q. 8. What are the publications of National Social Science Documentation Centre (NASSDOC)?

Ans. (i) Acquisition Update (Monthly).
(ii) Conference Alert (Quarterly).
(iii) Indian Diary of Events (Quarterly).
(iv) Paging Periodicals: Review of Contents (Bi-Monthly).
(v) Social Science Research Index (Irregular).
(vi) Social Science News: Index to select Newspapers in English (Monthly).
(vii) Samajik Vigyan Samachar (Monthly).

Q. 9. What are the publications of Defence Science Information and Documentation Centre (DESIDOC)?

Ans. (i) Defence Science Journal (Quarterly).
(ii) R&D Digest (Bi-Monthly).
(iii) R&D Bulletin (Quarterly).
(iv) DRDC Newsletter (Monthly).
(v) Popular Science and Technology (Half-Yearly).
(vi) DESIDOC Bulletin (Bi-Monthly).

Q. 10. Who publishes the weekly "Current Contents"?

Ans. Institute of Scientific Information (Philadelphia).

Q. 11. Who publishes the periodical "Monthly Abstracts of Statistics"?

Ans. Central Statistical Organisation, Government of India.

Q. 12. Who publishes the periodical "Biological Abstract"?

Ans. Biosciences Information Science, 1926.

Q. 13. Name the publishers who published the following Abstracting and Indexing publications?
(i) Chemical Abstracts.
(ii) Engineering Index.
(iii) Sociological Abstracts.
(iv) Humanities Index.
(v) Index Medicus.
(vi) Current Technology Index.
(vii) INIS Atom Index.
(viii) Library and Information Science Abstracts (LISA).
(ix) Indian Science Abstracts.
(x) Indian Dissertation Abstracts.
(xi) Agri Index.

Ans. (i) Chemical Abstracts (Chemical Abstracts Service, Columbus, USA), 1907: Weekly.
(ii) Engineering Index (Engineering Information Incorporation, New York), 1962.
(iii) Sociological Abstracts (Sociological Abstracts Inc. San Diago CA), 1953.
(iv) Humanities Index (H.W. Wilson Co., New York), 1974.
(v) Index Medicus—(US National Library of Medicine), 1879.
(vi) Current Technology Index (CIT)—(Library Association Publishing Limited, London), 1962: Monthly.
(vii) INIS Atom Index (International Nuclear Information System Vienna, Austria).
(viii) Library and Information Science Abstracts (LISA).
(ix) Indian Science Abstracts (Indian National Scientific Documentation Centre, Delhi), 1965: Monthly.
(x) Indian Dissertation Abstracts (The Indian Council of Social Science Research and Association of Indian Universities), 1973.
(xi) Agri Index (Food and Agriculture Organisation, AGRIS Co-ordination Centre, Rome), 1975.

Q. 14. Who has published the following current national bibliographies?
(i) Indian National Bibliography
(ii) Accession List: South Asia
(iii) Indian Science Abstracts
(iv) Press in India: Annual report on the press compiled by the Registrar of Newspapers for India.

Ans. (i) Indian National Bibliography—Central Reference Library, Calcutta, 1957.
(ii) Accession List: South Asia—Library of Congress, New Delhi, 1980.
(iii) Indian Science Abstracts—INSDOC, New Delhi, 1965.
(iv) Press in India: Annual report on the press compiled by the Registrar of Newspapers for India—Ministry of Information and Broadcasting, New Delhi, 1964.

Q. 15. Write the new name of "Reference Catalogue of Current Literature".

Ans. British Books in print form 1967.

Q. 16. Who started the "Reference Catalogue of Current Literature" and when?

Ans. Joseph Whitaker in 1874.

Q. 17. Name the organisation publishes "Indian Books in print".

Ans. Indian Bureau of Bibliographies, 1969 (by Sher Singh and S.N. Sadhu).

Q. 18. Which organisation publishes the "Brihad Hindi Granth Suchi"?

Ans. Bhartiya Granth Niketan, New Delhi (by Yashpal Mahajan and Krishna Mahajan).

Q. 19. Write the name of all publishers who published following bibliographies.

(i) Indian Publisher and Bookseller
(ii) Prakashan Samachar
(iii) Indian Book Reporter
(iv) Books on India: Supplement to Index India
(v) Indian Books: An Information Leaflet
(vi) Indian Books: A Bibliography of Indian Books
(vii) Indian Book Industry
(viii) Indian Books, 1974-75
(ix) Recent Indian Books.

Ans. (i) Indian Publishers and Bookseller—Popular Book Depot, Mumbai, 1951 (Monthly).
(ii) Prakashan Samachar—Raj Kamal Prakashan, Delhi, 1953 (Monthly).
(iii) Indian Books Reporter: Prabhu Book Service, Gurgaon, 1965 (Monthly).
(iv) Books on India: Supplement to Index India—Jaipur, 1967 (Annual).
(v) Indian Books: An Information Leaflet—Mukharjee Book House, Kolkata, 1968.
(vi) Indian Books: A Bibliography of Indian Books—Indian Bibliographic Centre, Varanasi, 1969 (Annual).
(vii) Indian Book Industry—Sterling, Delhi, 1969 (Monthly).
(viii) Indian Books, 1974-75: An Annual Bibliography—Today and Tomorrow, New Delhi, 1975.
(ix) Recent Indian Books—Federation of Publishers and Booksellers Association in India, New Delhi, 1975 (Quarterly).

Q. 20. Write the name of publishers, which have published the following Indexing and Abstracting.

(i) National Abstracting and Indexing Services
(ii) Japanese Periodical Index
(iii) Sri Lanka Science Index
(iv) Polish Technical and Economic Abstracts
(v) Korean Science Abstracts.

Ans. (i) National Abstracting and Indexing Service: INSDOC, New Delhi, 1965—12 issues/year.
(ii) Japanese Periodicals Index: National Diet Library, Tokyo, 1950—4 issues/year.
(iii) Sri Lanka Science Index: Natural Resources, Energy and Science Authority, Colombo, 1977—4 issues/year.
(iv) Polish Technical and Economic Abstracts: Institute Informacji, Maukowej Techniczneji Ekonomienej, Warsaw, 1951—4 issues/year.
(v) Korean Science Abstracts: Korean Institute of Economics and Technology, South Korea, 1969—6 issues/year.

Q. 21. Write the name of first Library Periodical in India. From where was it published?

Ans. Library Miscellany (Quarterly) published by State Library Dept., Baroda (1910-1913).

Q. 22. Write the full name of ABGILA. And who was the first editor?

Ans. Annals, Bulletin and Granthalaya of Indian Library Association (1949-53), S.R. Ranganathan.

Q. 23. Write the name of first editor of "Modern Librarian". And when was it published?

Ans. F. Monbrary Volte, 1930.

Q. 24. Write the name of most important indexing service published from Rajasthan University.

Ans. Index India, 1967 (Quarterly) (Social Science).

Q. 25. Write the name of indexing periodical published from New York, Subject on Library Science.

Ans. Library Literature, 1933.

Q. 26. Write the name of editor of "Library Herald".

Ans. Krishan Kumar, 1953.

Q. 27. Write the name of abstracting periodical in Library Science published from India.

Ans. Indian Library Science Abstracts (ILSA), IASLIC, 1962 (Quarterly).

Q. 28. Write the name of Library Science periodical published by the University of Chicago.

Ans. Library Quarterly.

Q. 29. Who had published the monthly journal "The Library World"?

Ans. J.D. Brown, 1898.

Q. 30. Write the name of British Picture Magazine of the 19th century that has survived to date.

Ans. Illustrated London News (1842).

Q. 31. Write the name of publishers who published the following periodicals.

(a) Indian Books, Monthly
(b) Indian Book Industry
(c) D.K. Newsletter (Fortnightly)
(d) Recent Indian Books (Quarterly)

Ans. (a) Indian Books Monthly—Mukharjee Book House, Kolkata.
(b) Indian Book Industry—Sterling Publishers, New Delhi.
(c) D.K. Newsletter (Fortnightly)—D.K. Publishers and Distributors, New Delhi.
(d) Recent Indian Books (Quarterly)—Federation of Publishers and Booksellers Association in India.

Q. 32. Write the name of publishers of 'Library and Information Science Abstracts'.

Ans. Library Association (UK)—Bi-Monthly.

Q. 33. Write the names of compilers of 'Current India' periodicals in English.

Ans. N.N. Gidwani and K. Navlani.

Q. 34. What is the arrangement of 'Publishers Trade List Annual'?

Ans. It is an alphabetical list of American publishers uniform sized catalogues.

Q. 35. Write the name of publishers who are publishing 'the index number of wholesale price in India'.

Ans. Office of the Economic Adviser to the Government of India.

Q. 36. Write the name of sources one should refer to for information on current periodicals in India.

Ans. (i) Annual Cumulative volumes of list of serials brought out as a part of Accession List: India.
(ii) Current Indian Periodicals: An Annotated Guide. Compiled by N.N. Gidwani, Jaipur.
(iii) Dictionary of Indian Scientific Periodicals (1976), INSDOC, New Delhi.
(iv) Nifor's Guide to Indian Periodicals 1955; National Information Service, Poona.
(v) Indian Periodicals in print by Gandhi, Lal and Agrawal; 1973 Vidya Mandal, Delhi.

Q. 37. Write the name of major newspaper Index for providing world news in English.

Ans. (i) The Time Index, Reading: Newspaper Archive Development, 1790.
(ii) The New York Times Index. New York Times Company, New York.

Q. 38. Write the name of three internationals digest published in English.

Ans. (i) Deadline Data on World Affairs, Greenwich.
(ii) Keesing's Contemporary Archives, Harlow.
(iii) Facts on File, New York, 1940.

Q. 39. Write the new title of Economic Abstracts published from Hague.

Ans. Key to Economic Science (since 1978).

Q. 40. Write the name of three major annuals published in the English speaking countries of the world that review the event of the prior year to dates.

Ans. (i) Britannica Book of the year (Encyclopedia Britannica), Chicago.
(ii) Annual Register, Longman (London).
(iii) The Americans Annual, Grolier (New York).

Q. 41. Write the name of journal and its periodicity and editor published by the Department of Library and Information Science, University of Delhi.

Ans. Journal of Library and Information Science, Vol. 1976, Bi-Annual, Chairman, Editorial Board: P.B. Mangla.

Q. 42. Write the name of publishers, which have the Indexing service.
(i) World Translation Index
(ii) Translation Register Index
(iii) Translation Bulletin
(iv) Transdex
(v) Commonwealth Index to unpublished Translations
(vi) Cumulative Index to English Translation

Ans. (i) It is published by the International Translations Centre—10 issues per year.
(ii) It is published by the special Libraries Association Translation Centre, Chicago.
(iii) It is published by the commission of the European Communities and Centre National de la Recherhe Scientific, France.
(iv) It is published by US-JPRS (Monthly).
(v) It is published by ASLIB, London.
(vi) It is compiled by UNESCO.

OBJECTIVE QUESTIONS

1. Journal of Documentation is published from (*NET Exam.* 1995)
(a) India (b) UK (c) USA (d) Canada

2. Indian Science Abstracts is being published by (*NET Exam.* 1995)
(a) Council of Scientific and Industrial Research (CSIR), India
(b) INSDOC
(c) DESIDOC
(d) National Science Library, New Delhi

3. Indian Library Science Abstracts is being published by (*NET Exam.* 1991)
(a) ILA (b) IASLIC
(c) IATLIS (d) INSDOC

4. Indian Library Association publishes (*NET Exam.* 1996)
(a) A Bulletin (b) A Newsletter
(c) Both (a) and (b) (d) Neither (a) nor (b)

5. National Index of Translation is published by (*NET Exam.* 1999)
(a) NASSDOC (b) DESIDOC
(c) SENDOC (d) INSDOC

6. Periodical publication 'Indian Science Abstracts' is (*NET Exam.* 1999)
(a) DESIDOC (b) INSA
(c) INSDOC (d) NISSAT

7. LIBRI is published from (*NET Exam.* 1995)
(a) Denmark (b) UK
(c) USA (d) Australia

8. Library Literature is published by (*NET Exam.* 1995)
(a) DESIDOC (b) H.W. Wilson
(c) INSDOC (d) R.R. Bowker

9. Indian National Bibliography is published by
(a) National Library, Kolkata
(b) Central Reference Library, Kolkata
(c) INSDOC, New Delhi
(d) NASSDOC, New Delhi

10. Who published the Statistical Abstracts?
(a) Central Statistical Organisation
(b) National Book Trust
(c) NCERT
(d) Statistical Office

11. "Facts of File" is weekly digest of
(a) Asian Events (b) African Events
(c) World Events (d) European Events

12. The National Union Catalogue of Scientific Serials in India was published by
(a) National Library (Kolkata)
(b) Central Reference Library
(c) INSDOC
(d) Delhi Public Library

13. Index India is published by
(a) Delhi Public Library
(b) Indian Library Association

(c) Rajasthan University Library
(d) National Library

14. Which of the following methods is user study on measuring the active like of periodicals? (*NET Exam.* 2001J)
(a) Survey (b) Citation analysis
(c) Interview (d) Case study

15. In the acquisition and control periodicals, Ranganathan devised a system which is denoted as (*NET Exam.* 2001D)
(a) Kardex (b) Three Card System
(c) Check list (d) Shelf list

16. "Journal of Librarianship" is the publication of (*NET Exam.* 2002D)
(a) ILA (b) ASLIB
(c) IFLA (d) LA(UK)

17. Periodical department has to function in close cooperation particularly with (*NET Exam.* 2002J)
(a) Reference and Documentation departments
(b) Circulation and Reference department
(c) Acquisition and Maintenance departments
(d) Technical and Acquisition department

18. ALIs Bulletin is a publication of (*NET Exam.* 2002J)
(a) Jawaharlal Nehru University, New Delhi
(b) Banaras Hindu University, Varanasi
(c) Indian Library Association
(d) University of Kerala, Trivandrum

19. Electronic Journal is one which is available (*NET Exam.* 2002J)
(a) Online
(b) Distributed via electronic network
(c) In CD-ROM format
(d) All of the above

20. Periodical department has to function in close cooperation particularly with (*NET Exam.* 2003D)
(a) Technical and Acquisition Department
(b) Circulation and Reference Departments
(c) Acquisition and Maintenance Departments
(d) Reference and Documentation Department

21. Centralised Acquisition of Periodical is the programme of (*NET Exam.* 2004J)
(a) NISCAIR (b) NASSDOC
(c) DESIDOC (d) NISSAT

22. Indian Press Index, New York Times Index and Newspaper Index are Indexing services devoted to (*NET Exam.* 2005)
(a) Newspaper (b) Periodical
(c) Journal (d) Report literature

23. Match the following: (*NET Exam.* 2004D)

Column A (Published Work)	**Column B (Year of Publication)**
(A) Publishers Weekly	1. 1872
(B) Psychological Abstracts	2. 1927
(C) Book Review Digest	3. 1905
(D) Chemical Abstract	4. 1907

Codes:	**A**	**B**	**C**	**D**
(a)	4	3	1	2
(b)	1	2	3	4
(c)	2	1	3	4
(d)	3	4	1	2

24. **Assertion (A):** User can have access to large number of E-Journals through consortia.
Reason (R): User are not aware of using web-resources. (*NET Exam.* 2006D)
Codes:
(a) (A) is false and (R) is true.
(b) (A) is true and (R) is false.
(c) Both (A) and (R) are true, but (R) is not the right explanation of (A).
(d) Both (A) and (R) are false.

25. An entry in Abstracting Journal consists of (*NET Exam.* 2006D)
(a) Bibliographic citation
(b) An abstract and bibliographic citation
(c) Annotation
(d) Bibliographic citation, an abstract and initials of the abstractor

26. Index Medicus is brought out as printed publication (*NET Exam.* 2010D)
(a) Quarterly (b) Monthly
(c) Weekly (d) Has ceased publication

27. JSTOR is an online system for archiving and accessing academic journals. It located in (*NET Exam.* 2010D)
(a) Germany (b) UK (c) USA (d) Budapest

28. Match the following: (*NET Exam.* 2007J)

List I	**List II**
(A) Journal of Librarianship	(i) Delhi
(B) Herald of Library Science	(ii) London
(C) Library Herald	(iii) New York
(D) Library Literature	(iv) Lucknow
	(v) Canada

Codes:	A	B	C	D
(a)	(ii)	(iv)	(i)	(iii)
(b)	(iv)	(iii)	(i)	(v)
(c)	(iii)	(ii)	(v)	(iv)
(d)	(ii)	(i)	(iv)	(iii)

29. Blog is a (*NET Exam.* 2007D)
(a) Offline journal (b) Internet journal
(c) Web Dictionary (d) Search Engine

30. "Publishers Weekly" is published by (*NET Exam.* 2011J)
(a) H.W. Wilson, New York
(b) R.R. Bowker, London
(c) American Library Association, Chicago
(d) Aslib, London

31. Magazines are suitable for (*NET Exam.* 2012D)
(i) Leisure and entertainment
(ii) Scholarly information
(iii) Popular information
(iv) Subject information
Codes:
(a) i, ii and iii are correct
(b) ii, iii and iv are correct
(c) i, iii are correct
(d) ii and iv are correct

32. E-Journal articles can be identified with the help of (*NET Exam.* 2012D)
(a) Digital Journal Identifier
(b) Journal Source Identifier
(c) Journal Article Identifier
(d) Digital Object Identifier

33. Library Herald is published from (*NET Exam.* 2011D)
(a) Kolkata (b) Bangalore
(c) Delhi (d) Lucknow

34. ETD database in India is maintained by (*NET Exam.* 2011D)
(i) Shodhgangotri (ii) Vidyanidhi
(iii) Shodhganga (iv) INDEST-AICTE consortium
Codes:
(a) (i) and (iii) are correct.
(b) (ii), (iii) and (iv) are correct.
(c) (ii) and (iii) are correct.
(d) (iii) and (iv) are correct.

35. One of the authorized users makes bulk downloading of a journal using robots and consequently licensor blocks access of the journals. What may be the most appropriate actions that librarian should initiate? (*NET Exam.* 2013J)
(i) Cancellation of authentication of the said user.
(ii) Asking the licensor for blocking up the access without prior information.
(iii) Investigate and take corrective measures
(iv) Notify user community of user restrictions
Codes:
(a) (ii) and (iv) are correct
(b) (ii) and (iii) are correct
(c) (i) and (iii) are correct
(d) (i) and (ii) are correct

36. Poor "accessibility" and less "affordability" of journal subscription in print era led to (*NET Exam.* 2013J)
(i) High allocation of funds for serials
(ii) Open access movements
(iii) Decrease in subscription of journals
(iv) E-Journal consortia subscription
Codes:
(a) (i) and (ii) are correct.
(b) (i), (ii) and (iv) are correct.
(c) (ii), (iv) are correct.
(d) (i), (ii) and (iii) are correct.

37. Which source would you consult to know the "Impact Factor" of journal publication? (*NET Exam.* 2012J)
(i) Web of science (ii) Science Direct
(iii) SCOPUS (iv) EBSCO
Codes:
(a) (i) and (iv) (b) (ii) and (iii)
(c) (iii) and (i) (d) (iii) and (iv)

38. Match the following: (*NET Exam.* 2012J)
List I
(A) Whitakers Almanac
(B) Ulrich International Periodical Directory
(C) National Union Catalogue of Scientific Serials in India
(D) Data India
List II
(i) Year of starting Publishers Weekly
(ii) Availability of V50 of Library Journal
(iii) Information of Discontinuation of New Encyclopedia Britannica
(iv) Astronomical Information

Codes:	A	B	C	D
(a)	(iv)	(i)	(ii)	(iii)
(b)	(ii)	(iv)	(i)	(iii)

(c)	(iii)	(ii)	(i)	(iv)
(d)	(i)	(iv)	(ii)	(iii)

39. Which of the following is a Bulletin Board Service on Internet? (*NET Exam.* 2012J)
(a) Picaso (b) Google talk
(c) Blog (d) ooVoo

40. CODEN is connected with (*NET Exam.* 2012J)
(a) Books (b) Serials
(c) Reports (d) Gray Literature

41. "Shodhganga" is repository of (*NET Exam.* 2012J)
(a) E-Resources (b) E-Thesis
(c) E-Journals (d) E-Books

42. **Assertion (A):** Users can have access to large number of e-journals. (*NET Exam.* 2012D)
Reason (R): Users are not aware of using e-journals.
Codes:
(a) (A) is true, but (R) is false.
(b) Both (A) and (R) are true but (R) is not the correct explanation of (A).
(c) (A) is false, but (R) is true.
(d) Both (A) and (R) are true and (R) is the correct explanation of (A).

43. Access to back volumes of E-Journals is known as (*NET Exam.* 2012D)
(a) Random Access (b) Perpetual Access
(c) Online Access (d) Restropective Access

44. Web of Science is (*NET Exam.* 2012D)
(a) A Citation Index (b) Bibliography
(c) An Abstracting service (d) All of these

45. **Assertion (A):** Present decade has accepted E-Journals as channels of fast communication.
Reason (R): E-publication have added enormous quantity of literature but affected the quality of research.(*NET Exam.* 2012D)
Codes:
(a) (A) is true, but (R) is false.
(b) (A) is false, but (R) is true.
(c) Both (A) and (R) are true and (R) is the correct explanation.
(d) Both (A) and (R) are true, but (R) is not a correct explanation.

46. "Data India" is published by (*NET Exam.* 2002D)
(a) NIC (b) NISCAIR
(c) Times of India (d) DESIDOC

47. Emerald full text Database is published from (*NET Exam.* 2009D)
(a) USA (b) Germany (c) France (d) UK

48. Emerald is the database of (*NET Exam.* 2008D)
(a) Gems and Jewellery Literature
(b) Material Science Literature
(c) Library and Information Science Literature
(d) Earth Science Literature

49. "Poole's Index to periodical Literature" was brought out by (*NET Exam.* 2013J)
(a) William Frederic (b) FW Lancaster
(c) Van Rijsbergen (d) HP Luhn

50. **Assertion (A):** INDEST conceived Gate as a customized gate for e-Journals subscribed by the member libraries. (*NET Exam.* 2013J)
Reason (R): J-Gate provide a common access platform for all its members to search and share resources subscribed by the member libraries.
Codes:
(a) Both (A) and (R) are true and (R) is the correct explanation.
(b) Both (A) and (R) are true but (R) is not the correct explanation.
(c) (A) is true, but (R) is false.
(d) (A) is false, but (R) is true.

51. Lotka's law deals with (*NET 17J ii paper*)
(a) Frequency of occurrence of words in a text.
(b) Productivity of authors in terms of scientific papers.
(3) Scattering of articles over different journals.
(d) Growth of articles in journals.

52. The license for accessing the 'Europa World of Learning Online' is available through (*NET 17J iii paper*)
(a) Routledge–(Taylor and Francis)
(b) SpringerOpen
(c) Sage Publications
(d) Elsevier

53. What is periodicity of 'Annals of Library and Information Studies' published by NISCAIR, India? (*NET 17J iii paper*)
(a) Monthly (b) Bi-monthly
(c) Quarterly (d) Bi-annual

54. 'Facet publishing' is a division of (*NET 17J iii paper*)

(a) American Library Association
(b) Canadian Library Association
(c) Chartered Institute of Library and Information Professionals
(d) International Federation of Library Associations

55. 'E-Shodh Sindhu' emerged by the merger of *(NET 16J iii paper)*

i. INDEST ii. INFONET
iii. NICNET iv. N-LIST

Codes:
(a) i, iii, iv are correct.
(b) ii, ii, iii are correct.
(c) ii, iii, iv are correct.
(d) i, ii, iv are correct.

56. Which of the following are not published by US National Library of Medicine? *(NET J16 iii paper)*

i. eMedicine ii. Pubmeth
iii. PubMed iv. Medline Plus

Codes:
(a) i and ii are correct.
(b) i and iv are correct.
(c) iii and iv are correct.
(d) ii and iv are correct.

57. 'Keesing's Record of World Events' is published from: *(NET 17 NOV iii paper)*

(a) London (b) France
(c) Germany (d) Japan

58. Arrange the following according to the year of first publication *(NET 15J iii paper)*

(i) Medical Subject Headings
(ii) Sears List of Subject Headings
(iii) Library of Congress Subject Headings
(iv) AGROVOC

Codes:
(a) ii, i, iv, iii (b) iii, ii, i, iv
(c) ii, i, iii, iv (d) i, iii, iv, ii

59. Match the following: *(NET 15J iii paper)*

List - I
(A) Indian Electronic Thesis and Dissertation Database
(B) Database of Indian Experts
(C) Indian Patent database
(D) Database of Indian Ancient Knowledge

List - II
(1) Ekaswa (2) TKDL
(3) Shodhganga (4) Vidwan

Codes:	**(A)**	**(B)**	**(C)**	**(D)**
(a)	(3)	(2)	(4)	(1)
(b)	(2)	(4)	(1)	(3)
(c)	(3)	(4)	(1)	(2)
(d)	(4)	(2)	(3)	(1)

60. **Assertion (A):** India's contribution to LIS literatures is decreasing.

Reason (R): Authors find it more convenient to get their articles published in open access journals. *(NET 13D iii paper)*

Codes:
(a) Both (A) and (R) are true.
(b) (A) is false, but (R) is true.
(c) Both (A) and (R) are false.
(d) (A) is true but (R) is false.

61. Which of the following are features of 'Open Journal System'? *(NET 14D iii paper)*

i. License to access content
ii. Access restricted to limited group
iii. Online submission
iv. Subscription module with delayed open access options

Codes:
(a) i and ii are correct.
(b) ii and iii are correct.
(c) iii and iv are correct.
(d) ii and iv are correct.

62. Arrange the following according to the procedural steps: *(NET 14D iii paper)*

i. Receipt of recommendations
ii. Preparing master card
iii. Checking titles of and bibliographical details
iv. Duplication checking from library catalogue

Codes:
(a) i, ii, iii, iv (b) i, iii, ii, iv
(c) iii, i, iv, ii (d) iv, iii, i, ii

63. Match the following publishers with the relevant databases: *(NET D14 iii paper)*

List – I	List – II
A. Elsevier	1. Academic search
B. Thomson Reuters	2. Aerospace & high technology
C. EBSCO	3. Scopus
D. ProQuest	4. Web of knowledge

Codes:	**A**	**B**	**C**	**D**
(a)	2	1	4	3
(b)	1	3	2	4

(c)	3	4	1	2
(d)	4	2	3	1

64. Arrange in sequence the following E-Journal Consortia in India according to their year of establishment: *(NET D15 iii paper)*
(i) National Knowledge Resource Consortium
(ii) IIM Library Consortium
(iii) Consortium for e-Resources in Agriculture
(iv) INDEST-AICTE Consortium
Codes:
(a) (iii), (i), (iv) and (ii)
(b) (i), (iv), (ii) and (iii)
(c) (ii), (iv), (iii) and (i)
(d) (iv), (ii), (i) and (iii)

65. Match the following: *(NET D15 iii paper)*
List - I
(A) Cumulative Books in Print
(B) Ulrich International Periodical Directory
(C) World of Learning
(D) Who's Who in India
List - II
(1) Bibliography of Periodicals
(2) Trade bibliography
(3) Biographical source
(4) Directory

Codes:	**(A)**	**(B)**	**(C)**	**(D)**
(a)	(2)	(1)	(4)	(3)
(b)	(1)	(2)	(3)	(4)
(c)	(3)	(1)	(4)	(2)
(d)	(1)	(3)	(4)	(2)

66. Match the following: *(NET 15J ii paper)*
List - I
(A) Annals of Library and Information Studies
(B) Journal of Information Management
(C) Herald of Library Science
(D) Library Herald
List - II
(1) S.R.E.L.S, Bangalore
(2) Delhi Library Association
(3) NISCAIR, Delhi
(4) P.N. Kaula Endowment, Lucknow

Codes:	**(A)**	**(B)**	**(C)**	**(D)**
(a)	(2)	(3)	(4)	(1)
(b)	(3)	(1)	(4)	(2)
(c)	(3)	(2)	(1)	(4)
(d)	(1)	(3)	(4)	(2)

67. Index Indiana, an index to Indian Periodical Literature is being compiled by *(NET 17J iii paper)*
(a) Central Reference Library, Kolkata
(b) National Library of India
(c) NISCAIR
(d) IASLIC

68. 'Open Journal System' is an example of which of the following open access models? *(NET 17J iii paper)*
(a) Green (b) Red
(c) Gold (d) Platinum

69. When was the final 'ISBD Consolidation Edition' published by IFLA? *(NET 17J iii paper)*
(a) 2008 (b) 2009 (c) 2010 (d) 2011

70. Match the following: *(NET 17J iii paper)*
List – I
(A) Portico (B) Lockss
(C) Clockss (D) Chorus
List – II
(1) Preserves scholarly publications in dark archives to be accessed under emergent situation
(2) Non-profit service that allows libraries to collect e-contents for digital preservation
(3) Non-profit digital preservation service for participating libraries
(4) Clearing house for the open resources of U S

Codes	**A**	**B**	**C**	**D**
(a)	1	2	3	4
(b)	4	3	2	1
(c)	2	4	1	3
(d)	3	2	1	4

71. Match the following: *(NET 14D ii paper)*

List – I	**List – II**
A. ETC	1. UK
B. NTC	2. India
C. BLLD	3. USA
D. NISCAIR	4. Netherland

Codes:	**A**	**B**	**C**	**D**
(a)	4	3	1	2
(b)	2	1	3	4
(c)	3	4	2	1
(d)	1	2	4	3

72. An e-resource consortium 'CeRA' is working in the field of *(NET 16J iii paper)*
(a) Agriculture (b) Astronomy
(c) Astrophysics (d) Anthropology

73. Journalseek is an: *(NET 16J iii paper)*

(a) Online database covering academic journals articles
(b) Online database covering abstracts
(c) Online database of freely available journal information
(d) Subscription agent for freely available journals

74. Which of the following are the International Cooperative Serials Control Program? *(NET 13D iii paper)*

(i) CONSER (ii) BIBCO
(iii) SERLINE (iv) CATLINE

Codes:
(a) (i) & (ii) are correct.
(b) (ii) & (iii) are correct.
(c) (i) & (iii) are correct.
(d) (ii) & (iv) are correct.

75. Identify the correct sequence according to year of first publication. *(NET D15 ii paper)*
(a) Library and Information Science Abstract, Biological Abstract, Chemical Abstract
(b) Chemical Abstract, Biological Abstract, Library and Information Science Abstract
(c) Biological Abstract, Chemical Abstract, Library and Information Science Abstract
(d) Chemical Abstract, Library and Information Science Abstract, Biological Abstract

76. **Assertion (A):** Most of the institutions around the world use "impact factor" measuring institutional productivity.

Reason (R): All the article published in an "Impact factor" journal will be of equal quality. *(NET D 15 ii paper)*

Codes:
(a) Both (A) and (R) are true
(b) (A) is true but (R) is false
(c) (A) is false but (R) is true
(d) Both (A) and (R) are false

77. According to APA Style Manual, a section at the end of a paper that includes information that is too detailed for the text of the paper itself and would "burden the reader" or be "distracting" or "in appropriate" is called: *(NET 17 NOV iii paper)*

(a) Appendix (b) Bibliography
(c) References (d) Tables

78. Match the following: *(NET D15 ii paper)*

List-I	List-II
(A) Indcat	(1) Access for e-resources
(B) Shodhganga Consortium	(2) Digital Library
(C) N-list	(3) Indian ETD repository
(D) UGC Infonet	(4) Online Union Catalogue of Indian Universities

Codes:	(A)	(B)	(C)	(D)
(a)	(3)	(2)	(4)	(1)
(b)	(2)	(1)	(3)	(4)
(c)	(1)	(4)	(2)	(3)
(d)	(4)	(3)	(1)	(2)

79. Match the following *(NET 18J)*

List - I	List - II
(A) Library Journal	(i) Reed Business Information
(B) Library Quarterly	(ii) Emerald Group Publishing Ltd.
(C) Library Review	(iii) John Hopkins University Press
(D) Library Trends	(iv) University of Chicago Press

Codes:	(A)	(B)	(C)	(D)
(a)	(i)	(ii)	(iii)	(iv)
(b)	(iv)	(i)	(iii)	(ii)
(c)	(i)	(iv)	(ii)	(iii)
(d)	(iv)	(iii)	(ii)	(i)

80. **Assertion (A):** Inclusion of DOAJ implies the quality of and open access journals.

Reason (R): DOAJ is and online directory that indexes and provides access to open access and peer viewed journals. Besides DOAJ has tightened the listing criteria. *(NET 18J)*

Codes:
(a) Both (A) and (R) are true
(b) Both (A) and (R) are false
(c) (A) is false, but (R) is true
(d) (A) is true but (R) is false

81. **Assertion (A):** The Mendeley is one of the most preferred online reference managers which cam store bibliographic records as well as full text documents and help in creating bibliographical references in any popular citation style like APA, MLA, or Chicago style.

Reason (R): Web-based solution related to online reference management have become freely available to the global researches engaged in collaborative research project. *(NET 18J)*

Codes:
(a) both (A) and (R) are false
(b) both (A) and (R) is true
(c) (A) is false and (R) is true
(d) (A) is true but (R) is false

82. **Assertion (A):** Dr Engune Garfields original invention still continues to serve as a reliable and efficient guide to the sprawling world of research. *(NET 18J)*

Reason (R): Garfield was not only honoured for his work in developing the field of Citation Analysis, but also his subsequent contribution in founding ISI (1960) that developed and launched SCI (1964) consequently led to the development of numerous citation databases of first order including 'Web of Science', all of which brought him an idiomatic identity in the research would till the date.

Codes:
(a) (A) is true but (R) is false
(b) (A) is false, but (R) is true
(c) both (A) and (R) are true
(d) Both (A) and (R) are false

ANSWER SHEET

1. (d)	2. (b)	3. (b)	4. (c)	5. (d)	6. (c)	7. (c)	8. (b)	9. (b)
10. (a)	11. (c)	12. (c)	13. (c)	14. (b)	15. (a)	16. (d)	17. (a)	18. (d)
19. (d)	20. (d)	21. (a)	22. (d)	23. (b)	24. (c)	25. (b)	26. (b)	27. (c)
28. (d)	29. (b)	30. (b)	31. (c)	32. (d)	33. (c)	34. (c)	35. (d)	36. (c)
37. (c)	38. (a)	39. (c)	40. (b)	41. (b)	42. (b)	43. (b)	44. (a)	45. (d)
46. (a)	47. (d)	48. (c)	49. (a)	50. (a)	51. (b)	52. (a)	53. (c)	54. (c)
55. (d)	56. (a)	57. (a)	58. (b)	59. (c)	60. (b)	61. (c)	62. (b)	63. (c)
64. (c)	65. (a)	66. (b)	67. (a)	68. (d)	69. (d)	70. (d)	71. (a)	72. (a)
73. (c)	74. (c)	75. (b)	76. (b)	77. (a)	78. (d)	79. (c)	80. (a)	81. (b)
82. (c)								

Chapter 12
Important Personalities

(Full names of the personalities in the field of Library Science and its allied fields.)

1. A. Neelameghan - Arashanapallai Neelameghan
2. A.D. Dickinson - Asa Don Dickinson
3. A.J. Walford - Arthur John Walford
4. A.P. Srivastava - Anand Prakash Srivastava
5. B.I. Palmer - Bernard Ira Palmer
6. B.S. Kesavan - Bellary Shamanna Kesavan
7. C.A. Cutter - Charles Ammi Cutter
8. C.G. Viswanathan - Caduveti Gurusubrahmanya Viswanathan
9. D.N. Marshall - Dara Nusserwanji Marshall
10. D.R. Kalia - Desh Raj Kalia
11. Dr. L. Mudaliar - Dr. Lakshmana Swamy Mudaliar
12. E.A. Savage - Ernest Albert Savage
13. E.C. Richardson - Ernest Cushing Richardson
14. Fremont Rider - Arthur Fremont Rider
15. G. Bhattacharya - Ganesh Bhattacharya
16. G. Rao Ekbote - Gopal Rao Ekbote
17. H. Fayol - Henry Fayol
18. H.E. Bliss - Henry Evelyn Bliss
19. H.P. Luhn - Hans Peter Luhn
20. H.W. Wilson - Halsey William Wilson
21. J.D. Brown - James Duff Brown
22. J. Mills - Jack Mills
23. J.C. Brunet - Jacques Charles Brunet
24. J.C.M. Hanson - James Christian Meinich Hanson
25. J.S. Sharma - Jagdish Saran Sharma
26. K.S. Hingwe - Krishnaji Shankar Hingwe
27. K.A. Isaac - Kadapuram Abraham Isaac
28. L.R. McColvin - Lionel Roy McColvin
29. M.E. Sears - Minnie Earl Sears
30. M.R. Kumbharo - Mahendragonda Rudragouda Kumbharo
31. Melvil Dewey - Melville Louis Kossuth Dewey
32. N.N. Gidwani - Narain Nanikram Gidwani
33. P.B. Mangla - Pramod Bhushan Mangla
34. P.N. Kaula - Prithvi Nath Kaula
35. Paul Otlet - Paul Marie-Ghislain Otlet
36. R.R. Bowker - Richard Rogers Bowker
37. R.S. Parkhi - Raghunath Shatanand Parkhi
38. S.C. Bradford - Samuel Clement Bradford
39. S.R. Bhatia - Sant Ram Bhatia
40. S.R. Ranganathan - Shiyali Ramamrita Ranganathan
41. W.A. Borden - William Alanson Borden
42. W. Greg - Water Greg
43. W.W. Bishop - William Warner Bishop
44. W.C.B. Sayers - William Charles Berwick Sayers
45. W.F. Poole - William Frederick Poole
46. W. Hulme - Wyndham Hulme
47. W.S. Jevons - William Stanley Jevons

Chapter 13
Important Dates in Library Science

1694- Newspapers started appearing and circulation increased rapidly when the government censorship was removed.

1725- The first Circulation Library was established in Edinburgh.

1768-71 The first edition of *Encyclopedia Britannica* was published in three volumes.

1800- Library of Congress established (USA).

1823- Members formed into a body called Glasgow Mechanics Institute.

The Peter Borough Municipal Council made a provision in their budget to set up a free Public Library.

1836- 21st March—Establishment of Public Library, Calcutta.

1837- 14th March—Birth of C.A. Cutter.

1841 Henri Fayol was born.

1848- John Jacob Astor, a businessman bequeathed $4,00,000 in his will to establish a reference Library in New York City.

1850- 14th August—A red letter day in the annals of British Library development.

Edward-Edward had taken over as the Librarian of Manchester Public Library.

1851- 14th Dec.—Birth of Melvil Dewey at New York.

1852 Roget's Thesaurus.

1856 Fredric Winslow Taylor was born.

1857 First edition of Oxford English Dictionary was published

1862- 6th Nov.—Birth of James Duff Brown.

1867- The first Copyright Act was passed.

1870- Another Reference Library was opened in New York.

1876- Dewey Decimal Classification, first edition was published.

1876 American Library Association (ALA) was founded.

Rules for Dictionary Catalogue published (1st edition) by C.A. Cutter.

1877- 5th Oct.—The Library Association (UK) was founded.

1879- Expansive Classification was published by C.A. Cutter.

1884- Establishment of free public Enoch Pratt Library at Baltimore.

1885- Dewey Decimal Classification, second edition was published.

1887- Establishment of free Public Newberry Library at Chicago.

1887 Melvil Dewey started the school of Library Science in USA.

1888- Dewey Decimal Classification, third edition was published.

1891- C.A. Cutter devised Expensive Classification.

1892- 9th August—Birth of Dr. S.R. Ranganathan, but in official record 12th of August has come into use as his date of birth.

1894- Establishment of free Public John Crerar Library at Chicago.

1895- First International Conference on Bibliography was held at Brussels.

1895 Brown charging system started.

1895 Establishment of International Federation for Information and Documentation.

1902- Library of Congress Classification First outline of class Z published.

1903- Imperial Library established at Calcutta.

1905- Universal Decimal Classification Scheme was published in French by Paul Otlet and La Fontaine.

1906- The Public Libraries development movement started from Baroda State.

J.D. Brown published the first edition of his subject classification. Baroda Library Movement started by the Sayaji Rao Gaekwad.

1909 Peter Druker was born.

1910- Library Association formed in the Baroda State.

1910 A.W. Borden start a refresher course for Librarian in India.

1911 W. Borden start from America to India for revival of Public Library.

1914- First Association formed in Andhra Pradesh whose name was Andhra Desa Library Association.

1915- Adam Report submitted about the working of Public Libraries in England.

1919- Dewey Decimal Classification, 10th edition was published edited by May Seymour.

1919- Establishment of free Public Henry E. Huntington Library at San Marino.

1920- Canegie Trust donated more than $50,000,000 for construction of library building at New York.

1922- Dewey Decimal Classification, 11th edition was published.

1924- Dr. S.R. Ranganathan was appointed as a Librarian in Madras University.

1926- Association of Special Libraries and Information Bureaux (ASLIB) was founded.

1927- Kenyon Report was submitted about the working of Public Libraries in England.

Bengal Library Association formed.

1928- The Five Laws of Library Science were enunciated.

1929- International Federation of Library Association and Institution (IFLA) was founded.

The fourteenth edition of *Encyclopedia Britannica* published.

1930- The selection of basic principle of reading materials for Library was enunciated.

1932- Dewey Decimal Classification, 13th edition was published edited by J.D. Fellows.

1933- The Indian Library Association founded at Calcutta, now located at New Delhi.

1933- First edition of Colon Classification was published.

1934- Classified Catalogue Code (CCC) was published by S.R. Ranganathan.

1935- Bibliographic Classification was published.

1936- The first Survey was undertaken by the Library Association in Britain.

1939- 10th March—The Delhi Library Association was formed.

1939-40 First Well-known Committee on Regional Public Libraries was the Library Development Committee, Bombay, headed by A.A.A. Fyzee.

1942- Dewey Decimal Classification, 14th edition was published edited by Constantin Mazney.

1946- United Nations Educational, Scientific and Cultural Organisation (UNESCO) was established.

1948- The Imperial Library was renamed as the National Library, India.

1951- Dewey Decimal Classification, 15th Revised edition was published edited by Milton J. Ferguson.

1951- 27th Oct.—Inauguration of Delhi Public Library.

DDC 15th edition was published.

1952- Indian National Scientific Documentation Centre (INSDOC) was established.

1953- The UGC was established in India and was made a statutory body in November by an act of Parliament 1956.

1954- The Delivery Books Act was passed.

1955- The Indian Association of Special Libraries and Information Centre (IASLIC) was founded.

Government constituted a National Bibliographical Committee, B.S. Kesavan was the Chairman.

1956- Delivery of Books was amended to include in it "The Delivery of Books and Newspapers" (Public Library Act).

1957- A Library Committee was appointed under the Chairmanship of Dr. S.R. Ranganathan.

Padamshri awarded to Dr. S.R. Ranganathan by the President of India. The Indian National Bibliography and its first issue was released.

1958- Defence Science Information and Documentation Centre (DESIDOC) was established.

1958- First Ph.D. in Library and Information Science in India.

1958- Dewey Decimal Classification, 16th edition was published

1959- The report was published by the University Grant Commission about Universities and College Libraries.

1961- A Review Committee on Library Science was appointed under the Chairmanship of Dr. S.R. Ranganathan.

International Classification was first published by Fremont Rider. Sharda Ranganathan Endowment established.

International Conference on Cataloguing principles held in Paris.

1962- Documentation Research Training Centre (DRTC), Bangalore was inaugurated.

1962 Dr. S.R. Ranganathan was appointed as a National research professor of Library Science.

1963-64 The UGC of India introduced a new scheme of "Book Bank".

1964-66 In July 1964, the Government of India appointed Education Commission under the Chairmanship of Prof. D.S. Kothari.

1965- Library Legislation Act implemented in the State of Mysore.

1966- Machine Readable Catalogue (MARC) was started.

1967- The Parry Committee Report published.

Machine Readable Catalogue (MARC) project completed.

Library Legislation Act implemented in the State of Maharashtra.

1969 The term "Bibliometrics" was coined by Alan Pritchard.

1970- National Social Science Documentation Centre (NASSDOC) established.

1971- Dewey Decimal Classification, 18th edition was published; edited by Benjamin A. Custer.

1971- The International Conference on Cataloguing Principle held in Paris.

1972- 22nd May—Raja Ram Mohan Roy Foundation (RRRLF) was established.

27th September—Dr. S.R. Ranganathan died at Bangalore.

1973- The fifteenth edition of Encyclopedia Britannica published as the "New Encyclopedia Britannica".

1974- A Library Reorganising Committee was appointed at Tamil Nadu.

1976- In Andhra Pradesh, a Committee was appointed by the government under the Chairmanship of Justice Gopal Rao Ekbote.

1977- National Information System for Science and Technology (NISSAT) was established.

1979- The British Library was established by enact of the Parliament.

1979- 19th Edition Dewey Decimal Classification scheme published edited by Benjamin A. Custer.

1979- Library Legislation Act implemented in the State of West Bengal.

1983- 24th December—The UGC appointed a committee under the Chairmanship of R.C. Mehrotra to consider the revision of pay scale, carrier, professional development and service condition of the teacher in the university.

1985 CD-Rom was prepared.

1985- The development of the culture, Ministry of Human Resource Development, Government of India appointed a Committee in October 1985—a Committee of a senior Library Scientist and other specialist with the Prof. D.P. Chattopadhyaya as a Chairman to prepare a draft document on National Policy on Library and Information System.

1985 CDS/ISIS software was developed.

1986- In the month of May National Policy on education, announced by the Govt. of India.

The National Book Policy was prepared.

On 31st May, the National Policy on Information System Committee submitted the report.

1987 7th edition of CC was published

1986- Dewey Decimal Classification, 20th edition was published edited by Dr. J.P. Camaromi.

1988- The UGC constituted a Committee on National Network System under the Chairmanship of Prof. Yash Pal.

Library Legislation Act implemented in the State of Manipur.

1989- Library Legislation Act implemented in the State of Haryana.

1989 Kerala Public Libraries Act.

1993 Library Legislation Act implemented in the State of Goa.

1993 Mizoram Public Libraries Act.

1996- Dewey Decimal Classification, 21st edition was published.

1997 Green Stone Library software was developed.

2000 EPrints Software was developed.

2000 KOHA Software was developed.

2000 SOUL Software was developed by INLIBNET.

2002 DSpace Software was developed.

2007 NEWGENLIB Software was developed.

2007 Dewey Decimal Classification, 22nd edition was published.

2001 Gujarat Public Libraries Act.

2005 Uttarakhand Public Libraries Act.

2005 Uttar Pradesh Public Libraries Act.

2006 Rajasthan Public Libraries Act.

2007 Bihar Public Libraries Act.

2007 Chhattisgarah Public Libraries Act.

2007 Pondicherry Public Libraries Act.

2009 Arunachal Pradesh Public Libraries Act.

2011 Dewey Decimal Classification, 23rd edition was published edited by Miss John S. Mitchell.

Chapter 14
Plagiarism

Plagiarism can be defined as **"wrongful appropriation"** and **"stealing publication"** of another author's "language, thoughts, ideas, creativity, work or expressions" and the representing them as own original work.

Plagiarism is the use or close imitation of the language and ideas of another author and representation of them as one's own original work. The intentional plagiarism refers to using someone's ideas or results without citing the source, using someone's ideas or results without using quotation marks, even though he/she cites the source and using someone's ideas or results without crediting the source. The accidental plagiarism is when the author does not know what is considered as plagiarism and he/she can't think of a better way to say it and so copy sentences, phrases, or even sentence structure from the original without using quotation marks and in the event while preparing the notes he/she does not put exact wording in quotation marks and so he/she plagiarizes without realizing it.

Plagiarism is considered as an academic dishonesty and betraying of journalistic ethics. It is a subject to sanctions such as penalties, suspension, expulsion from school or work, substantial fines and even incarceration. The modern concept of plagiarism as immoral and originality as an ideal emerged in Europe, during the Romantic movement in 18th century.

In general, Plagiarism is not only a crime, but like forging and fraud that can be punished in a court for prejudices caused by copyright breach, violation of ethical rights, or wrongdoings. In academia and industry, it is a major ethical offense. Plagiarism and copyright abuse overlap upto some extent, but actually they are not same ideas, and many types of plagiarism do not constitute copyright breach, which is defined by copyright law and may be arbitrated by courts.

Plagiarism might not be the same in all countries. Some countries like India and Poland consider plagiarism to be a misconduct, and there have been cases of people being imprisoned for plagiarizing. In other instances, plagiarism might be the complete opposite of "academic dishonesty," in fact some counties find the act of plagiarizing a professional's work flattering. Students who move to the United States from countries where plagiarism is not glowered upon often find the changeover difficult.

ETYMOLOGY

In the 1st century, the use of the Latin word *"plagiarius"* (literally "kidnapper") to denote stealing someone else's work was pioneered by the Roman poet Martial, who complained that another poet had "kidnapped his sections". *Plagiary*, a derivative of *plagiarus*, was introduced into English in 1601 by scriptwriter Ben Jonson during the Jacobean Era to describe someone guilty of literary theft.

Derived form of plagiarism was introduced into English language in 1620. The Latin plagiārius, "kidnapper", and plagium, "kidnapping", have the root plaga ("snare", "net"), based on the Indo-European root-plak, "to weave".

TYPES OF PLAGIARISM

1. Legal Aspects

Although plagiarism in some contexts is considered theft or stealing, the concept does not exist in a legal sense, still the use of someone else's work in order to gain academic credit may meet some legal definitions of fraud. In short, it is said, "if you cannot write in your own words then you should always give credit to the original author.

Plagiarism is not the same as copyright breach. In many aspects both the terms are same, Plagiarism can be defined as a false claim of authorship irrespective of material is taken from copyright protected or from the open source. Copyright breach is a violating the rights of a copyright holder, whose material is restricted by copyright and is used without his/her legal consent. Thus, plagiarism is considered a moral offense against the plagiarist's audience (for example, a reader, listener, or teacher).

2. In Academics

Within academics, plagiarism by students, professors, or researchers is considered academic fraudulence or academic dishonesty, and wrongdoers are subject to academic disapproval, including expulsion. Some institutions use plagiarism detection software to expose potential plagiarism and to deter students from plagiarizing. However, plagiarism detection software does not provide exact outcomes and there are loopholes in these systems. Some universities take this issue of academic integrity by providing students with detailed orientations, required writing courses, and clearly articulated honor codes. Indeed, there is a virtually uniform understanding among college students that plagiarism is wrong. Nevertheless, each year students are brought before their institutions' disciplinary boards on charges that they have misused sources in their schoolwork. However, the practice of plagiarizing by use of sufficient word substitutions to elude detection software, known as rogeting, has rapidly evolved as students and unethical academics seek to stay ahead of detection software.

No universally adopted definition of academic plagiarism exists; however, this section provides several definitions to exemplify the most common characteristics of academic plagiarism.

According to Bela Gippacademic plagiarism encompasses: "The use of ideas, concepts, words, or structures without appropriately acknowledging the source to benefit in a setting where originality is expected."

The definition by B. Gipp is an abridged version of Teddi Fishman's definition of plagiarism, which proposed five elements characteristic of plagiarism. According to T. Fishman, plagiarism occurs when someone:

(i) Uses words, ideas, or work products
(ii) Attributable to another identifiable person or source
(iii) Without attributing the work to the source from which it was obtained
(iv) In a situation in which there is a legitimate expectation of original authorship
(v) Stanford defines plagiarism as the "use, without giving reasonable and appropriate credit to or acknowledging the author or source, of another person's original work, whether such work is made up of code, formulas, ideas, language, research, strategies, writing or other form."
(vi) Yale views plagiarism as the "...use of another's work, words, or ideas without attribution," which includes "...using a source's language without quoting, using information from a source without attribution, and paraphrasing a source in a form that stays too close to the original."
(vii) Princeton describes plagiarism as the "deliberate" use of "someone else's language, ideas, or other original (not common-knowledge) material without acknowledging its source."
(viii) Oxford College of Emory University characterizes plagiarism as the use of "a writer's ideas or phraseology without giving due credit. "Brown defines plagiarism as "... appropriating another person's ideas or words (spoken or written) without attributing those word or ideas to their true source."
(ix) The U.S. Naval Academy defines plagiarism as "the use of the words, information, insights, or ideas of another without crediting that person through proper citation."

Forms of Academic Plagiarism

Different classifications of academic plagiarism forms have been proposed. Many classifications follow a behavioral approach, i.e., they seek to classify the actions undertaken by plagiarists.

For example, a 2015 survey of teachers and professors by Turnitin, identified 10 main forms of plagiarism that students commit:

- Submitting someone's work as their own.
- Taking passages from their own previous work without adding citations (self-plagiarism).
- Re-writing someone's work without properly citing sources.
- Using quotations but not citing the source.
- Interweaving various sources together in the work without citing.
- Citing some, but not all, passages that should be cited.
- Melding together cited and uncited sections of the piece.
- Providing proper citations, but failing to change the structure and wording of the borrowed ideas enough (close paraphrasing).
- Inaccurately citing a source.
- Relying too heavily on other people's work, failing to bring original thought into the text.

3. Journalism

In journalism, plagiarism is considered a breach of journalistic ethics, and reporters caught plagiarizing typically face disciplinary measures ranging from suspension to termination of employment. Some individuals caught plagiarizing in academic or journalistic contexts claim that they plagiarized unintentionally, by failing to include quotations or give the appropriate citation. While plagiarism in scholarship and journalism has a centuries-old history, the development of the Internet, where articles appear as electronic text, has made the physical act of copying the work of others much easier.

Ways to Minimize Plagiarism

There are various ways by which plagiarism can be minimized. Some of the ways are given below

(i) Verbatim copying without proper citation
(ii) Syntax-preserving plagiarism
(iii) Synonym substitution
(iv) Technical disguise (e.g. using identically looking glyphs from another alphabet)
(v) Semantics-preserving plagiarism
(vi) Translation
(vii) Paraphrase
(viii) Idea-preserving plagiarism
(ix) Appropriation of ideas or concepts
(x) Reusing text structure
(xi) Ghostwriting
(xii) Collusion (typically among students)
(xiii) Contract cheating

Sanctions for Student Plagiarism

In the academic world, plagiarism by students is usually considered a very serious offense that can result in punishments such as a failing grade on the particular assignment, the entire course, or even being expelled from the institution. The seriousness with which academic institutions address student plagiarism may be tempered by a recognition that students may not fully understand what plagiarism is.

A 2015 study showed that students who were new to university study did not have a good understanding of even the basic requirements of how to attribute sources in written academic work, yet students were very confident that they understood what referencing and plagiarism are. The same students also had a lenient view of how plagiarism should be penalized.

For cases of repeated plagiarism, or for cases in which a student commits severe plagiarism (e.g., purchasing an assignment), suspension or expulsion may occur. There has been historic concern about inconsistencies in penalties administered for university student plagiarism, and a plagiarism tariff was devised in 2008 for UK higher education institutions in an attempt to encourage some standardization of approaches.

Codes of Ethics

Some academic journals have codes of ethics that specifically refer to self-plagiarism. For example, the *Journal of International Business Studies*. Some professional organizations like the Association for Computing Machinery (ACM) have created policies that deal specifically with self-plagiarism. Other organizations do not make specific reference to self-plagiarism such as the American Political Science Association (APSA).

The organization published a code of ethics that describes plagiarism as "...deliberate appropriation of the works of others represented as one's own." It does not make any reference to self-plagiarism. It does say that when a thesis or dissertation is published "in whole or in part", the author is "not ordinarily under an ethical obligation to acknowledge its origins." The American Society for Public Administration (ASPA) also published a code of ethics that says its members are committed to: "Ensure that others receive credit for their work and contributions," but it makes no reference to self-plagiarism.

Factors that Justify Reuse

Pamela Samuelson, in 1994, identified several factors she says excuse reuse of one's previously published work, that make it not self-plagiarism She relates each of these factors specifically to the ethical issue of self-plagiarism, as distinct from the legal issue of fair use of copyright, which she deals with separately. Among other factors that may excuse reuse of previously published material Samuelson lists the following:

- The previous work must be restated to lay the groundwork for a new contribution in the second work.
- Portions of the previous work must be repeated to deal with new evidence or arguments.
- The audience for each work is so different that publishing the same work in different places is necessary to get the message out.
- The author thinks they said it so well the first time that it makes no sense to say it differently a second time.

Samuelson states she has relied on the "different audience" rationale when attempting to bridge interdisciplinary communities. She refers to writing for different legal and technical communities, saying: "there are often paragraphs or sequences of paragraphs that can be bodily lifted from one article to the other. And, in truth, I lift them." She refers to her own practice of converting "a technical article into a law review article with relatively few changes—adding footnotes and one substantive section" for a different audience.

Samuelson describes misrepresentation as the basis of self-plagiarism. She also states "Although it seems not to have been raised in any of the self-plagiarism cases, copyrights law's fair use defense would likely provide a shield against many potential publisher claims of copyright infringement against authors who reused portions of their previous works."

Along with the rise in the cases of plagiarism, concept of checking and detecting plagiarism is continuously increasing. To detect plagiarism, there are many softwares are available along with many free online websites are available. Some of them are given below.

1. Dupli Checker

This is one of the most effective free plagiarism detection tools on the Internet. While it doesn't have a fancy interface, it certainly gets the job done well. It is free of charge and user-friendly in nature.

2. Copyleaks

This cloud-based authentication platform enables you to track how eLearning content is being used all around the Internet. It is basically used for education and business purposes.

3. PaperRater

A multi-purpose free plagiarism detection tool that is used in over 140 countries. It consists of three tools in one software—Proofreader & Grammar Check, Vocabulary Builder, Plagiarism Checker.

4. Plagiarisma

Basic and easy-to-use, multi-purpose plagiarism detection tool that is used by students, teachers, writers, as well as various members of the literary industry. It is used in 190+ countries. Copy and Paste or type your text in the appropriate field, provide a URL, or upload a file from your computer. Supported file types include: TXT, HTML, RTF, DOC, DOCX, XLS, XLSX, PDF, ODT, EPUB, FB2, PDB.

5. Turnitin

Turnitin is a multi purpose software which promote academic integrity, streamline grading and feedback, deter plagiarism, and improve student outcomes. It is used among 190+ countries specially in plagiarism detection.

6. URKUND

URKUND is an automatic text-recognition system made for detecting, preventing and handling plagiarism, regardless of language. We are passionate about helping schools, universities and organisations to encourage original writing and have done so for 20 years. Read about how Urkund works.

URKUND is a completely automated system against plagiarism (Anti-plagiarism software) and is being successfully used at universities and colleges all around the world. URKUND's system checks all documents against three central source areas:

(a) The Internet
(b) Published material such as Journals, Books, etc.
(c) Previously submitted student material (e.g. memoranda, case studies and examination

University Grant Commission (UGC) has recommended that URKUND should be used as official Plagiarism detecting software in the universities. Universities which come under section 12(B)/2f of UGC Act and eligible for funding from UGC, will be getting the software free of cost from INFLIBNET Centre. According to a UGC notice, all universities in India got the final subscription to access the Swedish anti-plagiarism software 'URKUND' from September 1, 2019.

References

https://en.wikipedia.org/wiki/Plagiarism

https://www.prepostseo.com/plagiarism-checker

https://www.urkund.com/

NET Exam 2018

1. Creative common offers CCO (CC-Zero) for
   (a) Vendors (b) Publishers
   (c) Copyright holders (d) Users
2. According to S.R. Ranganathan, reference service provided using a chain of books, periodicals and materials is called as
   (a) Long Range Reference Service.
   (b) Short Range Reference Service.
   (c) Reach-me-down Service.
   (d) Information and referral Service.
3. Who was the first Librarian of the Imperial Library, India?
   (a) J.A. Chapman
   (b) John MacFarlane
   (c) Khan Bahadur M.A. Asadulla
   (b) Harinath De
4. Which of the following canon implies, according to Dr. S.R. Ranganathan that each class number should represent one and only subject or isolate idea?
   (a) Canon of Homonym
   (b) Canon of Mnemonics
   (c) Canon of Relativity
   (d) Canon of Hierarchy
5. Vidya Mitra, integrated e-content portal of INFLIBNET is a web-based portal consisting of all e-content developed under
   (a) ICSSR Data Service.
   (b) Swayam – Prabha.
   (c) Unnat Bharat Abhiyan.
   (d) NME-ICT.
6. In the context of user studies, a Librarian's study on "How well the human computer networks interaction works" can be categorized as
   (a) Physical approach
   (b) User-centred approach
   (c) Cognitive approach
   (d) Philosophical-analytical approach
7. On which of the following themes does "The Europa World of Learning 2017" contain introductory essays?
   (a) Accreditation
   (b) Academic freedom
   (c) The role of gender in access to and participation in higher education.
   (d) The role of higher education in national development.
8. Identify from the following which publication is not excluded from Indian National Bibliography
   (a) Maps
   (b) First issue of a new periodical.
   (c) Musical scores.
   (d) Ephemerals.
9. Decimal number '100' is represented in binary as
   (a) 01100100 (b) 00100111
   (c) 11101100 (d) 01010011
10. A set of best practices for publishing and interlinking structured data on the web is known
    (a) Web data (b) Distributed data
    (c) Linked data (d) Unmarked data
11. Copyright Office, Govt. of India functions under the Ministry of
    (a) Law and Justice
    (b) Culture
    (c) Information and Broadcasting
    (d) Commerce and Industry
12. In spiral of scientific method, the 'Hooke's Law' is an example
    (a) Empirical phase
    (b) Deductive phrase
    (c) Verification phrase
    (d) Hypothesizing phrase
13. Who said "Management is the art of getting things done through people"?

(a) Lillian Gilbreth (b) Mary Parker Follett.
(c) Henry Mintzberg (d) F.W. Taylor.

14. Who developed information literacy logo?
(a) IFLA/UNESCO (b) LC/OCLC
(c) IFLA/ALA (d) ALA/ACRL

15. Which of the following models of communication is also ABX model of communication?
(a) George Gerbner's model of communication
(b) The odore M. MacLean's model of communication
(c) Westley and MacLean's model of communication
(d) Wilbur Schramm and Osgood model of communication

16. In which year did IFLA launch 'International Advocacy Programme' (IAP)?
(a) 1996 (b) 2012 (c) 2016 (d) 2010

17. In PRECIS 'f' and 'g' in secondary operators represent
(a) Special classes of action
(b) Coordinate concepts
(c) Extra core concepts
(d) Core concepts

18. "Touch point" end-user discovery service is provided by
(a) OCLC (b) LC (c) SLA (d) ALA

19. UNIMARC is contribution of
(a) OCLC (b) UNESCO
(c) IFLA (d) LC

20. = 00 in UDC denotes
(a) Multilingual documents
(b) Untranslated documents
(c) Translated documents
(d) Artificial languages

21. Which of the following are the characteristics of Google's 'featured snippets' in search?
(1) Full text answer to a query.
(2) Quick direct answer to a query.
(3) Extracted from a web page.
(3) Displayed at the bottom of a search.
Codes:
(a) (1) and (2) are correct.
(b) (2) and (3) are correct.
(c) (2) and (4) are correct.
(d) (1) and (4) are correct.

22. Identify the correct Sound File Formats.
(1) MOV (2) WAV (3) MID (4) MPG
Choose the correct answer from the code given below:
Codes:
(a) (2) and(3) are correct.
(b) (1) and (2) are correct.
(c) (3) and (4) are correct.
(d) (1), (2) and (3) are correct.

23. Identify the independent variables in the statement "Will students who are taught by a team of three teachers learn more science than students taught by one individual teacher"
(i) One teacher. (ii) Learn more science.
(iii) Taught. (iv) Three teachers.
Choose the correct answer from the code given below:
Codes:
(a) (i) and (iii) are correct.
(b) (i) and (iv) are correct.
(c) (i) and (ii) are correct.
(d) (ii) and (iii) are correct.

24. Identify from the following the correct salient traits of "Invisible College"
(i) It is based on Francis Bacon's principle that "Knowledge is power".
(ii) It aims to acquire knowledge through experimental investigation.
(iii) It is not to be seen as a precursor to the Royal Society, UK.
(iv) It is a club of intellectuals with less than 14 core members.
Codes:
(a) (iii) and (iv) are correct.
(b) (ii) and (iii) are correct.
(c) (ii) and (iv) are correct.
(d) (i) and (ii) are correct.

25. Empty Digit means a digit
(i) With ordinal value.
(ii) Without semantic value.
(iii) Without ordinal value.
(iv) With semantic value.
Codes:
(a) (i) and (ii) are correct.
(b) (ii) and (iii) are correct.
(c) (iii) and (iv) are correct.
(d) (i) and (iii) are correct.

26. Identify the correct features of the Classification Research London (CRG) from the

(i) CRG was one of the most significant contributors to sociological research and theory.
(ii) The theoretical work of the group involved in the study of facet analysis, relational operators and theory of integrative levels.
(iii) It is the basis of the dynamics theory of Ranganathan.
(iv) CRG was interested in first piecing together individual elements and then determining the areas of knowledge they form.

Choose the correct answer from the code given below:

Codes:
(a) (ii) and (iv) are correct.
(b) (i) and (ii) are correct.
(c) (iii) and (iv) are correct.
(d) (i) and (iii) are correct.

27. Which of the following are Object-based-logical data models?
(i) Hierarchical model.
(ii) Network model.
(iii) Entity relationship model.
(iv) Functional model.

Choose the correct answer from the code given below:

Codes:
(a) (i) and (iv) are correct.
(b) (ii) and (iii) are correct.
(c) (i) and (iii) are correct.
(d) (iii) and (iv) are correct.

28. Which of the following are open access LIS journals from India?
(i) SRELS Journal of Information Management.
(ii) Annals of Library and Information Studies, NISCAIR.
(iii) Journal of Library and Information Science, DLIS, Delhi University.
(iv) DESIDOC Journal of Library and Information Technology.

Choose the correct answer from the code given below:

Codes:
(a) (i) and (iv) are correct.
(b) (ii) and (iii) are correct.
(c) (ii) and (iv) are correct.
(d) (i) and (ii) are correct.

29. Identify the correct objectives of an Enterprise Information System (EIS) from the following
(i) To increase employee productivity.
(ii) To advance the cost of IT and optimize the manual input of data.
(iii) To maximum duplication of company data and demote the work quality.
(iv) To ensure greater employee collaboration and efficiency.

Choose the correct answer from the code given below:

Codes:
(a) (ii) and (iv) are correct.
(b) (i) and (ii) are correct.
(c) (i) and (iv) are correct.
(d) (ii) and (iii) are correct.

30. Which among the following are the characteristics of 'informative abstracts'?
(i) Orientation to serve specific group.
(ii) Detailed information about content of the original.
(iii) May not need to consult the original.
(iv) Reviews the document.

Choose the correct answer from the code given below:

Codes:
(a) (i) and (iii) are correct.
(b) (ii) and (iii) are correct.
(c) (ii) and (iv) are correct.
(d) (iii) and (iv) are correct.

31. Which of the following documents on information literacy are developed by IFLA?
(i) Guidelines for information literacy assessment.
(ii) Information literacy guidelines and competencies for undergraduate.
(iii) Guidelines for information literacy for lifelong learning.
(iv) Framework for information literacy for higher education.

Choose the correct answer from the code given below:

Codes:
(a) (iii) and (iv) are correct.
(b) (i) and (ii) are correct.
(c) (ii) and (iii) are correct.
(d) (i) and (ii) are correct.

32. Identify the features of 'HTML'
(i) Ease of creating new references.
(ii) Users' interactivity.
(iii) Ease of tracing references.

(iv) Ease of customizing documents.

Choose the correct answer from the code given below:

Codes:

(a) (i), (ii) and (iv) are correct.
(b) (ii), (iii) and (iv) are correct.
(c) (i), (iii) and (iv) are correct.
(d) (i), (ii) and (iii) are correct.

33. Which of the following entities have been introduced by Functional Requirements for Subject Authority Records (FRASAR) working group?

(i) Strings (ii) Nomen
(iii) Thema (iv) Integers

Choose the correct answer from the code given below:

Codes:

(a) (i) and (ii) are correct.
(b) (i) and (iii) are correct.
(c) (iii) and (iv) are correct.
(d) (ii) and (iii) are correct.

34. Which of the following are free and open source Content Management Systems?

(i) Text pattern (ii) Concrete 5
(iii) Content verse (iv) Kentico

Choose the correct answer from the code given below:

Codes:

(a) (ii) and (iv) are correct.
(b) (i) and (ii) are correct.
(c) (i) and (iii) are correct.
(d) (ii) and (iii) are correct.

35. Which of the following are the different types of longitudinal study?

(i) Cohort study (ii) Correlational study
(iii) Panel study (iv) Trend study

Choose the correct answer from the code given below:

Codes:

(a) (ii), (iii) and (iv) are correct.
(b) (i), (iii) and (iv) are correct.
(c) (i), (ii) and (iv) are correct.
(d) (i), (ii) and (iii) are correct.

36. Which of the following are considered as standard channels of scholarly communication?

(i) Handbooks (ii) Wikis
(iii) Working papers (iv) Research report

Choose the correct answer from the code given below:

Codes:

(a) (ii) and (iv) are correct.
(b) (i) and (iii) are correct.
(c) (i) and (iv) are correct.
(d) (iii) and (iv) are correct.

37. Which of the following statements are true to define cost-benefit analysis?

(i) Evaluation of alternatives in relation to their costs.
(ii) Maintaining in the present performance level while reducing the costs of operating the system.
(iii) Holding operating costs constant while raising the average performance level.
(iv) Rank variant alternatives appropriate to a given set of objectives.

Choose the correct answer from the code given below:

Codes:

(a) (i) and (iii) are correct.
(b) (i) and (iv) are correct.
(c) (ii) and (iii) are correct.
(d) (iii) and (iv) are correct.

38. Which of the following can be categorised as administrative roles of an LIS professional?

(i) Knowledge organizer.
(ii) Resource allocator.
(iii) Disseminator of information.
(iv) Subscription negotiator.

Choose the correct answer from the code given below:

Codes:

(a) (i) and (iii) are correct.
(b) (i) and (iv) are correct.
(c) (ii) and (iv) are correct.
(d) (ii) and (iii) are correct.

39. Chi-square test is used by researchers to test which of the following?

(i) Judging the significance of several measures.
(ii) Test the significance of population variation.
(iii) Test the significance of the difference amongst more than two sample mean at the same time.
(iv) Test the significance of association between two attributes.

Choose the correct answer from the code given below:

Codes:

(a) (i) and (ii) are correct.
(b) (ii) and (iv) are correct.
(c) (ii) and (iii) are correct.
(d) (iii) and (iv) are correct.

40. Which of the following are sample errors?
(i) Framing errors (ii) Process errors.
(iii) Response errors (iv) Tabulation errors.
Choose the correct answer from the code given below:
Codes:
(a) (i) and (ii) are correct.
(b) (ii) and (iv) are correct.
(c) (i) and (iii) are correct.
(d) (iii) and (iv) are correct.

41. Match the following reference questions with corresponding service:
List I
(1) In which country was acupuncture originated?
(2) What measures are taken by the Government of India for control of Malaria in the last decade?
(3) How will you find out 'Ignited Minds' by A.P.J Abdul Kalam in the library?
(4) Asking of a list of newly added books to the library
List II
(i) Current awareness service.
(ii) Long Range reference service.
(iii) Ready reference service.
(iv) User orientation.
Codes:
(a) (1)- (iii) (2) - (i) (3) - (ii) (4) - (iv)
(b) (1)- (ii) (2)- (iii) (3)- (i) (4)- (iv)
(c) (1)- (iii) (2)-(ii) (3)- (iv) (4)- (i)
(d) (1)- (iv) (2)-(iii) (3)- (ii) (4)- (i)

42. Match the following characteristics with their notation as they appear in Table 1 K (Common auxiliaries of general characteristics) in UDC, standard edition.
List I
(1) 02 (2) 03 (3) 04 (4) 05
List II
(i) Common auxiliaries of Materials
(ii) Common auxiliaries of Persons and Personal Characteristics
(iii) Common auxiliaries of Properties
(iv) Common auxiliaries of Relations, Processes and Operations
Codes:
(a) (1)-(i) (2)-(ii) (3)-(iii) (4)-(iv)
(b) (1)-(iv) (2)-(iii) (3)-(i) (4)-(ii)
(c) (1)-(ii) (2)-(iii) (3)–(i) (4)-(iv)
(d) (1)-(iii) (2)-(i) (3)-(iv) (4)-(ii)

43. Match the following numerical values, used as collection indicators, with their respective depth levels as defined in the IFLA Guidelines on Acquisition and Collection Development.
List I
(1) 0 (2) 1 (3) 3 (4) 5
List II
(i) Comprehensive level
(ii) Study or Instructional Support Level
(iii) Minimal Information Level
(iv) Out of Scope
Codes:
(a) (1)-(ii) (2)-(iv) (3)-(iii) (4)-(i)
(b) (1)-(i) (2)-(ii) (3)-(iii) (4)-(iv)
(c) (1)-(iii) (2)-(ii) (3)-(i) (4)-(iv)
(d) (1)-(iv) (2)-(iii) (3)-(ii) (4)-(i)

44. Match the following terms with their corresponding explanations.
List I
(1) Compound Subject (2) Complex Subject
(3) Micro Subject (4) Spot Subject
List II
(i) Subject of small extension and great intension
(ii) A subject with a basic subject and one or more isolate ideas as component subjects
(iii) Subject of very tiny extension and enormous intension
(iv) Subject formed by coupling two or more subjects
Codes:
(a) (1)-(ii) (2)-(iv) (3)-(i) (4)-(iii)
(b) (1)-(i) (2)-(iii) (3)-(ii) (4)-(iv)
(c) (1)-(iii) (2)-(i) (3)-(iv) (4)-(ii)
(d) (1)-(iv) (2)-(i) (3)-(ii) (4)-iii)

45. Match the following memory measurement units with their corresponding equivalence.

List I	List II
(1) 1024 EB	(i) 1 BB
(2) 1024 ZB	(ii) 1 ZB
(3) 1024 YB	(iii) 1 GpB
(4) 1024 BB	(iv) 1 YB

Codes:

(a) (1)-(ii) (2)-(iv) (3)-(i) (4)-(iii)
(b) (1)-(i) (2)-(iii) (3)-(ii) (4)-(iv)
(c) (1)-(iii) (2)-(iv) (3)-(i) (4)-(ii)
(d) (1)-(ii) (2)-(i) (3)-(iii) (4)-(iv)

46. Match the following types of abstracts with their respective function.

List I

(1) Critical abstract (2) Indicative abstract
(3) Informative abstract (4) Slanted abstract

List II

(i) Oriented to serve a specific group
(ii) Comprehensive description of the document
(iii) Alerts the user with content of the document
(iv) Evaluates the document

Codes:

(a) (1)-(iii) (2)-(ii) (3)-(iv) (4)-(i)
(b) (1)-(iv) (2)-(iii) (3)-(ii) (4)-(i)
(c) (1)-(i) (2)-(iv) (3)-(iii) (4)-(ii)
(d) (1)-(ii) (2)-(iii) (3)-(i) (4)-(iv)

47. Match the following books with their authors.

List I

(1) Classification, Theoretical and Practical
(2) A Manual of Classification
(3) A Modern Outline of Library Classification
(4) Principles of Book Classification

List II

(i) E.W. Hulme (ii) J. Mills
(iii) E.C. Richardson (iv) W.C.B. Sayers

Codes:

(a) (1)-(ii) (2)-(i) (3)-(iv) (4)-(iii)
(b) (1)-(iv) (2)-(iii) (3)-(ii) (4)-(i)
(c) (1)-(i) (2)-(ii) (3)-(iii) (4)-(iv)
(d) (1)-(iii) (2)-(iv) (3)-(ii) (4)-(i)

48. Match the following types of management with corresponding library operational activity.

List I

(1) Total Quality Management
(2) Change Management
(3) Risk Management
(4) Participative Management

List II

(i) Taking measures for occupational health of library staff
(ii) Teamwork on digital library project
(iii) Analysis of user feedback operations
(iv) Introducing RFID for library circulation

Codes:

(a) (1)-(iii) (2)-(iv) (3)-(i) (4)-(ii)
(b) (1)-(ii) (2)-(iii) (3)-(i) (4)-(iv)
(c) (1)-(iv) (2)-(ii) (3)-(iii) (4)-(i)
(d) (1)-(i) (2)-(iii) (3)-(iv) (4)-(ii)

49. Match the following colour codes by JISC funded ROMEO project with their respective standardised approach to different rights.

List-I

(1) Blue (2) Gold (3) Green (4) Yellow

List-II

(i) Archiving of pre and post print
(ii) Can archive post-print
(iii) Can archive pre-print
(iv) Open access publishing

Codes:

(a) (1) (iv) (2) (iii) (3) (ii) (4) (i)
(b) (1) (ii) (2) (i) (3) (iv) (4) (iii)
(c) (1) (ii) (2) (iv) (3) (i) (4) (iii)
(d) (1) (i) (2) (ii) (3) (iii) (4) (iv)

50. Match the following ISO standard with their respective fields

List-I

(1) ISO 2146:2010 (2) ISO TR 11219:2012
(3) ISO11620:2014 (3) ISO16642:2017

List-II

(i) Computer applications in technology-terminology mark up frame work
(ii) Library performance indicator
(iii) Registry services for libraries and related organization
(iv) Qualitative conditions and basic statistics for library buildings

Codes:

(a) (1) (iii) (2) (i) (3) (iv) (4) (ii)
(b) (1) (i) (2) (ii) (3) (iii) (4) (iv)
(c) (1) (iv) (2) (ii) (3) (iii) (4) (i)
(d) (1) (iii) (2) (iv) (3) (ii) (4) (i)

51. Match the following quality assessment measures with corresponding explanation

List-I	List-II
1. Effectiveness	(i) Deriving best practices
2. Efficiency	(ii) Value provided
3. Benchmark	(iii) Desired result provided
4. Impact	(iv) Cost effectiveness

Codes:

(a) (1) (ii) (2) (i) (3) (iii) (4) (iv)
(b) (1) (iv) (2) (iii) (3) (ii) (4) (i)
(c) (1) (iii) (2)(iv) (3) (i) (4) (ii)
(d) (1) (ii) (2) (i) (3) (iv) (4) (ii)

52. Match the following management approaches with the person associated with it.

List-I	List-II
(1) Administrative	(i) Hugo Munsterberg
(2) Behavioural	(ii) Henry Fayol
(3) Quantitative	(iii) Peter Drucker
(4) Composite	(iv) Herbert A Simon

Codes:

(a) (1) (i)	(2) (iii)	(3) (ii)	(4) (iv)
(b) (1) (ii)	(2) (i)	(3) (iv)	(4) (iii)
(c) (1) (iii)	(2) (ii)	(3) (iv)	(4) (i)
(c) (1) (iv)	(2) (iii)	(3) (i)	(4) (ii)

54. Match the following awards with the association that instituted them

List-I

(1) Prof. Kula best librarian award
(2) Prof. Joginder Singh Ramdev Life time achievement award
(3) Librarian of the year award
(4) A.S. Raizada memorial young Information scientist award

List-II

(i) IATLIS (ii) IASLIC
(iii) SIS (iv) ILA

Codes:

(a) (1) (iv)	(2) (i)	(3) (ii)	(4) (iii)
(b) (1) (ii)	(2) (iii)	(3) (iv)	(4) (i)
(c) (1) (i)	(2) (iv)	(3) (iii)	(4) (ii)
(d) (1) (iii)	(2) (ii)	(3) (i)	(4) (iv)

54. Match the following in the context of a digital library

List-I

(1) Migration (2) Refreshing
(3) Emulation (4) Digital sustainability

List-II

(i) Replicating the functionally of an obsolete system
(ii) Transfer of data between two types of same storage system
(iii) Concerned with longevity of digital information
(iv) Transferring data two newer system

Codes:

(a) (1) (i)	(2) (iii)	(3) (ii)	(4) (iv)
(b) (1) (iii)	(2) (iv)	(3) (ii)	(4) (i)
(c) (1) (ii)	(2) (iii)	(3) (iv)	(4) (i)
(d) (1) (iv)	(2) (ii)	(3) (i)	(4) (iii)

55. Match the following motivation theories of management with their corresponding profounder

List-I

(1) Hierarchy of needs theory
(2) Motivation Hygiene theory
(3) Learned Need Theory
(4) Expectancy theory

List-II

(i) Victor Vroom (ii) David McClelland
(iii) Abraham Maslow (iv) Frederic Herzberg

Codes:

(a) 1.(iv)	2.(ii)	3.(iii)	4.(i)
(b) 1.(iii)	2.(i)	3.(iv)	4.(ii)
(c) 1.(iii)	2.(iv)	3.(ii)	4.(i)
(d) 1.(iii)	2.(ii)	3.(iv)	4.(i)

56. Match the following information literacy models with their developers

List-I	List-II
(1) Big 6 model	(i) Trvor Bond
(2) Eight WS Model	(ii) Mike Eisenberg and Bob Berkowitz
(3) PLUS Model	(iii) James Herring
(4) SAUCE Model	(iv) Annette Lamb

Codes:

(a) (1) (ii)	(2) (iii)	(3) (iv)	(4) (i)
(b) (1) (i)	(2) (ii)	(3) (iii)	(4) (iv)
(c) (1) (ii)	(2) (iv)	(3) (iii)	(4) (i)
(d) (1) (iii)	(2) (ii)	(3) (iv)	(4) (i)

57. Match the following types of knowledge Discovery in Database (KDD) with their respective activity

List-I

(1) Text mining (2) Web usage mining
(3) Web content mining (4) Web structure mining

List-II

(i) Aggregate related items
(ii) Structuring the input deriving patterns
(iii) Discovering hyper links for ranking
(iv) Discover patterns of visited page

Codes:

(a) (1) (i)	(2) (iii)	(3) (ii)	(4) (iv)
(b) (1) (iii)	(2) (ii)	(3) (iv)	(4) (i)
(c) (1) (iv)	(2) (i)	(3) (iii)	(4) (ii)
(d) (1) (ii)	(2) (iv)	(3) (i)	(4) (iii)

58. Match the following information phrase with their appropriate descriptions

List-I

(1) Information hunger
(2) Information appetite
(3) Information pollution
(4) Information poor

List-II

(i) Motivation or addiction to learning new Information

(ii) Excessive word count and details that make it harder for People to extract useful information

(iii) Less access to information and vulnerable to all kind of pressures

(iv) Eager to discuss and learn information in a group

Codes:

(a) (1) (i) (2) (iv) (3) (ii) (4) (iii)
(b) (1) (i) (2) (iii) (3) (ii) (4) (iv)
(c) (1) (iv) (2) (ii) (3) (i) (4) (iii)
(d) (1) (ii) (2) (i) (3) (iv) (4) (iii)

59. Match the following character position with their respective descriptions as given in MARC 21

List-I	List-II
(1) 00-04	(i) Record length
(2) 06	(ii) Type of record
(3) 07	(iii) Kind of Data
(4) 08	(iv) Type of control

Codes:

(a) (1) (iv) (2) (ii) (3) (i) (4) (iii)
(b) (1) (ii) (2) (i) (3) (iii) (4) (iv)
(c) (1) (i) (2) (ii) (3) (iii) (4) (iv)
(d) (1) (iii) (2) (ii) (3) (iv) (4) (i)

60. Match the following modes of information of subjective with their corresponding subject

List-I	List-II
(1) Lamination	(i) Management science
(2) Loose Assemblage	(ii) Astrophysics
(3) Distillation	(iii) Arteries of arms
(4) Fusion	(iv) Statistical analysis for railway manager

Codes:

(a) (1) (i) (2) (iii) (3) (iv) (4) (ii)
(b) (1) (ii) (2) (iv) (3) (i) (4) (iii)
(c) (1)(iii) (2) (iv) (3) (i) (4) (ii)
(d) (1) (iii) (2) (ii) (3) (iv) (4) (i)

51. Arrange the following steps of change process as mentioned by John Kotter

(i) Creating vision for change
(ii) Creating urgency
(iii) Removing obstacies
(iv) Forming a powerful coalition

Choose the correct answer from the code below

Codes:

(a) (ii) (iv) (i) (iii)
(b) (i) (ii) (iii) (iv)
(c) (ii) (iii) (iv) (i)
(d) (i) (iii) (ii) (iv)

62. Arrange the following library automation software according to the year of their first

(i) e-Granthalaya (ii) New Genlib
(iii) Soul (iv) Koha

Codes:

(a) (iii) (i) (ii) (iv)
(b) (i) (ii) (iii) (iv)
(c) (ii) (iii) (i) (iv)
(d) (ii) (i) (iv) (iii)

63. Arrange the following steps of procedure for classifying a simple book as mentioned in CC

(i) Title in Kernel terms
(ii) Expressive title
(iii) Title in Facet Numbers
(iv) title in standard terms

Codes:

(a) (i) (ii) (iii) (iv)
(b) (ii) (iv) (i) (iii)
(c) (ii) (i) (iv) (iii)
(d) (i) (ii) (iv) (iii)

64. Arrange the following terms letter by letter

(i) Lead Compounds (ii) Leadership
(iii) Leading edges (iv) Lead oxide

Codes:

(a) (i) (iii) (iv) (ii)
(b) (i) (ii) (iii) (iv)
(c) (i) (iv) (iii) (ii)
(d) (ii) (i) (iv) (iii)

65. Arrange the following steps in ascending orders of the year of enactment of their respective public library

(i) Manipur (ii) Lakshadweep
(iii) Karnataka (iv) Arunachal Pradesh

Codes:

(a) (iii) (i) (ii) (iv)
(b) (ii) (iv) (iii) (i)
(c) (iv) (i) (ii) (iii)
(d) (i) (ii) (iii) (iv)

66. Arrange the following pillars of SCONUL Seven pillars of Information Literacy Models

(i) Plan (ii) Manage
(iii) Gather (iv) Scope

Codes:

(a) (iv)	(i)	(iii)	(ii)
(b) (iii)	(iv)	(i)	(ii)
(c) (iv)	(iii)	(i)	(ii)
(d) (i)	(iv)	(ii)	(iii)

67. Arrange the following book authored by S.R. Ranganathan in order of the year of first publication
   (i) Headings and Canons
   (ii) Elements of Library classification
   (iii) Prolegomena to Library Classification
   (iv) Philosophy of library classification

Codes:

(a) (iii)	(i)	(ii)	(iv)
(b) (ii)	(iii)	(i)	(iv)
(c) (iii)	(ii)	(iv)	(i)
(d) (iv)	(iii)	(i)	(ii)

68. Arrange the following associations according to ascending order of their year of establishment.
   (i) ILA (ii) ALA (iii) CILIP (iv) IFLA

Codes:

(a) (i)	(iii)	(iv)	(ii)
(b) (iv)	(i)	(ii)	(iii)
(c) (ii)	(iii)	(i)	(iv)
(d) (ii)	(iv)	(i)	(iii)

69. Arrange the following libraries according to their year of establishment
   (i) Bibliotheque Publique (Pondicherry (New Roma in Rolland Library
   (ii) Connemara Public Library, Madras
   (iii) Asafia Public Library, Hyderabad (New State Central Library, Hyderabad
   (iv) Public Livraria, Panaji, Goa (New Krishnadas Shama Central Library)

Codes:

(a) (iii)	(ii)	(iv)	(i)
(b) (iv)	(iii)	(i)	(ii)
(c) (i)	(iv)	(iii)	(ii)
(d) (i)	(ii)	(iii)	(iv)

70. Arrange the following components in the order of their significance as stated by E.J. Coats
   (i) Material (ii) Part
   (iii) Action (iv) Thing

   Choose the correct answer from the code given bellow

Codes:

(a) (iv)	(ii)	(i)	(iii)
(b) (ii)	(i)	(iii)	(iv)
(c) (i)	(iii)	(iv)	(ii)
(d) (iii)	(ii)	(iv)	(i)

71. Arrange the following metadata standards in order of their year of development
   (i) Resource Description and Access
   (ii) Resource Description and Framework
   (iii) Metadata Object Description Scheme
   (iv) Text Encoding Initiative

   Choose the correct answer from the code given bellow

Codes:

(a) (ii)	(iv)	(i)	(iii)
(b) (iv)	(ii)	(iii)	(i)
(c) (iii)	(i)	(iv)	(ii)
(d) (ii)	(iii)	(i)	(iv)

72. Arrange the following important international events according to the date and month of their observation every year by UNESCO
   (i) World teacher's day
   (ii) International day for the universal access to Information
   (iii) International Literacy day
   (iv) World Book and Copyright Day

   Choose the correct answer from the code given below

Codes:

(a) (ii)	(iii)	(i)	(iv)
(b) (iv)	(i)	(ii)	(iii)
(c) (ii)	(i)	(iii)	(iv)
(d) (iv)	(iii)	(ii)	(i)

73. Arrange the following four stage of Carol Kuhlthau (1991) six stage model of information search process
   (i) Formulation (ii) Selection
   (iii) Collection (iv) Exploration

   Choose the correct answer from the code given below

Codes:

(a) (i)	(ii)	(iii)	(iv)
(b) (iii)	(ii)	(i)	(iv)
(c) (iv)	(iii)	(ii)	(i)
(d) (ii)	(iv)	(i)	(iii)

74. Arrange the following Indexing techniques according to their year of origin

(i) COMPASS (ii) SLIC
(iii) KWIC (iv) Systemic Indexing

Choose the correct answer from the code given bellow

Codes:

(a) (iv)	(iii)	(ii)	(i)
(b) (iv)	(ii)	(i)	(iii)
(c) (i)	(iii)	(iv)	(ii)
(d) (ii)	(i)	(iii)	(iv)

75. Arrange the following web mails according to the first year of launching
(i) Yahoo mail (ii) Hush mail
(iii) G mail (iv) Proton mail

Choose the correct answer from the code given bellow

Codes:

(a) (i)	(ii)	(iii)	(iv)
(b) (iii)	(i)	(iv)	(ii)
(c) (iv)	(iii)	(ii)	(i)
(d) (ii)	(iii)	(ii	(iv)

76. **Assertion (A):** Compound term in thesaurus are more exact and specific than single term used in combination to represent the same concept.

Reason (R): Compound term are able to prevent false drops and to ensure good precision. In the context of these two statements, which of the following is correct.

Codes:
(a) Both (A) and (R) are true
(b) Both (A) and (R) false
(c) (A) is true, but (R) is false
(d) (A) is false, but (R) is true

77. **Assertion (A):** The newly emerging libraries are being designed to become active agents of learning.

Reason (R): Participative new media tools and learning common are transforming the library physical and virtual spaces into collaborative work areas.

Codes:
(a) (A) is false but (R) is true
(b) Both (A) and (R) is true
(c) (Both (A) and (R) are false
(d) (A) is true but (R) is false

78. **Assertion (A):** Researchers in the behavioural science can describe variable in ration scale form.

Reason (R): Ration scale have an absolute or true zero measurement.

In the context of two statement which one of the following one is correct

Codes:
(a) (A) is false but (R) is true
(b) (A) is true but (R) is false
(c) (Both (A) and (R) are true
(d) both (A) and (R) false

79. **Assertion (A):** Patents provide incentives to individuals by recognizing their creativity

Reason (R): Patent provides patents owner with life time protection for their inventions

Codes:
(a) Both (A) and (R) are falls
(b) (A) is true, but (R) is false
(c) Both (A) and (R) are true
(d) (A) is false, but (R) is true

80. **Assertion (A):** The emergence of information economy, in an interdependent world played an insignificant role in the development of transborder dataflow.

Reason (R): Most of the data transmitted in transborder dataflow belong to business and finance using both publicly and privately available channels.

Codes:
(a) (Both (A) and (R) are falls
(b) (A) is false , but (R) is true
(c) Both (A) and (R) are true
(d)(A) is true, but (R) is false

81. **Assertion (A):** In an information economic society much of the returns to information are distributive.

Reason (R): Private returns to information can often exceed social returns.

In the context of these two statements which one of the following is correct?
(a) Both (A) and (R) are true
(b) (A) is true , but (R) is false
(c) (A) is false but (R) is true
(d) (Both (A) and (R) are false

82. **Assertion (A):** Employers of library and information personnel remain responsible for providing staff development programme and support for continuing education.

Reason (R): Professional and continuing education of the librarian is indispensable to ensure adequate services.

In the context these two statements which one of the following is correct?

Codes:

(a) Both (A) and (R) are false
(b) (A) is false, but (R) is true
(c) (A) is true but (R) is false
(d) (Both (A) and (R) are true

83. **Assertion (A):** Users, more or less, have same access points and can broaden up or narrow down their search, both in OPAC and Card Catalogue.

Reason (R): In OPAC almost every single part of the bibliographic record is accessible through keyword searching which is traditional counterpart cannot.

In the context these two statements which one of the following is correct?

Codes:

(a) (A) is false but (R) is true
(b) Both (A) and (R) is false
(c) Both (A) and (R) are true
(d) (A) is true but (R) is false

84. **Assertion (A):** IFLA advocates for copyright reform at WIPO.

Reason (R): Outdated copyright laws prevent libraries from performing their basic functions.

In the context these two statements which one of the following is correct?

Codes:

(a) (A) is false but (R) is true
(b) Both (A) and (R) is false
(c) Both (A) and (R) are true
(d) (A) is true but (R) is false

85. **Assertion (A):** In Unicode, the character encoding reflect the way the coded character set is mapped to bytes for manipulation in a computer.

Reason (R): Unicode is a standard that defines all the characters needed for writing the majority of living languages in use on computer.

In the context these two statements which one of the following is correct?

Codes:

(a) (A) is false but (R) is true
(b) Both (A) and (R) is false
(c) (A) is true but (R) is false
(d) Both (A) and (R) are true

86. **Assertion (A):** e-Shodhsindhu develop a formidable collection of e-journals, e-journals archives and e-books on perpetual access basis.

Reason (R): Perpetual access facilities the participating university libraries to access all journals right from their first issue.

In the context these two statements which one of the following is correct?

Codes:

(a) (A) is false but (R) is true
(b) (A) is true but (R) is false
(c) Both (A) and (R) are true
(d) Both (A) and (R) is false

87. **Assertion (A):** All LIS journals published in India are rigorously peer reviewed.

Reason (R): Peer reviewing is seen as a key quality control mechanism for reputed journal to keep it amongst the best in subject field.

In the context these two statements which one of the following is correct?

Codes:

(a) Both (A) and (R) is false
(b) (A) is false but (R) is true
(c) (A) is true but (R) is false
(d) Both (A) and (R) are true

88. **Assertion (A):** PRECIS was originally developed by the British National Bibliography replacing the chain indexing, to provide the subject index for UK/MARC record.

Reason (R): Chain index was not successful for production of subject index by computer.

In the context these two statements which one of the following is correct?

Codes:

(a) (A) is false but (R) is true
(b) Both (A) and (R) are true
(c) (A) is true but (R) is false
(d) Both (A) and (R) is false

89. **Assertion (A):** Consider for example that "A" write down "7" on paper with small font size

and uses FAX machine to transfer the page to "B". "B"sees a distorted "7"and decodes as "9".

Reason (R): Disruptive functioning of FAX machine.

In the context these two statements which one of the following is correct?

Codes:

(a) (A) is true but (R) is false
(b) Both (A) and (R) are true
(c) Both (A) and (R) is false
(d) (A) is false but (R) is true

90. **Assertion (A):** Resource Description and Access (RDA) lacks potential to revolutionize library catalogue in spite of its expansive element sets and vocabularies.

Reason (R): RDA is primarily designed as a content standard.

In the context these two statements which one of the following is correct?

Codes:

(a) (A) is true but (R) is false
(b) Both (A) and (R) are true
(c) Both (A) and (R) is false
(d) (A) is false but (R) is true

91. **Assertion (A):** All the main classes enumerated in Colon Classification, Ed. 6 are coordinate.

Reason (R): CC has secured the mutual exclusiveness of the classes by avoiding the overlapping of subdivisions.

In the context these two statements which one of the following is correct?

Codes:

(a) (A) is true but (R) is false
(b) Both (A) and (R) are true
(c) (A) is false but (R) is true
(d) Both (A) and (R) is false

92. **Assertion (A):** Social tagging technique used in some libraries allows students to tag books and other information resources with their own search terms.

Reason (R): Introducing social tagging methods to the traditional library settings usually helps to improve patron use of library and acquire knowledge.

In the context these two statements which one of the following is correct?

Codes:

(a) (A) is false but (R) is true
(b) (A) is true but (R) is false
(c) Both (A) and (R) are false
(d) Both (A) and (R) is true

93. **Assertion (A):** The entry element in Leading Section has the potency to decide the position of any entry among the various entries in a catalogue.

Reason (R): The potency entries sorted letter by letter or digit by digit goes on increasing rightwards and upwards.

In the context these two statements which one of the following is correct?

Codes:

(a) Both (A) and (R) are false
(b) (A) is true but (R) is false
(c) (A) is false but (R) is true
(d) Both (A) and (R) is true

94. **Assertion (A):** Infringement of copyright of digital materials is not a concern for rights owners.

Reason (R): The cost of copying electronic resources are trivial and the copies can be easily disseminated.

In the context these two statements which one of the following is correct?

Codes:

(a) Both (A) and (R) are false
(b) Both (A) and (R) are true
(c) (A) is false but (R) is true
(d) (A) is true but (R) is false

95. **Assertion (A):** In Colon Classification Ed. 6 Posteriorising Common Isolate "Profession (b)" is an Energy Common Isolate.

Reason (R): It is a manifestation of action.

In the context these two statements which one of the following is correct?

Codes:

(a) Both (A) and (R) are true
(b) (A) is false but (R) is true
(c) Both (A) and (R) are false
(d) (A) is true but (R) is false

Read the passage given below and answer the questions based on your understanding of the passage:

School lunches are a common topic when Japanese reminiscence about their school life. There is even a small museum in the Ministry of Education, Culture, Sports, Science and Technology in Japan (MEXT) where the typical school lunches of each generation are replicated. This exhibition receives favourable reviews from visitors, who make comments like, "It was great for conversation with my child", and "It brought back memories of those days". In Japan "eating from the same pot" signifies fellowship and bonds, and this phrase can be applied all around the country in the case of school lunches. This article looks into the school lunch service, which the Japanese hold so close to their hearts.

Modern school lunch services are widely defined as any sustenance given to children under school administration, but in Japan, it originated from local civilian effort to provide lunch for poor children at the end of the 19th century. Later on, before and during world wars, school lunches were recommended by the Ministry of Education (MOE) as a way of improving the physical health of school children. Starting from the more accessible major cities, school lunches were provided with the goal of reaching out to as many children as possible, but it was only after the establishment of the School Lunch Law, proclaimed and enacted in 1954 under reconstruction following World War II, that the Japanese school lunch program gained lawful authority and was provided nationwide.

The beginning of charity school lunch services in Japan can be traced in 1889, where lunches were provided by a Buddhist confederation for poverty-stricken children in an elementary school in Tsuruoka City, Yamagata Prefecture. The majority of school lunches in the *Meiji* (1868-1912) and *Taisho* (1912-1926) periods were limited to impoverished children and had the effect of encouraging them to attend school. Several examples were also seen in Akita, Shizuoka, Iwate and other prefectures, which were funded by school or district budgets as well as private donations. The meal usually consisted of a white-rice ball and miso (soya bean paste), with occasional pickled vegetables, or hot soups. In a documentary photo, recipient children can be seen eating in the corner of the school kitchen, while better- off classmates ate their packed home- made lunches in the classrooms.

96. Who was the first beneficiary to avail the charity school lunch service provided by Buddhist confederation for proverty-stricken children in Japan in 1889?
    (a) Higher Secondary students in Tsuruoka City, Yamagata Prefecture
    (b) Elementary School in Tsuruoka City, Yamagata Prefecture
    (c) Higher Secondary Schools in Meiji and Taisho
    (d) Upper Primary School in Akita, Shizuoka, Iwate
97. From where was the concept of 'modern school lunch' originated in Japan?
    (a) The efforts of the local civilians
    (b) MOE, Japan
    (c) Private School Management
    (d) Human Rights Organizations
98. What was the key goal of introducing school lunches by the MOE in Japan?
    (a) To control starvation
    (b) To worsen the physical health of school children
    (c) To reach out to as many children as possible
    (d) To improve the quality of primary education
99. What does the meal in school lunch usually contain?
    (a) Tempura, a Japanese fried snack
    (b) White-rice ball and miso with occasional picked vegetables, or hot soups
    (c) A ball of sushi and sashimi with vinegar mix (made with sugar and salt)
    (d) A ball of Ramen noodles served in a soy sauce or miso soup
100. What does the phrase, "eating from the same pot" signify in Japan?
    (a) Stretch to each other's heart
    (b) Fellowship and bonds
    (c) Fellowship and unfetter
    (d) Famishment

ANSWER SHEET

1. (c)	2. (a)	3. (b)	4. (b)	5. (b)	6. (b)	7. (c)	8. (c)	9. (a)
10. (c)	11. (a)	12. (d)	13. (d)	14. (a)	15. (c)	16. (d)	17. (a)	18. (b)
19. (d)	20. (c)	21. ((d)	22. (a)	23. (d)	24. (b)	25. (a)	26. (d)	27. (c)
28. (c)	29. (b)	30. (c)	31. (a)	32. (c)	33. (c)	34. (d)	35. (c)	36. (a)
37. (b)	38. (c)	39. (d)	40. (a)	41. (c)	42. (c)	43. (c)	44. (a)	45. (c)
46. (b)	47. (b)	48. (a)	49. (c)	50. (d)	51. (c)	52. (d)	53. (b)	54. (d)
55. (b)	56. (a)	57. (d)	58. (a)	59. (d)	60. (d)	61. (d)	62. (d)	63. (b)
64. (b)	65. (a)	66. (a)	67. (c)	68. (d)	69. (a)	70. (a)	71. (c)	72. (c)
73. (b)	74. (a)	75. (c)	76. (d)	77. (b)	78. (a)	79. (c)	80. (c)	81. (c)
82. (b)	83. (c)	84. (d)	85. (a)	86. (b)	87. (b)	88. (b)	89. (b)	90. (a)
91. (b)	92. (d)	93. (d)	94. (a)	95. (a)	96. (b)	97. (a)	98. (c)	99. (b)
100. (b)								

NET Exam June 2019

1. **Assertions (A):** E-Granthalaya is a freely available software.

   Reason (R): E-Granthalaya can be customized depending upon the requirement of libraries.

   In the context of the above two statements, which one of the following is true?

   (a) (A) is true but (R) is false
   (b) (A) is false but (R) is true
   (c) Both (A) and (R) are false
   (d) Both (A) and (R) are true

2. Which are the display elements of 'PRECIS'?

   (1) Qualifier (2) Call Number
   (3) Display (4) Lead

   Choose the correct answer from the following options given below:

   (a) (1), (2) and (3) (b) (1), (2) and (4)
   (c) (1), (3) and (4) (d) (2), (3) and (4)

3. Which of the following are included in the process of Big 6 Model of Information Problem of Solving Skills advocated by Carrie A. Lowe and Michael B. Eisenberg?

   (1) Task definition, information seeking strategies, location and address
   (2) Survey, feedback and compliance
   (3) Use of information, synthesis, evaluation
   (4) Analysing, prioritizing and reporting

   Choose the correct answer from the option given below

   (a) (1) and (2) are correct
   (b) (2) and (4) are correct
   (c) (1) and (3) are correct
   (d) (3) and (4) are correct

4. Which of the following components is NOT included in LAMP?

   (a) Linux (b) Apache
   (c) MySQL (d) Pearl

5. The rejection of a null hypothesis, when it is true, is known as

   (a) Hypothesis of difference
   (b) Hypothesis of association
   (c) Type-I error
   (d) Type-II error

6. Identify the persons NOT associated with the development of UDC:

   (1) S.R. Ranganathan (2) Paul Otlet
   (3) H.E. Bliss (4) Henry La Fontaine

   (a) (1) and (3) are correct
   (b) (1) and (2) are correct
   (c) (3) and (4) are correct
   (d) (2) and (4) are correct

7. Identify the key salient features of 'private library' from the following:

   (1) A library gives access to general public
   (2) A library belonging to an individual
   (3) A library not supported by taxation
   (4) A library having statuary support

   Choose the correct answer from the options given below:

   (a) (2) and (4) are correct
   (b) (1) and (2) are correct
   (c) (2) and (3) are correct
   (d) (1) and (3) are correct

8. Which of the following are the standard for the encoding records?

   (1) ONIX (2) SGML
   (3) W3C (4) MARC 21

   Choose the correct answer given below:

   (a) (1), (2) and (3) (b) (1), (2) and (4)
   (c) (2), (3) and (4) (d) (1), (3) and (4)

9. Which of the following tool search seamlessly across a wide range of local and remote content, provide relevance ranked result and has the ambitious goal of providing s single point entry into library collection

   (a) Web scale discovery
   (b) Web reference services
   (c) Union catalogue
   (d) Web opac

10. Who is the author of the book *The Third Wave*?
    (a) Daniel Bell (b) Alvin Toffler
    (c) W.R. Ashby (d) Robert T. Craig
11. Match the List-I with List-II
    List-I (Author)
    (A) George Kingsley Zifp
    (B) Samuel Clement Bradford
    (C) Alfred James Lotka
    (D) Theodore Besterman
    List-II (Works)
    (i) Documentation
    (ii) The Beginning of Systematic Bibliography
    (iii) Human Behaviour and Principle of Least Effort
    (iv) Element of Mathematical Biology

    Choose the correct option from those given below:
    (a) (1)-(iv), (2)-(i), (3)-(ii), (4)-(iv)
    (b) (1)-(iii), (2)-(i), (3)-(iv), (4)-(ii)
    (c) (1)-(i), (2)-(iii), (3)-(ii), (4)-(iv)
    (d) (1)-(ii), (2)-(iii), (3)-(iv), (4)-(i)
12. The function of a firewall is to
    (a) Filter the IP packet
    (b) Open part to all IP
    (c) Enable user privacy
    (d) Enable anonymous surfing
13. **Assertion (A):** Students are the among the most prolific users of Social Networking Sites (SNS).

    Reason (R): Social networking sites always help in fulfilling their academic information needs.
    (a) (A) is true but (R) is false
    (b) (A) is false but (R) is true
    (c) Both (A) and (R) are false
    (d) Both (A) and (R) are true
14. Match List-I with List-II:
    List-I
    (1) Web portal
    (2) Website
    (3) Vertical Web portal
    (4) Horizontal Web portal
    List-II
    (i) Personal login and single access point
    (ii) Enables users to see aggregated data from multiple applications
    (iii) No login required
    (iv) Focus on a specific application or business function enabling users to see, edit and contribute

    Choose the correct option from those given below:
    (a) (1)-(i); (2)-(iii); (3)-(iv); (4)-(ii)
    (b) (1)-(iii); (2)-(i); (3)-(iv); (4)-(ii)
    (c) (1)-(iv); (2)-(iii); (3)-(i); (4)-(ii)
    (d) (1)-(ii); (2)-(iii); (3)-(i); (4)-(iv)
15. Which of the following is a collaborative network of reference librarians?
    (a) Worldcat (b) INFLIBNET
    (c) QuestionPoint (d) Global Scholar
16. Match List-I with List-II:
    List-I (Formats of presenting information)
    (1) Electronic (2) Print
    (3) Face to face (4) Tele-conferencing
    List-II (Relevant naratives)
    (i) In-person meetings, personal discussions
    (ii) Telemeetings, technophobes, videographic meet
    (iii) Social media, e-mail, website banners, pay-per-click ads
    (iv) Brochures, fliers, ads, catalogues, reports, memos or letters

    Choose the correct option from those given below:
    (a) (1)-(iii); (2)-(iv); (3)-(i); (4)-(ii)
    (b) (1)-(iv); (2)-(iii); (3)-(i); (4)-(ii)
    (c) (1)-(ii); (2)-(iv); (3)-(i); (4)-(iii)
    (d) (1)-(i); (2)-(iv); (3)-(iii); (4)-(ii)
17. Which of the following consists of a series of rectangles drawn next to each other without any space between them, each representing the frequency of a category or subcategory?
    (a) Line diagram
    (b) Histogram
    (c) Pie chart
    (d) Cumulative frequency polygon
18. A customized website (often based on restrictions of domain articles) that immerses information from a wide array of sources in a consistent and unified manner is known as
    (a) a collection of interlinked web pages
    (b) online portal
    (c) web portal
    (d) website
19. LOCKSS has been initiated by

(a) MIT Libraries
(b) Stanford University
(c) University of Waikato
(d) Cambridge University

20. Which of the following States in North-East region have enacted library legislation?
(1) Mizoram (2) Manipur
(3) Nagaland (4) Assam
Choose the correct answer from the options given below:
(a) (1) and (2) (b) (2) and (3)
(c) (1) and (3) (d) (3) and (4)

21. Match List-I with List-II:
List-I (Class of IP)
(1) Class A IP (2) Class B IP
(3) Class C IP (4) Class D IP
List-II (Supporting coverage)
(i) Supports small networks with fewer than 256 devices
(ii) Reserved for multicast groups
(iii) Supports large networks with many devices
(iv) Supports medium-sized networks
Choose the correct option from those given below:
(a) (1)-(ii); (2)-(i); (3) (iv); (4)-(iii)
(b) (1)-(ii); (2)-(i); (3)-(iii); (4)-(iv)
(c) (1)-(iii); (2)-(iv); (3)-(ii); (4)-(i)
(d) (1)-(iii); (2)-(iv); (3)-(i); (4)-(ii)

22. Which Council has developed Leadership in Energy and Environmental Design (LEED) rating system?
(a) United States Green Building Council
(b) United Kingdom Green Building Council
(c) Canadian Green Building Council
(d) Indian Green Building Council

23. Identify the frequency of occurrence and the analysis of co-occurrence of descriptors assigned to journal articles:
(a) Co-word analysis (b) Word analysis
(c) h-index (d) g-index

24. In studying the relationship between smoking and cancer, if you assume that smoking is a cause of cancer and many factors affecting the relationship, such as number of cigarettes, the duration of smoking affect the extent of which smoking might cause cancer.
In the above example, the duration of smoking is which kind of variable?
(a) Intervening variable
(b) Extraneous variable
(c) Independent variable
(d) Dependent variable

25. According to UDC Scheme. (Abridged English 3rd Edition) symbol = in table of auxiliaries indicates.
(a) Common auxiliary's of language
(b) Common auxiliaries of place
(c) Common auxiliaries of time
(d) Common auxiliaries of point of view

26. Which of the following V's associated with Big Data is concerned with the integrity of data?
(a) Volume (b) Velocity
(c) Variety (d) Veracity

27. **Assertion (A):** All academic libraries provide their services on mobile platform.
Reason (R): Academic community demands more library services through mobile app.
In the context of the above two statements, which one of the following is true?
(a) Both (A) and (R) are true
(b) Both (A) and (R) are false
(c) (A) is false but (R) is true
(d) (A) is true but (R) is false

28. **Assertion (A):** "Big deal' is a licensed package of journals that costs less to the subscriber.
Reason (R): The package usually includes some less relevant titles.
In the context of the above two statements, which one of the following is true?
(a) (A) is true but (R) is false
(b) (A) is false but (R) is true
(c) Both (A) and (R) are true
(d) Both (A) and (R) are false

29. Who among the following coined the term Li-fi?
(a) F.W. Lancaster (b) Tim O'Relley
(c) Harold Hass (d) Mary Parker Follett

30. "Internet Governance Guide for Libraries" is a publication of
(a) ALA (b) IFLA
(c) UNESCO (d) OCLC

31. E-journal article can be identified with the help of
(a) Digital Open Identifier
(b) Journal Source Identifier
(c) Journal Article Identifier
(d) Digital Object Identifier

32. Which of the following are NOT the techniques of ranking scale?
(1) Paired comparison
(2) Open ended question
(3) Equal-appearing interval method
(4) Response analysis
Choose the correct answer from the options given below
(a) (2), (3) and (4) (b) (1), (2) and (3)
(c) (1), (3) and (4) (d) (1), (2) and (4)

33. 'A number in DDC without meaning in itself, but used to introduce examples of the topic' is known as
(a) class number (b) book number
(c) hook number (d) collection number

34. Multiplexing is used in
(a) Packet switching (b) Circuit switching
(c) Data switching (d) Protocol switching

35. NDL-India is developed and maintained by
(a) IIT, Guwahati (b) IIT, Chennai
(c) IIT, Roorkee (d) IIT, Kharagpur

36. "Diffusion of innovation" theory is proposed by
(a) Judy Smith (b) Eric Dezenhall
(c) Feter Drucker (d) Everett Rogers

37. Which is NOT the part of Maslow's hierarchy of need?
(a) Esteem need (b) Basic need
(c) Security need (d) Psycho-physical need

38. The easiest way to bring Internet video to one's desktop or download is known as
(a) flogging (b) podcasting
(c) vodcasting (d) blogging

39. Match List-I with List-II:
List-I
(1) Cost effectiveness (2) Cost-benefit analysis
(3) Cost analysis (4) Unit cost
List-II
(i) Cost of product/service rendered by organisation
(ii) Determined by dividing the allotted cost of subsystem by its actual number of operations
(iii) Relationship between the benefits of product service and cost providing it
(iv) Relationship between level of performance and the cost involved in achieving the level
Choose the correct option from those given below
(a) (1)-(iv); (2)-(iii); (3)-(i); (4)-(ii)
(b) (1)-(i); (2)-(ii); (3)-(iv); (4)-(iii)
(c) (1)-(ii); (2)-(iii); (3)-(iv); (4)-(i)
(d) (1)-(iii); (2)-(iv); (3)-(ii); (4)-(i)

40. 'Information Outlook' is a bi-monthly online magazine published by
(a) IFLA (b) ALA (c) SLA (d) CILIP

41. According to S.R. Ranganathan, if any conflict arises between the canons and/or principles, it is resolved by an appeal to
(a) The Theories (b) The Rules
(c) The Five Laws (d) The Postulates

42. HaaS is also known as
(a) SaaS (b) IaaS (c) PaaS (d) NaaS

43. **Assertion (A):** Non-participant observation technique is used as a primary data collection tool.
Reason (R): In non-participant observation technique, the researcher influences the subject of the study to get primary data.
In the context of the above two statements, which one of the following is true?
(a) (A) is true but (R) is false
(b) (A) is false but (R) is true
(c) Both (A) and (R) are false
(d) Both (A) and (R) are true

44. Which of the search engines is merged with ScienceDirect?
(a) CiteSeerX (b) AltaVista
(c) Dogpile (d) Scirus

45. Which of the following information-seeking behaviour model explains the activities, viz., starting, chaining, browsing, monitoring, etc.?
(a) Wilson's nested model
(b) Ellis's model

(c) Darvin's model
(d) Kuhlthau's model

46. The term 'Epigraph' means
(a) a motto or brief introduction prefixed to a book
(b) spine of a book
(c) essence of a subject
(d) a pamphlet

47. Match List-I with List-II:
List-I
(1) Yearbooks (2) Directory
(3) Almanac (4) Handbook
List-II
(i) Annual publication listing a set of events forthcoming in next year
(ii) Information about events of previous year
(iii) Contains instructions or advice about a particular subject
(iv) A list of facts that contains an alphabetical index of names and addresses of persons or organizations
Choose the correct option from those given below:
(a) (1)-(iv); (2)-(ii); (3-(iii); (4)-(i)
(b) (1)-(ii); (2)-(iv); (3)-(iii); (4)-(i)
(c) (1)-(i); (2)-(iv); (3-(iii); (4)-(ii)
(d) (1)-(ii); (2)-(iv); (3)-(i); (4)-(iii)

48. Match List-I with List-II:
List-I
(1) Independent variable
(2) Dependent variable
(3) Extraneous variable
(4) Intervening variable
List-II
(i) Change variable
(ii) Outcome/effect variable
(iii) Confounding variable
(iv) Affecting cause and effect relationship
Choose the correct option from those given below:
(a) (1)-(ii); (2)-(i); (3)-(iv); (4)-(iii)
(b) (1)-(i); (2)-(ii); (3)-(iv); (4)-(iii)
(c) (1)-(iii); (2)-(iv); (3)-(i); (4)-(ii)
(d) (1)-(iv); (2-(iii); (3)-(ii); (4)-(i)

49. Match List-I with List-II:
List-I (Awards)
(1) Best Retired Librarian Award
(2) S.M. Ganguli Award
(3) S.P. Narang Research Promotion Award
(4) Young Scientist Award
List-II (Library Associations in India)
(i) SIS (ii) IASLIC (iii) ILA (iv) IATLIS
Choose the correct option from those given below:
(a) (1)-(i); (2)-(iii); (3)-(iv); (4)-(ii)
(b) (1)-(iv); (2)-(ii); (3)-(iii); (4)-(i)
(c) (1)-(ii); (2)-(iii); (3)-(iv); (4)-(i)
(d) (1)-(iii); (2)-(ii); (3)-(iv); (4)-(i)

50. Who among the following have developed the initial version of SPSS?
(1) Norman Nie (2) C. Hadlai Hull
(3) Dale H. Bont (4) John Chambers
Choose the correct answer from the options given below:
(a) (2), (3) and (4) (b) (1), (2) and (3)
(c) (1), (2) and (4) (d) (1), (3) and (4)

51. In which year 'Webster's Third New International Dictionary of the English Language' was published?
(a) 1961 (b) 1965 (c) 1970 (d) 1971

52. Who propounded 'minimum, middling and maximum theories' in reference service?
(a) C.M. Winchell (b) James I. Wyer
(c) Samuel Rothstein (d) D.W. Lewis

53. "Law of Parsimony' belongs to the
(a) postulates (b) nomative principles
(c) rules (d) canons

54. Any act by a conservator that involves a direct interaction between the conservator and the cultural material is called
(a) archive conservation
(b) instrumentive conservation
(c) preventive conservation
(d) interventive conservation

55. In binary number system, digit '22' is represented by
(a) 10111 (b) 11000
(c) 00111 (d) 10110

56. Match List-I with List-II:
List-I
(1) FORSA (2) NKRC
(3) HELNET (4) CeRA
List-II
(i) Science and Technology
(ii) Medicinal Science

(iii) Agriculture
(iv) Astrophysics

Choose the correct option from those given below:

(a) (1)-(i); (2)-(iii); (3)-(iv); (4)-(ii)
(b) (1)-(ii); (2)-(i); (3)-(iii); (4)-(iv)
(c) (1)-(iv); (2)-(i); (3)-(ii); (4)-(iii)
(d) (1)-(iii); (2)-(ii); (3)-(iv); (4)-(i)

57. Arrange the following information systems in ascending order according to their year of establishment:

(1) INIS (2) AGRIS
(3) MEDLARS (4) INSPEC

Choose the correct answer from the options given below:

(a) (2), (1), (3), (4) (b) (4), (3), (1), (2)
(c) (1), (3), (4), (2) (d) (3), (4), (1), (2)

58. Who has developed 'Bibexcel'?

(a) Olle Persson (b) Chris Argyris
(c) Vroom (d) Frederick Herzberg

59. Match List-I with List-II:

List-I (e-depository)	List-II (Year of establishment)
(1) PMC	(i) 1999
(2) KB e-Depot	(ii) 2005
(3) Portico	(iii) 2000
(4) LOCKSS	(iv) 2003

Choose the correct option from those given below:

(a) (1)-(iii); (2)-(iv); (3)-(ii); (4)-(i)
(b) (1)-(iv); (2)-(ii); (3)-(i); (4)-(iii)
(c) (1)-(ii); (2)-(iii); (3-(iv); (4)-(i)
(d) (1)-(ii); (2)-(iv); (3)-(i); (4)-(iii)

60. Arrange the correct sequence of the sections of main entry in CCC (Ed. 5):

(1) Title section (2) Leading section
(3) Note section (4) Accession number

Choose the correct answer from the options given below:

(a) (2), (3), (4), (1) (b) (2), (1), (3), (4)
(c) (1), (2), (3), (4) (d) (1), (3), (2), (4)

61. i10-index was created by

(a) Scimago Journal and Country Rank
(b) Web of Science
(c) Scopus
(d) Google Scholar

62. Which of the following are the parts of MARC record structure?

(1) Check digit (2) Leader
(3) Directory (4) Record terminator

Choose the correct answer from the options given below:

(a) (1), (3) and (4) (b) (1), (2) and (4)
(c) (1), (2) and (3) (d) (2), (3) and (4)

63. ZOTERO is a

(a) Library management tool
(b) Statistical analysis tool
(c) Serials management tool
(d) Bibliographic reference management tool

64. In data transfer process, which of the following has multiple bridges between differ parts?

(a) Firewalls (b) Switching packets
(c) Hubs (d) Softwares

65. Choose the key characteristics of 'Augmented Reality' (AR) system in library settings as identified by Sharon Maria S., Esposo-Betan and Jonathan F. Santos in their studies

(1) Combines real and virtual
(2) Non-reciprocative and non-interactive application
(3) Registered 3D
(4) Interactive real time

Choose the correct answer from the options given below

(a) (1), (2) and (3) are correct
(b) (2), (3) and (4) are correct
(c) (1), (3) and (4) are correct
(d) (1), (2) and (4) are correct

66. Arrange the following library softwares in ascending order according to their year of launching:

(1) Php-MyLibrary (2) ABCD
(3) Koha (4) NewGenLib

Choose the correct answer from the options given below:

(a) (3), (1), (2), (4) (b) (3), (2), (1), (4)
(c) (3), (4), (1), (2) (d) (3), (1), (4), (2)

67. The protocol used to provide security to e-mails is known as

(a) POP (b) PGP
(c) SNMP (d) TCP

68. Which software is used by INFLIBNET Access Management Federation (INFED) for authenticating authorized users to access the resources?
(a) Koha (b) Php-MyLibrary
(c) Shibboleth (d) NewGenLib

69. Under RRRLF (Financial) Assistance Matching Scheme, assistance will be shared on matching basis between RRRLF and North Eastern States at the ratio
(a) 80 : 20 (b) 90 : 10
(c) 50 : 50 (d) 60 : 40

70. Arrange the following principles of management given by Henri Fayol in proper sequence
(1) Division of work
(2) Unity of command
(3) Discipline
(4) Authority and responsibility

Choose the correct answer from the options given below:
(a) (1), (3), (4), (2) (b) (1), (4), (3), (2)
(c) (2), (3), (4), (1) (d) (3), (4), (1), (2)

71. **Assertion (A):** Indian National Bibliography is not a comprehensive source of Indian publications.

Reason (R): National Library of India, Kolkata is entitled to receive one copy of each Indian publication under Delivery of Books Act.

In the context of the above two statements, which one of the following is true?
(a) (A) is true but (R) is false
(b) (A) is false but (R) is true
(c) Both (A) and (R) are true
(d) Both (A) and (R) are false

72. A design that seeks to control conditions within which persons are observed and analyzed is known as
(a) experimental design
(b) exploratory design
(c) survey design
(d) case study design

73. Who introduced the concept of Information Encountering (IE) into the Information Behaviour Literature in 1997?
(a) S. Erdelez (b) P. Vakkari
(c) R. Savolainen (d) B. Dervin

74. Delphi method is related to
(a) conservation method
(b) forecasting process based on panel of experts
(c) planning of disaster management
(d) method of recording bibliographic data

75. Which ISBN element identifies the particular publisher or imprint?
(a) Registrant element
(b) Publication element
(c) Registration group element
(d) Check digit

76. Which of the following are non-probability sampling techniques?
(a) Purposive (b) Convenience
(c) Snowball (d) Simple random

Choose the correct answer from the options given below:
(a) (1), (2) and (4) (b) (2), (3) and (4)
(c) (1), (3) and (4) (d) (1), (2) and (3)

77. Match List-I with List-II:

List-I
(1) Repeaters (2) Gateways
(3) Routers (4) Switches

List-II
(i) Allows similar networks to communicate
(ii) Allows data to be transferred within the network
(iii) Help in strengthening the signals
(iv) Allows dissimilar networks to communicate

Choose the correct option from those given below:
(a) (1)-(ii); (2)-(iii); (3)-(iv); (4) (i)
(b) (1)-(iv); (2) (iii); (3)-(ii); (4)-(i)
(c) (1)-(iii); (2)-(iv); (3)-(i); (4)-(ii)
(d) (1)-(iii); (2)-(i); (3)-(iv); (4)-(ii)

78. Arrange the following States in ascending order of the year of enactment of the respective Public Library Acts:
(1) Arunachal Pradesh (2) Uttar Pradesh
(3) Haryana (4) Orissa

Choose the correct answer from the options given below:
(a) (4), (3), (2), (1) (b) (3), (4), (2), (1)
(c) (2), (4), (3), (1) (d) (1), (3), (2), (4)

79. Arrange the following social networking tools according to their year of launching in ascending order:

(a) Twitter (b) Facebook
(c) LinkedIn (d) Pinterest

Choose the correct answer from the options given below:

(a) (2), (4), (1), (3) (b) (4), (2), (1), (3)
(c) (3), (2), (1), (4) (d) (1), (3), (2), (4)

80. In the formation of subjects, 'progressive decrease of extension and increase of intention of a basic subject' is known as
(a) lamination (b) denudation
(c) dissection (d) loose assemblage

81. Identify the characteristics of 'fugitive material' from the following:
(1) Material printed in limited quantities
(2) Material having perpetual value
(3) Usually of immediate interest at the time of publication
(4) Materials not related to any programme or processed publications

Choose the correct answer from the options given below:

(a) (1) and (3) (b) (1) and (2)
(c) (2) and (3) (d) (3) and (4)

82. Identify the penalty in case of plagiarism at Level 2 in Academic and Research Publications as per UGC (Promotion of Academic Integrity and Prevention of Plagiarism in Higher Education Institutions) Regulation, 2018:
(a) No penalty
(b) Shall be denied a right to one annual increment
(c) Shall be denied a right to two successive annual increments
(d) Shall be denied a right to three successive annual increments

83. The bit number as defined in IP Address in Internet Protocol Version 4 is
(a) 16 (b) 128 (c) 64 (d) 32

84. Which of the following are parts of 'SCONUL' Seven Pillars of Information Literacy Model?
(1) Gather (2) Scope
(3) Preserve (4) Present

Choose the correct answer from the options given below:

(a) (2), (3) and (4) (b) (1), (3) and (4)
(c) (1), (2) and (4) (d) (1), (2) and (3)

85. World Intellectual Property Organisation (WIPO) is an agency of
(a) ALA (b) IFLA
(c) UNESCO (d) United Nations

86. Arrange the following libraries according to their year of foundation:
(1) Khuda Bakhsh Library, Patna
(2) Raja Library, Rampur
(3) Delhi Public Library, Delhi
(4) National Library of India, Kolkata

Choose the correct answer from the options given below:

(a) (2), (1), (4), (3) (b) (1), (2), (3), (4)
(c) (3), (1), (2), (4) (d) (2), (3), (1), (4)

87. Identify the components of "WAMP' given below:
(1) Adobe (2) Web (3) MySQL (4) Pearl

Choose the correct answer from the options given below:

(a) (1) and (2) (b) (2) and (3)
(c) (3) and (4) (d) (1) and (4)

88. Arrange the following meta search engines in ascending order according to their year of launching
(1) SeerX (2) Skyscanner
(3) Kayak (4) Metacrawler

Choose the correct answer from the options given below:

(a) (4), (2), (3), (1) (b) (4), (1), (2), (3)
(c) (1), (2), (4), (3) (d) (1), (4), (3), (2)

89. Book Order Vigilance Pad (BOVP) was suggested by
(a) Paul Otlet (b) Michael Gorman
(c) Henry Fayol (d) Melvil Dewey

90. Which of the following Public Library Acts does NOT have the provision of Library Cess?
(1) Kerala (2) Karnataka
(3) West Bengal (4) Maharashtra

Choose the correct answer from the options given below:

(a) (3) and (4) (b) (2) and (4)
(c) (1) and (2) (d) (1) and (3)

Comprehension: Read the passage given below and answer the questions based on your understanding of the passage:

When you travel around the world, you see tremendous variation in the standard of living. The average income in a rich country, such as the United States, Japan, or Germany, is more than ten times the average income in a poor country, such as India, Indonesia, or Nigeria. These large differences in income are reflected in large differences in the quality of life. People in richer countries have better nutrition, safer housing, better healthcare, and longer life expectancy as well as more automobiles, more telephones, and more televisions. Even within a country, there are large changes in the standard of living over time. In the United States over the past century, average income as measured by real GDP (gross domestic product) per person has grown by about 2 percent per year. Although 2 percent might seem small, this rate of growth implies that average income doubles every 35 years. Because of this growth, most Americans enjoy much greater economic prosperity than did their parents, grandparents, and great grandparents.

Growth rates vary substantially from country to country. In recent history, some East Asian countries, such as Singapore, South Korea, and Taiwan, have experienced economic growth of about 7 percent per year, at this rate, average income doubles every 10 years. Over the past two decades, China has enjoyed an even higher rate of growth—about 12 percent per year, according to some estimates. A country experiencing such rapid growth can, in one generation, go from being among the poorest in the world to being among the richest. By contrast, in some nations in sub-Saharan Africa, average income has been stagnant for many years. Zimbabwe has had one of the worst growth experiences: From 1991 to 2011, income per person fell by a total of 38 percent.

What explains these diverse experiences? How can rich countries maintain their high standard of living? What policies should poor countries pursue to promote more rapid growth and join the developed world? These are among the most important questions in macroeconomics. As the Nobel-Prize-winning economist Robert Lucas put it, "The consequences for human welfare in questions like these are simply staggering: Once one starts to think about them, it is hard to think about anything else."

91. In USA, average income of a person is measured by
    (a) average GDP (b) real GDP
    (c) GNP (d) direct tax index
92. The country which enjoyed a higher rate of growth of 12% per year according to some estimates is
    (a) USA (b) Zimbabwe
    (c) Nigeria (d) China
93. The reason as to why Americans enjoy much greater economic prosperity than did their parents is
    (a) growth in average income
    (b) better nutrition and health care
    (c) growth in govt. jobs
    (d) growth in agriculture and its effective reform
94. The subject domain in which Robert Lucas has acclaimed recognition is
    (a) Chemistry (b) Nuclear Physics
    (c) Economics (d) Agriculture
95. The country which had experienced worst growth from 1991 to 2011 as income per person fell by a total of 38 percent during the above period is
    (a) Brazil (b) Zimbabwe
    (c) China (d) USA
96. What led the use of fire and smoke signals?
    (a) Large message over a short distance
    (b) An abridged message to war fighters
    (c) Short message over a large distance
    (d) Both short and large messages over a large distance
97. Who conducted a series of experiments on "Semaphore Telegraph"?
    (a) Marco Polo (b) Claude Shannon
    (c) Claude Chappe (d) William Francis
98. What is replaced by amplifiers and antennas in the present scenario?
    (a) Regenerative repeaters (b) Telegraph
    (c) Smoke signal (d) Lenses
99. Heliography was first used in
    (a) Ancient Greece (b) China
    (c) France (d) United States of America

100. What is heliography?
   (a) Using signal minor to reflect sunlight
   (b) Communication with a messenger on foot or on horseback
   (c) Semaphore telegraph
   (d) Maritime communication

ANSWER SHEET

1. (d)	2. (c)	3. (c)	4. (d)	5. (c)	6. (a)	7. (a)	8. (b)	9. (a)
10. (a)	11. (d)	12. (a)	13. (a)	14. (c)	15. (a)	16. (a)	17. (d)	18. (b)
19. (a)	20. (c)	21. (b)	22. (a)	23. (d)	24. (c)	25. (a)	26. (b)	27. (a)
28. (c)	29. (d)	30. (c)	31. (d)	32. (d)	33. (b)	34. (c)	35. (d)	36. (b)
37. (a)	38. (c)	39. (b)	40. (c)	41. (d)	42. (b)	43. (c)	44. (d)	45. (b)
46. (a)	47. (c)	48. (b)	49. (a)	50. (b)	51. (b)	52. (c)	53. (b)	54. (d)
55. (d)	56. (c)	57. (d)	58. (b)	59. (a)	60. (c)	61. (d)	62. (d)	63. (d)
64. (a)	65. (c)	66. (d)	67. (c)	68. (b)	69. (d)	70. (b)	71. (b)	72. (d)
73. (a)	74. (b)	75. (c)	76. (c)	77. (b)	78. (c)	79. (d)	80. (b)	81. (a)
82. (c)	83. (a)	84. (b)	85. (d)	86. (b)	87. (b)	88. (d)	89. (a)	90. (a)
91. (b)	92. (d)	93. (a)	94. (c)	95. (b)	96. (c)	97. (c)	98. (b)	99. (a)
100. (a)								

NET Exam December 2019

1. KB e-depot is maintained by
   (a) National Library of India
   (b) National Library of Netherlands
   (c) National Library of Germany
   (d) Library of Congress, USA
2. An attempt to make a computer resource unavailable to its intended user is called
   (a) Denial-of-service attack
   (b) Virus attack
   (c) Worm attack
   (d) Bot-net attack
3. Which of the following is an example of 'Information Padding'?
   (a) Inclusion of a source in the bibliography which is relevant to your work and duly consulted
   (b) Inclusion of a source in the bibliography though not consulted, but required for further reading
   (c) Adding of necessary words or information to a speech or piece of work making the same more shorter
   (d) Adding of gratuitous and impertinent words or information to a work or piece of writing or speech extraneously making the same more longer
4. Which of the following information seeking behaviour model explains the activities, viz. initiation, selection, exploration, formulation, collection and presentation?
   (a) Kuhlthau's Model (b) Ellis' Model
   (c) Willson's Model (d) Krikelas Model
5 Which of the following is an example of 'microblogging'?
   (a) Word press (b) Blogspot
   (c) Live journal (d) Twitter
6. Research in Progress' database developed by INFLIBNET is known as
   (a) Vidyanidhi (b) Shodhganga
   (c) Shodhgangotri (d) NDL
7. Identify the points related to Edward Deming's 14-points philosophy of TQM
   (i) Fair Wages
   (ii) Division of Labour
   (iii) Break Down Barriers
   (iv) Eliminate Exhortation
   Choose the correct answer from the following options:
   (a) (iii) and (iv) are correct
   (b) (i) and (ii) are correct
   (c) (i) and (iii) are correct
   (d) (ii) and (iv) are correct
8. Match the following:
   List - I
   (1) Barcode Technology
   (2) RFID Technology
   (3) QR code
   (4) Biometric Technology
   List - II
   (i) Ray Theories Ray tag
   (ii) Sir William Herschel
   (iii) Norman Joseph Woodland and Bernard Silver
   (iv) Denson Wave
   Choose the correct answer from the following options:
   (a) (1)-(ii), (2)-(iv), (3)-(i), (4)-(iii)
   (b) (1)-(iii), (2)-(i), (3)-(iv), (4)-(ii)
   (c) (1)-(iv), (2)-(iii), (3)-(i), (4)-(ii)
   (d) (1)-(iv), (2)-(i), (3)-(ii), (4)-(iii)
9. Ex-Libris is an example of which type of cloud computing?
   (a) Software as a service
   (b) Infrastructure as a service
   (c) Platform as a service
   (d) Network as a service
10. Which of the following technologies use electronic waves at radio frequency for data transmission?
   (a) Li-fi (b) Wi-fi
   (c) Optical cables (d) Twisted pairs
11. **Assertion (A):** Glossary is an alphabetical list of technical terms on a particular subject.
   Reason (R): There is no difference between discipline-specific terms and general terms.

In the context of these two statements, which one of the following is true?
(a) (A) is false, but (R) is true
(b) (A) is true, but (R) is false
(c) Both (A) and (R) are true
(d) Both (A) and (R) are false

12. **Assertion (A):** Web search engines get their information by crawling from site to site.
Reason (R): The "Spider" checks for the standard file name spider. Avi, addressed to it before sending certain information back to be indexed.
In the context of these two statements, which one of the following is true?
(a) (A) is true, but (R) is false
(b) (A) is false, but (R) is true
(c) Both (A) and (R) are false
(d) Both (A) and (R) are true

13. 'Altmetric' is not related to
(a) A record of bibliographic data on a subject
(b) A record of attention
(c) A measure of dissemination
(d) An indicator of influence and impact

14. Match the following:
List - I
(1) Fundamentals of Reference Service
(2) Introduction to Reference Works
(3) Reference Service
(4) Guide to Reference Books
List - II
(i) A.J. Walford
(ii) S.R. Ranganathan
(iii) F.N. Cheney and W.J. Williams
(iv) William A. Katz
Choose the correct answer from the following options:
(a) (1)-(ii), (2)-(i), (3)-(iv), (4)-(iii)
(b) (1)-(iii), (2)-(iv), (3)-(i), (4)-(ii)
(c) (1)-(iv), (2)-(ii), (3)-(iii), (4)-(i)
(d) (1)-(iii), (2)-(iv), (3)-(ii), (4)-(i)

15. Which Network protocol is involved in the execution of ping?
(a) TCP (b) ARP
(c) ICMP (d) BOOTP

16. INFOTERA is a global environmental information network of
(a) UNDP (b) UNISIST
(c) UNEP (d) OECD

17. Conservative, moderate and liberal theories of reference service are propounded by
(a) S.R. Ranganathan (b) James I. Wyer
(c) W.A. Katz (d) Krishan Kumar

18. Universal Bibliographic Control and International MARC (UBCIM) is a core activity of
(a) IFLA (b) UNESCO
(c) OCLC (d) ALA

19. Which of the following publications are excluded from the scope of Indian National Bibliography?
(i) Maps
(ii) Guide to textbooks
(iii) First issue of a new periodical
(iv) Musical scores
Choose the correct answer from the following options:
(a) (i), (ii) and (iii) are correct
(b) (i), (iii) and (iv) are correct
(c) (ii), (iii) and (iv) are correct
(d) (i), (ii) and (iv) are correct

20. Dublin Core Metadata Element set version 1.1 consists of
(a) Fifteen elements (b) Eighteen elements
(c) Twenty elements (d) Twenty-two elements

21. Which of the budget methods emphasizes on identification of program objectives and the measurement of results?
(a) ZBB (b) Line Budgeting
(c) Item budgeting (d) PPBS

22. Which of the following 'Change Management Model' has three stages namely, unfreezing, changing and refreezing?
(a) Mary Parker Follett's Model
(b) Kurt Lewin's Model
(c) Henry Mintzberg's Model
(d) Lillion Gilberth's Model

23. Bibframe 2.0 organises bibliographic information into three core levels of abstraction. Choose the correct answer from the options given below
(a) Work, Instance, Item
(b) Work, Item, Agents
(c) Work, Agents, Events
(d) Events, Instance, Subjects

24. Arrange the following phases of Six Sigma in their correct sequence

(i) Define (ii) Measure
(iii) Analyze (iv) Improve

Choose the correct answer from the following options:

(a) (i), (iii), (iv) and (ii)
(b) (i), (ii), (iii) and (iv)
(c) (iii), (i), (ii) and (iv)
(d) (iii), (iv), (i) and (ii)

25. "Haptics" is a form of non-verbal communication that uses
(a) Facial expression
(b) Touch-to-communicate
(c) Interpersonal space
(d) Interpretation of symbols

26. The g-index was proposed by
(a) Jorge Hirsch (b) Bill Smith
(c) Leo Egghe (d) Olle Persson

27. In universal decimal classification (Abridged English 3rd edition) symbol "..." indicates
(a) Relation sign
(b) Common auxiliaries of place
(c) Common auxiliaries of Race and Nationality
(d) Common auxiliaries of Time

28. Match the following types of questions with corresponding explanations:

List - I
(1) Ranking item questions
(2) Ambigous questions
(3) Dichotomous questions
(4) Structural questions

List - II
(i) When the language of questions is such that it may be interpreted in more than one way
(ii) When answer to a question has been preconceived and classified into possible groups
(iii) Questions are given to record the preference of the respondent
(iv) When reply to a question is given in form of one of the two alternatives

Choose the correct answer from the following options:

(a) (1)-(iii), (2)-(i), (3)-(iv), (4)-(ii)
(b) (1)-(ii), (2)-(iii), (3)-(iv), (4)-(i)
(c) (1)-(i), (2)-(ii), (3)-(iii), (4)-(iv)
(d) (1)-(iv), (2)-(ii), (3)-(i), (4)-(iii)

29. Which of the following are Web-Zine?
(i) E-mail Magazine
(ii) E-conference
(iii) On-line Bulletin
(iv) Electronic News Letter

Choose the correct answer from the following options:

(a) (i), (iii) and (iv) are correct
(b) (i), (ii) and (iii) are correct
(c) (ii), (iii) and (iv) are correct
(d) (i), (ii) and (iv) are correct

30. Annual publication, listing a set of events forthcoming in the next year is known as
(a) Almanac (b) Yearbook
(c) Directory (d) Handbook

31. What is the range for getting Gold level of certification under leadership in Energy and Environmental Design (LEED)?
(a) 40 - 49 (b) 50 - 59
(c) 60 -79 (d) 80 +

32. Arrange the following States in ascending order of the year of enactment of their respective public Library Acts
(i) Kerala (ii) Chhattisgarh
(iii) Goa (iv) Uttarakhand/Uttaranchal

Choose the correct answer from the following options:

(a) (i), (iii), (iv), (ii) (b) (ii), (iii), (i), iv)
(c) (iv), (i), (ii), (iii) (d) (iii), (iv), (i), (ii)

33. **Assertion (A):** As the level of Recall decreases, the precision increases.

Reason (R): Recall and Precision are not always inversely correlated.

In the context of these two statements, which one of the following is true?

(a) (A) is false, but (R) is true
(b) (A) is true, but (R) is false
(c) Both (A) and (R) are true
(d) Both (A) and (R) are false

34. Duraspace provides cloud-based services related to
(i) D-space (ii) NewGen Lib
(iii) E-Prints (iv) Fedora Commons

Choose the correct answer from the following options:

(a) (i) and (ii) are correct
(b) (ii) and (iii) are correct
(c) (iii) and (iv) are correct
(d) (i) and (iv) are correct

35. Which of the following consortium supports e-resources exclusively for health sciences?
(a) CeRA (b) HELINET
(c) FORSA (d) NKRC

36. 'Index Indiana' is
(a) An index to Indian language periodical literature
(b) An index to library science literature only
(c) An index to English Language literature
(d) An index to Reference material

37. The UK Committee on RDA (UKCOR) aims to:
(i) Represent the interests of LIS professional community of third world countries with regard to RDA
(ii) Contribute to the RDA development program and to the maintenance and governance of RDA
(iii) Ensure that representatives of the RDA European region are briefed on the position of the UK Community regarding all aspects of governance, development and maintenance of RDA
(iv) Support implementation and development of RDA in UK

Choose the correct answer from the following options:
(a) (i), (ii) and (iii) are correct
(b) (ii), (iii) and (iv) are correct
(c) (i), (iii) and (iv) are correct
(d) (i), (ii) and (iv) are correct

38. Arrange the following Library Associations according to ascending order of their year of establishment
(i) IFLA (ii) SLA
(iii) CILIP (iv) ALA

Choose the correct answer from the following options:
(a) (iv), (ii), (i), (iii) (b) (ii), (iv), (i), (iii)
(c) (iv), (i), (ii), (iii) (d) (iii), (ii), (iv), (i)

39. CANMARC and US-MARC are merged together with
(a) CCF (b) UNIMARÇ
(c) UK-MARC (d) MARC-21

40. According to S.R. Ranganatan "Wherever telescoping of array is done, the canon of Hierarchy is violated". This violation is deliberately done to satisfy
(a) Law of Parsimony
(b) Law of Local Variation
(c) Law of Symmetry
(d) Law of Interpretation

41. Patent information system is located at
(a) Kanpur (b) Lucknow
(c) Nagpur (d) Hyderabad

42. Which of the following steps are involved in the selection of documents for digitization?
(i) Checking for copyright
(ii) Checking the research significance of the document
(iii) Checking for price
(iv) Checking the condition of document

Choose the correct answer from the following options:
(a) (i), (ii) and (iii) are correct
(b) (i), (iii) and (iv) are correct
(c) (i), (ii) and (iv) are correct
(d) (ii), (iii) and (iv) are correct

43. **Assertion (A):** Big Data is a product of data being generated constantly, automatically, and rapidly.

Reason (R): Due to the omnipresence of personal computing devices and smart phones, individuals generate massive amount of data through e-commerce, e-communication, social media, online searches and GPS Navigation.

In the context of these two statements, which one of the following is true?
(a) (A) is true, but (R) is false
(b) (A) is false, but (R) is true
(c) Both (A) and (R) are true
(d) Both (A) and (R) are false

44. ISBD was created and is maintained by
(a) OCLC (b) UNESCO
(c) IFLA (d) Library of Congress

45. Which layer of the OSI Medel is mostly concerned with the syntax of the data?
(a) Session layer (b) Presentation layer
(c) Network layer (d) Data link layer

46. Who proposed 'General System Theory of Communication'?
(a) Robert T. Craig
(b) W.R. Ashby
(c) Shannon and Weaver
(d) Ludwig Von Bertalanffy

47. Physical arrangement of computers in a Network is called
(a) Topology (b) Routing
(c) Bandwidth (d) Switching

48. Which digital library software was developed at Cornell University?
(a) FEDORA (b) E-Prints
(c) GSDL (d) D-Space

49. Loss of signal power as light travel down the fibre is called
(a) Attenuation (b) Propagation
(c) Scattering (d) Interpretation

50. Who was the first Librarian of National Library of India after independence?
(a) K.M. Asadullah (b) D.R. Kalia
(c) B.S. Kesavan (d) Kalpana Dasgupta

51. Identify the committee charged with the responsibility for Indian standards related to libraries
(a) Z-39 (b) TC-46
(c) BIS-LIB (d) MSD-5

52. Match the following number of List - 1: Standard Subdivisions of Dewey Decimal Classification (19th Edition) with their correct terms:

List - I
(1) 0202 (2) 0142 (3) 06 (4) 071

List - II
(i) Organizations and management
(ii) Synopses
(iii) Schools and Courses
(iv) Etymology

Choose the correct answer from the following options:
(a) (1)-(iv), (2)-(iii), (3)-(ii), (4)-(i)
(b) (1)-(ii), (2)-(i), (3)-(iii), (4)-(iv)
(c) (1)-(ii), (2)-(iv), (3)-(i), (4)-(iii)
(d) (1)-(iii), (2)-(ii), (3)-(i), (4)-(iv)

53. Match the following:

List - I
(1) OCLC (2) INIS
(3) IFLA (4) MEDLARS

List - II
(i) The Hague, Netherlands
(ii) Washington DC, USA
(iii) Viena, Austria
(iv) Dublin, Ohio

Choose the correct answer from the following options:
(a) (1)-(iv), (2)-(iii), (3)-(i), (4)-(ii)
(b) (1)-(ii), (2)-(i), (3)-(iii), (4)-(iv)
(c) (1)-(iii), (2)-(ii), (3)-(iv), (4)-(i)
(d) (1)-(iii), (2)-(i), (3)-(ii), (4)-(iv)

54. Identify the electronic depository in which Librarians of the participating institutions have the right to put their words in managing the depository
(a) Portico (b) LOCKSS
(c) CLOCKSS (d) PubMed

55. Which of the following is a technique of non-probability sampling?
(a) Judgemental sampling
(b) Simple Random Sampling
(c) Stratified Random Sampling
(d) Cluster Sampling

56. **Assertion (A):** INFLIBNET provides electronic document delivery service to all types of libraries in India.

Reason (R): Due to inadequate ICT infrastructure, most of the libraries are not in a position to provide electronic document delivery service, to their clientele.

In the context of these two statements, which one of the following is true?
(a) Both (A) and (R) are true
(b) (A) is true, but (R) is false
(c) Both (A) and (R) are false
(d) (A) is false but (R) is true

57. Which are the factors responsible for deterioration of Library Materials?
(i) Biological Factor
(ii) Electromagnetic Factor
(iii) Chemical Factor
(iv) Environmental Factor

Choose the correct answer from the options given below:
(a) (i), (ii) and (iv) are correct
(b) (i), (iii) and (iv) are correct
(c) (ii), (iii) and (iv) are correct
(d) (i), (ii) and (iii) are correct

58. 'Indian Library Review' is a blog of
(a) IASLIC (b) NISCAIR
(c) INFLIBNET (d) National Library of India

59. Under RRRLF Financial Assistance Matching scheme, assistance is shared on matching

basis between RRRLF and developed States as per the given ratio
(a) 70 : 30 (b) 60 : 40
(c) 90 : 10 (d) 50 : 50

60. Which of the following routes is critical in CPM?
(a) Shortest route
(b) Longest route
(c) Routes having simple activities
(d) Routes having less important activity

61. Arrange the correct sequence of the following facets of Book Number according to Colon Classification (sixth reprint edition)
(i) Language Number (ii) Volume Number
(iii) Copy Number (iv) Form Number
Choose the correct answer from the following options:
(a) (i), (iv), (ii) and (iii)
(b) (i), (ii), (iii) and (iv)
(c) (iv), (i), (iii) and (ii)
(d) (i), (iii), (ii) and (iv)

62. Match the following:
List - I
(1) Judgemental Sampling
(2) Snowball Sampling
(3) Cluster Sampling
(4) Simple Random Sampling
List - II
(i) Based on ability of the researcher to divide the sampling population into groups
(ii) Selecting a sample using networks
(iii) Each element in the population is given on equal and independent chance of selection
(iv) Identification of person who can provide the best information
Choose the correct answer from the following options:
(a) (1)-(iv), (2)-(ii), (3)-(i), (4)-(iii)
(b) (1)-(iii), (2)-(iv), (3)-(ii), (4)-(i)
(c) (1)-(ii), (2)-(i), (3)-(iii), (4)-(iv)
(d) (1)-(i), (2)-(ii), (3)-(iv), (4)-(iii)

63. Who among the following are the editors of ALA Glossary of Library and Information Science Fourth Edition?
(i) Michael Levine-Clark
(ii) Philip Babcock Gove
(iii) Toni M. Carter
(iv) L.M. Harrod
Choose the correct answer from the following options:
(a) (i) and (ii) are correct
(b) (ii) and (iii) are correct
(c) (i) and (iii) are correct
(d) (i) and (iv) are correct

64. Identify the publication years of different editions of AACR
(i) 1967 (ii) 1970 (iii) 1978 (iv) 1988
Choose the correct answer from the following options:
(a) (i), (ii) and (iv) are correct
(b) (i), (ii) and (iii) are correct
(c) (ii), (iii) and (iv) are correct
(d) (i), (iii) and (iv) are correct

65. The concept of 'Information Encountering' (IE) was introduced in the domain information behaviour literature by Sanda Erdelez in 1997, where she proposed a conceptual framework for facilitating systematic study of IE. Identify the three key elements proposed by Erdelez in her study
(i) Characteristics of the information user
(ii) Characteristics of information seeking habit
(iii) Characteristics of information environment
(iv) Characteristics of encountered information
Choose the correct answer from the following options:
(a) (i), (ii) and (iv) are correct
(b) (ii), (iii) and (iv) are correct
(c) (i), (ii) and (iii) are correct
(d) (i), (iii) and (iv) are correct

66. Which of the following are not the publications of Ministry of Information and Broadcasting, Government of India?
(i) Economic and Political Weekly
(ii) University News
(iii) Yojana
(iv) Vigyan Pragati
Choose the correct answer from the following options:
(a) (i), (ii) and (iii) are correct
(b) (i), (iii) and (iv) are correct
(c) (i), (ii) and (iv) are correct
(d) (ii), (iii) and (iv) are correct

67. There is no significant difference in the proportion of male and female librarians in the study population is an example of

(a) Hypothesis of point prevalence
(b) Null-hypothesis
(c) Hypothesis of association
(d) Hypothesis of difference

68. Which of the following are the high-level classes or entities in the BIBFRAME model?
(i) Work (ii) Instance
(iii) Item (iv) Author
Choose the correct answer from the following options:
(a) (i), (ii) and (iii) are correct
(b) (i), (ii) and (iv) are correct
(c) (i), (iii) and (iv) are correct
(d) (ii), (iii) and (iv) are correct

69. What is 'Epilogue' in a thesis?
(a) First Chapter (b) Final Chapter
(c) Title Page (d) Appendix

70. Arrange the following information networks according to their year of launching
(i) NICNET (ii) NKN
(iii) INFLIBNET (iv) ERNET
Choose the correct answer from the following options:
(a) (ii), (iii), (i), (iv) (b) (i), (iv), (iii), (ii)
(c) (iii), (iv), (ii), (i) (d) (i), (iii), (ii), (iv)

71. Identify the former Librarians of National Library of India from the names given below
(i) D.N. Banerjee (ii) Kalpana Dasgupta
(iii) R.K. Dasgupta (iv) K.M. Asadullah
Choose the correct answer from the following options:
(a) (i) and (ii) are correct
(b) (ii) and (iv) are correct
(c) (i) and (iii) are correct
(d) (iii) and (iv) are correct

72. In data transfer process, which of the following is used for strengthening the signals
(a) Firewalls (b) Hubs
(c) Switching packets (d) Repeater

73. Arrange the following according to their increasing storage capacity
(i) Exabyte (ii) Zettabyte
(iii) Petabyte (iv) Yottabyte
Choose the correct answer from the following options:
(a) (iv), (ii), (i), (iii) (b) (iii), (i), (ii), (iv)
(c) (iii), (i), (iv), (ii) (d) iv), (iii), (i), (ii)

74. Match the following notation of second summary of DDC (19th Edition) with their correct terms:
List - I
(1) 110 (2) 120 (3) 160 (4) 170
List - II
(i) Ethics (Moral Philosophy)
(ii) Epistemology Causation, Human kind
(iii) Meta Physics
(iv) Logic
Choose the correct answer from the following options:
(a) (1)-(iv), (2)-(iii), (3)-(ii), (4)-(i)
(b) (1)-(iii), (2)-(ii), (3)-(i), (4)-(iv)
(c) (1)-(ii), (2)-(iii), (3)-(iv), (4)-(i)
(d) (1)-(iii), (2)-(ii), (3)-(iv), (4)-(i)

75. The method of communication in which transmission takes place in both the directions, but only in one direction at a time is called
(a) Simplex (b) Full Duplex
(c) Half Duplex (d) Two-wire Circuits

76. **Assertion (A):** The 'Schedule tool' of survey method helps the researcher to get information mostly from illiterates respondents.
Reason (R): In the schedule method, the onus of filling up of the questionnaire usually lies with the respondents.
In the context of these two statements, which one of the following is true?
(a) (A) is true, but (R) is false
(b) Both (A) and (R) are true
(c) (A) is false, but (R) is true
(d) Both (A) and (R) are false

77. Identify the services of OCLC from the following:
(i) Infoport (ii) OJAS
(iii) First search (iv) Question point
Choose the correct answer from the following options:
(a) (i) and (ii) are correct
(b) (ii) and (iv) are correct
(c) (i) and (iii) are correct
(d) (iii) and (iv) are correct

78. Match the following authors with their corresponding books.

List - I

(1) A. Broadfield (2) J.H. Shera
(3) Pierce Butler (4) James Thomson

List - II

(i) *The Foundations of Education for Librarianshi*
(ii) *A Philosophy of Librarianship*
(iii) *Library Power: A New Philosophy of Librariat*
(iv) *Introduction to Library Science*

Choose the correct answer from the following options:
(a) (1)-(i), (2)-(iii), (3)-(iv), (4)-(ii)
(b) (1)-(iv), (2)-(i), (3)-(iii), (4)-(ii)
(c) (1)-(iii), (2)-(i), (3)-(iv), (4)-(ii)
(d) (1)-(ii), (2)-(i), (3)-(iv), (4)-(iii)

79. Which of the following are network protocols?
(i) UDP (ii) SMTP (iii) TCP (iv) Telnet
Choose the correct answer from the following options:
(a) (i), (ii) and (iv) are correct
(b) (ii), (iii) and (iv) are correct
(c) (i), (iii) and (iv) are correct
(d) (i), (ii) and (iii) are correct

80. Who is the creator of 'R' statistics?
(a) Dale H. Bent and H.E. Garrett
(b) Norman H. Nie and C. Had
(c) Ross Inaka and Robert Gentleman
(d) Harold Cramer and John C.

81. Which of the following are Reference Style Management tools?
(i) Stata (ii) Ref works
(iii) Mendeley (iv) Zotero
Choose the correct answer from the following options:
(a) (i), (ii) and (iii) are correct
(b) (ii), (iii) and (iv) are correct
(c) (i) and (ii) are correct
(d) (i) and (iv) are correct

82. Who popularized the term 'Bibliomania'?
(a) Ted Nelson
(b) Thomas Frognall Dibdin
(c) George Kingsley Zipf
(d) Theodore Besterman

83. Who authored the book entitled *Putting Knowledge to Work*?
(a) Pauline Atherton (b) HermanM.Weisman
(c) S.C. Bradford (d) J.S. Brown

84. Identify the name of 'Editor-in-Chief' of Dewey Decimal Classification and Edition 23
(a) P. Green (b) J. Martin
(c) Joan S. Mitchell (d) A. Kent

85. The UK Committee on RDA (UKCOR) is support
(i) CILIP (ii) The British Library
(iii) OCLC (iv) UNESCO
Choose the correct answer from the following options:
(a) (i) and (iii) are correct
(b) (ii) and (iv) are correct
(c) (i) and (iv) are correct
(d) (i) and (ii) are correct

86. Arrange the following layers of Tiwana's KMS Architecture in order
(i) Interface layer
(ii) Application layer
(iii) Access and Authentication layer
(iv) Collaborative, Intelligence and Filtering
Choose the correct answer from the following options:
(a) (ii), (iii), (iv), (i) (b) (iv), (ii), (iii), (i)
(c) (i), (iii), (iv), (ii) (d) (iii), (iv), (i), (ii)

87. **Assertion (A):** Consortia-based subscription of online resources nowadays has become a practice in most of the University Libraries in India.

Reason (R): Spiraling cost of publications, optimal utilization of resources at least efforts and cost coupled with growing expectations of users, have made such subscription redundant.

In the context of these two statements which one of the following is true?
(a) (A) is false, but (R) is true
(b) (A) is true, but (R) is false
(c) Both (A) and (R) are true
(d) Both (A) and (R) is false

88. Who introduced the term 'Literary Warrant'?
(a) S.R. Ranganathan (b) Wyndham Hulme
(c) Melvil Dewey (d) J.D. Brown

89. Match the following protocols with their creators:

List - I

(1) HTTP (2) SHTTP

(3) FTP (4) SMTP

List - II

(i) Eric Rescoria and Allan M. Schiffman

(ii) Tim Berners-Lee

(iii) Robert E. Kahn and Vintcerf

(iv) Abhay Bhusan

Choose the correct answer from the following options:

(a) (1)-(ii), (2)-(iv), (3)-(i), (4)-(iii)

(b) (1)-(ii), (2)-(iii), (3)-(i), (4)-(iv)

(c) (1)-(ii), (2)-(i), (3)-(iv), (4)-(iii)

(d) (1)-(iv), (2)-(i), (3)-(ii), (4)-(iii)

90. Which of the following devices is used to connect different network segments and manage the traffic between them?

(a) Switch (b) Gateway

(c) Bridge (d) Repeater

Read the passage given below and answer the questions which follow.

Science provides the answer as to how to perform certain operations in order to secure given ends. But such knowledge is a two-edged sword. The same processes that led to the manufacture of aniline dyes set in motion physiological processes that ended in death for many of those who helped manufacture the dyes. The development of superior methods of keeping records, basic to the growth of social science, may also be the means of strenghtening the grip of a repressive political dictatorship. Today the use of radioactive-isotope therapy promises much for the reduction of disease, but these isotopes are products of the same scientific knowledge which produced the atomic bomb and which has made possible the even more destructive hydrogen bomb. Science as a method gives power, but this is a power which may be used for disapproved as well as approved ends.

Science, then can (1) offer a method of solving problems, i.e., of achieving values; (2) offer *alternative* methods, so that relative costs can be calculated; (3) provide a means for predicting what the order consequences of a given course of action may be. If, for example, it is desired to clear a slum, it is good to be able not only to predict the financial and emotional costs of the specific program but also to know what other effects the slum clearance will have upon the community. This is a task to which only the scientific method may be successful applied.

Since science operates as a technique of problem solving, and since problems in this sense are formulated upon the basis of vaue judgements, then it is clear science and values are interrelated.

91. Which destructive product is made up by the use of radioactive - isotope?

(a) Machine Gun (b) Hydrogen Bomb

(c) Robot (d) Pistol

92. What is the benefit of 'Radioactive Isotope Therapy'?

(a) Reduction of anxiety

(b) Reduction of stress

(c) Reduction of disease

(d) Reduction of psycho-fear

93. Which kind of process led to death for many who helped manufacture of the dyes?

(a) Motion physiological process

(b) Electromechanical process

(c) Cognitive process

(d) Psychological process

94. Which of the following strengthens the grip of a repressive political dictatorship?

(a) Superior method of keeping records

(b) Static in growth of social sciences

(c) Inferior method of documentation

(d) Fair political practice

95. Problems are formulated upon the basis of

(a) Market survey (b) Value Judgment

(c) Review of literature (d) Pilot study

Read the following passage carefully and answer the questions that follow.

The term User Education is used interchangeably with 'library instruction', 'library orientation' and 'bibliographic instruction'. Neelameghan distinguishes user education, user orientation and user assistance. Roberts and Blandy prefer a broad term: library instruction. User education is a comprehensive service and a process of making the user self-reliant in locating, sorting and repacking information. This process may require two strategies: for general exposure, and for specific subject oriented—bibliographic instruction. The first visit to the library is mostly casual and in a sense this requires more frequent meetings with the user.

By the 1850s, US librarians instructed patrons on library use Samuel Greens attempt to initiate a reference desk in the public library in the 1870s, Louis Shore's library-college movement in the 1920s and Patricia Knapp's Montieth College programme in the 1960s are all significant. In 1949 the three-stage user education programme proposed by the UK library association's University and Research Section was a landmark. Ranganathan prescribed the role of an intermediary as a user-friendly reference librarian. Boon Fjallbrant and Stevenson Hopkins, Roberts and Blandy and others have made extensive historical assessments. Progress was slow, partly due to the problem of defining its place in the services; it was lost in the informational function or reference service. While lectures, tours and seminars are traditional methods, programmed learning, teaching machines, audiovisual tools and computer assisted learning (CAL) are the recent advances. User education is not merely a library tour or a brochure, it includes searching databases (local and global) and generally making the user less dependent on others.

A variety of media are used. One-to-one instruction is simple but expensive. Orientation by informal tour is traditional and effective, but it is time-consuming and too general, and can cause boredom. Printed materials (leaflet, handout) describe services, tools and search strategies, but need frequent revision and may not be used. Displaying of posters, diagrams, etc. can teaching skills, but requires a mediator. In workbooks, the audience is involved, which enables learning at the individual's pace and the educator can know the effect of learning.

96. What is Roberts and Blandy's most preferred term for 'User Education'?
    (a) Library orientation
    (b) Bibliographic instruction
    (c) Library instruction
    (d) User assistance
97. What are the traditional methods of imparting user education?
    (a) Lectures, tours and seminars
    (b) Teaching machines
    (c) Audio-visual tools
    (d) Programmed learning
98. Three stage of user education programme was proposed by
    (a) S.R. Ranganathan
    (b) University and Research Section, UK Library Association
    (c) Samuel Green
    (d) Indian Library Association
99. User education as a service aims to
    (a) Aid in understanding non-bibliographic instruction
    (b) Use appropriate referral source
    (c) Rely upon intermediary service
    (d) Make the user self-reliant in locating, sorting and repackaging information
100. Which of the following type of 'user-instruction' is relatively a costly proposition and less time consuming?
    (a) One to many instruction
    (b) Informal tour
    (c) One to one instruction
    (d) Classroom instruction

ANSWER SHEET

1. (b)	2. (a)	3. (d)	4. (a)	5. (d)	6. (c)	7. (a)	8. (b)	9. (a)
10. (b)	11. (b)	12. (a)	13. (a)	14. (d)	15. (c)	16. (c)	17. (b)	18. (b)
19. (d)	20. (a)	21. (d)	22. (b)	23. (a)	24. (b)	25. (b)	26. (c)	27. (d)
28. (a)	29. (a)	30. (a)	31. (c)	32. (a)	33. (b)	34. (d)	35. (b)	36. (a)
37. (b)	38. (a)	39. (d)	40. (a)	41. (c)	42. (c)	43. (c)	44. (c)	45. (b)
46. (d)	47. (a)	48. (a)	49. (a)	50. (c)	51. (d)	52. (c)	53. (a)	54. (c)
55. (a)	56. (d)	57. (b)	58. (d)	59. (d)	60. (b)	61. (a)	62. (a)	63. (c)
64. (d)	65. (c)	66. (c)	67. (b)	68. (a)	69. (b)	70. (b)	71. (b)	72. (d)
73. (b)	74. (d)	75. (c)	76. (a)	77. (d)	78. (d)	79. (d)	80. (c)	81. (b)
82. (b)	83. (a)	84. (c)	85. (d)	86. (c)	87. (b)	88. (b)	89. (c)	90. (c)
91. (b)	92. (c)	93. (a)	94. (a)	95. (b)	96. (c)	97. (a)	98. (b)	99. (d)
100. (c)								